SPEECH COMMUNICATIONS

IEEE Press
445 Hoes Lane, P.O. Box 1331
Piscataway, NJ 08855-1331

Technical Reviewers

Joseph P. Campbell, Jr., *U.S. Department of Defense and Johns Hopkins University*
M. A. Kohler, *U.S. Department of Defense*
Joseph Picone, *Mississippi State University*
Kuldip Paliwal, *Griffith University, Brisbane, Australia*
Hynek Hermansky, *Oregon Graduate Institute*
Sadaoki Furui, *Tokyo Institute of Technology, Japan*

Books of Related Interest from the IEEE Press . . .

DISCRETE-TIME PROCESSING OF SPEECH SIGNALS: A Classic Reissue
John R. Deller Jr., John H. L. Hansen, and John Proakis
2000   Hardcover   936 pp   IEEE Order No. PC5826   ISBN 0-7803-5386-2

HUMAN MOTION ANALYSIS: Current Applications and Future Directions
A volume in the TAB-IEEE Press Book Series—Design and Applications
Edited by Gerald F. Harris and Peter A. Smith
1996   Hardcover   480 pp   IEEE Order No. PC4648   ISBN 0-7803-1111-6

SPEECH COMMUNICATIONS

Human and Machine

Second Edition

Douglas O'Shaughnessy
Université du Québec
Institut National de la Recherche Scientifique
INRS-TÉLÉCOMMUNICATIONS

The Institute of Electrical and Electronics Engineers, Inc., New York

This book and other books may be purchased at a discount
from the publisher when ordered in bulk quantities. Contact:

IEEE Press Marketing
Attn: Special Sales
445 Hoes Lane
P.O. Box 1331
Piscataway, NJ 08855-1331
Fax: +1 732 981 9334

For more information about IEEE Press products, visit the
IEEE Press Home Page: http://www.ieee.org/press

Printed in the United States of America

10   9   8   7   6   5   4   3   2   1

P95
.074
2000

ISBN 0-7803-3449-3
IEEE Order Number PC4194

Library of Congress Cataloging-in-Publication Data

O'Shaughnessy, Douglas, 1950–
    Speech communications : human and machine / Douglas O'Shaughnessy.
    —2nd ed.
        p. cm.
    Includes bibliographical references and index.
    ISBN 0-7803-3449-3
    1. Oral communication.   2. Speech processing systems. I. Title.
P95.074 2000
302.2'244—dc 21   99-28810
                                                                            CIP

To my beloved wife
Annick

Contents

Preface

This book is intended to provide readers with an overview of speech communication in its wide-ranging aspects, from a discussion of how humans produce and perceive speech to details of computer-based speech processing for diverse communications applications. Unlike other books in the field of speech, this one takes a broad view of speech communication, at times sacrificing some technical depth for breadth, so that readers may see the relationships between parts of the communication process that are often dealt with separately. A cohesive, even-handed discussion of speech production and perception (both human and machine) should help readers understand speech communication better than is possible with other texts.

In addition to a detailed description of human speech production and perception, readers will learn about current techniques to analyze, code, recognize, and synthesize speech. They will gain an understanding of the limits of current technology, as well as see future directions for speech research.

While this text should serve students in an introductory course on speech communication or processing, additional material is included throughout the book to aid more advanced readers. Sections that may be easily omitted in a one-semester course are noted with a double dagger (‡). For space reasons, the finer mathematical details of some speech processing algorithms have been omitted. Ample references are provided that enable interested readers to find these details quickly. Thus, readers should not expect to find program listings or detailed algorithms here, but rather should read the book to understand speech processing and how particular applications of interest fit into the broader picture of speech communication.

This is not to say that the book is unsophisticated mathematically. On the contrary, to understand many aspects of speech communication, mathematical description is imperative. Nonetheless, such detail is kept to the minimum necessary for adequate understanding. Readers not familiar with engineering mathematics should not be discouraged, since the necessary basic mathematical principles are reviewed in Chapter 2 in a way that presumes little prior knowledge. Indeed, although there are many cross-references between chapters and sections, readers with little mathematical background should find the book quite useful simply by skipping over equations (or even entire sections) that seem hard to follow.

It is unnecessary to read the book from the beginning to understand it. The chapters have a logical order, but it is not necessary to understand all preceding chapters before reading a chapter of particular interest. For example, readers interested primarily in speech synthesis could commence directly with Chapter 9 and refer to earlier chapters as they meet references to concepts of speech production or coding with which they were not familiar.

INTENDED AUDIENCE

Speech communication is an interdisciplinary subject. Although much of the research material for the book comes from engineering literature (e.g., IEEE journals), a wide variety of sources is employed (especially for Chapters 3–5). The book is directed primarily at an engineering audience (e.g., to a final-year undergraduate or graduate course in electrical engineering or to those in speech research), but it should also be accessible to linguists, phoneticians, psychologists, audiologists, computer scientists, and systems engineers. Linguists view speech in terms of language description; they characterize languages via phonemes and intonation and note differences and similarities in how different languages convey messages. Phoneticians examine the relationships between phonemes, their articulation, and their acoustic properties. Psychologists deal in perception, noting the relationships between acoustic properties of signals (e.g., speech) and what people hear and understand. Audiologists deal with disorders of the hearing system and often use sounds other than speech in their work. Speech communication is treated as a programming problem by computer scientists; using artificial intelligence techniques, they seek to simulate the human actions of producing and understanding speech signals or to represent speech in an efficient fashion for transmission. Systems engineers have similar objectives and use similar tools as the computer scientists, but tend to be more concerned with questions of efficiency and practicality, whereas scientists seek more to understand the communication process. By simultaneously including both technical detail and basic explanations about speech communication, this book should address the concerns of all researchers involved in speech, as well as interest the student wishing an introduction to the field.

Since the book covers a wide field, it should be useful as a reference text. In it, readers will find an introduction to virtually any subject of relevance to speech communication. By examining its up-to-date reference list, readers can quickly locate references for further details. To facilitate such reference searches, the list contains major information sources that should be available in most scientific or engineering libraries, such as textbooks, journals, and a few conference proceedings. Relatively inaccessible sources, such as technical reports and references with abstracts only, have been avoided where possible.

It is always difficult to write a book for an audience to include both students (from both engineering and other disciplines) and professionals. I have attempted to satisfy both groups with this book, but of necessity I have had to compromise. For students, the book is highly tutorial, does not presume any prior knowledge about speech communication, presents topics in a sequence that is relatively easy to follow, and provides problems at the end of most chapters. For researchers, the coverage of the book is complete in virtually all aspects of speech communication, the list of references is large and up-to-date [the most important references, and those of tutorial nature, are noted by an asterisk (*)], and new developments are put into the perspective of older, classical results. As a result, students may find the text at times too detailed, while professionals may wish for more detail in areas that interest them. I believe, however, that I have struck a good compromise: researchers, by using the reference list, should be able to locate further detail quickly, while one-semester students may skip over sections noted with a double dagger (‡).

Finally, this second edition has more details on major developments in speech processing between 1987 and 1999, for example, among others, on CELP, HMMs, and neural networks. A related major development of the 1990s has been the massive interest in the Internet (World Wide Web). In response, I have included a large list of relevant Web sites for speech information. I will update this information periodically at the Web site for this book, http://www.inrs-telecom.uquebec.ca/users/spchwww/English/persons/dougo/book.html

Douglas O'Shaughnessy
Université du Québec
Institut National de la Recherche Scientifique
INRS-TÉLÉCOMMUNICATIONS

Acknowledgments

I wish to thank my fellow researchers at INRS-Telecommunications and Bell-Northern Research (now Nortel Technologies, Inc.), in particular Dr. Paul Mermelstein for many fruitful discussions related to speech communication and specifically for his help in editing the first edition of the book. Drs. Greg Bielby, Vishwa Gupta, and Gérard Bailly assisted me with specific chapters related to their expertise. For reading the draft from the student's point of view with many helpful comments, I would like to thank my graduate students, David Bernardi and Hesham Tolba. Michel Héon helped with the spectrograms. I thank also several external reviewers for many helpful comments, which led to better organization of several chapters; in particular, I thank Dr. Joe Campbell, Dr. Jared Bernstein, Prof. Richard Stern, Prof. Ralph Ohde, Dr. Robert Gray, and the late Dr. Dennis Klatt. While many people assisted in the creation of this book, I had the final say on its contents and therefore I am responsible for any erroneous statements. Finally, I would like to thank INRS, for allowing me the freedom to write this book and furnishing the necessary facilities. I specifically thank Prof. Michael Ferguson of INRS for much assistance with the TeX text and graphic system by which this book was prepared.

Douglas O'Shaughnessy
Université du Québec
Institut National de la Recherche Scientifique
INRS–TÉLÉCOMMUNICATIONS

Acronyms in Speech Communications

A/D   analog-to-digital conversion
ADM   adaptive delta modulation
ADPCM   adaptive differential pulse code modulation
AGC   automatic gain control
ALSR   average localized synchronized rate
AMDF   average magnitude difference function
ANN   artificial neural network
APC   adaptive predictive coding
APCM   adaptive pulse code modulation
AR   autoregressive model of LPC
ASI   automatic speaker identification
ASR   automatic speech recognition
ASV   automatic speaker verification
ATC   adaptive transform coding
ATN   augmented transition network
BP   back-propagation
CELP   code-excited linear prediction
CSR   continuous speech recognition
CVSD   continuously variable slope delta modulation
CWR   connected-word recognition
CZT   chirp z-transform
D/A   digital-to-analog conversion
dB   decibel (dB)
DFT   discrete Fourier transform
DM   delta modulation
DPCM   differential pulse code modulation
DSI   digital speech interpolation
DSP   digital signal processing
DTW   dynamic time warping
EMG   electromyography
F-ratio   performance measure for speaker recognition
FFT   fast Fourier transform
FIR   finite-duration impulse response
F0   fundamental frequency
GMM   Gaussian mixture model
HMM   hidden Markov model
Hz   Hertz
IC   integrated circuit
IIR   infinite-duration impulse response
IWR   isolated word recognition
JND   just-noticeable difference
LMS   least mean squares LPC method
Log-PCM   logarithmic pulse code modulation
LPC   linear predictive coding
LS   least-squares estimation
LSF   line spectral frequency
LSP   line spectral pair
MA   moving average model of LPC
MBE   multiband excitation LPC
ML   maximum likelihood
MMSE   minimum mean-square estimation
MPLPC   multipulse-excited LPC
NN   nearest-neighbor rule for distance comparison
PARCOR   partial correlation LPC

PCM   pulse code modulation
PSOLA   pitch-synchronous overlap-and-add
PST   post-stimulus time histogram
Q   ratio of a resonance center frequency to
bandwidth
QMF   quadrature mirror filter
RAM   random access memory
RELP   residual excited linear prediction
ROM   read-only memory
RPE   regular-pulse excitation
SBC   sub-band coding
SIFT   simple inverse-filtering pitch detection
SNR   signal-to-noise ratio

STC   sinusoidal transform coding
TASI   time assignment speech interpolation
TDHS   time domain harmonic scaling
UELM   unconstrained endpoints, local
minimum DTW method
UWA   unsupervised without averaging clustering
VFR   variable frame rate
VLSI   very large scale integration technology
VOT   voice onset time
VQ   vector quantization
VSELP   vector self-excited linear prediction
ZCR   zero crossing rate

Important Developments in Speech Communications

1779 Mechanical speech synthesis
1876 Invention of the telephone
1922 Electrical speech synthesis
1924 Speech analysis by formants
1939 Vocoder
1946 Invention of Spectrogram device
1952 Delta modulation
1953 Analysis of phonemes by distinctive features
1957 Speech synthesis by formants
1959 Time assignment speech interpolation
1960 Acoustical theory of speech production
1962 Computer speech synthesis with digital filters
1964 Cepstral analysis
1967 Linear predictive coding of speech
1970 Adaptive delta modulation
1970 Dynamic time warping for speech recognition

1973 Adaptive differential pulse code modulation
1975 Markov models for speech recognition
1976 Sub-band coding
1977 Adaptive transform coding
1978 Large scale integrated circuit speech synthesizer
1980 Vector quantization for speech coding
1982 Multipulse-excited linear prediction
1985 Code-excited linear prediction
1986 Artificial neural networks for speech recognition
1986 Pitch-synchronous overlap-and-add synthesis
1987 Language models for speech recognition
1992 TIMIT database on CD-ROM
1995 Language identification

1

Introduction

1.1 WHAT IS SPEECH COMMUNICATION?

Speech communication is the transfer of information from one person to another via *speech*, which consists of variations in pressure coming from the mouth of a speaker. Such pressure changes propagate as *waves* through air and enter the ears of listeners, who decipher the waves into a received message. Human communication often includes gestures, which are not not part of speech, such as head and hand movements; such gestures, though normally part of face-to-face communication, are not considered in this book. The chain of events from the concept of a message in a speaker's brain to the arrival of the message in a listener's brain is called the *speech chain* [1]. The chain consists of a speech production mechanism in the speaker, transmission through a medium (e.g., air), and a speech perception process in the ears and brain of a listener.

In many applications of speech processing (italicized below), part of the chain is implemented by a simulation device. Automatic *synthesis* or generation of speech by algorithm (by computer) can simulate the speaker's role, except for generation of the original message, which usually comes in the form of a text (furnished by a computer user). In automatic speech or speaker *recognition*, an algorithm plays the listener's role in decoding speech into either an estimate of the underlying textual message or a hypothesis concerning the speaker's identity. Speech *coders* allow replacing the analog transmission medium (e.g., air or telephone lines) with a digital version, modifying the representation of the signal; in this way, speech can be efficiently stored and transmitted, often without noise problems and with enhanced security.

1.2 DEVELOPMENTS IN SPEECH COMMUNICATION

While many of the developments affecting speech communication have occurred in the last few decades, the basic tools for speech analysis are founded in mathematics, e.g., Fourier analysis, developed many decades ago. A basic understanding of how we produce speech has

1

existed for hundreds of years (e.g., mechanical speech synthesizers existed in the 1700s), but detailed knowledge of audio perception is fairly recent (e.g., Békésy's experiments on the basilar membrane in the 1940s). Modern speech research started in the 1930s, when the practical digital transmission method of *pulse-code modulation* (PCM) was developed and when a mechanical synthesizer called the Voder was demonstrated. The invention of the *sound spectrograph* in 1946 spurred much speech analysis work, since it allowed practical displays of the acoustic output of the vocal tract.

Viewing individual sounds or *phonemes* as composed of discrete, distinctive features originated in the 1950s and spurred development of electronic speech synthesizers, e.g., the Pattern Playback. More efficient digital speech coding in the form of delta modulation was developed at this time as well. Fant's benchmark work on speech acoustics appeared in 1960 [2], beginning a decade of much speech research, during which speech was first synthesized by computer and the important analysis techniques of the *cepstrum* and *linear prediction* were introduced.

The early 1970s saw development of time-adaptive speech coding as well as a big increase in speech recognition work, including the Advanced Research Projects Agency (ARPA) speech understanding project [3] and the use of dynamic programming in matching templates from different speech signals. *Digital signal processing* as a discipline saw much development [4]. In the late 1970s, more complex speech systems such as *subband* and *adaptive transform* coders appeared. Large-scale integrated circuits made their appearance in the form of one-chip speech synthesizers, and stochastic methods became accepted for speech recognition (e.g., *hidden Markov models*).

The major developments of the 1980s included single-chip digital signal processors, the use of *vector quantization* for low-rate speech coding, the search for better excitation models for speech synthesis (e.g., *multipulse excitation*), the use of auditory models in speech applications based on hearing experiments using speechlike stimuli, and the use of language models to aid speech recognition.

The 1990s have seen widespread acceptance of speech coders, synthesizers and recognizers, as computational power has continued to increase substantially while costs decrease. While the pace of major breakthroughs has slowed in recent years (e.g., the last significant new paradigm introduced in speech processing was the use of neural networks in the late 1980s), research continues unabated, because current speech products are far from ideal.

1.3 OUTLINE OF THE BOOK

The book is divided into two main parts: the first deals with the way **humans** generate and interpret speech, and the second examines how **machines** simulate human speech performance and how they code speech for efficient transmission. The first part is further subdivided into chapters on speech production, general audition, and speech perception. The second part has six chapters, three describing analysis, coding and enhancement of speech, one examining speech synthesis, and two on recognition (speech and speaker). The following sections briefly describe the different domains of scientific study found in speech communication research.

1.3.1 Production of Speech

Chapter 3 examines the first link in the speech chain: production. After a brief introduction, Section 3.2 discusses the organs of the *vocal tract* that a speaker uses to produce speech, from the viewpoint of their functions. The relationships between the positioning and motion of these organs and the sounds of a language (using English as the basic example) are the subject of Section 3.3. Since the speech wave or *acoustic signal* is of prime importance in all practical applications, Section 3.4 discusses how each sound can be simply described by a set of acoustic features observable in the speech signal's waveform or frequency *spectrum*.

Modeling aspects of human behavior during speech communication is of major interest, both to understand the speech process better and to suggest ways of simulating human speech tasks by machine. Thus, Sections 3.5 and 3.6 model vocal tract behavior in relation to time and frequency aspects of the speech signal. First, the tract is *modeled* by means of electrical circuits and transmission lines, to understand how the reflection of waves inside the tract causes different speech frequencies to be amplified or attenuated, depending on the shape of the tract. Then practical digital filters used in speech synthesis are introduced. The final two sections of Chapter 3 examine two major sources of difficulties in speech analysis: *coarticulation* and *intonation*; the former refers to variations in speech sounds due to context, and the latter denotes variations in the tone, length, and intensity of sounds.

1.3.2 Sound Perception

Aspects of human speech perception are divided into two chapters. Chapter 4 deals with the conversion of speech waves (and other sounds) into auditory nerve patterns, including elementary *auditory psychophysics*. Chapter 5 examines the relationships between the acoustic features of sounds and what listeners perceive. After a brief introduction, Section 4.2 discusses how the organs of the ear convert acoustic speech waves into electrical signals on the *auditory nerve*. Questions of how intense and long a sound must be to be heard are discussed in Section 4.3, along with aspects of *pitch* perception and the perceptual effects of one sound on another. While this section deals with simple sounds (e.g., clicks and tones), Section 4.4 extends these ideas to examine auditory responses to speech signals.

High-quality synthetic speech requires accurate modeling of aspects of the speech signal that are important perceptually. Since the identity of a sound in natural speech is signaled in a complex way through many redundant cues, Section 5.2 examines the difficulty of determining perceptually-important speech features when using synthetic speech stimuli. Section 5.3, which analyzes different speech perception models and theories, is followed by a summary of the results of perception experiments for vowels (Section 5.4) and consonants (Section 5.5). How intonation is used to segment continuous speech and highlight specific words is the subject of Section 5.7, preceded by a discussion of the utility of timing in speech. Miscellaneous aspects of speech perception (e.g., issues of adaptation, dichotic listening, distortions) end Chapter 5.

1.3.3 Speech Analysis

Whereas Chapters 3–5 focus on how humans utilize speech, the remaining chapters address applications of speech communication that typically involve digital computers. Chapter 6, an introduction to the application chapters, notes the key elements of automatic speech analysis. Chapter 7 investigates how speech signals can be coded for efficient transmission, Chapter 8 explores ways to improve distorted speech, Chapter 9 examines how speech is generated synthetically, and Chapters 10 and 11 consider techniques for extraction of the message and of the speaker's identity, respectively, from a speech signal.

The basic representation of a speech signal in a digital computer requires limiting the spectral bandwidth of the signal (e.g., 0–4 kHz), sampling it at a certain corresponding rate (e.g., 8000 samples/s), and storing each sample with an adequate resolution, e.g., 12 bits (*binary digits*) each. Eliminating frequencies in speech above, say, 4 kHz causes a slight degradation in speech quality or naturalness, but has little effect on information content. For many communication applications, preserving the intelligibility of the speech is paramount, and some degradations in quality are acceptable. Besides *intelligibility* (being able to understand the speech message), certain information about the speaker (e.g., identity and mood) is usually important to retain in coded speech; often, low-rate coders preserve intelligibility while sacrificing such speaker information.

Digital signal representations of sufficient bit rate can be converted back into speech without significant loss of quality (other than the unavoidable loss of high frequencies in the original bandlimiting). From the perspective of information transmission, however, using almost 100,000 bits/s of speech is very wasteful because each second of speech typically contains 12 distinct sounds, from a inventory of about $32 = 2^5$ linguistic units called *phonemes*, which suggests an actual information rate of about 60 bit/s. Speech contains information other than the simple sequence of sounds, however, since listeners can infer speaker identity and emotion as well as assign a linguistic structure to each utterance. Nonetheless, simple speech coding can theoretically be improved by a factor of about 1000 by extracting appropriate features from the signal rather than using elementary sampling.

Chapter 6 examines the basic techniques of *parameter* and *feature* extraction from speech, which is of direct use to coding and recognition and of indirect use to synthesis. Since a speech signal changes its characteristics for each new sound, speech analysis must be performed on short *windowed* segments for which the vocal tract is assumed in most cases to be essentially fixed (Section 6.2). Certain relevant features (e.g., energy and periodicity) can be observed directly in the time-domain display of a speech signal (Section 6.3). To accurately distinguish sounds, however, requires a spectral analysis (Section 6.4).

The important technique of *linear predictive* (LP) analysis is the subject of a detailed Section 6.5, including: (a) the basic LP model in terms of the two traditional block analysis methods (autocorrelation and covariance), (b) the relationship of spectral modeling resolution to the order of the LP model, (c) adaptive and lattice filters, and (d) the effects of the size of the analysis window.

Cepstral analysis, a general signal processing technique with specific application to speech (mostly recognition), is examined in Section 6.6. Other recent developments in analysis (e.g., wavelets) are explored in Section 6.7. The difficult task of pitch estimation is described in Section 6.8. Issues of *robustness* against distortions are the subject of Section 6.9. Chapter 6 ends with a discussion of how extracted features can be smoothed in time, to represent the speech signal more efficiently while still permitting adequate reconstruction of the speech.

1.3.4 Speech Coding

Solving the problem of reducing the bit rate of a speech representation, while preserving the quality of speech reconstructed from such a representation, continues in

Chapter 7. It builds on the fundamental procedures of Chapter 6 and addresses the tradeoffs of quality, coding rate, and algorithmic complexity. Fundamentals of linear and logarithmic *quantization* of speech are described in Section 7.2, noting how coding rate can be reduced by using basic amplitude statistics of speech signals. Section 7.3 gives an overview of the aspects of speech that are exploited in coders that reconstruct the signal sample by sample. Section 7.4 describes measures to evaluate speech quality. Sections 7.5–7.8 describe waveform coders that operate directly on the time signal. Various coding schemes exploit different properties of speech: (a) its average intensity changes slowly with respect to the sampling rate (Section 7.5), (b) it has primarily low-frequency energy and is adequately parameterized in the short term by simple models (Section 7.6), (c) it is often periodic (Section 7.7), and (d) its spectral components vary in perceptual importance (Section 7.8).

Section 7.9 deals with many aspects of linear predictive coding (LPC), ranging from simple differential PCM to the standard LPC *vocoding* method, which separates two sources of information in the speech signal (the *excitation* and the *frequency response* of the vocal tract) for efficient manipulation and transmission. Among the topics covered are: how the basic LPC parameters can be transformed into equivalent but more efficient representations, how the nonstationarity of speech affects the transmission rate of LPC, how the basic *all-pole* LPC model can be enhanced at the cost of extra complexity, and how we can trade transmission rate for quality via use of more complex excitation models.

Section 7.10 describes filtering approaches to coding (where more perceptually important frequency ranges are assigned more bits), including a *frequency-transform* method (which directly codes a spectrum) and methods that code speech harmonics directly. While LPC dominates vocoding methods, alternative vocoders (e.g., channel vocoding) are noted in Section 7.11.

Most speech coders transmit time or frequency samples as independent (scalar) parameters, but coding efficiency can be enhanced by eliminating redundant information within blocks of parameters and transmitting a single index code to represent the entire block, i.e., *vector quantization* (Section 7.12). Section 7.13 examines network aspects of speech transmission: when many speech signals are mixed with data and sent over a network where traffic varies with time, tradeoffs of speech quality and network availability arise.

1.3.5 Speech Enhancement

Chapter 8 examines how to increase the quality of degraded speech signals. Speech is often distorted by background noise (or other speech) and/or by poor transmission conditions. Various filtering or other processing techniques can reduce the distortion effects, rendering the signal easier to listen to. If noisy speech can be captured via several microphones, its intelligibility can even be raised. Sections 8.1 and 8.2 give an introduction to the problem, and Section 8.3 describes the types of interfering sounds we must deal with. The major enhancement methods are summarized in Section 8.4, and then discussed in more detail: (a) subtracting estimates of noise from noisy spectral amplitudes (Section 8.5), (b) filtering out the distortion (e.g., *adaptive noise cancellation*) (Section 8.6), (c) suppressing energy between speech harmonics (*comb filtering*) (Section 8.7), and (d) resynthesis of the speech after vocoder modeling (Section 8.8).

1.3.6 Speech Synthesis

Chapter 9 examines automatic generation of speech. Section 9.2 introduces the major aspects of speech synthesis: the size of the stored speech unit to be concatenated, the method of synthesis (which usually follows a coding method from Chapter 7), and the difference in output quality between *voice response* systems of very limited vocabulary and *text-to-speech* systems that accept unrestricted text input. Section 9.3 represents the bulk of Chapter 9, giving details for articulatory, formant, and LPC synthesizers. The three major reasons for limits on synthetic speech quality are discussed: simplistic models for excitation, intonation, and spectral time behavior. Section 9.4 examines the difficulty of simulating natural intonation. Section 9.5 discusses how to simulate different speaking voices, and Section 9.6 notes research progress for languages other than English. Performance in speech recognizers and in many speech coders can be measured objectively (i.e., via the percentage of words recognized correctly, or via signal-to-noise ratios); however, there is no objective way to evaluate speech synthesizers (Section 9.7). Chapter 9 ends with a section on specialized hardware for synthesis.

1.3.7 Speech and Speaker Recognition

The other side of human–machine communication via speech is automatic recognition, where either the textual message (Chapter 10) or the speaker's identity (Chapter 11) is extracted or verified from the speech signal. Chapter 10 starts with the view of speech identification as a *pattern recognition* task, where the input signal is reduced to a set of parameters or features, which in turn are compared to *templates* or models in memory to find the one with the best match. Sections 10.3 and 10.4 detail the initial stages of recognition: normalizing the signal, and extracting parameters and features from the data. When comparing an N-parameter model of an unknown input utterance (of, for example, a word) with a stored model of a known utterance, *distance measures* should reflect how well each parameter separates models for different words in N-dimensional space (Section 10.4).

Section 10.5 looks at the problems of comparing utterance representations to evaluate their similarity. A lengthy Section 10.6 examines the many sources of variability in speech, and how recognizers accommodate this variability. As an example, consider speech spoken with different durations or speaking rates: linearly normalizing all templates to the same duration often leads to poor comparisons, so nonlinear normalization through hidden Markov models (HMMs) or *dynamic time warping* is often used. State networks are commonly used in recognition as models of the sequence of acoustic events in speech. Each state in a network represents an acoustic event (e.g., a sound, a word), and the transition from state A to state B is labeled with the probability that event B follows event A in the sentences or words of the vocabulary. Section 10.7 continues the discussion of speech variability, in noting how recognizers can *adapt* to variability due to different speakers and recording conditions.

The use of statistics of sequences of words in text occurs in *language models* for speech recognition (Section 10.8). As constraints are relaxed on speakers (e.g., allowing use of wider vocabularies or speaking without frequent pauses), issues of computation time and memory become significant. This leads to ways to optimize the large *search space* in speech recognition.

Discriminating between phonetically similar words is often difficult for many recognizers. Nonlinear techniques using *artificial neural networks*, based on simple models of the human brain, are capable of more precise discrimination than HMMs, but do poorly on handling temporal variations (Section 10.10). Future systems will likely integrate the current stochastic recognition methods (e.g., HMMs) with *expert system* approaches (Section 10.11). Chapter 10 ends with a brief section describing available commercial recognizers.

Speaker identification is the subject of Chapter 11, whose first two sections briefly introduce the problem and distinguish between *recognition* (selecting one out of N known speakers) and *verification* (deciding whether a speaker is who he claims to be). The methodology of speaker identification, examined in Section 11.3, has many similarities and some differences compared with speech recognition techniques. If the speaker utters a text known to the system, the methods can be very similar; however, if the training and testing utterances use different texts, simple template matching is not possible. Section 11.4 describes common features extracted from speech signals that help distinguish speakers; some are based on physiological traits of vocal tracts, while others measure dynamic variations such as speaking style. Section 11.5 investigates the design of speaker identification systems, e.g., how data are collected and how the use of telephone speech affects system performance. Section 11.6 describes the related tasks of identifying the language being spoken and the accent of the speaker. The chapter ends with a comparison of how well humans and machines can identify speakers.

1.4 OTHER TOPICS

While the book surveys most major aspects of speech communication, of necessity certain areas are emphasized at the expense of others. For example, the developmental aspects of speech production and perception are not discussed. The interested reader is referred to reviews on biological development [5] as well as on phonetic and linguistic development [6, 7]. Also omitted for space reasons are discussions of impaired production and perception, that is, how the human speech mechanisms function in people with speech and hearing organs that are abnormal due to disease or injury [8].

2

Review of Mathematics for Speech Processing

One common factor among the chapters to follow is the concept of a *speech signal*, which mathematically represents speech, the acoustic output of a speaker's efforts. Human speakers and machine synthesizers produce speech signals, while human listeners and machine recognizers receive and analyze such signals. Because the analysis, processing, and synthesis of signals are the keys to much of speech communication, this chapter develops the mathematical tools necessary to understand signals and their manipulations. It is written as a concise review for an electrical or systems engineer, but should also be useful for readers who have little engineering background (such readers would also find basic calculus and linear algebra texts useful). The key mathematical concepts necessary for signal analysis are relatively few, and deal primarily with how to represent the energy components of signals in both time and frequency. The sections below attempt to summarize key ideas about energy, spectra, probability, and some circuit theory, all with the view toward speech applications.

2.1 MATHEMATICAL PRELIMINARIES

Before analyzing signals, we must start with a few basic definitions, concerning real and complex numbers, ways to graphically display complex numbers, and the means to arithmetically manipulate sets of numbers. Such issues appear in all types of speech processing.

2.1.1 Number Representations

Signals are typically defined in terms of quantities known as *variables*, e.g., amplitude and time. Such variables are often *continuous*, taking on any value from the set of real numbers, both positive and negative. For many applications, it is convenient to discuss pairs of real numbers as *complex numbers*. Any complex number can be expressed as $c = a + jb$, where a and b are real numbers and j is the unit *imaginary* number, defined as the square root of -1. The *complex conjugate* of c, denoted $c^* = a - jb$, is of interest because both cc^* and $c + c^*$ are purely real. Graphically, a complex number c can be viewed on a two-dimensional plot of *rectangular coordinates* (real number *axes*), often labelled *domain x* and *range y*, where the horizontal x axis extends infinitely in both negative and positive directions and represents the real part a. The vertical y axis, at a right angle to the x axis, has similar infinite extent and represents b, the imaginary part of c (Figure 2.1).

A circular or *polar coordinate* number representation is often useful. Both rectangular and polar systems use the same perpendicular axes and locate each number c at the same point, but the polar system interprets c in terms of the length and angle of a line *vector* drawn between the point c and the graph *origin* (where the axes cross, i.e., at $c = 0$). Relating the two coordinate systems,

$$c = a + jb = |c|e^{j\theta}, \tag{2.1}$$

where $|c|$ is the *magnitude* of c (the length of the vector) and θ (the *phase* of c) is its angle with respect to the x axis. (See below for $e = 2.1718\ldots$ and Euler's Rule.)

Consider forming a right triangle with the line vector to c and vertical and horizontal projections from c to each of the axes. The two representations of a complex c in terms of two real numbers, (a, b), and $(|c|, \theta)$, are related geometrically (via the Pythagorean theorem):

$$|c|^2 = a^2 + b^2 \qquad \text{and} \qquad \tan\theta = b/a, \tag{2.2}$$

where of course the *exponent* 2 means $a^2 = a \times a$. (Also $a^{-3} = 1/(a \times a \times a)$ and $a^{2/3} = a^2/a^3$.) As for trigonometric functions (e.g., sines and tangents), $\sin\theta = b/c$, $\cos\theta = a/c$, $\tan\theta = a/b$, $\cot\theta = b/a$, $\sec\theta = c/a$ and $\csc\theta = {'}c/b$.

2.1.2 Matrix Arithmetic

Most mathematical operations in this book involve manipulation of pairs of numbers or functions (e.g., addition, multiplication). While such *scalar* arithmetic is generally adequate, sometimes insight and computational efficiency are enhanced by grouping sets of numbers that must undergo the same operation. An ordered set of N numbers is called an N-dimensional *vector*. The set may be displayed vertically as a *column vector* or horizontally as a *row vector*; each is considered the *transpose* of the other. For example, using lowercase

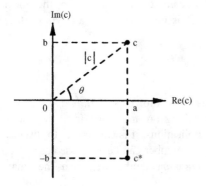

Figure 2.1 Representing a complex number on rectangular and polar coordinates. A complex number c and its conjugate c^* are plotted, with their real-number components noted.

letters in **boldface** notation to represent column vectors, consider a general three-dimensional vector:

$$\mathbf{x} = \begin{bmatrix} x_1 \\ x_2 \\ x_3 \end{bmatrix} \quad \text{and} \quad \mathbf{x}^T = [x_1 \quad x_2 \quad x_3],$$

where T indicates a transpose and x_i (for $i = 1, 2, 3$) are the *elements* of the vector.

Vectors are special cases of a more general set of numbers called a *matrix*, which groups numbers in a rectangular arrangement of rows and columns. An M-by-N matrix, having M rows and N columns, contains MN elements. Using boldface capital letters for matrices, we have

$$\mathbf{X} = \begin{bmatrix} x_{11} & x_{12} & x_{13} & \cdots & x_{1N} \\ x_{21} & x_{22} & x_{23} & \cdots & x_{2N} \\ \cdots & & & & \\ x_{M1} & x_{M2} & x_{M3} & \cdots & x_{MN} \end{bmatrix},$$

where x_{ij} are matrix elements with i indicating the row and j the column. Transposing an M-by-N matrix creates an N-by-M matrix, where x_{ji} replaces each x_{ij}:

$$\mathbf{X}^T = \begin{bmatrix} x_{11} & x_{21} & x_{31} & \cdots & x_{M1} \\ x_{12} & x_{22} & x_{32} & \cdots & x_{M2} \\ \cdots & & & & \\ x_{1N} & x_{2N} & x_{3N} & \cdots & x_{MN} \end{bmatrix}.$$

A column vector of N elements is simply an N-by-1 matrix, while its transposed row vector is a 1-by-N matrix.

Matrices and vectors can undergo mathematical operations similar to scalar operations, subject to certain dimensional restrictions. Typically, addition and subtraction of matrices involve pairwise operations between parallel elements, resulting in an output matrix of dimensions equal to those of the inputs. Thus, only matrices of identical dimensions may be added or subtracted. Consider two $M \times N$ matrices $\mathbf{X}$ and $\mathbf{Y}$:

$$\mathbf{X} - \mathbf{Y} = \begin{bmatrix} x_{11} - y_{11} & x_{12} - y_{12} & x_{13} - y_{13} & \cdots & x_{1N} - y_{1N} \\ x_{21} - y_{21} & x_{22} - y_{22} & x_{23} - y_{23} & \cdots & x_{2N} - y_{2N} \\ \cdots & & & & \\ x_{M1} - y_{M1} & x_{M2} - y_{M2} & x_{M3} - y_{M3} & \cdots & x_{MN} - y_{MN} \end{bmatrix}.$$

Multiplication of matrices usually is interpreted differently from forming element products pairwise. Matrix multiplication is not commutative (i.e., $\mathbf{XY} \neq \mathbf{YX}$) and requires that the number of columns in the first multiplicand equal the number of rows in the second. The product matrix $\mathbf{Z}$ of $\mathbf{X}$, an $L \times M$ matrix, and $\mathbf{Y}$, an $M \times N$ matrix, is $L \times N$ and has elements $z_{ij} = \sum_{k=1}^{M} x_{ik} j_{kj}$, i.e.,

$$\mathbf{Z} = \mathbf{XY} = \begin{bmatrix} x_{11}y_{11} + \cdots + x_{1M}y_{M1} & x_{11}y_{12} + \cdots + x_{1M}y_{M2} & \cdots & x_{11}y_{1N} + \cdots + x_{1M}y_{MN} \\ x_{21}y_{11} + \cdots + x_{2M}y_{M1} & x_{21}y_{12} + \cdots + x_{2M}y_{M2} & \cdots & x_{21}y_{1N} + \cdots + x_{2M}y_{MN} \\ & & & \cdots \\ & & & \cdots \\ x_{L1}y_{11} + \cdots + x_{LM}y_{M1} & x_{L1}y_{12} + \cdots + x_{LM}y_{M2} & \cdots & x_{L1}y_{1N} + \cdots + x_{LM}y_{MN} \end{bmatrix},$$

where $\sum_{k=1}^{M} x_k = x_1 + x_2 + x_3 + \cdots + x_M$.

The (multiplicative) *inverse* $\mathbf{Y}^{-1}$ of an $M \times N$ matrix $\mathbf{Y}$ is an $N \times M$ matrix defined such that $\mathbf{Y}\mathbf{Y}^{-1} = \mathbf{I}$, where $\mathbf{I}$ is an $M \times M$ *identity* matrix whose only nonzero elements are all ones and lie on the *main diagonal* (from upper left to lower right):

$$\mathbf{I} = \begin{bmatrix} 1 & 0 & 0 & \cdots & 0 \\ 0 & 1 & 0 & \cdots & 0 \\ 0 & 0 & 1 & \cdots & 0 \\ 0 & 0 & 0 & \ddots & 0 \\ 0 & 0 & 0 & \cdots & 1 \end{bmatrix}.$$

To divide a matrix $\mathbf{X}$ by another matrix $\mathbf{Y}$, we instead multiply $\mathbf{X}$ by $\mathbf{Y}^{-1}$. This is analogous to scalar division, where the division of a by b can be expressed as $a/b = ab^{-1}$, and $bb^{-1} = b/b = 1$.

The *determinant* $|\mathbf{X}|$ of a square $N \times N$ matrix $\mathbf{X}$ may be viewed intuitively as its scalar "magnitude" and is defined recursively in terms of component $(N - 1) \times (N - 1)$ matrices $\mathbf{X}_i$:

$$|\mathbf{X}| = \sum_{i=1}^{N}(-1)^{i+1}x_{1i}|\mathbf{X}_i|,$$

where $\mathbf{X}_i$ is obtained by eliminating the top row and the ith column of $\mathbf{X}$, e.g.,

$$\mathbf{X}_2 = \begin{bmatrix} x_{21} & x_{23} & x_{24} & \cdots & x_{2N} \\ x_{31} & x_{33} & x_{34} & \cdots & x_{3N} \\ \cdots & & & & \\ x_{M1} & x_{M3} & x_{M4} & \cdots & x_{MN} \end{bmatrix}.$$

Finally, a square matrix $\mathbf{X}$ is called *positive-definite* if $\mathbf{y}^T\mathbf{X}\mathbf{y} > 0$ for all $\mathbf{y} \neq \mathbf{0}$, a matrix of zeros.

2.2 SIGNALS AND LINEAR SYSTEMS

A *signal* is a function of time that specifies a unique value or *amplitude* for every instant of time. Such functions are described by a correspondence or *mapping*, relating one set of numbers (the independent variable, e.g., time) to another set (the dependent variable, e.g., amplitude). *Continuous* or *analog* signals map a real-valued continuous-time domain into a range of real or complex amplitudes. Notationally, $x(t)$ denotes both a signal in general and its value at any specific time t, where t may be any real number from $-\infty$ to $+\infty$. The time origin ($t = 0$) is usually defined relative to some event, such as the start of some speech activity. Speech signals, as portrayed (e.g., on an oscilloscope) by converting acoustic pressure at the mouth into variations in voltage via a microphone, are continuous in time and real-valued. The simplest representation of a signal is its *time waveform*, which displays a two-dimensional plot of the signal (amplitude) value on the y axis and time on the x axis (Figure 2.2).

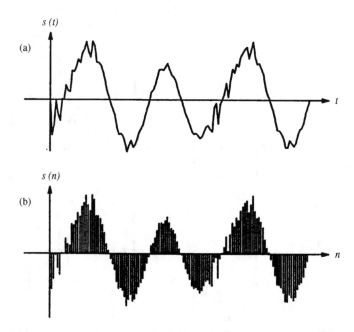

Figure 2.2   Time waveform of a continuous speech signal and its sampled (discrete-time) version (see Section 2.5 for a discussion of sampling).

2.2.1 Simple Signals

Because speech signals have complicated waveforms, they are usually analyzed in terms of simpler component signals. Examples of the latter are steps, impulses, sinusoids, and exponentials (Figure 2.3). A *step* has value zero for negative time and unity for positive time:

$$u(t) = \begin{cases} 0 & \text{for } t < 0 \\ 1 & \text{otherwise.} \end{cases} \tag{2.3}$$

The derivative of a step, an *impulse* $\delta(t)$, is a useful mathematical function having two properties: (a) $\delta(t) = 0$ for all $t \neq 0$, and (b) unit area ($\int \delta(t)dt = 1$). While an impulse is not physically realizable, it may be considered as the limit of a very narrow pulse whose width is inversely proportional to its height.

While an introduction to calculus is beyond the scope of this book, think of *integrals* and *derivatives* as inverse functions, where $\int_a^b x(t)dt$ = the area enclosed between vertical lines $t = a$ and $t = b$ and between $x(t)$ and the x axis (the area below the x axis counts negatively). If integral $y(t) = \int_{-\infty}^{t} x(s)ds$, then derivative $dy/dt = x(t)$; e.g., if $y(t)$ is the location of a car at time t, then $x(t)$ is its velocity.

Sinusoidal signals are periodic, oscillating functions of special interest owing to their simple spectral properties. A *periodic* signal repeats itself every cycle or *period* of T seconds (i.e., $p(t) = p(t + T)$). The *fundamental frequency* or repetition rate of such a signal is $F = 1/T$ in cycles/s or Hertz (Hz), or $2\pi/T$ in radians/s.* When a sinusoidal signal is associated with transmission, the distance it propagates during one period is called a

---

* Following standard abbreviations, s = second, ms = millisecond, m = meter, g = gram, cm = centimeter, and so on.

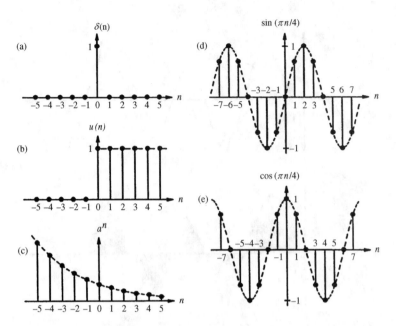

Figure 2.3 Time waveforms of an (a) impulse, (b) step, (c) exponential, (d) sine, and (e) cosine. Dashed lines show continuous-time signals; filled dots with vertical bars note corresponding discrete-time signals.

wavelength $\lambda = c/F$, where c is the signal speed (3×10^8 m/s for electrical or optical signals, but only 340 m/s for sound in air).

A sinusoid of frequency F is described in terms of sines and cosines, which are related as follows:

$$\sin(2\pi F t) = \cos(2\pi(F t - 0.25)).$$

The 0.25 term refers to a $\frac{1}{4}$-cycle delay between a sine and its cosine, i.e., a $90°$ *phase shift*. Consider a clock with one hand rotating at a uniform rate of $360°$ (a full cycle) every T seconds: if we take a line through 3 and 9 o'clock as an x axis, the projection of the tip of the hand onto this axis (e.g., a in Figure 2.1) would describe a sine waveform if the hand starts at 12 o'clock at $t = 0$. The projection (b in Figure 2.1) on the y axis (i.e., a line through 12 and 6 o'clock) describes a cosine. Treating each hour on the clock as $30°$, the relative rotation of the hand at $t = 0$ denotes the phase shift of the sinusoid. Other *transcendental functions*, besides sines and cosines, are defined as follows:

$$\tan(t) = \frac{\sin(t)}{\cos(t)}, \qquad \cot(t) = \frac{1}{\tan(t)},$$

$$\sec(t) = \frac{1}{\cos(t)}, \qquad \csc(t) = \frac{1}{\sin(t)}.$$

An *exponential* signal is one that increases (or decreases) in amplitude by a fixed percentage every time interval:

$$e(t) = a^t, \tag{2.4}$$

where a is called the *base*. Most often, a is either 10 or the natural constant $e = 2.71828\ldots$. For example, a natural exponential $e(t)$ with a *time constant* or *decay time* of τ seconds uniformly decays to 37% of its size $(1/e)$ every τ s:

$$e(t) = \exp(-t/\tau) = e^{-t/\tau}.$$

The inverse of an exponential is a *logarithm*: if $y = a^x$, then $x = \log_a(y)$.

Complex exponentials are related to sinusoids by Euler's theorem:

$$e^{j\theta} = \cos\theta + j\sin\theta, \tag{2.5}$$

where θ may be a function of time (see Equations (2.1) and (2.2)). This complex-valued exponential has a cosine as its real part and a sine of the same variable as its imaginary part. If $\theta = (2\pi F t) + \phi$, F is the frequency of the sinusoid or complex exponential, and ϕ is its *phase*. (In general, two physical or real signals may be combined for mathematical purposes to yield a complex-valued signal, as in Equation (2.5).)

From Equation (2.5) it follows that

$$\cos\theta = \frac{e^{j\theta} + e^{-j\theta}}{2} \qquad \text{and} \qquad \sin\theta = \frac{e^{j\theta} - e^{-j\theta}}{2j},$$

which suggests another set of functions called *hyperbolic functions*, for example:

$$\cosh(\theta) = \cos(j\theta) = \frac{e^{\theta} + e^{-\theta}}{2} \qquad \text{and} \qquad \sinh(\theta) = -j\sin(j\theta) = \frac{e^{\theta} - e^{-\theta}}{2}.$$

Many functions (e.g., sinusoids or exponentials) can be expressed as an infinitely long polynomial or *power series*:

$$f(y) = \sum_{k=0}^{\infty} \frac{f^{(k)}(0)}{k!} y^k,$$

where $k!$ (*k factorial*) is the product of all integers from 1 to k, and $f^{(k)}(0)$ is the kth derivative of $f(y)$ evaluated at $y = 0$. For example,

$$\sin(y) = y - \frac{y^3}{3!} + \frac{y^5}{5!} - \frac{y^7}{7!} \cdots. \tag{2.6}$$

Power series are especially useful for approximations when the terms in the series become increasingly smaller at higher powers of y; e.g., if $|y| < 1$, the ratio of the second and first terms in Equation (2.6) is $y^2/6 < 0.17$, the ratio of the third and first terms is $y^4/120 < 0.01$, etc., so that $\sin(y) \approx y - y^3/6$ to within $\pm 1\%$.

A signal may contain a large amount of information in the sense that many numbers or bits of information must be used to represent or reconstruct the signal. Signal processing often involves reducing signal information to a smaller set of features or parameters. One common signal feature is its *energy* E, which measures the signal intensity over a portion of time. The energy in a real signal $x(t)$ between times t_1 and t_2 is

$$E_x = \int_{t=t_1}^{t_2} x^2(t)dt.$$

2.2.2 Filtering and Convolution

Speech processing often employs *filters* to modify (e.g., attenuate or amplify), as a function of frequency, the energy in a signal. In their output or response, *lowpass* filters preserve only low-frequency components of an input signal, while *highpass* filters reduce energy at low frequencies. *Bandpass* and *bandstop* filters preserve or eliminate, respectively, signal components in specific ranges of frequencies. In this book, filters are assumed to be *linear*, which means that if inputs $x_1(t)$ and $x_2(t)$ yield $y_1(t)$ and $y_2(t)$, respectively, as outputs, then $Ax_1(t) + Bx_2(t)$ yields $Ay_1(t) + By_2(t)$ for all choices of constants A and B. We also typically assume *shift invariance* for nonadaptive filters; i.e., $x_1(t - T)$ yields $y_1(t - T)$ for all values of T.

A common measure of a filter is its *impulse response* $h(t)$, the output signal when we are given a simple impulse $\delta(t)$ as input. If the filter has *stationary* characteristics (i.e., not changing with time) and is linear, then the response $y(t)$ to a general input $x(t)$ is related to $h(t)$ through a commutative operation called *convolution* (denoted by $*$):

$$y(t) = x(t) * h(t) = \int_{\tau=-\infty}^{\infty} x(\tau)h(t - \tau)d\tau. \qquad (2.7)$$

While impulses do not exist physically, their extreme simplicity (nonzero at only one infinitesimally small time point) explains their common usage in mathematics.

2.3 FREQUENCY ANALYSIS

The aspects of speech signals that are most relevant to production and perception involve concepts of spectral frequency. When a speaker repeats a sentence, producing two utterances that sound identical, there are usually much larger differences in the two time waveforms than in corresponding spectral displays. In terms of time signals, speech analysis typically extracts only periodicity and energy measures. Much more relevant information can be obtained spectrally.

Periodic signals (e.g., vowels) are often analyzed in terms of sinusoidal components via *Fourier series*. Sinusoids are signals with energy at only one frequency, but each practical periodic signal $x_p(t)$ can be expressed as a linear combination of weighted sinusoids (noted here as complex exponentials, for convenience of simpler mathematical notation):

$$x_p(t) = \sum_{k=-\infty}^{\infty} c_k \exp(j2\pi kt/T), \qquad (2.8)$$

where T is the signal period and c_k is a (theoretically infinite) Fourier series of *coefficients* defined as

$$c_k = \int_{t=T_0}^{T+T_0} x_p(t) \exp(-j2\pi kt/T)dt,$$

where T_0 can be any constant. For the kth *harmonic* (multiple) of the fundamental frequency $1/T$, the complex-valued c_k notes the required amplitude and phase (see Equation (2.1)) of the sinusoidal component of frequency k/T Hz so that the sum of all the sinusoids equals $x_p(t)$. Periodic signals have a *discrete spectrum*, with energy only at multiples of the fundamental, where $|c_k|^2$ is the energy of the kth harmonic (see Figure 2.4).

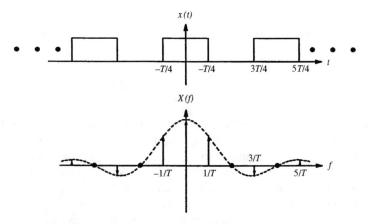

Figure 2.4   The time signal and discrete spectrum of a square wave (a simple periodic signal). The spectral envelope is $A \sin(\pi f T/2)/(\pi f T)$.

The role of the sinusoid or exponential in Equation (2.8) can be filled by other sets of *basis functions* $\phi_k(t)$ as long as they have the property of *orthogonality*:

$$\int_{t=T_0}^{T+T_0} \phi_i(t)\phi_j(t)dt = 0, \qquad \text{for all } i \neq j.$$

2.3.1 Fourier Transform

The principle of expressing time signals as sums of weighted sinusoids can be extended to *aperiodic* signals as well. Indeed, since all practical signals are of finite duration, we cannot limit our discussion to theoretical, periodic signals. The *Fourier transform* of a general signal $x(t)$ is

$$X(f) = \int_{t=-\infty}^{\infty} x(t)\exp(-j2\pi ft)dt. \qquad (2.9)$$

The Fourier transform is an invertible operation, with the inverse being

$$x(t) = \int_{f=-\infty}^{\infty} X(f)\exp(j2\pi ft)df. \qquad (2.10)$$

Thus no information is lost in these 1:1 reversible mappings. The transform of a filter's impulse response is called its *frequency response*.

Signals symmetric about their time or frequency origin (e.g., $x(t) = x(-t)$) are called *even*, while antisymmetric signals (e.g., $x(t) = -x(-t)$) are *odd*. If $x(t)$ is purely real, e.g., with physical signals such as speech, $X(f)$ is *conjugate symmetric* ($X(f) = X^*(-f)$) (its real part is even and its imaginary part is odd), and the frequency response is typically viewed only for positive frequencies.

The Fourier series can be viewed as a special case of the Fourier transform, if we allow $X(f)$ to have impulses. Using the series coefficients c_k, the Fourier transform of a periodic signal is

$$X_p(f) = \sum_{k=-\infty}^{\infty} c_k \delta(f - k/T).$$

Such a *discrete* spectrum is a weighted sequence or train of equally spaced impulses. From the similarity of Equations (2.9) and (2.10), we can infer that a periodic function in either the time or frequency domain has a transform that is a weighted impulse train. Thus, a periodic impulse train in time has a transform that is also a periodic impulse train. In particular, a uniform train of impulses, each of unit area and spaced at intervals of T s, transforms to another uniform impulse train, but with impulses spaced at intervals of $1/T$ Hz. This is an example of the inverse relationship between time and frequency: signals compact in one domain are proportionately spread out in the other.

Filtering or convolving two signals corresponds to multiplication of their Fourier transforms, i.e., if $y(t) = x(t) * h(t)$, then $Y(f) = X(f)H(f)$. This property is exploited when designing filters: a bandpass filter sets its response $H(f)$ to unity within desired frequency bands (ranges) and to zero for undesired frequencies. Another useful property of Fourier transforms is that a differentiated time signal $dx(t)/dt$ has a transform of $j2\pi f X(f)$.

2.3.2 Spectra and Correlation

The absolute value of a signal $x(t)$'s frequency response, $|X(f)|$, is called the *magnitude spectrum* or simply the spectrum of $x(t)$. For both filters and speech signals, the phase part $\theta(f)$ of $X(f) = |X(f)| \exp(j\theta(f))$ is often ignored as being much less important (for applications) than the spectrum. For signals with finite energy, the *power spectrum* $|X(f)|^2$ has a corresponding time-domain signal called the *autocorrelation*. Since $|X(f)|^2 = X(f)X^*(f)$, the inverse Fourier transform of $R(f) = |X(f)|^2$ is the convolution of $x(t)$ and $x^*(-t)$, which in the case of real signals ($x(t) = x^*(t)$) is

$$r(t) = \int_{\tau=-\infty}^{\infty} x(\tau)x(t + \tau)d\tau. \tag{2.11}$$

Autocorrelation $r(t)$ retains spectral information about $x(t)$ but loses phase detail; it effectively measures how similar $x(t)$ is to itself under different delays.

2.3.3 Laplace Transform: Poles and Zeros

The Fourier transform, a function of a real frequency variable f, is sometimes extended into two frequency dimensions via a *Laplace transform*:

$$X(s) = \int_{t=-\infty}^{\infty} x(t) \exp(-st)dt,$$

where s is complex-valued, $s = \sigma + j2\pi f$. Laplace transforms are primarily useful in explaining the spectral behavior of a signal. Many practical signals have Laplace transforms that are ratios of polynomials in s. For example, passive filters employing resistors, capacitors, and inductors connected in various series and parallel networks have input $x(t)$ and output $y(t)$ voltages and currents related by differential equations of the form

$$\sum_{k=0}^{N} a_k y^{(k)}(t) = \sum_{k=0}^{M} b_k x^{(k)}(t), \tag{2.12}$$

where $y^{(k)}(t)$ indicates the kth derivative of $y(t)$. Applying Laplace transforms to Equation (2.12), a *transfer function* relating input and output is

$$H(s) = \frac{Y(s)}{X(s)} = \frac{\displaystyle\sum_{k=0}^{M} b_k s^k}{\displaystyle\sum_{k=0}^{N} a_k s^k}. \tag{2.13}$$

The roots of the numerator and denominator polynomials are called *zeros* and *poles*, respectively, because $H(s)$ is zero at a zero frequency of the system and is infinitely large at a pole frequency. Evaluating $H(s)$ on the vertical axis (where $\sigma = 0$) of the s plane yields the Fourier transform $H(f)$. The magnitude $|H(f)|$ tends to dip or rise, respectively, as f nears a zero or a pole (e.g., as f approaches f_p, where $s = \sigma_p + j2\pi f_p$ is a pole or zero location). Such deviations are most pronounced when the pole or zero is close to the vertical axis and well away from opposite singularities (e.g., poles and zeros in proximity tend to cancel each other's effects).

2.4 CIRCUITS

In the past, most filters contained discrete components, e.g., resistors and capacitors. While signal analysis for today's digital filters does not require an understanding of the physical behavior of such components, in Chapter 3 it will be useful to model the vocal tract with such traditional elements, and thus a brief introduction to circuit theory follows.

Electrical circuits or networks consist of interconnections of elements and subnetworks, in which current flows from points of high voltage to points of low voltage (Figure 2.5). Often a reference voltage of zero is called *ground*. A typical component is linked to the network through wires at two or more *port* locations. Points at which components are connected are called *nodes*, and the sum of all currents flowing into each node equals the sum of those flowing out of that node (Kirchhoff's current law). If components are connected so that a closed loop is formed among nodes (i.e., current can flow from a node through components and back to the same node), the sum of voltage drops across the components in the loop is zero (Kirchhoff's voltage law).

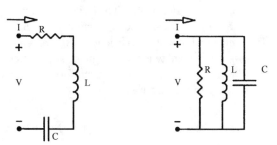

Figure 2.5   Simple *RLC* bandpass filters.

For two-port elements (e.g., resistors) (transistors have three ports), it is common to describe the relationship between the current I flowing through the element and the amount of voltage drop V from one port to the other. (In a case where the composition of a network is unknown, it may be called a *black box* and is usually described via V–I relationships among its ports.) By convention, V is obtained by subtracting the voltage at the port where current leaves from the voltage at the other port. A resistor has a simple linear V–I characteristic: $V = IR$, where R is a constant resistance with units of ohms. For a capacitor, $I = C\, dV/dt$, and for an inductor, $V = L\, dI/dt$, where the capacitance C (in farads) and the inductance L (in henries) are constants. In the latter cases, both voltage and current vary with time. Current is said to *lead* voltage in a capacitor and *lag* it in an inductor, where the phase differences are 90° in the case of sinusoidal signals.

Using Laplace transforms, the V–I functions can be expressed in the frequency domain: $I = CsV$ and $V = LsI$, since a time derivative multiplies the transform by s. Treating the ratio of voltage to current as an *impedance* Z to current flow, Z equals R for a resistor, $1/sC$ for a capacitor, and sL for an inductor. In *RLC* networks (i.e., circuits containing resistors, inductors and capacitors), inductors have low impedance at low signal frequencies, while capacitors have high impedance; the opposite occurs at high frequencies.

2.5 DISCRETE-TIME SIGNALS AND SYSTEMS

Physical signals (e.g., speech) are continuous in both time and amplitude; i.e., an *analog* $x_a(t)$ varies continuously, taking on a value from a (theoretically) uncountably infinite number of possible amplitudes at an uncountably infinite number of times t (i.e., amplitude and time values are real numbers). However, since virtually all applications of speech processing involve digital computers, which operate on discrete numbers at periodic clock cycles, continuous signals must be converted into number sequences. A *discrete-time sequence* $x(n)$ is defined to have a real (analog) value for every (discrete) integer value of n. To obtain a *digital signal*, the $x(n)$ values must also be quantized in amplitude via an analog-to-digital (A/D) converter, which represents each real $x(n)$ sample by a number selected from a finite set; e.g., for an 8-bit A/D converter, the set has $2^8 = 256$ numbers. Representing a real-valued sample by a digital sample adds distortion called *quantization noise*, which is inversely proportional to the size of the set of possible digital numbers used to represent a signal. This noise affects both signals and digital filter coefficients.

2.5.1 Sampling

The $x(n)$ sequence is typically obtained by *sampling* $x_a(t)$ at periodic intervals T (e.g., *clock cycles*): $x(n) = x_a(nT)$ (Figure 2.6). If $x_a(t)$ is lowpass filtered before sampling so that all its energy is below $0.5/T$ Hz, $x_a(t)$ can be perfectly reconstructed mathematically from the $x_a(nT)$ samples. (Reconstruction via a digital-to-analog (D/A) converter is imperfect due to practical limitations.) The *Nyquist theorem* requires that the sampling frequency $F_s = 1/T$ be greater than twice the highest signal frequency (having energy) to permit exact signal recovery. Sampling $x_a(t)$ at uniform time intervals T is equivalent to multiplying $x_a(t)$ by a uniform impulse train:

$$x_s(t) = x_a(t) \sum_{n=-\infty}^{\infty} \delta(t - nT) = \sum_{n=-\infty}^{\infty} x_a(nT)\delta(t - nT).$$

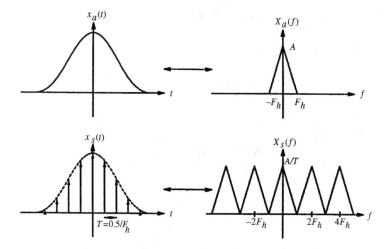

Figure 2.6 The time and frequency displays for sampling a section of a signal.

Since multiplication in one domain (e.g., time) corresponds to convolution in the other (frequency)

$$X_s(f) = X_a(f) * \frac{1}{T} \sum_{k=-\infty}^{\infty} \delta(f - k/T) = \frac{1}{T} \sum_{k=-\infty}^{\infty} X_a(f - k/T). \qquad (2.14)$$

If $X_a(f)$ is nonzero only for $|f| < 1/2T$, there is no *aliasing* (overlapping) in $X_s(f)$ of the copies of $X_a(f)$, which are repeated every $1/T$ Hz. Thus $X_a(f)$ (and hence $x_a(t)$) can be recovered by a simple lowpass filtering of $X_s(f)$ to eliminate all copies of $X_a(f)$ except that at zero frequency (i.e., the $k = 0$ copy in Eq. (2.14)) (Figure 2.6). Bandpass signals can also be efficiently sampled at low rates if the highest signal frequency is a multiple of the signal bandwidth; aliasing is avoided when $F_s \geq 2W$ for such signals with no energy below F_l Hz or above $F_l + W$ Hz.

Although sampling is restricted to signals of finite bandwidth (i.e., lowpass and bandpass), two basic continuous-time signals that contain high-frequency energy have discrete-time versions defined in similar fashion (see Figure 2.3). The discrete-time analog of a step $u(n)$ is zero for negative n and unity otherwise. The analog of an impulse, a *unit sample $\delta(n)$*, is zero except at $n = 0$, where it equals 1. A linear, shift-invariant filter is completely described by its unit-sample response $h(n)$. Passing a signal $x(n)$ through a filter of response $h(n)$ corresponds to discrete-time convolution, which is defined with summation replacing integration in Eq. (2.7), due to the discrete nature of the signals:

$$y(n) = x(n) * h(n) = h(n) * x(n) = \sum_{k=-\infty}^{\infty} x(k)h(n - k).$$

2.5.2 Frequency Transforms of Discrete-time Signals

For discrete-time signals, the Laplace transform is replaced by the z *transform*:

$$X(z) = \sum_{n=-\infty}^{\infty} x(n)z^{-n}, \tag{2.15}$$

where z is a complex frequency variable, usually defined in polar coordinates ($z = |z| \exp(j\omega)$), because the regions of the z plane for which the series in Equation (2.15) *converges* (i.e., sums to a finite value) involve circles in the z plane rather than the vertical lines in the s plane of Laplace transforms. For example, for an exponential $x(n) = a^n u(n)$ (often called "dying" if $|a| < 1$),

$$X(z) = \sum_{n=0}^{\infty} (az^{-1})^n,$$

which is a power series that converges to $1/(1 - az^{-1})$ if $|az^{-1}| < 1$ or $|z| > |a|$ (the region boundary is a circle of radius $|a|$). As in the continuous-time case, passing a discrete-time signal through a filter with unit-sample response $h(n)$ corresponds to multiplying the z transforms of the signal and $h(n)$.

By evaluating the z transform on a circle of unit radius ($z = \exp(j\omega)$ in Equation (2.15)) in the z plane, the *discrete-time Fourier transform* is obtained:

$$X(e^{j\omega}) = \sum_{n=-\infty}^{\infty} x(n)e^{-j\omega n}$$

because the vertical axis used in the s plane for continuous-time Fourier transforms maps into the z plane unit circle. For $x(n)$ obtained from the usual Nyquist sampling, the s and z planes are related by $z = \exp(sT)$, which maps horizontal strips of the s plane of frequency width $1/T$ into the entire z plane (Figure 2.7). Continuous-time frequencies f are mapped linearly into discrete-time radian frequencies ω by $\omega = 2\pi fT$. In discrete-time filters, "high" frequencies mean values of ω near π rad since $\omega = \pi$ corresponds to $1/2T$ Hz, the highest frequency represented with a sampling period of T without aliasing. For signals with energy above $1/2T$ Hz, aliasing corrupts $X(z)$ so that $X(s)$ cannot be recovered exactly. Other $s \leftrightarrow z$ mappings exist that avoid aliasing (e.g., the bilinear transformation, used in digital filter

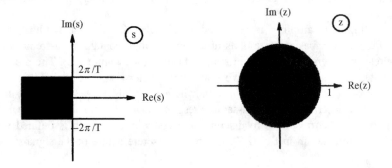

Figure 2.7   Illustration of a standard mapping between the s and z planes. The portion of one strip of the s plane that corresponds to the inside of the unit circle in the z plane is shaded.

design [1]), but this book assumes $z = \exp(sT)$, which corresponds to simple time-domain sampling and maps frequencies linearly.

Since the discrete-time Fourier transform is a continuous function of ω, it must be sampled for manipulation in digital computers. The *discrete Fourier transform* (DFT) serves this purpose:

$$X(k) = \sum_{n=0}^{N-1} x(n) \exp(-j2\pi kn/N). \tag{2.16}$$

Like the continuous-time Fourier transform, the DFT has an inverse of virtually identical form:

$$x(n) = (1/N) \sum_{n=0}^{N-1} X(k) \exp(j2\pi kn/N). \tag{2.17}$$

Equation (2.16) is called an N-point DFT because it accepts as input a sequence of only N samples (indexed in time n from 0 to $N-1$) and can be obtained from $X(e^{j\omega})$ by uniform sampling at $\omega = 2\pi k/N$ for $k = 0, 1, 2, \ldots, N-1$ (Figure 2.8). Due to the periodicity of $X(e^{j\omega})$, $X(k)$ is also periodic, with period N. Intuitively, the reason for limiting the DFT input to a finite range of N samples (which restricts the DFT to representing only a portion of an arbitrary time signal) is that N frequency samples $X(k), k = 0, 1, 2, \ldots, N-1$ can only model a signal with N degrees of freedom. Alternatively, sampling $X(e^{j\omega})$ every $2\pi k/N$ rad corresponds to convolving $x(n)$ with a unit-sample train of period N; aliasing and loss of accurate signal representation occur if $x(n)$ is not timelimited to N samples. If $x(n)$ is real-valued, the N DFT samples are conjugate symmetric, and only values for $k = 0, 1, 2, \ldots, N/2$ are normally displayed, since the other $(N/2) - 1$ samples are mirror images.

2.5.3 Decimation and Interpolation

Sometimes, speech processing manipulates one or more bandlimited portions of the discrete-time speech signal, instead of operating on the fullband speech. In such cases, it is computationally efficient to reduce the sampling and storage rate of the reduced-bandwidth signals. Since A/D conversion is relatively expensive compared to digital filtering, sampling rates are typically changed by manipulating discrete-time signals rather than by sampling a continuous-time signal several times at different rates.

Reducing the sampling rate of a signal $x(n)$ by a factor M is called $M:1$ *decimation*; increasing it is called $1:M$ *interpolation*. To decimate $x(n)$, we delete $M-1$ out of every M samples, i.e., $y(n) = x(Mn)$. This is equivalent to having sampled $x_a(t)$ originally every MT s

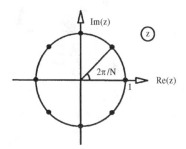

Figure 2.8 The frequencies at which the z transform is sampled to obtain an N-point discrete Fourier transform are noted in the case $N = 8$.

(assuming that $x(n) = x_a(nT)$). Aliasing problems arise unless $x(n)$ is sufficiently lowpass; in the range $|\omega| \leq \pi$, $X(e^{j\omega})$ must have energy limited to $|\omega| \leq \pi/M$ to avoid aliasing during $M:1$ decimation. This is readily seen by viewing the spectral effects of multiplying $x(n)$ by a unit-sample train of period M and then compressing the time axis: the first operation places copies of $X(e^{j\omega})$ every $2\pi/M$ rad, and the second expands the ω axis by a factor M (Figure 2.9). Typically, $x(n)$ is lowpass filtered prior to decimation since it is preferable to lose high-frequency information than to corrupt (via aliasing) information in the decimated signal.

Raising the sampling rate via interpolation is useful primarily to reconstruct fullband signals from several decimated signals (e.g., after they have been individually processed). To interpolate $x(n)$ by a factor M, a series of $M-1$ zero-valued samples is inserted after every original sample; that is, the time axis is expanded:

$$y(n) = \begin{cases} x(n/M) & \text{for } n = 0, \pm M, \pm 2M, \pm 3M, \ldots, \\ 0 & \text{otherwise} \end{cases}$$

Spectrally, interpolation compresses the ω axis by a factor M: $Y(e^{j\omega}) = X(e^{j\omega M})$ (Figure 2.10). Assuming that interpolation should be the inverse of decimation (i.e., except for the

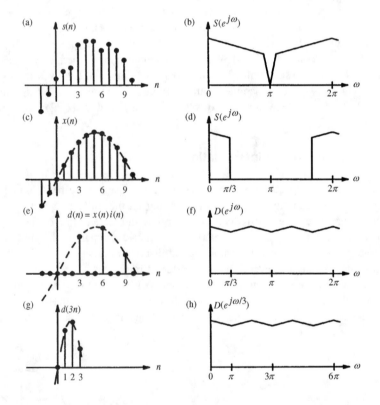

Figure 2.9 Decimation in the time and frequency domains: (a, b) a short section of a speech signal and its Fourier transform; (c, d) the same signals after lowpass filtering to preserve only $(1/M)$th of the original bandwidth ($M = 3$ is used to illustrate); (e, f) multiplying $x(n)$ by a uniform sample train $i(n)$ of period M aliases M copies of $X(e^{j\omega})$; (g, h) the time axis is compressed and the frequency axis expanded, both by the factor M.

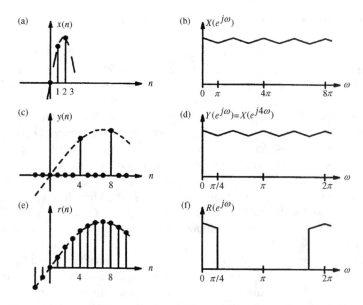

Figure 2.10   Interpolation in the time and frequency domains: (a, b) a signal $x(n)$ and its Fourier transform (for convenience, the final signals in Figure 2.9 are used); (c, d) expanding the time axis and compressing the frequency axis by a factor N (here, $N = 4$); (e, f) lowpass filtering with a cutoff of π/N rad preserves the shape of the original $x(n)$.

lowpass filtering prior to decimation to avoid aliasing, decimation followed by interpolation by the same factor should not change a signal), the zero-insertion operation must be followed by a lowpass filter with cutoff of π/M rad. This *interpolation filter* smooths the waveform, to have the same shape as the signal before interpolation. Viewed in terms of analog signals, interpolated discrete-time signals are *oversampled* beyond the Nyquist rate by a factor M.

The prior discussion assumes that M is an integer. To change sampling rates by a fractional factor, e.g., M/N, a signal is first interpolated ($M - 1$ zeros inserted after each sample), then lowpass filtered (with a cutoff of π/M or π/N, whichever is smaller), and finally only every Nth sample is retained.

2.6 FILTERS

Filters are the basic elements of most speech processing systems. In coding and recognition, speech analysis often selects, attenuates, or amplifies energy in certain frequency bands. Speech synthesizers frequently consist of filters, each simulating a vocal tract resonance. For the purposes of this book, a *filter* is a linear device that transforms an input signal into an output signal. A simple amplifier is a degenerate case of a filter that (theoretically) preserves phase and raises equally the amplitudes of all frequency components of an input signal. Nonlinear devices, e.g., rectifiers (which yield the magnitude of a signal, $y(t) = |x(t)|$), are used in some processing, but are not considered filters.

2.6.1 Bandpass Filters

For many applications, an ideal filter would pass certain frequencies without modification (i.e., have a *gain* of 1) and totally eliminate other frequencies (a gain of zero). Although such a filter cannot be realized physically, close approximations to the ideal are possible. Bandpass filters are usually designed so that (a) the gains in the passbands are within a certain percentage of unity, (b) the gains in the stopbands are below a certain small amount, and (c) the widths of the *transition bands* or *filter skirts* (the frequency ranges between stopbands and passbands) are small. Better filters have skirts with steeper slopes. Slopes are often expressed in decibels/octave (dB/oct), where *octave* is a doubling of frequency and *decibel* is a logarithmic unit of amplitude. An amplitude factor of A (e.g., a filter that amplifies a 6 V input into a $6A$ V output) corresponds to $20 \log_{10} A$ dB. When dealing with energy or power, which varies as the square of amplitude, a factor of $B = A^2$ means $10 \log_{10} B$ dB since $\log(A^2) = 2 \log A$. Logarithmic amplitude scales are common for representing signals of large dynamic range.

The frequency selectivity of a bandpass filter is sometimes noted by Q, the ratio of the center frequency of the passband to its *bandwidth*. Bandwidth is usually measured at *half-power points*, where the filter gain is $1/\sqrt{2}$ of its maximal gain (i.e., 3 dB lower); i.e., if $|H(f_c)| = C$ at the center f_c of the passband and the spectrum falls monotonically to a value of $C/\sqrt{2}$ at f_1 and f_2 (below and above f_c, respectively), the bandwidth is $(f_2 - f_1)$ Hz.

The simplest bandpass filter is a three-component RLC filter with the elements in a single path (in *series* or *cascade*) or with all elements connected to two nodes (in *parallel*) (see Figure 2.5). If we treat circuit voltage as an input and current as an output, gain is largest in a series circuit when impedance is minimal; *resonance* is said to occur at this frequency. (For parallel circuits, the current is viewed as input, and resonance occurs when impedance is maximal.) To evaluate impedance in terms of frequency f, replace s in the impedance formulas of Section 2.4 with $j2\pi f$. In series, the circuit impedance is $Z_s = R + j2\pi f L + 1/(j2\pi f C)$, while in parallel the relationship is described in terms of inverse impedances (*admittances*):

$$Y_p = \frac{1}{Z_p} = \frac{1}{R} + \frac{1}{j2\pi f L} + j2\pi f C.$$

The magnitudes of Z_s and Y_p are minimal near $f = (2\pi\sqrt{LC})^{-1}$.

2.6.2 Digital Filters

Continuous-time filters contain RLC elements, transistors, diodes, and other analog components. They tend to be bulky, hard to design precisely, and not easily modified. Implementations of discrete-time systems via digital computers, on the other hand, are increasingly compact. Advances in VLSI (very-large-scale integration) design continue unabated, following an informal *Moore's Law*: a doubling of available chip capacity about every 18 months. Digital processing is limited in precision only by the number of bits assigned to each signal sample, and programmable filters are easily modified. Most digital filters consist of only three elements: (1) an adding device that sums two inputs every clock cycle, (2) a multiplier that scales its single input by a constant factor every cycle, and (3) a delay that simply passes its input on as output after one cycle (Figure 2.11).

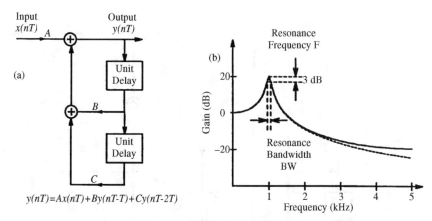

Figure 2.11   A digital bandpass filter: (a) implementation with adders, multipliers, and delays; (b) frequency responses of the digital filter (solid line) and a continuous-time counterpart (dotted line).

   Digital filters are typically displayed as flow diagrams with an input signal at a port on the left and an output on the right. Each multiplier appears as a circle or an arrow, labeled with the value of the multiplier coefficient or scale factor. An addition is shown as a circle with a plus sign or simply as a node with two (or more) inputs. A node with more than one output signifies that the signal is sent down multiple paths. A delay is usually noted as a box or arrow labeled z^{-1}, i.e., the z transform of a delayed unit sample (the unit-sample response of this delay "filter"). The transfer function relating the z transform of a filter's input to that of its output is thus easily determined from simple network evaluation.

2.6.3 Difference Equations and Filter Structures

   Signal behavior in continuous-time filters is often represented by differential equations (e.g., Equation (2.12)) because of the time-differential relationships of voltage and current in capacitors and inductors. These lead to transfer functions of ratios of polynomials in s (Equation (2.13)), which in turn facilitate spectral interpretation via poles and zeros. The parallel situation for discrete-time signals involves *difference equations* of the form

$$y(n) = \sum_{k=1}^{N} a_k y(n-k) + \sum_{k=0}^{M} b_k x(n-k), \tag{2.18}$$

where output $y(n)$ is the sum of N delayed and weighted output samples and $M+1$ delayed and weighted input samples. The *order* of the filter is the maximum of M and N, the number of feedforward and feedback paths. After being delayed k samples but before summing, each input and output sample is multiplied by a constant *coefficient*, a_k or b_k, respectively. Figure 2.12 shows two digital filters whose *direct-form* structure follows immediately from Equation (2.18). The series of delays is sometimes called a *delay line*, and the multiply branches are *taps*. In theory, filters in cascade can be reordered without affecting the overall input–output relationship because time convolution is commutative. Exchanging the order of the two subfilters in Figure 2.12(a) leads to the more efficient structure in Figure 2.12(b), which uses fewer delay elements or memory, without affecting the overall filter response.

   In practice, however, the effects of quantization noise are nonlinear, and filter ordering can be important. The noise arises from clipping or truncating the results of addition and

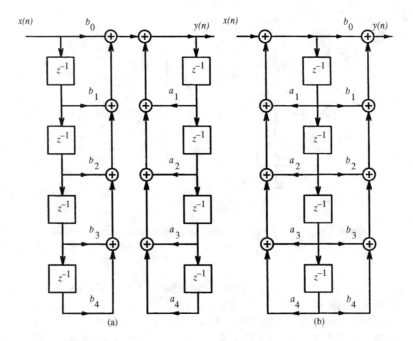

Figure 2.12   Two direct-form implementations of a fourth-order digital filter: (a) following the difference equation exactly; (b) with minimal use of delay elements.

multiplication to fit into finite-length computer registers. For example, the product of two 8-bit numbers contains 16 bits, whose least significant 8 bits must be dropped to fit into an 8-bit word for the next filter step. Distortion effects increase with the order of the filter. Thus, to minimize filter sensitivity to digital quantization, most applications strive to use first- and second-order filters. Second-order filters are necessary to keep the arithmetic simple because real-valued signals often have complex poles and zeros that occur in conjugate pairs; pairing them up in second-order filters allows all multipliers to be real.

High-order filters can be realized with low-order subfilters by placing the latter in cascade or in parallel (Figure 2.13). By taking z transforms of Equation (2.18), we obtain the transfer function of a general digital filter:

$$H(z) = \frac{Y(z)}{X(z)} = \left(\sum_{k=0}^{M} b_k z^{-k} \right) \bigg/ \left(-\sum_{k=1}^{N} a_k z^{-k} \right),   \tag{2.19}$$

where a_0 is assumed to be 1 for simplicity. By factoring the numerator and denominator polynomials into first- and second-order polynomials with real coefficients, $H(z)$ can be expressed as the product of ratios of polynomials of order no greater than two; e.g., if $M = N = 4$,

$$H(z) = \left(\frac{\sum_{k=0}^{2} c_{1k} z^{-k}}{1 - \sum_{k=1}^{2} d_{1k} z^{-k}} \right) \left(\frac{\sum_{k=0}^{2} c_{2k} z^{-k}}{1 - \sum_{k=1}^{2} d_{2k} z^{-k}} \right).$$

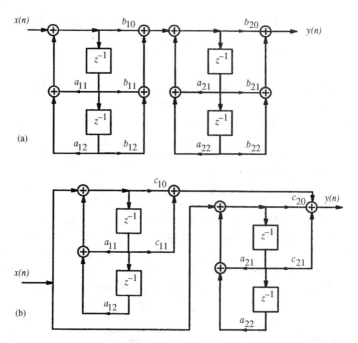

Figure 2.13   Examples of a fourth-order digital filter, implemented using second-order subfilters (a) in cascade and (b) in parallel.

Alternatively, a parallel set of second-order filters can be selected by factoring only the denominator and determining individual low-order polynomials for the numerator by a technique called *partial fraction expansion* [4]:

$$H(z) = \left(\frac{\sum\limits_{k=0}^{1} e_{1k}z^{-k}}{1 - \sum\limits_{k=1}^{2} d_{1k}z^{-k}} \right) + \left(\frac{\sum\limits_{k=0}^{1} e_{2k}z^{-k}}{1 - \sum\limits_{k=1}^{2} d_{2k}z^{-k}} \right).$$

Some applications require passing or attenuating a large number of equally spaced frequencies, e.g., harmonics in a periodic signal. Filters with many equally spaced passbands and stopbands are known as *comb filters*. In discrete-time filters, a delay line with M delays but only two taps, one at each end of the delay line, yields a simple approximation to a comb filter: $H(z) = 1 - z^{-M}$ has M zeros in the z plane, all on the unit circle and uniformly spaced every $2\pi/M$ rad. Thus a signal passing through such a filter will have energy attenuated at frequency multiples of $2\pi/M$ rad.

2.7 PROBABILITY AND STATISTICS

Communication is the transmission of information from one place to another. The receiver may have prior knowledge or statistics about the sent information, but the latter is not completely predictable. Describing information in terms of signals involves aspects of probability theory. Indeed, all aspects of speech communication have phenomena that are best determined probabilistically:

(a) In speech production, articulator muscles move in response to thousands of neural commands, which can only be coarsely related to the speech message being communicated; no two speech signals are exactly alike, due to minute statistical variations in muscle commands and execution.

(b) The auditory system converts acoustical vibrations from speech into neural firings in the inner ear in a partly random fashion.

(c) In coding, speech signals must be quantized for digital representations. Quantization effects are usually modeled as effectively adding random noise to the original signal. Modeling the time behavior and amount of energy in such noise requires elementary probability theory.

(d) Speech analysis (e.g., for automatic recognition) often requires averaging data for more efficient and robust speech representations. Measuring the variability of such data also helps to determine their reliability for use in making recognition decisions. Such estimation of averages and variances involves simple statistics.

(e) Speaker recognition can involve decisions based on statistics of many parameters extracted from speech signals. To measure the interdependence of these parameters, the concepts of joint and conditional probability are important.

2.7.1 Probability Densities and Histograms

A basic probability event involves an experiment that may have one of N possible outcomes. On any given trial of the experiment, the outcome is unpredictable but can be described statistically; e.g., when a fair die is tossed, there is a one-sixth chance for each of the six faces to appear. Letting X be the number of the face that appears, the *probability density function* (pdf) describing this experiment (Figure 2.14) is

$$\text{Prob}[X = x] = p_X(x) = \begin{cases} 1/6 & \text{for } x = 1, 2, 3, 4, 5, 6, \\ 0 & \text{otherwise.} \end{cases}$$

X is called a *random variable*, and the sum of all its probabilities is unity.

In many physical systems, the pdf of an experiment is not known but must be estimated from observations. If the experiment is repeated enough times, a statistical *histogram* approximates the actual pdf. A histogram plots the frequency of occurrence of an event as a function of some index of the event; in the case of a random variable X, X itself is the index. If a die is tossed exactly 6 times, the probability that each face appears once is less than 2% ($5!/6^5$); thus with few trials, a face might be incorrectly assumed to never occur. A histogram based on few trials is a poor approximation to the pdf. If, on the other hand, the die is tossed

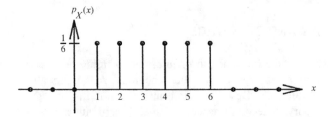

Figure 2.14 Probability density function for a toss of a fair die.

1000 times, it is very likely that each face will appear about 167 times (plus or minus a few), a more accurate percentage estimate.

In speech processing, the set of possible outcomes is often very large, unlike the simple six-outcome case of the die. A speech measurement at a given time (e.g., energy near a certain frequency) has a theoretically infinite number of possible values. Many probability densities are defined for *continuous* random variables, which may take on values of any real number, as opposed to *discrete* variables, which have nonzero probability only at discrete intervals (e.g., integers 1–6 in the die case). For a continuous random variable X, the probability of X having a specific outcome is usually infinitesimally small; so we talk instead of the probability of X occurring in a finite range called a *bin* (δ):

$$\text{Prob}[x \leq X < x + \delta] = \int_{\alpha=x}^{x+\delta} p_X(\alpha)d\alpha.$$

In practice, the finite resolution of all measuring devices limits the number of outcomes for continuous signals such as speech; for example, a measurement stored in an 8-bit register has only 256 ($= 2^8$) possibilities. A histogram with such a large number of values on the horizontal axis is hard to interpret. In such cases, the axis is usually compressed so that each plotted point represents a set of similar outcomes. For example, in the 8-bit case, the least significant 2 bits might be ignored, averaging contiguous sets of 4 points to plot only 64 values in the histogram. As the *bin width* increases from 1 to 4, the scale of the vertical axis (relative percentages) increases proportionately and the histogram becomes smoother in appearance. Bin widths are often 5–10% of the range, so that 10–20 classes are displayed.

2.7.2 Averages and Variances

The two most useful statistics of a random variable X are its *mean* or average, $\bar{X}$, and its *variance*, σ_X^2. $\bar{X}$ indicates the most typical value for X, and σ_X^2 measures how much variation X exhibits. Both values are defined in terms of a weighted average (weighted by the probability density), where $E(g(X)) = \overline{g(X)}$ is the average or *expected value* of a function g of the random variable X. Consider a discrete pdf $p_X(x)$ that is nonzero only at integer values of X:

$$E[g(X)] = \overline{g(X)} = \sum_{i=-\infty}^{\infty} g(i)p_X(i), \tag{2.20}$$

where $g(i)p_X(i)$ is evaluated for all possible integers i and the products summed. To calculate $\bar{X}$ from Equation (2.20), we simply use the identity function $g(X) = X$; for the variance σ_X^2, let $g(X) = (X - \bar{X})^2$. Thus the mean is the probability-weighted average of the set of outcomes for X, and the variance is a weighted average of the square of the deviation of X from its mean. The square root of the variance is called the *standard deviation* σ_X.

2.7.3 Gaussian Probability Density

Many physical measurements of probabilistic systems (e.g., speech production) tend to have histograms with most values relatively tightly clustered about a mean, with rapidly

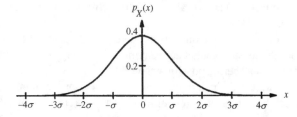

Figure 2.15 Plot of the Gaussian probability density. The peak value coincides with the mean, and one standard deviation is noted.

decreasing probability as the distance from the mean increases. Such systems are often modeled well by the *Gaussian density* (Figure 2.15)

$$p_X(X) = \frac{1}{\sqrt{2\pi}\sigma_X}\exp\left(\frac{-(X-\bar{X})^2}{2\sigma_X^2}\right),$$

which has the property that X is within one standard deviation of the mean on 68% of the trials and 95% within $\pm 2\sigma_X$. Each Gaussian has the nice property of being fully specified by just two numbers, its mean and variance. Although the Gaussian density employs a continuous random variable, it is easily applied to discrete random variables by dividing up the range for X into uniform bins (e.g., every y units of X) and defining a discrete random variable Z with density

$$p_Z(z) = \int_{\alpha=z-y/2}^{z+y/2} p_X(\alpha)d\alpha.$$

2.7.4 Joint Probability

Often probabilistic events are related to one another; e.g., if a speech signal has large amplitude at time t_1, it is likely to continue to be intense for times t_i soon afterward. Some events, however, have no effect on one another, and knowledge of one event yields no information about the other; i.e., the events are *independent*. The relationship between probabilistic events is often described by a *joint probability*: Prob[A, B] is the likelihood of events A and B both occurring.

The effect of one event on another is measured via *conditional probability*: Prob[$A|B$] is the probability of event A, given that event B occurs. A joint probability can be noted as the product of a conditional probability and the probability of the event the first probability is conditioned on:

$$\text{Prob}[A, B] = \text{Prob}[A|B]\text{Prob}[B] = \text{Prob}[B|A]\text{Prob}[A].$$

Bayes' rule follows directly:

$$\text{Prob}[A|B] = \frac{\text{Prob}[B|A]\text{Prob}[A]}{\text{Prob}[B]}.$$

If events A and B are independent,

$$\text{Prob}[A|B] = \text{Prob}[A] \quad \text{and} \quad \text{Prob}[B|A] = \text{Prob}[B],$$

$$\text{Prob}[A, B] = \text{Prob}[A]\text{Prob}[B].$$

These relationships hold as well for random variables.

2.7.5 Noise

In all electrical circuits and transmission systems, signals are corrupted by noise distortion, similar in effect and nature to the quantization noise in digital filters. Noise is usually modeled as a random signal that is added to the signal of interest; e.g., speech transmission over telephone lines typically is subject to additive, continuous low-level background noise as well as other dynamic distortions.

Probabilistic signals such as noise are extensions of random variables called *random processes*. Such a process $X(t)$ can be viewed either as a randomly chosen time signal or as an infinite series of random variables indexed on time t. In speech applications, noise is usually viewed as an additive signal, independent of the speech signal. Measuring the energy (as a function of frequency) in the noise component of a signal, relative to the energy in the speech part, is of prime interest. Fourier transforms cannot directly handle random signals, but instead operate on autocorrelations of such signals. The autocorrelation of a stationary random process $X(t)$ is

$$R_X(\tau) = E[X(t)X(t + \tau)],$$

where the expectation E treats $X(t)$ and $X(t + \tau)$ as random variables whose joint density can be obtained. $R_X(\tau)$ is a deterministic function and has the same interpretation as the autocorrelation of deterministic signals (Equation (2.11)). Its Fourier transform, the *power spectrum* $S_X(f)$, can be intuitively viewed as the square of the magnitude of the spectrum of a typical random signal.

Many cases of noise are modeled as *white noise*, $W(t)$, which has a flat power spectrum (i.e., constant $S_X(f)$), with equal energy at all frequencies. The inverse Fourier transform of a constant is an impulse ($R_W(\tau) = A\delta(\tau)$), which implies that samples of white noise at different times are uncorrelated and independent. Due to the mathematical simplicity of white noise, both quantization noise created in a speech coder and channel noise added during transmission are often viewed as white noise, even though such spectra are bandlimited in practice.

Integrating the power spectrum over a frequency range of interest yields a measure of the average energy in a random signal at those frequencies. The ratio of the average energy in an uncorrupted signal (e.g., speech prior to coding or transmission) to the average energy in noise that later distorts the signal is called the *signal-to-noise ratio* (SNR).

2.8 SUMMARY

Further detail on the subjects introduced in this review chapter can be found in references on the following topics: digital signal processing [1,2], probability [3], signals and systems [4], and linear algebra (matrices) [5].

3

Speech Production and Acoustic Phonetics

3.1 INTRODUCTION

Speech serves to communicate information from a speaker to one or more listeners. Mechanisms to produce speech in humans have evolved over many years, yielding a vocal system that is efficient in this information transfer and allows the speaker to use a minimum of effort. The speaker produces a *speech signal* in the form of pressure waves that travel from the speaker's head to the listener's ears. This signal consists of variations in pressure as a function of time and is usually measured directly in front of the mouth, the primary sound source (although sound also comes from the nostrils, cheeks, and throat). The amplitude variations correspond to deviations from atmospheric pressure caused by traveling waves. The signal is *nonstationary* (time-varying), changing characteristics as the muscles of the vocal tract contract and relax. Speech can be divided into *sound segments*, which share some common acoustic and articulatory properties with one another for a short interval of time. Since the speaker wishes to produce a sound sequence corresponding to the message to be conveyed, most major vocal tract movements have a voluntary basis. For each sound, there is a positioning for each of the vocal tract *articulators*: *vocal folds* (or *cords*), *tongue*, *lips*, *teeth*, *velum*, and *jaw* (Figures 3.1 and 3.7). Sounds are typically divided into two broad classes: (a) *vowels*, which allow unrestricted airflow in the vocal tract, and (b) *consonants*, which restrict airflow at some point and have a weaker intensity than vowels.

After a preparatory inhalation of air into the lungs, speech is produced as air is exhaled (speech while inhaling is very rare [1]). Changes in articulatory positions influence this *pulmonic egressive* airstream (so-called because the air leaves the lungs). Speech production can be viewed as a filtering operation in which a sound source excites a vocal tract filter; the source may be either periodic, resulting in *voiced* speech, or noisy and aperiodic, causing *unvoiced* speech. The voicing source occurs in the larynx, at the base of the vocal tract, where airflow can be interrupted periodically by vibrating vocal folds. The pulses of air produced by the *abduction* and *adduction* (opening and closing, respectively) of the folds generate a periodic excitation for the vocal tract. Roughly proportional to the glottal area, the pulse

35

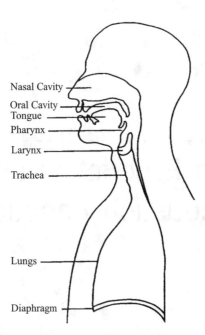

Nasal Cavity
Oral Cavity
Tongue
Pharynx
Larynx
Trachea
Lungs
Diaphragm

Figure 3.1 The speech organs. (After Sonesson [3], 1968, "The functional anatomy of the speech organs," *Manual of Phonetics*, B. Malmberg [North Holland: Amsterdam].)

volume (vs time) resembles half a sine wave, with the glottal closure more abrupt than its opening. Small deviations from a periodic, smooth pulse waveform (due to nonlinearities in the vocal tract) are likely an aspect of the naturalness of human speech (that synthesizers have difficulty replicating) [2].

Unvoiced speech is noisy due to the random nature of the signal generated at a narrow constriction in the vocal tract for such sounds. For both voiced and unvoiced excitation, the vocal tract, acting as a filter, amplifies certain sound frequencies while attenuating others.

As a periodic signal, voiced speech has spectra consisting of *harmonics* of the *fundamental frequency* of the vocal fold vibration; this frequency, often abbreviated F0, is the physical aspect of speech corresponding to perceived pitch. The harmonics are energy concentrations at multiples of F0. A truly periodic signal has a discrete-line spectrum, but since the vocal tract changes shape almost continually, voiced sounds are instead only locally *quasi-periodic* (almost periodic). Whether or not the speech signal is voiced, its characteristics (e.g., spectral amplitudes) are often relatively fixed or *quasi-stationary* over short periods of time (tens of milliseconds) as one sound is produced, but the signal varies substantially over intervals greater than the duration of a distinct sound (typically 80 ms).

Time waveform displays of speech (Figure 3.2) are used to discover aspects of the signal, e.g., its periodicity, the durations and boundaries of individual sounds, and amplitude relationships in sound sequences. Several important aspects of speech can be noted: (a) the quasi-periodicity of voiced speech during vowels and some consonants; (b) the wide range of amplitudes and frequency content in different sounds, e.g., vowels with large, low-frequency waveforms and fricatives with weak, high-frequency signals; (c) the tendency of the signal to gradually change pattern between sounds. Speech is not a sequence of steady-state sounds, abruptly changing from one to the next. The transition between most pairs of sounds is quite gradual; the signal slowly changes from the characteristics of one sound to those of the next. Even in cases of relatively sudden transitions, additional small signal changes often occur just before or after the abrupt discontinuity. Changes in the shape of the speech signal,

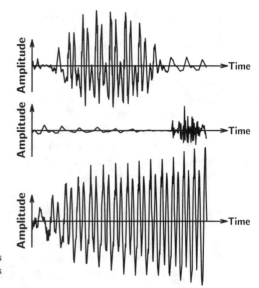

Figure 3.2 A speech signal corresponding to the words "the goo...." Each plot shows successive 100 ms segments.

whether gradual or abrupt, result from movements of the vocal tract articulators, which rarely stay fixed in position for more than 40 ms at a time (except perhaps in careful, slow speech).

This chapter is limited to human speech; a broader class of *vocalizations* includes sounds from animals and infants, which will not be discussed here. Section 3.2 describes the articulators; Section 3.3 explores the relationships between vocal tract configurations and the sounds they produce. Section 3.4 discusses the acoustic properties of phonemes. Section 3.5 details the mathematics relating speech signals and spectra to models of speech production; Section 3.6 formulates practical digital versions of these models. Section 3.7 addresses the effects of context on human speech production, and Section 3.8 examines intonation.

3.2 ANATOMY AND PHYSIOLOGY OF THE SPEECH ORGANS

Unlike the ear, which has evolved expressly for hearing, organs used in speech production share speech with other body functions (breathing, eating, and smelling) [3–6]. The multiple roles of these organs suggest that they may not have evolved to be as optimal a source (in a communication sense) as might have occurred if they were dedicated to speech. (To accommodate the complexities of speech, the human vocal tract is less efficient in breathing and eating than that of our ancestors.)

In electronic communications, an optimal source creates a signal with the least energy and shortest duration possible to convey information reliably, subject to the bandwidth and noise constraints of a transmission channel. Many parallels exist between electronic and human speech communication. Much of speech production can be interpreted in communication terms of minimizing effort ("energy" and time, in some sense), while maximizing perceptual contrast [7]. The bandwidth of human speech communication is approximately the frequency range up to 7 kHz, because both production and perception organs are most efficient at these low frequencies.

3.2.1 The Lungs and the Thorax

The speech organs can be divided into three main groups: lungs, larynx, and vocal tract (while the term *vocal tract* can refer to the whole system, our use includes only the supralaryngeal articulators) (Figure 3.1). The lungs are the source of an airflow that passes through the larynx and vocal tract, before leaving the mouth as pressure variations constituting the speech signal. Situated in the chest or *thorax* cavity, the lungs primarily serve breathing, inspiring and expiring a *tidal volume* of air (about 0.5 liter) every 3–5 s at rest. Normal exhaling takes about 60% of each breathing cycle. Breathing is accomplished primarily with the *diaphragm* at the bottom of the thorax; the contraction of the diaphragm expands the lungs, and relaxation of the diaphragm allows the elastic recoil of the lungs and ribs to expel air. *Intercostal* (rib) and abdominal muscles also aid breathing: the external intercostals pull the rib cage up and outward for inhaling, and internal intercostal muscles pull the ribs together to help exhalation. (The internal muscles of each organ lie entirely within the organ, whereas its external muscles connect the organ to other organs.) Airflow patterns differ for speaking and for normal breathing. Since all sounds in English (and most sounds in virtually all languages) are formed during expiration (*egressive* sounds), it is more efficient to spend greater time exhaling than inhaling—typical input:output ratios are 1:10, but they can be up to 1:30 in long-winded cases [4]. Speech while inspiring (e.g., gasps of surprise, infant cries) is much less efficient than egressive speech [8].

Much rarer *ingressive* sounds (e.g., clicks) are caused by inward airflow due to sucking actions (such as kissing) [1,9,10]. Closing off a section of the vocal tract at two locations and then causing the volume in such a cavity to increase creates a drop in pressure for the cavity with respect to the outside air. An abrupt release of the closure between the cavity and the outside air allows a sudden inward air movement causing a sound burst. *Ejectives* follow an opposite path: raising the larynx in such a closed system causes pressure build-up prior to an oral release [11].

Sound amplitude increases with airflow rate. To produce speech of several seconds, more than 0.5 l (500 cm^3) of air must be expelled. Typical resting lung volume is about 4–5 l for an adult male, of which about 1–2 *residual* liters cannot be expelled. The maximal difference (*vital capacity*) between fully inflated and deflated lungs is about 5 l in adult males (4 l for women) [12]. Ordinary speech employs up to half the vital capacity, while very loud speech uses as much as 80%. The *volume velocity* of air leaving the lungs is controlled by chest and abdominal muscles to be relatively constant at about 0.2 l/s during sustained sounds. This may require contraction of inspiration muscles during the first part of a long speech expiration (to delay lung collapse). More typically, utterances are short enough so that lung recoil need not be checked. Contracting expiration muscles can force air out past normal breathing levels for long utterances.

Conversational speech requires a relative lung pressure of about 10 cm H$_2$O (pressure is often measured in terms of the height of a column of water in an inverted vacuum tube suspended in a pool—roughly the pressure needed to blow into a straw immersed in such a depth of water). This compares to 1–2 cm H$_2$O during normal breathing. Even very loud speech sounds have a maximum pressure deviation of only about 20 cm H$_2$O (about 2 kPa), which is very small compared to atmospheric pressure (14.7 lb/in^2 or 976 cm H$_2$O at sea level, caused by the force of the atmosphere pulled by gravity toward the Earth; such pressure diminishes to half at 5.5 km altitude). (Aerodynamic power in speech is about 1 W, approximately 1% of the metabolic power of the body.) While air pressure in the lungs stays relatively constant during an utterance, airflow varies significantly due to time-varying obstructions in the larynx and vocal tract.

Starting from a *phonation threshold pressure* (the minimum lung pressure to maintain voicing), speech intensity increases 8–9 dB per doubling of excess pressure (with 2–3 dB of this due to less symmetry in glottal waveshape) [13]. A similar increase follows a doubling of F0, if pressure is proportional to the threshold. Vowel amplitude is also a function of the first resonance bandwidth and the spectral tilt of the vocal fold excitation [14].

3.2.2 Larynx and Vocal Folds (Cords)

Normal breathing creates little audible sound because air expelled by the lungs passes unobstructed through the vocal tract. As pressure varies, sound occurs when the airflow path is narrowly constricted or totally occluded, interrupting the airflow to create either turbulent noise or pulses of air. The source of most speech occurs in the *larynx* where vocal folds can obstruct airflow from the lungs (Figure 3.3). The larynx is a framework of four cartilages (thyroid, cricoid, arytenoid, and epiglottis) joined by ligaments and membranes; it connects the lungs to the vocal tract through a passage called the *trachea* (Figure 3.1). About 12 cm long and 1.5–2 cm in diameter, the trachea divides into two bronchial tubes for the lungs. The epiglottis serves to cover the larynx when food is intended to descend the alimentary tube to the stomach. Within the larynx are the vocal folds, a pair of elastic structures of tendon, muscles, and mucous membranes that lie in an anterior–posterior direction behind the *Adam's apple* (thyroid cartilage) [4]. The vocal folds are typically 15 mm long in men and about 13 mm in women, weigh about 1 g each, and vibrate about 1 mm. By means of various muscle contractions, the vocal folds can be varied in length and thickness and positioned in different configurations.

The anterior ends of the vocal folds are attached together to the thyroid cartilage, but the posterior (rear) ends are connected to two individual arytenoid cartilages, which can rock and slide so as to abduct or adduct the vocal folds. During normal breathing, the vocal folds remain sufficiently parted to allow free air passage without creating sound (for heavy breathing, they abduct farther for maximal airflow). If they are adducted sufficiently, airflow may be hindered enough to create a turbulent noise at the *glottis*, the variable opening

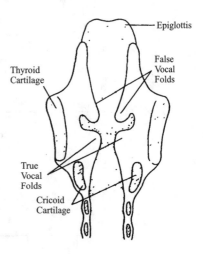

Figure 3.3 Larynx cross-section as viewed from the front.

between the vocal folds (about 8 mm wide at rest). Speech arising from such noise is called *whisper* or *aspiration* and is similar to sighing (it also corresponds to the phoneme /h/ in Table 3.1). Noise can be generated by the same mechanism farther up the vocal tract, at a narrow constriction involving either the tongue and the *palate* (roof of the mouth) or the lips and teeth. In such cases, *frication* noise generates *fricative* sounds, which are distinguished

TABLE 3.1   English phonemes and corresponding features.

Phoneme (IPA symbols)	Manner of articulation	Place of articulation	Voiced?	Example word
i	vowel	high front tense	yes	beat
I	vowel	high front lax	yes	bit
e	vowel	mid front tense	yes	bait
ε	vowel	mid front lax	yes	bet
æ	vowel	low front tense	yes	bat
ɑ	vowel	low back tense	yes	cot
ɔ	vowel	mid back lax rounded	yes	caught
o	vowel	mid back tense rounded	yes	coat
U	vowel	high back lax rounded	yes	book
u	vowel	high back tense rounded	yes	boot
ʌ	vowel	mid back lax	yes	but
ɝ	vowel	mid tense (retroflex)	yes	curt
ə	vowel	mid lax (schwa)	yes	about
ɑj (ɑI)	dipthong	low back → high front	yes	bite
ɔj(ɔI)	dipthong	mid back → high front	yes	boy
ɑw(ɑU)	dipthong	low back → high back	yes	bout
j	glide	front unrounded	yes	you
w	glide	back rounded	yes	wow
l	liquid	alveolar	yes	lull
r	liquid	retrofax	yes	roar
m	nasal	labial	yes	maim
n	nasal	alveolar	yes	none
η	nasal	velar	yes	bang
f	fricative	labiodental	no	fluff
v	fricative	labiodental	yes	valve
θ	fricative	dental	no	thin
δ	fricative	dental	yes	then
s	fricative	alveolar strident	no	sass
z	fricative	alveolar strident	yes	zoos
ʃ	fricative	palatal strident	no	shoe
3	fricative	palatal strident	yes	measure
h	fricative	glottal	no	how
p	stop	labial	no	pop
b	stop	labial	yes	bib
t	stop	alveolar	no	tot
d	stop	alveolar	yes	did
k	stop	velar	no	kick
g	stop	velar	yes	gig
tʃ	affricate	alveopalatal	no	church
dʒ	affricate	alveopalatal	yes	judge

from whisper in having mainly high-frequency energy (e.g., "Shhh!"). A noise source primarily excites the portion of the vocal tract in front of its source constriction, and the shorter cavities excited in frication lead to higher frequencies than for whisper. All sounds involving noise are *aperiodic*.

If the vocal tract or glottis is closed completely, airflow ceases and no sound emerges. A class of sounds called *stops* or *plosives* utilizes such airflow interruptions of 20–150 ms, with different acoustic aspects depending on whether the closure occurs at the glottis (vocal folds), in the vocal tract (tongue against palate; e.g., /t/), or at the lips (e.g., /p/). With the chest muscles continuing to attempt to expel air, pressure builds behind the closure until it is released by opening the occlusion.

3.2.2.1 Vocal fold motion during voiced sounds.

3.2.2.1 Vocal fold motion during voiced sounds. Fricative sounds employ a narrow vocal tract constriction, while plosive sounds close and release a full occlusion. A third and most important class of sounds is the *sonorant* sounds, which excite the vocal tract through periodic vocal fold vibration (e.g., /i,m/). Air leaving the lungs in sonorants is rapidly interrupted by periodic closing and opening of the vocal folds; the rate of vibration is the *fundamental frequency* (F0). The *fundamental period* or *pitch period* between successive vocal fold closures, $T_0 = 1/F0$, has an average value that varies with the size of the speaker's vocal folds, roughly $L/1.7$ ms, where L is the length (in mm) of the membranous portion of the folds (the nonvibrating, cartilagenous portion remains about 2 mm throughout life) [15]. Thus, infants have very short periods ($L = 2$ at birth), adult males long periods. (Again, the use of the term "period" does not indicate true repetition, but merely quasi-periodicity over intervals of tens of ms.)

Phonation (vibration of the vocal folds) occurs when (a) the vocal folds are sufficiently elastic and close together, and (b) there is a sufficient difference between subglottal pressure P_{sub} (below the glottis) and supraglottal pressure P_{sup} (above the glottis). Unlike voluntary muscle actions that occur in stop closures, vocal fold vibration is caused by both aerodynamics and the elasticity of muscle tissue, and is explained by the *myoelastic aerodynamic theory* of voicing [16]. Constant P_{sub} causes air to flow rapidly through the narrow glottal constriction of adducted (but not fully closed) vocal folds. Voicing typically uses $P_{sub} = 5$–15 cm H_2O and peak glottal airflow of 250–750 cm^3/s [17]. While fricatives employ a fixed vocal tract constriction, glottal constrictions usually involve elastic vocal folds, which move in response to airflow (Figure 3.4). A negative pressure develops in the glottis due to a *Bernoulli force* and closes the vocal folds in a sucking action.

The force can be explained in terms of conservation of energy. Air flowing through a tube has a constant sum of kinetic and potential energy at all points in the tube. Potential energy is proportional to air pressure, whereas kinetic energy follows the square of air velocity. As velocity increases in the narrow glottis, local pressure must drop. When a sufficient pressure difference exists across the glottis to cause a large airflow, a negative pressure develops in the glottis and forces the vocal folds to close. Glottal closure interrupts airflow, and a pressure gradient develops across the glottis, eventually building to a point where the vocal folds open again. In most voiced sounds, the vocal tract is relatively open and the average P_{sup} is at atmospheric pressure. During fricatives and especially stops, a significant pressure drop also develops at the vocal tract constriction, which lessens the net pressure drop across the glottis [19]. In voiced stops, F0 falls as the glottal pressure drop decreases, and vibration may cease completely if the vocal tract remains closed long enough. During voiced fricatives, the vocal folds relax to maintain vibration with less effort.

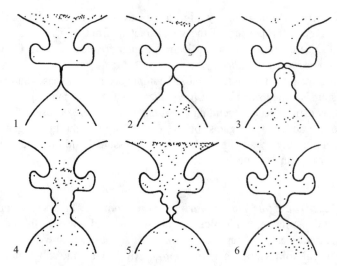

Figure 3.4 Schematic cross-sections of the larynx at six time intervals during a cycle of voicing. (After Vennard [18].)

Because lower portions of the vocal folds are more compliant than the upper parts, there is a time lag in which the lower portions close and open before the upper parts do. The vocal fold cycle of motion exhibits both vertical and horizontal components: (a) the folds move upward during closure as P_{sub} gradually forces the vocal folds apart and downward during the open phase before the lower portions of the vocal folds close again; (b) the folds tend to separate in the posterior glottis before the anterior portions part. This self-sustained oscillation is aided by the elastic recoil of the vocal folds, which tends to return them to their original adducted state. Maximal glottal area during voicing is about $20\,mm^2$ for men

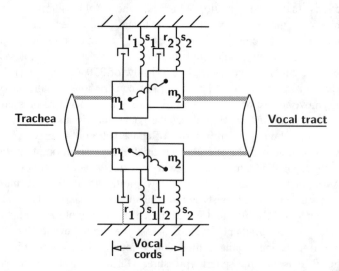

Figure 3.5 Two-mass vocal fold model, which accounts for phase effects between the upper and lower parts of the vocal folds. Each vocal fold is viewed as having two masses coupled by a spring, where each of the masses is attached to tracheal walls by a system consisting of a spring of stiffness s_i and a resistance device r_i. (After Flanagan [26].)

and $14\,mm^2$ for women. Vocal fold models range in complexity from simple one-mass models or two- and three-mass systems [20,21] (Figure 3.5) to a 16-mass system capable of modeling both vertical shear effects and lateral mucosal effects [22,23]. Nonlinear three-dimensional models of glottal vibration describe the pulsating jet air flow through a modulated orifice with deformable, compliant walls [24]. Many efforts are underway to improve glottal flow models (including the popular LF model) [2], which could have significant effects in lowering bit rate in speech coding [25].

3.2.2.2 Fundamental frequency of voicing vibrations.

3.2.2.2 Fundamental frequency of voicing vibrations.   Although vocal fold closures do not follow individual muscle contractions, muscle variations can change the characteristics of the quasi-periodic airflow. Variations in P_{sub} and vocal fold elasticity due to the muscles of the chest and larynx, respectively, cause changes in the waveshape of glottal air pulses, including their duration and amplitude, which lead to changes in perceived pitch and loudness. A doubling of P_{sub} raises output sound intensity by about 8–12 dB (speech is usually less than 90 dB, which is equivalent to 10 mW power at 0.5 m distance [13]). F0 exhibits some correlation with P_{sub}, increasing 2–7 Hz/cm H_2O [4], but F0 variations are primarily due to two laryngeal muscles (the *vocalis* of the vocal folds and the *cricothyroid*), which increase F0 by lengthening (up to about 4 mm) and tensing the vocal folds [27,28]. Rapid lowering of F0 may utilize both muscle relaxation and some active contractions of the *thyroarytenoid* and the (external) *sternohyoid* muscles [15]. F0 tends to increase slightly with tongue height, which may relate to greater tension on the vocal folds when the tongue is pulled upward [29]. A model attempts to use biomechanical principles to show how F0 varies under different muscle conditions [30].

Typical speech uses an F0 range of about an octave (doubling)—about 80–160 Hz for males—while singers often use a two-octave range. Most speakers are capable of two octaves but limit F0 variation in normal speech, because extremes of F0 require increased effort. Average F0 values of 132 Hz and 223 Hz for males and females, respectively [31], are in the lower parts of their ranges, which suggests that higher F0 requires more effort than low F0. Rapid F0 changes (more than 1 Hz/ms [32]) are possible because F0-adjusting laryngeal muscles respond very quickly, some in about 20 ms [33]. The switch between unvoiced and voiced sounds usually takes longer, about 100–200 ms; the abducting (*cricoarytenoid*) and adducting (*interarytenoid*, cricothyroid, and lateral cricoarytenoid) muscles are slower than the muscles controlling F0. When a stop occlusion is released into a voiced sound, the time from stop release (the start of the resulting sound burst) to the start of vocal fold periodicity is called the *voice onset time* (VOT). Aspiration often occurs during the VOT, while the vocal folds are being positioned for voicing. (A corresponding voice offset time is rarely examined [34].)

3.2.2.3 Types of phonation.

3.2.2.3 Types of phonation.   In addition to the normal *modal register* voicing just described, there are other *phonation types* [15] (sometimes called dysphonic), which may involve nonlinearities (and may be modeled via chaos theory [35]). *Breathy* or *murmur* phonation combines voicing and whispering by keeping a posterior portion of the glottis (between the arytenoid cartilages) open while anterior parts of the vocal folds vibrate (Figure 3.6); such glottal airflow has both periodic pulses and a noisy component similar to aspiration. *Creaky voice* is a rarer type of phonation in which the vocal folds are tightly adducted, allowing only a small part of the vocal folds to vibrate; such a voice sounds harsh and has an irregular F0 and low intensity. *Vocal fry* or *pulse register phonation* is the opposite of creaky voice in that the vocal folds are short, thick, and relaxed, leading to a very low and irregular

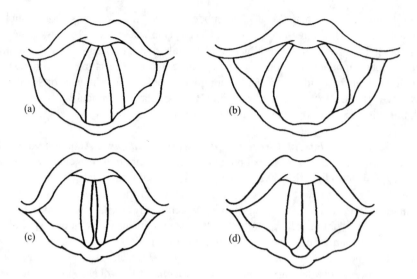

Figure 3.6 Pictures of the glottis, viewed from above during (a) normal breathing, (b) deep breathing, (c) voicing, (d) whisper. (After Sonesson [3], 1968, The functional anatomy of the speech organs, in *Manual of Phonetics*, B. Malmberg (ed) [North-Holland: Amsterdam].)

F0 (in the range 3–50 Hz). The effective mass of the vocal folds may increase by coupling with a second set of folds (called the ventricular or false vocal folds) above the vocal folds. Vocal fry, in which each glottal pulse may be long enough to be perceived separately, often occurs at the end of an utterance as lung pressure dies out and laryngeal muscles relax. The vocal folds are closed most of the time during fry, with each period having typically 1–3 overlapping pulses of 3–4 ms followed by a long closed phase of 11–27 ms [36].

Virtually all speech employs modal register voice, which is capable of wide variation in F0 (1.5 octaves) and amplitude, while exciting a 4–6-octave span of vocal tract frequencies. Besides pulse and modal registers, a third register, *falsetto* or *loft*, is often identified with high F0. In this register the vocal folds are so thin that the vertical and horizontal lag effects of modal register disappear and only central portions of the vocal folds vibrate. In falsetto the vocal folds often do not close completely, adding a breathy quality to the voice.

Natural glottal pulses are not truly periodic, exhibiting *jitter* and *shimmer*, which are period-to-period variations in duration and amplitude, respectively. Normal voices have jitter of 0.5–1.0% (e.g., 1 Hz) and shimmer of about 0.04–0.21 dB [37] (of which about 12% is due to heartbeats [38]). Such low-level variations are normally not directly perceptible, and roughness is heard only in speech with about 2% jitter or 1 dB shimmer. *Hoarse* voices are characterized by considerable deviation of the glottal signal toward aperiodicity. Hoarseness is often quantified in terms of the amount of aperiodic noise found in speech relative to its periodic components [39], but recent research suggests that hoarse voices have a loss of energy in the harmonics of F0 relative to the amplitude of the fundamental [40, 41]. Pathological voice qualities (e.g., breathiness and roughness) are difficult to quantify, but are often multidimensional and interrelated [42].

Besides the obvious correlation of vocal tract size with speech frequencies (i.e., smaller tracts having higher F0 and resonant frequencies), female speech tends to be more breathy, leading to wider bandwidths and steeper spectral slope [43]. Glottal flow and speech amplitude are greater for males, and the glottis remains open a smaller percentage of the pitch cycle, leading to higher speech energy, despite the fewer number of excitations (due to lower F0) [2].

3.2.3 Vocal Tract

The lungs provide the airflow and pressure source for speech, and the vocal folds often modulate the airflow to create sound, but the vocal tract is the most important component in speech production. A tubular passageway composed of muscular and bony tissues, the vocal tract provides the means to produce the many different sounds that characterize spoken language. The vocal tract has two speech functions: (1) it can modify the spectral distribution of energy in glottal sound waves, and (2) it can contribute to the generation of sound for *obstruent* (stop and fricative) sounds. Different sounds are primarily distinguished by their periodicity (voiced or unvoiced), spectral shape (which frequencies have the most energy), and duration. The vocal folds specify the voicing feature, and a sound's duration is the result of synchronized vocal fold–tract actions, but the major partitioning of speech into sounds is accomplished by the vocal tract via spectral filtering.

The vocal tract can be modeled as an acoustic tube with resonances, called *formants*, and antiresonances. (The formants are abbreviated Fi, where F1 is the formant with the lowest frequency.) Moving the articulators of the vocal tract alters the shape of the acoustic tube, which in turn changes its frequency response (the simple presence of the vocal tract boosts output speech intensity by 10–15 dB, as an impedance match between the glottis and free space beyond the lips [13]). As volumes of air and corresponding sound pressure waves pass through the vocal tract, certain frequencies are attenuated and others amplified, depending on the filter's frequency response. The vocal tract filter amplifies energy around formant frequencies, while attenuating energy around antiresonant frequencies between the formants. The resonances are due to the poles of the frequency response, while some spectral nulls are due to zeros of the response. In addition to studying laryngeal speech behavior, this chapter emphasizes aspects of vocal tract physiology and dynamics, and their effects on the acoustic phonetics of speech.

Figure 3.7(a) shows salient aspects of the vocal tract. In an adult male, the vocal tract is about 17 cm long from the glottis (1) to the lips (8), with cross-sectional area up to about 20 cm^2. After the larynx, air from the lungs passes through the *pharyngeal* and *oral cavities* in turn, eventually exiting at the *lips*. The boundary between these two cavities is at the uvula (6) because airflow at this point may enter the *nasal cavity* or pass into the oral cavity. The uvula is the tip of a movable tissue structure called the *velum* or *soft palate* (5), which is raised for most speech sounds, closing off the nasal cavity from receiving air. During breathing and nasal sounds, however, the velum lowers to allow air through the nostrils, in place of, or in addition to, airflow via the lips.

The vocal tract is often modeled as a chain of cylinders of varying cross-sectional area, but the actual shape is much more complex because its walls vary in shape [44]. The tongue, lower teeth, and lips are subject to much movement. The upper and posterior boundary of the vocal tract is relatively fixed (in relation to the head) but its composition is diverse: the rear of the pharynx is smooth and continuous, while the oral cavity roof consists of a flexible soft palate at its rear, followed by a stiff hard palate, and finally the upper lip and teeth. The nasal cavity is quite different, consisting of a labyrinth of passages lined with mucous tissue, with no movable structures under voluntary control. It has a large interior surface area compared to

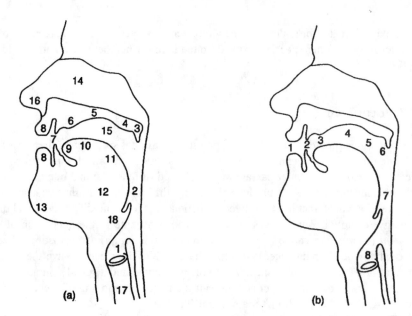

Figure 3.7 A cross-sectional view of the vocal tract. (a) Speech articulators: (1) vocal
folds, (2) pharynx, (3) velum, (4) soft palate, (5) hard palate, (6) alveolar
ridge, (7) teeth, (8) lips, (9) tongue tip, (10) blade, (11) dorsum, (12) root, (13)
mandible (jaw), (14) nasal cavity, (15) oral cavity, (16) nostrils, (17) trachea,
(18) epiglottis. (b) Places of articulation: (1) labial, (2) dental, (3) alveolar, (4)
palatal, (5) velar, (6) uvular, (7) pharyngeal, (8) glottal.

its volume (about $60\,\mathrm{cm}^3$, with individual sinuses less than $20\,\mathrm{cm}^3$) and acts as a highly
damped resonator, significantly attenuating the energy of sound waves that pass through (the
overall pharyngonasal volume is about $120\,\mathrm{cm}^3$) [45]. The opening between the nasal and
pharyngeal cavities is called the *velopharyngeal port*, and its size controls the amount of
acoustic coupling between the cavities and hence the amount of nasal emission; full opening
in an adult male is about $5\,\mathrm{cm}^2$. The opening at the nostrils is about $0.8\,\mathrm{cm}^2$.

3.2.3.1 Articulators. Structures in the vocal tract that move in the production of
different sounds are called *articulators*. In terms of the number of different sounds produced,
the most important articulators are the tongue and lips, but the velum and larynx also have
important speech roles. The primary function of the larynx is to control airflow through the
glottis, but the larynx can also be raised or lowered to alter the length of the vocal tract: (a) to
raise or lower, respectively, formant frequencies, (b) to enlarge the pharynx for longer vocal
fold vibration in voiced stops, or (c) to facilitate movement of the upper articulators connected
to the larynx. The jaw or *mandible* is considered an indirect articulator because it assists
positioning of the tongue and lips for many sounds.

The most visible articulators are the lips, a pair of muscular folds on the face that
function in two ways: (1) they effect a vocal tract closure or narrow slit when they are pressed
together or when the lower lip presses against the upper teeth; or (2) in varying degrees, they
either round and protrude (pucker) or spread and retract. Closure is usually accomplished by
moving the jaw and lower lip, while rounding is due to the *orbicularis oris*, the lip muscle,

which surrounds the lips. *Transverse* muscles entering the lips at the corners of the mouth retract and spread the lips.

Among the teeth, only the four front upper *incisors* seem important for speech. Dental obstruent sounds involve either the lower lip (e.g., /f/) or the tongue tip (e.g., /θ/) contacting these teeth. Behind the teeth on the upper wall of the oral tract is the hard palate, a dome-shaped structure consisting of four bones. Many speech sounds involve a constriction between it and the tongue (e.g., /t,s/). The *alveolar ridge* in the hard palate just behind the teeth provides a major contact point. The back of the vocal tract consists of the pharyngeal wall, which contains layers of horizontal muscles; relaxing these muscles and contracting *hyoid* muscles may enlarge the pharynx during voiced stops, but otherwise the pharynx is passive in speech production.

The most important and complex articulator, the tongue, consists of 12 interactive muscle pairs and some passive tissues. It can be divided into four components: tip or apex, blade, dorsum, and root. They are all part of the same muscular tongue structure but each can function independently to a certain degree. Since the tongue provides virtually all of the lower wall of the pharyngeal and oral tracts, and since the upper wall components (except the velum) have little freedom of movement, it is primarily tongue positioning that creates the many vocal tract shapes necessary to produce different speech sounds. The *tip* is the quickest and most agile part of the tongue; being thin and narrow, it can make and break contact with the palate up to nine times per second. The *dorsum* is the surface of the tongue, of which the anterior portion is called the *blade*; the tongue body or *root* positions the dorsum so that constrictions may be made at different locations in the vocal tract (Figure 3.8). The tongue is very flexible, capable of many different shapes (but limited in number [46]), and can move rapidly from one position to another, often in less than 50 ms. Almost completely composed of muscle, the tongue has *intrinsic* (internal) muscles that primarily change its shape, e.g., flattening it or curling its tip and edges. Among the *extrinsic* muscles (those attached to both the tongue and other structures), the *genioglossus* is the largest and is basically responsible for tongue height (up–down positioning) and lateral (anterior–posterior) position (Figure 3.9). Specifically, the vertical fibers of the genioglossus pull the tip down and back, its middle fibers flatten the dorsum, and the lower fibers move the root forward. Contraction of the *styloglossus* muscle pulls the root up and back, the *palatoglossus* raises and humps the dorsum, and the *hyoglossus* pulls the root down and back.

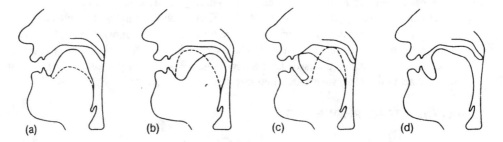

(a)   (b)   (c)   (d)

Figure 3.8 Typical articulatory positions for (a) a vowel, showing two tongue height positions; (b) a high vowel, showing front and back positions; (c) a stop, showing alveolar and velar places of articulation (for a nasal, the only difference is a lowered velum); and (d) an alveolar fricative.

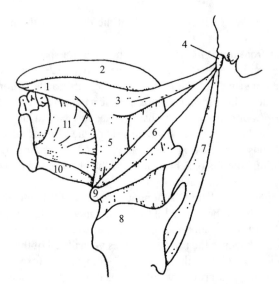

Figure 3.9 Diagram of the tongue, including extrinsic muscles (italicized) and related structures: (1) inferior longitudinal muscle (intrinsic), (2) dorsum, (3) *styloglossus* muscle, (4) styloid process of temporal bone, (5) *hyoglossus* muscle, (6) stylohyoid muscle, (7) stylopharyngeal muscle, (8) thyroid cartilage, (9) hyoid bone, (10) genio-hyoid muscle, (11) *genioglossus* muscle.

3.2.3.2 Articulator movement. Each articulator moves in response to neural commands to its intrinsic and extrinsic muscles. Commands from the brain descend along axon paths, eventually reaching muscle fibers that contract in response to an all-or-nothing neural firing. Most speech articulators have low fiber:neuron ratios, which allow relatively precise movements by controlling which fibers contract and how often they do so. Most muscles exist in antagonistic pairs, where movement in one direction occurs by contracting one muscle and/or relaxing the second, and motion in the opposite direction is caused by reversing the roles of the two muscles. Two types of motion are apparent in the speech organs: ballistic and controlled. In rapid *ballistic* motion, one muscle contracts and its antagonist relaxes. The motion stops only when the articulator hits another part of the vocal tract or reaches the end of its dynamic range and connective tissue arrests the motion. Closures of the vocal tract (e.g., lip closures or tongue motion toward the palate) are examples of ballistic motion [47].

During *controlled* motion, on the other hand, both antagonistic muscles contract to different degrees. Motion follows the muscle contracting more strongly, until the braking action of its antagonist grows strong enough to stop the articulator. Controlled movements are slower than ballistic ones, but they are necessary to achieve all vocal tract positions except closures. The behavior of antagonistic muscles can explain asymmetry in transition durations: in vowel–stop–vowel sequences (e.g., /ɑdɑ/), closure is often faster than opening because closure is ballistic whereas the transition to the ensuing vowel requires controlled movements. Most articulator movements toward a target position start as ballistic but become controlled as the target is neared or as muscle commands are issued for a new target. Peak velocity is often linearly related to displacement [48]. Movements are often less than 1 cm, at speeds up to 30 cm/s.

3.3 ARTICULATORY PHONETICS

Speech sounds can be analyzed from several points of view: articulatory, acoustic, phonetic, and perceptual. This section describes articulatory phonetics, which relates linguistic features of sounds to positions and movements of the speech organs. Knowledge in this area is limited by a lack of data on the motion of the vocal tract; visual and X-ray observation does not permit a complete dynamic three-dimensional model. Due to their dangers, full X-rays are no longer made, although old data are still useful [49]. X-ray microbeam experiments minimize the health risks by focusing very limited doses on lead pellets attached to the tongue, and have led to limited views of the vocal tract. Tongue shapes have also been determined through small coils on the tongue and electromagnetics or ultrasound [50,51]. Magnetic resonance imagery experiments provide good 3D data, but have been limited to the study of sustained speech sounds, due to their long acquisition times [52,53].

While humans can produce a very large number of sounds (within the constraints of the vocal tract), each language has a small set of abstract linguistic units called *phonemes* to describe its sounds. A phoneme is the smallest meaningful contrastive unit in the phonology of a language. The sounds associated with each phoneme usually have some articulatory gesture(s) or configuration in common. Each word consists of a series of phonemes corresponding to the vocal tract movements needed to produce the word. Except for homonyms, English words differ from each other in some aspect of their phonemic composition or stress pattern. Most languages have 20–40 phonemes (some have fewer, while a few have more than 100), which provide an alphabet of sounds to uniquely describe words in the language. The alphabet of phonemes is large enough to allow such differentiation; e.g., the set of words (including words not currently used in English but phonologically permissible) *heed, hid, ahead, hayed, had, hod, hawed, hoed, hood, who'd, hide, hud, howed, heard, hoyed* illustrates how the 15 *vowel* sounds of English are needed to distinguish words. Similarly, the set *thin, sin, fin, tin, pin, kin, din, lin, gin* shows how consonants can distinguish words.

Although languages vary widely in semantic and grammatical structure, they employ the vocal tract in similar ways. The vowel sounds /i,ɑ,u/ appear in most languages, but other sounds are particular to a few (e.g., the *th* sounds of English are relatively rare). Most of the examples of phonemes in this chapter concern English, but other languages are mentioned where the set of English sounds is too restrictive for a general discussion of speech production.

Phonemes may be associated with linguistic features or articulatory configurations [54]; e.g., the following discussion notes that the phoneme /s/ has the features unvoiced, fricative, and alveolar and that producing an /s/ involves an open glottis, a raised velum, and a single narrow constriction in the alveolar region. Evidence (although controversial [55]) for the psychological reality of phonemes is found in studies of speech errors, which usually involve substitution or exchange of phonemes [56,57]. Articulatory phonetics relates features for each phoneme to the positions and gestures of vocal tract articulators that produce them.

The physical sound produced when a phoneme is articulated is called a *phone*. Since the vocal tract is not a discrete system and can vary in infinitely many ways, an infinite number of phones can correspond to each phoneme. (Repeated pronunciations of the same phoneme by a single speaker differ from one another, but by a lesser degree than versions from different speakers.) The term *allophone* usually describes a class of phones corresponding to a specific variant of a phoneme, especially where various vocal tract shapes yield the same phoneme. For example, /k/ requires occlusion of the tongue dorsum with the roof of the mouth, but the range of permissible occlusion points is broad enough that significantly different allophones of /k/ occur. Preceding a front or back vowel, respectively, /k/ closure is sufficiently forward or back in the velar region to cause perceptible acoustic differences. Stop consonants tend to have more allophones than other phonemes; e.g., depending on context, alveolar stop phonemes may be either aspirated or unaspirated, voiced or unvoiced, long or short [58]. If, in a speech signal, one were to exchange allophones of a phoneme, intelligibility should not be affected, although the modified signal may sound less natural.

The transformation of phonemes into allophones involves *coarticulation*, a phenomenon by which the articulatory configurations of neighboring phonemes affect the articulation of each phoneme. Speech signals cannot be segmented into discrete phones with a simple 1 : 1

correspondence to phonemes. In many applications, speech is divided into segments whose boundaries are times of major spectral change, which usually correspond to major changes in vocal tract state (e.g., occlusion, narrow constriction, or onset/offset of voicing). Since a phoneme's features affect the speech signal beyond these times, however, they do not correspond to "phoneme boundaries" in a strict sense. The gestures associated with successive phonemes overlap so much that each phoneme's features often affect several preceding and ensuing phones. Further discussion of coarticulation is postponed until after we examine the features and gestures that characterize each phoneme.

Words are traditionally divided into phonological units called *syllables*. Each syllable has one vowel (or diphthong), which is its most intense sound and for which the vocal tract is most open. (A few "words" such as *psst*, *shh*, *tsk*, and *hmmm* have no vowel; their most intense sound is a either a fricative or a *syllabic nasal*.) Each syllable may contain consonants before and after the vowel; such consonants include glides, liquids, nasals, stops, fricatives, and affricates (Table 3.1). Vowel and consonant phonemes are classified in terms of manner and place of articulation and voicing. *Manner of articulation* concerns how the vocal tract restricts airflow: (a) completely stopping airflow by an occlusion creates a stop consonant; (b) vocal tract constrictions of varying degree occur in fricatives, liquids, glides, and vowels; and (c) lowering the velum causes nasal sounds. *Place of articulation* refers to the location in the vocal tract, usually in terms of the upper wall, of the most narrow constriction. Nominally, a phoneme is considered voiced if the vocal folds vibrate during its realization, but the following discussion shows that such an analysis is too simplistic.

3.3.1 Manner of Articulation

Manner of articulation is concerned with airflow: the path(s) it takes and the degree to which it is impeded by vocal tract constrictions. The largest class of English sounds is that of *vowels* and *diphthongs*, in which air flows (at rates of 100–200 cm^3/s) directly through the pharyngeal and oral cavities, meeting no constriction narrow enough to cause turbulent flow (frication). For vowels, the area of minimum constriction ranges from 0.3 to 2.0 cm^2 [17].

Glides are similar to high vowels but employ narrow vocal tract constrictions that, under conditions of unusually strong airflow, may cause frication; each glide is close in articulation to a high vowel (i.e., /j/–/i/ and /w/–/u/). *Liquids* too are similar to vowels but use the tongue as an obstruction in the oral tract, causing air to deflect around the tip or dorsum. In the liquid /l/ (also called a *lateral*), for example, the tip contacts the alveolar ridge and divides airflow into two streams on either side of the tongue. In syllable-initial position (before the vowel), /l/ is called *light* due to the tongue's small area of contact in the alveodental region. English uses a *dark* /l/, with greater contact area, for syllable-final laterals.

The *rhotic* liquid /r/ has a more variable articulation but generally involves either (a) the tongue tip pointing toward the alveolar ridge and often curling back (*retroflex*) or (b) a raised and "bunched" dorsum with secondary pharyngeal and labial constrictions [53,59,60]. The sides of the tongue also contact the upper molar teeth in /r/, restricting the airflow path. There are several allophones of /r/; e.g., prevocalic /r/ tends to have more lip rounding, a more advanced tongue, and less tongue grooving than /r/ in other positions. The English /r/ is a rare sound that can achieve the same acoustics with very different articulations, and is found in very few of the world's languages; in most languages where [r] exists, it is more like a fricative.

The velum is lowered during *nasal* sounds, which allows airflow through the nostrils. The only nasal phonemes in English are consonants, during which the oral tract is completely closed at the lips or with the tongue against the palate. Some languages (e.g., French) have *nasalized* vowels, in which air passes through both oral and nasal cavities. Vowels may be nasalized in English, but the distinction is allophonic and not phonemic (i.e., vowel identity does not change); French, on the other hand, has pairs of words that differ only in whether a vowel is nasalized.

All phonemes in the manner classes above (vowels, diphthongs, glides, liquids, and nasals) employ voicing and excite the vocal tract solely at the glottis; these continuous, intense, and periodic phonemes are also known as *sonorants*. The remaining *obstruent* phonemes (stops and fricatives) are weak and aperiodic, and each is primarily excited at its major vocal tract constriction.

Stop (*plosive*) consonants involve the complete closure and subsequent release of a vocal tract obstruction. The velum must be raised to prevent nasal airflow during closure. After a rapid closure, pressure builds up behind the occlusion (to about 6 cm H_2O, due to persistent lung pressure) and is suddenly released with a rush of air that creates a brief (e.g., 10 ms) acoustic *burst* or *explosion* (in the first few ms, the area increases at about 50 cm^2/s [61]). As the vocal tract widens and the vocal folds adduct in preparation for voicing in an ensuing sound, a period of noisy *aspiration* may occur before voicing starts. Closure for a stop occurs in the oral tract (except for the *glottal stop*, which closes the glottis for 30–60 ms).

Fricatives employ a narrow constriction in the oral tract, in the pharynx (more rarely), or at the glottis [9]. If pressure behind the constriction is high enough (e.g., 3–8 cm H_2O) and the passage sufficiently narrow (0.05–0.2 cm^2), airflow becomes fast enough (41 m/s) to generate turbulence at the end of the constriction [62]. Noise is generated when the *Reynolds number*, defined as vh/v (where v is air particle velocity, h is the width of the orifice, and $v = 0.15 \, cm^2/s$ is the viscosity of air), exceeds about 1800. The turbulence is due to random rotation of air molecules from eddies and vortices (about the size of h) at the constriction termination, where rapidly moving air molecules in the constriction abruptly slow down upon entering the cavity in front of the constriction. At low Reynolds numbers, airflow is *laminar* (smooth) and roughly parallel to the sides of the vocal tract.

In the case of *strident* fricatives, noise amplitude is enhanced by airflow striking a surface (e.g., the upper incisors during /s/ or / ʃ /) as it leaves the constriction. Frication ceases when the constriction widens enough to drop air velocity below about 13 m/s. Airflow for most fricatives is about 200–500 cm^3/s, while aspiration (including the phoneme /h/) uses 500–1500 cm^3/s [17]. (Airflow U through a constriction of area A is $U = A\sqrt{(2P/\rho)}$, where P is pressure and $\rho = 1.15 \, kg/m^3$ is the air density [61]).

Most phonemes (vowels, liquids, nasals, fricatives) are characterized by an articulatory position and can be sustained in steady state (until the speaker runs out of breath). Stops are *transient* consonants involving a sequence of articulatory events (closure followed by release). Glides are also transient because they are usually released into an ensuing vowel. As a succession of sounds, speech in general is transient; steady sounds constitute a small percentage of time in speech. Due to coarticulation and the freedom speakers have in articulating sounds (within the constraints that listeners understand the speech), there is much variability in speech signals; no two repetitions of the same word are exactly alike.

Certain phonemes may be viewed as having phoneme subsequences: diphthongs (vowel followed by a glide) and *affricates* (stop followed by a fricative). Phonological convention dictates that diphthongs and affricates be considered single phonemes, although there are also articulatory and acoustic justifications (e.g., an affricate usually has less duration than other stop + fricative sequences).

3.3.2. Structure of the Syllable

Words are composed of phoneme sequences called *syllables*, each having one vowel or diphthong as a nucleus. Consonants are affiliated with the syllable of an adjacent vowel, forming an *initial consonant cluster* of one or more consonants before the vowel and/or a *final consonant cluster* after the vowel. Syllable boundaries, which affect F0 and duration, can be ambiguous for consonants between two vowels (e.g., the word *tasty* could be divided ta/sty, tas/ty or tast/y). Certain rules of *sonority* hold in virtually all languages, however, facilitating boundary location. Sonority corresponds to the degree of vocal tract constriction: vowels are most sonorous, followed by glides, liquids, nasals, and then obstruents. Within a syllable, sonority and amplitude start low in initial consonants, increase to a peak during the vowel, and then fade during ensuing consonants. (In the case of successive syllables with adjacent vowels, an amplitude dip may not be evident.) If present in a syllable, a glide must be immediately adjacent to the vowel. The liquids /r,l/ (in that order) are the next closest to the vowel, after which may come a nasal consonant. Furthest away from the vowel are the least vowel-like sounds, the obstruents.

Fricatives and stops appear in many combinations at the beginning or end of a syllable, but most languages require that obstruents in a cluster have the same voicing feature. In a series of obstruents between two vowels, the voicing characteristic can change only once—at the syllable boundary. English allows initial and final clusters with up to three and four consonants, respectively (e.g., *sphere* /sfɪr/, *streak* /strik/; *texts*/tɛksts/, *helms*/hɛlmz/); it has more complex syllable structures than most languages. In French, for example, most syllables are *open*, i.e., they have no post-vowel consonants, and final clusters have at most three consonants. Many languages (e.g., Japanese) forbid consonant clusters, and many do not allow any consonant after the vowel (or limit severely the possible consonants). Many languages have a simple consonant + vowel structure for all syllables.

3.3.3 Voicing

Both types of obstruents, stops and fricatives, may be either voiced or unvoiced. For most unvoiced obstruents, an open glottis allows air to pass without impediment from the lungs to the vocal tract constriction. The glottal obstruents are necessary exceptions: (a) the fricative /h/ maintains a narrow glottal opening, generating (unvoiced) glottal noise that excites a relatively unconstricted vocal tract, (b) the stop /ʔ/ completely closes the glottis. Voiced fricatives have two sources of sound excitation, periodic glottal air pulses and noise at the vocal tract constriction, which cause the speech to have noise amplitude-modulated at the rate of F0. The glottal excitation in voiced fricatives is not uniformly periodic; the perception of voicing here depends primarily on periodicity (e.g., fricatives are judged as voiced if periodicity is absent for at least 60 ms [63]), but prosodic factors are also relevant [64].

For most sounds, P_{sub} is dissipated in one major pressure drop, either across the glottis (in most voiced sounds) or at a narrow vocal tract constriction (in unvoiced obstruents). Voiced obstruents, however, divide the pressure gradient in the vocal tract between the glottis and the constriction, which leads to decreased F0 (unless P_{sub} or vocal fold tension is raised) and weaker noise intensity than for unvoiced obstruents.

The voicing feature in most phonemes is a direct function of periodicity during the sounds. Due to the transient nature of stops, voicing there is more complex. In many languages (e.g., French and Spanish) and in certain dialects of English, periodicity is maintained during the closure of voiced stops. Since vibrating folds require air to enter the vocal tract behind the stop occlusion, the tract must expand until the occlusion is released. Sound is weakly radiated through the walls of the vocal tract. Vocal fold vibration can be prolonged (up to about 100 ms for a typical 10 ml volume expansion) by lowering the larynx, allowing the pharynx and/or cheeks to expand, and/or relaxing the vocal folds [65,66]. As the *intraoral* pressure builds behind the occlusion, however, the falling pressure drop across the glottis eventually causes voicing to cease. In most dialects of American English, such *prevoicing* before stop release occurs only in intervocalic stops. "Voiced stops" without prevoicing are distinguished from "unvoiced stops" by their relatively short VOTs: vocal folds adduct immediately after the voiced stop release, and voicing commences within 10–30 ms. Unvoiced stops typically have an aspiration period of 40–100 ms before voicing starts. Unvoiced and voiced obstruents are often described as "tense" and "lax," respectively, possibly reflecting a general difference in muscle tension. Intraoral pressure, for example, is about 1–2 cm H_2O higher during unvoiced than voiced stops, which causes more intense release bursts.

3.3.4 Place of Articulation

While manner of articulation and voicing partition phonemes into the broad categories used by most languages, it is the *place of articulation* (point of narrowest vocal tract constriction) that enables finer discrimination of phonemes. Languages differ considerably as to which places are used for phonemes within the various manner classes. Virtually all languages employ vowels, nasals, stops, and fricatives, but the number and choice of places of articulation within each class are highly variable across languages. Many languages use as few as 3–5 vowels, whereas English has 13 and French 15. English and French have only three distinct places of articulation for stops (ignoring the rare glottal stops), whereas other languages employ as many as six [9]. Even when two languages appear to use the same phoneme, slight variations in tongue positioning between the languages often yield different sounds.

3.3.4.1 Consonants. Place of articulation is most often associated with consonants, rather than vowels, because consonants use a relatively narrow constriction. Along the vocal tract, approximately eight regions or points are traditionally associated with consonant constrictions, as follows:

1. Labials: if both lips constrict, the sound is *bilabial*; if the lower lip contacts the upper teeth, it is *labiodental*.
2. Dental: the tongue tip or blade touches the edge or back of the upper incisor teeth (if the tip protrudes between upper and lower teeth, as in $/\theta/$, the sound is *interdental*).
3. Alveolar: the tongue tip or blade approaches or touches the alveolar ridge.
4. Palatals: the tongue blade or dorsum constricts with the hard palate; if the tongue tip curls up, the sound is *retroflex*.
5. Velar: the dorsum approaches the soft palate. Some linguists use the term *compact* for velars because their spectra concentrate energy in one frequency region.
6. Uvular: the dorsum approaches the uvula.
7. Pharyngeal: the pharynx constricts.
8. Glottal: the vocal folds either close or constrict.

Each language typically employs a relatively small subset of these places for phoneme discrimination. For example, English requires only five places to partition sounds into phoneme classes: labial, dental, alveolar, palatovelar, and glottal. Stops occur at four points: bilabial, alveolar, velar, and glottal. Fricatives occur at five locations: labiodental, dental, alveolar, palatal, and glottal. While seven separate place categories are implicated for the obstruents, five emerge by combining close categories that differ by manner of articulation. For example, English has palatal fricatives and velar stops, but no palatal stops or velar fricatives; thus a broad palatal/velar place can be defined for which the actual constriction would vary with manner of articulation.

While a consonant is classified by its point of narrowest constriction, some also have a secondary constriction. Common points for secondary articulation are the lips, hard palate, soft palate, and pharynx, for which sounds are *labialized, palatalized, velarized,* and *pharyngealized,* respectively; for example, /w/ is a velarized bilabial glide, and /r/ is often a pharyngealized retroflex liquid.

3.3.4.2 Vowels.   Despite their relatively open vocal tracts, vowels can nonetheless be distinguished by points of constriction, but additional information is required about the degree of constriction. Vowels are primarily described in terms of tongue position and lip rounding. Vowel "place of articulation" refers to a lip constriction and/or the horizontal position of the tongue body (forward, middle, or back); the tongue height and degree of lip rounding are also important factors. Mouth opening ranges typically from 1 to 5 cm^2 between the most rounded vowel /u/ and the most open /ɑ/. Most vowels in virtually all languages can be classified in binary terms for horizontal tongue position (front or back) and lip rounding (rounded or unrounded), although the degrees of positioning vary across vowels. (Norwegian's three high rounded vowels and Swedish's three high front vowels are exceptions.) Some vowels (e.g., the common /ɑ/) often occupy a mid-horizontal position, with no other low contrasting vowel; in English, /ɑ/ is "back", with /æ/ (much rarer in the world's languages) front and low. Two other English vowels are best classified as having a middle horizontal tongue position, but they are distinguished from other vowels by special features: /ɝ/ is rhotic (see below) and /ə/, the *schwa* vowel, is short and weak.

Vowel tongue height is more complex than other production dimensions, requiring at least four levels (in order of widening constriction): high (close), mid-high, mid-low, and low (open). All languages have vowels with at least two contrasting heights [67]. In English, all front vowels (/i,I,e,ε,æ/) and two back vowels (/ɑ,ʌ/) are unrounded, while the other back vowels (/ɔ,o,U,u/) are rounded (with the degree of rounding increasing with tongue height).

The vowels may be divided into *tense* and *lax* classes, depending on duration and on how far the tongue is displaced from a neutral, central position. Longer vowels with more extreme articulation positions are considered tense: /i,e,æ,ɑ,o,u,ɝ/. (In English, the shorter lax vowels /I,U,ʌ/ may not end a syllable, unless one occurs as a reduced pronunciation of a tense vowel.) An alternate place system classifies vowels into four categories depending on the location of major tongue constriction: (1) the hard palate for high front vowels (/i,e,ε/); (2) the soft palate for high back vowels (/u,U/); (3) the upper portion of the pharynx for low back vowels (/o,ɔ/); and (4) the lower portion of the pharynx for low vowels (/ɑ,æ, ʌ /) [68]. Vowels within each class can be further specified by the degree of constriction (e.g., /i/vs/ε/) and/or the degree of mouth opening (e.g., /o/vs/ɔ/).

Vowels are usually produced with the velum relatively closed, but about 20% of languages allow both oral and nasalized vowels. Because the nasal tract has higher impedance than the oral tract, airflow patterns are similar in both types of vowels, i.e., there is little flow through the nostrils. Coupling the nasal and oral cavities, however, has significant acoustic consequences that enable nasalized and oral vowels with the same place of articulation to be distinguished. While the velum must be lowered significantly for intended nasalization or be closed for obstruents, velar height is more variable during oral vowels and tends to be proportional to tongue height [69]. Low vowels with wide oral cavities tolerate a low velum because the impedance of the oral tract is low compared to that of the nasal tract, and little air enters the nasal cavity unless the velum is very low.

3.3.5 Phonemes in Other Languages

Except for trills [70] and ingressive sounds (those produced while sucking air into the lungs), English provides good examples of sounds used in various languages. Languages differ mostly in aspects of place of articulation: for a given voicing characteristic and manner of articulation, different languages have phonemes with different places of constriction in the vocal tract. Languages usually share phonemes such as the cardinal vowels /i,ɑ,u/ and /p,t,k/, but the actual vocal tract shapes are usually slightly different for these sounds in different languages. Languages rarely use all possible combinations of voicing and manner; e.g., in many languages, stops or fricatives may be voiced or unvoiced but not both. English is typical of most languages in voicing all nonobstruent sounds, but some languages even have unvoiced nasals (i.e., snorting sounds).

Languages usually differ most significantly in the set of vowels used. Many languages have only a few vowels; 25% of the world's languages (e.g., Spanish and Japanese) have only five vowels /i,e,ɑ,o,u/, many just have /i,ɑ,u/, and a few use only two vowels. Vowels are usually widely separated in the F1–F2 space to minimize perceptual confusion. In most languages, including English, lip rounding occurs for all back vowels, and not for front (or central) vowels. French and German allow front rounded vowels, while Russian and Turkish permit back unrounded vowels. (Like other high vowels, the front rounded vowel /y/ has a glide counterpart /ɥ/.) Such sounds are difficult for native English speakers to produce because they do not occur in English.

In most languages, vowel nasalization is nonphonemic; it occurs in vowels adjacent to nasal consonants and does not change the perceived identity of the vowel. In French, however, vowels with similar vocal tract shapes and formant frequencies cue different phonemes based on nasalization.

Many languages (but not English) employ duration and F0 directly to cue different phonemes. Long and short vowels are used contrastively in some languages (e.g., Estonian has three vowel durations). Languages such as Mandarin and Thai are called *tone languages* because different patterns of F0 cue different phonemes; e.g., the same syllable /mɑ/ has four completely different meanings in Chinese depending on whether F0 is high, low, rising, or falling. Swedish also employs grave and acute F0 accents as a reduced type of tone language.

3.3.6 Articulatory Models

A number of complex models have recently appeared for describing the way the vocal tract behaves, in terms of physiology, biomechanics, and muscle control. Such models usually accept inputs of muscle activation levels, and output kinematic variables describing vocal tract configuration (and eventually acoustics) [71,72].

3.4 ACOUSTIC PHONETICS

Having described the mechanics of speech production, we now turn to its acoustics. The relationships between phonemes and their acoustic realizations form the bases for many speech applications (e.g., recognition, synthesis) as well as for an understanding of speech perception. A later section will examine relationships between speech acoustics and aspects of articulatory models of the vocal tract. In light of the earlier discussion of the articulator mechanisms for different phonemes, this section investigates the waveform and spectral properties of speech sounds; we delay to Section 3.5 the mathematical justifications for the observed phenomena.

Acoustic phonetics treats the speech signal as the output of the speech production process and relates the signal to its linguistic input (e.g., a sentence). It considers the differentiation of sounds on an acoustic (not articulatory) basis. Since each phoneme can be articulated in different ways and by different vocal tracts, there is much variability in speech signals for the same phoneme. In the ensuing discussion, common acoustic aspects are described for each phoneme, and figures give example waveforms and spectra.

As we will see in Chapter 6, most speech analysis uses spectral displays, which show the distribution of speech energy as a function of frequency. The importance of spectral analysis is highlighted in Chapter 4, which shows that the ear effectively extracts spectral amplitudes from speech signals. While the speech waveform contains the information necessary for speech communication, the information is encoded in a form not subject to easy interpretation. Most acoustic–phonetic features are more apparent spectrally than in the time domain. The following discussion focuses on the dynamic behavior of formants and spectral regions of energy, which appear to be the primary acoustic cues to phonemes.

3.4.1 Spectrograms

A basic tool for spectral analysis is the wideband *spectrogram*, which is discussed further in Chapter 6. A spectrogram converts a two-dimensional speech waveform (amplitude/time) into a three-dimensional pattern (amplitude/frequency/time) (Figure 3.10). With time and frequency on the horizontal and vertical axes, respectively, amplitude is noted by the darkness of the display. Peaks in the spectrum (e.g., formant resonances) appear as dark horizontal bands [73]. Voiced sounds cause vertical marks in the spectrogram due to an increase in speech amplitude each time the vocal folds close. The noise in unvoiced sounds causes rectangular dark patterns, randomly punctuated with light spots due to instantaneous

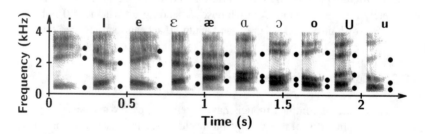

Figure 3.10 Spectrogram of short sections of English vowels from a male speaker. Formants for each vowel are noted by dots.

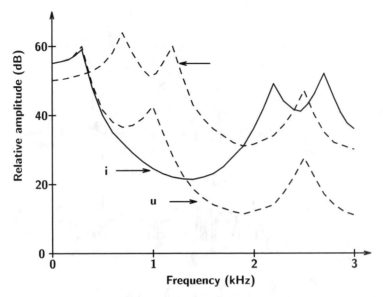

Figure 3.11 Cross-sections of spectra from the middle of English vowels of a male speaker, showing formants as spectral peaks.

variations in energy. Spectrograms portray only spectral amplitude, ignoring phase information, following the assumption that phase is relatively unimportant for many speech applications.

While analog spectrograms have a dynamic range (from white to black) of only about 12 dB, the digitally produced spectrograms in this book have a greater range. Spectrograms are used primarily to examine formant center frequencies. If more detailed information is needed about the spectrum (e.g., resonance bandwidths, relative amplitudes of resonances, depths of spectral nulls), individual spectral cross-sections (displays of amplitude vs frequency) must be analyzed (Figure 3.11). Despite these limitations, spectrograms furnish much information relevant to acoustic phonetics: the durations of acoustic segments, whether speech is periodic, and the detailed motion of formants. As will be explained in Chapter 6, wideband spectrograms employ 300 Hz bandpass filters with response times of a few ms, which yield good time resolution (for accurate durational measurements) but smoothed spectra. Smoothing speech energy over 300 Hz produces good formant displays of dark bands, where the center frequency of each resonance is assumed to be in the middle of the band (provided that the skirts of a resonance are approximately symmetric).

3.4.2 Vowels

Vowels (including diphthongs) are voiced (except when whispered), are the phonemes with the greatest intensity, and range in duration from 50 to 400 ms in normal speech. Like all sounds excited solely by a periodic glottal source, vowel energy is primarily concentrated below 1 kHz and falls off at about −6 dB/oct with frequency. Many relevant acoustic aspects of vowels can be seen in Figure 3.12, which shows brief portions of waveforms for five English vowels. The signals are quasi-periodic due to repeated excitations of the vocal tract by vocal fold closures. Thus, vowels have *line spectra* with frequency spacing of F0 Hz (i.e,

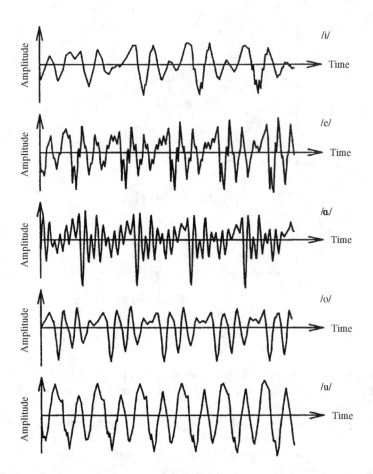

Figure 3.12 Typical acoustic waveforms for five English vowels. Each plot shows 40 ms of
a different vowel, which comprises about 5–6 pitch periods for this speaker.
Note the quasi-periodic nature of such voiced speech as well as the varying
spectral content for different vowels.

energy concentrated at multiples of F0). The largest harmonic amplitudes are near the low-formant frequencies.

Vocal fold excitations cause an abrupt signal increase once every period, after which amplitude decays exponentially with a time constant inversely proportional to the bandwidth of the formant(s) of highest energy (usually F1). F1 can be readily identified in time plots of many vowels as the inverse of the period of dominant oscillation within a pitch period. Front vowels in particular have a wide separation between F1 and F2, and the lowpass nature of the glottal source causes F1 to have much more energy than higher formants in these cases.

Vowels are distinguished primarily by the locations of their first three formant frequencies. Figure 3.10 shows spectrograms of typical vowel spectra, and Table 3.2 has mean formant values from a study of 32 male and 28 female speakers, who repeated twice ten monosyllabic nonsense words of the form /hVd/, where V was one of ten different vowels.

TABLE 3.2 Average formant frequencies (in Hz) for English vowels by adult male and female speakers from a classic study (see also [74] for a replication). (After Peterson and Barney [31].)

		/i/	/ɪ/	/ɛ/	/æ/	/ɑ/	/ɔ/	/ʊ/	/u/	/ʌ/	/ɝ/
F1	male	270	390	530	660	730	570	440	300	640	490
	female	310	430	610	860	850	590	470	370	760	500
F2	male	2290	1990	1840	1720	1090	840	1020	870	1190	1350
	female	2790	2480	2330	2050	1220	920	1160	950	1400	1640
F3	male	3010	2550	2480	2410	2440	2410	2240	2240	2390	1690
	female	3310	3070	2990	2850	2810	2710	2680	2670	2780	1960

Due to varying vocal tract shapes and sizes, formants vary considerably for different speakers; Figure 3.13 plots values for F1 and F2 for the ten vowels spoken by 60 speakers. There is much overlap across speakers, such that vowels with the same F1–F2 are heard as different phonemes when uttered by different speakers. Other aspects of the vowels (e.g., F0, upper formants, bandwidths) enable listeners to make correct interpretations. Each speaker keeps his vowels well apart in three-dimensional F1–F3 space. A plot of mean F1–F2 values for vowels shows a pattern called the *vowel triangle* (Figure 3.14), where the *point vowels* /i,ɑ,u/ have extreme F1–F2 values and most other vowels have formant values lying close to one of

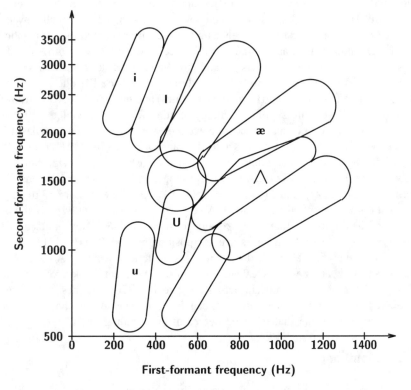

Figure 3.13 Plot of F1 vs F2 for vowels spoken by 60 speakers. (After Peterson and Barney [31].)

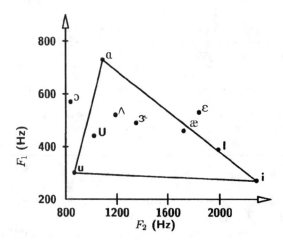

Figure 3.14 The vowel triangle for the vowels of Table 3.2.

the sides of the triangle: the /i/–/ɑ/ axis for the front vowels and the /u/–/ɑ/ axis for the back vowels. (For English, a "vowel quadrilateral" is more appropriate, including /æ/ as the fourth point vowel, but the relative infrequency of /æ/ in other languages has led to the tradition of a vowel triangle.) The vowel triangle has articulatory as well as acoustic interpretations: F1 decreases with tongue height, and F2 decreases as the tongue is shifted backward. Thus, the high front /i/ has the lowest F1 and highest F2 of all vowels, and the low vowel /ɑ/ has the highest F1. Vowels tend to have a more central tongue position laterally as tongue height decreases, and so the F2 difference between low vowels /æ/ and /ɑ/ is much less than between the high vowels /i/ and /u/. Vowel intensity decreases with tongue height over a 4–5 dB range. High vowels have little energy outside F1, due to a combination of a wide separation of F1 and F2 (from low F1 values) and the −6 dB/oct spectrum falloff, while lower vowels have more significant energy in other formants as well.

Although vowel formants occur on average every 1 kHz for adult males, F2 varies more than other formants. Table 3.2 notes a 460 Hz range for F1 (270–730 Hz) and a 1450 Hz range for F2 (840–2290 Hz). The range for F3 is also large (1690–3010 Hz), but eight of the ten vowels have F3 in a narrow 2240–2550 Hz range. In synthesis applications, F3 and higher formants are often kept fixed (e.g., F3 = 2500, F4 = 3500), except for F3 in /ɝ/ and perhaps /i/, with little perceptual degradation. A very low F3 (almost 1600 Hz) is the distinguishing aspect of the English rhotic vowel /ɝ/ and consonant /r/ [60]. Nonrhotic constrictions in the vocal tract only lower F3 from its average position by 200–300 Hz [75].

The values in Table 3.2 do not necessarily reflect standard American English, even though a large number of speakers are pooled. A recent revisit to this data notes that dialectical variation is significant across large regions [76]. The descriptions we use in this book reflect a common view of American English. The reader should be aware of large deviations in particular dialects, e.g., degree of lip rounding in /u/.

3.4.3 Diphthongs

There is some dispute over what constitutes a diphthong. The three diphthongs of Table 3.1 are universally accepted; they consist of a dynamic vowel sound in which the tongue (and lips) move between two vowel positions [77]. The three can be described as a vowel followed by a glide, but the articulators rarely attain the full constriction of a glide. The glide + vowel sequence /ju/ of Figures 3.15 and 3.16 is sometimes called a diphthong, but there are many other glide + vowel sequences (vs only three vowel + glide ones, all called diphthongs).

The vowels /e/ and /o/ in English are *diphthongized* (sometimes noted as /eʲ/ and /oʷ/, following formant trajectories for /ɛI/ and /ɔU/, respectively. Other European languages diphthongize these vowels to a much lesser extent (if at all). Part of a foreigner's accent when speaking English is often the result of an inadequate use of diphthongs; conversely, native English speakers are easily spotted by their inappropriate use of diphthongs in other languages. Diphthongs should not be confused with sequences of two vowels; e.g., the word *brake* has a diphthongized /e/, while *algebraic* has two vowels /eI/. The difference reflects the general rise + fall pattern of amplitude in syllables: amplitude falls during the glide portion of a diphthong, whereas the amplitude in a sequence such as /eI/ might dip only briefly, continuing strong for the second vowel.

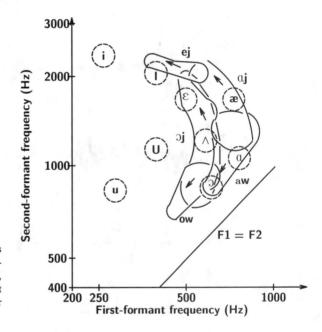

Figure 3.15 F1 and F2 time movements for diphthongs. The dashed circles indicate typical F1–F2 positions for vowels, and the solid contours enclose formant trajectories during diphthongs. (After Holbrook and Fairbanks [78].)

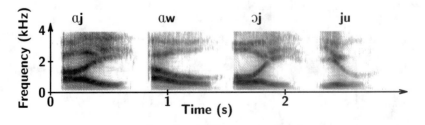

Figure 3.16 Spectrograms of four English diphthongs.

3.4.4 Glides and Liquids

Glides and liquids are sonorant consonants, very similar to vowels in that they have periodic, intense waveforms (Figure 3.17a) with most energy in the low formants (Figures 3.18a, b and 3.19a–d). They are weaker than vowels because they require a greater average constriction of the vocal tract, but airflow is rarely constrained enough to generate noise. Also known as *semivowels*, glides can be viewed as brief high vowels of greater constriction than corresponding vowels (/j/: /i/, /w/: /u/). Glides tend to be transient, sustaining a steady spectrum for much less time than vowels do [79].

The liquids /l,r/ have spectra very similar to vowels, but they are usually a few decibels weaker. The English /r/ causes F3 to descend much lower than for any other phoneme. In other languages, /r/ is quite variable, ranging from a velar or uvular fricative (both voiced and unvoiced) in French to a *trill* (rapid aerodynamic vibration) or even a single tap of the tongue tip in Spanish. The presence of multiple acoustic paths for /l/ (air passing on either side of the tongue tip) leads to an antiresonance in the F2–F4 region and a possible extra resonance near F4 [80]. The English /l/ is often characterized by a deep spectral null near 2 kHz and a

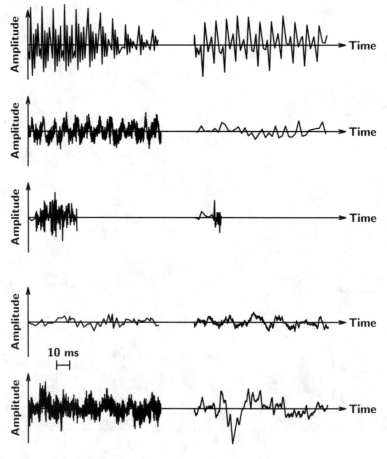

Figure 3.17 Typical acoustic waveforms for ten English consonants /l,n,ʒ,v,k,g,f,s,ʃ,z/.

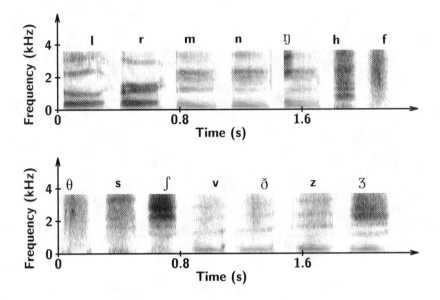

Figure 3.18 Spectrograms of 14 English steady-state consonants
/l,r,m,n,η,h,f,θ,s,∫,v,ð,z,ʒ/.

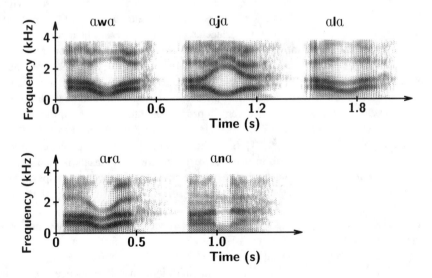

Figure 3.19 Spectrograms of English sonorants in vocalic contest:
/αwα, αjα, αlα, αrα, αnα/.

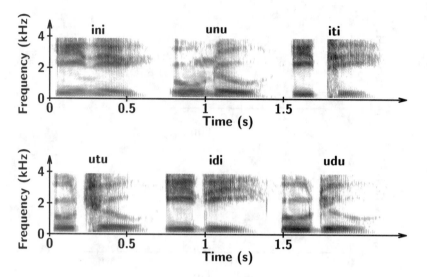

Figure 3.20 Spectrograms of English stops and nasals in vocalic context:
/ini,unu,iti,utu,idi,udu/.

high F3. Discontinuities appear in formant slopes when the tongue tip makes or breaks contact with the alveolar ridge.

3.4.5 Nasals

The waveforms of nasal consonants (called *murmurs*) resemble those of vowels (Figure 3.17b) but are significantly weaker because of sound attenuation in the nasal cavity. For its volume, the nasal cavity has a large surface area, which increases heat conduction and viscous losses so that formant bandwidths are generally wider than for other sonorants. Owing to the long pharyngeal + nasal tract (about 20 cm, vs a 17 cm pharyngeal + oral tract), formants occur about every 850 Hz instead of every 1 kHz. F1 near 250 Hz dominates the spectrum, F2 is very weak, and F3 near 2200 Hz has the second-highest formant peak (Figure 3.18c–e). A spectral zero, whose frequency is inversely proportional to the length of the oral cavity behind the constriction, occurs in the 750–1250 Hz region for /m/, in the 1450–2200 Hz region for /n/, and above 3 kHz for /η/ [81]. Since humans have relatively poor perceptual resolution for spectral nulls, discrimination of place of articulation for nasals is also cued by formant transitions in adjacent sounds (Figures 3.19e and 3.20). Spectral jumps in both formant amplitudes and frequencies coincide with the occlusion and opening of the oral tract for nasals.

The velum often lowers during a vowel preceding a nasal consonant, which causes nasalization of the vowel (Figures 3.19e and 3.20) (less often the nasalization continues into an ensuing vowel, if the oral tract opens before the velum closes). Vowel nasalization primarily affects spectra in the F1 region: an additional nasal resonance appears near F1 and the oral first formant weakens and shifts upward in frequency [82]; there is also less energy above 2 kHz [45].

3.4.6 Fricatives

As obstruents, fricatives and stops have waveforms (Figure 3.17c–j) very different from sonorants: aperiodic, much less intense, and usually with most energy at high frequencies (Figure 3.18f–n). The reduced energy is due to a major vocal tract constriction, where airflow is (relatively inefficiently) converted into noise much weaker than glottal pulses. The obstruents of English and many other languages may be either voiced or unvoiced. Since acoustic properties can vary significantly depending on voicing, unvoiced and voiced fricatives are discussed separately.

Unlike sonorants, in which the entire vocal tract is excited, unvoiced fricatives have a noise source that primarily excites the portion of the vocal tract anterior to the constriction, which results in a lack of energy at low frequencies. Unvoiced fricatives have a highpass spectrum, with a cutoff frequency approximately inversely proportional to the length of the front cavity. Thus the palatal fricatives are most intense, with energy above about 2.5 kHz; they have a large front cavity, since the constriction is a 10–12 mm wide groove behind the posterior border of the alveolar ridge [83]. With a groove 6–8 mm wide and further forward, the alveolar fricatives lack significant energy below about 3.2 kHz and are less intense. The labial and dental fricatives are very weak, with little energy below 8 kHz, due to a very small front cavity. The glottal fricative /h/ also has low intensity since the whisper noise source of the glottis is usually weaker than noise from oral tract constrictions, but energy appears at all formants since the full vocal tract is excited; in general, /h/ is a whispered version of the ensuing vowel.

Voiced fricatives have a double acoustic source, periodic glottal pulses and the usual frication noise generated at the vocal tract constriction. The nonstrident voiced fricatives /v/ and /ð/ are almost periodic, with few noise components, and resemble weak versions of a glide such as /w/. The fricatives /z/ and /ʒ/, on the other hand, usually have significant noise energy at high frequencies typical of /s/ and / ʃ /, respectively. In addition, they exhibit a *voice bar* (very-low-frequency formant) near 150 Hz and sometimes have weak periodic energy in the low formants typical of sonorants. The spectra of unvoiced fricatives are rarely characterized in terms of formants because low frequencies are not excited and the excited upper resonances have broad bandwidths. Since the glottal pulses of voiced fricatives may excite all resonances of the vocal tract, however, formants can characterize voiced fricatives.

3.4.7 Stops (Plosives)

Unlike other sounds, which can be described largely in terms of steady-state spectra, stops are transient phonemes and thus are acoustically complex (Figures 3.17i, j, 3.20 and 3.21). The closure portion of a stop renders the speech either silent (for most stops) or having a simple voice bar with energy confined to the first few harmonics (for some voiced stops). When present, the voice bar is due to radiation of periodic glottal pulses through the walls of the vocal tract; the throat and cheeks heavily attenuate all but the lowest frequencies.

The release of the vocal tract occlusion creates a brief (a few ms) explosion of noise, which excites all frequencies, but primarily those of a fricative having the same place of articulation. After the initial burst, turbulent noise generation (frication) continues at the opening constriction for 10–40 ms, exciting high-frequency resonances, as the vocal tract moves toward a position for the ensuing sonorant. Unvoiced stops average longer frication than do voiced ones (35 vs 20 ms) [84]. In voiced stops, vocal fold vibration either continues throughout the entire stop or starts immediately after the burst. The vocal folds are more

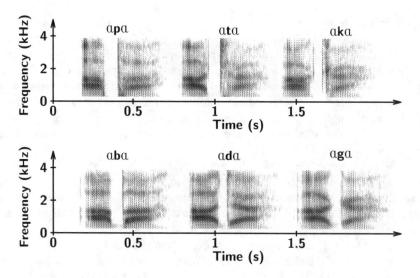

Figure 3.21 Spectrograms of the six English stops in vocalic context: /ɑpɑ,ɑtɑ,ɑkɑ,ɑbɑ,ɑdɑ,ɑgɑ/.

widely separated during the closure for unvoiced stops and begin to adduct only near the time of release. Before the vocal folds begin to vibrate, a condition suitable for whisper usually occurs at the narrowing glottis. In such *aspirated stops*, the whisper source excites the resonances of the vocal tract, which are moving toward positions for the ensuing sonorant for about 30 ms after the frication period [84].

Unaspirated stops have little periodic energy at low frequency in the first 20 ms after stop release. Voiced stops in English are not aspirated, nor are stops after fricatives in initial consonant clusters. Other languages permit the independent specification of aspiration and voicing, thus creating four classes of stops. Stops are identified on spectrograms as sounds with very little intensity (at most a voice bar) for 20–120 ms during occlusion, often followed by a brief noise burst. Stops at the end of a syllable are often *unreleased*, in that little burst is apparent, due to a relaxation in lung pressure or a glottal stop, which reduces oral pressure behind the stop occlusion.

Stops can be very brief between two vowels. Alveolar stops, in particular, may become *flaps* in which the tongue tip retains contact with the palate for only 10–40 ms. The shortest flaps occur between low vowels, where rapid ballistic motion is more feasible than between high vowels (due to the longer distance the tongue tip moves with low vowels) [58].

The burst release of alveolar stops is broadband, with energy primarily above 2 kHz. The peak for /t/ is usually near 3.9 kHz, but it drops to 3.3 kHz before rounded or retroflex vowels; peaks for /d/ are about 365 Hz lower than for /t/. The different allophones of /k/ lead to radically different burst spectra: a compact peak at about 2.7 kHz for /k/ before a front vowel and a lower-frequency peak with a secondary peak above 3 kHz before a back vowel (the lower peak averages 1.8 kHz before unrounded vowels and 1.2 kHz before rounded vowels) [84]. Alveolar and velar bursts average about 16 dB weaker than ensuing vowels, while labial bursts are the weakest (28 dB less than vowels). The acoustics of affricates resemble that of stop + fricative sequences [61].

3.4.8 Variants of Normal Speech

Common variants of normal speech are whisper, shout, and song. In whispered speech, the glottal periodic source for voiced speech is replaced by glottal frication (aspiration). Unvoiced obstruents are unaffected, but sonorants become unvoiced and decrease substantially in amplitude so that fricatives are louder than whispered vowels. At the other extreme of speech intensity is shouted voice, typically 18–28 dB louder than normal voice [85]. Both extremes suffer from decreased intelligibility, but for different reasons. In whisper, voiced and unvoiced obstruents are often confused. In shouting, the distinctions between many phonemes are sacrificed to increase amplitude so that the voice can be heard at a distance. Speakers often raise their voice intensity, without shouting, in inverse proportion to the distance from listeners (to compensate for the inverse square law of sound power radiating from the lips); F0 level also goes up (but not F0 range) and vowels lengthen [86,87]. Speakers also increase duration and intensity (among other factors) when faced with a noisy environment (the *Lombard effect*) [88,89].

Vowels, especially open vowels, dominate shouted speech in terms of duration. It is much easier to raise intensity for vowels than for obstruents, so shouting emphasizes vowels. Physiologically, the vocal tract tends to be more open for shouted than for normal voice, which raises F1 and general amplitude but alters the speech spectra. The main difference, however, occurs at the glottis, where increased subglottal pressure raises amplitude, and altered vocal fold tension reduces the duration of the open phase in vocal fold vibration (similar glottal changes occur in emotional or stressed speech [90]). The resulting sharper glottal air puffs resemble square pulses rather than the normal rounded shape and thus have more high-frequency energy. F0 also rises considerably, and formants tend to neutralize, deforming the vowel triangle [85].

Fundamentally, singing differs from normal voice mostly in intonation: (a) durations are modified to accomplish various rhythms, usually extending vowels (as in shouting) rather than consonants, and (b) F0 is held fixed for musical intervals corresponding to different notes, rather than allowed to vary continuously as in speech. However, singing is often correlated with increased intensity (e.g., in opera), and singers can modify their articulations to have up to 12 dB more intensity via a fourfold increase in airflow with the same lung pressure [13,91]. One such change is a lowered larynx in vowels, which appears to add a *singing formant* (also called *vocal ring*) at about 2.8 kHz, boosting energy by about 20 dB in the F3–F4 range, which is usually weak in normal voice [92]. This "formant" is actually a clustering of existing formants (F3–F5), and appears to relate to the narrow *epilarynx* tube (vocal tract right above the glottis). This tube is about 3 cm long and 0.5 cm^2 in area (vs 3 cm^2 in the pharynx); being about $\frac{1}{6}$ the length of the vocal tract, its quarter-wavelength resonance (see below) is about 3 kHz. Like the mouthpiece of a brass musical instrument, it matches a high glottal impedance to the lower impedance of the wider pharynx [93].

As we will see in Chapter 10, the style of speech significantly affects accuracy rates in automatic speech recognition. Spontaneous and conversational speech is the most difficult to recognize, due to its often faster rate, high use of words familiar to the listener, and frequent disfluencies. The latter include pauses at unexpected locations (e.g., within words), repetitions of portions of words, and filled pauses (e.g., "uhh" or "umm") [94]. At the other extreme, "hyperarticulate" or "clear" speech may be used when talking to computers or foreigners, on the assumption that such listeners cannot handle normal speech; such speech is slower with more pauses and fewer disfluencies [95].

Lastly, other human vocalizations include coughs and laughs. While not strictly speech, their analysis is relevant, especially in the context of speech recognition applications, where it would be useful to distinguish pertinent, linguistic sounds from other human sounds. Laughter usually consists of a series of 200–230 ms bursts of a breathy neutral vowel, often at higher F0 than normal speech [96]. Coughs are irregular, brief, broadband noise bursts.

3.5 ACOUSTIC THEORY OF SPEECH PRODUCTION

This section gives mathematical details for acoustic and electrical models of speech production that are suitable for many speech applications. Since more readers are familiar with electrical circuits than acoustics, electrical analogs of the vocal tract will be analyzed. Such analog models are further developed into digital circuits suitable for simulation by computer.

3.5.1 Acoustics of the Excitation Source

In modeling speech, the effects of the excitation source and the vocal tract are often considered independently. While the source and tract interact acoustically, their interdependence causes only secondary effects. Thus this chapter generally assumes independence. (Some recent literature examines in more detail these interactions, e.g., influences on formants due to the subglottal regions, and on glottal flow due to supraglottal load, which is raised by oral constrictions [2]).

In sonorant production, quasi-periodic pulses of air excite the vocal tract, which acts as a filter to shape the speech spectrum. Unvoiced sounds result from a noise source exciting the vocal tract forward of the source. In both cases, a speech signal $s(t)$ can be modeled as the convolution of an excitation signal $e(t)$ and an impulse response characterizing the vocal tract $v(t)$. Since convolution of two signals corresponds to multiplication of their spectra, the output speech spectrum $S(\Omega)$ is the product of the excitation spectrum $E(\Omega)$ and the frequency response $V(\Omega)$ of the vocal tract. This section models $e(t)$ and $E(\Omega)$ for different types of excitation.

Unvoiced excitation, either frication at a constriction or explosion at a stop release, is usually modeled as random noise with an approximately Gaussian amplitude distribution and a flat spectrum over most frequencies of interest. The flat range is about 2–3 octaves, centered on a frequency of $U/(5A^{3/2})$ (which equals typically 1 kHz), where A is the area of constriction generating the noise and U is its volume velocity [17]. White noise, limited to the bandwidth of speech, is a reasonable model; in this case, $|E(\Omega)|$ has no effect on $|S(\Omega)|$. The phase of $E(\Omega)$ is rarely analyzed because (a) spectral amplitude is much more important than phase for speech perception, and (b) simple models for random (unvoiced) $e(t)$ suffice for good quality in speech synthesis.

More research has been done on voiced than on unvoiced excitation because the naturalness of synthetic speech is crucially related to accurate modeling of voiced speech. It is difficult to obtain precise measurements of glottal pressure or volume velocity waveforms. Photography using mirrors at the back of the throat has shown how the glottal area behaves during voicing, but glottal airflow is not always proportional to glottal area because acoustic impedance varies during the voicing cycle (e.g., airflow follows the third power of glottal area for small areas [62]). Two methods to measure glottal signals employ *inverse filtering* or a *reflectionless tube* attached to the mouth.

In inverse filtering, an estimate $|\hat{V}(\Omega)|$ is made of $|V(\Omega)|$, using the observed $|S(\Omega)|$ and knowledge of articulatory acoustics. The excitation estimate then is simply

$$|\hat{E}(\Omega)| = \frac{|S(\Omega)|}{|\hat{V}(\Omega)|}.$$ (3.1)

A problem here is that errors are often made in estimating $|\hat{V}(\Omega)|$, and this estimate is often adjusted to yield a smooth $e(t)$, following preconceived notions of how glottal pulses should appear [97]. An alternative method extends the vocal tract with a long uniform tube attached to the mouth, which effectively flattens $|V(\Omega)|$ by preventing acoustic reflections that would otherwise cause resonances. The spectrum of the output of the long tube should be $|E(\Omega)|$ if the coupling at the mouth is tight and the entire system (vocal tract + tube) can be modeled as a long, uniform, hard-walled passageway. Since the vocal tract cross-sectional area is not uniform, however, certain distortions enter into $|\hat{E}(\Omega)|$, especially for narrowly constricted vocal tract shapes [98].

The glottal volume velocity $e(t)$ of voiced speech is periodic and roughly resembles a half-rectified sine wave (Figure 3.22). From a value of zero when the glottis is closed, $e(t)$ gradually increases as the vocal folds separate. The closing phase is more rapid than the opening phase (thus the glottal pulse is skewed to the right) due to the *Bernoulli force*, which adducts the vocal folds. A discontinuity in the slope of $e(t)$ at closure causes the major excitation of the vocal tract; i.e., a sudden increase in $|s(t)|$ (Figure 3.12) every glottal period occurs about 0.5 ms after glottal closure (sound travels from glottis to lips in 0.5 ms). The *duty cycle* or *open quotient* (ratio of open phase—both opening and closing portions—to full period) varies from about 0.4 in low-F0 shouts and *pressed voice* to above 0.7 in breathy, low-amplitude voices.

To analyze voiced excitation spectrally, assume that one period of $e(t)$ is a glottal pulse $g(t)$. Periodic $e(t)$ results in a line spectrum $|E(\Omega)|$ because (a) $e(t)$ can be modeled by the convolution of a uniform impulse train $i(t)$ with one pulse $g(t)$, and (b) $|E(\Omega)|$ is thus the product of a uniform impulse train $|I(\Omega)|$ in frequency and $|G(\Omega)|$. Since $e(t)$ and thus $i(t)$ are periodic with period $T = 1/F0$, both $|I(\Omega)|$ and $|E(\Omega)|$ are line spectra with F0 Hz spacing between lines. The relatively smooth function $g(t)$ leads to a lowpass $|G(\Omega)|$, with a cutoff frequency near 500 Hz and a falloff of about -12 dB/oct. Increased vocal effort for loud voices decreases the duty cycle of $e(t)$, causing more abrupt glottal closure, hence a less smooth $g(t)$ and more high-frequency energy in $|G(\Omega)|$.

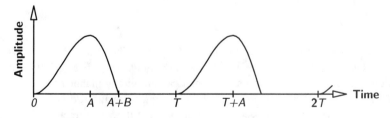

Figure 3.22 Simplfied glottal waveforms during a voiced sound.

3.5.2 Acoustics of the Vocal Tract

Except for a falloff with frequency, the amplitudes of the spectral lines in $|S(\Omega)|$ for voiced speech are determined primarily by the vocal tract transfer function $|V(\Omega)|$. A later section calculates $|V(\Omega)|$ for a number of simplified models of the vocal tract. This section uses a general model to analyze vocal tract acoustics heuristically in terms of resonances and antiresonances. In its simplest model, speech production involves a zero-viscosity gas (air) passing through a 17 cm long, hard-walled acoustic tube of uniform cross-sectional area A, closed at the glottal end and open at the lips. In practice, such modeling assumptions must be qualified: (a) vocal tract length varies among speakers (about 13 cm for women, and 10 cm for 8-year-old children) and even within a speaker's speech (protruding the lips or lowering the larynx extends the vocal tract); (b) the walls of the vocal tract yield, introducing vibration losses; (c) air has some viscosity, causing friction and thermal losses; (d) area A varies substantially along the length of the vocal tract, even for relatively neutral phonemes; (e) while glottal area is small relative to typical A values, the glottal end of the vocal tract is truly closed only during glottal stops and during the closed phases of voicing; (f) for many sounds, lip rounding or closure narrows the acoustic tube at the lips. The effects of each of these qualifications will be examined in turn, but we ignore them for now.

3.5.2.1 Basic acoustics of sound propagation. Sound waves are created by vibration, either of the vocal folds or other vocal tract articulators or of random motion of air particles. The waves are propagated through the air via a chain reaction of vibrating air particles from the sound source to the destination of a listener's ear. The production and propagation of sound follow the laws of physics, including conservation of mass, momentum, and energy. The laws of thermodynamics and fluid mechanics also apply to an air medium, which is compressible and has low viscosity.

In free space, sound travels away from a source in a spherical wave whose radius increases with time. When sound meets a barrier, diffractions and reflections occur, changing the sound direction (variations in air temperature and wind speed also affect the direction of travel). At most speech frequencies of interest (e.g., below 4 kHz), however, sound waves in the vocal tract propagate in only one dimension, along the axis of the vocal tract. Such *planar propagation* occurs only for frequencies whose wavelengths λ are large compared to the diameter of the vocal tract; e.g., for energy at 4 kHz,

$$\lambda = c/f = \frac{340\,\text{m/s}}{4000/\text{s}} = 8.5\,\text{cm}, \tag{3.2}$$

which exceeds an average 2 cm vocal tract diameter. (The speed of sound c is given for air at sea level and room temperature; it increases at about 0.6 m/s per °C [99], and is much higher in liquids and solids.) Due to its mathematical simplicity, planar propagation is assumed in this book, even though it is less valid at high frequencies and for parts of the vocal tract with large width. The initial discussion also assumes that the vocal tract is a hard-walled, lossless tube, temporarily ignoring losses due to viscosity, heat conduction, and vibrating walls.

Linear wave motion in the vocal tract follows the law of continuity and Newton's law (force equals mass times acceleration), respectively:

$$\frac{1}{\rho c^2}\frac{\partial p}{\partial t} + \text{div } \mathbf{v} = 0 \tag{3.3}$$

$$\rho\frac{\partial \mathbf{v}}{\partial t} + \text{grad } p = 0 \tag{3.4}$$

where p is sound pressure, $\mathbf{v}$ is the vector velocity of an air particle in the vocal tract (a three-dimensional vector describes 3D air space), and ρ is the density of air in the tube (about $1.2\,\text{mg/cm}^3$) [98]. In the case of one-dimensional airflow in the vocal tract, it is more convenient to examine the velocity of a volume of air u than its particle velocity v:

$$u = Av, \tag{3.5}$$

where A is the cross-sectional area of the vocal tract. In general, A, u, $\mathbf{v}$, and p are all functions of both time t and distance x from the glottis ($x = 0$) to the lips ($x = l$) (e.g., $l = 17\,\text{cm}$). Using volume velocity $u(x,t)$ and area $A(x,t)$ to represent $\mathbf{v}$ under the planar assumption, Equations (3.3) and (3.4) reduce to

$$-\frac{\partial u}{\partial x} = \frac{1}{\rho c^2}\frac{\partial(pA)}{\partial t} + \frac{\partial A}{\partial t}, \tag{3.6}$$

$$-\frac{\partial p}{\partial x} = \rho\frac{\partial(u/A)}{\partial t}. \tag{3.7}$$

For simple notation, the dependence on both x and t is implicit. While closed-form solutions to Equations (3.6) and (3.7) are possible only for very simple configurations, numerical solutions are possible by specifying $A(x,t)$ and boundary conditions at the lips (for the speech output) and at the sound source (e.g., the glottis).

3.5.2.2 Acoustics of a uniform lossless tube.
Analysis is simplified considerably by letting A be fixed in both time and space, which leads to a model of a steady vowel close to /ə/. Other steady sounds require more complex $A(x)$ functions, which are described later as concatenations of tube sections with uniform cross-sectional area. The analysis for a single long uniform tube applies to shorter tube sections as well. The tube is assumed straight, although actual vocal tracts gradually bend 90°, which shift resonant frequencies about 2–8% [100]. With A constant, Equations (3.6) and (3.7) reduce to

$$-\frac{\partial u}{\partial x} = \frac{A}{\rho c^2}\frac{\partial p}{\partial t} \quad\text{and}\quad -\frac{\partial p}{\partial x} = \frac{\rho}{A}\frac{\partial u}{\partial t}. \tag{3.8}$$

To obtain an understanding of the spectral behavior of a uniform tube, assume now that the glottal end of the tube is excited by a sinusoidal volume velocity source $u_G(t)$ and that pressure is zero at the lip end. Using complex exponentials to represent sinusoids, we have

$$u(0, t) = u_G(t) = U_G(\Omega)e^{j\Omega t} \tag{3.9}$$

$$p(l, t) = 0$$

where Ω is the radian frequency of the source and U_G is its amplitude. Since Equations (3.8) are linear, they have solutions of the form

$$p(x, t) = P(x, \Omega)e^{j\Omega t}$$
$$u(x, t) = U(x, \Omega)e^{j\Omega t}, \quad (3.10)$$

where P and U represent complex spectral amplitudes that vary with time and position in the tube. Substituting Equations (3.10) into equations (3.8) yields ordinary differential equations

$$-\frac{dU}{dx} = YP \quad \text{and} \quad -\frac{dP}{dx} = ZU, \quad (3.11)$$

where $Z = j\Omega\rho/A$ and $Y = j\Omega A/\rho c^2$ are the distributed acoustic impedance and admittance, respectively, of the tube. Equations (3.11) have solutions of the form

$$P(x, \Omega) = a_1 e^{\gamma x} + a_2 e^{-\gamma x}, \quad (3.12)$$

where the *propagation constant* γ is

$$\gamma = \sqrt{ZY} = j\Omega/c \quad (3.13)$$

in the lossless case (losses add real components to Z and Y, causing a complex γ). Applying boundary conditions (Equations (3.9)) to determine the coefficients a_i, we have the steady-state solutions for p and u in a tube excited by a glottal source:

$$p(x, t) = jZ_0 \frac{\sin(\Omega(l - x)/c)}{\cos(\Omega l/c)} U_G(\Omega)e^{j\Omega t}$$
$$u(x, t) = \frac{\cos(\Omega(l - x)/c)}{\cos(\Omega l/c)} U_G(\Omega)e^{j\Omega t}, \quad (3.14)$$

where $Z_0 = \rho c/A$ is called the *characteristic impedance* of the tube. Equations (3.14) note the sinusoidal relationship of pressure and volume velocity in an acoustic tube, where one is 90° out of phase with respect to the other. The volume velocity at the lips is

$$u(l, t) = U(l, \Omega)e^{j\Omega t} = \frac{U_G(\Omega)e^{j\Omega t}}{\cos(\Omega l/c)}. \quad (3.15)$$

The vocal tract transfer function, relating lip and glottal volume velocity, is thus

$$V(\Omega) = \frac{U(l, \Omega)}{U_G(\Omega)} = \frac{1}{\cos(\Omega l/c)}. \quad (3.16)$$

The denominator is zero at formant frequencies $F_i = \Omega_i/(2\pi)$, where

$$\begin{cases} \Omega_i l/c = (2i - 1)(\pi/2) \\ F_i = (2i - 1)c/(4l) \end{cases} \quad \text{for } i = 1, 2, 3, \ldots. \quad (3.17)$$

If $l = 17\,\text{cm}$, $V(\Omega)$ becomes infinite at $F_i = 500, 1500, 2500, 3500, \ldots$ Hz, which indicates vocal tract resonances every 1 kHz starting at 500 Hz. For a vocal tract with a length l other than 17 cm, these F_i values must be scaled by $17/l$. Linear scaling of formants for shorter vocal tracts of nonuniform area is only approximately valid because the pharynx tends to be disproportionately small as length decreases in smaller people [101,102].

    Similar analysis using Laplace transforms instead of Fourier transforms shows that $V(s)$ has an infinite number of poles equally spaced on the $j\Omega$ axis of the complex s plane, a pair of

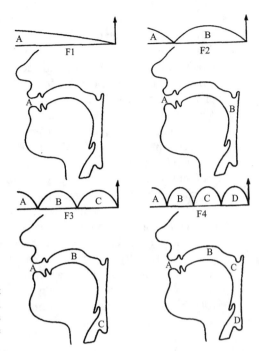

Figure 3.23 Spatial distribution of volume velocity at frequencies of the first four resonances of an ideal vocal tract having uniform cross-sectional area. Places of maximum volume velocity are noted in a schematic of the vocal tract.

poles for each resonance at $s_i = \pm j2\pi F_i$. Since a fixed acoustic tube is a linear time-invariant system, it is fully characterized by its frequency response $V(\Omega)$. The spectrum $S(\Omega)$ of the tube output is thus $U_G(\Omega)V(\Omega)$, for arbitrary excitation U_G as well as for the simple sinusoidal example of Equations (3.9).

A tube closed at one end and open at the other resembles an organ pipe and is called a *quarter-wavelength resonator*. The frequencies at which the tube resonates are those where sound waves traveling up and down the tube reflect and coincide at the ends of the tube. As an alternative to the lengthy derivation above, vocal tract resonances can be heuristically computed using only boundary conditions and the phase relationship of pressure and volume velocity. Formant frequencies match boundary conditions on pressure P (relative to outside atmospheric pressure) and net volume velocity U: a closed end of the tube forces $U = 0$, whereas $P \approx 0$ at an open end. P is 90° out of phase with U, much as voltage and current are at quadrature in transmission lines or in inductors and capacitors. Given the boundary conditions and the 90° phase shift, resonance occurs at frequencies F_i, $i = 1, 2, 3, \ldots$, where $|U|$ is maximum at the open end of the vocal tract and $|P|$ is maximum at the closed end. Such frequencies have wavelengths λ_i where vocal tract length l is an odd multiple of a quarter-wavelength (Figure 3.23):

$$l = (\lambda_i/4)(2i - 1), \qquad \text{for } i = 1, 2, 3, \ldots, \tag{3.18}$$

which leads to Equation (3.17).

3.5.2.3 Resonances in nonuniform tubes.   A uniform acoustic tube is a reasonable vocal tract model only for a schwa vowel. To determine formant frequencies for other sounds, more complex models must be employed. One approach that yields good models for many sounds follows *perturbation* theory. If the uniform tube is modified to have a constriction with slightly reduced diameter over a short length of the tube, the resonances perturb from their original positions. The degree of formant change is correlated with the length and narrowness of the constriction. Consider a resonance F_i with maxima in U and P at alternating locations along the tube. If the tube is constricted where U is maximum, F_i falls; if P is maximum there, F_i rises. In particular, a constriction in the front half of the vocal tract (i.e., between lips and velum) lowers F1, and a constriction at the lips lowers all formants. The effects on formants above F1 of constrictions not at the lips are complex due to the rapid spatial alternation of P and U maxima as frequency increases.

This phenomenon derives from simple circuit theory. The relationships of volume velocity U (acoustical analog of electrical current I) and pressure P (analog of voltage V) can be described in terms of impedances Z, involving resistance, inductance, and capacitance. As we will see later, modeling an acoustic tube by discrete elements (e.g., simple resistors, capacitors, and inductors) has severe drawbacks. A distributed model of impedances, as for a transmission line, is more appropriate for an acoustic tube.

The mass of air in a tube has an *inertance* opposing acceleration, and the compressibility of its volume exhibits a *compliance*. The inertance and compliance are modeled electrically as inductance and capacitance, respectively. The local distributed (per unit length) inductance L for a section of tube with area A is ρ/A, while the corresponding capacitance C is $A/\rho c^2$. Following transmission line theory [103], the characteristic impedance is

$$Z_0 = \sqrt{L/C} = \rho c/A. \qquad (3.19)$$

If A is a function of distance x along the tube, then wide and narrow sections of the tube will have large values of C and L, respectively.

In passive circuits such as the vocal tract, an increase in either inductance or capacitance lowers all resonant frequencies (e.g., the resonance of a simple LC circuit is $(2\pi\sqrt{LC})^{-1}$), but in varying degrees depending on the distribution of potential and kinetic energy. Perturbing a uniform tube with a slight constriction reduces A at one point along the tube. If at that place, for a given resonance F_i, U is large without the constriction, kinetic energy dominates and the change in L has a greater effect on F_i than do changes in C. Similarly, for those places where P is large, potential energy dominates and changes in C dominate F_i movement. Since reducing A raises L and lowers C, F_i increases if the constriction occurs where P is large and decreases where U is large [80].

Calculating the amount of formant change is left to a later section, but certain vocal tract configurations facilitate acoustic analysis. If the vocal tract can be modeled by two or three sections of tube (each with uniform area) and if the areas of adjacent sections are quite different, the individual tube sections are only loosely coupled acoustically, and resonances can be associated with individual cavities. Except for certain extreme vowels (e.g., /i,ɑ,u/), most vowels are *not* well represented by tube sections with abrupt boundaries; consonants, however, often use narrow vocal tract constrictions that cause $A(x)$ to change abruptly with x at constriction boundaries. Thus, resonant frequencies for most consonants and some vowels can be quickly estimated by identifying resonances of individual cavities, which avoids the mathematical complexities of acoustic interaction between cavities.

3.5.2.4 Vowel modeling.   The vowel /ɑ/ can be roughly modeled by a narrow tube (representing the pharynx) opening abruptly into a wide tube (oral cavity) (Figure 3.24a). Assuming for simplicity that each tube has a length of 8.5 cm, each would produce the same set of resonances at odd multiples of 1 kHz. Each tube is a quarter-wavelength resonator, since each back end is relatively closed and each front end is relatively open. At the boundary

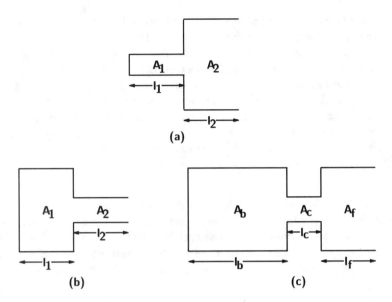

Figure 3.24 Two- and three-tube models for the vocal tract. In the two-tube case, the first tube section of area A_1 and length l_1 may be viewed as modeling the pharyngeal cavity, while the second section of area A_2 and length l_2 models the oral cavity. The first two models represent the vowels: (a) /ɑ/ and (b) /i/. The three-tube model (c) has a narrow section corresponding to the constriction for a consonant. (After Stevens [104].)

between the tube sections, the narrow back tube opens up, whereas the wide front tube finds its area abruptly reduced. If the change in areas is sufficiently abrupt, the acoustic coupling between cavities is small and the interaction between cavity resonances is slight. Since each tube is half the length of the vocal tract, formants occur at twice the frequencies noted earlier for the single uniform tube. Due to actual acoustic coupling, formants do not approach each other by less than about 200 Hz; thus F1 and F2 for /ɑ/ are not both at 1000 Hz, but rather F1 = 900, F2 = 1100, F3 = 2900, and F4 = 3100. Deviations from actual observed values represent modeling inaccuracies (e.g., a simple two-tube model is only a rough approximation to /ɑ/; nonetheless, this model gives reasonably accurate results and is easy to interpret physically.

The respective model for /i/ has a wide back tube constricting abruptly to a narrow front tube (Figure 3.24b). In this case, the back tube is modeled as closed at both ends (the narrow openings into the glottis and the front tube are small compared to the area of the back tube), and the front tube has open ends. These tubes are *half-wavelength resonators* because their boundary conditions are symmetrical: a tube closed at both ends requires U minima at its ends for resonance, whereas a tube open at both ends requires P minima at its ends. In both cases, the conditions are satisfied by tube lengths l that are multiples of half a resonance wavelength λ_i:

$$l = \frac{\lambda_i}{2}i \quad \text{and} \quad F_i = \frac{c}{\lambda_i} = \frac{ci}{2l}, \quad \text{for } i = 1, 2, 3, \ldots. \tag{3.20}$$

Thus, for /i/, both tubes have resonances at multiples of 2 kHz (again, in practice the formants of one tube are slightly below predicted values and those of the other are above, when the tubes have identical predicted resonances). Besides the formants of Equation (3.20), another resonance at very low frequency occurs for vocal tract models containing a large tube (e.g., the back cavity) closed at both ends. This corresponds to F1, which decreases from a value of 500 Hz in a one-tube model as a constriction is made in the forward half of the vocal tract. In the limiting case of a tube actually closed at both ends, F1 approaches a zero-frequency (infinite-wavelength) resonance, where the boundary conditions of minimal U at both ends are satisfied. In practice, F1 goes no lower than about 150 Hz, but many consonants and high vowels approach such F1 values. Back rounded vowels (e.g., /o,u/) can be modeled as having two closed tubes with a constricted tube between them; in such cases both F1 and F2 are relatively low.

   3.5.2.5 Consonant modeling.   A three-tube model appropriate for many consonants (Figure 3.24c) employs relatively wide back and front tubes, with a narrow central tube to model a vocal tract constriction. The back and central tubes are half-wavelength resonators (one closed at both ends, the other open at both ends), whereas the front tube is a quarter-wavelength resonator. Thus, three sets of resonances F_i can be defined:

$$\frac{ci}{2l_b}, \frac{ci}{2l_c}, \frac{c(2i-1)}{4l_f}, \qquad \text{for } i = 1, 2, 3, \ldots, \tag{3.21}$$

where l_b, l_c, l_f are the lengths of the back, central, and front tubes. Figure 3.25 shows how the front and back cavity resonances vary as a function of the position of the constriction, assuming a typical consonant constriction length l_c of 3 cm. The resonances of the

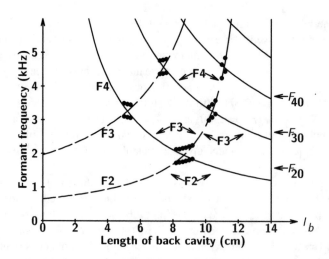

Figure 3.25 Formant frequencies as a function of the length of the back tube in the model of Figure 3.24(c), using 16 cm as the overall length of the three tubes and 3 cm as the constriction length. The dashed lines show the lowest two front cavity resonances, the solid lines the lowest four back cavity resonances. Dotted lines show the effect of a small amount of coupling between tubes, which prevents coinciding formant frequencies. The arrows at right note the formants (F2, F3, F4) of an unconstricted 16 cm long tube. (After Stevens [104] 1972 *Human Communication: A Unified View*, E. David and P. Denes (eds), reproduced with permission of McGraw-Hill Book Co.)

constriction occur at multiples of 5333 Hz and can be ignored in many applications that use speech of 4 or 5 kHz bandwidth.

Labial consonants have virtually no front cavity, and thus all formants of interest are associated with the long back tube, yielding values lower than those for a single uniform open tube. A model for alveolar consonants might use a 10 cm back tube and a 3 cm front tube; Figure 3.25 suggests that such consonants should have a back cavity resonance near 1.7 kHz for F2 and a front cavity resonance for F3 around 2.8 kHz. Alveolars are indeed characterized by relatively high F3 compared with average F3 values for vowels. Velar constrictions are more subject to coarticulation than labials or alveolars, but an 8.5 cm back tube and a 4.5 cm front tube is a good model that leads to close values for F2 and F3 near 2 kHz. The dominant acoustic characteristic of velars is indeed a concentration of energy in the F2–F3 region around 2 kHz. If the velar has a relatively forward articulation (e.g., if it is adjacent to a forward vowel), F2 is a back cavity resonance and F3 is affiliated with the front cavity. The opposite occurs if the velar constricts farther back along the palate, e.g., when the velar is near a back vowel. A similar effect occurs between F3 and F4 for alveolar and palatal fricatives: /s/ and / ʃ / might have 11 cm and 10 cm back tubes, respectively, which lead to a front cavity resonance of F3 for / ʃ / but of a higher formant for /s/.

The distinction between front and back tube resonance affiliation is important for obstruent consonants because speech energy is dominated by front cavity resonances. Frication noise generated just anterior to an obstruent constriction primarily excites the cavities in front of the constriction. Posterior cavities are usually acoustically decoupled from the noise source, until the constriction widens, at which point the noise ceases. Alveolars and front velars have dominant energy in F3, while F2 is prominent for back velars. Labial consonants with no front cavity to excite simply have low energy.

In stop + vowel production, the stop release is marked by a noise burst that excites primarily the front cavities, giving rise to different spectral content for different stops. A velar constriction provides a long front cavity, with a low resonance near 2 kHz (F2 or F3). Alveolar resonances are higher (F4 and F5) due to shorter front cavities. The spectrum of a labial burst is relatively flat and weak since there is essentially no front cavity to excite.

3.5.2.6 Resonances and antiresonances. Postponing technical details, we can heuristically estimate the frequencies of antiresonances (zeros) in fricatives using simple acoustic tube models. When a sound source has only one acoustic path to the output (the mouth), the vocal tract frequency response has only resonances (poles) and no zeros. For nasals and obstruents, however, multiple acoustic paths cause zeros in the transfer function. In the case of fricatives, noise generated at a constriction outlet may propagate into the constriction as well as toward the mouth. At frequencies where the impedance looking into the constriction is infinite, no energy flows toward the mouth, and thus the output speech has antiresonances.

A similar situation might be thought to occur at the glottis, i.e., sound energy could enter the lungs as well as the vocal tract. However, the glottal source is viewed as a volume velocity source, whereas frication noise is better modeled as a pressure source [62, but cf 105]. Zeros in voiced speech due to a glottal source are not considered part of the vocal tract response. Frication noise sources, on the other hand, have flat spectra with no apparent zeros. As a pressure source, the noise can be modeled in series with impedances due to the constriction and the front cavity. At those frequencies where the constriction impedance is infinite, no air flows and the output speech has no energy.

This circuit analog holds for pole estimation as well. At the boundary between tubes of a two-tube model of the vocal tract, the impedance Z_b looking back into the posterior tube is in parallel with Z_f looking forward into the front tube. In such a parallel network, resonances occur at frequencies where

$$Z_b + Z_f = 0. \tag{3.22}$$

For a tube closed or open at both ends, $Z = 0$ at frequencies where tube length is an even multiple of a quarter-wavelength; for a tube closed at one end and open at the other, $Z = 0$ where tube length is an odd multiple. If, on the other hand, tube length is an odd multiple in the first case or an even multiple in the second, then $Z = \infty$. (Mathematical justification for these observations is given later.) When the boundary between tube sections is not abrupt enough to view the end of a section as fully open or closed, Z takes on intermediate values, and resonances cannot be associated with a single tube (as Equation (3.22) suggests).

A simple two-tube model with abrupt section boundaries is valid for many fricatives, with a narrow back tube modeling the constriction and a wide front tube for the mouth cavity. The large pharyngeal cavity is ignored in such models because it is essentially decoupled acoustically from the frication excitation by the abrupt boundary between such a cavity and the constriction. The resonances of the pharyngeal cavity are canceled by its antiresonances in such cases. Thus, fricatives have resonances at frequencies where l_f is an odd multiple of a quarter-wavelength or l_c is a multiple of a half-wavelength. Conversely, zeros occur where l_c is an odd multiple of a quarter-wavelength. If alveolar fricatives /s,z/ are modeled with a 2.5 cm constriction and a 1 cm front cavity, a zero appears at 3.4 kHz and poles at 6.8 and 8.6 kHz, with the two lowest frequencies being due to the constriction [106]. Palatal fricatives present a longer l_c and thus lower values for the first pole-zero pair, whereas dental and labial fricatives have very short l_c and l_f, leading to very high pole and zero locations. Fricatives have little energy below the frequency of their first zero and have energy peaks near the first pole frequency. Thus, in the frequency range of primary interest below 5 kHz, fricative energy is only at high frequencies, with more energy for the strident fricatives, having longer constrictions and longer front cavities.

3.5.3 Transmission Line Analog of the Vocal Tract

Some insight can be gained into the spectral behavior of an acoustic tube by modeling it as a uniform lossless transmission line (T-line). Equations (3.8) (the acoustic wave equations)

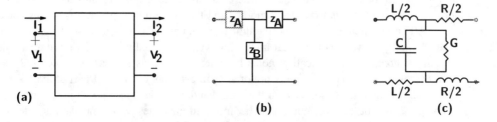

Figure 3.26 Two-port electrical network to model a length of uniform acoustic tube or transmission line: (a) "black box" showing input and output currents and voltages; (b) equivalent T-section two-port network; (c) realization of network with discrete components, which is valid if l is sufficiently small.

have a direct parallel with the behavior of voltage $v(x,t)$ and current $i(x,t)$ in a uniform lossless transmission line [103]:

$$-\frac{\partial i}{\partial x} = C \frac{\partial v}{\partial t} \quad \text{and} \quad -\frac{\partial v}{\partial x} = L \frac{\partial i}{\partial t}, \tag{3.23}$$

with the following analogies: current–volume velocity, voltage–pressure, line capacitance C–acoustic capacitance $A/\rho c^2$, and line inductance L–acoustic inductance ρ/A. (As above, all inductances and capacitances are distributed, i.e., per unit length of tube or transmission line.) The acoustic impedance $\rho c/A$ is analogous to Z_0, the *characteristic impedance* of a transmission line. Using only basic properties of T lines, we can easily calculate the frequency response of vocal tract models involving more than one acoustic tube in terms of T-line impedances. Consider a T-line section of length l as a two-port network, with voltages V_1 at the input and V_2 at the output and current I_1 into the T line and I_2 out (Figure 3.26a). As a passive network,

$$V_1 = Z_{11}I_1 + Z_{12}I_2 \quad \text{and} \quad V_2 = Z_{21}I_1 + Z_{22}I_2, \tag{3.24}$$

where Z_{11} and Z_{22} are the input and output impedances of the T line, respectively, and Z_{12} and Z_{21} are cross-impedances. By symmetry,

$$Z_{12} = -Z_{21} \quad \text{and} \quad Z_{11} = -Z_{22} \tag{3.25}$$

(the minus signs are due to the definition of I_2 as flowing out of the T line and I_1 into it). If I_2 is set to zero by leaving the output port as an open circuit, Z_{11} can be identified as the input impedance of an open-circuited T line [103]:

$$Z_{11} = Z_0 \coth(\gamma l), \tag{3.26}$$

where Z_0 and γ are from Equations (3.19) and (3.13). If V_2 is set to zero by making the output port a short circuit, Equations (3.24) give

$$Z_{21} = -Z_{22}\frac{I_2}{I_1} = Z_{11}\frac{I_2}{I_1},$$
$$V_1 = [Z_0 \coth(\gamma l)]I_1 + Z_{12}I_2. \tag{3.27}$$

In addition, V_1 can also be described via the input impedance of a short-circuited T line [103]:

$$V_1 = [Z_0 \tanh(\gamma l)]I_1. \tag{3.28}$$

Thus

$$Z_{21} = Z_0 \operatorname{csch}(\gamma l). \tag{3.29}$$

Under the assumption of zero pressure at the lips (Equation (3.9)) and using Equation (3.13), we obtain the tube transfer function for current (or volume velocity):

$$\frac{I_2}{I_1} = \frac{U_2}{U_1} = \frac{Z_{21}}{Z_{11}} = \frac{Z_0 \operatorname{csch}(\gamma l)}{Z_0 \coth(\gamma l)} = \frac{1}{\cosh(\gamma l)} = \frac{1}{\cos(\Omega l/c)}. \tag{3.30}$$

Thus, the same result for a lossless model of the vocal tract is obtained through T-line (Equation (3.30)) or acoustic analysis (Equation (3.16)).

It is often convenient in circuit theory to model a symmetric network as a T section. The impedances of Figure 3.26(b) can be easily determined from Equations (3.25), (3.29) and (3.26) and simple circuit theory to be

$$Z_a = Z_0 \tanh(\gamma l/2) \quad \text{and} \quad Z_b = Z_0 \operatorname{csch}(\gamma l). \tag{3.31}$$

If l is sufficiently small, the hyperbolic tangent and cosecant functions of Equation (3.31) can be approximated by the first terms in their power series expansions, e.g.,

$$\tanh(x) = x - \frac{x^3}{3} + \frac{2x^5}{15} - \cdots \approx x, \qquad \text{if } |x| = |\gamma l/2| \ll 1. \tag{3.32}$$

Discrete components can thus replace the complex impedances in Equation (3.31):

$$Z_a \approx Z_0 \frac{\gamma l}{2} = \frac{l}{2}(R + j\Omega L) \qquad \text{and} \qquad \frac{1}{Z_b} \approx \frac{\gamma l}{Z_0} = l(G + j\Omega C). \tag{3.33}$$

The last steps of equation (3.33) simply assign values R and G to the real parts of functions of γ and Z_0, and L and C to their imaginary parts, for the general case of a T line with loss. The earlier definition of γ in Equation (3.13) assumed a lossless case, for which G and R would be zero. R represents viscous loss, which is proportional to the square of air velocity, while G represents thermal loss, proportional to the square of pressure; both R and G also have components related to the mechanical losses of vibrating vocal tract walls [62]. The usual interpretation of R and L as resistors and inductors in series and of G and C as resistors and capacitors in parallel reduces Figure 3.26(b) to that of Figure 3.26(c) when l is small enough. The model using such discrete components in place of the usual distributed model is valid only if $|\gamma l| \ll 1$. Assuming a frequency F in a lossless system,

$$|\gamma l| = \Omega l/c = 2\pi Fl/c \ll 1. \tag{3.34}$$

To model frequencies F below 4 kHz, l must be much less than 1.4 cm. Thus an analog model of a 17 cm vocal tract using discrete components would require well over 20 T sections to accurately represent frequencies up to 4 kHz. A more practical analog representation would model each of the four resonances below 4 kHz separately, perhaps with an RLC network. The T-section model has the advantage of a close relationship to vocal tract shape (each impedance Z_a and Z_b for a short section of the vocal tract model would be specified by its local cross-sectional area), but building such a model is impractical. Indeed, all analog models are of little practical use because they are difficult to modify in real time, which is necessary to simulate time-varying speech. Models practical for speech simulation are discussed later.

3.5.3.1 Two-tube model.

An earlier heuristic analysis for two-tube vocal tract models was limited to configurations with very abrupt tube-section boundaries and decoupled acoustic cavities. Equations (3.24)–(3.33) permit a resonance analysis of a general two-tube model in which concatenated sections are modeled by T-line networks. A two-tube model can be viewed as a network in which two circuits are in parallel at the juncture between the two sections. At the juncture, the impedance Z_1 looking back into the first tube and Z_2 looking up into the second tube serve to model the effects of the two circuits. The poles of a general circuit with N parallel components are those frequencies where their admittances add to zero:

$$\sum_{i=1}^{N} Y_i = \sum_{i=1}^{N} \frac{1}{Z_i} = 0. \tag{3.35}$$

A circuit of only two parallel components can also be viewed as a series circuit, where poles occur at frequencies for which impedances add to zero. With either approach, the poles of a two-tube model satisfy

$$Z_1 = -Z_2. \tag{3.36}$$

Since the glottal opening is usually much smaller than A_1, the first tube (modeling the pharyngeal cavity) is assumed closed at the glottal end. In T-line analogs, an open circuit (zero current) models the closed end of an acoustic tube (zero volume velocity). Defining Z_{0i} as the characteristic impedance of tube section i ($Z_{0i} = \rho c/A_i$), Equation (3.26) gives

$$Z_1 = Z_{01} \coth(\gamma l_1) = -jZ_{01} \cot(\beta l_1), \tag{3.37}$$

where $\beta = \Omega/c$ in the lossless case. For unrounded phonemes, the mouth termination of the second tube is considered to be open, and the opening is modeled by a T-line short circuit. Thus, Equation (3.28) yields

$$Z_2 = Z_{02} \tanh(\gamma l_2) = jZ_{02} \tan(\beta l_2). \tag{3.38}$$

Combining Equations (3.36)–(3.38) gives

$$\cot(\beta l_1) = \frac{A_1}{A_2} \tan(\beta l_2). \tag{3.39}$$

Models for several sounds (e.g., /i, /ɑ/, ə/) allow $l_1 = l_2$, which facilitates an explicit solution of Equation (3.39) in terms of formants F_i:

$$F_i = \frac{c}{2\pi l} \cot^{-1} \sqrt{\left(\frac{A_1}{A_2}\right)} \qquad \text{for } i = 1, 2, 3, \ldots. \tag{3.40}$$

More general cases have easy graphical solutions at those frequencies for which plots of the tangent and cotangent curves of Equation (3.39) intersect (Figure 3.27). There are intersections every 1 kHz on average (most easily seen in Figures 3.27c and d). For a model in which $l_1 \approx l_2$ (e.g., Figure 3.27c), both curves have periods of about 2 kHz. For /ɑ/, $A_2 \gg A_1$ and pairs of resonances occur near odd multiples of 1 kHz; /i/ conversely has pairs of resonances near even multiples of 1 kHz.

3.5.3.2 Three-tube model for nasals.

The resonances for the three-tube model of Figure 3.24(c) are not as easily determined as for the two-tube case because two tube junctions must be considered. One approach, valid for a general model of N tube sections, determines the transfer function of N T-section circuits in series and then solves for the roots of its denominator [62]. For more insight, however, consider the three-tube model of Figure 3.28, which applies to nasal sounds. Since the nasal tube joins the rest of the vocal tract at the velum, the entire system can be modeled as three tubes (pharyngeal, nasal, and oral) joined at one point, with circuits for the three in parallel. The poles of such a model are specified by Equation (3.35) (using the notation of Figure 3.28):

$$\frac{1}{Z_p} + \frac{1}{Z_m} + \frac{1}{Z_n} = 0, \tag{3.41}$$

where $Z_p = -jZ_{0p} \cot(\beta l_p)$, $Z_m = -jZ_{0m} \cot(\beta l_m)$, and $Z_n = jZ_{0n} \tan(\beta l_n)$. The mouth and pharyngeal tubes have closed acoustic terminations, while the nasal tube is open. Its graphical solution is complex because of the interaction of three curves, but the dimensional similarity of the pharynx and nasal tubes allows a simplification. If $l_p = l_n = 10.5$ cm, each of $1/Z_p$ and $1/Z_n$ has periods of about 1.6 kHz and the function $1/Z_p + 1/Z_n$ has infinite values about every 800 Hz. The mouth tube for nasal consonants is often significantly shorter than the other tubes (e.g., 3–7 cm). A plot of the slowly varying $-1/Z_m$ vs the more rapid $1/Z_p + 1/Z_n$

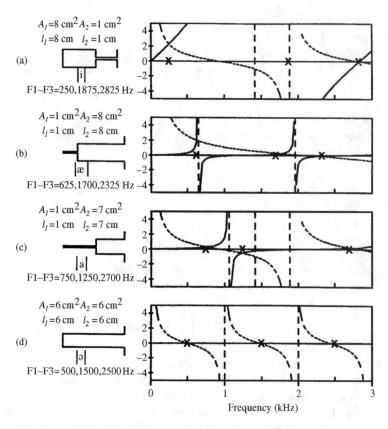

Figure 3.27 Two-tube approximations to vowels /i,æ,ɑ,ə/ and graphical solutions to their
formant frequencies using Equation (3.39). The solid lines are the tangent
curves, the dashed lines the cotangent curves; the vertical dashes note where
the curves attain infinite values. (After Flanagan [62].)

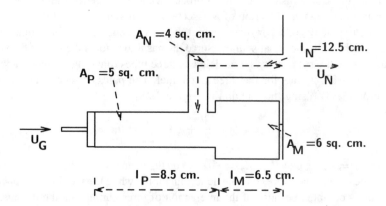

Figure 3.28 Three-tube vocal tract model for nasal consonants. Typical cross-sectional
area and length values are noted for the pharyngeal, nasal and mouth (oral)
cavities. The glottal source is modeled by a piston. Output volume velocity
U_n emerges from the nostrils. (After Flanagan [62].)

would note intersections roughly every 800 Hz, with additional intersections every period of $-1/Z_m$.

Nasal consonants are characterized by (a) formants every 800 Hz (due to the longer pharynx + nasal tube than the normal pharynx + mouth tube), (b) wider formant bandwidths, and (c) zeros in the spectrum [107]. When airflow from the lungs reaches the velum junction, it divides according to the impedances looking into the mouth and nasal tubes. Spectral zeros occur at frequencies where $Z_m = 0$, which results in no airflow into the nasal tube and thus no nasal speech output. Solving $Z_m = -jZ_{0m} \cot(2\pi F_i l_m/c) = 0$ for F_i yields zeros at odd multiples of $c/4l_m$. The mouth tube for /m/ is about 7 cm, which gives zeros at 1.2, 3.6, 6.0, ... kHz. Shorter tubes for /n/ and /ŋ/, about 5 and 3 cm, respectively, mean fewer zeros below 5 kHz: only one each at 1.7 and 2.8 kHz, respectively. Besides the poles due to the pharynx and nasal cavities, which occur every 800 Hz, nasal spectra have *pole-zero pairs* due to the mouth cavity; i.e., each zero is close in frequency to a mouth cavity pole.

Nasalized vowels are much stronger than nasal consonants because virtually all airflow passes through the relatively unconstricted oral cavity, which reduces the role of the lossy nasal cavity. In terms of the three-tube model, the major difference between nasalized vowels and consonants is that the mouth cavity has an open termination. Thus Z_m should be replaced by $jZ_{0m} \tan(\beta l_m)$ in Equation (3.41). The major difference in pole positions between oral vowels and their nasalized counterparts is a shift in F1 and an additional *nasal formant* near F1 [82]. Since much more sound exits the mouth than the nose in nasalized vowels, the nasal cavity is viewed as an acoustic side branch specifying zero frequencies (other small side branches off the vocal tract near the glottis, called piriform fossa, add spectral zeros near 4–5 kHz and slightly reduce lower formants [93,108]). The fixed nature of the nasal cavity suggests that zeros should not vary significantly for different nasalized vowels and should be found at frequencies F_i where

$$Z_n = jZ_{0n} \tan(2\pi F_i l_n/c) = 0, \qquad (3.42)$$

i.e., at odd multiples of about 1.7 kHz.

The transition from an oral vowel to a nasal consonant (and vice versa) may involve an intermediate nasalized vowel sound, as the velum lowers before (or raises after) oral closure. As the velum lowers, nasal pole-zero pairs are created with the nasal tract as a side resonator. When the mouth cavity closes, these pairs disappear and other pole-zero pairs due to the mouth cavity appear. The process reverses for the release of a nasal consonant.

3.5.3.3 Three-tube model for fricatives.
Unlike the previously modeled sonorants, virtually all obstruents have an excitation source in the oral cavity. From the noise source, sound waves at most frequencies flow out the mouth as speech, but some are trapped in cavities behind the source (via spectral zeros) and thus are not present in the speech output. This situation does not arise for sonorants, because the glottis closes at the primary excitation, forcing one-way airflow during the closed phase of voicing. While the poles of a transfer function for a system such as the vocal tract are independent of the location or type of excitation source, zeros are highly dependent on the source. In most unvoiced fricatives, the first few resonances (due to the back cavities) of the vocal tract have their spectral effects canceled by zeros.

The three-tube model of Figure 3.24(c) is appropriate for many fricatives. The noise excitation is usually modeled as a pressure source at the juncture of the constriction and the front tube (Figure 3.29). For /s/, typical model parameters would be $l_c = 2.5$ cm, $A_c = 0.2$ cm^2, and $A_b = A_f = 7$ cm^2. Due to the large A_b/A_c ratio, the back cavity is

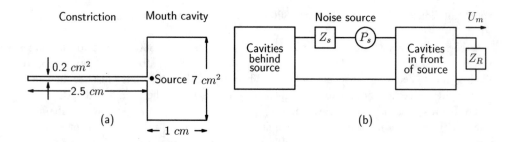

Figure 3.29 Production models for fricatives: (a) a simplified model of the vocal tract for /s/; (b) an equivalent circuit representation. (After Heinz and Stevens [106] and Flanagan [62].)

effectively decoupled from the noise source and can be ignored. From Equations (3.19), (3.28), and (3.36), the poles of the remaining two-tube system occur where

$$Z_c + Z_f = j\frac{\rho c}{A_c}\tan(\Omega l_c/c) + j\frac{\rho c}{A_f}\tan(\Omega l_f/c) = 0. \tag{3.43}$$

Since $A_f \gg A_c$, poles occur near frequencies where $Z_c = 0$ (half-wavelength resonances of the constriction) and where Z_f is very large (quarter-wavelength resonance of the front tube).

Zeros occur in the output speech spectrum where the impedance Z_c of the constriction is infinite because no airflow circulates at those frequencies in a series network such as that of Figure 3.29(b). $Z_c = jZ_{0c}\tan(2\pi F_i l_c/c)$ becomes infinite at odd multiples of $c/(4l_c)$ (i.e., when l_c is quarter-wavelength). For a 2.5 cm constriction, the first zero is at 3.4 kHz. As discussed earlier, palatal fricatives have longer values for l_c and l_f, resulting in lower-frequency zeros and poles, whereas /f,θ/ have much higher zeros and poles.

When the front tube is very short, its spectral effects can be ignored at most frequencies of interest. A two-tube version of Figure 3.24(c) ignoring the front tube permits investigation of the effects of the large cavity behind the constriction, especially during transitions to and from the fricative, where the back cavity is not fully decoupled acoustically. Most low-frequency poles are due to the back tube and occur near frequencies where $\cot(\beta l_b) = \infty$ (half-wavelength resonances at multiples of 1360 Hz for $l_b = 12.5$ cm), but poles also appear near frequencies where $\cot(\beta l_c) = \infty$ (half-wavelength resonances at multiples of 6800 Hz for $l_c = 2.5$ cm). The zeros can be shown [62] to solve

$$\tan(\beta l_b) = -\frac{A_c}{A_b}\tan(\beta l_c). \tag{3.44}$$

Since $A_b \gg A_c$ and $l_b \gg l_c$, most zeros occur where $\tan(\beta l_b) = 0$ and effectively cancel out the corresponding poles of the back cavity. The uncanceled zeros occur where $\tan(\beta l_c) = \infty$, i.e., l_c is an odd multiple of quarter-wavelength (e.g., 3.4 kHz in the example).

For some sounds (e.g., /f/), the noise source is close to the junction between the *back* tube and the constriction [62]. Using the same two-tube model as above, the poles do not change, but the zeros can be shown to occur where

$$Z_{0b}\csc(\beta l_b) = 0 \tag{3.45}$$

i.e., where l_b is a multiple of half-wavelength. Again, the back cavity poles are canceled by zeros.

3.5.3.4 Four-tube vowel model.

While a few vowels can be roughly approximated with only two tubes, others require at least three tubes due to a tongue constriction between the pharyngeal and oral cavities. Lip rounding can require a fourth short tube to model the lips (Figure 3.30). If the constriction length l_2 is kept fixed at 5 cm (the middle six points), F2 falls and F1 rises as the back length l_1 decreases. Note the similarity of Figures 3.30 and 3.25. In general, modeling accuracy improves as more (and shorter) tubes are employed, but complexity also increases with the number of tubes (Figure 3.31). Models of 2–4 tubes do not produce the spectra of natural sounds with great accuracy, but they have the advantage of insight into articulatory–acoustic relationships.

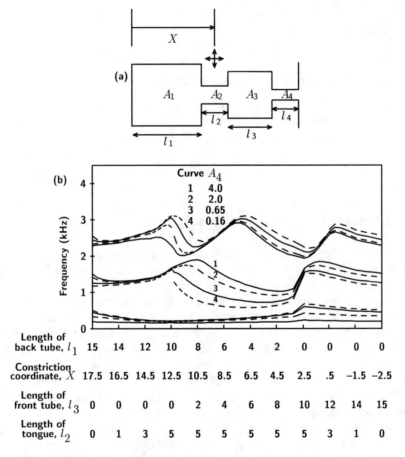

Curve	A_4
1	4.0
2	2.0
3	0.65
4	0.16

Length of back tube, l_1	15	14	12	10	8	6	4	2	0	0	0	0
Constriction coordinate, X	17.5	16.5	14.5	12.5	10.5	8.5	6.5	4.5	2.5	.5	−1.5	−2.5
Length of front tube, l_3	0	0	0	0	2	4	6	8	10	12	14	15
Length of tongue, l_2	0	1	3	5	5	5	5	5	5	3	1	0

Figure 3.30 Four-tube vocal tract model for vowels and their first three formants: (a) model in which the first three areas are fixed at $A_1 = A_3 = 8\,cm^2$ and $A_2 = 0.65\,cm^2$ and the lip length l_4 is fixed at 1 cm; (b) curves 1, 2, 3, and 4 represent mouth areas of 4, 2, 0.65, and 0.16 cm^2, respectively. The horizontal axis varies the lengths of the first three tubes. (After Fant [109] and Flanagan [62].)

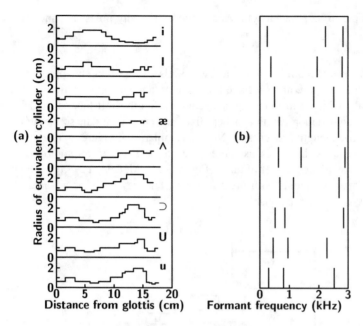

Figure 3.31 (a) The graphs show typical area functions for nine vowels, specifying the radius of consecutive $\frac{1}{2}$ cm long cylindrical sections of the vocal tract model; (b) corresponding measured formant frequencies. (After Stevens *et al.* [110].)

3.5.4 Effects of Losses in the Vocal Tract

Under the assumptions of a hard-walled tube containing a zero-viscosity gas, there are no losses in the vocal tract. Resonances and antiresonances have zero bandwidth (i.e., poles and zeros on the $j\Omega$-axis of the s plane or on the unit circle of the z plane), and electrical circuit models have no resistive components. In practice, however, losses are introduced at each step of the speech production process. When the glottis is open, a varying glottal impedance affects the spectrum of the glottal source. As air flows up the vocal tract, yielding walls react to pressure variations and vibrate, primarily at low frequencies due to the massive size of the walls. Viscous friction between the air and the walls, as well as heat conduction through the walls, causes energy loss. Big losses occur during nasals due to the large, yielding surface area of the nasal cavity. Finally, sound radiation at the lips adds significant energy loss. Viscous, thermal, and radiation losses occur primarily at high frequencies, since radiation losses are proportional to F^2 and the other two losses increase with $\sqrt{F}$ [62,111].

For the basic acoustic equations, terms would be added to Equation (3.6) to account for the volume velocity shunted by wall motion and to Equation (3.7) to account for viscous pressure drop [98]. Viewing losses in terms of formant bandwidths (which are proportional to the distance of the poles from the unit circle in the z plane), wall vibration is significant only below 2 kHz and dominates (along with glottal damping) the bandwidth of F1. Radiation losses dominate formant bandwidths above 2 kHz. Friction and thermal losses can be neglected below 3–4 kHz, except for nasals.

3.5.5 Radiation at the Lips

Up to now, we have ignored lip radiation and assumed that sound pressure at the lips was zero (e.g., an electrical short circuit or an open termination for an acoustic tube). In practice, the lips are more accurately modeled as an opening in a spherical baffle representing the head [112], where a lip impedance $Z_L(\Omega)$ describes the relationship of lip volume velocity $U_L(\Omega)$ and pressure $P_L(\Omega)$:

$$P_L(\Omega) = P(l, \Omega) = Z_L(\Omega)U_L(\Omega) = Z_L(\Omega)U(l, \Omega). \tag{3.46}$$

$Z_L(\Omega)$ can be modeled as a parallel RL (resistor–inductor) circuit, which acts as a highpass filter with a cutoff frequency near 6 kHz. The L reactance models the effective mass of vibrating air at the lips. Thus Z_L behaves like a differentiator: very small at low frequencies and growing at 6 dB/oct over frequencies of interest. A similar radiation effect occurs for nasal consonants, where sound radiates out the nostrils. The combination of vocal tract resonances (Equation (3.30)) and losses (including radiation) produces the typical vocal tract transfer function of Figure 3.32. Actual speech spectra also include the effects of excitation.

3.5.6 Model of Glottal Excitation

During the closed phase of voiced excitation, the vocal folds are shut, and the model of an electrical open circuit or a tube with a closed termination is accurate. Maximal glottal area during voicing is sufficiently small compared with the pharyngeal area to justify use of the same model even during the open phase for high frequencies. At low frequencies, however, a better model employs a glottal volume velocity source with a parallel glottal impedance $Z_G(\Omega)$, which is the ratio of the transglottal pressure head to the mass flow rate of air [24]. $Z_G(\Omega)$ acts as a series RL circuit, whose impedance increases at 6 dB/oct above a certain break frequency. As with yielding vocal tract walls, $Z_G(\Omega)$ has its primary effects on the lowest formants, broadening their bandwidths. $Z_G(\Omega)$ is not a fixed impedance but oscillates with the vocal folds. This is most visible in the decay rate of a vowel waveform, which is dominated by the bandwidth of F1 (and F2, if F1 and F2 are close). The main vocal tract excitation occurs at vocal fold closure, after which $Z_G(\Omega)$ is infinite and the F1 bandwidth is

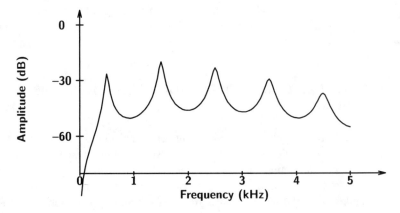

Figure 3.32 Frequency response for a uniform vocal tract relating lip pressure to glottal volume velocity.

small; when the vocal folds open, $Z_G(\Omega)$ decreases, widening F1, and the speech wave oscillations damp out more rapidly than when the vocal folds are closed [111].

Most speech models assume that the vocal tract and glottal source can be manipulated independently and have separate acoustic effects. For frequencies near F1, however, the vocal tract impedance is comparable to the high glottal impedance, and significant source–tract interaction occurs [62]. Furthermore, sounds with a narrow vocal tract constriction produce a pressure drop at the constriction sufficient to affect the glottal source. The load of the vocal tract impedance skews glottal pulses away from a symmetric waveform and toward a more rapid closing phase [113]. Accurate modeling of vocal fold behavior may lead to improved quality in speech synthesis [114,115]. For most sounds and frequencies, however, source–tract independence is a good approximation that permits independent analyses of the glottal and supraglottal systems.

3.5.7 Quantal Theory of Speech Production

The relationship between speech spectra and the vocal tract shapes that produce them is highly nonlinear. Large articulatory movements sometimes cause small acoustic effects, and other small movements yield large changes in formants. One theory of speech production [116] holds that sounds have evolved to take advantage of articulatory positions that can vary to a degree without causing large acoustic variations; e.g., spectra for the vowels /i,ɑ/ correlate well with simple two-tube models, for which small changes in tube length have little effect on formant locations. Evidence for this *quantal* theory comes from both speech production and perception [68]. Changes in the manner of articulation often relate to the narrowness of a vocal tract constriction, while place of articulation relates to the position of the constriction along the vocal tract. Since changes in manner have larger acoustic effects than do changes in place, evidence that vertical tongue positioning is more accurate than horizontal location [117] supports the quantal theory.

The point vowels /i,ɑ/, governed by one constriction, exhibit acoustic stability (i.e., steady formants) over a relatively wide range of constriction positions, while the acoustics is still highly sensitive to the degree of constriction, although motor commands show a quantal (nonlinear) relationship with the degree [118]. The latter is not evident for /u/, which exploits two constrictions (lips and pharynx) to control the formant patterns.

Revisions of this theory of speech production (*theory of enhancement*) hypothesize that: (1) *distinctive features* represent well the sounds of languages (with groups of such features simultaneously forming phoneme segments), (2) the acoustic manifestations of a subset called *primary features* are more salient, and (3) features with varying degrees of strength can enhance each other [54].

3.6 PRACTICAL VOCAL TRACT MODELS FOR SPEECH ANALYSIS AND SYNTHESIS

Analog speech production models employing electrical circuits or T lines are useful for understanding the behavior of airflow and pressure in the vocal tract and for predicting spectral resonances and antiresonances. For automatically generating speech, however, these models are too cumbersome, and digital models are invariably employed. One type of practical model is based directly on vocal tract shape, while another derives from the time and spectral behavior of the output speech signal and is only indirectly based on articulation. We examine the *articulatory model* first and the *terminal-analog model* later.

3.6.1 Articulatory Model

A digital articulatory model of the vocal tract is an extension of earlier lossless multi-tube models, e.g., the two- and three-tube models that facilitated resonance analysis. For simplicity, the effects of vibration, friction, and thermal losses are included only in the glottal and lip termination models. Consider a model of N lossless cylinders of lengths l_i and cross-sectional areas A_i concatenated in series, where i runs from 1 at the glottal end to N at the lips (Figure 3.33). N is typically 8–12, which allows more accurate articulatory representation than is possible with only 2–3 tubes. For some sounds, however, even 1.4 cm sections (as with $N = 12$) are not short enough to yield accurate models.

Earlier, we interpreted the basic laws of acoustics spectrally and established models relating vocal tract shape to the impedances of uniform tube sections or T lines. Whether heuristically relating tube or T line lengths to resonance wavelengths or explicitly solving for resonances in complex impedance relationships of vocal tract transfer functions, the spectral approach gave little insight into the time-domain behavior of sound waves. The most common digital model for the vocal tract, however, is based on time signal relationships.

3.6.1.1 Traveling waves. Returning to the basic acoustic laws for a time-domain interpretation, recall that Equations (3.8) hold for a lossless uniform acoustic tube and thus are followed in each of the N tube sections for the current model. To find the volume velocity $u_i(x, t)$ in the ith tube, combine Equations (3.8) into a second-degree equation:

$$\frac{\partial^2 u}{\partial x^2} = \frac{1}{c^2}\frac{\partial^2 u}{\partial t^2}, \tag{3.47}$$

which has a solution of the form

$$u_i(x, t) = u_i^+(t - x/c) - u_i^-(t + x/c), \tag{3.48}$$

where x is measured from the glottal end of each tube ($0 \le x \le l_i$). The pressure $p_i(x, t)$ has a similar solution, which can be expressed in terms of Equation (3.48) as

$$p_i(x, t) = \frac{\rho c}{A_i}[u_i^+(t - x/c) + u_i^-(t + x/c)]. \tag{3.49}$$

The functions $u_i^+(t - x/c)$ and $u_i^-(t + x/c)$ represent traveling waves of volume velocity moving up and down the ith tube (to the right and left in Figure 3.33), respectively.

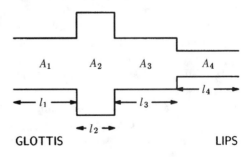

Figure 3.33 Model of the vocal tract using a concatenation of four lossless cylindrical acoustic tubes, each of length l_i and uniform cross-section area A_i.

Boundary conditions between sections are due to physical conservation principles, which specify continuity in both time and space for both $p_i(x, t)$ and $u_i(x, t)$. At the boundary between sections i and $i + 1$,

$$u_i^+(t - \tau_i) - u_i^-(t + \tau_i) = u_{i+1}^+(t) - u_{i+1}^-(t), \tag{3.50}$$

where $\tau_i = l_i/c$ is the time for a sound wave to propagate through the ith section. The left side of Equation (3.50) is the net volume velocity $u_i(l_i, t)$ at the left edge of the boundary, while the right side corresponds to $u_{i+1}(0, t)$ at the right edge. The parallel result for pressure is

$$\frac{\rho c}{A_i}[u_i^+(t - \tau_i) + u_i^-(t + \tau_i)] = \frac{\rho c}{A_{i+1}}[u_{i+1}^+(t) + u_{i+1}^-(t)]. \tag{3.51}$$

In an analogy to T lines, when a traveling wave in a uniform tube meets a discontinuity in area, part of the wave propagates to the next section and part is reflected back. Propagation is 100% only if the impedance of the next section matches that of the current section, i.e., if the sectional areas are the same or if the tube is terminated in a load impedance identical to the characteristic impedance of the present tube. This relationship is clarified by solving Equations (3.50) and (3.51) for the outgoing waves in terms of the incident waves:

$$u_{i+1}^+(t) = \beta_i u_i^+(t - \tau_i) + r_i u_{i+1}^-(t)$$
$$u_i^-(t + \tau_i) = -r_i u_i^+(t - \tau_i) + \phi_i u_{i+1}^-(t), \tag{3.52}$$

where

$$r_i = \frac{A_{i+1} - A_i}{A_{i+1} + A_i} = \frac{Z_{0i} - Z_{0i+1}}{Z_{0i} + Z_{0i+1}},$$

$$\beta_i = \frac{2A_{i+1}}{A_{i+1} + A_i} = 1 + r_i, \tag{3.53}$$

$$\phi_i = \frac{2A_i}{A_{i+1} + A_i} = 1 - r_i.$$

The term r_i is called the *reflection coefficient* between sections i and $i + 1$ because it indicates how much of the wave traveling to the left (i.e., down the vocal tract) is reflected back to the right. The magnitude of r_i is bounded by unity and is equal to unity only when one of the areas at a boundary is zero or infinite; the entire volume velocity wave is reflected back when it meets a closed end of a tube (e.g., $r_0 = 1$ during the closed phase of glottal vibration) or when it meets the lip juncture ($r_N = -1$, ignoring lossy radiation effects). Reflection in the case of an open termination changes the sign of the wave. β_i and ϕ_i represent the amounts of the waves propagated past the boundary for the two traveling waves.

Equations (3.53) can be expressed in a flow graph (Figure 3.34) where the wave transit times τ_i become delay elements, labeled arrows denote multiplications, and circular nodes represent the addition of signals on incident paths. An N-tube model of the vocal tract would have N pairs of delay elements and $N - 1$ junctions, each characterized by a reflection coefficient. The glottal and lip boundaries, however, need further investigation.

3.6.1.2 Lip and glottal junctions.

The lip junction is relatively easy to analyze. There is no incident downward wave u_{N+1}^- since the upward wave u_N^+, once past the lip juncture, meets no further obstacles and is not reflected back. Instead of a tube impedance Z_{N+1} at the

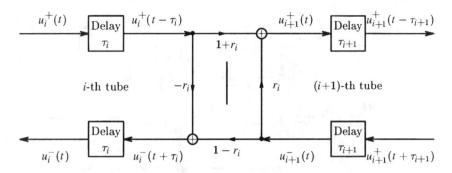

Figure 3.34 Signal-flow diagram of the boundary between two lossless tubes. The boxes represent delay elements of the noted duration.

lips, u_N^+ sees the radiation load impedance Z_L of Equation (3.46). Thus the reflection coefficient for the final lip juncture is

$$r_L = \frac{(\rho c/A_N) - Z_L}{(\rho c/A_N) + Z_L}. \tag{3.54}$$

Complex Z_L can be handled by using frequency-domain versions of the preceding equations or by using differential equations (e.g., the inductive component of a radiation load relates u_L and p_L by a first-order differential equation). Losses leading to finite formant bandwidths are often implemented via Z_L.

Modeling the glottal termination as a volume velocity source $U_G(t)$ in parallel with an impedance Z_G, we obtain the net volume velocity into the first tube section:

$$u_1^+(t) - u_1^-(t) = u_G(t) - \frac{p_1(t)}{Z_G} = u_G(t) - \frac{Z_{01}(u_1^+(t) + u_1^-(t))}{Z_G}, \tag{3.55}$$

where $p_1(t)$ is the pressure at the left end of the first tube. Solving for $u_1^+(t)$, we have

$$u_1^+(t) = \frac{1 + r_G}{2} u_G(t) + r_G u_1^-(t), \quad \text{where} \quad r_G = \frac{Z_G - Z_{01}}{Z_G + Z_{01}} \tag{3.56}$$

has the usual reflection coefficient interpretation. The $(1 + r_G)/2$ term of Equation (3.56) equals $Z_G/(Z_G + Z_{01})$, which illustrates that the amount of U_G propagated into the first tube follows the usual "current divider" function of parallel impedances Z_G and Z_{01}. Earlier analysis showed Z_G, like Z_L, to be a complex function of frequency; for simplicity, however, many practical applications use real approximations for both Z_G and Z_L.

3.6.1.3 Digital interpretations. A complete vocal tract model using three tubes is shown in Figure 3.35. If we choose r_1 and r_2 according to Equation (3.53), the network can produce a volume velocity speech signal $U_L(t)$ for any three-tube model with areas A_1, A_2, and A_3. (For tubes of different lengths, it suffices to use the appropriate delay in each section.) The frequency response of such a system is readily obtained from basic flow-graph or circuit theory, where a delay of τ seconds has a Fourier transform of $\exp(-j\Omega\tau)$ or a Laplace transform of $\exp(-s\tau)$. Solving for the roots of the numerator and denominator polynomials in such a Laplace transfer function yields the zeros and poles of the model, respectively, which coincide with the heuristic and spectral analyses of earlier sections.

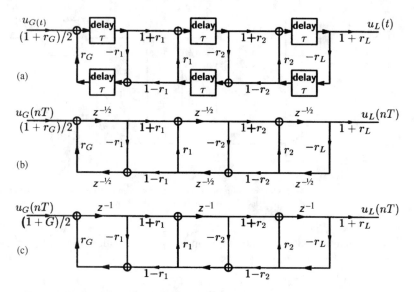

Figure 3.35 Signal-flow diagrams for a lossless model of the vocal tract using three tube sections of equal length and different uniform cross-sectional areas: (a) analog system, (b) equivalent discrete-time system, (c) system of part (b) modified to reduce the number of delay components.

Since the flow graph of Figure 3.35(a) contains only additions, multiplications, and delays, it can be easily converted into a discrete-time or digital model. The only restriction is that the delay times for all tubes must be a multiple of some time unit T that corresponds to the clock cycle of the discrete-time model. Since operations in such a model occur every T seconds, the delays are represented by shift registers or memories where an input sample is held for an integral number of cycles before being output. The most common implementation assumes equal tube lengths $l_i = l$ (Figure 3.35) so that T can be a multiple of $\tau = l/c$. If the number N of tubes is large enough, such an assumption does not hinder modeling complex vocal tract shapes.

Consider an impulse excitation for $u_G(t)$ in a model of N tubes, each of length l. Energy from this impulse first reaches the output $U_L(t)$ after $N\tau$ ms, and then every 2τ ms (the round trip for an impulse due to two reflections within each tube) thereafter. If the sampling period T of the discrete-time model is set to 2τ, however, the system of Figure 3.35(b) results since z^{-1} is the z transform of a unit delay; it is nonetheless a good choice to minimize computation because the two half-delays in each section can be merged into one unit delay (Figure 3.35c) without serious consequences to the output. The delay around any closed loop path is the same for the two cases of Figures 3.35(b) and (c). The only significant difference is that the delay between input and output is twice that of the original model. Since $N\tau = 0.5$ ms for a typical vocal tract, doubling the delay adds a mere 0.5 ms, which is irrelevant even in real-time applications.

Another important factor in choosing T is the bandwidth of the speech to be represented in discrete time. Before speech is sampled every T seconds, it must be lowpass filtered to eliminate energy above $1/(2T)$ Hz. For a 5 kHz bandwidth, T must be less than 0.1 ms.

Ignoring radiation effects, the transfer function [119] for an N-tube model is

$$H(z) = \frac{U_L(z)}{U_G(z)} = \frac{1 + r_G}{2} \frac{z^{-N/2} \prod_{i=1}^{N}(1 + r_i)}{1 - \sum_{i=1}^{N} a_i z^{-1}}, \tag{3.57}$$

where a_i are coefficients that depend on r_i (cf Chapter 6). $H(z)$ has N poles and no zeros (other than trivial ones at $z = 0$). In general, most of the N poles occur in complex conjugate pairs, which represent formants, but some wide-bandwidth poles contribute to spectral shaping.

$H(z)$ has no zeros because it is based on a model with one path from the excitation to the output and no side branches. We have not derived corresponding versions of Figure 3.35 for the nasal and fricative models of Section 3.5, because the all-pole model is capable of producing waveforms that are very similar to actual nasals and fricatives (the reflection coefficients in such cases would, of course, not correspond to the vocal tract shapes that produce natural sounds). Further discussion of the utility of all-pole models is postponed to Chapter 6.

In the implementation of Figure 3.35(c), each junction requires four multiplications and two additions. Since each multiply involves a simple factor r_i (i.e., $\pm r_i$ or $1 \pm r_i$), straightforward manipulation of the circuit allows alternative models with less computation. There are, for example, standard two- and one-multiply versions of these junctions, which require 3–4 additions, however [119]. Multiplication operations usually require an order of magnitude more computation than additions in microprocessors; thus practical implementations minimize multiplies. Other implementation factors must be considered, however, such as control of computation and quantization effects. Digital filters differ from discrete-time models in that signals and coefficients have finite resolution (e.g., 16-bit numbers); some of the resulting nonlinear quantization effects are discussed in Chapter 7.

3.6.2 Terminal-Analog Model

We will see in Chapter 7 that the articulatory model of the last section is very useful for speech coding, but we now turn to another practical model of speech production that will be exploited in Chapter 9. Due to the complexity of the vocal tract and the difficulty of obtaining precise data on articulatory motion and cross-sectional areas, most speech applications concentrate on modeling the acoustic aspects of speech rather than the vocal tract dynamics that produce it. *Terminal-analog* models attempt to represent the speech production process in terms of its (terminal) output. The fact that different vocal tract shapes may produce the same sound is irrelevant to terminal-analog models. Virtually all speech coders and all practical synthesizers are of this type, where the systems attempt to faithfully code and/or reproduce either the speech waveform or its amplitude spectrum. Even the applications that use the articulatory model above do not attempt to determine actual vocal tract areas, but use the model only to find reflection coefficients that produce appropriate speech. The (incorrect) lumping of all losses at the ends of the vocal tract, for simplicity, leads to area estimates that often differ considerably from actual values [120].

In the most common terminal-analog system, a spectral vocal tract model $H(z)$ and radiation model $R(z)$ are excited by a discrete-time glottal excitation $u_G(n)$, which is switched between a voiced and an unvoiced source (Figure 3.36). The unvoiced noise source has a flat spectrum and is often modeled by a simple random number generator. Periodic (voiced)

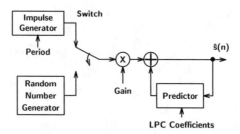

Figure 3.36 Typical terminal-analog model of speech production.

excitation employs a train of impulses exciting a lowpass filter $G(z)$ to produce a waveform with an amplitude spectrum similar to those of glottal signals. This excitation system, also used with articulatory models, is flawed in that voiced fricatives cannot be correctly represented since noise and periodic excitation are mutually exclusive. Since /v,δ/ have only a small noise component and since the lack of a voice bar for /z, 3/ causes little perceptual degradation, the simplicity of the model has nonetheless led to widespread acceptance. While $u_G(n)$ is identified as a glottal signal, it represents frication excitation equally well if $H(z)$ is modified to correspond to a fricative spectrum.

In most terminal-analog models, the vocal tract transfer function has an all-pole form (rewriting Equation (3.57)), where G specifies the speech amplitude and where the poles of $H(z)$ occur at p_i, $i = 1, 2, \ldots, N$:

$$H(z) = \frac{G}{1 - \sum_{i=1}^{N} a_i z^{-i}} = \frac{G}{\prod_{i=1}^{N}(1 - p_i z^{-1})}. \tag{3.58}$$

To model each formant in the speech spectrum, a pair of poles p_i, p_i^* is needed (where * indicates the complex conjugate). A typical pair of poles in $H(s)$ at $-\sigma_i \pm j2\pi F_i$ in the s plane maps into the z plane at $\exp(-\sigma_i T \pm j2\pi F_i T)$, where F_i is the formant frequency and σ_i/π is its bandwidth. Since the vocal tract is a stable system, all poles are inside the unit circle in the z plane.

To simulate a speech sound with this terminal-analog model, the spectrum of the sound must be analyzed to determine the positions of enough poles in Equation (3.58) so that $H(z)$ is a close match. This usually involves analyzing the first few formants as well as specifying poles for a reasonable glottal spectrum.

The radiation component is often modeled by a simple first difference:

$$R(z) = 1 - z^{-1}, \tag{3.59}$$

corresponding to the +6 dB/oct spectrum of $R(\Omega)$ for frequencies of interest. The speech spectrum $S(\Omega)$ is the product of the spectra for the excitation, the vocal tract response, and the radiation effect:

$$S(\Omega) = E(\Omega)V(\Omega)R(\Omega). \tag{3.60}$$

The global trend for $|S(\Omega)|$ is specified by $|E(\Omega)R(\Omega)|$ because the formant peaks of $|V(\Omega)|$ tend to have similar amplitudes. For voiced speech, $|E(\Omega)|$ typically falls off at $-12\,\text{dB/oct}$, which results in a net $-6\,\text{dB/oct}$ decay for $|S(\Omega)|$ when the radiation effect is considered. (The amount of the falloff is proportional to the glottal duty cycle; thus, high frequencies are emphasized in shouted voice but are attenuated in breathy voice.) In the case of a noise source, $|E(\Omega)|$ has a $-6\,\mathrm{dB/oct}$ falloff, which results in a flat spectral trend for $|S(\Omega)|$ (ignoring the local effects of $|V(\Omega)|$).

3.7 COARTICULATION

Speech production involves a sequence of articulator gestures timed so that certain key aspects of vocal tract shape occur in an order corresponding to the intended phoneme sequence. Gestures for successive phonemes overlap in time so that the vocal tract shapes during a phone are highly dependent on the phone's context. The phenomenon of coarticulation involves changes in the articulation and acoustics of a phoneme due to its phonetic context. The most direct evidence of coarticulation occurs at the articulatory level and is measured by visual observation (photography, X-ray radiography, resonance imagery) or observation of muscle activity (electromyography, EMG) [121]. Due to the difficulty of obtaining such data and to the fact that acoustic (instead of articulatory) effects tend to be more important for speech applications, coarticulation is often examined indirectly from its acoustic and perceptual effects. Furthermore, individual EMG (hence muscular) activations do not directly reflect specific higher-level commands.

Because different phonemes have varied requirements for the articulators, there is much freedom in the timing and degree of vocal tract movements. When an articulator gesture for a sound does not conflict with those of a preceding phoneme, the articulator may move toward or adopt a state appropriate for the latter phoneme during the former. Such *forward coarticulation* is called *anticipatory* or *right-to-left* (R–L) because a target for a phoneme (on the "right") induces motion in an articulator during a prior phone (on the "left"). Such anticipation implies either that some articulators for a phoneme start moving (perhaps a fixed time [122–124]) earlier than others or that planning for speech production scans ahead so that each articulator may move towards its next required state as soon as the last phone that needs it has finished. Evidence seems to indicate that the latter is more likely and that a feature for one phoneme spreads over preceding phones. For example, lip rounding for a vowel usually commences during preceding nonlabial consonants; the formant lowering that the rounding imposes does not cause these consonants to be perceived differently. Indeed, there is much perceptual evidence that listeners expect such anticipatory coarticulation [125]. Some coarticulation is likely centrally planned (especially anticipatory effects), while some can be explained by properties of the peripheral speech apparatus.

Although coarticulation is not symmetric in time, the same articulatory freedom that allows R–L coarticulation also permits backward *carryover* or *left-to-right* (L–R) coarticulation, in which some of a phoneme's features persist into ensuing phones. This is most obvious for formant transitions during vowels after a consonant, which are heavily influenced by the consonant [125]. The effects of coarticulation often extend across syllable and syntactic boundaries. L–R coarticulation appears to be a low-level phenomenon in speech production, closer in origin to vocal tract movements than to speech planning in the brain. They are usually ascribed to the mechanical inertia of articulators, whereas R–L coarticulation appears to involve a more active look-ahead planning. Both cases involve the communication principle of least effort: it likely requires less muscle effort to move an articulator gradually toward a target over several phones than to force its motion into a short time span "between phonemes"; similarly, letting an articulator gradually return to a neutral position over several phones is easier than using a quick motion right after the phone that needed it. (The peak velocity of an articulator is likely a good measure of biomechanical effort [126].)

The planning of vocal tract movement by the central nervous system is likely to be organized by coordinating several muscle groups (both agonist and antagonist pairs), rather than controlling individual muscles. Such "coordinative structures" must exist at levels high enough to deal simultaneously with uncoupled articulators such as the larynx and lips, since a perturbation of the lips affects glottal behavior [127].

3.7.1 Where Does Coarticulation Occur?

A phone is usually associated with a phoneme when all the articulators needed for the phoneme are in proper position. The phone "ends" when one or more articulators move (often abruptly) toward positions for the next phoneme and thus cause acoustic changes in the speech signal. Intuitively, one might say [122] that a phoneme's "articulation period" exceeds its "acoustic period" because the gestures for a phoneme start during a preceding phone and finish during an ensuing one. The times of largest acoustic change between phones, identified as phone boundaries, are usually associated with changes in manner of articulation, which often involve vocal tract constriction. Except for sequences of sonorants without major constrictions, the motion of articulators directly involved in a phoneme's constriction specify the boundaries of its phone, while other articulators are freer to coarticulate. Phonemes with a labial constriction allow the tongue to coarticulate, and lingual phonemes permit labial coarticulation, e.g., the lip-rounding feature of a labial spreads to adjacent lingual consonants.

Not all articulators coarticulate in all contexts. Coarticulation occurs in varying degrees depending on context. The motion of articulators from positions for one phoneme to those for the next leads to different vocal tract movements depending on the phoneme sequence; thus the speech signal during such transitions is affected by context. The most obvious cases involve formant transitions before and after oral tract closure for stops and nasals, which provide primary cues to their place of articulation. In other cases, however, the amount of coarticulation may depend on speaking style and rate. Classical steady-state positions and formant frequency targets for many phonemes are rarely achieved in actual speech. Indeed, many models emphasize the importance of dynamic articulatory gestures and suggest that transitions, not steady-state targets, may be the units of speech production [128]. One theory assumes that movement arises from changes in neural control variables that shift equilibrium points in the motor system [129]. *Undershooting* of articulators (and hence of formant transitions) moving toward phoneme targets occurs most often when one speaks rapidly [130,131]. Coarticulation effects beyond immediately adjacent phones are not required for fluent speech production, but they aid in reducing the speaker's effort.

Acoustic variability, such as changes in duration or formant frequencies across different phones for the same phoneme, can be separated into inherent variability and effects of context. Comparing segments in identical phonetic contexts, a speaker produces variations (standard deviations) on the order of 5–10 ms in phone durations and 50–100 Hz in F1–F3. Variations in different contexts beyond these amounts can be attributed to coarticulation.

While the mechanisms may differ between vocal tract articulators and the glottis (vocal folds), coarticulation also seems to apply to F0; e.g., F0 patterns in tone languages show significant modifications in context [132].

3.7.2 Coarticulation Effects for Different Articulators

To explain coarticulation, it helps to identify six relatively independent articulators: glottis, velum, tongue body, tongue tip, lips, and jaw. The glottis controls the presence of voicing and acts as a constrictor for /h/. Glottal coarticulation may include delays in the onset and offset of voicing; e.g., the boundaries between unvoiced fricatives and sonorants can be associated with the times of onset/offset of either voicing or frication, which do not always coincide. Variations in voice onset time (VOT) after a stop release are other examples of glottal coarticulation. VOT (a) increases as stop place of articulation occurs more posterior in the oral tract (Figure 3.37) (e.g., velars have the longest VOTs); (b) increases with the height of the ensuing vowel [1]; and (c) is longer before sonorant consonants than before vowels [84,133]. The first effect is due to vocal tract motion away from the stop closure, preserving frication conditions (i.e., a narrow constriction) longer for velars than for labials. In the latter

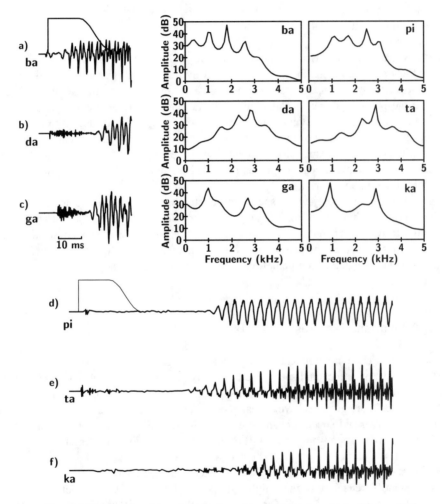

Figure 3.37 Examples of waveforms and spectra sampled at the release of three voiced and unvoiced stops into the vowels /ɑ/ and /u/. The 26 ms analysis time window used to calculate the spectra is superimposed on waveforms (a) and (d). The smooth spectra are derived from pre-emphasized linear prediction analysis (see Chapter 6). Note the long VOT for the unvoiced stops, especially the velar. Note also the increase in burst intensity for place of articulation further posterior in the vocal tract. (After Blumstein and Stevens [134].)

two cases, ensuing sounds with more vocal tract constriction delay voice onset because they preserve some intraoral pressure behind the constriction, which lowers the available pressure drop across the glottis.

Like the glottis (with the exception of /h/), the velum is not involved in oral tract constrictions that primarily specify manner of articulation and hence is relatively free to coarticulate. The velum is closed during most speech but often lowers well in advance of a nasal consonant, causing the spread of nasalization to adjacent phones (especially in the anticipatory direction). While nasal consonants require both a lowered velum and an occluded oral tract, the nasal phone is associated with the period of the occlusion. The velum is typically lowered before oral closure and raised after oral opening. Nasalization of adjacent phones is blocked only when a raised velum is essential (i.e., in obstruents or where nasalization would specify another phoneme, such as in French vowels, which have nasalized counterparts).

Vocal tract constrictions involve tongue and lip articulators. When one articulator constricts for a phoneme, the others are relatively free to coarticulate (if they do not cause an additional constriction). The constricting articulator may also coarticulate to a limited degree when the point or shape of constriction for the phoneme is flexible. Vowels, for example, exhibit considerable coarticulation in which the tongue is displaced toward targets for preceding or ensuing phonemes. Phonemes requiring a complex lingual constriction (e.g., the strident fricatives, especially palatals) allow little tongue coarticulation [135], whereas the occlusion location for velar stops has sufficient freedom to allow coarticulation (e.g., front and back allophones for /k,g/).

The role of the jaw in speech production is to position the tongue and lips for the appropriate amount of tongue height and lip rounding. Just as the tongue body and tip are not truly independent articulators and therefore limit each other's ability to coarticulate, the jaw has limited coarticulation due to its connections to the lips and tongue. Nonetheless, the jaw may exhibit coarticulation into a preceding phone and up to two ensuing phones [125].

3.7.3 Invariant Features

While coarticulation causes significant problems for automatic speech recognition (Chapter 10), its effects aid speech perception (Chapter 5). Most phonemes can be identified by portions of the speech signal from the middle (e.g., steady-state portion) of their phones. Some articulatory gestures have a clear acoustic effect; e.g., a narrow constriction of the vocal tract causes a rapid spectral change, usually lowering F1 to near 200 Hz. Acoustic cues to place of articulation, however, are often complex, involving formant frequencies and amplitudes. Coarticulation, in particular, often complicates the relationship between place and spectrum. Certain sounds have simple place cues; e.g., place in strident fricatives is cued by the cutoff frequency in their highpass spectra. Except for undershoot, vowels in general seem to resist coarticulation. The schwa vowel however is highly coarticulated, virtually assimilating with its phoneme neighbors (its traditional, but perhaps misplaced, status as a neutral vowel at the center of the vowel triangle notwithstanding) [136].

For stops, nasals, and weak fricatives, however, the speech signal during most of the phoneme gesture is often inadequate (too weak in the case of obstruents and too similar in the case of nasals) for reliable place perception. Place is primarily cued in these phones by spectral transitions that occur before and after oral tract closure. Coarticulation causes these transitions to be complex functions of phonetic context, however, which has led to the search for *invariant acoustic features* for place of articulation [137–139].

Invariance may be found in spectral transitions (primarily F2 and F3) to and from stops, but the stop burst spectrum may also be a sufficient cue to place. When the spectra of stop bursts are examined (e.g., using 26 ms windows starting at stop release) (Figure 3.37), labials tend to have diffusely falling or flat spectra, alveolars have diffusely rising patterns, and velars exhibit compact spectra (Figure 3.38) [134,140]. The labels *diffuse* and *compact* refer to the absence or presence, respectively, of one prominent spectral peak. Velars, alone in their excitation of a low-frequency front-cavity resonance, provide the only case of a single strong spectral peak, while the other stops show several peaks, with spectrum either generally rising (alveolars) or falling (labials).

This analysis also applies to the release of nasal consonants, despite the lack of a release burst, if we examine one glottal period (with a 6 ms window) exactly at the release. About 80% of all stop bursts, in both consonant–vowel (CV) and vowel–consonant (VC) syllables, and of nasal releases can be correctly characterized using templates based on the patterns described above (Figure 3.38) [134]. The procedure is considerably less successful for spectra sampled at the vowel offset in VC syllables. (Furthermore, the templates are such that spectra can satisfy more than one template simultaneously, and 70% of alveolar nasals fit both diffuse templates.)

Certain cues to stop place appear to be invariant but may be too small for reliable use in perception. The durations of both F1 transition (from release to vowel steady state) and VOT are relatively long for velars and short for labials; the differences, however, are often less than can be consistently resolved perceptually, suggesting that such place cues are only secondary. It is likely that the primary place cues vary with context; e.g., one study showed that F2–F3 patterns were able to correctly classify place in 97% of initial voiced stops in stressed syllables if the vowel context was known, but in only 68% of the cases when context was ignored [75]. Invariant cues were found only for alveolars, where formant transitions into different vowels seemed to arise from *loci* (constant starting positions) at 1.8 kHz for F2 and 2.6 kHz for F3. The idea of a locus as a target for formant transitions derives from perceptual experiments using synthetic speech: transitions heard as the same phoneme tend to "point toward" fixed loci depending on the place of articulatory constriction [141]. Applying locus theory to acoustic analysis of natural speech, however, appears to require modification of the

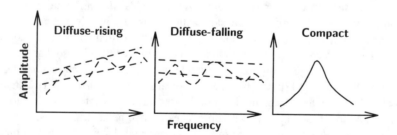

Figure 3.38 Guidelines for spectral templates to characterize stop bursts for alveolar, labial, and velar places of articulation, respectively. The diffuse templates require a spread of peaks at least 500 Hz apart to be within a 10 dB range of either rising or falling parallel lines. Alveolars must have a high peak above 2.2 kHz; labials must have a peak below 2.4 kHz. Velars have a single gross peak in the range 1.2–3.5 kHz (peaks closer than 500 Hz count as one). (After Blumstein and Stevens [134].)

perceptual loci. The perceptual F2 locus for labials was 720 Hz, but two loci at 1645 Hz (for front vowels) and 1090 Hz (for back vowels) model natural speech better (although a single locus at 2337 Hz suffices for F3) [75].

3.7.4 Effects of Coarticulation on Duration

Duration is an implicit parameter of coarticulation. Coarticulation is usually described in terms of (a) spatial effects on articulator motion or (b) the degree of acoustic effects (e.g., formant undershoot), but sometimes the effects are primarily temporal [142]. The simplest coarticulation effects are rapid, involving the movements of articulators responsible for vocal tract constrictions of successive phonemes; the durations of longer coarticulation effects may relate to how fast articulator muscles can contract. Duration, however, can also be explicitly specified by phonetic context. If phones are assigned "inherent" base durations related to their length in "neutral" phonetic contexts, durational deviations may be attributed to coarticulation. Consonants generally have shorter durations in clusters, in part due to shorter articulatory distances for the relatively closed vocal tract during consonants (i.e., vowel–consonant alternations require opening and closing the tract) [133]. Low vowels are typically longer than high vowels because the slow jaw must be moved (maximum jaw speed is about 20 cm/s, with typical acceleration less than that of gravity [126]). Stressed vowels are longer before voiced than before unvoiced consonants and longer before fricatives than before stops [143]. Some of these effects may be due, at least in part, to learned phonological variation (to aid communication) rather than to mechanical coarticulation only.

3.7.5 Models for Coarticulation

To explain the wide range of coarticulation phenomena, several models have been proposed. They typically represent each phoneme with a set of features or articulatory targets, which may spread to adjacent phones as long as the features/targets for such phones do not conflict with the spreading ones. In one view, speech production is a series of vowel-to-vowel articulations on which consonant articulations are superimposed [47,144,145]. (Some models limit the articulation base to stressed vowels, with consonants and unstressed vowels superimposed.) Vowels tend to use large muscles that are less complex and less precise in timing than the muscles for consonants. As examples of long-duration coarticulation, lip rounding and nasalization involve slow-acting muscles, which are not needed for many phonemes. One version of this model [146] views coarticulation as a "coproduction" of "coordinative structures" of muscles functionally grouped together so that the vocal tract may attain articulatory target positions for different phonemes. Research on *compensatory speech* supports this view [147]: when a person speaks with an artificial constraint (e.g., with clenched teeth or an object in the mouth), the articulators tend to deviate from normal positions so that the output speech approaches normal acoustics. In a similar coarticulation model, the articulatory gestures for successive phonemes have a constant amount of temporal overlap, although different articulators for a phoneme may start motion at different times (e.g., large, slow muscles commence before faster muscles when both are needed) [122]. Such coproduction models, with their view of uniform overlapping gestures, contrast with "look-ahead" or "feature-migration" models, which view anticipatory coarticulation as allowing features (e.g., lip rounding) to spread far ahead via planning and have a different mechanism for carryover coarticulation (e.g., inertia).

Linear regressions of F2 transitions in CV syllables (called *locus equations* [148]) have shown promise in modeling coarticulation and in the search for invariant features. Labial stops have steeper slopes than alveolars, suggesting stronger coarticulatory influence of lip closure on the tongue position for an ensuing vowel. As in the older locus theory, velars need two regression lines (one with a flat slope for front vowels, having little coarticulation, and a steep one for back vowels). Comparisons with VC syllables suggest that CV F2 transitions are more precisely controlled than for VCs, which dovetails with the view that CVs are more dominant in speech communication [148]. (Locus equations do not seem to provide invariant features across different manners of articulation [149].)

Most researchers support the notion that auditory feedback is important for production—that control of production is directed toward auditory goals [150]. Speakers economize their effort when the context permits (e.g., less clear speech among friends), while articulating more clearly under more stressful conditions. Supporting evidence includes the Lombard effect and the deterioration of speech with deafness [151] (or when disrupting audition). While some think that articulatory goals replace auditory ones after language acquisition [152], compensation experiments (e.g., putting a bite block or tube in the mouth) show that speakers can radically adjust their articulators to accomplish the acoustic goals needed for speech communication [153,154].

The *task-dynamic* model [155,156] suggests that coordination of articulators ("vocal tract variables" specifying constriction locations and degrees) is paramount, rather than vocal tract shapes. A related theory describes gestures both spatially and temporally [152]; such gestural theories are based in articulation, while other theories integrate acoustics and perception as other factors influencing speech production. The degree to which individual speakers consistently use different articulatory strategies [157] supports this theory. *Motor task* models based on vocal tract shapes correlate well with actual tract movements [158]. The increasing analysis of large databases of speech (e.g., TIMIT) has led to better models of speech variability [159].

3.8 PROSODY (SUPRASEGMENTALS)

This chapter has concentrated so far on the *segmentals* of speech, acoustic aspects of speech signals that help identify each acoustic segment (phone) with a phoneme. Each phone's segmentals derive primarily from vocal tract movements during its articulation and concern dynamics of a sound's spectral envelope (e.g., formants). Other relevant aspects of speech called *suprasegmentals* or *prosody* have domains of interpretation well beyond phone boundaries. Prosody concerns the relationships of duration, amplitude, and F0 of sound sequences. Pronunciations of a word can have substantially varied prosody without affecting the word's identity: phones can be long or short, loud or soft, and have various pitch patterns. In general, segmentals cue phoneme and word identification, while prosody primarily cues other linguistic phenomena. Prosody assists word recognition, however, especially in tone languages, where different F0 patterns superimposed on identical segment sequences cue different words. Even in English, there are definite relationships between phonemics and prosody: some phones inherently are longer, have more amplitude, or have higher F0 than others. Nonetheless, the suprasegmentals are relatively free in many languages to cue aspects of a linguistic message besides phonemics.

Highlighting *stressed* syllables against a background of unstressed syllables is a primary function of prosody. Details of stress perception are examined in Chapter 5; stressed syllables are longer, more intense, and/or have F0 patterns that cause them to stand out against unstressed syllables. A word is considered "stressed" if its *lexically stressed syllable* (so marked in dictionary entries) has sufficient acoustic marking to be perceived as stressed. Prosody also serves several syntactic purposes: (a) segmenting long utterances into smaller phrasal or clausal units, (b) noting the relationships between such phrasal units, and (c) indicating whether an utterance is a question expecting a yes/no answer. The emotional state and identity of the speaker are also reflected in prosody; e.g., utterances reflecting anger, fear, or sorrow are typically longer than in normal speech [160,161]. Emotions can even be cued with relatively short words [162]. Speakers often adjust their prosody to make speech clearer (e.g., slower, louder) in the presence of noise or following loss of hearing (indicating the importance of auditory feedback in aspects of speech production) [163].

The many degrees of freedom that prosody has leads to large interspeaker variability, especially across accents [164]. Intonation is often the last aspect of speech production a foreign speaker masters in learning a new language.

3.8.1 Duration

Conversational speech employs 150–250 word/min, including pauses, which average about 650 ms each [165]. Phone durations vary considerably due to factors such as speaking style (reading vs conversation), stress, the locations of pauses and of word and syllable boundaries, place and manner of articulation, and rhythm [166–170]. A typical syllable duration is about 200 ms, with stressed vowels averaging 130 ms and other phones about 70 ms. Phone durations vary widely for phonemes with different features (especially for phonemes of different manner of articulation); e.g., schwa vowels are typically 45 ms, whereas diphthongs in conversation average 180 ms [171]. Vowels average about 30 ms longer than sonorant consonants, which in turn are about 5 ms longer than obstruents. Diphthongs are about 75 ms longer than vowels, and tense vowels exceed lax and schwa vowels by about 60 ms; unvoiced stops tend to be about 15 ms longer than voiced stops [165]. In read speech, syllable-initial consonants are about 20 ms longer than consonants that terminate a syllable, and unvoiced fricatives are about 40 ms longer than voiced ones [133].

The difference in style between read and conversational speech can have significant durational effects; e.g., typically half of conversation time consists of pauses, compared to only 20% in read speech. Three durational phenomena common in read speech do not seem to occur in conversation [172]: (1) phrase-final lengthening, (2) polysyllabic shortening, and (3) consonantal effects on preceding vowels. (1) The final syllable of major *phrases* (word sequences grouped together by syntax) in English tends to be up to 200 ms longer than syllables in other positions. (2) Average syllable duration tends to decrease with more syllables in a word. The relative shortening of syllables in polysyllabic words in read speech may relate to communication efficiency: words with many phonemes are easier to identify than short words, which could allow spending less time per phoneme without risking perceptual mistakes. (3) Vowels are longer before voiced consonants than before unvoiced ones [171,173]. Vowels lengthen before voiced consonants in many languages, but the effect appears to be largest in English prepausal read speech (up to 100 ms lengthening) [171]. In conversation, such lengthening appears to be limited to tense vowels before voiced stops [165]. English nasal consonants also tend to be much longer before voiced than before unvoiced stops; e.g., nasals in *limp*, *lint* and *link* are briefer than those in *dimmed* or *pinned* (e.g., 35 ms vs 95 ms [133]). Phonological redundancy may explain this nasal effect: the place of articulation feature is the same for both phonemes in nasal + unvoiced stop clusters, so perception of nasalization in /I/ (without requiring a long nasal consonant) is sufficient to cue the /m-n-ŋ/ distinction in the unvoiced context.

Both voiced and unvoiced speech exhibit a general *prepausal lengthening* of the last few syllables just prior to a pause, in which most phones (but not stops) lengthen compared with nonpausal contexts. The final prepausal syllable typically doubles in duration, while earlier syllables have lesser lengthening. The effect has been attributed to a slowing down of speech in anticipation of a pause, aiding perceptual cues to syntactic boundaries, and/or additional time needed to accomplish large F0 movements that often occur in prepausal speech. In read speech, similar lengthening often occurs at syntactic boundaries without pauses. There is some evidence for rhythmical patterns in read speech: one study of Swedish notes a tendency for durations of phones (62.5 ms average), unstressed syllables (125 ms), stressed syllables (250 ms), interstress intervals (500 ms) and pauses (0.5 and 1.0 s) to be multiples of each other [174].

When compared to single consonants in syllables, consonants in clusters tend to shorten in general; e.g., consonant durations in CCV or VCC syllables are shorter than those in CVC syllables, even for clusters containing a syllable boundary [172]. Some of these effects can be attributed to shorter articulatory distances in clusters, but others are more likely to have a phonological basis. A study of stressed monosyllabic words in read speech found that consonants in clusters shorten about 15 ms for articulatory reasons, with the largest changes occurring in word-initial sonorants [133]. Following an obstruent, /w/ shortened 70 ms and other sonorants shortened 35–55 ms or 25 ms following an unvoiced or voiced obstruent, respectively. In the unvoiced case, the shortening was compensated by an increase of 15–25 ms in aspiration between the obstruent release and voice onset in the sonorant.

Unvoiced stops in initial /s/ + stop clusters are unaspirated, thus resembling voiced stops. They cannot be confused with voiced stops, because English does not allow voicing to change between the initial /s/ and an ensuing stop. The fact that voicing cannot change inside clusters may account for a tendency to lengthen consonants in final clusters, while initial cluster consonants shorten. If the extra duration of initial consonants is a cue to syllable boundaries, it is less necessary in clusters that often block boundary possibilities; e.g., the /n/ in "a near … " is longer than in "an ear … ," possibly to cue the word boundary, but in "a sneer … " the initial /s/ forces /n/ to be part of the second syllable, and /n/ shortens.

Because there appears to be a certain rhythm to stressed syllables in English, it is known as a *stress-timed* language; i.e., there is some regularity in the duration between onsets of stressed syllables. Other languages (e.g., French, Japanese), which have a lesser tendency to reduce unstressed syllables, are often called *syllable-timed*, in which syllables (or "morae" in Japanese) are supposedly regularly spaced. Evidence for either position (i.e., regular spacing of stresses or syllables) is weak in terms of speech production [175], although the percept seems to be there.

3.8.2 Effects of Stress and Speaking Rate

The durations of phones are heavily influenced by stress and speaking rate. As noted above, stressed syllables are longer than unstressed ones. Stress primarily affects vowel duration, whereas syllable-final consonants have little stress variation; durations typically differ 10–20 % between stressed and unstressed syllables. Stressed syllables are usually found in words considered important by the speaker for proper communication of a message. *Function words* (e.g., prepositions, articles, conjunctions, pronouns) are rarely stressed, while most *content words* (nouns, verbs, adverbs, adjectives) are stressed. Words unexpected by the listener or new to a conversation (*new information*) typically are stressed. Infrequently used words have longer durations than common words [172].

When a person speaks more slowly than normal, pauses account for about 80% of the durational increase (about 55% are new pauses and 25% are extensions of pauses at the normal rate) [165]. At rates faster than normal, all durations shorten about 30% [176], but the effect in English may be nonlinear. In read speech, unstressed syllables shorten more than stressed ones [143], vowels more than consonants, and unvoiced stops more than voiced ones [177]. Some studies, however, suggest a more linear relationship (especially in conversational speech [165]) at the acoustic level [176] or the EMG level [178]. Many of the durational contrasts that may help cue phonemics at slow and normal rates tend to neutralize at fast rates [179]. For example, /b/ and /w/ can be distinguished by the rate at which the labial constriction is opened (a rapid transition cues /b/), but the /b/ transition is resistant to rate changes whereas /w/ shortens with increasing rate [180].

Each phone may have a minimal "incompressible" duration related to the speed of its articulators [171]. When subject to several shortening phenomena (e.g., a cluster consonant in an unstressed, polysyllabic word at a fast speaking rate), the net effect of all shortenings is less than the sum of all the individual effects. However, durations in such cases tend toward an asymptote longer than can be explained on articulatory grounds [179]. In modeling duration, there has been no agreement whether rules for lengthening or shortening should be expressed absolutely or in percent and whether the rules should combine by addition or multiplication [171,179].

Although increases in speaking rate and decreases in stress both shorten duration, rate changes appear to have few effects on F0 and formants, whereas stress affects both formants and prosody [178]. Decreases in stress reduce F0 variation and centralize formants, suggesting that articulator movement decreases in unstressed syllables. Unstressed English vowels tend toward the center of the vowel triangle [181]: tense vowels become lax, lax vowels tend toward schwa, and vowels may even become very brief and devoiced. In polysyllabic words, some vowels resist reduction despite lack of stress (e.g., in *constitutionalize*, the first and third syllables have secondary and main stress, respectively, and their vowels cannot reduce, while the other vowels may reduce, except the final one in this case—such unstressed, unreduced vowels are often diphthongs).

Rate increases tend to decrease the time phones spend in steady state; while the speed of articulators increases at very fast rates, more often articulators are simply displaced shorter distances [182], e.g., a smaller transition toward a glide target in a diphthong. One study of dorsum motion found that the ratio of maximum velocity to displacement was proportional to speaking rate [183].

3.8.3 Fundamental Frequency (F0)

F0 provides speakers with a tool of significant power to communicate information other than phonemics, especially in nontone languages (e.g., English), where F0 is virtually independent of segmentals [184,185]. Phone duration has only one degree of freedom to cue information, but F0 trends (reflecting tension in the larynx) may change several times in a single phone and thus F0 may signal stress or syntactic information via both its relative value and its slopes. Most phones have a simple rising or falling F0 pattern, but a single phone may contain a rise + fall + rise.

The F0 contour over an utterance may be viewed as a superposition of effects, ranging from global (sentential) to local (segmental) [186]. The global basis for F0 in many utterances is flat, although most read utterances have a downward trend called *declination* after the first stressed word [187]. The declination pattern is often reset at major syntactic boundaries in long utterances and is sometimes associated with *breath groups* (inspirations often increase prior to long utterances [12]), although the correlation of F0 and subglottal pressure is weak. In most English utterances, F0 starts at a medium level, rises rapidly on the first stressed syllable, declines during ensuing words, and finally falls to a very low level at the end. Questions anticipating a yes/no answer deviate from this pattern: F0 tends to decline at a much slower rate during the question and then to rise to a very high value at the end [188].

Upon this global F0 base are found phrase-level rise + fall obtrusions, sometimes called *hat patterns* if the terminating F0 fall is delayed for a few syllables. In typical English phrases, F0 rises on the first stressed syllable and falls on the final one. Phrases that are not sentence-final are often marked by a *continuation rise* in F0 on their last syllable or two. Thus an F0 rise on a lexically stressed syllable cues its word as important and signals the start of a syntactic unit; a rise on an unstressed syllable (especially if followed by a pause) cues the end of a unit; a sharp fall cues the last stressed syllable in a unit; level or slightly falling F0 is the default for other syllables.

For syllables with unvoiced consonants, F0 is interrupted when voicing ceases. In such cases, an F0 rise "on" a syllable includes any upward jump in F0 during a preceding unvoiced interval, while a fall includes any F0 drop in an ensuing unvoiced period. In stressed syllables, F0 tends to jump to a higher level if the syllable has an initial unvoiced consonant than if it starts with a vowel or voiced consonant. The high F0 at the initiation of voicing is likely related to the adducting motion of the vocal folds, which causes the initial periods to be short. Voiced consonants tend to show a small dip in F0, presumably resulting from a decreased glottal pressure drop due to the consonantal constriction of the vocal tract. Assuming a carryover coarticulation from consonant to vowel, the effect is best explained in terms of slack vocal folds for voiced consonants (to aid vibration under low pressure conditions) and stiff vocal folds for unvoiced consonants (to prevent vibration) [189].

Figure 3.39 illustrates a number of F0 effects: (a) the word *that* has a larger F0 stress rise when it acts as an adjective (3.39a) than as a simple function word; (b) *fish*, *true*, and the

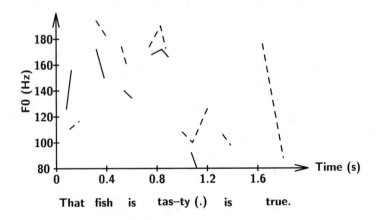

Figure 3.39 Contours of F0 as a function of time for two utterances: (a) "That fish is tasty" (solid lines) and (b) "That fish is tasty is true" (dashed lines). Straight lines were fit to the actual F0 data during the high-amplitude portions of each syllable.

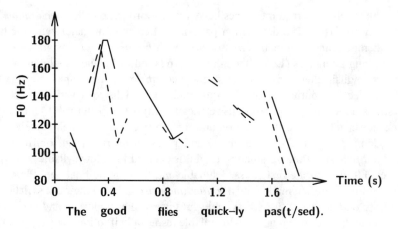

Figure 3.40 F0-contours for (a) "The good flies quickly passed" (solid lines) and (b) "The good flies quickly past" (dashed lines).

first syllable of *tasty* have both F0 stress rises and falls, but the rises exceed the falls when introducing a phrase rather than finishing one; (c) the second syllable of *tasty* shows a typical continuation rise (Figure 3.39b); (d) F0 during the *is* words exhibits the declination effect; and (e) "That fish is tasty" in Figure 3.39(b) suggests a hat pattern.

Potential syntactic ambiguities are usually resolved by word or conversational context, but prosody assists in many cases [190,191]. For example, phrases of the "*A* or *B* and *C*" type could be segmented before or after the *B* word (i.e., *B* and *C* together or *A* alone vs either *A* or *B* accompanies *C*, respectively). Placing a pause and/or a continuation rise after *A* or *B* resolves the ambiguity, as would putting an F0 rise or fall on *B* (in the latter case, a fall on *B* groups "*A* or *B*" together). In Figure 3.40, the rapid stress F0 fall on either *flies* or *good* cues the end of the first syntactic phrase and resolves its ambiguity. Note also the complexity of the F0 pattern on *good* in Figure 3.40(b).

As a final example, Figure 3.41 contrasts the terminal F0 rise of yes/no questions (" . . . steak?") with the fall on other questions that (like declarative sentences) exhibit terminal fall

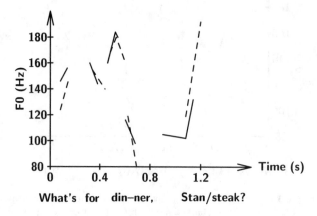

Figure 3.41 F0 contours for (a) "What's for dinner, Stan?" (solid lines) and (b) "What's for dinner, steak?" (dashed lines).

("... dinner?"). Both sentences here end with "tag" words. Figure 3.41(b) displays two questions, the first with a terminal fall ("... dinner?"), the second with a rise ("... steak?"). Figure 3.41(a) asks only one question but adds the vocative *Stan*, which is associated with an F0 pattern starting low and then rising abruptly at the end. Always occurring at the end, the rise in a vocative contour is thus easily distinguished from a stress rise that occurs early in the syllable.

3.9 CONCLUSION

This chapter has examined the mechanisms and acoustics of human speech production, noting the physiology and movements of the vocal tract, as well as the acoustic–phonetic relationships of speech communication. It has concentrated on normal production, and omitted (for space reasons) aspects specific to child speech [192], aging [193], and speech disorders [57,194].

PROBLEMS

P3.1. Draw a diagram of the vowel triangle, giving the approximate positions of the basic 11 English vowels. Explain the significance of such a diagram in terms of acoustics and physiology.

P3.2. Briefly explain the difference between nasal consonants and fricative consonants in terms of (a) how they are produced physically and (b) their acoustic characteristics. What aspects of a fricative's vocal-tract shape determine the shape of its speech spectrum?

P3.3. Using the two-tube lossless model of the vocal tract in Figure 3.24, find (to the nearest 10 Hz) the formant resonance frequencies when (i) $A_1 = 5\,cm^2$, $l_1 = 17\,cm$, $A_2 = 0$, $l_2 = 0$; (ii) $A_1 = 6\,cm^2$, $l_1 = 8.5\,cm$, $A_2 = 3\,cm^2$, $l_2 = 8.5\,cm$; (iii) $A_1 = 3\,cm^2$, $l_1 = 6\,cm$, $A_2 = 6\,cm^2$, $l_2 = 11\,cm$.

(a) In each case, which phoneme does the model approximate best?

(b) In case (ii), if A_2 shrinks to near zero, how would the resonance frequencies change?

(c) How does the speech spectrum change if all areas are scaled proportionally?

(d) If a short constriction is made at the lips, how would the spectrum change?

(e) In case (ii), at what times would an impulse exciting the left, glottal end of the model cause outputs at the right, lip end?

(f) In case (ii), what is the acoustic impedance, looking up into the oral cavity, from a point midway in this vocal tract model?

P3.4. Assume an infant with a vocal tract length of 8.5 cm and a fundamental frequency of 400 Hz utters a vowel sound with a vocal tract of uniform cross-sectional area. Give a detailed sketch of the spectral amplitude as a function of frequency, up to 4 kHz, noting specifically the formant locations.

P3.5. Using the three-tube lossless model of the vocal tract in Figure 3.24, draw a network flow diagram, using delay elements and reflection coefficients, for the case where $A_1 = 0.8\,cm^2$, $l_1 = 10\,cm$, $A_2 = 0.2\,cm^2$, $l_2 = 2\,cm$, $A_3 = 0.6\,cm^2$, $l_3 = 5\,cm$. Include glottal and lip effects.

4

Hearing

4.1 INTRODUCTION

Speech communication is the transmission of information from the brain of a speaker to that of a listener via a speech signal. Chapter 3 dealt with the first part of this process, and now we examine how the signal entering a listener's ears is converted into a linguistic message. Two processes are involved: *audition* or *hearing*, which registers the speech sounds in the brain, and *speech perception*, which decodes the speech message from the neural representation of the sounds. Audition is the subject of this chapter, and speech perception is discussed in Chapter 5. Much technical detail is known about the audition process, in which pressure variations in the outer ear are converted into neural firings on the auditory nerve. The mechanisms by which the brain translates these neural firings into a linguistic message are much less understood. This chapter examines the functioning of the organs of the ear, at the anatomical and physiological levels, whereas Chapter 5 explores the *psychoacoustics* of the hearing process. Psychoacoustics is the study of auditory perception at the psychological level, relating acoustic signals to what the human listener perceives. We will limit ourselves to normal hearing, and not discuss hearing disorders [1], cochlear implants [2], or other hearing aids [3].

4.2 ANATOMY AND PHYSIOLOGY OF THE EAR

The human speech production and hearing mechanisms are likely to have evolved in parallel, each system taking advantage of properties of the other. The ear is especially responsive to those frequencies in the speech signal that contain the most information relevant to communication (i.e., in the 200–5600 Hz range). The listener can discriminate small differences in time and frequency found in speech sounds in this frequency range. Indeed, parts of the ear aid perception by amplifying sound energy at speech frequencies, which may partially compensate for the decline with frequency in voiced speech energy above 400 Hz.

Many of the phenomena discussed in this chapter have been explored in detail for the auditory systems of animals. While humans, alone among animals, can talk (although animals can produce noises, and some birds can replicate speech sounds), virtually all animals can hear. Human audition is very similar to that for other mammals, and shares many features with the auditory systems of birds. There are important differences; e.g., cochlear hair cells, when damaged by loud sounds, regenerate with time in birds, but not in mammals [4]. Another difference is that of size: mammals larger than humans have bigger auditory structures, and hence are more sensitive to lower sound frequencies (and vice versa for smaller animals; e.g., bats can hear to 200 kHz). Given the danger of experiments on live human auditory systems, most results below derive from animal studies.

The ear is composed of three sections: the outer ear, middle ear, and inner ear (Figure 4.1) [5–11]. The outer ear directs speech pressure variations toward the eardrum, where the middle ear transforms these variations into mechanical motion. The inner ear converts these vibrations into electrical firings in the auditory neurons, which lead to the brain.

4.2.1 Outer Ear

The external, visible part of the outer ear, called the *pinna*, funnels sound waves into the ear canal (or *external auditory meatus*). The pinna (a cartilaginous flap of skin) helps in sound localization [13], and by its asymmetric shape makes the ear more sensitive to sounds coming from in front of the listener than to those coming from behind. The meatus, an air-filled cavity open at one end (pinna) and closed at the other (eardrum), acts as a quarter-wavelength resonator. The canal in an adult is about 2.7 cm long (and about 0.7 cm in diameter); thus the first resonance is near 3 kHz. This resonance amplifies energy in the 3–5 kHz range by up to 15 dB [14], which likely aids perception of sounds having significant information at these high frequencies (e.g., obstruents). The resonance is fairly broad because the ear canal has yielding walls and especially a pliant eardrum.

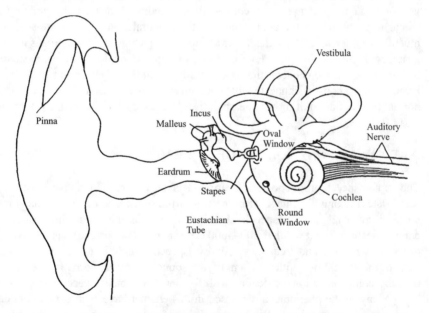

Figure 4.1   The structure of the peripheral auditory system. (After Lafon [12], 1968, The functional anatomy of the speech organs, *Manual of Phonetics.*, B. Malmberg (ed) [North-Holland: Amsterdam].)

4.2.2 Middle Ear

The eardrum (*tympanic membrane*) marks the beginning of the middle ear, an air-filled cavity of about 6 cm^3 that contains the tiny ossicular bones (*malleus* or *hammer*, *incus* or *anvil*, and *stapes* or *stirrup*). These three dense bones linearly transmit eardrum vibrations to the *oval window* membrane of the inner ear. The middle ear accomplishes an impedance transformation between the air medium of the outer ear and the liquid medium of the inner ear [15]. The acoustic impedance of the inner ear fluid is about 4000 times that of air. This impedance mismatch is such that, without the transformer effect of the ossicles, all but 0.1% of the pressure waves hitting the eardrum would be reflected back, with little energy entering the inner ear. There is an increase in sound pressure within the middle ear (peaking at about 20 dB near 1 kHz [16]), partly due to a lever action in the ossicles but mostly due to the difference in surface area between the large eardrum and the small area on the oval window that the stapes contacts. The vibrating area of the eardrum is approximately 55 mm^2, compared to the stapes area of 3.2 mm^2. For a given force on the eardrum, the concentration of area through the middle ear raises the effective pressure (force per unit area) at the input to the inner ear. Spectrally, the middle ear acts as a lowpass filter with attenuation of about -15 dB/oct above 1 kHz.

The middle ear also protects the delicate inner ear against very strong sounds. As sound intensity increases, the stapes motion changes from a pumping action to one of rotation, so that inner ear oscillations do not increase proportionally with sound levels. When low-frequency sounds of more than 85–90 dB reach the eardrum, the middle ear muscles contract in an *acoustic reflex* to attenuate pressure transmission by up to 20 dB [14, 17]. The reflex has a latency of approximately 60–175 ms and activates only for frequencies below 2 kHz, thus providing little protection for impulsive sounds. Voicing in the speaker's vocal tract activates his own acoustic reflex, perhaps to avoid overloading the hearing mechanism while talking. Pressure is equalized between the outer and middle ear via the eustachian tube, which leads to the nasopharynx. Unequal pressure, sometimes felt in air travel, hinders proper eardrum vibration and causes discomfort.

4.2.3 Inner Ear

The *cochlea*, a tube filled with a gelatinous fluid called *endolymph* and located in the inner ear, transforms mechanical vibrations at its oval window input into electrical excitation on its neural fiber outputs. The tube is coiled in a snail-shaped spiral of about 2.5 turns. Two membranes and a thin *bony shelf* divide the interior of the cochlea along its 35 mm length, creating three separate tunnels of lymphatic liquid. The largest chamber (54 mm^3), the *scala vestibuli*, is separated from the small middle cavity, the *cochlear duct* or *scala media* (7 mm^3), by the delicate *Reissner's membrane* (Figure 4.2). Between the cochlear duct and the *scala tympani* (37 mm^3) is the sturdy *basilar membrane*.

The stapes of the middle ear attaches to the scala vestibuli through the oval window membrane, all of which vibrate in response to sound pressure entering the ear. Since the walls of the cochlea are hard bone and the liquid is incompressible, oval window vibrations cause motion in the flexible cochlear membranes. Perilymph (much thinner than the endolymph elsewhere in the inner ear) from the scala vestibuli can enter the scala tympani via a small opening (the *helicotrema*) at the apex (interior) of the cochlea. Pressure in the scala tympani can be relieved by the round window membrane at the basal end of the cochlea.

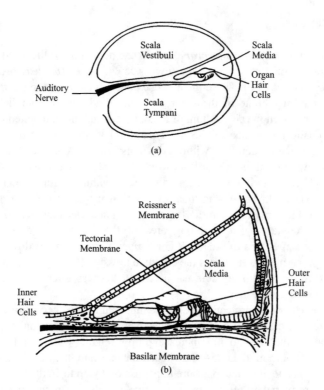

Figure 4.2 Structural and anatomical features of the cochlea: (a) cross-section of the cochlea; (b) the structures within the scala media.

The cochlea has a cross-sectional area of about $4\,mm^2$ at its base near the stapes and tapers gradually to about $1\,mm^2$ at its apex. The basilar membrane is 32–35 mm long, increasing from a width of 0.04 mm at its base to 0.5 mm at the apex. On the basilar membrane lies the organ of Corti, which contains about 30,000 sensory *hair cells*, arranged in several rows along the length of the cochlea. The endings of the auditory nerve terminate on these hair cells, each of which has about 40–140 hairs (stereocilia grouped in a bevelled shape and suspended in the endolymph) that bend (about 1 nm) from vibrations in the basilar and tectorial membranes (Figure 4.2b), causing neural *firings* (electrical potentials) to propagate in the auditory nerve. The *inner hair cells* (IHCs) lie in a single row of about 5000 cells, on which nearly 95% of the nerve fibers terminate, while the more numerous *outer hair cells* (OHCs) form several rows and share the remaining nerve fibers; OHCs and IHCs have different response characteristics.

Stimulus-dependent electrical potentials in the organ of Corti consist of an alternating waveform called the *cochlear microphonic* (which resembles the input acoustic signal) and an offset value ($-60\,mV$) known as the *summating potential* (due to different concentrations of sodium and potassium ions in the two lymph fluids). OHCs are primarily responsible for the cochlear microphonic, while IHCs generate the summating potential [6, 18–20]. The tips of the OHCs are embedded in the tectorial membrane (Figure 4.2b), whereas the IHCs barely make contact with it. One theory holds that the OHCs are moved directly by the basilar membrane, while the IHCs respond to the velocity of the basilar membrane through the viscous drag of fluid around them [5]. The OHCs are sensitive to bending across the basilar membrane, whereas the IHCs react to motion along the membrane.

The OHCs are motile, thus lengthening and shortening due to *efferent* nerve fiber messages from the brain (the *afferent* fibers send *to* the brain), which increase auditory sensitivity, hence causing sharper responses. The OHCs thus control the IHC responses, but do not send information themselves [14, 21].

After leaving the cochlea, neural information follows an ascending pathway to the brain. In turn, the auditory firings pass through (and are recoded in) the cochlear nucleus, the trapezoid body, the superior olivary complex, the lateral lemniscus, the inferior colliculus, and finally the medial geniculate body, before entering the cerebral brain cortex [22]. Firings arriving at the cochlear nucleus are processed by two types of neurons: *onset chopper units* extract precise temporal features, while *transient chopper units* get spectral information [23]. The former respond strongly to the onsets of high-frequency tones; the latter have small range, but avoid saturation due to inhibitory inputs from high-threshold fibers over a wide range.

Such a system occurs for most mammals, and a similar system is found in birds (despite their evolutionary divergence 300 million years ago). Both groups separately developed specialized hair-cell populations arranged across the width of a sensory epithilium (e.g., the basilar membrane in mammals). The avian basilar papillae differ from the mammalian organ of Corti in being much shorter, yet having similar numbers of hair cells.

4.2.4 Basilar Membrane (BM) Behavior

Since the basilar membrane (BM) varies gradually in tautness and shape along its length, its frequency response varies accordingly. The BM is stiff and thin at the basal end, but compliant and massive at the apex (the ratio of stiffness between ends exceeds 100). Each location along the BM has a *characteristic frequency* (CF), at which it vibrates maximally for a given input sound. For a specific location, the response curve (as a function of the vibration frequency of the oval window) is that of a bandpass filter with almost constant Q (fixed ratio of center frequency to bandwidth) (Figure 4.3a). Because of this constant-percentage bandwidth, frequency resolution along the basilar membrane is best at low frequencies. A hair cell linked with a high-CF location on the BM fires in response to a broader set of frequencies than does a low-CF hair cell.

The response curve has a similar shape when BM vibration is shown as a function of distance from the stapes along the membrane, using a tone (a sound of single frequency) input. For every input frequency, there is a point on the BM of maximal vibration. This point, measured in distance from the apex of the BM, is roughly proportional to the logarithm of the sound frequency (Figure 4.3b).

When a tone excites the oval window, pressure is applied to the entire cochlea at once, causing the BM to vibrate at the same frequency as the input. Since the velocity of sound in cochlear fluid is 1600 m/s and the cochlea is only 35 mm long, there is essentially no phase delay in pressure along the BM. Whether sound reaches the cochlea through the bones of the head or through the ear canal, the resulting BM motion is similar because of this simultaneous application of pressure. The motion of the BM, in response to a sinusoidal pressure, is that of a traveling wave, progressing from the base to the apex. The characteristics of the wave are due entirely to the properties of the BM and are not related to the source location of the oval window. There is no obvious reflection at the apex or any standing wave structure. The speed

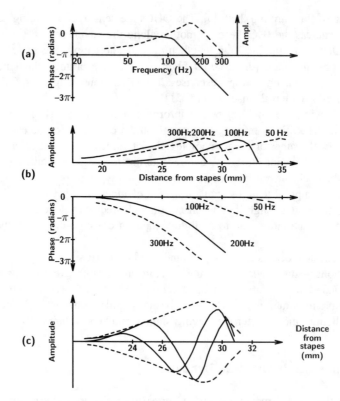

Figure 4.3 Displacement of the BM due to an input sound: (a) the phase (solid line) and
amplitude (dashed line) of BM vibration, at 33 mm from the stapes; (b) phase
and amplitude envelopes for four tones at low frequencies; (c) the amplitude
envelope (dashed lines) and two waves (solid lines) of a 200 Hz vibration
separated by 90°. These curves were based on experiments using human
cadaver ears and very intense sounds; live human ears exhibit sharper curves
(e.g., higher Q). (After von Békésy [24].)

of the wave decreases as it travels: very rapid at the base, about 15 cm/ms in the middle of the
BM, and about 1 cm/ms at the apex. At any point along the BM, the motion is periodic, with
a period equal to that of the sound excitation. The traveling wave reaches a maximum
amplitude at the point on the BM whose CF matches the input frequency. Each section of the
BM vibrates sinusoidally in time, with a phase delay (with respect to the oval window
vibration) proportional to the distance between the two points (Figure 4.3c). Since the basal
end is thin and stiff, the maximum of the traveling wave occurs there for high-frequency
inputs; the apex responds maximally to low-frequency tones. Only very-low-frequency inputs
(less than 20 Hz) cause sufficient BM motion near the helicotrema to move liquid back and
forth between the scala vestibuli and scala tympani.

In response to an impulsive sound, e.g., a click (having short duration, with energy at all
frequencies of interest), each point along the BM responds at its own CF, commencing
vibration in phase with the input pulse (after a certain propagation delay) (Figure 4.4). Unless
the input pulse is repeated, the BM vibration dies out in time, ranging from a rapid decay at
the base (less than 1 ms) to slow decay at the apex (several ms). The wave progressively loses

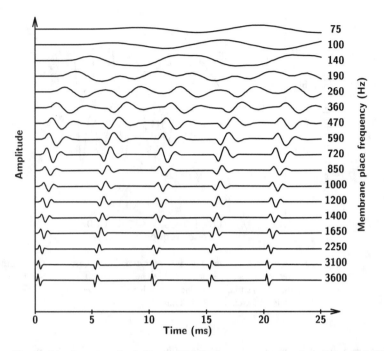

Figure 4.4 Computer simulation for BM displacement as a function of time and CF (noted along the ordinate); each trace is the response for a different point (separated by 0.5 mm) along the basilar membrane to alternating positive and negative sound pulses of 100 μs duration at a rate of 200 pulses/s. (After Flanagan [8].)

its high-frequency components as it travels toward the helicotrema; this motion has been modeled using filters [25].

4.2.5 Electrical Activity in the Auditory Neurons

The hair cells in the organ of Corti are connected to the brain via the eighth cranial (auditory) nerve, which is composed of nerve cells (*neurons*). The neurons "fire" (an "all-or-nothing" 0.5–1.0 ms *spike* or pulse deviation from resting potential) in response to bending and shearing forces (of about 100 nm) experienced by the hair cells to which they are attached. The tension on the hair cells (which act as capacitor plates) alters their electrical conductance, which influences the release of a chemical substance, which in turn causes the attached neuron to fire [26]. (The helicotrema relieves any static pressure that might cause the basilar membrane to deform, and bend the hair cells, in the absence of sound.)

Studies of hearing in cats and monkeys, who have similar auditory mechanisms to humans, show distinct firing patterns in response to simple click and tone stimuli. Without sound stimuli, each neuron fires in a random, spontaneous sequence at average rates of 10–50/s. In the presence of sound, neurons also act stochastically, but spikes are more likely at certain times than at others, depending on the intensity and frequencies of the sound input. Each nerve fiber follows a *tuning curve* that plots, as a function of tone frequency, the sound intensity necessary to raise its firing rate above the low, spontaneous rate (Figure 4.5). The V-shaped curve for each neuron indicates a CF, at which a tone of minimal amplitude will raise

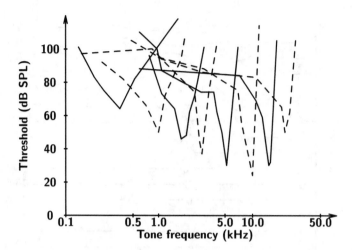

Figure 4.5 Representative tuning curves of cat auditory fibers, for eight different frequency regions. For each fiber, the frequency threshold is a function of stimulating frequency. The curves have been arbitrarily positioned on the ordinate for clarity. (After Evans [33].)

the tendency for that neuron to fire. These CFs correspond well to the mechanical behavior of the basilar membrane, at the point where the neuron contacts the BM. The frequency-selective nature of auditory fibers in the cochlea provides a *tonotopic organization*, mapping sound frequency into place information along the BM, which is preserved in varying degrees in the ascending neural pathway to the brain (at least as far as the inferior colliculus) [27]. Several models for the neural activity patterns exist [28–31], including ones in software [32].

The tuning curves resemble inverted forms of the bandpass filters of Figure 4.3(b), with approximately constant Q at frequencies above 500 Hz. They are more sharply defined (about 200 dB/oct above the CF and 60 dB/oct for frequencies just below the CF) than the BM responses. This sharpening (sometimes called a *second filter effect*) appears to be due to nonlinear active amplification via the motile outer hair cells (OHCs) [34, 35], especially as frequency increases [36]. Resulting *otoacoustic emissions* (OAEs) are weak sounds (usually < 0 dB) in the outer ear that originate in the inner ear, most likely from rapid length changes in the OHCs, which normally derive from changes in the IHCs. Such active feedback enhances the selectivity of the tuning curves, and appears to be unique to primates. When two tones (at frequencies $f_1 < f_2$) enter the ear, distortion products are generated at $nf_1 - f_2$ ($n = 2, 3, \ldots$) [37], of which the one for $n = 2$ is strongest. Such OAEs are easily observable in humans (although not audible by humans themselves) and give a useful tool to analyze inner ear behavior and to detect ear disorders. This phenomenon is also studied subjectively through combination tones at the same distortion product frequencies.

For a specific fiber, plots of average spikes/s as a function of frequency resemble inverted tuning curves, for low and medium sound amplitudes (Figure 4.6). However, at high intensity, such plots become trapezoidal, where maximal firing rates are achieved over a broad range of frequencies above and below the fiber's CF. The broadening of these contours indicates a *recruitment* of adjacent neurons to fire, whose CFs are near but not identical to the stimulus frequency. When sound intensity reaches the upper limit of a neuron's range, its firing rate "saturates" and does not increase further in response to higher amplitudes.

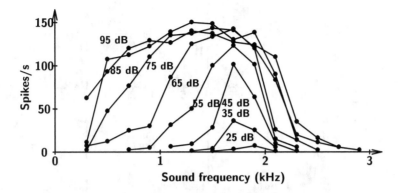

Figure 4.6   Firing rates as a function of the frequency of a stimulus tone for an auditory
nerve fiber in a squirrel monkey, plotted for eight different sound intensities
(25–95 dB) (iso-intensity contours). The fiber's CF is 1700 Hz. (After Rose *et
al.* [43].)

Saturation rate varies among neurons, but sustained firing rates above 300/s are rare. The
range of pure tone intensities for which the firing rate of a given neuron varies with intensity
is only about 20–40 dB, and the range of thresholds for most neurons at a given CF is only
about 20 dB. *Low-threshold fibers* have a small dynamic range (about 20 dB) and high
spontaneous rates (50/s), while other fibers have thresholds 15 dB higher, a wider range
(40 dB), and low spontaneous rates (15/s) [23].

This suggests a maximum range of 60 dB in which the integrated firing rate increases
with sound intensity. The timing patterns of neural firings, however, relate to intensities over a
much wider range (> 80 dB) in sounds more complex than tones [38]. A small minority of
fibers (about 9%) [39] have dynamic ranges greater than 60 dB, which could help explain the
wide range of perceived sounds, but a more likely interpretation is that the timing patterns, as
well as the average number, of firings affect perceived loudness [40–42].

4.2.5.1 Timing of neural firings.   The properties of a nerve fiber are often measured
using histograms of spikes, in response to many click and tone stimuli over long durations.
These displays show the number of firings at specific time delays with respect to each other or
to the sound stimulus: *post-stimulus histograms* record the delay relative to the initiation of
the stimulus, *period histograms* show the delay relative to the (sometimes arbitrarily defined)
"start" of each period in a periodic stimulus, and *interval histograms* display the times
between successive firings (Figure 4.7). These histograms have shown that firings tend to be
synchronized with displacements of the basilar membrane in a certain direction. When the
BM vibrates sinusoidally with sufficient amplitude, a nerve fiber tends to fire on synchronous
half-cycles of the movement at the point where the fiber is attached. Histograms of the times
of the spikes (synchronized to the period of the sound stimulus) closely resemble half-wave
rectified versions of the BM movement near the neuron (Figure 4.8). There also appears to be
a form of automatic gain control (with an approximate response time of 20 ms), by which
loud and soft stimuli yield very similar timing histograms; i.e., higher probability of neural
firing at peaks in the sound waveform, relatively independent of its amplitude.

In response to input clicks, preferred firing times are well modeled by a delay plus a
multiple of the inverse of the fiber's CF. The delay (up to 3 ms at the BM apex) is well

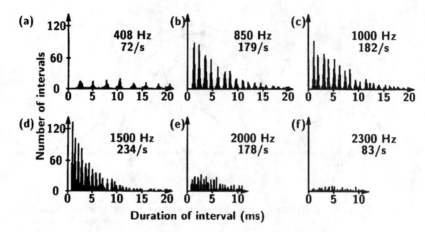

Figure 4.7   Interval histograms of a fiber with a 1.6 kHz CF. The average response rate in spikes/s is indicated for six different 1 s tone burst excitations (at 80 dB). (After Rose *et al.* [43].)

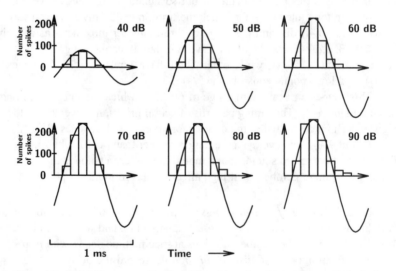

Figure 4.8   Period histograms of a fiber activated by a low-frequency tone. Each plot is fitted with a sinusoid corresponding to the stimulus frequency, with varying amplitude but fixed phase. The bin width or horizontal (time) resolution in this figure is coarse compared with that of Figure 4.7. (After Rose *et al.* [43].)

modeled by the propagation time for a traveling wave from the stapes to the hair cell in question. Several firings in response to one click are possible, depending on the click's intensity. With tone stimuli, the spikes tend to occur at intervals of multiples of the period of the input tone. In each case, there is some time jitter (usually less than 1 ms) in the actual firing times; i.e., the intervals between firings are not perfect multiples of the BM period. Each neuron normally fires just prior to maximal membrane displacement.

Neurons have a latency period of 1–3 ms in which, having once fired, a neuron cannot fire again, no matter how intense the stimulus. Thus at low frequencies of BM motion (e.g., below 1 kHz), a neuron could fire on each half-cycle of a sinusoidal vibration, and the spikes would be time-synchronized (*phase-locked*) to a tonal sound input. At higher frequencies, the latency period is too long to allow such synchronous firings, although a set of adjacent neurons would exhibit an average synchronous pattern. Above about 4–5 kHz, phase locking disappears due to the smearing in time caused by jitter, which becomes comparable in range to the fundamental period. With an input of two sinusoids, phase locking in a fiber may occur with one or both tones, depending on their relative intensities and how close their frequencies are to the fiber's CF [5].

4.2.6 Adaptation

An auditory neuron can fire at rates up to 1000/s for short periods of time in response to a sudden loud stimulus, but if the sound remains, the neuron *adapts* slowly and decreases its firing rate by about half (exponentially with a time constant τ of about 40 ms, relatively independent of signal level). Most of the decay occurs in the first 15–20 ms after stimulus onset (especially at high stimulus intensities) [44, 45]. When the stimulus is removed, the firing rate falls to near zero and then exponentially increases back to the spontaneous rate characteristic of the neuron (the recovery time constant is about 2.5τ, and is larger for neurons with lower spontaneous rates [46]). This behavior can be explained in terms of depletion and regeneration of the chemical transmitter substance in the hair cells associated with the neuron. Adaptation is more pronounced and has a more complex form for neurons higher in the auditory nervous system than for those in the cochlea. Such adaptation suggests that the brain may interpret sound intensities and some spectral information from changes in firing patterns rather than from steady-state patterns. There may be two classes of auditory neurons: one that responds primarily to steady-state sounds and another that fires more often when the stimulus is of rapidly changing frequency. This sensitivity of the latter class to change in frequency persists over a wider range of sound intensities than is the case for the steady-state neurons. Indeed, the sensitivity is more pronounced near normal sound levels such as in speech (*physiological levels*) than at levels near the hearing threshold. This contrasts with steady-state neurons, which often have saturated firing rates at physiological levels. Neurons in the cochlear nucleus and at higher levels exhibit recoding of the cochlear firings, in that they often respond in a complex fashion with respect to the sound stimulus, e.g., responding only to the start or end of a stimulus [5].

4.3 SOUND PERCEPTION

The primary questions in sound perception [5, 47] concern what sounds are perceptible, what a person hears, and how different sound components affect or interfere with one another. Whether a sound can be heard depends on its intensity and spectrum; we discuss perceptibility in terms of hearing thresholds. What a person hears in response to a sound is a more complicated question, and we will initially limit our discussion to how a sound's structure relates to its perceived pitch. Finally, we address the complex question of *masking* or interference. The behavior of the ear in response to simple tones is relatively straightforward, but most sounds are dynamic and have many spectral components. The cochlear processes of basilar membrane vibration and neural firings are highly nonlinear, with the result that perception of sound energy at one frequency is dependent on the distribution of sound energy at other frequencies as well as on the time course of energy before and after the sound.

4.3.1 Auditory Psychophysics

Auditory psychophysics is concerned with the resolving power of audition. Basic sounds such as tones and clicks are often used as acoustic stimuli. How well listeners can discriminate the timing and frequencies of such sounds is likely relevant to speech perception. However, experiments using stimuli closer to speech (than clicks and tones) lead to a more direct correspondence between the acoustic aspects of a speech signal and how it is perceived. Asked to discriminate two similar sounds resembling speech, listeners may utilize linguistic knowledge, attempting to label the stimuli as different linguistically (e.g., as representing different phonemes). Alternatively, they may simply listen for some salient difference in timing or spectral content. Listeners are much better at discriminating two sounds than at labeling them; e.g., they can distinguish tones near 100 Hz to within 1 Hz accuracy, but cannot consistently group such tones into fine categories such as 100, 101, 102, ... Hz. A typical listener, in ordering a set of ten tones at 1 Hz intervals from 100 to 109 Hz, must listen to them in pairs, each time deciding which is higher.

4.3.2 Thresholds

The ear is capable of hearing sounds over a wide frequency range, from about 16 Hz to 18 kHz. (This range of about 10 octaves is much larger than that for vision—about 0.7 oct, from infrared to ultraviolet.) Sounds of frequency below 1 kHz or above 5 kHz require significantly more energy to be heard than those in the 1–5 kHz range (Figure 4.9). The intensity of a sound is measured in terms of sound pressure level (SPL) in units of decibels (dB). The reference level for SPL is an intensity of 10^{-16} W/cm^2 (0.0002 dyn/cm^2 or μbar of pressure) at a frequency of 1 kHz, which corresponds to 0 dB. At the extreme frequencies of the audible range, sounds can be perceived only over a narrow amplitude range, whereas at the frequencies where the ear is most sensitive (1–5 kHz), sounds are detectable over a range of more than 100 dB (which slightly exceeds the 90 dB range for vision).

The minimum intensity at which sounds can be perceived is called the *auditory* or *hearing threshold*, which rises sharply with decreasing frequency below 1 kHz and with increasing frequency above 5 kHz. This spectral bandpass effect is due both to the filtering action of the outer and middle ear and also to the smaller number of hair cells toward extreme CFs. Loud sounds can actually be *felt* in the ear, which leads to two other thresholds: of feeling (the intensity at which a sound is felt) and of pain (intensity causing pain). These upper thresholds are much less variable with frequency than the auditory threshold is; e.g., the pain threshold is near 120–140 dB for all frequencies in the auditory range, whereas the auditory threshold varies over a 100 dB range. Speech normally occupies only a portion of the range between the thresholds of hearing and pain (known as the *auditory field*). With frequencies ranging from 100 Hz up to perhaps 8 kHz, speech has amplitudes between 30 and 90 dB (measured at a distance of 1 m from the lips). Since speech has dynamic intensity, we can define a slowly varying *speech level* that reflects the peak SPL over periods of the order of a second. Speech perception is optimal when peak amplitudes are in the 60–70 dB range.

The auditory threshold remains almost constant across most speech frequencies; e.g., between 700 and 7000 Hz the hearing threshold stays within ±3 dB of 0 dB. While the threshold increases substantially above 7 kHz, speech energy at such high frequencies is significantly present only for fricatives and has little effect on either speech intelligibility or naturalness. The threshold is more relevant for frequencies below 700 Hz, which is the region of the first formant as well as the fundamental frequency and its most intense harmonics. At

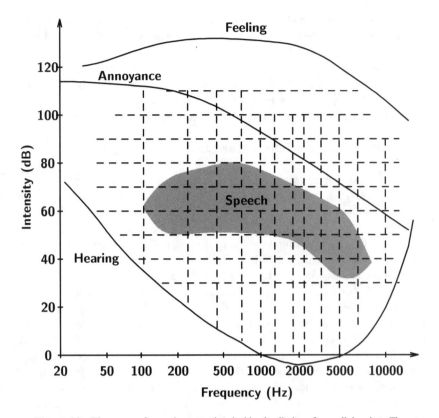

Figure 4.9 The areas of speech perception inside the limits of overall hearing. The partition grid corresponds to the auditory differential limen (Section 4.4) of pitch and loudness under the influence of wideband noise. The lowest curve is also known as an audiogram and can vary by up to 20 dB in individual listeners of normal hearing. (After Winckel 1968 Acoustical foundations of phonetics, B. Malmberg (ed) in *Manual of Phonetics*, Amsterdam: North-Holland [48].)

an average F1 of 500 Hz, the hearing threshold is elevated by about 10 dB compared to the F2–F3 regions. A typical F0 at 100 Hz needs almost 40 dB more intensity to be heard than harmonics at higher frequencies. For vowel sounds at *physiological levels* (those typical of speech), all the harmonics are normally audible (but not equally loud) up through F4, with harmonics between formants at higher frequencies sometimes falling below audibility. However, as speech amplitude is reduced, e.g., in quiet speech, it is likely that the fundamental and its first few harmonics are lost perceptually. These frequencies are not crucial to intelligibility since, for example, speech is understood over the telephone network, which severely attenuates frequencies below 300 Hz. While irrelevant for intelligibility, frequencies below 300 Hz contribute to naturalness, and their lack is one aspect of the quality limitations of telephone speech.

The hearing threshold concerns the detectability of steady tones. If the sound duration is less than 0.3 s, the threshold is elevated since overall energy becomes important for perceiving short stimuli. For wideband noise, sounds under 0.3 s, the threshold increases about 3 dB for each halving of duration [47]. In tones with changing frequency (*tone glides*) and very short duration (50 ms), the hearing threshold can be higher by up to 5 dB for falling than for rising tones [49, 50]. This can be relevant for transition sounds in speech, where most spectral movement at phoneme boundaries occurs over durations of less than 50 ms. It is difficult to extrapolate the audibility of speech sounds from these tone thresholds because hearing is a nonlinear process; the detectability of a sound consisting of many spectral components is not a simple function of the detectability of its components.

4.3.3 Just-Noticeable Differences (JNDs)

Most psychophysical experiments use sounds that differ along one or more acoustic dimensions (e.g., intensity or F0) but are otherwise identical. Listeners are asked whether two successive sounds are identical (*AX* procedure: does *X* sound the same as *A*?), or are presented with three sounds and asked which of two of the sounds resembles most the third (*ABX* or *AXB* procedure: does *X* sound closest to *A* or *B*?). The first technique is most common and yields a plot of percentage "different" responses as a function of the acoustic difference. If the acoustic dimension varied is perceptually relevant, the plot typically goes from a low percentage ("same") to a high percentage ("different") monotonically as the acoustic difference increases. The acoustic value at which 75% of responses are "different" is normally selected as the *just-noticeable difference* (JND) or *difference limen*. In the second procedure (*ABX* or *AXB*), *X* is the same as either *A* or *B*, and the number of correct identifications increases as the difference between *A* and *B* increases; the point where subjects correctly identify 75% of the stimuli is the JND. An alternative procedure, which tends to yield smaller JND values, asks listeners to adjust some parameter of a sound to resemble a reference sound; the standard deviation of selected parameter values provides the JND [51]. JNDs are relevant for both speech perception and coding: JNDs measure the resolving power of the ear and the limits of audition, and suggest how precisely speech parameters need to be quantized for transmission.

Due to the frequency variation in auditory thresholds, the perceptual loudness of a sound is specified via its relative intensity above the threshold. A sound's loudness is often defined in terms of how intense a reference 1 kHz tone must be, to be heard as equally loud as the sound. Loudness units are called *phons* and are identical to dB for tones near 1 kHz. At speech frequencies, equal-loudness contours parallel the hearing threshold curve (Figure 4.9). At low frequencies, however, 1 dB can have the effect of two phons (Figure 4.10). The JND for loudness is essentially constant at about 0.5–1.0 dB for noise bursts, but varies for tones: ranging from 0.3 dB in optimal conditions (e.g., a 60 dB tone at 1 kHz) to more than 1 dB at low intensities; they also increase with frequency at low levels [52]. Greater JNDs are found at very high intensities [53] or with durations less than 250 ms [47]. Sounds of equal intensity increase in loudness with duration up to about 200 ms. Another measure of loudness is the *sone*, by which a doubling of loudness is equivalent to an intensity increase of about 10 dB.

Below 1 kHz, two equally intense tones must differ by about 1–3 Hz to be distinguished in frequency. At higher frequencies, the JND is progressively larger (e.g., at 8 kHz, it is 100 Hz) [47, 55]. The JND increases substantially if the sound is weak or brief, i.e., less than 20 dB above threshold or shorter than 100 ms. Over the entire auditory field, there are about 1600 distinguishable frequencies and 350 such intensities, leading to about 300,000 tones of different combinations of frequency and intensity that can be distinguished by listeners in pairwise tests [48, 56]. People in general cannot, however, identify so many tones in isolation;

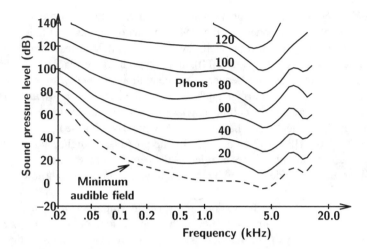

Figure 4.10 Equal-loudness contours as a function of tone frequency. (After Robinson and Dadson [54].)

they must be heard in successive pairs. (Those few who possess "absolute pitch," and thus have the musical ability to name tones without context, do not appear to have smaller JNDs [57].)

The figures above are valid for sounds lasting more than 100–200 ms; the ear is less sensitive with shorter sounds. For example, there are 850 distinguishable frequency levels for tones of more than 250 ms, but only 120 levels for 10 ms tones. Similarly, the number of discriminable intensities is halved as duration decreases to 10 ms. Other sounds are less precisely perceived than tones; e.g., for narrowband noise bursts, only 132 frequency steps and 120 intensities can be distinguished, which represents only 5% of the number of distinguishable tones.

4.3.4 Pitch Perception

Distinguishing two tones (or other periodic sounds) is usually done through *pitch*, the perception of the "basic" frequency of a sound. Pitch is usually affiliated with periodic sounds, and most closely corresponds to the fundamental rate of sound vibration; it is however much more complicated than a simple acoustic:perceptual mapping of F0:pitch. A sound is said to have a certain pitch if it can be reliably matched to a tone by adjusting the tonal frequency (usually using a 40 dB sine) [58]. Sounds lacking periodicity can be said to differ in *timbre* [59], e.g., /s/ has brighter timbre than /ʃ/ because /s/ has most energy at higher frequencies; timbre reflects a sound's spectral envelope.

Information relevant to a sound's perception can be obtained from the rates and timing of neural firings at different locations along the basilar membrane. A sound's loudness may be perceived in proportion to the overall rate of neural firings, but spectral perception is more complex. The *timing* or *volley* theory holds that low frequencies, e.g., those corresponding to the first harmonics of the fundamental frequency (F0) in speech, are perceived in terms of time-synchronous neural firings from the BM apex. The *place* theory, on the other hand, suggests that, especially for higher frequencies such as those in the formants of speech, spectral information is decoded via the BM locations of the neurons that fire most [6].

Thus there are two types of pitch: the "normal" pitch corresponding to the inverse of the fundamental period of the sound (F0), and a "spectral" (or place) pitch corresponding to timbre (e.g., /u/ with its low-frequency concentration of energy sounds lower in spectral pitch than does /i/). The normal pitch is also called *residue* or *virtual* pitch since it is perceived even when the F0 component is absent [60]. For example, in speech over the telephone, the fundamental and harmonics below 300 Hz are absent, yet a pitch corresponding to an F0 of 100 Hz would be detected by the presence of higher harmonics separated by 100 Hz each. Virtual pitch can be regarded as the perceived repetition frequency of a periodic sound and is apparently determined by the positions of about the eight lowest harmonics [61, 62].

The harmonics in the F1 region are especially important for pitch perception. Even though pitch is most naturally associated with temporal repetition, pitch perception seems to follow spectral measures (e.g., harmonics) more closely than changes in the time signal; in particular, changes in the phases of harmonics do not affect pitch but change waveform structure [63]. When speech is simulated with one sinusoid per formant ("sinusoidal speech," with three tones centered at three formant frequencies), unnatural speech results, but pitch usually follows the tone at the F1 frequency [64]. Phase is less important than other perceptual factors, but listeners can distinguish a phase shift of 2–4° in one harmonic of a complex tone when phases are set to zero (but not when randomized) [65].

Some sound stimuli give conflicting pitch cues. For example, short clicks of alternating polarity every 5 ms have an F0 of 100 Hz but a pulse rate of 200 pulses/s. The BM displacement resolves each pulse in time at its basal, high-frequency end, and associated neurons fire in cycles of 200/s [8]. However, the apical end vibrates sinusoidally near 100 Hz, leading to time-synchronous neural firings there at F0. When there are sufficient time-synchronous firings at the base (usually the case for F0 above 100 Hz), they dominate the perception of pitch. At lower rates, even the apical end of the BM resolves the pulses in time, and the perceived pitch corresponds to the pulse rate, not F0. The same results occur with complex waveforms whose phase is inverted every half-period, which suggests that neural time patterns are insensitive to phase inversions in low-frequency stimuli [66].

Such ambiguous pitch seems to arise mostly when a stimulus has a small number of high-frequency harmonics within a critical band (see below), leading to *unresolved* harmonics (i.e., ones interacting within a single auditory filter) [60, 67]. Indeed, the F0 JND increases with the frequency of the lowest harmonic in such sounds.

The place theory is supported by the varying frequency sensitivity with displacement along the BM and by the tonotopic organization of neurons in the auditory pathway to the brain. The maximal vibration of a specific BM location in response to a tone could be signaled to the brain by a pathway "labeled" cognitively with the tone frequency. The timing theory instead presumes that the central nervous system can convert timing patterns into pitch. This theory is limited to low and middle physiological frequencies because the synchronization of spikes to tonal inputs disappears above 4–5 kHz (due to latency effects), whereas the place theory cannot explain the high pitch resolution of the ear to low frequencies. It is likely that both processes operate in parallel, with one or the other dominant depending on the frequency and type of sound [68]. One theory holds that spectral selectivity in the cochlea serves to separate broadband sounds into a number of channels, within which temporal analyses are performed [69]. Another recent model uses inhibitory gating neurons [70].

4.3.5 Masking

An important aspect of hearing is the phenomenon of *masking*, by which the perception of one sound is obscured by the presence of another. Specifically, the presence of one sound raises the hearing threshold for another sound, for sounds heard either simultaneously or with a short intervening delay. Simultaneous sounds cause *frequency masking*, where a lower-frequency sound generally masks a higher-frequency one (such masking can be directly related to speech recognition in low-frequency noise [71]). Sounds delayed with respect to one another can cause *temporal masking* of one or both sounds. Masking is the major nonlinear phenomenon that prevents treating the perception of speech sounds as a summation of responses to their tone and bandlimited noise components. In some speech coding applications, quantization noise that arises in the coding process can be distributed across frequencies to take advantage of masking effects, such that the noise may be masked by high speech energy in the formant regions. Masking involving tones (e.g., harmonics in speech) and noise is thus especially relevant.

Classic masking experiments show the effect of one tone on another as a function of the frequency separation between them [61, 72]. With a stimulus consisting of two tones above the threshold of hearing, a listener tends to hear only the lower-frequency tone in certain conditions. If one tone is fixed at 1200 Hz and 80 dB, a second tone below 800 Hz can be heard as low as 12 dB. However, when that second tone is within 100 Hz of 1200 Hz, it needs at least 50 dB to be heard. This masking effect remains for higher frequencies as well: at least 40 dB is required for the second tone (up to 4 kHz) to be perceptible. In general, low frequencies tend to mask higher frequencies, with the largest effects near harmonics of the low-frequency masker.

Masking effects are usually described with functions of a *masked threshold* (the energy a masked signal needs to be heard) or the *amount of masking* (the additional energy needed to hear the signal in the presence of the masker) as a function of signal frequency (Figure 4.11). Such *psychophysical tuning curves* are obtained using simple perceptual experiments and provide analogs to the tuning curves of auditory fibers [73]. The actual inhibition of neural firings caused by a masker can be displayed via *suppression areas* superimposed on tuning curves (usually just outside the curve's skirts), which indicate the amplitude required, as a function of frequency, for a tone to act as a suppressor. The mechanism for such suppression may be saturation [74].

When tones are used as both signal and masker, the analysis is complicated by beats and combination tones, which can change masked thresholds by more than 10 dB near the frequencies of the difference tones; e.g., in response to tones at f_1 and f_2 Hz ($f_1 < f_2$), the inner ear appears to generate perceivable combination tones at $f_2 - f_1$ Hz and $f_1 + n(f_1 - f_2)$ Hz (for integer n) [6, 76].

Against a background of narrowband masking noise, a *probe tone* near the center frequency f of the noise must have an elevated intensity to be heard (Figure 4.12). This masked threshold elevation is assumed to measure the activity produced by the masker in neurons with CFs at f. The probe is detected only if it produces more activity than the masker alone. There is an upward (frequency) spread of masking at high-intensity levels due to the asymmetry of neural tuning curves. Since tuning curves have less steep skirts (especially for high intensities) on the low-frequency side of a CF, a masker has more effect on tones above its frequency than on those below it. The asymmetry of masking tends to disappear and even to reverse below signal levels of 40 dB [77], but this latter phenomenon is of little relevance to speech except in very quiet environments.

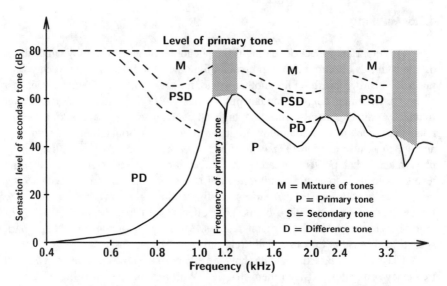

Figure 4.11 Different sensations produced by a two-tone stimulus. The primary tone at 1200 Hz, 80 dB above auditory threshold, is fixed, while the secondary tone varies in frequency (horizontal axis) and intensity (vertical axis). Below the solid curve, the secondary tone is masked (not heard); above it, beats and various combinations of tones are heard. (After Fletcher [74].)

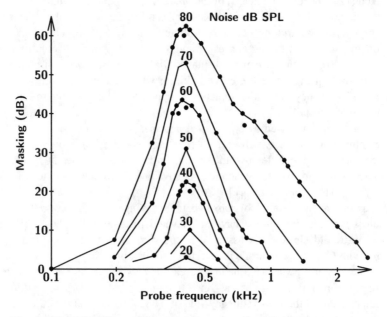

Figure 4.12 The masking pattern produced by a narrow band (365–455 Hz) of noise. The elevation in hearing threshold of a probe tone is shown as a function of the probe frequency. (After Egan and Hake [72].)

A 1 kHz tone in a narrow band of noise becomes inaudible when it is 2–6 dB below the noise level, but for the tone instead to completely mask the noise, it must be 24 dB higher than the noise [78, 79]. This asymmetry is due to the way humans perceive tones: small variations in tone amplitude or frequency, such as caused by small amounts of added noise, can easily be heard in the otherwise repetitious tone signal, whereas small spectral variations in noise, e.g., from a low-level tone in the midband of this noise, easily escape detection in the unpredictable noise. Since (undesired) quantization noise in speech coders tends to be broadband and (desired) vowel harmonics are similar to tones, this perceptual asymmetry is relevant in the design of speech coders.

4.3.6 Critical Bands

Many masking phenomena can be explained in terms of ranges of sound frequencies known as *critical bands*. A critical band can be related to a bandpass filter whose frequency response corresponds roughly to the tuning curves of auditory neurons. A critical band defines a frequency range in psychoacoustic experiments for which perception abruptly changes as a narrowband sound stimulus is modified to have frequency components beyond the band. When two competing sound signals pass energy through such a critical-band filter, the sound with the higher energy within the critical band dominates the perception and masks the other sound. The amount of masking is approximately equal to the total amount of masker energy (above the auditory threshold) within the critical band of the probe [80]. A band of noise kept at constant spectral level, while its bandwidth (and energy) is increased, is heard with constant loudness until the critical bandwidth is attained. Thereafter, noise loudness increases as neurons, presumably, from adjacent critical bands fire in response to the broader-band noise. (This model is not fully valid for time-varying signals, whose masking effects are more complex [81].)

The shapes of critical-band filters have been determined in experiments using broad-band low- or high-pass noise to mask a tone. As the cutoff frequency of a lowpass noise is increased past the tonal frequency f, more noise energy enters the critical-band filter centered at f (the critical band to which the tone perception corresponds). By varying the relative amplitudes of the noise and the tone, the masked threshold is found as a function of the noise cutoff frequency, which provides one definition of the shape of a critical-band filter. The filters are nearly symmetric on a linear frequency scale, with very sharp skirts, which range from 65 dB/oct for critical bands at 500 Hz to over 100 dB/oct at 8 kHz [82]. Below 500 Hz, critical bandwidth is roughly constant at about 100 Hz. For higher frequencies, it increases with frequency (roughly logarithmically above 1 kHz), reaching bandwidths of 700 Hz near 4 kHz. The filters are approximately constant Q (i.e., bandwidth proportional to frequency) at frequencies above 1 kHz ($Q \approx 5$–6). One-third- or one-sixth-octave filters are often used as critical-band models [31]. The increasing bandwidth with frequency means better temporal resolution at higher frequencies (since wider filters have shorter time constants), which is confirmed up to 10 kHz [83].

Critical-band filters have symmetric shapes only for sound levels below about 45 dB; at higher amplitudes, bandwidth increases due to a flattening of the lower-frequency skirt of the filter. This corresponds well with the flattening of neural tuning curves at low frequencies as amplitude increases above a certain level, and with the asymmetry of masking (upward spread), which apparently occurs only at sufficiently high sound intensities.

Critical bandwidths correspond approximately to 1.5 mm spacings (1200 primary nerve fibers) along the BM, suggesting that a set of 24 bandpass filters (having bandwidth increasing with frequency) would model the BM well. A perceptual measure, called the *Bark scale* or critical-band rate, relates acoustical frequency to perceptual frequency resolution, in which one Bark covers one critical bandwidth. An analytical expression [84] mapping frequency f into critical-band rate z is

$$z = 13 \tan^{-1}\left(0.76\frac{f}{\text{kHz}}\right) + 3.5 \tan^{-1}\left(\frac{f}{7.5\,\text{kHz}}\right)^2. \tag{4.1}$$

In a similar measure called the *mel scale*, the mapping is approximately linear in frequency up to 1 kHz and logarithmic at higher frequencies, e.g.,

$$m = 2595 \log_{10}(1 + f/700), \tag{4.2}$$

although simpler representations may be valid (e.g., $m = f/(af + b)$ [85]). Using equivalent rectangular bandwidths (ERBs) is yet another related approach [86].

Loudness sensation appears to depend on the total sum of auditory nerve fiber activity. The loudness of a sound can be approximated by summing the contributions from each of 24 critical-band filters, raised to the 0.23 power [76]. (This 0.23 compression factor appears in other sound perception phenomena, such as the additivity of spectrally nonoverlapping maskers: when two such maskers are combined, masking effects can be substantially larger than predicted by a linear model, but adding the effects after an exponential compression provides a good model [87], e.g., a modified power-law model [88].) The output of each filter is calculated by convolving the spectral density of the input sound with a BM *spreading* function having lower and upper skirts of +25 and −10 dB per critical band, respectively [78]. (The upper skirt flattens to −5 dB per critical band for loud stimuli, which results in an upward spread of masking for intense sounds.)

Neural spectrograms have been proposed [89] using bandpass filter analysis, with bandwidths equal to critical bands, rather than fixed as in traditional spectrograms. Such an *inner spectrum* (as seen by the auditory nerve), however, is not easy to interpret (in terms of traditional spectrogram viewing). To remedy this, (a) low-frequency filters could have double the critical bandwidth (to eliminate the effect of harmonics moving between filters as F0 changes), and (b) high-frequency filters could have slightly larger bandwidths ($Q = 4$) to make the patterns similar for wide ranges of F0 (e.g., for men and women).

4.3.7 Nonsimultaneous or Temporal Masking

Masking extends in time as well as across frequencies [90]. Successive signals with energy in the same critical band can interfere with each other's perception if the intervening delay is sufficiently short; e.g., a noise signal will mask an ensuing tone burst in the same critical band if the noise has sufficient energy. (Note that tonal bursts are not true tones, only at one frequency, due to their limited duration.) The noise energy needed to mask the tone increases with: (1) the delay between the end of the noise and the tone onset, and (2) the tone duration. This *forward* masking is most effective if the tone burst starts within 10 ms of the noise offset; the effect (in terms of decibels of masking) decreases with time to nil beyond about a 200 ms delay. Short masker durations are less effective than those longer than 100 ms [91]. The effect is weaker than simultaneous masking, i.e., an increase in masker intensity has a greater masking effect when the two signals co-occur than when one follows the other.

Backward masking also occurs, e.g., a short tone burst is not heard when followed immediately by sufficient noise within the tone's critical band. Backward masking falls off rapidly with time and has the effect only with delays less than 20 ms. Nonetheless, it is a strong phenomenon: a short tone burst ending 1 ms before noise onset can experience 60 dB of masking (i.e., require 60 dB more amplitude to be heard than without the masker), whereas the same pulse 1 ms after noise offset is limited to 30 dB of masking.

Since simultaneous and forward masking are effective only when the two signals enter the same ear and occupy the same limited frequency range, they likely involve peripheral auditory processes using *temporal integration* of energy [92] (e.g., modeled by correlograms [32]). Such integration accounts for the fact that sounds of varying duration can appear equally loud [93]. Neuron fatigue has been suggested to explain forward masking because firing rates for a tone are reduced in proportion to the intensity of a preceding sound (within the same critical band) and in inverse proportion to the time delay between the sounds. Backward masking, which can occur contralaterally (masker in one ear, test signal in the other) and at wider frequency ranges than critical bands [6], likely involves a blocking phenomenon, in which the auditory processing of a tone burst is interrupted by an ensuing loud noise if the noise arrives before the tone perception is completed. The time delays at which backward masking can occur suggest blocking at higher levels of auditory processing than the cochlea. However, the relatively sharp tuning curves for auditory neurons correspond to long response times, so cochlear responses to nonsimultaneous stimuli could still overlap at the basilar membrane [94].

The masker bandwidth has a direct effect on forward masking: assuming a masker of bandpass noise having a fixed spectral level (W/Hz), as the bandwidth (and hence energy) increases, the threshold for detecting an ensuing tone first increases and then decreases after a noise bandwidth called the *rollover bandwidth* is attained. Increasing the noise bandwidth initially produces more neural activity within the critical band of the tone, thus raising the amount of energy needed to hear the tone [95]; as bandwidth exceeds the critical band, neural activity within the band is decreased by the stimulation of neighboring suppression bands. This *lateral suppression* effect is instantaneous but is normally not evident in simultaneous masking since both the masker and tone signal should be suppressed equally (except for low-level simultaneous suppression [96]). A masker preceding a tone is subject to its own masking effects when its bandwidth exceeds a critical band, lowering its effectiveness in masking an ensuing tone.

One problem in interpeting nonsimultaneous masking is that listeners, in attempting to detect sounds, may use sound aspects other than energy within critical bands. In particular, short probe sounds are often used, and these sounds necessarily are not simply narrowband. Short tone bursts have most energy concentrated near the tone frequency, but the percentage of a burst's energy outside a given bandwidth is inversely proportional to signal duration. Such *energy splatter* can lead to *off-frequency listening*, in which a listener detects a probe signal from its energy away from the center frequency (when the masker is sufficiently narrowband) [97]. Listeners may also be sensitive to *quality differences* between the signal and masker, involving temporal structure as well as spectral composition.

Forward masking can operate conversely: a masker with a spectral notch (missing frequencies among a broadband noise) enhances perception at the notch frequency after the masker is removed. For example, listeners often have difficulty discriminating ("hearing out") harmonics in a complex sound of several harmonically related tones, but not when the sound is preceded by a masker containing all the harmonics of the signal except the one of interest [98]. Enhanced perceptibility at the notch frequency appears to result from the masking of adjacent frequencies by the masker. This suppression phenomenon is related to the fact that in simultaneous masking, as more components are added to a masker, the masked threshold usually increases, but with certain configurations of forward masking the addition of a second masker can decrease masking effects [99, 100].

Psychophysical tuning curves (PTCs) describing the masked threshold are sharper in forward masking than in simultaneous masking. This difference has led to numerous proposals for additional tuning mechanisms in the ear such as the second-filter effect and off-frequency listening. PTCs are often assumed to reflect neural tuning curves and hence to measure the frequency selectivity of the auditory system, although PTCs appear to be variable under different experimental conditions [101].

4.3.8 Origins of Masking

While most evidence of masking has come from psychoacoustic experiments, masking patterns are also readily evident in auditory nerve firings [69]. Changes in the average firing rate of auditory neurons due to the addition of a masker correspond directly to patterns of psychoacoustic masking. Masking levels have also been directly related to changes in synchronized firing rates [102], which will be noted below as relevant to speech perception.

Because masking patterns appear to change little over a wide range of masker levels, masking seems to have its origin at the basilar membrane level. The lack of saturation effects in masking phenomena appears to rule out masking origins above the hair cell level since neural firings are subject to saturation. Masking cannot be due to neural inhibition because it occurs with little latency delay, does not adapt with time, and does not affect spontaneous discharge rates. One theory suggests that masking arises in the neuroelectric processes of hair cell firings or in the cochlear microphonics near the tectorial membrane [102]. BM motion, at least at low sound levels, appears to be linear (however, see [103]), suggesting nonlinear transformations of the sound information in the organ of Corti.

4.3.9 Release from Masking (‡)

Given the importance of masking in sound perception, much recent research has explored its mechanisms in detail. In particular, masking can be affected by sounds distant in time or frequency, e.g., by *modulation detection interference* (MDI), in which the threshold for detecting amplitude modulation (AM) in a sound can be substantially raised (e.g., 10–15 dB) by AM at a distant frequency [104]. It is unlikely that audition exploits autocorrelation directly (despite the spectral behavior of the cochlea, which is often modeled with reverse correlation functions [105]), but some auditory cells respond to AM [60].

Thus the ability to hear a sound in the presence of a simultaneous masker can be affected by additional sounds spectrally distant. When the masker and maskee have the same amplitude envelope, masking thresholds are reduced (*comodulation masking release* (CMR)) [106]. Similar threshold reductions occur if the extra sound is coherent. Acoustic coherence may come from sounds with synchronous onsets/offsets or from harmonic relations [62]; e.g., a formant filled with noise syncronized with normal higher formants gives coherence, even in the absence of harmonic relations [107]. Unlike MDI, CMR depends on the target–masker frequency separation (and seems to have limited effects in normal speech conditions), and hence may reflect local-frequency processing (vs global MDI effects).

Such *release from masking* can occur in different ways. In *two-tone suppression*, adding a second tone to a tonal masker at a frequency 10–20% higher improves the audibility of a masked tone, which may involve both mechanical BM phenomena and neural inhibition [108]. In *signal enhancement* (also called *overshoot* or *temporal decline of masking*), a simultaneously masked sound is easier to hear (by about 10–15 dB) if its onset is delayed relative to that of the masker [108]. Such phenomena vary significantly across different subjects.

A related phenomenon is release from broadband masking of speech by modulating the noise [109]; sinusoidal modulation at 10–20 Hz allows significant low-noise intervals of about the duration of a phoneme, thus raising intelligibility (at lower rates, many phonemes are entirely masked, and at higher rates, the reduced-noise "windows" are too short to help perception). Such "glimpsing" experiments have been extended to modulating the frequency range as well (i.e., gating the noise on/off in both time and frequency), in which masking release occurs when the spectrum is divided into 2–4 bands (but not 8) [110].

4.3.10 Sound Localization (‡)

Using differences in the sound arriving at one's two ears can allow one to localize where a sound is originating. Such an ability is important for safety, as well as for paying attention to one sound in the presence of others. Interaural differences in level and timing allow estimation in one dimension (*lateralization*): the horizontal direction from which a sound comes (it arrives first and louder at the closer ear). Spectral cues, due to filtering by the pinna, which emphasizes sound from a forward direction, also help in localization, especially in estimating location in the vertical plane (where interaural cues do not help) or when one ear is blocked [13]. The interaural JND (the smallest delay between ears giving a perceived change of direction for a sound) is about 0.05 ms, corresponding to a 5° change of direction [58]. (This is much smaller than the typical temporal resolution of 2 ms monaurally.) One can detect a 2° change directly in front, but the JND increases to 10° on the side.

Until recently, most audio applications have involved monaural (e.g., telephone handset) or stereo listening conditions. Increasing interest in virtual reality environments has shown the need for a better 3D (three-dimensional) understanding of sound perception. Binaural headphones are often used to simulate sounds from different directions, using interaural time and level differences. However, such experiments often yield sound "images within the head," but closer to one ear than the other, rather than coming from outside the head. With an interaural level difference exceeding 30 dB, the image is heard only in the ear with the stronger signal; a JND for displacement is 1–2 dB [58]. The "law of the first wavefront" is a general observation that we tend to localize in terms of where the first sound comes from, even if later echos are stronger (unless they arrive > 50 ms later). When pinna filtering and a "head transfer function" are taken into consideration, a *virtual auditory space* can be simulated for better 3D effects [111, 112].

4.4 RESPONSE OF THE EAR TO COMPLEX STIMULI

Auditory studies using stimuli more complex than simple clicks and tones, e.g., frequency sweeps and wideband noise, have shown that firing patterns for such sounds cannot be easily extrapolated from results for simpler sounds. For example, there appear to be two classes of neurons in the cochlear nucleus: those that respond best to steady-state or slowly varying sounds and those that respond best to rapidly changing sounds [69]. Such a division is not evident in the primary auditory neurons, but higher-level processing in the cochlear nucleus apparently can help in recoding the information in transient sounds. The neural processing that a listener uses for simple sounds may be different from that used for more complex sounds.

4.4.1 Speech Stimuli (‡)

In response to steady-state synthetic vowels and fricatives, high firing rates have been found in neurons whose CFs correspond to frequencies of high energy (e.g., formants) [113, 114]. Complicating factors arise in the form of suppression of firing in high-frequency neurons due to high energy in the first formant. Other nonlinearities include saturation effects: the firing patterns in many neurons tend to saturate above 60 dB SPL, which limits frequency resolution along the basilar membrane. It may be that certain neurons with low spontaneous activity and high firing thresholds (compared to other neurons, those with spontaneous rates below 18/s have thresholds elevated by about 10 dB) do not saturate at these levels [115] and thus preserve a firing rate profile distinctive for different speech sounds. In any event, saturation is a problem only for vowels and sonorants since fricatives and stop bursts are usually 10–20 dB less intense than vowels, leading to few saturated neurons.

Interspike intervals as well as place information seem to be relevant in decoding speech. Since most speech energy is below 5 kHz, neural firings are phase-locked following the temporal envelope of the speech filtered by the neuron's tuning curve; the firings appear to phase-lock to formant frequencies over a large range of sound levels. Synchrony to harmonics not near formants is suppressed more as speech intensity increases [116], with the net effect of enhancing formants. In response to synthetic consonant–vowel (CV) stimuli, individual neurons with a CF near a moving formant frequency are able to track its changing frequency, in that the average intervals between firings vary inversely with the formant frequency [117, 118]. Cochlear nonlinearities appear to emphasize the dominant formant frequency in neural synchronized firing rates [119].

A measure called the *average localized synchronized rate* (ALSR) has been related to dynamic formant patterns in CV ([120]; see [121] for similar measures, such as the *synchronization index*). The ALSR computes the Fourier transform of post-stimulus time histograms of 20 ms speech segments with a typical resolution of 50 Hz and averages the spectrum at each frequency over those fibers whose CFs are within ±0.25 octave of the frequency. Although its utility at higher levels in the auditory chain is in doubt [122], the ALSR provides a measure of the average firing rates as a function of place along the basilar membrane while also reflecting the degree of phase locking of the neural firings. The fine spectral structure of the speech (pitch harmonics, if voiced) is preserved in the ALSR. Since neural firings are thought to arise from rectified BM vibration, the time signal chosen for Fourier analysis is usually a compound histogram that sums together post-stimulus time histograms at half-period delays in response to periodic stimuli of opposite polarity. Rate-difference measures simpler than the ALSR seem to suffice for vowel discriminability [123].

4.4.2 Masking Due to Complex Stimuli (‡)

The masking patterns (tone threshold elevations as a function of frequency) caused by steady-state synthetic vowels resemble the vowel spectra, with the first 2–3 formants clearly represented [124]. The formants are more obvious in the patterns of forward masking than in those of simultaneous masking, which suggests that lateral suppression serves to enhance spectral contrasts in speech. Masking is unaffected when the phases of the individual harmonics of the masker are changed, suggesting that the temporal structure of a vowel masker has no effect on the thresholds of an ensuing tone.

Short tone glides (< 200 ms), which are very simple models of formant transitions, cause less masking than tones with equivalent energy if the glide range extends beyond a critical band. For a given duration and intensity, glides have broader spectra than tones; when masking a tone, only the masker energy within the tone's critical band has an effect, integrated over about 250 ms [80]. Thus, tone glides over wide frequency ranges have less masking effects than narrower-band signals, but are capable of masking a wider frequency range.

While it is difficult to integrate all the results from different masking studies, we can nonetheless attempt to find a simple model for masking relevant to speech. Consider whether a particular spectral component (e.g., a harmonic) in a speech sound is perceptible. This will depend primarily on sound components nearby in frequency and in time. Since simultaneous masking is stronger than temporal masking, the primary concern is whether nearby harmonics (within a critical band) are more intense than the harmonic of interest. In addition, formant frequencies below a harmonic of interest will mask such a high-frequency harmonic beyond the range of a single critical band. In normal CVs, strong F1 energy can hinder stop place identification, since place cues reside in weaker, higher-frequency regions [125].

For a spectral component in a weak sound immediately following a strong sound (e.g., a fricative after a vowel), forward masking may obscure the initial portion of the weak sound. The formants in a vowel (even at high frequencies) may have enough energy to mask an ensuing brief, nonstrident fricative. The audibility of a simple sound after a vowel has been simulated by examining the masking of a tone following a sound complex of ten equal-amplitude harmonics [126]. First, at low frequencies, masking can be as much as 10 dB less for a probe tone between harmonics of the masker than for one at a harmonic frequency; this suggests that noise away from harmonics will be more noticeable than nearby noise. Second, as the tone duration increases from 10 to 40 ms, the amount of masking decreases by about 0.3 dB/ms (to about 15 dB, given a masker of 71 dB). Thus, shorter sounds are more subject to masking following a vowel; the longer a sound lasts, the more likely it can be heard.

Backward masking could play a role in the perception of consonants followed by (intense) vowels. Stop bursts are typically 30 dB weaker than ensuing vowels, and occur within the range of backward masking (especially for voiced stops with short VOTs). The detectability of the bursts is normally not in question [127], but perhaps perception of place of articulation is affected by masking. The stop place is usually identified through spectral transitions at and right after the stop release. Strong vowel formants could mask brief, weak frication energy during the burst and aspiration period to cause phonemic confusion (especially in the presence of background noise).

4.4.3 Adaptation (‡)

Adaptation refers to changing sensitivity in response to a continued stimulus, and is likely a feature of the mechanoelectrical transformation in the cochlea, which allows better hearing in noisy conditions. When compared to measures such as the ALSR, spectral profiles of average firing rates are more subject to adaptation effects and display less information concerning formants and pitch. Many speech sounds are characterized by sudden changes in amplitude and spectra. Adaptation effects in neurons may serve to emphasize such transitions in the patterns of neural firings [128]. For example, the rise time of a noise burst can determine whether a fricative or an affricate is perceived; a slow onset of 40 ms leads to fricative perception, whereas a sudden 1 ms onset causes an affricate to be heard. Sudden onsets cause brief, large increases in neural firings that do not occur with more gradual amplitude changes. Most neurons have limited dynamic response ranges to steady-state sounds, typically going from spontaneous firing rates to saturation with stimulus changes of about 25 dB. The neural dynamic range for transient sounds with sudden onsets is greater by about 10–15 dB. Thus, the ear may be well tuned to provide information to the brain about transients of the type common in plosives, fricatives, and perhaps nasals.

Adaptation likely plays a role in sudden spectral changes as well as in sudden amplitude changes. Neurons with CFs in a range where energy is significant for one sound often do not exhibit large changes in firing patterns in response to large spectral and amplitude changes for a following sound. For example, for /ma/, low-CF neurons do not increase firing at the onset of /a/, which is louder than /m/, because these neurons adapt to the low-frequency energy in /m/. The higher-CF neurons, however, will respond in normal fashion to the presence of energy at the higher frequencies in /a/ [44].

At typical speech levels, single-formant stimuli cause varied firing patterns, depending on the proximity of the neuron's CF to the formant frequency. Near the formant, the neurons fire near saturation level at times synchronous with the formant frequency. For neurons whose CF is distant from the formant, the neurons tend to saturate only at the start of each pitch period, where the stimulus has maximum intensity. In these synthetic speech stimuli, the onset of a pitch period is sudden; for a brief time at the start of each pitch period, the spectrum is fairly broad (as in a click stimulus), and these latter neurons respond as to a click. Thus the fundamental pitch period is easily visible in the firing patterns. Since their CFs are distant from the formant, these latter neurons tend to fire at times related to both the formant frequency and the neuron's own CF.

The addition of broadband noise to synthetic vowels typically reduces the neural firing rates but does not strongly affect their timing patterns [114]. Thus formant frequency information could be decoded from the intervals between neural spikes, even in the presence of moderate noise. Even with intense vowels (causing spikes at saturated rates), most auditory fibers fire in synchrony with intervals inversely related to one of the first 2–3 formants. Such patterns are robust in noise and distinctive since they differ from broadband noise response, which causes firings at intervals related to the neural CF.

4.4.4 Just-Noticeable Differences (JNDs) in Speech

Consider speech from a synthesizer in which one formant frequency is varied in steady-state vowel stimuli. The formant frequency JND is in the range 1.5–5% [8, 129], e.g., about 14 Hz for F1. Listeners are less sensitive when dynamic vowels, with changing spectra more typical of natural speech, are used; e.g., JNDs are 9–14% for symmetric formant trajectories in 200 ms CVC syllables [130]. However, simultaneous parallel movement of F1 and F2 halve JNDs [131]; resonance bandwidths also affect JNDs [132]. These JNDs give lower bounds to the formant resolution necessary when synthesizing vowels, because it is not necessary to simulate natural formant behavior more accurately than it can be heard in such ideal, controlled circumstances. Listeners usually can distinguish simple speech stimuli with more precision than in normal speech perception.

Typical JNDs for formant amplitudes are 1.5 dB for F1 (the most intense and perceptually most prominent formant) and about 3 dB for F2. Varying only one harmonic in a vowel spectrum yields amplitude JNDs ranging from about 2 dB for those in the middle of F1 or F2 to more than 13 dB for harmonics in spectral valleys between formants. (Similar results are found for complex tones [133].) The large JNDs in regions of relatively low amplitude are likely due to masking effects and suggest that speech synthesizers should concentrate on modeling well the spectral content of natural vowels near the formant frequencies. Spectral accuracy between formants seems to be much less perceptually important than accuracy at formant peaks.

Since formants typically encompass several harmonics, it could be that listeners identify the formant frequency as that of the loudest harmonic. Studies have shown, however, that the perceived frequency follows a weighted average of adjacent harmonics, with minimal change in perceived vowel quality as F0 (and thus harmonic spacing) is changed [134]. This appears to be true even at very high values of F0, e.g., in soprano singing, where only 1–2 harmonics occur in each formant bandwidth [135]. Finally, perception of center frequencies for formants is largely independent of spectral detail beyond the three strongest harmonics of a formant [136].

Formant bandwidths are poorly discriminated compared to their center frequencies; listeners can only note differences of 20–40% in the bandwidths of F1–F2. In experiments with harmonic complexes in which only two harmonics per formant were increased above an otherwise-constant level, only a 2 dB elevation was needed for good vowel discrimination [137]. Synthesizers often take advantage of such poor formant bandwidth resolution and use fixed-bandwidth formants, especially for the less perceptually relevant higher formants. Time variation of bandwidths is primarily important for nasal phonemes.

Using steady-state synthetic vowels, the JND for monotonic F0 is 0.3–0.5% [8], or less than 1 Hz [138]. The JND is larger for high than for low vowels, presumably due to the masking of more harmonics by the lower-frequency F1 in high vowels. In vowels with either (more natural) dynamic F0 [139] or background noise [140], the JNDs were an order of magnitude larger. This suggests that, while F0 should be coded precisely to match natural speech in certain circumstances, the more common uses of F0 to signal stress and syntactic groupings could allow less accurate modeling. Subjects are most accurate in perceiving rising vs falling pitch with stimuli of longer duration [141]. Changes in F0 of less than 5 Hz, or those during voiced segments of less than 50 ms, are likely perceived as average, level pitches [142]. Differences in F0 of less than a quarter octave are unlikely to be useful in linguistic communication [143].

Noise sounds in fricatives and stops tend to have broadband spectra, with many irregularities in an otherwise locally flat spectrum. JND studies have shown that listeners cannot hear spectral peaks in such noise with $Q < 5$, or spectral notches with $Q < 8$. Thus most spectral irregularities in obstruent consonant spectra are likely perceptually irrelevant. Fricatives have been well modeled acoustically in terms of two high-frequency poles (with Q's of 5–13) and one lower-frequency zero (with Q of 2–4). The location of the lowest-frequency pole appears to be of greatest perceptual importance; it specifies the cutoff frequency of the highpass frication noise, which determines place of articulation perception.

The abruptness in time with which a phoneme begins or ends is often a cue to phonemic or allophonic contrast; e.g., /ʃ/ is distinguished from /č/ by the rate of noise onset (/č/ having a relatively abrupt onset). A rise (or decay) time for phoneme onsets (or offsets), defined as the transition time from 10% to 90% of peak intensity expressed in decibels, varies from 10 to 150 ms in typical speech. The JND is about 25–30%, which suggests that discrimination is too poor to reliably cue more than two phonetic categories (e.g., abrupt vs smooth) [144, 145].

Related to JND experiments is a study of perceptual distance among similar vowels [146] (see also [147, 148]), in which aspects of a synthetic /æ/ were varied and listeners judged pairs of vowels as to how different they sounded. Formant bandwidth changes appeared to affect perception primarily through their effects on formant amplitudes. The valleys between formants were less important than formant peaks, but small-amplitude changes at very low frequencies (the first and second harmonics) caused large perceptual distances. Total elimination of harmonics between formants was ignored unless the spectral notch removed energy very close to a formant or at very low frequencies. Setting the phases of the harmonics to zero or to random values resulted in large perceptual effects (e.g., harsh speech), which suggests a temporal component to speech perception since an auditory analysis in the ear that provides only an amplitude spectrum would be insensitive to phase. Auditory phase insensitivity is likely limited to small amounts of phase distortion. It may be that the ear primarily discriminates phase within each critical band and that speech degradation is perceived only when large phase differences occur between harmonics within a critical band.

In masking, when the task is not simply to detect one signal in the presence of another but rather to identify some aspect of the signal, the term *recognition masking* is used. Signal threshold is higher in such recognition tasks; e.g., to understand a speech signal amid background noise typically requires 10–12 dB more intensity than to simply note the presence of the speech. *Speech reception thresholds* serve to measure intelligibility [149].

4.4.5 Timing

Time plays a major role in speech perception; thus the temporal resolution of the ear is crucial. Two brief clicks are perceived monaurally as one, unless separated by at least 2 ms. Similarly, the onsets of two signals must differ by at least 2 ms for a listener to hear them as different [80]. To identify the order of two such signals, however, about 17 ms of separation are needed. This temporal order identification threshold decreases for stimuli durations less than 300 ms, but can double as stimulus rise times increase from 10 to 100 ms (both typical values for speech sounds) [150]. Detecting a temporal gap in a narrowband sound (vs a wideband click) requires increasing gap duration as the center frequency of the sound decreases (22.5 ms at 200 Hz), perhaps due to longer impulse response times of the basilar membrane at locations with lower CFs (i.e., the narrower bandwidths lead to more ringing in the time response) [151]. The equivalent window durations of auditory filter models are 4–5 ms [152].

Sounds with onsets faster than 20 ms are heard as abrupt *plucks* rather than gliding *bows* [153]. For these and other reasons (e.g., the maximum rise time for a stimulus onset yielding an overshoot in auditory neural firings is about 20 ms), 20 ms is often used as an integration time typical of auditory processing. (The question of auditory time constants is difficult to assess, since for sound detectability the ear appears to integrate energy over 200 ms, whereas durations as short as 2 ms are relevant in some masking experiments [92, 154].)

To note the order in a set of sequential short sounds, each sound must be about 125–200 ms long. Listeners cannot identify the order of a repeating sequence of four 200 ms steady-state vowels, but have no problem with even shorter vowels if the vowels have gradual onsets and offsets with 50 ms pauses intervening [155]. People use rhythmic sound sequences, in which amplitude regularly rises and falls, for perceptual segmentation. A lack of transitions apparently disrupts perceptual processing; normal speech contains many such transitions, permitting speech to be perceived at rates up to 40–50 phonemes/s [156], although 12 phonemes/s is a more typical rate.

Short sounds near the threshold of hearing must exceed a certain intensity–time product to be perceived. This value is roughly constant (for a given sound frequency) over the approximate range of 10–200 ms. The lower time limit is likely related to critical-band effects (e.g., a 10 ms tone burst has a half-power bandwidth of 100 Hz—approximately a critical band), while the upper limit may reflect some unit of auditory processing time. The values for the auditory threshold described in Section 4.3 apply to sounds longer than 200 ms. Peripheral auditory analysis also operates under a time–frequency tradeoff in which the product of time resolution and frequency resolution stays essentially constant within certain limits. Spectral resolution is limited to critical bandwidths (about a quarter to a third octave), while timing is smoothed through a window of several ms. Thus, the ability to finely discriminate tone bursts decreases as the burst duration becomes smaller, and conversely fine timing discrimination is possible only for broadband signals. Similarly, successive short sounds are best resolved in time when they have energy in identical frequency bands [157]. In sound perception, the auditory system appears to *tune* its focus of attention to the frequency range of highest energy; this focus frequency changes only in response to a sound with primary energy at another frequency. The ability to discriminate is best when successive sounds do not require much movement of this focus. Such discrimination appears also to trade off spectral and temporal cues within frequency ranges of an octave and over intervals of 120 ms [158].

Although timing is very important in speech production to obtain natural speech, little research has been done on duration JNDs in utterances of more than a few syllables. Listeners are known to be more sensitive to durational changes in vowels than to changes in consonants [159]. Natural speech timing is based more on events at the syllable level than at the phoneme level [160] (i.e., changes in syllable durations are more noticeable than changes in adjacent phonemes that leave the syllable with the same duration). Typical stressed vowels can be varied over a 40 ms range without deviating from what listeners consider "normal." Durational JNDs for natural speech generally range from 10 to 40 ms [138], although some authors have found shorter values [161]. It has been argued that, while listeners may tolerate a deviation of up to 100 ms in a single segment within an utterance, the average durational deviation over all phonemes should be less than 10 ms [162]. JNDs vary with (a) the absolute duration of the segment (Weber's law is roughly followed, i.e., JNDs are directly proportional to overall segment durations); (b) the syllable position within a word (JNDs are smaller in word-initial than in word-final syllables); and (c) word position within a sentence [163]. The wide range of JND values obtained in different studies may be explained by examining the experimental paradigms. In many studies, the same word or sentence is repeated many times, so that a listener develops a stable psychological reference pattern, which hones his ability to hear small differences. Large values for JNDs tend to be found in studies that compensate for this adaptation effect.

4.4.6 Separating Sound Sources

Humans often hear several simultaneous sound sources, and attempt to recognize important aspects of each source. This is important for identifying potential dangers, and for deciding to which source to pay primary attention. We do well at focusing on one source (e.g., one voice in a crowded room), while still being able to pay secondary attention to other sources (e.g., background listening with limited comprehension, to enable us to switch attention when needed). How we do this segregation of multiple sound sources involves issues of perceptual streaming. It is likely that paying attention to different sound sources in an *auditory scene* has two stages: an initial, data-driven automatic feature-extraction process and then a higher cognitive process [164–167].

4.5 CONCLUSION

An understanding of how the ear transforms speech into auditory information is important in many applications of speech processing. To the extent that speech recognition systems simulate human auditory processes, knowledge of which aspects of the speech signal are perceptually important should guide system development. Since synthetic speech is destined for human ears, the time and frequency resolution of the ear provides guidelines in synthesizer design; it is important for high-quality synthetic speech to follow natural speech in those aspects that are perceptually important. In speech coding, the information preserved in a narrow bandwidth transmission should eliminate redundancies and take advantage of the masking properties of auditory perception.

This chapter discussed the structure and mechanics of the ear from the perspective of signal transmission. How time and frequency information in speech is transformed into a linguistic message in the brain is well understood only up to the point of primary auditory neural firings. The 30,000 cochlear hair cells and their attached neurons code sounds in a complex fashion related to the time and frequency components of the sounds. How the higher levels of the auditory system treat sound information coded in the neural firings remains a subject of long-term research. In bridging the gap between neural firings and speech perception, basic elements of auditory psychophysics were discussed. The perceptibility of a sound component in the context of neighboring sound components (nearby in time or in frequency) was discussed in terms of thresholds and masking effects. The next chapter continues to examine the auditory process, specifically looking at how speech sounds are heard and transformed into linguistic units, discovering the acoustic aspects of speech that are linguistically relevant.

PROBLEMS

1. Two narrow bands of noise of equal bandwidth are centered at 250 Hz and 1000 Hz, respectively.
   (a) If their intensities are kept equal to each other but gradually increased from a very low value, which will be heard first? Explain.
   (b) The bandwidth of the noise centered at 250 Hz is now increased in steps while keeping its power density (energy per unit frequency) constant. How would this change the results of part (a)?

2. Two short noise bursts (centered at 1 kHz) are separated in time by 600 ms. A 10 ms tone burst at 1 kHz occurs between the two noise bursts. Sketch the threshold amplitude for hearing the tone burst, as a function of the delay of the tone burst onset to the end of the first noise burst. Explain.

3. Trace the path of perception for a simple 200 Hz sine wave from the outer ear to the neural firings in the cochlea, in terms of where the energy undergoes conversion and how the inner ear behaves for such a stimulus. How would the situation change for a 3000 Hz sine wave of equal amplitude?

4. Consider two neurons, one attached to the basal end of the basilar membrane and the other near the apex.
   (a) Describe the likely times that these two neurons might fire, in response to (i) a click and (ii) a sinusoidal tone.
   (b) Explain why the effects of masking are asymmetrical in frequency.

    (c) Explain why critical bands are not uniform in frequency width.

    (d) What effects do the outer and middle ear have on the firing of neurons in the cochlea? Explain.

    (e) Describe the critical-band phenomena in hearing.

5. Assume the ear receives a sound consisting of a periodic train of very brief rectangular pulses (clicks). The pulses arrive every N ms, but every fourth one is negative (the other three in each period have positive sign).

    (a) What pitch is perceived? Note how the pitch might change nature for different ranges of N.

    (b) Explain this pitch perception in terms of how the basilar membrane reacts to the stimulation.

    (c) Add a train of bandpass noise bursts to the stimulus. Relative to the timing of the original train, when should the noise bursts occur and what frequency range must they occupy to mask the perception of the original pulse train?

6. Consider a 5 ms tone burst and a 100 ms noise burst, both with frequencies centered at 2 kHz.

    (a) If they have similar amplitudes, by how much time must one signal be delayed with respect to the other before both signals are distinctly heard?

    (b) If they occur simultaneously but the bandwidth of the noise is decreased from 1000 Hz to 50 Hz, how does that affect the intensity the tone must have to be heard in the presence of the noise?

7. A 1 kHz tone at 40 dB SPL is used to mask one of two tones separately, one at 750 Hz, the other at 1500 Hz.

    (a) What are the intensity levels at which the tones are just audible above the masking tone?

    (b) The two masked tones are now adjusted to 10 dB SPL; which tone will appear louder (the one at 750 Hz or at 1500 Hz)?

    (c) The intensity of the 1000 Hz masker is now reduced to 20 dB SPL, while the levels of the 750 Hz and 1500 Hz masked tones are unchanged. Which tone appears louder now?

8. Why is the just-noticeable difference (JND) for intensity smaller for a tone than for a vowel, while the JND for fundamental frequency is bigger for a tone than for a vowel?

5

Speech Perception

5.1 INTRODUCTION

While much is known about audition, which converts speech signals into patterns of auditory nerve firings, the mechanisms by which the brain translates these firings into a linguistic message are much less understood [1]. Speech perception research usually views a listener as a *black box*, an entity without analyzable parts. In experiments, acoustic stimuli are played to listeners via earphones or loudspeakers, and the listeners respond to questions about the stimuli. Such questions involve detectability of sounds, discrimination among stimuli, and identification of stimuli using linguistic categories.

The chapter is divided into sections examining perceptually relevant aspects of speech, models of speech perception, vowel perception, consonant perception, intonation perception, and finally some miscellaneous topics. Section 5.2 notes that speech contains multiple, redundant acoustic cues to the perception of phonemes and their component features. In estimating the perceptual importance of these interactive cues, control is virtually impossible with natural speech; however, synthetic speech often omits minor cues, which leads to intelligible but unnatural speech stimuli.

Examples of some of the many proposed models for general speech perception are described in Section 5.3, including *active* models that directly relate speech production to perception and *passive* models that view these processes separately. The nonlinear mapping between acoustic cues and perception is exemplified by *categorical perception*, where equal changes along an acoustic continuum can lead to widely varying perceptual effects. There is no consensus on the best speech perception model, mostly due to the difficulty of designing tests to evaluate a model's validity.

Vowel perception (Section 5.4) is relatively simple since the positions of the first three formants relate directly to perceiving different vowels. The contextual nature of perception is nonetheless apparent for vowels. People weigh context heavily in making phoneme decisions. Directly, context changes perception via coarticulation; indirectly, certain aspects of the speech signal (e.g., speaking rate, average intensity and pitch, typical formant locations), both before and after a section of interest, influence phonemic judgments.

Unlike vowel perception, consonant perception (Section 5.5) is an area of continuing controversy. While the acoustic cues to discrimination of manner of articulation are understood, the search continues for *invariant cues* to the features of voicing and place of articulation. The distinction between voiced and unvoiced consonants lies not simply in detecting periodicity, but also in such diverse cues as voice onset time and formant transitions. The acoustic similarity of stops with different place features has led to much discussion of the relative merits of formant transitions vs burst frequency location.

The importance of duration as a cue to phoneme perception is noted in Section 5.6. While duration is usually not a primary cue to phonemic distinctions, durational changes have significant effects. To the extent that duration influences phoneme decisions, the speaking rate acts as an additional indirect influence. Duration, F0 and intensity are the acoustic cues of prosody (Section 5.7), which help to segment utterances into smaller linguistic units, identify the units' syntactic functions, and highlight important words. Because of the many ways that prosody can be manipulated, even in short utterances, the psychoacoustic relationships of intonation remain an active area of research.

5.2 PERCEPTUALLY IMPORTANT FEATURES OF SPEECH SIGNALS

Experiments on the intelligibility of bandpass-filtered speech in a noisy background, using measures such as the articulation index [2, 3], have shown that the 200–5600 Hz frequency range contributes most to speech perception. This range matches the frequencies of greatest auditory sensitivity and highest speech energy, and suggests that in language evolution the phonemes that are easily produced and perceived by human speech organs survived. Key perceptual aspects of a speech signal are more evident when represented spectrally (e.g., by the Fourier transform of the signal) than in the time domain. Temporal speech properties that are perceptually relevant, e.g., the amplitude envelope (which cues syllable structure, rhythm, and prosody), can be readily obtained from a spectrogram.

The importance of different frequency ranges can be measured by how speech perception is affected when they are omitted or obscured by noise. If frequencies below 1 kHz are filtered out of the speech signal, confusions occur in voicing and manner of articulation for weak obstruents [4] (e.g., /p/ vs /b/ vs /v/). If frequencies above 1.2 kHz are eliminated instead, errors occur primarily in place of articulation (e.g., /p/ vs /t/). Additive broadband noise causes few voicing errors, some stop-fricative confusions, but mostly errors in place of articulation. (Small-room reverberation, with delays near 800 ms, causes mostly place errors, likely due to multiple reflections acting as speech-shaped masking noise [5].) Masking experiments suggest that noise with a flat spectral level obscures frequencies with low energy, e.g., in the upper formant regions or during phoneme transitions when energy is changing rapidly. Since place of articulation is cued both in high-frequency bursts and in the F2–F3 region (in contrast to voicing cues in the strong F1 region), place perception suffers the most in broadband noise.

These results follow the view that (a) voicing is perceived through harmonic structure (which is strongest at low frequencies, but normally present at least up to 3 kHz), (b) manner cues are strongest at low frequencies, and (c) place cues are found mostly above 1 kHz (especially in the F2 region). Similarity judgments of consonants rate phonological features of manner, voicing, and place in decreasing order of importance, which reflect their robustness in noise. These features are important because they represent a recoding stage of speech information that seems to be retained in short-term auditory memory more readily than are other aspects of the speech signal.

5.2.1 Synthetic vs Natural Speech

Listeners use more than acoustic information when interpreting a spoken message. Their familiarity with the speaker and subject of the conversation aids perception. When available, visual cues (e.g., facial gestures) also assist [6]; indeed, for deaf people, lipreading provides the main cues. Thus, perception experiments must be carefully controlled to demonstrate a direct relationship between a variation in an acoustic stimulus and a perceptual effect. Since there are so many variables in the production of natural speech, perceptual experiments often use synthetic stimuli produced by computer. Automatic speech synthesis can provide stimuli resembling natural speech, as well as accurate control impossible with human speakers.

Extending the results of perceptual experiments using synthetic stimuli to natural speech perception, however, is not straightforward. Listeners may not interpret acoustic cues in synthetic speech the same way they do for natural speech. A synthetic speech experiment shows that listeners *can* interpret certain acoustic variations linguistically, but it does not prove that such a process is relevant for natural speech perception. It is nonetheless usually assumed that, if the synthetic stimuli are sufficiently close to natural speech, the perceptual results represent a valid model for natural speech. Unfortunately, most reports of perceptual experiments include few objective comments on the naturalness of their synthetic speech.

The problem is especially acute when simplistic models lead to synthetic speech significantly different from natural speech. For example, classical studies of place of articulation in plosives used stimuli with two steady formants and either a bandlimited burst of noise or formant transitions [7, 8]; natural plosives have more complex closure releases in terms of varying energy at different frequencies, and only severely bandlimited natural vowels have just two formants. It is likely that listeners respond to natural speech in ways similar to responses given to simplified synthetic speech, but in cases where the acoustic cues for a particular linguistic feature (e.g., place of articulation) are complex and interrelated, simplified experiments run the risk of demonstrating only how listeners react to distorted speech (from which some of the acoustic cues normally utilized have been removed). Synthetic speech generally provides the major acoustic cues needed for perception, while often omitting minor, redundant cues that enrich natural speech.

5.2.2 Redundancy in Speech

Speech is highly redundant; e.g., infinite peak clipping of the signal (i.e., reducing it to a binary waveform) eliminates virtually all amplitude information, yet listeners can still understand such distorted 'speech'. As another example, eliminating all frequencies either above or below 1.8 kHz still allows 67% of all syllables to be correctly identified [9]. Unlike visual perception of a scene in which discrete objects are discerned, speech perception involves decoding auditory signals in which the (linguistically discrete) phonemes are realized as overlapping acoustic events. The perception of a phoneme is usually dependent on context; i.e., the acoustic signal before and after the actual articulation of the phoneme is crucial to its perception. Speech perception is also highly dependent on forms of context other than the coarticulation of time-adjacent acoustic sounds. Listeners adjust their perceptual framework to fit expectations about the incoming speech signal, often anticipating it from their knowledge of the speaker, the context of the conversation, and their general knowledge. Thus we often can understand speech in extremely noisy conditions when it comes from someone we know, but not from a stranger. Words with ambiguous phonetic cues tend to be perceived under the assumptions that they are meaningful words, consistent with the semantic context of the rest of the sentence, and that the speaker usually maintains a constant speaking rate [10].

The redundant cues of speech aid perception in adverse circumstances, e.g., a noisy environment or a speaker with a foreign accent. Speakers usually exploit this redundancy, articulating clearly [11] when needed, but speaking rapidly and casually in informal conversations. Perception experiments have tried to determine the nature of these cues in the speech signal; in particular, acoustic–phonetic cues are sought that may be invariant to context or speaker. Sufficient cues have been discovered that can describe much about the perception of phonemes within a language, but the cues often vary with respect to phonetic context, stress, and speaking rate. Listeners may be born with or develop certain *feature detectors*, which could be invoked to classify speech sounds into linguistic categories that differ by one or more features.

5.3 MODELS OF SPEECH PERCEPTION

Speech perception involves several stages of analysis: auditory, phonetic, phonological, lexical (word), syntactic, and semantic. These could be viewed as serial processes, in which the speech signal is transformed at each stage into a more refined representation, eventually ending with a linguistic message. However, some stages must occur in parallel (perhaps simultaneously) with feedback, to correct low-level (e.g., phonemic) misinterpretations using more global (e.g., sentential or contextual) knowledge and also to allow low-level processes the option of delayed decisions when the signal does not provide sufficient information. The following sections review common speech perception models.

5.3.1 Categorical Perception

Finding and measuring which acoustic aspects of an auditory signal are relevant for perceptual discrimination provide a useful characterization of audition (*auditory psychophysics*). Labeling sound stimuli, on the other hand, as members of a class of linguistically relevant sounds (e.g., as phonemes) is a concern of auditory psycholinguistics. Categorizing a sound according to some linguistic criterion that one has learned is a convenient way to discriminate sounds that resemble speech, but is limited to categories with which the listener is familiar. One cannot use linguistic knowledge to distinguish two sounds that do not resemble phonemes, nor two sounds that resemble the same phoneme. In general, acoustic criteria are used to distinguish sounds, but linguistic knowledge can assist perceptual resolution when two sounds straddle a linguistic boundary (e.g., when such sounds can be perceived as having different linguistic features); e.g., a listener can detect a 1 Hz difference between two tones but cannot label or order such tones separately because they have no linguistic meaning.

Like most physical stimuli, most sounds (including many speech sounds) are perceived on a continuous scale; i.e., as their physical aspects slowly change, the sounds are gradually perceived as being different. Certain stimuli appear to be perceived in categorical or psycholinguistic fashion, where the ability to discriminate two stimuli depends mainly on the ability to label them as different linguistically [12]. For such sounds, there are ranges along a physical continuum in which large physical changes yield no perceived difference (all the stimuli are labeled as identical); in other ranges a small physical change causes a large perceived difference (a new label). The effect of *voice onset time* (VOT) on initial stop voicing is one example (Section 5.5): for very short or long VOTs, listeners hear voiced or unvoiced stops, respectively, and are not able to distinguish small changes in VOT. However, at the boundary (near 30 ms of VOT for English) listeners can detect 10 ms changes because they result in a labeling change for the stimulus between voiced and unvoiced.

Categorical perception normally presumes that discrimination of stimuli *within* a category should be at *chance level*, i.e., that performance is equivalent to guessing one out of N trials correct in a forced-choice test with N alternatives. However, well-practiced subjects usually can distinguish such stimuli above chance level, while exhibiting yet higher discriminating ability for stimuli straddling the category boundaries. Most evidence in favor of categorical perception has used the *ABX* paradigm, in which the listener judges whether the third (X) of three stimuli presented in sequence is more similar to A or to B. The phenomenon may be due to categoric memory rather than categorical perception, since the delay in hearing X after A and B may require short-term memory storage in terms of categorical features [13]. When subjects rate speech sounds along a continuum, perceptual resolution is primarily continuous, with perhaps enhanced discriminability between stimuli across a phoneme boundary.

Rather than preserving many aspects of A and B in short-term memory, the listener may simply identify A and B as specific phonemes (where possible) and then recognize X as being in the phoneme class of A or B. If phoneme decisions are not feasible, perhaps the listener represents a sound as a set of features, which is simpler to retain in memory than a complex time–frequency pattern. Enhanced discrimination between sounds near a phonetic boundary is evidence for *phonetic processing* of speech. If (more general) psychoacoustic processing were used in speech perception, discriminability would follow direct acoustic factors, independent of phonetic categories [14]. Vowels are generally viewed as not subject to categorical perception [15].

5.3.2 Distinctive Features

A linguistic approach to phoneme classification uses a set of *distinctive features*. Rather than consider phonemes as minimal units of language, a small set of orthogonal (often binary) properties or features can classify both phonemes [16] and other levels of phonology and phonetics [17]. Such features as *voiced, labial–alveolar–velar, nasal, fricative*, etc., are based on acoustics and articulation, not on perception. Nonetheless, since phoneme confusions correlate well with these features (e.g., sounds in distorted conditions are more often confused in proportion to the number of features they share), distinctive features have been widely used in perception studies. Of particular relevance here are time-varying acoustic cues during phones that lead to phonemic perception; how such cues relate to the perception of phonemes and their assigned distinctive features is discussed below.

The role of formants in speech perception has been widely debated. It is clear that (a) formants are useful in describing the acoustics of speech production, (b) simple formant information is preserved in auditory neural firing patterns, and (c) formant movements cause direct perceptual effects. However, formants per se are not necessarily the most important spectral cues to speech perception, nor do they provide invariant cues in many phonetic contexts. Gross spectral shape, rather than formant locations, may furnish better explanations of perceptual phenomena. There is no evidence that speech perception tracks formants; indeed, the difficulty of automatic formant tracking [18], even by trained phoneticians using spectrograms, is evidence that the ear interprets speech in ways other than by simply following the trajectories of F1–F3. Perceived vowel distance, in terms of how different two vowels sound, does not follow a linear measure of formant separation [19]. It is more likely that the auditory system does a more general spectral analysis, in which formants play an important but indirect role in shaping spectra, especially for periods of speech where formants are not readily distinct (e.g., in voiced–unvoiced transitions). In this view, the listener recognizes spectral patterns while identifying phoneme sequences or distinctive features. These patterns can often be efficiently described in terms of formants, but the specific presence of formant detectors in auditory processing is unlikely.

A similar debate exists over the presence of speech-specific auditory detectors of phonetic features. Evidence for feature analyzers comes from perceptual confusion studies [4], cross-adaptation [20], the perception of stimuli with conflicting acoustic cues [21], and categorical consonant perception [22, 23]. However, these studies merely suggest the *possibility* of phonetic feature detectors. Much of the research on selective adaptation (see Section 5.8) has attempted to prove the existence of feature detectors, yet what those studies actually show is that certain perceptual contrasts change with fatigue [24]. There is no proof that speech-specific features exist in the early stages of speech perception, and perception based on more elementary spectral aspects of speech is a reasonable alternative; e.g., speech production errors tend to manipulate entire phonemes rather than only component features [25]. Distinctive features describe well the organization of languages and possible phonetic contrasts in production and perception, but it is not clear that the features are directly used either by the speaker at the articulatory level or by the listener at the acoustic level. More likely are general innate property detectors found in all mammals [26], although there may be innate linguistic "knowledge" in newborn infants that predisposes humans to language [17]. Infants from many language backgrounds appear to categorize sounds into groups that can be characterized by distinctive features.

Speech perception is a specialized aspect of the general human ability to seek and recognize patterns. The processes of speech perception and production are likely to have evolved in parallel. Sounds easily produced by the vocal tract, capable of consistent differentiation with minimal effort by the speaker, while presenting at the same time similar acoustic patterns across different speakers, were likely those sounds chosen for verbal communication. The capability of the hearing mechanism to consistently perceive and discriminate these sounds from different speakers must be a dominant factor in language evolution.

5.3.3 Active Models

Many models of speech perception have been proposed to account for the diverse results of experiments with different methodologies. Listeners use the speech signal to decode information about the vocal tract configurations and movements that produced the signal [27, 28]. One controversial suggestion is that there is a special *speech mode* of listening that is invoked when a listener first hears (or expects to hear) speech [29, 30]; a listener then pays more attention to speech-specific parameters (e.g., formants) than normally. An alternative *motor theory* of perception states that listeners decode incoming speech by unconsciously producing an internal articulatory version of the speech to compare to the actual speech [29]. This theory presumes a close mapping between phonemes and their corresponding articulatory commands, in which invariant patterns could be found for phonemes independent of context. According to this view, the lack of invariance at the acoustic level is due to coarticulation and results from overlapping articulatory commands for successive phonemes.

Electromyographic recordings of articulator muscle activity, however, show that invariance in motor commands is limited to higher cognitive levels, at best.

In a related theory called *analysis by synthesis*, the listener unconsciously produces a "synthetic" version of the input speech based on a coarse auditory analysis (Figure 5.1). If the two versions match, the analysis is considered successful; if they do not match, more refined processing of the input is necessary. Such a dual-process model incorporates both top-down and bottom-up cognitive processes in speech perception, and hypothesizes that the listener decodes details about the speech signal only to the extent that he cannot predict them from context. A highly redundant conversation between friends in a quiet room requires little acoustic decoding, whereas a chance conversation on a noisy street involving strange dialects relies heavily on bottom-up acoustic analysis.

Categorical perception is often cited [31] as evidence for a dual-process model of speech perception, with a bottom-up auditory process and a top-down phonetic process. The auditory process interprets the speech signal in terms of acoustic features and stores them in short-term auditory memory; the phonetic process yields phoneme perception based on the features in auditory memory. The theory holds that sounds that are perceived categorically are coded in terms of features which disappear rapidly from auditory memory and are recoded phonetically for the longer term, whereas continuously perceived sounds have more lasting features in auditory memory. This theory remains controversial [13, 24, 32–34].

Categories are often interpreted via their purported boundaries, i.e., the ability to distinguish two sounds would depend on whether they lie on opposite sides of a boundary separating them in some sort of phonetic space. An alternative *prototype theory* holds that long-term memory contains speech prototypes and that sounds can be judged on how "good" they are as category exemplars [35]. (*Working memory* available for speech understanding appears to decline with age [36].) A related *perceptual magnet* effect may occur only in humans, unlike categorical perception, which humans share with animals; the latter would be

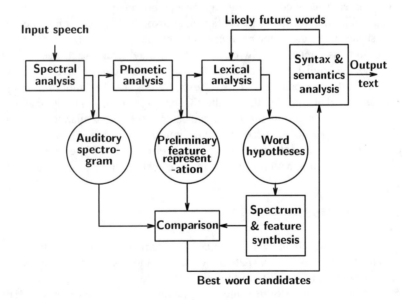

Figure 5.1 Simplified block diagram of an analysis-by-synthesis model of speech perception. Memory buffers are represented by circles.

found in an early auditory processing stage of perception, while humans exploit a later phonetic stage. (Such an effect may however simply relate to better discrimination across, rather than within, phonetic categories [37].)

Listeners may recognize words by matching aspects of the acoustic input to patterns stored in their *lexical dictionary* [38]. Recognition involves cognitive processes other than simply matching auditory patterns, however. The listener utilizes context to anticipate future words. If a word cannot be immediately recognized, the following words often help. This presumes a short-term acoustic memory (of about 200–300 ms [39]) in which spectral information about running speech is temporarily stored, perhaps in the form of features representing a partial decoding of the signal. It is necessary to store phonetic details of at least a syllable's duration, since consonant and vowel perception use interdependent, parallel perception processes that, due to coarticulation, often involve acoustic detail over several phonemes. Transient acoustic information in this memory may be lost unless it is quickly recoded into a more compact phonetic form for longer-term memory. The latter memory (termed a *precategorical acoustic store* [40]) is useful when a listener must *backtrack*, i.e., after misinterpreting acoustic cues. Experiments examining intelligibility in background noise suggest that long-term memory has a duration of about seven syllables [41]. (This number of syllables may be related to a general limitation on memory; psychology tests often show that only about seven concepts can be retained in memory unless one imposes a cognitive structure.)

There is evidence that word recognition may not require the identification of individual phonemes as an intermediate step: (a) listeners have quicker reaction times to words than to phonemes [42], (b) word onsets can sometimes be identified by *allophonic* variations (variants in spectral patterns of a phone depending on context, which still cue the same phoneme) [43], (c) clicks superimposed on speech tend to be heard at word boundaries [44]. Most word boundaries in fluent speech are not marked acoustically (a glottal stop between a word ending in a vowel and a word starting with a similar vowel is an exception), and the few that are marked usually coincide with a syntactic boundary.

For multisyllabic words, perception may involve syllables as intermediate processing units. Listeners make use of the phonological constraints of syllable context in perception. For example, in consonant clusters within a syllable, only certain sequences of consonants are permissible: (a) English requires that obstruents within a cluster have common voicing, i.e., all voiced or all unvoiced (e.g., "*steps*," "te*xts*," "do*gs*"); (b) in initial /s/+stop clusters, the stop is considered unvoiced (although the VOT is very short); and (c) in final nasal+unvoiced stop clusters, the consonants must have the same place of articulation (e.g., "li*mp*," "li*nt*," "li*nk*"). Words that violate these and other limitations are judged as nonsense words more quickly than words that conform. Perception of words is easier if they are less confusable with other words, i.e., words with few neighbors in lexical or phonetic space are easier to identify [45].

5.3.4 Passive Models

The active models for speech perception assume that perception involves direct access to speech production processes. Alternative passive models make no reference to articulation and assume a direct mapping from acoustic features to phonetic categories (see Figure 5.2). A speech signal (A) is transformed into firing patterns in the auditory nerve (B) and is coded directly into distinctive auditory features (C), which in turn permit recognition of linguistic units (D) at the level of phonemes and larger units. The auditory patterns at C are

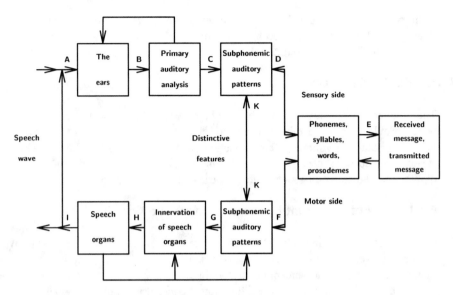

Figure 5.2 Hypothetical model of brain functions in speech perception and production. (After Fant [46].)

subphonemic, i.e., involve features at the level of acoustic events (e.g., stop bursts) and could deal with identification of periodicity or of speech energy at different frequencies. Any analysis-by-synthesis is invoked, after the speech has been converted into linguistic units of phonemes or words (E). In motor theories, speech production is an integral part of perception, but for passive models production provides a parallel process, which can interact indirectly with perception through distinctive features (K).

One such model [47] is based on speech recognition systems. Listeners, in decoding speech into words, may generate lexical hypotheses directly from a spectral representation without identifying phonetic segments. Acoustic–phonetic knowledge and word-boundary phonology can be precompiled into a network of spectral templates capable of handling the listener's entire lexicon. Phonetic segments and phonological rules would assist only in the network compilation (developed as one learns the language) and not in direct analysis of speech. Acknowledging that speech perception often involves both top-down cognitive processes (word hypotheses predicted from syntactic and semantic context) and bottom-up analyses (identifying words directly from the speech signal), this model [48] concentrates on bottom-up processes. Listeners' knowledge about phonological phenomena (e.g., coarticulation, palatalization, missing and added segments, etc.) can be precompiled into network form. Spectral movement between phonemes is coded via *diphones*, involving transitions between presumed steady states of successive phonemes. To the extent that phonological phenomena extend beyond diphones, larger context-sensitive allophones may be necessary [49].

Both active and passive models provide material for interesting speculation about speech perception, but experiments to critically evaluate models are difficult to design. It is unlikely that a model with many states and paths would correspond to actual mental processes during natural speech perception. Many perception theories assume direct relationships (e.g., invariant features) between the discrete domain of phonology (e.g., words, syllables, phonemes) and either (or both) of the physical domains (articulatory and auditory) [23]. The active models assume that simple relationships exist at the gestural level [12, 28] or the auditory level [50]. While there is clearer evidence for the importance of auditory objects (than gestural invariants) in speech perception, ample experimental evidence shows difficulties with any theory that assumes simple phonological relationships [51].

5.4 VOWEL PERCEPTION

The production of steady-state vowels can be described in terms of static vocal tract shapes, which provide prototype *targets* when vowels are articulated in words. The perception of vowels in isolation (without the coarticulation effects of neighboring phones) is based on their steady-state spectra, usually interpreted in terms of the locations of F1–F3 [52]. For diphthongs, the endpoint steady states appear to be important [53].

5.4.1 Perceived Formant Location in Synthetic Vowels

A systematic variation of F1 and F2 (following vowel triangle positions) in two-formant synthetic vowel stimuli can create distinguishable versions of all English vowels (although including F3 aids in the perception of certain vowels, such as /ɝ/) (see Figure 3.10). Rear vowels, having low values for F2 and therefore a concentration of energy below 1 kHz, can be perceived with only one broad low-frequency formant in the F1–F2 region. Front vowels have so much separation between F1 and F2 as to require two individual resonances in synthetic stimuli. Multidimensional scaling analyses have shown that F1 and F2 are two good orthogonal dimensions to separate the vowels, on both perceptual and production grounds [54].

One way to evaluate the perceptual relevance of spectral peaks is to ask listeners to move the formant (called F1′) in a one-formant synthetic "vowel" so that it sounds similar to a two-formant (F1 and F2) stimulus. They locate F1′ about midway between F1 and F2 if the latter are separated by less than 3.0–3.5 bark (1 bark = 1 critical band). (This frequency distance has been successfully applied to multispeaker vowel recognition [55].) If F1 and F2 are more widely separated, F1′ is located close to one of the actual formants [56]. This suggests a form of spectral integration, where a *center-of-gravity* of energy concentration within a range of a few bark is a prime perceptual correlate. When listeners are asked to adjust the formant frequencies (F1′, F2′) of two-formant synthesized vowels to perceptually match more natural three- and four-formant vowels, they usually locate one formant (F1′) in the vicinity of F1 and place F2′ near either F2 or F3, depending on the major concentration of spectral energy [57]. The exact placement of F2′ appears to be a complicated function of F1–F4 locations that involves critical-band spectral resolution of the ear. Such experiments note the difficulty of extending results obtained with two-formant stimuli to normal speech perception, even though virtually all vowels can be identified based on their F1–F2 alone.

5.4.2 Context Normalization

A specific set of formants in a synthetic vowel does not guarantee unambiguous phoneme perception. Listeners, familiar with the speech of many talkers, have expectations about F0 and formants. High-pitched vowels are presumed to come from female (or child) vocal tracts [58, 59], which are shorter than adult male vocal tracts and thus have higher formant frequencies. When one hears a voice with an F0 of 100 Hz, one expects it to have formants spaced roughly every 1 kHz [60]. With an F0 of 200 Hz, one expects formants shifted up 10–15%, corresponding to typical female voices. As a result, two vowels with the same formants may be perceived as closely related but distinct phonemes if F0 is sufficiently different in each. The perceptual shift due to F0 is similar to the types of errors found in normal vowel perception: confusions between vowels with similar formants, e.g., between /I/ and /i/. (Issues of speaker recognition will be addressed in Chapter 11; we know relatively little about how individual voices are represented in perception and memory [61, 62].)

The mapping from phones (with their varied acoustic correlates) to individual phonemes at the phonological level is likely to be accomplished by analyzing auditory patterns over sections of speech corresponding roughly to syllables. Since the same phoneme produced by different vocal tracts yields different spectral patterns and formant frequencies, speech perception must use some form of normalization, by which different acoustic realizations are interpreted as the same phonetic unit [63]. A linear scaling of formant frequencies with (perceived) vocal tract length provides a reasonable first-order approximation, but is not fully adequate because different-sized vocal tracts are not simply scaled versions of one another. (For example, the ratio of male to female vocal tract dimensions is greater for the pharynx than the oral cavity: a typical adult female has a pharynx 2 cm shorter than a male's, but the female's oral cavity is only 1.25 cm shorter.) Listeners are likely to interpret acoustic patterns based on preliminary assumptions (e.g., visual cues of the speaker, when available) and on an analysis of the initial speech from the speaker (e.g., the point vowels /i,α,u/ may provide a reference formant space to infer the acoustic patterns of other phonemes). Formant normalization may be an automatic process, involving cues of both F0 and formant spacing [64, 65]. F3 and higher formants are relatively constant for a given speaker and may provide a reference to evaluate the variations in F1–F2. However, there is sufficient information in the spectra of very short vowel segments to uniquely identify them with little context needed [66].

5.4.3 Coarticulation Effects

When vowels are produced in typical contexts (i.e., not in isolation), they coarticulate with adjacent sounds. Formants undershoot their "targets" and are otherwise modified by the phonemic context. Perception of such vowels seems to depend on a complex auditory analysis of the formant movements before, during, and after the vowel. In CVC (consonant–vowel–consonant) syllables, if the middle 50–65% of the vowel is excised and played to listeners, they perform worse in phoneme identification than if the CV and VC transitions (containing the other 35–50% of the vowel) are heard instead [67]. Short portions of the CV and VC transitions often permit identification of the vowel when a large part of the vowel is removed [68, 69]. The importance of spectral transitions in coarticulated vowel perception is clear, but it is uncertain how listeners utilize the spectral information [70].

Given that vowel formants are modified in consonantal context, it might be expected that vowels are less well identified in a CVC context. Such is usually found with synthetic stimuli [71], but naturally produced vowels in certain contexts are identified more accurately than in isolation, even in multispeaker experiments [72]. It appears that vowels in continuous speech are specified by dynamic acoustic parameters and that these spectral patterns over the course of a syllable are used in vowel perception.

"Target" theories of vowel perception hold that the essential cues reside in an asymptotic spectrum approached toward the middle of the vowel, while other theories focus attention on the whole complex of acoustic events in the transitions. Initial CV and final VC transitions specify formant trajectories whose asymptotes approximately correspond (perhaps after a transformation to compensate for undershoot) to static vowel targets [29].

While spectra dominate in vowel perception, temporal factors also affect phoneme identification; e.g., lax and tense vowels, respectively, tend to be heard with slow and fast formant transitions. Indeed, speech is perceived well when temporal envelope information is preserved, while spectral detail is replaced by a few broad bands of noise [73].

Formant transitions, in addition to helping cue phoneme identification, aid in auditory stream integration or continuity [74]. Synthetic speech without such transitions, linking vowels with low-frequency energy to high-frequency fricatives and noise bursts, tends to be perceived as two separate sound streams. Inadequate modeling of formant transitions may lead to fricatives being heard as isolated hisses superimposed on the rest of the synthetic speech.

5.5 CONSONANT PERCEPTION

Consonants are traditionally classified by the features of voicing and manner and place of articulation. Perception of manner is related to gross spectral distribution of speech energy and to periodicity, while cues for place pertain to finer aspects of the spectrum. Consonant voicing is simply related to periodicity for fricatives, but has several interrelated cues for stops. Among the distinctive features, those dealing with manner of articulation are the simplest to explain. The voicing and place of articulation features, on the other hand, involve complex interactions of several acoustic cues and continue to be researched.

5.5.1 Perception of the Manner of Articulation Feature

Manner perception concerns acoustic cues that permit the listener to classify speech into the following categories: vowels (including liquids), glides, nasals, stops, and fricatives. A vowel is heard when the sound is periodic with sufficient amplitude and duration and a strong formant structure (i.e., the lower formants excited with relatively narrow bandwidths). Glides can usually be distinguished from vowels through weaker amplitude, briefer durations, and a greater tendency toward dynamic spectral patterns. Nasals can be distinguished from vowels by their weaker amplitude, wider bandwidths, and higher concentration of energy at low frequencies. Stops are heard when a period of silence interrupts the speech signal, especially when followed by a short burst of noise. Sounds with high-frequency noise of sufficient duration are perceived as fricatives. The crucial cues that separate these manner classes involve amplitude, duration, general formant structure, and the balance between low-frequency voiced energy and high-frequency frication. Whether a sound is harmonically structured with no noise (vowels, glides, and nasals) or it has an aperiodic component (stops and fricatives) is the basic manner cue.

The most common confusions due to perceptual errors in manner of articulation involve the nonstrident voiced fricatives /v,δ/ and voiced stops (especially /b/) and to a lesser extent their unvoiced counterparts (/f,θ,p/) [4]. The nonstrident fricatives are sufficiently weak that they are often hard to distinguish from a stop, especially a labial stop, which is usually weakly released and has formant transitions similar to those of the labial and dental fricatives.

5.5.1.1 Glides.   Each consonant involves a constriction in the vocal tract. The timing of transitions to and from such a constriction influences consonant perception; e.g., when steady formants are preceded by linearly rising formants, one hears /b/ if the transition is short and /w/ if more than 40 ms [75]. With very long transitions (>100 ms), a sequence of vowels is heard, the first being /u/. In all cases, an initial low formant pattern signals labial

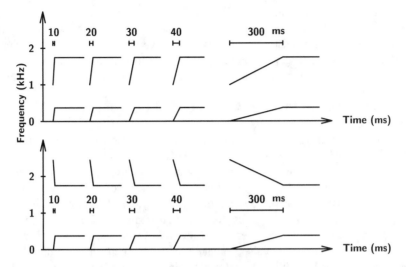

Figure 5.3 Spectrographic patterns with different transition durations. The first four patterns in each row show how the initial transition was varied. At the right is a complete stimulus pattern, with the longest transition. (After Liberman *et al.* [75].)

articulation, but the transition duration specifies the manner feature. When falling formants are used, /g/, /j/, and /i/ are successively heard as the transition duration increases (Figure 5.3). When the transition is rapid, a (prior) stop is detected; further lengthening of the transition approaches the more gradual articulation of glides. Extending the transition of a glide beyond its normal value leads to the perception of two vowels. The amplitude envelope (rapid rise for stops, gradual rise for glides) is also a critical acoustic property for the contrast of continuant (glide) vs noncontinuant (stop) [76].

The glides /j,w/ can be reasonably approximated with only two formants since their spectra are quite similar to the vowels /i,u/, respectively. The liquids /l,r/, however, require a third formant to be perceived: a low F3 for the retroflex /r/ and a high F3 for the lateral /l/.

5.5.1.2 Nasality feature. Acoustic cues for the perception of nasal consonants include abruptly lower intensity (compared to vowels) and an additional, distinctive low-frequency resonance (the *nasal murmur*) at about 250 Hz. Acceptable nasals can be synthesized with the murmur extending (via coarticulation) into adjacent sonorants by about 50 ms. Often the murmur is accompanied by a spectral zero between it and F1, with about 100 Hz separating the nasal pole and zero [77]. Wide bandwidths and a relative lack of energy at high frequencies also contribute to the perception of *nasality*. In vowel+nasal sequences, the vowel becomes gradually nasalized as the nasal approaches, with widening bandwidths and the introduction of antiresonances. Nasality is especially strongly perceived in response to a wider and weaker first formant (relative to oral vowels).

Due to the multiplicity of cues to nasality [78], some perceptual studies have used articulatory synthesizers, which directly model the lowering of the velum. The amount of acoustic coupling of the nasal tract to the oral tract governs nasality but results in diverse acoustic cues that are difficult to specify in a formant-based synthesizer. For example, listeners compensate for ensuing vowel height when perceiving nasality (e.g., whether the

154

Chapter 5 ■ Speech Perception

consonant in a CV stimulus was /d/ or /n/) [79]; this follows production phenomena in which velum height is proportional to vowel height (i.e., more nasal coupling for lower vowels). Among English listeners, nasality is perceived categorically with consonants, but not with vowels; Hindi listeners exhibit categorical perception in vowels as well [80]. (Hindi, like French and unlike English, uses nasality in vowels phonemically.)

5.5.2 Perception of Place of Articulation of Consonants

Acoustic cues to the perception of consonant place reside primarily in the spectral transitions between the consonant and adjacent phones. For continuants, the steady-state consonant spectrum is also of major importance. For example, distinguishing among the fricatives is mostly based on the amplitude and spectrum of the frication noise [81]. Strong amplitude indicates a rear place (e.g., /s,ʃ/), while weak frication signals a forward place (e.g., /f,θ/). The cutoff frequency for the high-frequency frication energy distinguishes alveolar and palatal fricatives: energy at a lower frequency cues the palatal.

Steady-state spectra are also primary cues for distinguishing among /l,r,w,j/; e.g., in syllable-initial position, /r/ and /w/ can be distinguished by the separation of F2 and F3 (/w/ having the wider spacing) [82]. However, for stops and the forward fricatives, spectral transitions are more reliable cues to place perception [83]. In prevocalic stops: (1) velar bursts are more effective at signaling place than other bursts, (2) formant transitions for /b/ are better than for /d/, (3) the burst dominates before front vowels, while transitions are more important before other vowels, (4) unvoiced bursts are more important than voiced ones, (5) transitions are more useful than gross cues (e.g., spectral tilt) [84]. Weak continuant consonants are primarily distinguished by spectral transitions at phoneme boundaries, but the nasal murmur contributes as well to place perception in nasals [85]. The liquids /l,r/ are distinguished through F3 position and the abruptness of F1 motion (the tongue-palate contact in /l/ leads to abrupt formant motion, especially at release) [86].

Like most phonetic distinctions, place perception involves multiple acoustic cues. Articulatory adjustments necessary to change perception from one phonetic category to another cause changes along several acoustic dimensions (e.g, spectrum, duration, amplitude, F0) [87]. Perceiving a change of phonetic category may be the net effect of several acoustic cues. Individual cues can be ranked according to their perceptual effect, when the other cues are kept constant. *Primary cues* provide the dominant perceptual effects, causing a phonetic effect even in the presence of conflicting *secondary cues*. The latter can cause the same phonetic percept as primary cues, but only when the primary cues cooperate or are ambiguous. *Trading relationships* among cues can be quantified by varying the cues in synthetic speech in opposite directions so that their perceptual effects cancel; e.g., sufficient variation in one acoustic cue may cause a change in phonemic perception, but then a change in another cue restores the original phoneme. Some view this as evidence that different acoustic cues can act as independent phonetic carriers of information [31], while others explain it on psychoacoustic grounds [14].

5.5.2.1 Stop+vowel stimuli. In the case of unreleased plosives in VC (vowel+conso-nsonant) syllables, spectral transitions provide the sole place cues. For released plosives in CV syllables, the situation is more complex since place cues occur in: the spectrum of the burst release and during the ensuing aspiration period, and (if followed by a voiced phoneme) the aspiration duration, as well as in spectral transitions during adjacent phones. Early research [7] found evidence of a *starting locus* of F2 for each of /b,d,g/ in the perception of two-formant CV stimuli. With F1 having a 50 ms rising transition (typical of all voiced stops), if F2 started at 1.8 kHz, /d/ was heard, whereas an initial 720 Hz caused /b/ perception. A 3 kHz start yielded /g/ for most ensuing vowels, but for high and mid-rear vowels, a much lower locus was necessary. In general, one can say that rising F2 indicates a labial stop, relatively flat F2 tends to be heard as alveolar, and a falling F2 yields velar perception. In all cases, it is necessary, however, to eliminate the first 50 ms of the F2 transition (so that the transition "points to" the locus rather than actually starting there); otherwise different stops are heard (Figure 5.4).

Another early study used steady-state two-formant stimuli (representing vowels) preceded by a brief narrowband noise burst at various frequencies. Figure 5.5 shows that listeners heard /t/ with high-frequency bursts and /p/ with low-frequency bursts. In a large mid-frequency region (720–2880 Hz), however, place perception involved an interaction of burst frequency with the ensuing vowel formant frequencies. When the burst was at or just above the ensuing F2, listeners heard /k/; otherwise, a /p/ tended to be heard.

The extension of these results to natural speech (with more than two formants) is unclear. Many two-formant CV stimuli lack naturalness and provide listeners with ambiguous phonetic cues. For CV stimuli from natural speech, stop bursts and ensuing formant transitions may have equivalent perceptual weight and act in complementary fashion depending on context [88]. When formant transitions are brief, due to short articulator movements (e.g., with a lingual stop followed by a high vowel) or to anticipatory coarticulation (e.g., labial stop before a rounded vowel), the release burst lies near the major spectral peak of the following vowel and contributes significantly to place perception. Conversely, when formant transitions are extensive, the burst is distinct from the vowel spectral peaks, and the formant transitions are more important for stop place perception. In VCV stimuli, the CV

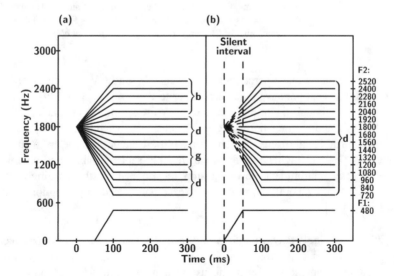

Figure 5.4 Formant patterns of two-formant CV stimuli, illustrating the locus principle. Both diagrams use an initial F2 locus of 1.8 kHz. (a) Different voiced stops are perceived when the F2 transitions actually start at the locus and move toward F2 targets for different vowels; (b) the initial 50 ms of the F2 transition is omitted (and the F1 transition delayed), and all patterns are perceived as starting with /d/. (After Delattre *et al.* [7].)

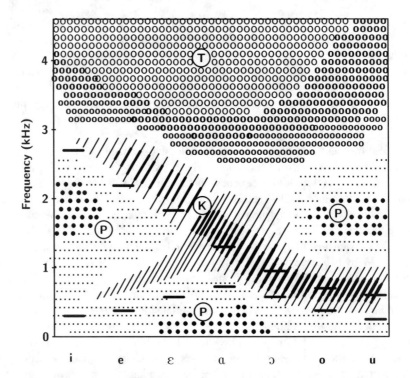

Figure 5.5 Listeners' identification as /p,t,k/ in response to synthetic CV stimuli of a
noise burst followed by a steady two-formant vowel. The vertical axis
indicates burst frequency, while different vowels are displayed horizontally.
In each column, the two bars note the positions of F1 and F2. The size of the
symbol (circles for /t/, slanted lines for /k/, dots for /p/) indicates the
relative number of listener responses. (After Cooper *et al.* [8].)

transition dominates place perception; i.e., if the VC and CV transitions provide conflicting
place cues, listeners perceive place according to the CV transition [89].

Finally, although the primary cues to place are spectral, VOT and amplitude also play a
role. When F2 and F3 transitions give ambiguous cues in synthetic CV stimuli, VOT duration
can distinguish labial from alveolar stops [90]. Changes in spectrum amplitude at high
frequencies (F4 and higher formants) can reliably separate labial and alveolar stops: when
high-frequency amplitude is lower at stop release than in the ensuing vowel, labials are
perceived [91]. In general, more intense release bursts lead to perception of alveolars rather
than labials [92].

5.5.2.2 Static onset vs dynamic spectral transitions. Certain aspects of spectral
patterns of releases in voiced stops appear to distinguish place of articulation. The
concentration or spread of energy (diffuse vs compact) and whether the main spectral trend
is rising, flat, or falling with frequency have been suggested as crucial spectral cues [22, 23,
93]. Manipulating burst spectra and initial formant frequencies in synthetic CV stimuli led to
unambiguous place identification when the onset spectrum was either diffuse-falling (/b/),
diffuse-rising (/d/), or compact (/g/) (see Figure 3.38). Stimuli with spectra not fitting any of
the three categories yielded equivocal responses from listeners. When the stimuli were

truncated to 10–46 ms versions of the original CV syllables (starting at stop release), place identification was good, even when the noise burst was eliminated and when the second and higher formants held steady.

Thus the gross properties of the spectrum during the initial 10–20 ms of a stop consonant provide important cues to place perception. When the initial spectrum is ambiguous (e.g., diffuse but flat), listeners apparently utilize formant transitions to distinguish place. Such transitions temporally link the primary place cues in the stop release to the slowly varying vowel spectrum, with no abrupt spectral discontinuities after the stop release. In this view, the formant patterns act as secondary cues, which are invoked when the primary cues of the release spectrum are ambiguous.

The performance of this model was evaluated by comparing listeners' judgments of place in isolated CV syllables with the model's predictions based on the initial CV spectra. The model achieved 85% accuracy for CV syllables, but only 76% for VCs; furthermore, nasal consonants performed more poorly. One problem with this model is that the proposed templates involve fixed *loci*, which is at variance with earlier experiments [7]. The templates emphasize static acoustic features rather than dynamic ones, and much other evidence points to the relevance of spectral changes [94]. Dynamic aspects of the CV over the initial 40 ms are likely crucial for stop perception [95]. For example, velar stops are poorly identified (73%) on a basis of only the first 20 ms of natural CV stimuli, and when stimuli contain cues conflicting between onset spectra and formant transitions, listeners apparently rely more on the dynamic cues [96]. The relevant cues may not reside in the formant transitions per se, but in other time-dependent spectral features, e.g., VOT, spectral tilt, presence of mid-frequency spectral peaks, abruptness of energy onset at high frequencies, and onset of a prominent low-frequency peak [97]. Labial and alveolar/dental stops can be distinguished by a metric involving relative change in energy at high and low frequencies between burst and voice onset: the labials show equal or less change at low frequencies than at high frequencies [98]. Formant transitions, however, seem to be the most important cues for stop place perception [99], e.g., *locus equations* (straight-line regression fits to critical points in formant transitions) [100].

5.5.2.3 Interaction of cues.

Perception of place of articulation and other consonant features are interdependent. In synthetic voiced stops and nasals, place can be reliably cued by F2–F3 transitions, but the boundaries on formant continua between labials and alveolars are not the same for stops as for nasals [101]. The same holds for voiced stops and weak voiced fricatives [102]. Such interactions between place and manner perception appear to occur at the phonetic (and not auditory) level since place boundary shifts can occur with identical acoustic stimuli perceived differently as to manner (due to ambiguous manner cues) [103]. One possibility to explain the shift in the case of stops and fricatives is that slightly different places of articulation are involved: /b/ is a bilabial with an extreme forward place of articulation and /d/ has a constriction farther to the rear than either /f/ or /θ/, which have intermediate constriction points. Thus the perceptual boundary along an acoustic continuum of F2 and F3 is likely to be different for stops and fricatives.

Coarticulation appears to affect perception in various ways. Normally the distinction between /s/ and /ʃ/ follows the steady-state frication energy: energy at lower-frequency cues /ʃ/. (Since these fricatives differ only in the place feature, discriminating between the two is done by place perception.) Formant transitions to and from the fricative provide secondary cues, due to the coarticulation of the fricative with adjacent phonemes. When a fricative with spectrum ambiguous between /s/ and /ʃ/ is followed by a rounded vowel or an unrounded vowel, listeners tend to hear /s/ or /ʃ/, respectively [104]. The effect occurs with synthetic stimuli and also when naturally spoken phonemes are concatenated with synthetic ones. Similar perceptual shifts along stop continua occur when a stop ambiguous between /t/ and /k/ is preceded by either /s/ or /ʃ/ [105] and when a stop ambiguous between /d/ and /g/ is preceded by /l/ or /r/ [106]. These effects exhibit a form of *perceptual compensation* for the presumed coarticulation that occurs in natural speech production. For example, in the context of a rounded vowel, natural fricative spectra are shifted lower, and listeners expect to hear lower-frequency energy in a fricative adjacent to a rounded vowel; thus they shift their perceptual boundary so as to hear /s/ with more low-frequency energy than occurs next to an unrounded vowel. The fricative-vowel effect shrinks in proportion to the temporal separation between frication offset and ensuing vowel onset and also varies with the presumed sex of the synthetic voice, both of which imply that listeners use tacit knowledge of speech production during speech perception. These phenomena could be due to auditory contrast or nonsimultaneous masking, but a phonetic interpretation is more likely, in which the listener integrates disparate acoustic cues (frication noise and formant transitions) in phoneme identification.

5.5.3 Perception of Voicing in Obstruents

The linguistic feature *voiced* is used to distinguish the voiced class of obstruents /b,d,g,v,δ,z,ʒ/ from the unvoiced class /p,t,k,f,δ,s,ʃ/. For obstruents, *voiced* does not simply mean "having vocal cord vibration." Phonemic perception of the voiced/unvoiced distinction in stops and fricatives is correlated with a diverse set of acoustic properties. Fricatives provide the simpler case, with voicing usually perceived when the speech signal is periodic during the steady portion of the fricative. If vocal cord vibration produces enough energy at the fundamental and low harmonics (the *voice bar* on spectrograms), voiced fricatives are heard, at least for syllable-initial fricatives. Voicing perception in syllable-final fricatives (which have weaker periodicity) involves multiple cues; e.g., the duration of frication affects its voicing perception: shorter fricatives tend to be heard as voiced, and vice versa [107].

5.5.3.1 Syllable-final obstruents. One voicing cue for both stops and fricatives in syllable-final position is the duration of the preceding vowel. Given that many syllable-final "voiced" obstruents have little vocal cord vibration, the primary cues may be durational: voicing is perceived more often when the prior vowel is long and has a higher durational proportion of formant steady state to final formant transition [108]. The ratio of vowel duration to consonant duration in VCs has also been proposed to distinguish final consonant voicing since final voiced obstruents tend to be shorter than unvoiced counterparts; however, the data favor consonant and vowel durations as independent voicing cues [109]. It is not the physical duration of a preceding vowel that determines consonant voicing, but rather its perceived length; e.g., equal-duration vowels are perceived to be longer when F0 varies rather than remains monotonic [110]. Thus, with VC durations ambiguous as to consonant voicing, voiced identifications increase with F0 variation during a synthesized vowel [111]. Because F0 patterns do not vary consistently before voiced and unvoiced stops, caution must be used in generalizing this last result (and others) to natural speech.

English stop voicing perception is complex, in part because most voiced stops consist primarily of silence during the closure interval, with the voice bar much less in evidence than in other languages. Therefore, the obvious cue of vocal cord vibration is less available to distinguish stop voicing. However, even in other languages where voiced stops are truly "voiced" (vocal cord vibration throughout the oral closure), the situation remains far from simple. In French vowel+stop sequences, the duration of the closure, the duration and intensity of voicing, and the intensity of the release burst, as well as the preceding vowel duration, all affect voicing perception [112].

While most English voiced stops show little periodic structure, in VC contexts the glottal vibration in the vowel usually continues into the initial part of a voiced stop, whereas voicing terminates abruptly with oral tract closure in unvoiced stops. This difference in voice offset timing appears to be a primary cue to voicing perception in final English stops [113]. When a naturally produced syllable ending in a voiced stop has enough "voicing" removed (by substituting silence for periods of the speech signal) around the VC boundary, the corresponding unvoiced stop is heard. Since removing glottal periods from the vowel effectively lowers the durational V:C ratio, such an effect cannot be due to the primary cue of duration noted above. Rather, acoustic analyses of the stimuli reveal that unvoiced stops tend to be heard with high F1 offset frequencies and short amplitude–decay times, suggesting rate of voicing offset as the crucial cue.

5.5.3.2 Syllable-initial stops.

Voicing in syllable-initial stops involves interactions between temporal factors (VOT and the timing of the F1 transition) and spectral aspects (intensity and shape of the F1 transition). It has been argued [114] that the diverse acoustic cues available for voicing perception in stops are all due to laryngeal timing with respect to the oral tract closure and that the listener integrates the varied acoustic cues into one voicing decision, based on the implicit knowledge that they arise from a common articulatory source. The primary cue seems to be VOT: a rapid voicing onset after stop release leads to voiced stop perception, while a long VOT cues an unvoiced stop. Along a continuum of VOT, the voiced–unvoiced boundary is near 30 ms, with shifts of about 5–10 ms lower or higher for labial or velar stops, respectively [101]. Thus perception appears to compensate for production: in natural speech, VOT decreases with the advancement of place of articulation, and in perception longer VOTs are needed to hear an unvoiced stop as the constriction moves farther back.

A secondary cue to initial stop voicing is the value of F1 at voicing onset [115]: lower values cue voiced stops. This again follows speech production since F1 rises in CV transitions as the oral cavity opens from stop constriction to vowel articulation. Thus, F1 rises during the aspiration period and is higher at voicing onset after longer VOTs. The duration and extent of the F1 transition significantly affect stop voicing perception [116], whereas the behavior of the higher formants has little effect. Natural stop+vowel sequences do not always have a clear boundary between the end of aspiration and the onset of voicing (e.g., voicing often starts in F1 while higher formants still have aperiodic structure). Confining periodic energy to the fundamental for the first 30 ms of voicing has little effect on perceived stop voicing, but more voiced stops are heard if voicing starts simultaneously in all formants (rather than just in F1) [117].

A third cue to stop voicing is aspiration intensity. The perceptual salience of VOT may not reside in duration but in integration of aspiration energy. Listeners may utilize VOT differences as voicing cues, not in terms of timing judgments but rather via detection of presence vs absence of aperiodic aspiration [33]. Many psychoacoustic experiments note the salience of energy integrated over time; e.g., equally loud stimuli can trade duration for amplitude, with integrated energy being the perceptually relevant parameter. Thus, listeners may judge a stop to be unvoiced if they hear enough aspiration after stop release rather than using direct temporal cues.

Finally, when the primary acoustic cues to voicing are ambiguous, spectra and F0 can affect voicing perception in CV sequences [90]. Recall that, when an obstruent is released into a vowel, F0 starts relatively high if the consonant is unvoiced, and low if voiced. When VOT is ambiguous as to voicing in synthetic stimuli, rising F0 at stop release cues stop voicing, and falling F0 signals an unvoiced stop [118]. However, the F0 cue is easily overridden by VOT in normal circumstances.

The secondary voicing cues trade with VOT; e.g., changes in F1 onset values can shift the voiced–unvoiced boundary along a VOT continuum. Before open vowels, a 1 Hz change in F1 onset is perceptually equivalent to a 0.11 ms change in VOT [119]. Similarly, a VOT decrease of 0.43 ms is equivalent to a 1 dB increase in aspiration intensity [120]. This sensory integration of spectral and temporal cues to make phonetic decisions does not appear to be restricted to speech sounds [121].

5.6 DURATION AS A PHONEMIC CUE

Hearing utterances of syllables in isolation, listeners can distinguish phonemes with very short stimuli. If normal isolated vowels are cut back so that only the first few periods are presented, listeners can identify (above chance levels) tongue advancement and height features based on the first 10 ms alone, but they need 30 ms to distinguish the tense–lax feature [122]. The stop place of articulation in CVs can be identified based on the first 10 ms after release, but the voicing feature requires about 22 ms (voicing in velar stops requires the longest duration, 29 ms). It appears that longer portions of the stimuli are needed to discriminate certain phonemes, namely those whose distinguishing features involve timing as well as spectra: duration is crucial for the tense–lax vowel distinction and voicing in stops (VOT), but tongue advancement (place of articulation) and height can be specified by the spectra of the first 10 ms. Trading relationships may exist in durational perception at other levels [123].

5.6.1 Manner Cues

Unlike some languages (e.g., Swedish and Japanese), English does not use duration directly as a phonemic cue, in the sense that phonemes differ only by duration and not spectrally. Nonetheless, with synthetic speech, duration alone can cause phonemic distinctions, which suggests that duration can be a secondary phonemic cue utilized when a primary cue is ambiguous; e.g., in the word *rabid*, the /b/ closure duration is normally short; if the closure is artificially prolonged, *rapid* is heard. The tendency for unvoiced sounds to be longer than voiced sounds apparently affects perception. Since the stop follows the stressed vowel here, VOT is a reduced voicing cue, being short in both voiced and unvoiced cases. Thus, the cues for voicing may be found in the durational balance between the stop and the preceding vowel [124].

Similarly, when enough silence is added after /s/ in *slit*, it sounds like *split*. In normal /sp/ clusters, the /p/ release is weak; thus the lack of a burst (in the extended version of *s_lit*) is insufficient to deter the perception of a stop. Normally a short, silent interval (about 10 ms) intervenes between the cessation of frication in a fricative+sonorant cluster and the onset of voicing. When this duration exceeds about 70 ms, the listener apparently decides that the interval is too long for a transition between phonemes and must itself be a stop phoneme. Silence duration interacts in a trading relation with spectral cues in signaling the presence of a stop here. The amount of duration necessary to hear a stop is greater if the formant transitions are more appropriate for *slit* than for *split* (conflicting cues) [125]. Stop duration also trades with (a) burst amplitude and duration in *say–stay* continua (e.g., *stay* is heard with a very short stop closure if the stop release burst is strong enough) [126] and (b) glottal pulsing in the perception of voicing in stops [127].

5.6.2 Place Cues

An apparent secondary cue for place perception in stop consonants in stressed CV contexts is the duration of VOT. Due to coarticulation, labial stops have the shortest VOTs, while velar stops have the longest, with bigger differences (of about 40 ms) occurring in unvoiced stops. Labial stops permit tongue movement in anticipation of the ensuing vowel, which allows more rapid voicing onset since the vocal tract attains a proper vowel configuration more rapidly than for alveolars or velars. The velars have the longest VOTs, presumably because the tongue body moves slowly (compared to the tongue tip, used in alveolars) and because the tongue body usually must move for an ensuing vowel.

Place perception in stops is affected not only by the duration of VOT but also by closure duration in some cases. Stop closures tend to be longer for labials than for alveolars or velars, and the listener's tacit knowledge of this production fact appears to affect perception: longer stops are biased toward labial perception [92]. As another example, if a silence interval of 100–200 ms occurs between two synthetic vowels and formant transitions are ambiguous as to place, listeners tend to hear two separate stops (i.e., VCCV) [128]. If the initial VC transition specifies one stop, an ambiguous CV transition is perceived as a different stop, presumably because the listener expects two different stop consonants with a silence interval of sufficient duration between two vowels. If the silence interval is short ($\leqslant 25$ ms), the CV transition dominates in place perception of one stop [129]. If the silence is greater than 200 ms, a pause instead tends to be perceived.

5.6.3 Speaking Rate Effects

In virtually all situations where duration can function as a phonemic cue, its effect is relative to speaking rate [10, 130]. Segment durations both before and after a given phoneme affect that phoneme's recognition when duration is a critical identification cue [131]. For example, with an acoustic continuum /ba/–/wa/ where the duration of the initial formant transitions cues the manner of articulation, longer transitions are needed to hear /wa/ as the syllable is lengthened [132]. As syllable duration is increased from 80 to 300 ms, the /b/–/w/ boundary increases from transitions of 28 ms to 44 ms. Listeners apparently judge the abruptness of the transition in relation to speaking rate or syllable duration, assuming slower average transitions with slower speaking rates. The effect is nonlinear, most likely because duration is not the only cue to phonemic identity and because rate changes do not affect all speech events equally. The effect also appears to be local; i.e., the durations of adjacent phonemes have much more perceptual effect than phonemes more distant [133]. Finally, the effect tends to shrink under conditions closely approximating natural speech [134].

Coarticulation and formant undershoot are dependent on timing, with the percentage of time that vowels have steady-state formants decreasing as speaking rate increases. Listeners apparently compensate for coarticulation in interpreting different formant patterns in CVC contexts (with different consonants) as the same vowel. They also seem to compensate for speaking rate since identical syllables preceded by syllables spoken at different rates cause varying vowel perception [135, 136]. In hearing a syllable excised from a sentence, listeners assume the syllable was spoken in isolation with relatively long duration and little presumed formant undershoot, and thus they tend to misidentify the vowel. If the syllable is placed in a context where the speaking rate is different from the original utterance, listeners interpret the inserted syllable accordingly, judging the vowel duration and amount of formant undershoot in proportion to what would normally occur at the new speaking rate. Since duration is a secondary cue to vowel perception (i.e., some vowels with ambiguous formant cues are heard as tense if long and lax if short [136]), it is not clear whether listeners normalize vowel perception based on anticipated duration or formant undershoot.

Similar speaking rate effects occur in consonant perception. If the closure duration of /p/ in *topic* is lengthened, listeners hear *top pick*, but the boundary threshold is a function of the contextual speaking rate. At faster rates, a given rendition is more likely heard as *top pick* [137]. Similar results occur for *slit–split* [133]. The VOT boundary for voicing perception in stop+vowel syllables can be shifted by up to 20 ms through manipulations of speaking rate [138]; similar effects occur with the duration of the burst release [139]. Voicing perception is most affected by the durations of the immediately adjacent context of the stop and can be cued equally through the steady-state durations of neighboring vowels or the durations of consonant transitions [138]. Furthermore, the effect of preceding context decreases as a function of the duration of any silence gap that occurs just prior to the stop. Finally, the phonemic effect of speaking rate is primarily due to the articulation rate (syllables per second) rather than the proportion of time spent in pauses, even though both factors contribute to the overall perception of speaking rate [132].

Compensations for speaking rate are not always straightforward. The distinction between fricative and affricate (e.g., *shop, chop*) is cued by the duration of frication, the duration of any preceding silence, and onset characteristics of the noise [32]. A normal trading relationship is found between the duration of silence and frication: long frication tends to cue a fricative, while long silence cues an affricate [140]. When contextual speaking rate is varied, however, more silence is needed to hear the affricate at faster rates. One possible explanation is that, as speaking rate changes, frication duration normally changes more than silence duration, and the listener perceptually compensates for the overall effect of rate and also uses inherent knowledge of which acoustic segments vary more or less with rate changes. Silence duration may be perceived differently when cueing a manner distinction rather than a voicing distinction.

5.7 INTONATION: PERCEPTION OF PROSODY

Thus far this chapter has concentrated on how listeners perceive and discriminate individual sounds. Another important aspect of speech perception concerns prosody, whose domain of variation extends beyond the phoneme into units of syllables, words, phrases, and sentences. The perception of rhythm, intonation, and stress patterns helps the listener understand the speech message by pointing out important words and by cueing logical breaks in the flow of an utterance. The basic functions of prosody are to segment and to highlight. Cues in rhythm and intonation patterns notify the listener of major syntactic boundaries, which help one to mentally process speech units smaller than the entire sentence. The alternation of stressed and unstressed syllables identifies the words that the speaker considers important to understand the speech message and also helps in word comprehension (via placement of lexical stress).

Besides segmenting utterances, prosody signals other aspects of syntactic structure. In many languages, a question requesting a yes/no answer from a listener ends with an intonation rise. There are usually cues in the choice of words or word order that also signal that the utterance is a question (e.g., subject–verb inversion: "*Has Joe* studied?"). However, sometimes the only cue lies in the intonation (e.g., "Joe has studied?"). Intonation can also signal whether (a) a clause is main or subordinate, (b) a word functions as a vocative or an appositive, (c) the utterance (or a list of words) is finished.

While prosody usually helps a listener segment utterances perceptually, it can also serve as a continuity guide in noisy environments. This *prosodic continuity* function is very useful when there are several competing voices and the listener attempts to follow a specific voice. Experiments with two equal-amplitude voices have shown that listeners use intonation continuity and separation of pitch to follow one voice [141]. Even if two voices are presented binaurally through earphones and periodically switched between ears, listeners find it easiest to concentrate on one voice if its F0 range differs from the other voice and if the F0 contour is reasonably smooth (especially at the times when the voices switch between ears). Aspects of phase also seem to play a role in identifying simultaneous vowels [59].

Prosody also provides cues to the state of the speaker; attitudes and emotions are primarily signaled through intonation. F0 and amplitude patterns vary with emotions [142], emotions often raise F0 and amplitude levels and their variability [143, 144], increased F0 range sounds more "benevolent" [145], and emotions (e.g., anger, sorrow, and fear) cause changes in F0, timing, articulation precision, average speech spectrum, and waveform regularity of successive pitch periods [146, 147].

Prosody is so important to normal speech perception that communication can occur even with severely distorted segmentals [148]: if speech is spectrally rotated so that high-frequency energy appears at low frequency and vice versa, segmental information is effectively destroyed. Nonetheless, subjects can converse under such conditions by exploiting the preserved aspects of F0, duration, and amplitude.

5.7.1 Stress: Lexical and Sentential

There are two levels of stress in speech: lexical (word) stress, and sentential (phrase) stress. At the word level, one syllable in each word is inherently marked to receive stress, but only certain of these syllables in each utterance (i.e., those in words with sentential stress) actually receive prosodic variations that perceptually cue stress. In many languages, one syllable in each polysyllabic word pronounced in isolation receives more emphasis than the others; this syllable is considered to be lexically stressed (e.g., "comp*u*ter"). (For long words, there may also be another stressed syllable with secondary stress.) The correct lexical stress pattern is as important to the identification of a spoken word as the use of the proper sequence of phonemes. A speaker with a foreign accent often misplaces lexical stress, which may make words with the same sequence of phonemes sound entirely alien to native listeners. In some languages, lexical stress is completely predictable; e.g., every word in French is stressed on its final syllable. Other languages have tendencies toward stress on a certain syllable position (e.g., the first syllable in English) but have no fixed pattern in general.

When spoken as an isolated "word" or in a simple list of words, each lexically stressed syllable has the acoustic cues leading to stress perception. However, in normal utterances the speaker selects a subset of words to highlight and does not stress the others (whose lexically stressed syllables then are prosodically very similar to the non–lexically stressed syllables). Typically, the speaker stresses words that provide *new information* to the listener, in the sense that the listener must pay most attention to words least likely to be anticipated from prior conversational context. When speakers attempt to make a contrast with some prior concept, they stress the relevant words, sometimes to the extent of stressing syllables normally considered not lexically stressed (e.g., "I said *in*volve, not *re*volve!").

5.7.2 Acoustic Correlates of Stress

Stress perception follows the perceived attributes of pitch, loudness, length, and articulation precision. For each of these four perceptual features there is a corresponding acoustic correlate: F0, amplitude, duration, and *vowel timbre*, respectively. Vowel timbre (or spectrum) is not always included as a suprasegmental since it directly relates to segmental or phoneme perception, but it has an indirect effect on stress perception (e.g., stress tends to raise energy more at higher frequencies [149]).

The mapping between physical acoustics and perceived prosody is neither linear nor one-to-one among the four features; e.g., variations in F0 are the most direct cause of pitch perception, but amplitude and duration also affect pitch. In vowels, spectral content has a slight pitch effect: at the same F0 and intensity, low vowels yield about 2% higher pitch than high vowels [150]. Pitch varies monotonically with F0, but the mapping is closer to logarithmic than linear [151]; similar comments hold for length and loudness. F0 is often reported in Hz (linear scale) or tones (logarithmic; 12 semitones = 1 tone = an octave), but a more accurate measure is the *ERB-rate* scale (e.g., syllables tend to be heard as equally prominent with F0 movements that are equivalent on this scale [152]).

In comparing two phonemically identical syllables, one is heard as more stressed than the other if it has higher amplitude, longer duration, higher or more varied F0, and/or formants farther away from average values. While one usually thinks of stress as binary (i.e., a syllable is stressed or unstressed), stress is actually a relative feature along a continuum. Listeners can discriminate many levels of stress, in the sense that they can order a set of several syllables from least to most stressed, by making repeated pairwise comparisons. On isolated presentation, however, listeners seem unable to consistently group syllables into more than three stress classes (i.e., unstressed, weakly stressed, and strongly stressed).

Stress cannot be heard on a time scale smaller than that of the syllable (e.g., one cannot stress only a vowel or a consonant, but rather the entire syllable containing a vowel and its adjacent consonants). Nonetheless, the vowel likely contributes most to stress perception since it generally occupies the largest durational part of the syllable, forms the loudest component, and is voiced (thus having pitch). During a syllable, there are many ways to vary F0, duration, and amplitude, thereby leading to a complex relationship between stress and its acoustic correlates. Which of the correlates is most important for stress and how they trade in cases of conflicting cues are questions of interest.

English has certain words that are identical phonemically but that function as different parts of speech depending on which syllable is stressed (e.g., "*ex*port," noun; "ex*port*," verb). (This follows a trend toward nouns having their first syllable lexically stressed and verbs their last.) Experiments with synthetic speech can control all aspects other than F0, amplitude, and duration in exploring how stress is related to these acoustic features [153–156]. Other studies examine natural speech for noun–verb pairs [157, 158], nonsense CVCV words [159], sentences [160, 161], and even paragraphs [162]. Due to the diversity of experiments, it is difficult to compare results, but the consensus is that F0 is most important for stress in English, that duration is secondary, and that amplitude ranks third. (Vowel timbre has rarely been systematically tested as a stress correlate, other than to note that F1 and F2 in vowels tend toward their average values—the middle of the vowel triangle—as the vowels become less stressed [158].) This ranking was determined by testing the strength of each cue in the presence of conflicting cues (e.g., *export* was heard as a noun when the first syllable had high F0, even though the second syllable was long and loud). Typically, F0, duration, and amplitude are measured from both noun and verb versions of the words, and then each parameter is allowed to vary over its range between the two cases. The test cases in other languages are, of course, different, but for languages that admit syllables of varying stress, the acoustic correlates are quite similar to those for English [151]. F0 change, rather than high F0 [159], is a more likely indicator of stress across languages, especially in cases like Danish, in which a stressed syllable immediately *follows* an F0 fall [163]. Upward obtrusions in F0 are heard as more stressed than downward movements [155]. English listeners tend to hear utterance-initial syllables more often as stressed, probably due to an implicit F0 rise at the start of each utterance [164].

One problem with measuring the relationship between F0 and stress is the many possibilities for F0 contours during a syllable. While each phone in a syllable has only a single duration, F0 in naturally spoken phones is not limited to a simple average value, but can have patterns as complex as rise+fall+rise (each with a different range) within a single vowel. In comparing syllables with level F0 patterns, the one with the higher F0 is perceived as more stressed, but changing F0 usually invokes more stress perception than flat F0, even when the average F0 over the syllable is lower than the flat F0 contour. A F0 rise early in a syllable cues stress better than a late rise [165].

Another difficulty in these experiments involves the inherent values for F0, amplitude, and duration, which vary phonemically as well as with the position of a phoneme in the utterance. Each phoneme has its own inherent average duration and intensity. Vowels have more amplitude and duration than consonants; low vowels have more intensity than high vowels; nonstrident fricatives are weaker than strident fricatives, etc. Thus in synthesizing a word like *export*, one cannot give each phoneme the same duration and amplitude without rendering the speech unnatural; e.g., vowels such as /ɑ/ and /i/ can sound equally loud even though their intensities are quite different [166]. F0 also varies phonemically in stressed syllables: high vowels have higher F0 than low vowels (by about 5–10 Hz), and in CV contexts F0 in the vowel starts higher if the consonant is unvoiced than if it is voiced.

Phoneme position is important for F0, duration, and amplitude. The tendency for F0 to fall gradually throughout an utterance spoken in isolation (the case for most prosodic experiments) affects perception [167]. Syllable-initial consonants tend to be longer than syllable-final consonants [168]. Amplitude tends to fall off during the final syllable of an utterance [169], which can especially affect short utterances (e.g., two-syllable words).

A technique called *reiterant speech* can eliminate much of the phonemic variation in the analysis of intonation [170]. A speaker thinks of a sentence and pronounces it with its proper intonation while replacing all syllables with repetitions of one syllable, e.g., /mɑ/. Instead of pronouncing a sentence like "Mary had a little lamb," the speaker says "Mama ma ma mama ma," with the rhythm and stress of the original sentence. This enables the analysis of F0, duration, and amplitude, based on stress and syntactic phenomena, without the interference of phonemic effects [171]. A major (and risky) assumption here is that prosody is unaffected when pronouncing one sentence while thinking of another, however closely related they may be.

5.7.3 Perception of Syntactic Features

As the domain of analysis increases from syllables and words to phrases and sentences, the perceptual effects of prosody shift from the highlighting effects of stress to syntactic features. The primary function of prosody in these larger linguistic units lies in aiding the listener to segment the utterance into small phrasal groups, which simplifies mental processing and ultimate comprehension. Monotonic speech (i.e., lacking F0 variation) without pauses usually contains enough segmental information so a listener can understand the message, but it is fatiguing to listen to. Since the objective of speech communication is to facilitate the transfer of information from speaker to listener, the speaker usually varies rhythm and intonation to help the listener identify major syntactic structures.

5.7.3.1 Segmentation.   In normal sentential utterances, the speaker develops a rhythm of stressed and unstressed syllables. Certain languages (e.g., English and German) have been called *stressed-timed* because stressed syllables tend to occur at regular time intervals. Other languages (e.g., French and Japanese) are *syllable-timed* because each syllable tends to have equal duration. In both cases, the phenomenon is more perceptual than acoustical since physical measurements of duration vary considerably from the proposed isochronies [172]. The production regularity may exist not at the acoustic level but at the articulatory level, in terms of muscle commands for stressed syllables coming at regular intervals [27]. Nonetheless, there are acoustic differences between the two types of languages: stress-timed languages significantly reduce the durations of unstressed syllables compared to stressed ones, while syllable-timed languages do so to a much lesser extent.

The rhythm, whether stress-timed or syllable-timed, is often interrupted at major syntactic boundaries, as well as when the speaker hesitates. In many languages the speaking rate (measured in phonemes/s) slows down just prior to a major syntax break, whether or not a pause occurs at the break [173]. *Prepausal lengthening* of the last one or two syllables in a syntactic group is usually greater if a pause actually follows, but the lengthening itself is often sufficient to signal a break in rhythm to a listener. In English, major syntactic boundaries are usually cued by F0 as well. At sentence-internal boundaries, F0 often rises briefly on the syllable immediately prior to the break. Such short rises (on the order of 10–30 Hz for a typical male voice) are called *continuation rises* [174, 175] because they signal the listener that the sentence has not finished and that the speaker does not wish to be interrupted.

Finally, most languages vary F0, duration, and amplitude at the end of an utterance. The last few syllables typically are lengthened relative to the rest of the utterance, and the last few phonemes frequently have diminishing amplitude. F0 usually falls, often sharply, at the end of most sentences, to the lowest value in the entire utterance. The depth of the F0 fall is often correlated with the perception of *finality*. Exceptions occur when the speaker is ready to say something else and, in the case of yes/no questions, where F0 instead rises rapidly on the last word in the sentence, often to the highest level in the utterance. In perceptual experiments with synthetic speech, listeners associate low and falling F0 with declarative statements, high and rising F0 with yes/no questions, and level terminal F0 with talking to oneself (when speaker and listener are the same, the need for intonational syntax cues diminishes!) [176, 177].

5.7.3.2 Resolving syntactic ambiguity.   One common paradigm to establish some relationships between syntax and intonation concerns syntactically ambiguous sentences, having words phonemically identical yet with different meanings depending on intonation. Examples are "The good flies quickly passed/past" (is *flies* a noun or a verb?) and "They fed her dog biscuits" (did she or her dog eat?). Such situations are usually resolved by conversational context, but these sentences provide a viable method to evaluate the segmentation effects of intonation. Inherently ambiguous coordinate constructions also have been investigated, e.g., "Sam and Joe or Bob went" (did one or two people go?) and "A plus B times C" (which comes first: multiplication or addition?). Since English allows many words to act as both adjective and noun, many three-word phrases can also be ambiguous (e.g., "light house keeper"). In all these cases, the ambiguity can be resolved through segmentation; placement of a perceptual break through intonation suffices [178]. A break located before or after *flies* or *dog* will decide whether *good flies* and *dog biscuits* are syntactic units; likewise for *Joe, B,* and *house* in the examples above. The assumptions are that normal rhythm and intonation act to group words into logical phrasal units and that interruptions in the prosody will override the default groupings, forcing perceived boundaries at intonation junctures.

F0, duration, and amplitude each serves as a boundary marker in this fashion [179]. Duration is the most reliable cue [180, 181], in the form of pauses and prepausal lengthening, which often occur at major syntactic breaks. Insertion of 150 ms pauses is sufficient to shift the perception from one syntactic interpretation to another. From a rhythmic point of view, an English utterance consists of similar-duration *feet*, which are the intervals between the successive onsets of stressed vowels. When a foot containing a potential boundary is lengthened (whether by pause insertion, prepausal lengthening, or lengthening of other phonemes) in ambiguous sentences, listeners tend to hear a break [182].

Amplitude is a less reliable boundary cue. Its use as a boundary cue appears related to stress: part of a natural juncture cue is often an increase in stress on the last word prior to the break. This word normally has longer duration and larger F0 movement, which raise its stress. Amplitude tends to rise a few decibels just prior to a major syntactic break and then drop down a few decibels right after the break. However, when F0 and duration cues are neutral or in conflict with this amplitude cue, boundary perception is weak.

Ambiguities concerning word boundary placement are less consistently marked and make less use of F0 movement than other syntactic cases. For example, *a name* vs *an aim* or *gray tie* vs *great eye* are phonemically identical but can be resolved through intonation juncture cues [183]. Duration again seems to be the primary cue, with longer (and stronger) consonants at potential word boundaries suggesting that the consonant follows the boundary, and vice versa. Spectral differences can also be prominent here: word boundaries appear to affect formant transitions in complex fashion. In the latter example pair above, how strongly the /t/ is released is a strong cue to the word boundary since word-final plosives are often unreleased.

Sometimes syntactic ambiguity can be resolved using stress alone. In sentences of the form "John likes Mary more than Bill," *Bill* can act as either the subject of a deleted phrase ("Bill likes Mary") or the object ("John likes Bill"). The interpretation can be shifted by stressing *John* or *Mary*, respectively [184]. Listeners tend to hear a parallel structure and assume that the deleted words were unstressed; e.g., if *John* is stressed, listeners assume that *John* and *Bill* are from parallel positions in successive clauses (subjects) and that *Mary* acts as the object of both clauses and has been deleted in the second clause since it is repeated information.

Since the syntactic effects of intonation occur over relatively broad speech domains, it has been difficult to construct simple controlled perceptual experiments. The few tests that have been done have varied widely in technique. Usually only duration is varied, by inserting pauses or linearly expanding phoneme durations on either side of a possible syntactic boundary. Since F0 and amplitude variations involve contours over time, they are typically replaced as whole patterns, using a vocoder. The effects of stress have been readily examined using two-syllable utterances, but the effects of syntax usually require longer sentences. Given the multiplicity of patterns available for F0, duration, and intensity over long sentences, much research remains to be done in understanding the relationships of syntax and intonation.

5.7.4 Perceptually Relevant Pitch Movements

Because of the complex relationship between F0 and linguistics, F0 has been virtually ignored in speech recognition systems, and most speech synthesizers have at best rudimentary F0 variations such as the declination line and obtrusions for stressed syllables. A major problem has been to determine what is perceptually relevant in the F0 contour, i.e., to separate the linguistic aspects of F0 movement from free variation having no perceptual effect on intelligibility or naturalness. For example, F0 contours can be smoothed (via lowpass filtering) to a large extent without perceptual effect [185]. Only gross F0 movements (e.g., large rises and falls) appear to be important perceptually, with listeners more sensitive to rises than falls [186]. Perception of the slope of an F0 contour may also be important since listeners can detect changes in slope as small as 12 Hz/s in synthetic vowels [187]. Pitch perception is most influenced by F0 during high-amplitude portions of an utterance (i.e., during the vowels), and F0 variations during consonants (which are often irregular) appear to be mostly disregarded [188]. F0 interruptions due to unvoiced consonants do not seem to have much effect on pitch perception: similar intonation is perceived whether F0 moves continuously through a voiced consonant or jumps during an unvoiced consonant [175].

Some Dutch researchers have attempted to model the infinite number of F0 contours by concatenations of short F0 patterns taken from a set of about 12 prototypes [175]. They found that large F0 movements are not perceived in certain contexts and suggest that listeners interpret intonation in terms of recognizable patterns or perceptual units. The declination effect appears to be important, even though most listeners are not conscious of declining pitch. The actual F0 contour can apparently be replaced without perceptual effect by a standard declination line with superimposed sharp rises and falls. F0 rises early in a syllable or falls late in a syllable correlated with perceived stress on the syllable, while late rises and early falls were heard as unstressed. A *hat pattern* can describe many syntactic phrases, in which F0 rises early on the first stressed syllable in a phrase, then declines slowly at a high level, and finally falls to a low level late in the last stressed syllable of the phrase.

5.8 OTHER ASPECTS OF SPEECH PERCEPTION (‡)

This chapter has discussed the major psychoacoustic aspects of phoneme and intonation perception as well as general models of speech perception. This last section describes additional topics that have not received as intense research attention.

5.8.1 Adaptation Studies

Speech perception is often analyzed in terms of thresholds, in which sounds with an acoustic aspect on one side of a physical boundary are perceived as being in one category while sounds on the other side are perceived differently. Such boundaries can be shifted temporarily by *selective adaptation*. A sound is repeatedly played to a listener; this adapting stimulus usually has some characteristics of the sounds whose threshold is being examined. For example, plosive voicing in English /tɑ/–/dɑ/ can be cued by VOT, with a threshold near 30 ms. If a listener hears many repetitions of /tɑ/ and then some stimuli along a

/tɑ/ − /dɑ/ continuum, the perceptual boundary typically shifts toward the adapting stimulus (e.g., the person will hear /dɑ/ more often due to the contrast with the adapting stimulus). Such a phenomenon is usually explained in terms of a fatiguing of linguistic feature detectors in the brain (see [24, 189] for opposing viewpoints, however). Selective adaptation must involve central, rather than peripheral, auditory processing because it occurs with adapting and test stimuli presented to different ears. Perceptual biases similar to those caused by selective adaptation are also found in *anchor* experiments, in which an anchor stimulus is heard more often than others, causing listeners to shift their normal perceptual frame of reference [190]. Clearly, listeners make perceptual judgments based on contextual contrasts in speech (e.g., accuracy in discriminating sounds in a foreign language depends on whether such sounds are contrastive in one's native language [191]).

5.8.2 Dichotic Studies

The auditory nerves for each ear are connected contralaterally to the opposite side of the brain. The right ear and left brain hemisphere perceive many speech sounds more accurately than the left ear. However, specialized speech processors are not exclusively found in the left hemisphere, nor is the *right ear advantage* a simple phenomenon restricted to speech. If speech in only one ear is masked by noise, the other ear compensates to keep intelligibility high.

Individual listeners show large variations in this phenomenon for a given sound, but groups of listeners on average demonstrate consistent patterns across several sounds [192]. Ear advantage is not affected by speech vs nonspeech, the overall duration of sequential sounds, or the presence of formant transitions. Rather, the bandwidth and complexity (in terms of the number of dynamic auditory dimensions) of the sounds, as well as the rate of change within the sound, affect ear advantage. Some studies have used dichotic presentation of speechlike stimuli to explore different levels of speech perception. Since some auditory processing occurs in each ear, while some happens only at higher levels (after the auditory nerves from each ear merge), and since phonetic processing probably occurs only in the brain, splitting apart speech sounds into separate stimuli in different ears is a viable technique for examining the hierarchy of sound perception. For example, how formant transitions in different ears merge into one perceptual speech image is in debate [193].

5.8.3 Phase Effects

The ear appears to be relatively insensitive to phase variations in the sound stimulus, as long as group delay variations are less than a few milliseconds [194]. Randomizing the phase angles in a short-time Fourier transform of speech has less perceptual effect than changing its amplitude spectrum. In particular, time-invariant linear phase transformations of an acoustic signal entering the inner ear cannot be heard. Many speech synthesizers take advantage of this phenomenon by using a simple excitation source whose harmonics all have zero phase. However, while time-invariant phase distortion is relatively unimportant perceptually, time-varying phase affects the naturalness of a speech signal [195], as evidenced by the lower quality of most synthetic speech.

When synthetic vowel-like stimuli with identical formants and harmonics but differing via phase in the time waveform are matched with natural vowels, different phonemes may be perceived if the formants are ambiguous between the two vowels [196]. Similarly, formant frequency glides typical of /ej/ and /uw/ (diphthongization) can be heard, without actual formant movement, when time structure is varied [197].

5.8.4 Word and Syllable Effects

That linguistic context and the effects of coarticulation are important in speech perception is evident from tests where words excised from normal conversations are played in isolation to listeners: only about half the words are identified without the supporting context [198]. (About 1 s of continuous speech is necessary to avoid perceptual degradation.) Listeners hear "what they want to hear" in cases where linguistic context does not assist perception [199]. Sentences in a noisy background are more easily understood if they make syntactic and semantic sense; thus adjacent words help identification of words in sentences [200, 201]. When certain phonemes in an utterance are replaced by noise bursts of corresponding amplitude and duration, listeners are unable to locate the timing of the noise intrusion and do not perceive that a phoneme is missing [202, 203]. Similarly, intelligibility of speech passed through two narrowband filters at widely spaced frequencies is good [204]. Such *phonemic restoration* [205] suggests that one can use context to "hear" phonemes not actually present, suppressing actual auditory input information.

When listeners are asked to indicate when they hear a specific phoneme, they react more quickly to target phonemes in words easily predicted from context. English, with its stressed syllables approximately rhythmically spaced, permits faster reaction times in stressed syllables than in unstressed ones, but only in sentences where the stressed syllables can be predicted from context [206]. Listeners are likely to focus their attention at rhythmic intervals on these anticipated stressed words, thus permitting a cyclic degree of attention, which is less perceptually demanding than constant attention to all words [207].

One theory proposes that words are perceived one at a time, with the recognition of each word locating the onset of the next one in the speech stream [208]. *Shadowing* experiments are cited in which subjects try to repeat what they hear as quickly as possible. Typical running delays of 270–800 ms suggest that listeners treat syllables or words as processing units [209]. These experiments support the perceptual importance of the start of the word, if one notes that mispronunciations are perceived more easily at the beginning than later in a word and that reaction times are faster to mispronunciations in later syllables within a word. Further evidence for syllables as perceptual units is found in reaction-time experiments where listeners respond more quickly to syllable than to phoneme targets, implying that phonemes are identified only after their syllable is recognized. Finally, speech alternated rapidly between ears over headphones may be disruptive to perception when switching occurs near the syllabic rate [210]. Although syllables and words appear to be important perceptual units, we most likely understand speech not word by word, but rather in phrasal units that exploit stress and prosodic structure [211].

5.8.5 Perception of Distorted Speech

Speech can be distorted in many ways, leading to loss of speech quality (in terms of lower intelligibility or naturalness, increased annoyance [212], or vocal roughness [213]). It was noted earlier that adding noise, bandpass filtering, or clipping the signal reduces the intelligibility of speech; Chapter 7 will examine the perception of speech under digital coding distortions. Degradations from noise or echos seem to be mostly due to less evident temporal envelope modulations, but distorted fine structure is also a factor [214]. Decreased perception due to loss of spectral detail (found in practice in some echoic or noise situations) has been explored by smearing formants: averaging across 250 Hz (as in wideband spectrograms) has little effect, but smearing across 700–2000 Hz is equivalent to a 13–16 dB loss [215]. Similarly, smearing that simulates a significant expansion of auditory filters primarily affects perception only in noise [216].

Normal conversation has a level around 60 dB, but increases by about 20 dB in shouted voice, where perceptual accuracy decreases. In a quiet background, intelligibility of isolated shouted words can decrease up to 13% [217]. The decrease reaches about 30% in noisy environments; noise must be lowered 10–15 dB for shouts to achieve the same intelligibility for normal voice. Most errors concern obstruent consonants that are relatively weak in shouts because shouting raises the amplitude of voiced sounds more than unvoiced sounds.

5.8.6 Speech Perception by the Handicapped

In evaluating the speech perception process, this chapter has assumed that the listener has normal hearing. If instead a listener has a hearing impairment, e.g., some loss of reception of certain frequencies of sound, then devices such as hearing aids may assist speech perception. (Gradual elevation of the speech reception threshold is normal in the aging process, up to 1 dB/yr [36].) When there is some auditory reception in the 300–3000 Hz range, a simple amplifier with gain matching the hearing loss suffices (although masking by the amplified sounds may cause side effects). If, however, some frequency range is entirely absent, aids may shift relevant speech energy to other frequencies within the remaining range of hearing [218]. This latter approach is not always successful since the user must adapt to new, unnatural sounds and learn to understand them as replacing normal perceived speech.

For the fully deaf, lipreading can be a method of receiving partial information about speech. Phoneme distinctions that rely on front–rear tongue position (e.g., velar–alveolar consonants, front vs rear vowels) are not easily discerned this way, however. Alternatively (and exclusively for the blind–deaf), tactile aids can transform speech into a three-dimensional display that can be felt [219]. Normally, a simple spectral display indicates the amount of speech energy within a small number of frequency bands, similar to a wideband spectrogram with a raised surface showing amplitude. A pitch detector may also be integrated into the display. Such spectral and prosodic information can also be displayed visually for the sighted deaf [220]. Finally, if adjacent to the talker, a blind–deaf person can feel the talker's face to obtain information such as lip and jaw movement, airflow, and laryngeal vibration [221].

5.9 CONCLUSION

While the basic aspects of speech psychoacoustics are well understood, many details remain to be explored for a complete model of speech perception. One indication of the state of our knowledge is the quality of synthetic speech generated by rule, which is usually intelligible but far from natural. Perception research has often been based on knowledge of human speech production and resulting formant models of synthesis. These models lead to a good understanding of first-order effects (i.e., primary acoustic cues to perception) but often leave secondary factors vague. Thus, much research into perception currently is investigating areas where production models are inadequate. In particular, the search for invariant cues to phoneme perception is active for voicing and place of articulation features. Since production models of coarticulation (and context effects in general) are less well advanced than models of isolated phone production, much perceptual research continues for the effects of context. Contextual effects beyond the syllable especially are still poorly understood; thus considerable research remains unfinished in the prosodic area, where intonation acts over long time spans. Compared to prosody, the relatively good understanding of phoneme perception reflects the fact that most phonemic cues are local (i.e., confined to a short section of the speech signal).

PROBLEMS

P5.1. Speech over telephone lines is limited to the 300–3300 Hz frequency band. What phonemes are distorted most? Explain, giving examples of confusions that would be expected among words over the telephone.

P5.2. Explain the difference between categorical and continuous perception. Give an example using stop consonants, describing a typical experiment and its results.

P5.3. Consider filtering speech with a bandpass filter, eliminating all energy below X Hz and above Y Hz.
   (a) What is the smallest range of frequencies (X, Y Hz) that would allow all English phonemes to be distinguished? Explain.
   (b) If $X = 1$ kHz and $Y = 2$ kHz, explain which phonemes would be most confused with one another.

P5.4. (a) Which phonemes are most easily confused with /b/? Explain.
   (b) If a two-formant synthetic vowel with F1 = 600 Hz and F2 = 1300 Hz is preceded by a short burst of noise, at what frequency should the noise be located to hear /b/, /d/, and /g/, respectively?
   (c) In natural speech, which acoustic features enable a listener to discriminate among /b/, /d/, and /g/?

P5.5. Models of speech perception vary in many ways:
   (a) What acoustic aspects of speech are considered most important?
   (b) How does timing affect the perception of phonemes?
   (c) Is the speech production process necessarily involved in perception?

P5.6. List acoustic cues useful for distinguishing voicing in prevocalic stops.

P5.7. Why is place perception less reliable than manner perception?

6

Speech Analysis

6.1 INTRODUCTION

Earlier chapters examined the production and perception of natural speech, and described speech-signal properties important for communication. Most applications of speech processing (e.g., coding, synthesis, recognition) exploit these properties to accomplish their tasks. This chapter describes how to extract such properties or features from a speech signal $s(n)$—a process called *speech analysis*. This involves a transformation of $s(n)$ into another signal, a set of signals, or a set of parameters, with the objective of simplification and data reduction. The relevant information in speech for different applications can often be expressed very compactly; e.g., a 10 s utterance (requiring 640,000 bits in basic coding format) typically contains about 120 seconds and 20–30 words (codable as text in a few hundred bits). In speech analysis, we wish to extract features directly pertinent for different applications, while suppressing redundant aspects of the speech. The original signal may approach optimality from the point of view of human perception, but it has much repetitive data when processed by computer; eliminating such redundancy aids accuracy in computer applications and makes phonetic interpretation simpler. We concentrate here on methods that apply to several applications; those that are particular to only one will be examined in later chapters.

For speech storage or recognition, eliminating redundant and irrelevant aspects of the speech waveform simplifies data manipulation. An efficient representation for speech recognition would be a set of parameters which is consistent across speakers, yielding similar values for the same phonemes uttered by various speakers, while exhibiting reliable variation for different phonemes. For speech synthesis, the continuity of parameter values in time is important to reconstruct a smooth speech signal; independent evaluation of parameters frame-by-frame is inadequate. Synthetic speech must replicate perceptually crucial properties of natural speech, but need not follow aspects of the original speech that are due to free variation.

This chapter investigates methods of speech analysis, both in the time domain (operating directly on the speech waveform) and in the frequency domain (after a spectral transformation of the speech). We want to obtain a more useful representation of the speech signal in terms of parameters that contain relevant information in an efficient format. Section 6.2 describes the tradeoffs involved in analyzing speech as a time-varying signal. Analyzers periodically examine a limited time range (*window*) of speech. The choice of duration and shape for the window reflects a compromise in time and frequency resolution. Accurate time resolution is useful for segmenting speech signals (e.g., locating phone boundaries) and for determining periods in voiced speech, whereas good frequency resolution helps to identify different sounds. Section 6.3 deals with time-domain analysis, and Section 6.4 with spectral analysis. The former requires relatively little calculation but is limited to simple speech measures, e.g., energy and periodicity, while spectral analysis takes more effort but characterizes sounds more usefully.

Simple parameters can partition phones into manner-of-articulation classes, but discriminating place of articulation requires spectral measures. We distinguish speech *parameters* that are obtained by simple mathematical rules but have relatively low information content (e.g., Fourier coefficients) and *features* that require error-prone methods but yield more compact speech representations (e.g., formants, F0). Many speech analyzers extract only parameters, thus avoiding controversial decisions (e.g., deciding whether a frame of speech is voiced or not). *Linear predictive analysis* does both: the major effort is to obtain a set of about 10 parameters to represent the spectral envelope of a speech signal, but a voicing (feature) decision is usually necessary as well. Section 6.5 is devoted to the analysis methods of linear predictive coding (LPC), a very important technique in many speech applications.

The standard model of speech production (a source exciting a vocal tract filter) is implicit in many analysis methods, including LPC. Section 6.6 describes another method to separate these two aspects of a speech signal, and Section 6.7 treats yet other spectral estimation methods. The excitation is often analyzed in terms of periodicity (Section 6.8) and amplitude, while variations in the speech spectrum are assumed to derive from vocal tract variations. Finally, Section 6.9 examines how continuous speech parameters can be derived from (sometimes noisy) raw data.

The analysis technique in this chapter can be implemented digitally, either with software (programs) or special-purpose hardware (microprocessors and chips). Analog processing techniques, using electronic circuitry, can perform most of the tasks, but digital approaches are prevalent because of flexibility and low cost. Analog circuitry requires specific equipment, rewiring, and calibration for each new application, while digital techniques may be implemented and easily modified on general-purpose computers. Analyses may exceed *real time* (where processing time does not exceed speech duration) on various computers, but advances in VLSI and continued research into more efficient algorithms will render more analyses feasible without computational delay.

6.2 SHORT-TIME SPEECH ANALYSIS

Speech is dynamic or time-varying: some variation is under speaker control, but much is random; e.g., a vowel is not truly periodic, due to small variations (from period to period) in the vocal cord vibration and vocal tract shape. Such variations are not under the active control of the speaker and need not be replicated for intelligibility in speech coding, but they make speech sound more natural. Aspects of the speech signal directly under speaker control (e.g., amplitude, voicing, F0, and vocal tract shape) and methods to extract related parameters from the speech signal are of primary interest here.

During slow speech, the vocal tract shape and type of excitation may not alter for durations up to 200 ms. Mostly, however, they change more rapidly since phoneme durations average about 80 ms. Coarticulation and changing F0 can render each pitch period different from its neighbor. Nonetheless, speech analysis usually assumes that the signal properties change relatively slowly with time. This allows examination of a *short-time window* of speech to extract parameters presumed to remain fixed for the duration of the window. Most techniques yield parameters averaged over the course of the time window. Thus, to model dynamic parameters, we must divide the signal into successive windows or *analysis frames*, so that the parameters can be calculated often enough to follow relevant changes (e.g., due to dynamic vocal tract configurations). Slowly changing formants in long vowels may allow windows as large as 100 ms without obscuring the desired parameters via averaging, but rapid events (e.g., stop releases) require short windows of about 5–10 ms to avoid averaging spectral transitions with steadier spectra of adjacent sounds.

6.2.1 Windowing

Windowing is multiplication of a speech signal $s(n)$ by a window $w(n)$, which yields a set of speech samples $x(n)$ weighted by the shape of the window. $w(n)$ may have infinite duration, but most practical windows have finite length to simplify computation. By shifting $w(n)$, we examine any part of $s(n)$ through the movable window (Figure 6.1).

Many applications prefer some speech averaging, to yield an output parameter contour (vs time) that represents some slowly varying physiological aspects of vocal tract movements. The amount of the desired smoothing leads to a choice of window size trading off three factors: (1) $w(n)$ short enough that the speech properties of interest change little within the window, (2) $w(n)$ long enough to allow calculating the desired parameters (e.g., if additive noise is present, longer windows can average out some of the random noise), (3) successive windows not so short as to omit sections of $s(n)$ as an analysis is periodically repeated. The last condition reflects more on the *frame rate* (number of times per second that speech analysis is performed, advancing the window periodically in time) than on window size. Normally, the frame rate is about twice the inverse of the $w(n)$ duration, so that successive windows overlap (e.g., by 50%), which is important in the common case that $w(n)$ has a shape that de-emphasizes speech samples near its edges (see Section 6.4).

The size and shape of $w(n)$ depend on their effects in speech anlaysis. Typically $w(n)$ is smooth, because its values determine the weighting of $s(n)$ and *a priori* all samples are equally relevant. Except at its edges, $w(n)$ rarely has sudden changes; in particular, windows

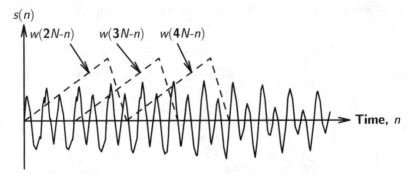

Figure 6.1 Speech signal $s(n)$ with three superimposed windows, offset from the time origin by $2N$, $3N$, and $4N$ samples. (An atypical asymmetric window is used for illustration.)

rarely contain zero- or negative-valued points since they would correspond to unutilized or phase-reversed input samples. The simplest common window has a rectangular shape $r(n)$:

$$w(n) = r(n) = \begin{cases} 1 & \text{for } 0 \leq n \leq N - 1 \\ 0 & \text{otherwise.} \end{cases} \qquad (6.1)$$

This choice provides equal weight for all samples, and just limits the analysis range to N consecutive samples. Many applications trade off window duration and shape, using larger windows than strictly allowed by stationarity constraints but then compensating by emphasizing the middle of the window (Figure 6.2); e.g., if speech is quasi-stationary over 10 ms, a 20 ms window can weight the middle 10 ms more heavily than the first and last 5 ms. Weighting the middle samples more than the edge relates to the effect that window shape has on the output speech parameters. When $w(n)$ is shifted to analyze successive frames of $s(n)$, large changes in output parameters can arise when using $r(n)$; e.g., a simple energy measure obtained by summing $s^2(n)$ in a rectangular window could have large fluctuations as $w(n)$ shifts to include or exclude large amplitudes at the beginning of each pitch period. If we wish to detect pitch periods, such variation would be desired, but more often the parameters of interest are properties of vocal tract shape, which usually vary slowly over several pitch periods. A common alternative to Equation (6.1) is the Hamming window, a raised cosine pulse:

$$w(n) = h(n) = \begin{cases} 0.54 - 0.46 \cos\left(\dfrac{2\pi n}{N-1}\right) & \text{for } 0 \leq n \leq N - 1 \\ 0 & \text{otherwise.} \end{cases} \qquad (6.2)$$

or the very similar Hanning window. Tapering the edges of $w(n)$ allows its periodic shifting (at the frame rate) along $s(n)$ without having effects on the speech parameters due to pitch period boundaries.

6.2.2 Spectra of Windows: Wide- and Narrow-band Spectrograms

While a window has obvious limiting effects in the time domain, its effects on speech spectra are also important. Due to its slowly varying waveform, $w(n)$ has a frequency response of a lowpass filter (Figure 6.3). As example windows, the smooth Hamming $h(n)$ concentrates more energy at low frequencies than does $r(n)$, which has abrupt edges. This

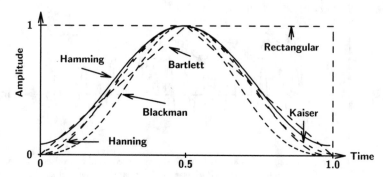

Figure 6.2 Common time windows, with durations normalized to unity.

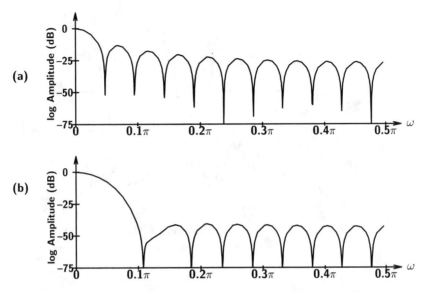

Figure 6.3 Magnitude of Fourier transforms for (a) rectangular window, (b) Hamming window.

concentration helps preserve the integrity of spectral parameters obtained from windowed signals, since $x(n) = s(n)w(n)$ corresponds to a convolution of spectra:

$$X(e^{j\omega}) = \frac{1}{2\pi} \int_{\theta=0}^{2\pi} S(e^{j\theta})W(e^{j(\omega-\theta)})d\theta. \tag{6.3}$$

To minimize distortion in the output spectral representation, $W(e^{j\omega})$ should have a limited frequency range and a smooth shape; e.g., an ideal lowpass filter (rectangular frequency pulse) strictly limits the frequency range and has a constant value. The output spectrum $X(e^{j\omega})$ is a smoothed version of $S(e^{j\omega})$, where each frequency sample is the average of its neighbors over a range equal to the bandwidth of the lowpass filter. A window with a rectangular spectrum has (usually undesirable) edge effects in frequency (as did $r(n)$ above for time); e.g., for voiced speech, $X(e^{j\omega})$ fluctuates as harmonics are included/excluded in the convolution process, depending on the interaction between the filter bandwidth and the speech F0.

An ideal lowpass filter is not a feasible window, due to its infinite duration. Practical windows however are flawed in not having strictly limited frequency ranges: each sample in $X(e^{j\omega})$ is not only the (desired) average of a range of $S(e^{j\omega})$ but also has contributions from many other frequencies. This undesirable behavior can be limited by concentrating most of $W(e^{j\omega})$ in a *main lobe* centered at zero frequency. Since the Hamming $H(e^{j\omega})$ is closer to an ideal lowpass filter than $R(e^{j\omega})$ (Figure 6.3), the former yields a better $X(e^{j\omega})$, more closely approximating the original $S(e^{j\omega})$. For a given window duration (a critical factor in computation and time resolution), however, $h(n)$ acts as a lowpass filter with twice the bandwidth of the rectangular $r(n)$ and thus smooths the speech spectrum over a range twice as wide (thus reducing the spectral detail) (Figure 6.4).

A properly smoothed output spectrum is often preferred; e.g., wideband spectrograms and formant detectors need spectral representations that smooth the fine structure of the

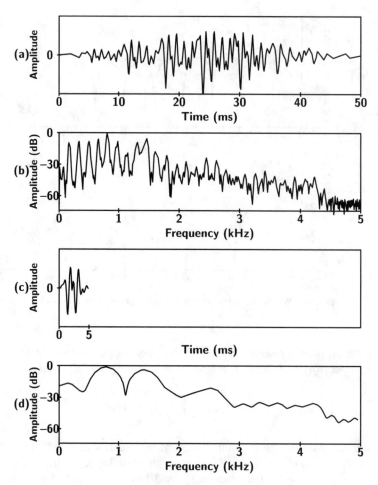

Figure 6.4 Time signals and spectra of a vowel: (a) signal multiplied by a 50 ms Hamming
window; (b) the corresponding spectrum (note that harmonic structure is
strongest at low frequencies); (c) signal multiplied by a 5 ms Hamming
window; (d) its corresponding spectrum.

harmonics while preserving formant structure, which varies more slowly with frequency. For
a given shape of window its duration is inversely proportional to its spectral bandwidth; the
choice of window duration trades off time and frequency resolution. Traditional *wideband
spectrograms* use a window of about 3 ms (fine time resolution, showing amplitude variations
within each pitch period), which corresponds to a bandwidth of 300 Hz and smooths the
harmonic structure (unless $F0 > 300$ Hz) (Figure 6.4).

    Narrowband spectrograms, on the other hand, use a window with a 45 Hz bandwidth
and thus a duration of about 20 ms. This allows a resolution of individual harmonics (since
$F0 > 45$ Hz) (Figure 6.4) but smooths the signal in time over a few pitch periods. The latter
spectral displays are good for F0 estimation, while wideband representations are better for
viewing vocal tract parameters, which can change rapidly and do not need fine frequency
resolution.

For windowing of voiced speech, a rectangular window with a duration of one pitch period (and centered on the period) produces an output spectrum close to that of the vocal tract impulse response, to the extent that each pitch period corresponds to such an impulse response. (This works best for low-F0 voices, where the pitch period is long enough to permit the signal to decay to low amplitude before the next vocal cord closure.) Unfortunately, it is often difficult to reliably locate pitch periods for such *pitch-synchronous* analysis, and system complexity increases if window size must change dynamically with F0. Furthermore, since most pitch periods are indeed shorter than the vocal tract impulse response, a one-period window truncates, resulting in spectral degradation.

For simplicity, most speech analyses use a fixed window size of longer duration, e.g., 25 ms. Problems of edge effects are reduced with longer windows; if the window is shifted in time without regard for pitch periods in the common *pitch-asynchronous* analysis, the more periods under the window the less the effects of including/excluding the large-amplitude beginning of any individual period. Windows well exceeding 25 ms smooth rapid spectral changes (relevant in most applications) too much. For F0 estimation, however, windows must typically contain at least two pitch periods; so pitch analysis uses a long window—often 30–50 ms.

Recent attempts to address the drawbacks of a fixed window size include more advanced frequency transforms (e.g., wavelets—see below), as well as simpler modifications to the basic DFT approach (e.g., the 'modulation spectrogram' [1], which emphasizes slowly varying speech changes around 4 Hz, corresponding to approximate syllable rates, at the expense of showing less rapid detail).

6.3 TIME-DOMAIN PARAMETERS

Analyzing speech in the time domain has the advantage of simplicity in calculation and physical interpretation. Several speech features relevant for coding and recognition occur in temporal analysis, e.g., energy (or amplitude), voicing, and F0. Energy can be used to segment speech in automatic recognition systems, and must be replicated in synthesizing speech; accurate voicing and F0 estimation are crucial for many speech coders. Other time features, e.g., zero-crossing rate and autocorrelation, provide inexpensive spectral detail without formal spectral techniques.

6.3.1 Signal Analysis in the Time Domain

Time-domain analysis transforms a speech signal into a set of parameter signals, which usually vary much more slowly in time than the original signal. This allows more efficient storage or manipulation of relevant speech parameters than with the original signal; e.g., speech is usually sampled at 6000–10,000 samples/s (to preserve bandwidth up to 3–5 kHz), and thus a typical 100 ms vowel needs up to 1000 samples for accurate representation. The information in a vowel relevant to most speech applications can be represented much more efficiently: energy, F0, and formants usually change slowly during a vowel. A parameter signal at 40–100 samples/s suffices in most cases (although 200 samples/s could be needed to accurately track rapid changes such as stop bursts). Thus, converting a speech waveform into a set of parameters can decrease sampling rates by two orders of magnitude. Capturing the relevant aspects of speech, however, requires several parameters sampled at the lower rate.

While time-domain parameters alone are rarely adequate for most applications, a combined total of 5–15 time- and frequency-domain parameters often suffice.

Most short-time processing techniques (in both time and frequency) produce parameter signals of the form

$$Q(n) = \sum_{m=-\infty}^{\infty} T[s(m)]w(n - m). \tag{6.4}$$

The speech signal $s(n)$ undergoes a (possibly nonlinear) transformation T, is weighted by the window $w(n)$, and is summed to yield $Q(n)$ at the original sampling rate, which represents some speech property (corresponding to T) averaged over the window duration. $Q(n)$ corresponds to a convolution of $T[s(n)]$ with $w(n)$. To the extent that $w(n)$ represents a lowpass filter, $Q(n)$ is a smoothed version of $T[s(n)]$.

Since $Q(n)$ is the output of a lowpass filter (the window) in most cases, its bandwidth matches that of $w(n)$. For efficient manipulation and storage, $Q(n)$ may be decimated by a factor equal to the ratio of the original sampled speech bandwidth and that of the window; e.g., a 20 ms window with an approximate bandwidth of 50 Hz allows sampling of $Q(n)$ at 100 samples/s (100:1 decimation if the original rate was 10,000 samples/s). As in most decimation operations, it is unnecessary to calculate the entire $Q(n)$ signal; for the example above, $Q(n)$ need be calculated only every 10 ms, shifting the analysis window 10 ms each time. For any signal $Q(n)$, this eliminates much (mostly redundant) information in the original signal. The remaining information is in an efficient form for many speech applications.

In addition to the common rectangular and Hamming windows, the Bartlett, Blackman, Hann, Parzen, or Kaiser windows [2, 3] are used to smooth aspects of speech signals, offering good approximations to lowpass filters while limiting window duration (see Figure 6.2). Most windows have finite-duration impulse responses (FIR) to strictly limit the analysis time range, to allow a discrete Fourier transform (DFT) of the windowed speech and to preserve phase. An infinite-duration impulse response (IIR) filter is also practical if its z transform is a rational function; e.g., a simple IIR filter with one pole at $z = a$ yields a recursion:

$$Q(n) = aQ(n - 1) + T[s(n)]. \tag{6.5}$$

IIR windows typically need less computation than FIR windows, but $Q(n)$ must be calculated at the original (high) sampling rate before decimating. (In real-time applications, a speech measure may be required at every sample instant anyway). FIR filters, having no recursive feedback, permit calculation of $Q(n)$ only for the desired samples at the low decimated rate. Most FIR windows of N samples are symmetric in time; thus $w(n)$ has linear phase with a fixed delay of $(N - 1)/2$ samples. IIR filters do not permit simple delay compensation.

6.3.2 Short-Time Average Energy and Magnitude

$Q(n)$ corresponds to short-time energy or amplitude if T in Equation (6.4) is a squaring or absolute magnitude operation, respectively (Figure 6.5). Energy emphasizes high amplitudes (since the signal is squared in calculating $Q(n)$), while the amplitude or magnitude measure avoids such emphasis and is simpler to calculate (e.g., with fixed-point arithmetic, where the dynamic range must be limited to avoid overflow). Such measures can help segment speech into smaller phonetic units, e.g., approximately corresponding to syllables or phonemes. The large variation in amplitude between voiced and unvoiced speech, as well as smaller variations between phonemes with different manners of articulation, permit segmentations based on energy $Q(n)$ in automatic recognition systems. For isolated word recognition,

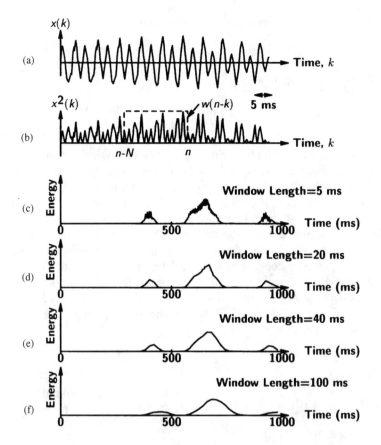

Figure 6.5 Illustration of the computation of short-time energy: (a) 50 ms of a vowel, (b)
the squared version of (a), with a superimposed window of length N samples
delayed n samples, (c–f) energy function for a 1 s utterance, using rectangular
windows of different lengths.

such $Q(n)$ can aid in accurate determination of the endpoints of a word surrounded by pauses.
In speech transmission systems that multiplex several conversations, this $Q(n)$ can help detect
the boundaries of speech, so that pauses need not be sent.

6.3.3 Short-Time Average Zero-crossing Rate (ZCR)

Normally, spectral measures of speech require a Fourier or other frequency transformation or a complex spectral estimation (e.g., linear prediction). For some applications, a simple
measure called the zero-crossing rate (ZCR) provides adequate spectral information at low
cost. In a signal $s(n)$ such as speech, a *zero-crossing* occurs when $s(n) = 0$, i.e., the waveform
crosses the time axis or changes algebraic sign. For narrowband signals (e.g., sinusoids), ZCR
(in zero-crossings/s) is an accurate spectral measure; a sinusoidal has two zero-cross-
ings/period, and thus its F0 = ZCR/2.

For discrete-time signals with ZCR in zero-crossings/sample,

$$F0 = (ZCR * F_s)/2, \tag{6.6}$$

for F_s sample/s.

The ZCR can be defined as $Q(n)$ in Equation (6.4), with

$$T[s(n)] = 0.5|\text{sgn}(s(n)) - \text{sgn}(s(n-1))| \qquad (6.7)$$

where the algebraic sign of $s(n)$ is

$$\text{sgn}(s(n)) = \begin{cases} 1 & \text{for } s(n) \geq 0 \\ -1 & \text{otherwise,} \end{cases} \qquad (6.8)$$

and $w(n)$ is a rectangular window scaled by $1/N$ (where N is the duration of the window) to yield zero-crossings/sample, or by F_s/N to yield zero-crossings/s. This $Q(n)$ can be heavily decimated since the ZCR changes relatively slowly with the vocal tract movements.

The ZCR can help in voicing decisions. Most energy in voiced speech is at low frequency, since the spectrum of voiced glottal excitation decays at about -12 dB/oct. In unvoiced sounds, broadband noise excitation excites mostly higher frequencies, due to effectively shorter vocal tracts. While speech is not a narrowband signal (and thus the sinusoid example above does not hold), the ZCR correlates well with the average frequency of major energy concentration. Thus high and low ZCR correspond to unvoiced and voiced speech, respectively. A suggested boundary is 2500 crossings/s, since voiced and unvoiced speech average about 1400 and 4900 crossings/s, respectively, with a larger standard deviation for the latter (Figure 6.6).

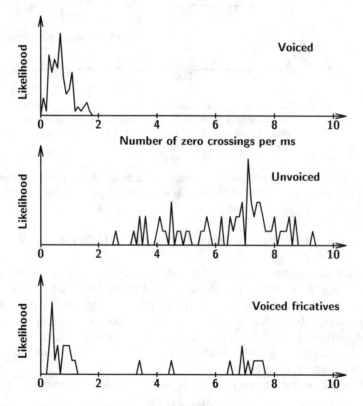

Figure 6.6 Typical distribution of zero-crossings for voiced sonorants, for unvoiced frication, and for voiced frication.

For vowels and sonorants, the ZCR corresponds mostly to F1, which has more energy than other formants. Interpreting ZCR is harder for voiced fricatives, which have both periodic energy in the voice bar at very low frequency and unvoiced energy at high frequency. This, of course, is a problem for all voiced/unvoiced determination methods; a binary decision using a simple threshold test on the ZCR is inadequate. Depending on the balance of periodic and aperiodic energy in voiced fricatives, some are above the threshold (e.g., the strident /z/) and others (e.g., /v/) are below. This problem is also language-dependent; e.g., English appears to have relatively weak voice bars, while French has strong ones.

Unlike short-time energy, the ZCR is highly sensitive to noise in the recording environment (e.g., 60 Hz hum from a power supply) or in analog-to-digital (A/D) conversion. Since energy below 100 Hz is largely irrelevant for speech processing, it may be desirable to highpass filter the speech in addition to the normal lowpass filtering before A/D conversion.

The ZCR can be applied to speech recognition. If speech is first passed through a bank of bandpass filters, each filter's output better resembles a narrowband signal, whose frequency of major energy concentration the ZCR easily estimates. Such a frequency could be a single harmonic (for filter bandwidths less than F0) or a formant frequency (for bandwidths of about 300–500 Hz). A bank or eight filters covering the 0–4 kHz range provides a simple set of eight measures, which could replace a more complex spectral representation (e.g., a DFT) in some applications.

6.3.4 Short-Time Aurocorrelation Function

The Fourier transform $S(e^{j\omega})$ of speech $s(n)$ provides both spectral magnitude and phase. The time signal $r(k)$ for the inverse Fourier transform of the energy spectrum $(|S(e^{j\omega})|^2)$ is called the *autocorrelation* of $s(n)$. $r(k)$ preserves information about harmonic and formant amplitudes in $s(n)$ as well as its periodicity, while ignoring phase (as do many applications), since phase is less important perceptually and carries much less communication information than spectral magnitude. $r(k)$ has applications in F0 estimation, voiced/unvoiced determination, and linear prediction.

The autocorrelation function is a special case of the cross-correlation function,

$$\phi_{sy}(k) = \sum_{m=-\infty}^{\infty} s(m)y(m-k), \tag{6.9}$$

which measures the similarity of two signals $s(n)$ and $y(n)$ as a function of the time delay between them. By summing the products of a signal sample and a delayed sample from another signal, the cross-correlation is large if at some delay the two signals have similar waveforms. The range of summation is usually limited (i.e., windowed), and the function can be normalized by dividing by the number of summed samples.

When the same signal is used for $s(n)$ and $y(n)$, Equation (6.9) yields an autocorrelation. It is an even function ($r(k) = r(-k)$), it has maximum value at $k = 0$, and $r(0)$ equals the energy in $s(n)$ (or average power, for random or periodic signals). If $s(n)$ is periodic in P samples, then $r(k)$ also has period P. Maxima in $r(k)$ occur for $k = 0$, $\pm P$, $\pm 2P$, etc., independently of the absolute timing of the pitch periods; i.e., the window does not have to be placed synchronously with the pitch periods.

The *short-time* autocorrrelation function is obtained by windowing $s(n)$ and then using Equation (6.9), yielding

$$R_n(k) = \sum_{m=-\infty}^{\infty} s(m)w(n-m)s(m-k)w(n-m+k). \qquad (6.10)$$

Equivalently, the product of speech $s(n)$ with its delayed version $s(n-k)$ is passed through a filter with response $w(n)w(n+k)$ (time index n indicates the position of the window). Equation (6.10) is evaluated for different values of k depending on the application. For linear prediction (Section 6.5), $R_n(k)$ for k ranging from 0 to 10–16 are typically needed, depending on the signal bandwidth. In F0 determination, $R_n(k)$ is needed for k near the estimated number of samples in a pitch period; if no suitable prior F0 estimate is available, $R_n(k)$ is calculated for k from the shortest possible period (perhaps 3 ms for a female voice) to the longest (e.g., 20 ms for men). With a sampling rate of 10,000 samples/s, the latter approach can require up to 170 calculations of $R_n(k)$ for each speech frame, if a pitch period resolution of 0.1 ms is desired.

Short windows minimize calculation: if $w(n)$ has N samples, $N-k$ products are needed for each value of $R_n(k)$. Proper choice of $w(n)$ also helps; e.g., using a rectangular window reduces the number of multiplications; symmetries in autocorrelation calculation can also be exploited (see LPC below). While the duration of $w(n)$ is almost directly proportional to the calculation (especially if $N \gg k$), there is a conflict between minimizing N to save computation and having enough speech samples in the window to yield a valid autocorrelation function: longer $w(n)$ give better frequency resolution. For F0 estimation, $w(n)$ must include more than one pitch period, so that $R_n(k)$ exhibits periodicity and the corresponding energy spectrum $|X_n(e^{j\omega})|^2$ resolves individual harmonics of F0 (see Figure 6.4). Spectral estimation applications (e.g., LPC) permit short windows since harmonic resolution is unimportant and the formant spectrum can be found from a portion of a pitch period.

For F0 estimation, an alternative to using autocorrelation is the average magnitude difference function (AMDF) [4]. Instead of multiplying speech $s(m)$ by $s(m-k)$, the

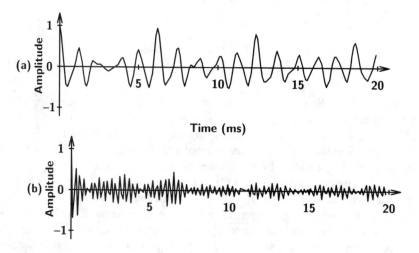

Figure 6.7 Typical autocorrelation function for (a) voiced speech and (b) unvoiced speech, using a 20 ms rectangular window ($N = 201$).

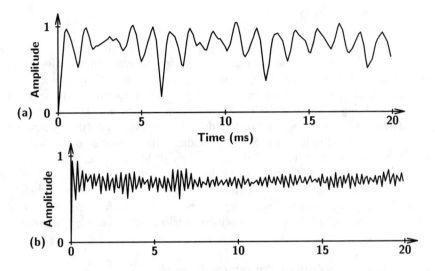

Figure 6.8 AMDF function (normalized to 1.0) for the same speech segments as in Figure 6.7.

magnitude of their difference is taken:

$$\text{AMDF}(k) = \sum_{m=-\infty}^{\infty} |s(m) - s(m - k)|. \tag{6.11}$$

Since subtraction and rectification are much simpler operations than multiplication, the AMDF is considerably faster. Where $R_n(k)$ peaks for values of k near multiples of the pitch period (Figure 6.7), the AMDF has minima (Figure 6.8).

Some speech recognition applications have used a simplified version of the autocorrelation [5]:

$$\psi(k) = \sum_{m=-\infty}^{\infty} \text{sgn}(s(m))s(m - k). \tag{6.12}$$

Replacing $s(m)$ by its sign in Equation (6.9) eliminates the need for multiplications and reduces the emphasis that $r(k)$ normally places on the high-amplitude portions of $s(n)$.

6.4 FREQUENCY-DOMAIN (SPECTRAL) PARAMETERS

The frequency domain provides most useful parameters for speech processing. Speech signals are more consistently and easily analyzed spectrally than in the time domain. The basic model of speech production with a noisy or periodic waveform that excites a vocal tract filter corresponds well to separate spectral models for the excitation and for the vocal tract. Repeated utterances of a sentence by a speaker often differ greatly temporally while being very similar spectrally. Human hearing appears to pay much more attention to spectral aspects of speech (e.g., amplitude distribution in frequency) than to phase or timing aspects. Thus, spectral analysis is used to extract most parameters from speech.

6.4.1 Filter-Bank Analysis

One spectral analysis method (popular due to real-time, simple, and inexpensive implementations) uses a *filter bank* or set of bandpass filters (either analog or digital), each analyzing a different range of frequencies of the input speech. Filter banks are more flexible than DFT analysis since the bandwidths can be varied to follow the resolving power of the ear, rather than being fixed, as in DFTs. Furthermore, many applications require a small set of parameters describing the spectral distribution of energy, especially the spectral envelope. The amplitude outputs from a bank of 8–12 bandpass filters provide a more efficient spectral representation than a more detailed DFT. Filters often follow the bark scale, i.e., equally spaced, fixed-bandwidth filters up to 1 kHz, and then logarithmically increasing bandwidth. One-third-octave filters are also common. Certain speech recognition systems use two levels of spectral analysis, a coarse filter bank with only a few filters for preliminary classification of sounds, followed where necessary by a more detailed analysis using a larger set of narrower filters.

6.4.2 Short-Time Fourier Transform Analysis

As the traditional spectral technique, Fourier analysis provides a speech representation in terms of amplitude and phase as a function of frequency. Viewing the vocal tract as a linear system, the Fourier transform of speech is the product of the transforms of the glottal (or noise) excitation and of the vocal tract response. For steady-state vowels of fricatives, the basic (infinite-time) Fourier transform could be used by extending or repeating sections or pitch periods of the speech ad infinitum. However, speech is not stationary, and thus short-time analysis using windows is necessary.

The short-time Fourier transform of a signal $s(n)$ is often defined as

$$S_n(e^{j\omega}) = \sum_{m=-\infty}^{\infty} s(m)e^{-j\omega m} w(n - m). \tag{6.13}$$

If ω is considered fixed, the transform has an interpretation as $Q(n)$ in Equation (6.4), where the transformation T corresponds to multiplication by a complex exponential of frequency ω, which has the spectral effect of rotating energy through a frequency shift of ω rad. Assuming $w(n)$ acts as a lowpass filter, $S_n(e^{j\omega})$ is a time signal (a function of n), describing the amplitude and phase of $s(n)$ within a bandwidth equivalent to that of the window but centered at ω rad. Repeating the calculation of $S_n(e^{j\omega})$ at different ω of interest yields a two-dimensional representation of the input speech: an array of time signals indexed on frequency, each noting the speech energy in a limited bandwidth about the chosen frequency.

A second interpretation of $S_n(e^{j\omega})$ views n as fixed, thus yielding the Fourier transform of $s(m)w(n - m)$, the windowed version of $s(m)$ using a window shifted to a time n with respect to the speech. This calculation could be repeated for successive n to produce an array of Fourier transforms index on time n, each expressing the spectrum of the speech signal within a window centered at time n.

For computational purposes, the DFT is used instead of the standard Fourier transform, so that the frequency variable ω only takes on N discrete values (N = the window duration, or *size*, of the DFT):

$$S_n(k) = \sum_{m=0}^{N-1} s(m)e^{-j2\pi km/N} w(n - m). \tag{6.14}$$

(In practice, each frame of speech samples $s(m)$ is shifted by the time delay n to align with a start at $m = 0$, allowing a simple N-sample window $w(m)$ to replace $w(n - m)$, and the fast Fourier transform or FFT is used to implement the DFT [6]. Since the Fourier transform is invertible, no information about $s(n)$ during the window is lost in the representation $S_n(e^{j\omega})$, as long as the transform is sampled in frequency sufficiently often (i.e., at N equally spaced values of ω) and the window $w(n)$ has no zero-valued samples among its N samples. The choice of N is thus crucial for short-time Fourier analysis. Low values for N (i.e., short windows and DFT's of few points) give poor frequency resolution since the window lowpass filter is wide, but they yield good time resolution since the speech properties are averaged only over short time intervals (see Figure 6.4). Large N, on the other hand, gives poor time resolution and good frequency resolution.

Assuming a rectangular window $w(n) = r(n)$ and viewing the main spectral lobe of $R(e^{j\omega})$ as its bandwidth, common choices are a 3.3 ms *wideband* window (300 Hz bandwidth) for good time resolution or a 22 ms *narrowband* window (45 Hz bandwidth) for good frequency resolution. The time–frequency tradeoff in resolution is related to window shape. Finite-duration windows theoretically have energy at infinitely high frequencies, but most is concentrated in a lowpass bandwidth. The abrupt $r(n)$ in particular has much of its energy beyond the main lobe of the lowpass filter. While the problem is reduced for other windows, frequency range and window duration cannot be completely limited simultaneously. Viewed as a time signal, $S_n(e^{j\omega})$ primarily notes energy components around frequency $\omega F_s/2\pi$ Hz but has contributions beyond the main lobe bandwidth in varying degree, depending on the window shape.

Alternatives to the rectangular $r(n)$ are common in spectral analysis due to $r(n)$'s high proportion of energy outside the main lobe and despite its narrow main lobe, which provides good frequency resolution for a short-time window. It is preferable to use another window with an appropriate increase in window duration to achieve the same frequency resolution, rather than accept the frequency distortion due to poor lowpass filtering. The allowable window duration is limited by the desired time resolution, though, which usually corresponds to the rate at which spectral changes occur in speech (e.g,. as rapidly as 5–10 ms). Any single spectral representation usually does not contain enough information for all speech processing applications. Short windows serve for formant analysis and segmentation, where good time resolution is important and where the smoothing of spectral harmonics into wider-frequency formants is desirable. Long windows are good for harmonic analysis and F0 detection, where individual harmonics must be resolved.

Because it retains sufficient information to completely reconstruct the windowed speech $x(n)$, the short-time Fourier transform is not economical for representing speech, in terms of the number of data samples. For fixed ω, $S_n(e^{j\omega})$ is a time signal of bandwidth roughly equal to that of the window and must be sampled at the Nyquist rate of twice the highest frequency. For fixed-time n, $S_n(e^{j\omega})$ is a Fourier transform to which an appropriate sampling rate in *frequency* may be calculated by applying the Nyquist theorem through the duality of the Fourier transform and its inverse. Since common windows are strictly "timelimited," $S_n(e^{j\omega})$ must be sampled at twice the window's "time width"; e.g., with a rectangular window of N samples and speech at F_s samples/s, the main spectral lobe occupies the range $0-F_s/N$ Hz. Thus each time function $S_n(e^{j\omega})$ must be sampled at $2F_s/N$ samples/s, and N time functions must be retained at N uniformly spaced frequencies from $\omega = 0$ to 2π. Since speech $s(n)$ is real, $S_n(e^{j\omega})$ is conjugate symmetric, and therefore the latter function need be retained only for $\omega = 0$ to π. However, since the Fourier transform is complex-valued, the net requirements are $2F_s$ real-valued samples/s, which is twice the original sampling rate. With the Hamming and other windows, coding rates are even higher because of the larger bandwidths for the same window durations.

The short-time Fourier transform is thus not directly used for efficient coding, but as an alternative speech representation that has simpler interpretation in terms of the speech production and perception processes. Chapter 7 will explore coding applications that exploit data reduction of $S_n(e^{j\omega})$ while limiting speech quality degradation. More economical representation of speech parameters is achieved when the transform is subsampled below the Nyquist rate. This does not permit exact reconstruction of the speech waveform, but the ear is very tolerant of certain changes in speech signals that are more easily exploited in spectral form than in the time domain.

6.4.3 Spectral Displays

For decades a major speech analysis tool has been the *spectrogram*, or sound spectrograph, which provides a three-dimensional representation of short speech utterances (typically 2–3 s). The short-time Fourier transform $S_n(e^{j\omega})$ is plotted with time n on the horizontal axis, with frequency ω (from 0 to π) on the vertical axis (i.e., $0-F_s/2$ in Hz), and with magnitude indicated as degrees of shading (weak energy below one threshold shows as white, while very strong energy is black; the range between the two displays a varying amount of gray) (Figure 6.9). Since the transform phase is often of little interest, only the magnitude of the complex-valued $S_n(e^{j\omega})$ is displayed, typically on a logarithmic scale (following the dynamic range of audition). In the past, spectrograms used analog filtering, transferring electrical energy to Teledeltos paper through an electromechanical operation [7]; the dynamic range of such paper was only about 12 dB, which nonetheless was adequate to study most formant behavior. Recent computer-generated spectrograms are much more flexible.

Wideband spectrograms display individual pitch periods as vertical striations corresponding to the large speech amplitude each time the vocal cords close (Figure 6.9a). Voicing can be easily detected visually by the presence of these periodically spaced striations. Fine time resolution here permits accurate temporal location of spectral changes corresponding to

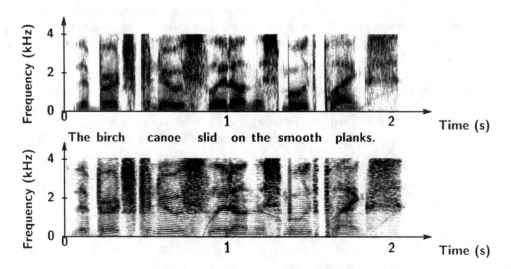

Figure 6.9 (a) Wideband and (b) narrowband spectrograms of a sentence.

vocal tract movements. The wide filter bandwidth smooths the harmonic amplitudes under each formant across a range of 300 Hz, displaying a band of darkness (of width proportional to the formant's bandwidth) for each formant. The center of each band is a good estimate of formant frequency.

Narrowband spectrograms display separate harmonics instead of pitch periods, and are less useful for segmentation because of poorer time resolution (Figure 6.9b). Instead they aid anlaysis of F0 and vocal tract excitation. A traditional, but tedious, way to estimate F0 is to divide a low-frequency range (e.g., 0–2 kHz, chosen due to the presence of strong formants) by the number of harmonics there. Due to limited range on spectrograms or to filtering of the speech (e.g., in the telephone network), however, harmonics are often invisible (i.e., their weak energy shows as white).

Since the amplitude of voiced speech falls off at about −6 dB/oct, dynamic range is often compressed prior to spectral analysis so that details at weak, high frequencies may be visible. *Pre-emphasizing* the speech, either by differentiating the analog speech $s_a(t)$ prior to A/D conversion or by differencing the discrete-time $s(n) = s_a(nT)$, compensates for falloff at high frequencies. If speech is to be reconstructed later using data from pre-emphasized speech, the final synthesis stage requires the inverse operation of *de-emphasis* or integration, which restores the proper dynamic range. The most common form of pre-emphasis is

$$y(n) = s(n) - As(n - 1), \qquad (6.15)$$

where A typically lies between 0.9 and 1.0 and reflects the degree of pre-emphasis. Effectively, $s(n)$ passes through a filter with a zero at $z = A$. The closer the zero to $z = 1$, the greater the pre-emphasis effect. The attenuation at frequencies below 200 Hz can be large, but such low frequencies are rarely of interest in spectral analysis applications.

The −6 dB/oct falloff applies only to voiced speech, since unvoiced speech tends to have a flat spectrum at high frequencies. Ideally, pre-emphasis should be applied only to voiced speech. In practice, however, the slightly degraded analysis of pre-emphasized unvoiced speech does not warrant limiting pre-emphasis only to voiced speech. Most applications use pre-emphasis throughout the entire speech signal and limit its effects on unvoiced speech by choosing a compromise value for A (e.g., 0.9).

6.4.4 Formant Estimation and Tracking

An assumption for much speech analysis is that the signal can be modeled as a source exciting a time-varying vocal tract filter. The source is either the quasi-periodic puffs of air passing through the glottis or broadband noise generated at a constriction in the vocal tract. The vocal tract filter response normally varies slowly because of constraints on movements of the tongue and lips, but it can change rapidly at articulator discontinuities (e.g., when a vocal tract passage closes or opens). The spectrum of voiced speech is the product of a line spectrum (harmonics spaced at F0 Hz) and the vocal tract spectrum. The latter is a slowly varying function of frequency, with an average of one formant peak/kHz.

The behavior of the first 3–4 formants is of crucial importance in many applications, e.g., formant vocoders (voice coders), some speech recognizers, and speech analysis leading to formant-based synthesis. Typical methods to estimate formant center frequencies and their bandwidths involve looking for peaks in spectral representations from short-time Fourier transforms, filter bank outputs, or linear prediction [8–11]. Such *peak-picking* methods appear to be accurate to within ±60 Hz for the first and second formants, but simple Fourier transforms allow an accuracy of only ±110 Hz for F3 [12]. This compares to errors of ±40 Hz for manual measurements of spectrograms. For dynamic formants, wideband spectrograms (e.g., with a 6 ms analysis window) allow accurate tracking, especially pitch-synchronously [13].

The automatic tracking of formants is difficult, despite the typical spacing of formants every 1 kHz (for a vocal tract 17 cm long), the limited range of possible bandwidths (30–500 Hz), and the generally slow formant changes. Occasional rapid spectral changes limit the assumption of formant continuity. In oral vowel and sonorant sequences, formants smoothly rise and fall, and are readily followed via spectral peak-picking. Acoustic coupling of the oral and nasal cavities during nasals causes abrupt formant movements as well as the introduction of extra formants. Zeros in the glottal source excitation or in the vocal tract response for lateral or nazalized sounds also tend to obscure formants. Many sounds have two formants close enough that they appear as one spectral peak (e.g., F1–F2 in /o, ɑ/, F2–F3 in /i/). Continuity constraints can often resolve these problems but are frequently thwarted by nasal and obstruent consonants, which interrupt the formants and abruptly alter the spectral distribution of energy. During obstruents, the sound source excites only a forward portion of the vocal tract; thus F1 and often F2 have little energy.

One way to track formants is to estimate speech $S(z)$ in terms of a ratio of z polynomials, solve directly for the roots of the denominator, and identify each root as a formant if it has a narrow bandwidth at a reasonable frequency location. This process can be precise but expensive since the polynomial often has order greater than 10 to represent 4–5 formants (see however a recent fixed-point algorithm [14]). Another approach [15–17] uses phase information to decide whether a spectral peak is a formant. In evaluating $S(z)$ along the unit circle $z = \exp(j\omega)$, a large negative phase shift occurs when ω passes a pole close to the unit circle. Since formants correspond to complex–conjugate pairs of poles with relatively narrow bandwidths (i.e., near the unit circle), each spectral peak having such a phase shift is a formant. The phase shift approaches $-180°$ for small formant bandwidths.

When two formants may appear as one broad spectral peak, a modified DFT can resolve the ambiguity. The *chirp z transform* (CZT) (named after a *chirp*, or signal of increasing frequency) calculates the z transform of the windowed speech on a contour inside the unit circle. Whereas the DFT samples $S(z)$ at uniform intervals on the unit circle, the CZT can follow a spiral contour anywhere in the z plane. It is typically located near poles corresponding to a spectral peak of interest and is evaluated only for a small range of frequency samples. Such a contour can be much closer to the formant poles than for the DFT; thus the CZT can resolve two poles (for two closely spaced formants) into two spectral peaks (Figure 6.10). Because formant bandwidths tend to increase with frequency, the spiral contour often starts near $z = \alpha$, just inside the unit circle (e.g., $\alpha = 0.9$), and gradually spirals inward with increasing frequency $\omega_k = 2\pi k/N$ ($z_k = \alpha\beta^k \exp(j\omega_k)$, with β just less than 1). This contour follows the expected path of the formant poles and eliminates many problems of merged peaks in DFT displays. CZT algorithms can reduce the amount of calculation necessary, approaching that of the DFT, by taking advantage of the spiral nature of the contour in the z plane [18].

Formant trackers have great difficulty when F0 exceeds formant bandwidths, e.g., F0 > 250 Hz [12], as in children's voices. Harmonics in such speech are so widely separated that only one or two constitute each formant. Thus, most spectral analyzers tend to label the most prominent harmonic as the formant, which is erroneous when the center frequency is not a multiple of F0. An analysis using critical band filters, rather than formants, has been more successful in classifying children's vowels [19].

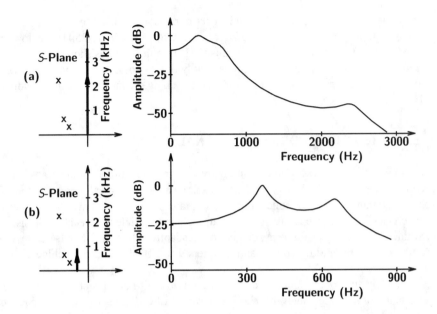

Figure 6.10 Improved frequency resolution obtained by using the chirp z-transform (After
Schafer and Rabiner [9].)

6.4.5 Other Spectral Methods (‡)

While formants are widely viewed as important spectral measures for much of speech
processing, the difficulty of reliably tracking them has led to related measures. One recent
analysis method passes speech through a bank of bandpass filters, and then calculates an
autocorrelation of each bandpass power spectrum; following the mel scale, the subband filters
have increasing bandwidth with frequency [20]. Another method uses principal components
analysis on 16 filter outputs, reducing speech information to as little as two dimensions,
which correspond roughly to F1–F2 (but do not require formant tracking) [21].

6.4.6 Energy Separation (‡)

Following recent evidence of significant amplitude and frequency modulations (AM
and FM) within pitch periods (due to nonlinear air flows in the vocal tract), an Energy
Separation Algorithm (ESA) was developed to analyze these modulations [22]. Each formant
is viewed as an AM–FM signal $x(t) = a(t)\cos(\phi(t))$ with AM $a(t)$ and a time-varying
frequency $f(t) = (1/2\pi)d\phi(t)/dt = f_c + f_m(t)$, with oscillation $f_m(t)$ around the formant center
f_c. An "energy operator" is defined as $\Psi(x(t)) = (dx(t)/dt)^2 - x(t)(d^2x(t)/dt^2)$ (in discrete
time: $\Psi_d(x(n)) = (x(n))^2 - x(n-1)x(n+1)$). Under some reasonable assumptions on bandwidths and deviations, it can be shown that $f(t) \approx (1/2\pi)\sqrt{\Psi(dx(t)/dt)/\Psi(x(t))}$ and
$|a(t)| \approx \Psi(x(t))/\sqrt{\Psi(dx(t)/dt)}$ [22]. In discrete time, estimations of the envelope and
instantaneous frequency only require simple manipulations of a 5-sample moving window
[23].

An iterative ESA converges quickly if given good initial estimates for f_c, but requires
another form of formant tracker for the initial values. A simulation of what humans do for

estimating formants from narrowband spectrograms uses local minima and maxima in harmonic amplitudes over a range of frequencies B, where B is 250 Hz at low frequency and extends to 750 Hz for the high formants [23]. This method has shown significant AM and FM in formants within pitch periods, presumably due to nonlinearities in vocal tract air flow. The ESA method also provides reliable formant tracking, including good bandwidth estimates [11].

6.5 LINEAR PREDICTIVE CODING (LPC) ANALYSIS

As a model for speech, a popular alternative to the short-time Fourier transform is linear predictive coding (LPC). LPC provides an accurate and economical representation of relevant speech parameters that can reduce transmission rates in speech coding, increase accuracy and reduce calculation in speech recognition, and generate efficient speech synthesis. Chapter 7 examines applications of linear prediction in adaptive differential pulse-code modulation (ADPCM) systems and LP coders, and Chapters 9 and 10 show man–machine applications of LPC.

LPC is the most common techniques for low-bit-rate speech coding and is a very important tool in speech analysis. The popularity of LPC derives from its compact yet precise representation of the speech spectral magnitude as well as its relatively simple computation. LPC has been used to estimate F0, vocal tract area functions, and the frequencies and bandwidths of spectral poles and zeros (e.g., formants), but it primarily provides a small set of speech parameters that represent the configuration of the vocal tract. LPC estimates each speech sample based on a linear combination of its p previous samples; a larger p enables a more accurate model. The weighting factors (or LPC *coefficients*) in the linear combination can be directly used in digital filters as multiplier coefficients for synthesis or can be stored as templates in speech recognizers. LPC coefficients can be transformed into other parameter sets for more efficient coding. We examine below how to calculate the parameters, and also examine spectral estimation via LPC.

LPC has drawbacks: to minimize analysis complexity, the speech signal is usually assumed to come from an all-pole source; i.e., that its spectrum has no zeros. Since actual speech has zeros due to the usual glottal source excitation and due to multiple acoustic paths in nasals and unvoiced sounds, such a model is a simplification, which however does not cause major difficulties in most applications. Nonetheless, some efforts have been made to modify all-pole LPC to model zeros as well.

6.5.1 Basic Principles of LPC

LPC provides an analysis–synthesis system for speech signals [24, 25]. The synthesis model consists of an excitation source $U(z)$ providing input to a spectral shaping filter $H(z)$, yielding output speech $\hat{S}(z)$. Following certain constraints, $U(z)$ and $H(z)$ are chosen so that $\hat{S}(z)$ is close (in some sense) to the original speech $S(z)$. To simplify the modeling problem, $U(z)$ is chosen to have a flat spectral envelope so that most relevant spectral detail lies in $H(z)$. A flat spectrum is a reasonable assumption for $U(z)$ since the vocal tract excitation for unvoiced sounds resembles white noise. For voiced sounds, the source is viewed as a uniform sample train, periodic in N samples (the pitch period), having a line spectrum with uniform-area harmonics (below we discuss problems of viewing a uniform line spectrum as "flat"). The vocal cord puffs of air, which are normally viewed as the excitation for the vocal tract in voiced speech, can be modeled as the output of a glottal filter whose input is the sample train. The spectral shaping effects of the glottis and the vocal tract are thus combined into one filter $H(z)$.

To simplify obtaining $H(z)$ given a speech signal $s(n)$, we assume the speech to be stationary during each window or frame of N samples. This allows the $H(z)$ filter to be modeled with constant coefficients (to be updated with each frame of data). $H(z)$ is assumed to have p poles and q zeros in the general *pole-zero* case, i.e., a synthetic speech sample $\hat{s}(n)$ can be modeled by a linear combination of the p previous output samples and $q + 1$ previous input samples of an LPC synthesizer:

$$\hat{s}(n) = \sum_{k=1}^{p} a_k \hat{s}(n - k) + G \sum_{l=0}^{q} b_l u(n - l), \tag{6.16}$$

where G is a gain factor for the input speech (assuming $b_0 = 1$). Equivalently,

$$H(z) = \frac{\hat{S}(z)}{U(z)} = G \frac{1 + \sum_{l=1}^{q} b_l z^{-l}}{1 - \sum_{k=1}^{p} a_k z^{-k}}. \tag{6.17}$$

Most LPC work assumes an all-pole model (also known as an *autoregressive*, or AR, model), where $q = 0$. (Any zeros at $z = 0$ are ignored here, because such zeros do not change the spectral magnitude and add only linear phase, since they result from simple time delays.) An all-zero model ($p = 0$) is called a *moving average* (MA) model since the output is a weighted average of the q prior inputs. The more general, but less popular, LPC model with both poles and zeros ($q > 0$) is known as an autoregressive moving average (ARMA) model. We assume here the AR model. If speech $s(n)$ is filtered by an inverse or *predictor* filter (the inverse of an all-pole $H(z)$)

$$A(z) = 1 - \sum_{k=1}^{p} a_k z^{-k}, \tag{6.18}$$

the output $e(n)$ is called an *error* or *residual* signal:

$$e(n) = s(n) - \sum_{k=1}^{p} a_k s(n - k). \tag{6.19}$$

The unit sample response for $A(z)$ has only $p + 1$ samples and comes directly from the set of LPC coefficients: $a(0) = 1$, $a(n) = -a_n$ for $n = 1, 2, \ldots, p$. To the extent that $H(z)$ adequately models the vocal tract system response, $E(z) \approx U(z)$. Since speech production cannot be fully modeled by a p-pole filter $H(z)$, there are differences between $e(n)$ and the presumed impulse train $u(n)$ for voiced speech (Figures 6.11 and 6.12). If $s(n)$ has been recorded without phase distortion [26] and if the inverse filtering is done carefully (e.g., pitch-synchronously), an estimate of the actual glottal waveform can be obtained after appropriate lowpass filtering of $e(n)$ (to simulate the smooth shape of the glottal puff of air) [27, 28].

6.5.2 Least-squares Autocorrelation Method

Two approaches are often used to obtain a set of LPC coefficients a_k characterizing an all-pole $H(z)$ model of the speech spectrum. The classical *least-squares* method chooses a_k to minimize the mean energy in the error signal over a frame of speech data, while the *lattice*

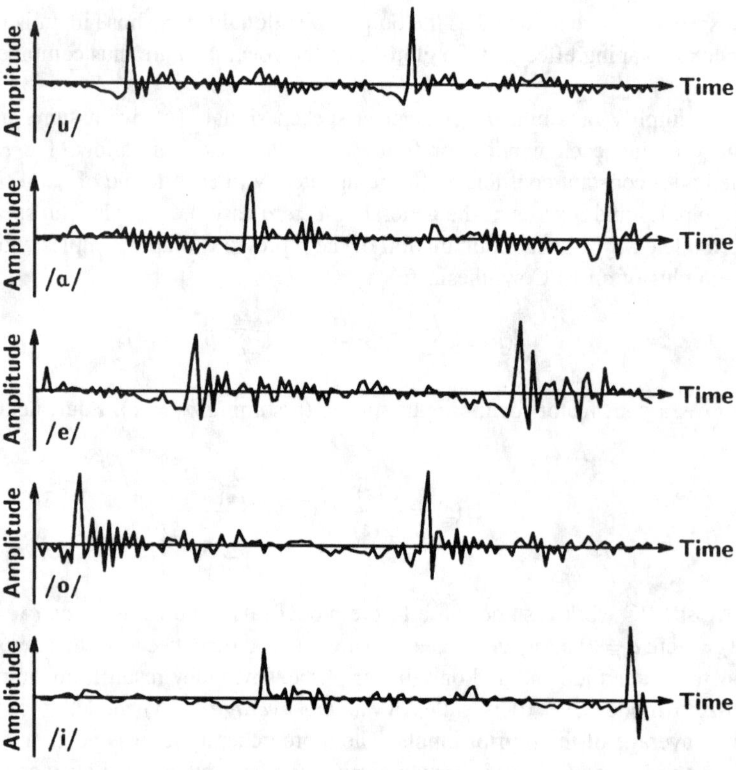

Figure 6.11 Examples of pre-emphasized speech signals and their corresponding prediction error signals for five vowels /u, ɑ, e, o, i/.

approach permits instantaneous updating of the coefficients (at the expense of extra computation). In the former technique, either $s(n)$ or $e(n)$ is windowed to limit the extent of the speech under analysis. The first of two least-squares techniques is the data-windowing or *autocorrelation* method, which multiplies the speech by a Hamming or similar time window

$$x(n) = w(n)s(n) \tag{6.20}$$

so that $x(n)$ has finite duration (N samples, typically corresponding to 20–30 ms). Thus $x(n) = 0$ outside the range $0 \leq n \leq N - 1$. As in other speech analyses, $s(n)$ is assumed to be stationary during each window. LPC equally considers all speech samples within each frame; thus for nonstationary speech, the LPC coefficients describe a smoothed average of the signal.

Let E be the error energy:

$$E = \sum_{n=-\infty}^{\infty} e^2(n) = \sum_{n=-\infty}^{\infty} \left[x(n) - \sum_{k=1}^{p} a_k x(n-k) \right]^2, \tag{6.21}$$

where $e(n)$ is the residual corresponding to the windowed signal $x(n)$. The values of a_k that minimize E are found by setting $\partial E / \partial a_k = 0$ for $k = 1, 2, 3, \ldots, p$. This yields p linear

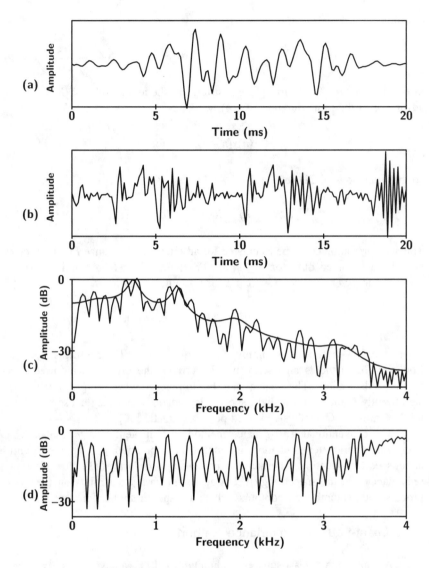

Figure 6.12 Signals and spectra in LPC via the autocorrelation method using 12 poles: (a) 20 ms of an /ɑ/ vowel from a male speaker at 8000 samples/s (using a Hamming window); (b) residual error signal obtained by inverse LPC filtering the speech (magnified about 3 times); (c) speech spectrum with the smooth LPC spectrum superimposed; and (d) spectrum of the error signal (note the different amplitude scales for parts c and d).

equations

$$\sum_{n=-\infty}^{\infty} x(n-i)x(n) = \sum_{k=1}^{p} a_k \sum_{n=-\infty}^{\infty} x(n-i)x(n-k), \qquad \text{for } i=1,2,3,\ldots,p, \qquad (6.22)$$

in p unknowns a_k. Recognizing the first term as the autocorrelation $R(i)$ of $x(n)$ and taking advantage of the finite duration of $x(n)$, we have

$$R(i) = \sum_{n=i}^{N-1} x(n)x(n-i), \qquad \text{for } i=1,2,3,\ldots,p, \qquad (6.23)$$

so that Equations (6.22) reduce to

$$\sum_{k=1}^{p} a_k R(i-k) = R(i), \qquad \text{for } i=1,2,3,\ldots,p. \qquad (6.24)$$

The autocorrelation could be calculated for all integers i, but since $R(i)$ is an even function, it need be determined only for $0 \le i \le p$. From Equations (6.21) and (6.24), the minimum residual energy or *prediction error* E_p for a p-pole model is

$$E_p = R(0) - \sum_{k=1}^{p} a_k R(k), \qquad (6.25)$$

where the first term $R(0)$ is simply the energy in $x(n)$. For synthesis, setting $G^2 = E_p$ in Equation (6.16) yields an energy match between the original windowed speech and the synthesized version. The match can be imprecise when output pitch periods overlap significantly (yielding only slight speech degradation), but may cause overflows [29] when implementing LPC synthesis in fixed-point arithmetic [30].

The conventional least-squares method is equivalent to a *maximum likelihood* (*ML*) approach to parameter estimation; it simplifies computation, but ignores certain information about speech production. Alternative *maximum a posteriori* (*MAP*) methods exploit better the redundancies in the speech signal, but at a high cost. Constraints on the MAP estimation process (e.g., smooth time contours) which aid speech applications are feasible [31].

6.5.3 Least-Squares Covariance Method

An alternative least-squares technique of LPC analysis, the *covariance* method, windows the error $e(n)$ instead of $s(n)$:

$$E_p = \sum_{n=-\infty}^{\infty} e^2(n)w(n). \qquad (6.26)$$

Setting $\partial E/\partial a_k = 0$ again to zero leads to p linear equations

$$\sum_{k=1}^{p} a_k \phi(i,k) = \phi(0,i), \qquad 1 \le i \le p, \qquad (6.27)$$

where

$$\phi(i,k) = \sum_{n=-\infty}^{\infty} s(n-k)s(n-i)w(n) \qquad (6.28)$$

is the covariance function for $s(n)$. Usually the error is weighted uniformly in time via a simple rectangular window of N samples, and Equation (6.28) reduces to

$$\phi(i, k) = \sum_{n=0}^{N-1} s(n-k)s(n-i), \qquad \text{for } 0 \le (i, k) \le p. \tag{6.29}$$

The autocorrelation R and covariance ϕ functions are quite similar, but they differ in the windowing effects. The autocorrelation method uses N (Hamming) windowed speech samples, whereas the covariance method uses no window on the speech samples. The former thus introduces distortion into the spectral estimation since windowing corresponds to convolving the original short-time $S(e^{j\omega})$ with the frequency response of the window $W(e^{j\omega})$. Since most windows have lowpass spectra, the windowed speech spectrum is a smoothed version of the original, with the extent and type of smoothing dependent on the window shape and duration. The covariance method avoids this distortion, but requires knowledge of $N + p$ speech samples ($s(n)$ for $-p \le n \le N - 1$ in Equation (6.29)).

6.5.4 Computational Considerations

In the autocorrelation method, the p linear equations (Equation (6.24)) to be solved can be viewed in matrix form as $\mathbf{R}A = \mathbf{r}$, where $\mathbf{R}$ is a $p \times p$ matrix of elements $\mathbf{R}(i, k) = R(|i - k|)$, $(1 \le i, k \le p)$, $\mathbf{r}$ is a column vector $(R(1), R(2), \ldots, R(p))^T$, and A is a column vector of LPC coefficients $(a_1, a_2, \ldots, a_p)^T$. Solving for the LPC vector requires inversion of the $\mathbf{R}$ matrix and multiplication of the resultant $p \times p$ matrix with the $\mathbf{r}$ vector. A parallel situation occurs for the covariance approach if we replace the autocorrelation matrix $\mathbf{R}$ with the $p \times p$ covariance matrix $\P$ of elements $\P(i, k) = \phi(i, k)$ and substitute the $\mathbf{r}$ vector with a ϕ vector $(\phi(0, 1), \phi(0, 2), \ldots, \phi(0, p))$. Calculation of the minimum residual error E_p can also be expressed in vector form as the product of an extended LPC vector

$$\mathbf{a} = (1, -a_1, -a_2, \ldots, -a_p), \tag{6.30}$$

with either the $\mathbf{r}$ or ϕ vector augmented to include as its first element the speech energy ($R(0)$ or $\phi(0, 0)$, respectively). The extended LPC vector contains the $p + 1$ coefficients of the LPC inverse filter $A(z)$.

Redundancies in the $\mathbf{R}$ and $\P$ matrices allow efficient calculation of the LPC coefficients without explicitly inverting a $p \times p$ matrix. Both matrices are symmetric (e.g., $\phi(i, k) = \phi(k, i)$); however, $\mathbf{R}$ is also Toeplitz (all elements along a given diagonal are equal), whereas $\P$ is not. As a result, the autocorrelation approach is simpler ($2p$ storage locations and $O(p^2)$ math operations) than the basic covariance method ($p^2/2$ storage locations and $O(p^3)$ operations, although this can be reduced to $O(p^2)$ operations [32]). ($O(p)$ means "of the order of p" and indicates approximation.) If $N \gg p$ (often true in speech processing), then computation of the $\mathbf{R}$ or $\P$ matrix ($O(pN)$ operations) dominates the overall calculation. (N often exceeds 100, while p is about 10.) Assuming the $\P$ matrix is positive definite (generally true for speech input), its symmetry allows solution through the square root or Cholesky decomposition method [33], which roughly halves the computation and storage needed for direct matrix inversion techniques.

The additional redundancy in the Toeplitz **R** matrix allows the more efficient Levinson–Durbin recursive procedure [25, 33], in which the following set of ordered equations is solved recursively for $m = 1, 2, \ldots, p$:

$$k_m = \frac{R(m) - \sum_{k=1}^{m-1} a_{m-1}(k)R(m-k)}{E_{m-1}}, \tag{6.31a}$$

$$a_m(m) = k_m, \tag{6.31b}$$

$$a_m(k) = a_{m-1}(k) - k_m a_{m-1}(m-k) \quad \text{for } 1 \leq k \leq m-1, \tag{6.31c}$$

$$E_m = (1 - k_m^2)E_{m-1}, \tag{6.31d}$$

where initially $E_0 = R(0)$ and $a_0 = 0$. At each cycle m, the coefficients $a_m(k)$ (for $k = 1, 2, \ldots, m$) describe the optimal mth-order linear predictor, and the minimum error E_m is reduced by the factor $(1 - k_m^2)$. Since E_m, a squared error, is never negative, $|k_m| \leq 1$. This condition on the *reflection coefficients* k_m, which can be related to acoustic tube models, also guarantees a stable LPC synthesis filter $H(z)$ since all the roots of $A(z)$ are then inside (or on) the unit circle in the z plane. The negatives of the reflection coefficients are called *partial correlation*, or PARCOR, coefficients. The k_m rarely have magnitude equal to unity since that would terminate the recursion with $E_m = 0$ and yield $H(z)$ poles on the unit circle, a marginally stable situation. Unlike the covariance method, the autocorrelation method, even when not calculating the reflection coefficients directly, guarantees a stable synthesis filter when using infinite-precision calculation.

One radical way to reduce calculation in LPC analysis is to center-clip and infinite-peak clip the speech signal before LPC processing. Clipping is useful for F0 estimation as a means to simplify the speech signal, eliminating formant detail while preserving periodicity. If the clipping level is lowered to about 20% of its value in F0 estimation, formant detail is also preserved, yet the signal may be simplified to contain only values of -1, 0, and $+1$. Calculating the autocorrelation matrix for LPC using such a signal involves no multiplications, which greatly reduces computation. Some supplementary multiplications must be done, however, to find the LPC gain since clipping destroys energy information. The cost for such efficiency is that synthetic LPC spectra differ from the original by about 2 dB [34], which can be significant.

6.5.5 Spectral Estimation via LPC

Parseval's theorem for the energy E of a discrete-time signal (e.g., the error signal $e(n)$) and its Fourier transform is

$$E = \sum_{n=-\infty}^{\infty} e^2(n) = \frac{1}{2\pi} \int_{\omega=-\pi}^{\pi} |E(e^{j\omega})|^2 \, d\omega. \tag{6.32}$$

Since $e(n)$ can be obtained by passing speech $s(n)$ through its inverse LPC filter $A(z) = G/H(z)$, the residual error can be expressed as

$$E_p = \frac{G^2}{2\pi} \int_{\omega=-\pi}^{\pi} \frac{|S(e^{j\omega})|^2}{|H(e^{j\omega})|^2} \, d\omega. \tag{6.33}$$

Obtaining the LPC coefficients by minimizing E_p is equivalent to minimizing the average ratio of the speech spectrum to its LPC approximation. Equal weight is given to all frequencies, but $|H(e^{j\omega})|$ models the peaks in $|S(e^{j\omega})|$ better than its valleys (Figure 6.12c) because the contribution to the error E_p at frequencies where the speech spectrum exceeds its LPC approximation is greater than for the opposite condition. The LPC all-pole spectrum $|H(e^{j\omega})|$ is limited, by the number p of poles used, in the degree of spatial detail it can model in $|S(e^{j\omega})|$. For a typical $p = 10$, at most five resonances can be represented accurately. A short-time voiced-speech spectrum, with rapid frequency variation due to the harmonics as well as the slower variations due to the formant structures, cannot be completely modeled by such an $|H(e^{j\omega})|$. Locating the (smooth) LPC spectrum well below the (ragged) speech spectrum (to model spectral valleys well) would cause large contributions to the overall error at spectral peaks. $|H(e^{j\omega})|$ tends to follow the spectral envelope of $|S(e^{j\omega})|$ just below the harmonic peaks, which balances small errors at peak frequencies with larger errors in valleys (which contribute less to E_p). Thus, the valleys between harmonics are less well modeled than the harmonic peaks, and valleys between formants (including those due to zeros in the vocal tract transfer function) are less accurately modeled than formant regions. The importance of good formant modeling has been underlined recently by suggested modifications to LPC to emphasize narrow bandwidth components in the spectral model [35].

6.5.5.1 Pre-emphasis. Many analysis methods concentrate on the high-energy portions of the speech spectrum. It is nonetheless clear that relatively weak energy at high frequencies is often important in many applications. To help model formants of differing intensity equally well, input speech energy is often raised as a function of frequency prior to spectral analysis (e.g., LPC) via pre-emphasis. The degree of pre-emphasis is controlled by a constant α, which determines the cutoff frequency of the single-zero filter through which speech effectively passes. This reduces the dynamic range (i.e., "flattens" the speech spectrum) by adding a zero to counteract the spectral falloff due to the glottal source in voiced speech. The pre-emphasis and radiation zeros approximately cancel the falloff, giving formants of similar amplitudes. In speech coding, the final stage of synthesis must contain a *de-emphasis* filter $1/(1 - \beta z^{-1})$ to undo the pre-emphasis. With values of α and β of typically about 0.94, pre-emphasis acts as a differentiator, while de-emphasis performs integration. In addition to making spectral analysis more uniform in frequency, pre-emphasis reduces a signal's dynamic range, facilitating some fixed-point implementations [24].

Usually β is chosen equal to α so that the de-emphasis exactly cancels the pre-emphasis effects, but when α is near unity, a slight mismatch often yields higher-quality speech. Such common high values for α locate the pre-emphasis zero at very low frequency, causing significant attenuation in the region below F1, which in turn is poorly matched by the usual LPC analysis. Frequently, LPC spectra overestimate gain at these low frequencies. By allowing $\beta < \alpha$ (e.g., 0.74 and 0.94, respectively), this mismatch can be reduced, while having little effect on the formant spectra [36]. Whereas intelligibility depends little on frequencies below F1, much energy is present there in voiced speech, and a proper spectral match is important for naturalness.

6.5.5.2 Order of the LPC model. In the LPC model, the choice of the order p is a com-promise among spectral accuracy, computation time/memory, and transmission bandwidth (the last being relevant only for coding applications). In the limit as $p \to \infty$, $|H(e^{j\omega})|$ matches $|S(e^{j\omega})|$ exactly (Figure 6.13), but at the cost of memory and computation. In general, poles are needed to represent all formants (two poles per resonance) in the signal bandwidth plus an additional 2–4 poles to approximate possible zeros in the spectrum and general spectral shaping (e.g., the standard for 8 kHz sampled speech is 10 poles [37]). The

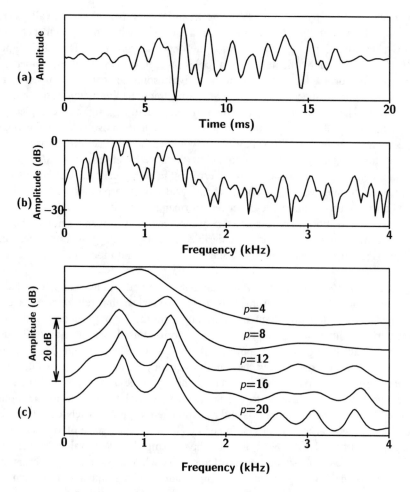

Figure 6.13 Signals and spectra in LPC for 20 ms of an /α/ vowel at 8000 samples/s: (a) time waveform, (b) speech spectrum, (c)–(g) LPC spectra using 4, 8, 12, 16, and 20 poles, respectively.

latter effects come mostly from the spectra of the glottal waveform and lip radiation, but zeros also arise from nasalized and unvoiced sounds. It is usually unnecessary to add more poles to the model for nasals, despite the extra nasal formants in such speech, since high-frequency formants in nasals have wide bandwidths and so little energy that their accurate spectral modeling is unimportant.

The all-pole LPC model can handle zeros indirectly; e.g., a zero at $z = a$ ($|a| < 1$) can be exactly represented by an infinite number of poles:

$$(1 - az^{-1}) = \frac{1}{1 - \sum_{n=1}^{\infty}(az^{-1})^n}. \qquad (6.34)$$

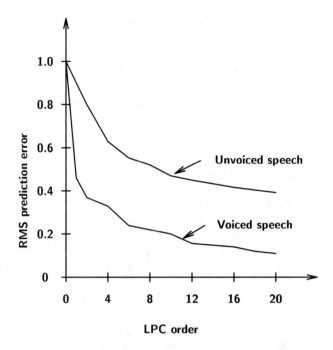

Figure 6.14 Normalized prediction error as a function of the LPC model order. (After Atal and Hanauer [39].)

Evaluating on the unit circle ($z = e^{j\omega}$), we can approximate the infinite-order denominator with a finite number of terms (e.g., M) and hence a finite number of poles. The high-order terms in Equation (6.34) can be ignored if $a^M \ll 1$. Wide-bandwidth zeros (i.e., those with small $|a|$) are more accurately modeled with a few poles than are zeros whose bandwidths are comparable to those of the formants. It is generally (but not universally [38]) assumed that 2–4 poles can handle the zeros and other glottal effects, given the ear's greater sensitivity to spectral peaks than valleys.

The prediction error energy E_p is often used as a measure of the accuracy of an LPC model. The *normalized prediction error* (i.e., divided by the speech energy), $V_p = E_p/R(0)$ (see Equation (6.31d)), decreases monotonically with predictor order p (Figure 6.14) (i.e., each additional pole improves the model). For voiced speech, after having enough poles to model the formant structure (e.g., $p = 10$), additional poles do little to improve the spectral fit (as measured by V_p), but they add significantly to the computation (and to bit rate, for vocoders). Unvoiced speech yields larger V_p because its excitation signal is spread out in time. The usual calculation of LPC coefficients ignores $u(n)$ in Equation (6.16). (The effects of $u(n)$ for voiced speech are small for a small analysis frame located in the middle of a pitch period, but this requires a period detector to find the F0 epochs before LPC analysis.) Unvoiced $u(n)$ has relatively constant energy over the analysis frame; in voiced speech, $u(n)$ has energy concentrated at the start of each pitch period (primarily when the vocal cords close), allowing $u(n)$ to be ignored for most of the speech samples. Thus, the LPC model is a better fit to voiced speech because ignoring $u(n)$ is valid for more time samples in Equation (6.21) for voiced speech. Some algorithms exploit this distinction by basing voiced–unvoiced decisions on the relative V_p (high, unvoiced; low, voiced).

A recent proposal to account for $u(n)$ in the LPC representation of voiced speech suggests modifying the spectral coefficients at the synthesis stage, to make the original speech and the corresponding synthetic speech more similar. Specifically, the first $p + 1$ autocorrelation coefficients $R(i)$ should be identical for the two signals, except for the interference of multiple excitations in $u(n)$ for the speech within the frame of analysis. In the case of voices with high F0 (leading to more excitations per frame), two iterations modifying the LPC coefficients to guarantee the $R(i)$ match lead to significant improvements in synthetic speech quality [40].

6.5.6 Updating the LPC Model Sample by Sample

We earlier described the *block estimation* approach to LPC analysis, where spectral coefficients are obtained for each successive frame of data. Alternatively, LPC parameters can be determined sample by sample, updating the model for each speech sample. For real-time implementation (e.g., echo cancellation in the telephone network [41]), this reduces the delay inherent in the block approach, where typical frame lengths of 20–30 ms cause 10–15 ms delays. Chapter 7 notes that ADPCM with feedback adaptation requires an instantaneous method for updating its predictor, based only on transmitted residual samples. Feedforward ADPCM allows block LPC estimation, but feedback ADPCM with its minimal delay and lack of side information does not. In instantaneous LPC estimation, a recursive procedure is necessary to minimize computation. Each new sample updates some intermediate speech measure (e.g., a local energy or covariance measure), from which the LPC parameters are revised. Recalculating and inverting the covariance matrix for each speech sample, as in the block methods, is unnecessary.

6.5.7 Transversal Predictors

The two basic ways to implement a linear predictor are the *transversal* form (i.e., direct-form digital filter) and the *lattice* form. The transversal predictor derives directly from Equation (6.16) and updates N LPC coefficients $a_k(n)$ (the kth spectral coefficient at time n) as follows:

$$a_k(n+1) = va_k(n) + (1 - v)a_k^* + G_k(n+1)e(n+1), \tag{6.35}$$

where a^* is a target vector of coefficients that is approached exponentially in time (depending on the damping factor v) during silence (i.e., when the LPC error $e(n) = 0$) and G is an "automatic gain control" vector (based on the N previous speech samples) that controls the model adaptation. The *gradient* or *least-mean-square* (LMS) approach assigns simple values to G:

$$G_k(n) = \frac{\hat{s}(n-k)}{C + \sum_{i=0}^{N-1} w^i \hat{s}^2(n-i-1)}, \tag{6.36}$$

where the denominator is simply a recent speech energy estimate (with weighting controlled by a damping factor w) and C is a constant to avoid division by zero during silence. Alternatives to the gradient approach, e.g., the *Kalman algorithm*, trade more computation for G against more accurate LPC coefficients [2, 42].

6.5.8 Lattice LPC Models

The *lattice* method for LPC typically involves both a *forward* and a *backward* prediction [43]. (These should not be confused with feedforward and feedback adaptation of waveform coders.) Block LPC analysis uses only forward prediction (i.e., the estimate $\hat{s}(n)$ is based on p prior samples of $s(n)$), but the estimation can be done similarly from p ensuing samples in a form of backward "prediction." Consider $a_m(n)$ to be the unit-sample response of a fixed $A_m(z)$, the inverse LPC filter for a block of data at the mth stage of the Durbin recursion (Equation (6.31)) (i.e., for an m-pole model). The usual (forward) error signal $f_m(n)$ is the convolution of $s(n)$ with $a_m(n)$. Applying Equation (6.31c),

$$f_m(n) = s(n) * a_{m-1}(n) - k_m s(n) * a_{m-1}(m - n),\qquad(6.37)$$

whose first term is the forward error from an $(m - 1)$th predictor and whose second term is a parallel backward error. Assigning $b_m(n)$ to this backward error yields a recursion formula:

$$f_m(n) = f_{m-1}(n) - k_m b_{m-1}(n - 1),\qquad(6.38)$$

where

$$b_m(n) = s(n) * a_m(m - n) = \sum_{l=n-m}^{n} s(l)a_m(m - n + l).\qquad(6.39)$$

Shifting index l by $n - m$ samples and noting that $a_m(0) = 1$ (from Equation (6.18)), we obtain

$$b_m(n) = s(n - m) - \sum_{l=1}^{m} a_m(l)s(n - m + l),\qquad(6.40)$$

which has the interpretation of predicting sample $s(n - m)$ from m ensuing samples of $s(n)$ (note the similarity to Equation (6.19)). The same set of $m + 1$ samples is involved in both the forward prediction of $s(n)$ and the backward prediction of $s(n - m)$. The recursion formula for the mth stage of backward prediction can be derived in similar fashion:

$$b_m(n) = b_{m-1}(n - 1) - k_m f_{m-1}(n).\qquad(6.41)$$

The recursion Equations (6.38) and (6.41) lead to the lattice flow diagram of Figure 6.15(a), with initial conditions of $f_0(n) = b_0(n) = s(n)$; i.e., using no predictor gives an "error" equal to the speech signal itself. The corresponding synthesis filter in Figure 6.15(b) can be derived directly from the same recursion equations by viewing Equation (6.38) as

$$f_{m-1}(n) = f_m(n) - k_m b_{m-1}(n - 1).\qquad(6.42)$$

The lattice synthesizer has the same form as one of the vocal tract models in Chapter 3, viewed as a lossless acoustic tube of p sections of equal length with uniform cross-sectional area A_m within each section. The reflection coefficients k_m could specify the amount of plane wave reflection at each section boundary:

$$k_m = \frac{A_m - A_{m-1}}{A_m + A_{m-1}}.\qquad(6.43)$$

Efforts to relate these k_m (obtained from speech) to corresponding vocal tract areas, however, have met with only limited success because (a) natural vocal tracts have losses, and (b) standard models using k_m must locate all losses at the glottal or labial ends [44]. If glottal

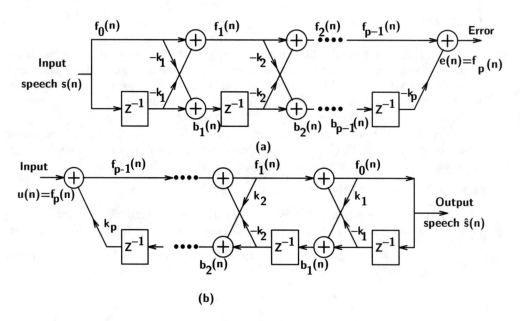

Figure 6.15 Lattice filters: (a) inverse filter $A(z)$, which generates both forward and backward error signals at each stage of the lattice; (b) synthesis filter $1/A(z)$.

pressure can be measured (e.g., through skin accelerometers attached to the throat) in addition to the speech signal, then accurate vocal tract shapes can be determined automatically [45].

Applying z transforms to Equation (6.37), we have

$$F_m(z) = S(z)[A_{m-1}(z) - k_m z^{-m} A_{m-1}(z^{-1})]. \quad (6.44)$$

If $S(z)$ is temporarily considered as unity (i.e., to find the filter's unit-sample response, using $s(n) = \delta(n)$), then $F_m(z) = A_m(z)$, yielding a recursion formula for the mth stage of the LPC inverse filter via the reflection coefficients:

$$A_m(z) = A_{m-1}(z) - k_m z^{-m} A_{m-1}(z^{-1}). \quad (6.45)$$

Minimizing the forward energy over an appropriate time window, Equation (6.38) gives

$$k_{m+1}^f = \frac{E[f_m(n) b_m(n-1)]}{E[b_m^2(n-1)]}, \quad (6.46)$$

where $E[\ ]$ means expectation (averaging), k_m^f denotes the reflection coefficient obtained using forward error minimization at the mth stage of LPC lattice analysis, and k_{m+1}^f is equal to the ratio of the cross-correlation between the forward and backward errors to the backward error energy. Equivalently, minimizing the backward error energy leads to

$$k_{m+1}^b = \frac{E[f_m(n) b_m(n-1)]}{E[f_m^2(n)]}, \quad (6.47)$$

the ratio of the cross-correlation to the forward error energy. The disadvantage of both approaches is that neither guarantees that $k_m < 1$ for all m, although it can be shown that either k_m^f or k_m^b must be so bounded for each m.

For instantaneous adaptation of LPC coefficients obtained via the lattice approach, the Itakura and Burg methods [33, 46] are popular. The Itakura method follows directly from the Levinson–Durbin recursion and defines the reflection coefficients as

$$k_m = \frac{E[f_{m-1}(n)b_{m-1}(n-1)]}{\{E[f_{m-1}^2(n)]E[b_{m-1}^2(n-1)]\}^{1/2}},$$ (6.48)

i.e., the partial correlation between forward and backward error signals, normalized by their energies. As PARCOR coefficients, the $k_m \leq 1$, thus guaranteeing stable synthesis filters (even when using quantized coefficient values and finite-wordlength computation [24]).

Windowing the error instead of the speech signal suggests an adaptive method to update the model sample by sample. The Burg technique minimizes

$$E_m = \sum_{n=-\infty}^{\infty} w(n)[f_m^2(n) + b_m^2(n)],$$ (6.49)

where the $w(n)$ error window could be rectangular (as in the Itakura method) or shaped so that more recent speech samples are weighted more heavily, e.g., simple real-pole filters of the form

$$W(z) = \frac{1}{(1 - \beta z^{-1})^L}.$$ (6.50)

(Good-quality speech results when $L = 3$ and $\beta = 1 - (100L/F_s)$ [47].) This leads to reflection coefficients involving the ratio of the cross-correlation between the forward and backward errors to the average of the two error energies:

$$k_m = \frac{\displaystyle\sum_{n=-\infty}^{\infty} w(n)f_{m-1}(n)b_{m-1}(n-1)}{\dfrac{1}{2}\displaystyle\sum_{n=-\infty}^{\infty} w(n)[f_{m-1}^2(n) + b_{m-1}^2(n-1)]}.$$ (6.51)

Coefficient magnitudes are bounded by unity if $w(n) > 0$ (over its finite duration). Figure 6.16 illustrates how the reflection coefficients for time $n + 1$ can be obtained from the immediately prior error samples. The filter memories for $W(z)$ retain the necessary information about earlier speech samples in the window. See [2, 48] for alternative *least-squares* (LS) approaches. Two-bit (16 kbit/s) ADPCM with fourth-order adaptive prediction performs best with the LS lattice approach, which yields SEGSNR of 15 dB, about 1–2 dB better than nonadaptive or other adaptive methods [2].

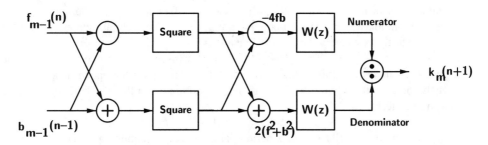

Figure 6.16 Adaptive estimation of reflection coefficients (only the *m*th stage of *p* identical stages is shown).

Traditional lattice methods, updating the LPC parameters every sample, require $5p$ multiplication operations per speech sample (where p is the LPC order), compared to p multiplies/sample in calculating the autocorrelation or covariance matrices in the block approaches. (This assumes that each sample is used in one matrix calculation, i.e., in nonoverlapping blocks of data, and ignores the matrix inversion for $N \gg p$, which adds $O(p^2)$ or $O(p^3)$ multiplies.) Similarly, three memory locations per sample (to store the forward and backward errors, and the speech) are needed in the lattice approach, compared with one location per sample for the other methods. More efficient techniques, however, exist, for block-lattice LPC analysis, making that approach computationally comparable to other block estimation LPC [46].

6.5.9 Window Considerations

Both window size N and order p should be small to minimize calculation in LPC analysis. However, since p is usually specified by the speech bandwidth, only N allows any flexibility to trade off spectral accuracy and computation. Due to windowing distortion, the autocorrelation LPC window must include at least two pitch periods for accurate spectral estimates (20–30 ms typically, to guarantee two periods even at low F0). In the lattice and covariance methods, the lack of signal windowing theoretically allows windows as short as $N = p$, but spectral accuracy usually increases with larger N. The major difficulty with short windows concerns the unpredictability of the speech excitation signal $u(n)$. The LPC model predicts a speech sample based on p prior samples, assuming that an all-pole vocal tract filter describes the signal. It makes no attempt to deconvolve $s(n)$ into $h(n)$ and $u(n)$ and cannot distinguish vocal tract resonances and excitation effects. The poles of the LPC model correspond primarily to vocal tract resonances but also account for the excitation disturbance.

Most LPC analysis is done pitch-asynchronously, i.e., without regard for F0; e.g., adaptive lattice techniques evaluate for every sample, and block methods usually examine the sets of N samples which are shifted periodically by N or $N/2$ samples. This leads to poorer spectral estimation when pitch epochs (the large initial samples of periods, which are unpredictable for small p) are included during an analysis frame. The problem is worse when N is small because some analysis frames are then dominated by poorly modeled excitation effects. Spectral accuracy improves if N is large enough to contain a few pitch periods, because the LPC model is good for speech samples in each period after the first p (i.e., after the first p samples, $s(n)$ is based on prior samples that all include the effects of the major pitch excitation). Use of a rectangular window to evaluate the error signal pitch-asynchronously leads to fluctuating spectral estimates, with the size of the variations inversely related to window length. They can be reduced by using a smooth (e.g., Hamming) window to weight the error in Equation (6.28) [49], at the cost of some increased computation. Another possible solution which trades off computation for improved spectral estimates, is to eliminate from the analysis window those speech samples $s(n)$ that lead to values of $e(n)$ exceeding a specified threshold [50]. These large-error samples (usually near pitch epochs) degrade the spectral estimates the most. This approach does not need a pitch epoch locator as in pitch-synchronous methods, but uses less efficient algorithms than the standard autocorrelation or covariance techniques do.

These problems can be partly avoided by *pitch-synchronous analysis*, where each analysis window is fully within a period. This, however, requires an accurate F0 estimator since short windows yield poor spectral estimation for frames improperly placed. The extra computation required for (sometimes unreliable) epoch location has deterred most LPC analysis from using short windows. For rapidly changing speech, however, accurate estimates require pitch-synchronous techniques [51]. Here, the covariance method is typically used since (unlike the autocorrelation method) it requires no explicit window that would distort the signal significantly over short frame analyses of less than one pitch period. The standard Burg method does not perform well with short windows because its use of both forward and backward errors presumes similar energy in the two residuals [52]. A modified Burg technique, which weights the instantaneous LPC error with a tapered window prior to error minimization, yields spectral estimates approaching those of the covariance method, except that formant bandwidths are underestimated [53].

6.5.10 Modifications to Standard LPC

The standard forms of all-pole LPC analysis, minimizing the energy in the error signal over a time window, are simple and computationally efficient. However, their spectral estimates are flawed due to inherent limitations in the procedure. Zeros in the speech spectrum can only be approximately modeled by poles, and their presence causes the pole estimates to deviate from actual formant values. Not accounting for vocal tract excitation in pitch-asynchronous LPC analysis leads to vocal tract estimates that vary with the fine structure of the speech spectrum. Such structure depends on environmental noise and the choice of analysis window as well as on the actual vocal tract excitation. Placement of the analysis window not aligned with a pitch period causes variation in LPC parameters even during stationary speech [54], which can cause warbling in LPC speech.

The problem of poor spectral estimation is especially acute for high-F0 voices, where several pitch impulses occur in a typical analysis frame and few harmonics are available to define the center frequencies and bandwidths of the crucial F1–F2 formants. When one harmonic dominates a formant, LPC often incorrectly places a pole frequency to coincide with the harmonic. Synthesis based on such parameters is usually poor when F0 deviates from its original values, as when F0 is quantized or when an alternate F0 counter is used.

Basic LPC analysis weighs high-amplitude frequencies (e.g., harmonic peaks) more than spectral valleys, which corresponds well with perceptual resolution. For high-F0 voices, however, the weighting could be adjusted to improve spectral estimates and vocoder speech quality. One could compress the amplitude of the speech spectrum before LPC analysis (e.g., by taking its cube root) [55]. This, however, may require a preliminary DFT and inverse DFT on the windowed speech signal (before and after the root operation, respectively) to obtain a transformed autocorrelation signal for LPC analysis. In a vocoder application, two more DFTs in the synthesis stage would be needed to compensate for the spectral distortion of the analysis stage.

A less costly way is to identify the harmonic peaks (through F0 estimation and a peak picking operation on the speech spectrum) and to transform the ragged speech spectrum $|S(e^{j\omega})|$ (with ripples due to the fine structure of the harmonics) into a smooth approximation of the vocal tract spectrum $|H(e^{j\omega})|$ via parabolic interpolation of the peaks [55]. Such a transformation preserves the basic shape of the spectral envelope, eliminating most of the fine-structure interference. After an inverse DFT, the resulting autocorrelation function can be used as input to standard autocorrelation method LPC analysis. For high-F0 voices, this approach improves spectral estimation and speech quality at the cost of extra computation.

Another approach, called *Perceptual Linear Prediction* (PLP), is useful for speech recognition. It follows some auditory phenomena in modifying basic LPC, e.g., using a critical-band power spectrum with a logarithmic amplitude compression. The spectrum is multiplied by the equal-loudness curve and raised to the power 0.33 to simulate the power law of hearing [56, 57]. Seventeen critical-band (CB) filters equally-spaced in Bark z,

$$z = 6 \log \left(\frac{f}{600} + \sqrt{\left(\frac{f}{600}\right)^2 + 1} \right),$$

map the range 0–5 kHz into 0–17 Bark. Each CB is simulated by a spectral weighting,

$$c_k(z) = \begin{cases} 10^{z-y_k} & \text{for } z \le y_k, \\ 1 & \text{for } y_k < z < y_k + 1, \\ 10^{-2.5(z-y_k-1)} & \text{for } z \ge y_k + 1, \end{cases}$$

where z_k are the center frequencies (roughly, $1, 2, \ldots 17$ Bark) and $y_k = z_k - 0.5$ (the zeroth filter is arbitrarily set equal to the first filter). The 10 dB/Bark roll-off for low frequencies and -25 dB/Bark roll-off for high frequencies matches typical CB filters. A fifth-order PLP can suppress speaker-dependent aspects of the speech spectrum, leading to improved speech recognition.

A related auditory-based analysis method called *Ensemble-Interval Histograms* (EIH) models synchrony phenomena with 85 cochlear filters equally spaced in log-frequency in the 200–3200 Hz range. It has seen some success in speech recognition. Another similar technique is the *correlogram*, which shows a series of short-time autocorrelations of auditory-neuron firing rates [58]. The ERB-scale (equivalent rectangular bandwidth) is yet another frequency scale of practical relevance, motivated by auditory phenomena [59].

In noisy conditions, doing LP analysis on part of the autocorrelation vector (rather than on the speech itself) has been shown to yield more robust parameters. One version of this method [60] models the magnitude spectrum of a one-sided (i.e., causal) autocorrelation (this involves the Hilbert transform); the benefit comes from an enhancement of peaks in the spectrum, at the expense of noise-corrupted valleys. Basic LPC models peaks rather than valleys, due to the use of the mean square error as a criterion; this method raises the spectrum to the second power, emphasizing the peaks even more. It and a related method (short-time modified coherence) [61] require more computation than basic LPC.

6.5.11 Emphasizing Low Frequencies

Standard LPC weighs all frequencies in the speech spectrum equally, although lower frequencies are better resolved by the ear and are more important for speech intelligibility than are higher frequencies. LPC modeling could be improved by combining subband coding (see Chapter 7) with LPC, which allows LPC analyses of different orders to model different frequency ranges according to their perceptual importance. *Selective linear prediction* [25] models the F1–F3 frequency range with the standard 2 poles/kHz (plus 2–3 poles for general shaping) and relies on only a few poles for the higher frequencies, where formant structure is of less importance (Figure 6.17). The filtering problems of subband coding, however, reduce the advantages of this approach.

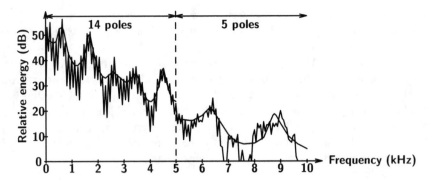

Figure 6.17 Speech spectrum (ragged line) and LPC spectrum (smooth line), corresponding to a 14-pole LPC analysis in the 0–5 kHz region and a 5-pole analysis in
the 5–10 kHz region. (After Makhoul [25] © IEEE.)

Other ways to emphasize low frequencies in LPC analysis include modifying the error
function or warping the frequency axis (as in PLP) following the perceptually based mel or
Bark scale. Minimizing the standard LPC error treats all frequencies equally; attempts to
utilize a frequency-weighted error without substantially increasing computation have been
partially successful [54, 62]. If frequency is warped with an all-pass transformation (a
standard procedure in designing digital filters [6]), DFTs and inverse DFTs are not needed,
thus reducing additional computation [63]. Such frequency-warping, however, appears to
yield improved speech quality only for very-low-order LPC vocoders (e.g., $p < 8$ for 4.8 kHz
bandwidth speech). In standard LPC analysis, too low an order causes perceptually important
lower formants to be inadequately modeled; but in frequency-warping LPC, the low-
frequency range takes on increased significance in proportion to the degree of the warping.
Frequency warping appears useful only where bit rate constraints impose a low order on the
LPC model.

In some applications, the behavior of the LPC inverse filter $A(e^{j\omega})$ is of concern at high
frequencies, where very high gain is possible if most of the energy near $\omega = \pi$ has been
eliminated during the lowpass filtering of the original analog speech (prior to A/D
conversion). In some coders, a predictor $P(e^{j\omega}) = 1 - A(e^{j\omega})$ is usually placed in a feedback
loop around a quantizer, which filters coarsely quantized speech samples. The quantization
adds broadband noise (including energy around $\omega = \pi$) to the input of the predictor filter,
which yields an output with unwarranted large gains at high frequencies. One solution is to
add a small amount of highpass noise to the digitized speech for input to the LPC analysis
(ideally the noise spectrum should be the complement of the A/D lowpass filter spectrum)
[49]. The noise is used only in determining $A(z)$, not in the actual waveform coding.

6.5.12 Pole-Zero LPC Models

Almost all applications of LPC use the all-pole (AR) model. By not modeling zeros
directly, the analysis equations (e.g., Equation (6.24)) are linear and have symmetries that
reduce computation. Pole-zero (ARMA) models require solution of nonlinear equations to
obtain the optimal set of parameters [64]. Since the quality of ARMA speech is only slightly
better than AR speech [65], pole-zero modeling is rarely used for coding. ARMA has
however shown good results in formant and voicing estimation [66], and can handle lossy

vocal tract models [67]. It has also been suggested for processing noisy speech [68], since the all-pole AR model is less valid in noise. Faster special-purpose hardware may increase use of ARMA in the future [69].

Approaches to ARMA modeling may trade off strict optimality in spectral representation and computation time. For instance, one method involves a two-step procedure that locates the poles first by a standard AR technique and then models the spectral *inverse* of the residual signal with a second AR model [70]. The residual after the first AR model presumably contains the effects of the zeros; thus, inverting its spectrum provides the input for a second all-pole modeling. Solving for the poles and zeros sequentially is efficient but does not guarantee that the pole-zero locations obtained would be those of a simultaneous, optimal solution.

A major difficulty in ARMA modeling is determining the order of the model, i.e., how many poles and zeros to use. A poor choice of model order leads to inaccurate estimation of both poles and zeros [71]. One study of 4.8 kHz male speech suggests using ten poles for voiced sounds and only five poles for unvoiced consonants, plus three zeros for the latter and five zeros for nasals [72]. The magnitude spectrum of any type of speech with 4 kHz bandwidth can be very accurately modeled with a *high-order* all-pole model, e.g., 40–50 poles [73]. In such a model, strong harmonics are directly approximated by pairs of poles. One may decompose such a high-order model $C(z)$ into low-order polynomials:

$$C(z) = \sum_{k=1}^{r} c_k z^{-k} = \frac{Q(z)}{P(z)}, \qquad (6.52)$$

where $Q(z)$ represents the zeros and $P(z)$ represents the poles, both with order much less than $r \approx 45$. Assuming p poles and q zeros, the problem reduces to solving $p + q$ linear equations involving the high-order LPC coefficients c_k, with a cross-correlation between the high-order residual signal and the original speech, and autocorrelations of the speech and the error signals [73]. Requiring 4–7 times as much computation as AR analysis, this ARMA method yields accurate results.

6.6 CEPSTRAL ANALYSIS

In speech analysis we usually estimate parameters of an assumed speech-production model. The most common model views speech as the output of a linear, time-varying system (the vocal tract) excited by either quasi-periodic pulses or random noise. Since the easily observable speech signal is the result of convolving excitation with vocal tract sample response, it would be useful to separate or "deconvolve" the two components. While unfeasible in general, such deconvolution works for speech because the convolved signals have very different spectra.

One step in *cepstral* deconvolution transforms a product of two spectra into a sum of two signals. If the resulting summed signals are sufficiently different spectrally, they may be separated by linear filtering. The desired transformation is logarithmic, in which $\log(EV) = \log(E) + \log(V)$, where E is the Fourier transform of the excitation waveform and V is the vocal tract response. Since the formant structure of V varies slowly in frequency compared to the harmonics or noise in E, contributions due to E and V can be linearly separated after an inverse Fourier transform.

6.6.1 Mathematical Details of Cepstral Analysis

Consider a simple signal $x(n) = a^n u(n)$ and its z transform $X(z) = 1/(1 - az^{-1})$, with a pole at $z = a$ and a zero at $z = 0$. For $\log(X(z))$ in a power series,

$$\log(X(z)) = \sum_{n=1}^{\infty} \frac{a^n}{n} z^{-n}, \qquad \text{if } |z| > |a|. \tag{6.53}$$

(A similar expansion holds for $n < 0$, if the region of convergence is $|z| < |a|$.) The *complex cepstrum* $\hat{x}(n)$ (the circumflex notation is often used to denote cepstra) is the inverse transform of $\log(X(z))$. In this example,

$$\hat{x}(n) = -\frac{a^n}{n} u(n - 1) \tag{6.54}$$

by simple inverse z transform, term by term. Thus $x(n)$ retains its exponential form in $\hat{x}(n)$, except for a more rapid decay due to the $1/n$ factor.

Because the logarithm of a product equals the sum of the individual log terms, a more complicated z transform consisting of several first-order poles and zeros results in a complex cepstrum that is the sum of exponential terms, each decaying with the extra $1/n$ factor. Since $\log(1/A) = -\log(A)$, the only difference between the effect of a pole and that of a zero in the complex cepstrum is the sign of the power series. The equal treatment of poles and zeros is an advantage for cepstral modeling (vs all-pole LPC).

For a more general $X(z)$ (e.g., speech) that converges on the unit circle, poles p_k and zeros z_k inside the unit circle contribute linear combinations of p_k^n/n and $-z_k^n/n$, for $n > 0$, while corresponding poles a_k and zeros b_k outside the unit circle contribute summed terms of the form $-p_k^n/n$ and z_k^n/n, for $n < 0$. The complex cepstrum is of infinite extent, even if $x(n)$ has finite duration. However, given a stable, infinite-duration $x(n)$, $\hat{x}(n)$ decays more rapidly in time than the original $x(n)$:

$$|\hat{x}(n)| < \alpha \frac{\beta^{|n|}}{|n|}, \qquad \text{for } |n| \to \infty, \tag{6.55}$$

where α is a constant and β is the maximum absolute value among all $p_k, z_k, 1/a_k$, and $1/b_k$ (which corresponds to the closest pole or zero to the unit circle).

For speech, the closest pole involves F1, which has relatively narrow bandwidth and dominates the rate of amplitude decay in most pitch periods. While many periods in speech $s(n)$ have time constants about 10–30 ms, the $1/n$ factor in Eq. (6.54) causes $\hat{s}(n)$ to decay rapidly within a few milliseconds of $n = 0$. This is in distinct contrast to the excitation component $e(n)$ of voiced speech $s(n)$, which may be viewed as the convolution of a sample train $e(n)$ (where $N =$ pitch period) and the vocal tract response $v(n)$ (including glottal effects). Using Fourier transforms (for convergence when using impulse signals), recall that $E(e^{j\omega})$ is a uniform train of impulses with frequency spacing of $2\pi/N$. Taking the logarithm of the Fourier transform affects only the areas of the impulses, not their spacing. Thus the complex cepstrum $\hat{e}(n)$ retains the same form as $e(n)$, i.e., a sample train of period N. Since $S(z) = E(z)V(z)$, $\log(X(z)) = \log(E(z)) + \log(V(z))$ and $\hat{s}(n) = \hat{e}(n) + \hat{v}(n)$. With $\hat{v}(n)$ decaying to near zero over its first few milliseconds and $\hat{e}(n)$ being nonzero only at $n = 0, \pm N, \pm 2N, \pm 3N, \ldots$, the two functions are easily separated via a rectangular window. A suitable boundary for that window would be the shortest possible pitch period, e.g., 3–4 ms.

The duration and shape of the speech analysis window $w(n)$ can have a significant effect on the cepstrum. The simple discussion above must be modified, since the signal under analysis is

$$x(n) = s(n)w(n) = [e(n) * v(n)]w(n). \tag{6.56}$$

Much research has assumed that Equation (6.56) can be approximated by

$$x(n) \approx [e(n)w(n)] * v(n), \tag{6.57}$$

which is valid for impulsive $e(n)$ (as in voiced speech) only if

$$w(n) \approx w(n + M), \tag{6.58}$$

where M is the effective duration of $v(n)$. Unfortunately, typical cepstral analysis windows tend to violate Equation (6.58). As a result, the vocal tract contribution to the cepstrum is repeated every pitch period and is subject to a double sinc-like distortion [74]. Applications using the windowed cepstrum should compensate for this distortion and should employ a cepstral window no larger than half the expected pitch period to avoid aliasing.

6.6.2 Applications for the Cepstrum

Applications for cepstral analysis occur in speech vocoders, spectral displays, formant tracking (Figure 6.18), and F0 detection [75]. Samples of $\hat{x}(n)$ in its first 3 ms describe $v(n)$ and can be coded separately from the excitation. The later is viewed as voiced if $\hat{x}(n)$ exhibits sharp pulses spaced at intervals typical of pitch periods, and the interval is then deemed to be $1/F0$. If no such structure is visible in $\hat{x}(n)$, the speech is considered unvoiced. The Fourier transform of $\hat{v}(n)$ provides a "cepstrally smoothed" spectrum, without the interfering effects of $e(n)$ (see Figure 6.18).

In practice, the complex cepstrum is not needed; the real cepstrum suffices, defined as the inverse transform of the logarithm of the speech magnitude spectrum:

$$c(n) = \frac{1}{2\pi} \int_{\omega=0}^{2\pi} \log|X(e^{j\omega})|e^{j\omega n}\, d\omega. \tag{6.59}$$

For real signals $x(n)$, $c(n)$ is the even part of $\hat{x}(n)$ because

$$\hat{X}(e^{j\omega}) = \log(X(e^{j\omega})) = \log|X(e^{j\omega})| + j\arg[X(e^{j\omega})] \tag{6.60}$$

and the magnitude is real and even, while the phase is imaginary and odd. In cepstral speech coding, as in other coding techniques (see Chapter 7), the phase may be discarded for economy, at the risk of some degradation in output speech quality.

To render the cepstrum suitable for digital algorithms, the DFT must be used in place of the general Fourier transform in Equation (6.59):

$$c_d(n) = \frac{1}{N}\sum_{k=0}^{N-1} \log|X(k)|e^{j2\pi kn/N} \qquad \text{for } n = 0, 1, \ldots, N-1. \tag{6.61}$$

Replacing $X(e^{j\omega})$ with $X(k)$ is equivalent to sampling the Fourier transform (multiplication by an impulse train) at N equally spaced frequencies from $\omega = 0$ to 2π. Including the inverse DFT, the net effect is to convolve the original $c(n)$ with a uniform sample train of period N:

$$c_d(n) = \sum_{i=-\infty}^{\infty} c(n + iN). \tag{6.62}$$

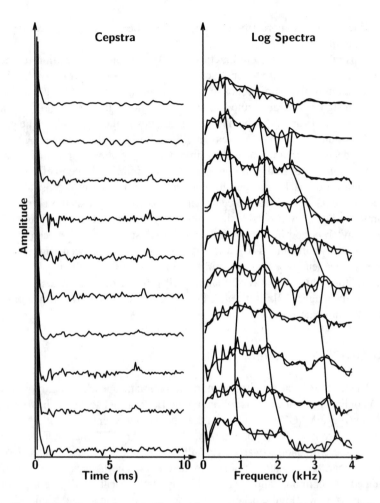

Figure 6.18 Automatic formant estimation from cepstrally smoothed log spectra. (After Schafer and Rabiner [9].)

Thus, the "digital" version $c_d(n)$ of the cepstrum contains copies of $c(n)$, at intervals of N samples. The resulting aliasing is not important if N, the duration of the DFT analysis window, is large enough. N is usually a few hundred samples, which more than suffices to eliminate any aliasing problem in the $\hat{v}(n)$ part of the cepstrum. The $\hat{e}(n)$ components for voiced speech extend into the high time range of $c(n)$, though, and may cause aliasing problems for $c_d(n)$. Typically, however the analysis frame contains a few pitch periods that are sufficiently nonidentical to cause the impulses in $\hat{e}(n)$ to be of lower amplitude as n increases. This minimizes the interference of aliased copies of $c(n)$ on the copy of interest near $n = 0$.

The cepstrum has not been popular for speech coding due to its computational complexity. Two DFTs and a logarithm operation are needed to obtain $c(n)$, which is windowed to separate $\hat{v}(n)$ and $\hat{e}(n)$. Then inverse operations (two more DFTs and an exponential) reconstruct $v(n)$, which is convolved at the synthesis stage with a synthetic $e(n)$ to generate output speech. In addition, good-quality speech has required coding up to 3 ms of

$c(n)$, which involves more stored samples/s of speech than other coding approaches, for comparable quality.

Cepstral analysis is more practical for F0 or formant estimation (especially in speech recognition) since response reconstruction is unnecessary. A further application for cepstra is the elimination of fixed-time echos in speech signals, e.g., in the telephone network. An echo in a speech signal $x(n)$ can be modeled as convolution with $\delta(n) + A\delta(n - N)$, where A is the percentage of echo and N is the number of samples in the echo delay. The effect is similar to that of periodic $e(n)$ samples exciting $v(n)$, with the echo introducing into $c(n)$ a set of impulses, decaying in amplitude with time n and spaced at intervals of N samples. A comb filter, with notches located at multiples of N, can eliminate the echo effects in $c(n)$, which can then be converted back into speech, much as in the manner of a cepstral speech coder. This procedure works best when the echo delay N is fixed (so that the comb filter need not be dynamic) and when N is outside the range where $c(n)$ would be significantly nonzero; e.g., an echo at a pitch period interval would result in whispered output speech after comb filtering.

Several modifications to basic cepstral analysis have been suggested. One claims to overcome a tendency for the cepstrum to overestimate formant bandwidths, and accounts for some auditory traits in a way similar to PLP [76]. "Root cepstral analysis" also has some potential advantages [77]. Lastly, an LPC spectrum is often used in Equation (6.61) instead of a DFT, to eliminate F0 effects.

6.6.3 Mel-Scale Cepstrum

The most popular analysis method for automatic speech recognition uses the cepstrum, with a nonlinear frequency axis following the Bark or mel scale. Such *mel-frequency cepstral coefficients* c_n (MFCCs) provide an alternative representation for speech spectra which incorporates some aspects of audition. An LPC or DFT magnitude spectrum S of each speech frame is frequency-warped (to follow the bark or critical-band scale) and amplitude-warped (logarithmic scale), before the first 8–14 coefficients c_n of an inverse DFT are calculated. A common approach [78] simulates critical-band filtering with a set of 20 triangular windows (Figure 6.19), whose log-energy outputs are designated X_k; if M cepstral coefficients are desired, they are

$$c_n = \sum_{k=1}^{20} X_k \cos\left[n\left(k - \frac{1}{2}\right) \frac{\pi}{20} \right] \qquad \text{for } n = 1, 2, \ldots, M. \qquad (6.63)$$

These windows are sometimes called filters, but they simply weight spectral $S(i)$ values across a frequency index i (i.e., they do not filter time signals).

The initial c_0 coefficient represents the average energy in the speech frame and is often discarded (amplitude normalization); c_1 reflects the energy balance between low and high frequencies, positive values indicating sonorants and negative values for frication. (This is due to the cosine weighting in the final IDFT of the cepstral calculation: for c_1, the one-period cosine weights the lower half of the log spectrum positively and the upper half negatively.) For $i > 1$, c_i represent increasingly fine spectral detail (as the cosine with i periods weights shorter frequency ranges (corresponding to $0.25F_s/i$ Hz) alternately positively and negatively). As with LPC a_k, no simple relationship exists between c_i and formants; e.g., in speech with four formants, a high c_2 suggests high energy in F1 and F3 and low energy in F2 and F4, but such a relationship is only approximate when the formants deviate from their average positions.

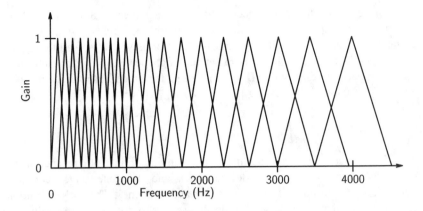

Figure 6.19 Filter bank for generating mel-based cepstral coefficients. (After Davis and
Mermelstein [78] © IEEE.)

6.7 OTHER SPECTRAL ESTIMATION METHODS (‡)

Since the spectral distribution of speech energy as a function of both time and frequency is
widely considered to be the most important factor in speech production and perception,
analysis applications search for efficient time–frequency representations (TFRs). The Fourier
Transform (FT) and related spectral measures, such as LPC and the cepstrum, are by far the
most common TFRs. This is due to their mathematical simplicity, ease of computation, and
easy interpretation. Spectrographic displays show clearly where energy is concentrated in
two-dimensional time–frequency plots. However, the use of a fixed window for each display
leads to an obligatory compromise for resolution between time and frequency (e.g., good time
and poor frequency resolution in wideband spectrograms). Some alternative TFRs have been
explored for speech analysis to avoid this compromise, at the cost of some loss of ease of
interpretation.

6.7.1 Karhunen–Loeve Transform (KLT)

The objective of speech analysis is usually to reduce the dimensionality of an input
signal vector, while retaining the pertinent information of the vector for applications such as
coding or recognition. Relatively simple transformations such as the FT or LPC are most
common. However, as computers increase in capacity, more complex algorithms become
feasible. The KLT has the advantage of being optimal in compressing a vector, but is
expensive in computation. For KLT, an N-dimensional speech vector $\mathbf{X}$ is converted to a set
of N eigenvectors ϕ_j and N corresponding weights (eigenvalues) λ_j. The λ_j can be rank-
ordered in terms of the relative energy (and thus perceptual importance) of each ϕ_j (the ϕ_j act
as basis functions). The FT is a special case of the KLT, where ϕ_j are harmonically related
sinusoids (where F0 corresponds to the frame length). The more general KLT allows different
ϕ_j for each frame of data, which usually yields a much more efficient choice of basis
functions. As a result, the speech frame can be very compactly represented by a few
eigenvectors. As an example, suppose the input vector is one pitch period of a voiced speech
signal; the KLT would likely select damped sinusoids (corresponding to the formants) as
eigenvectors, and the eigenvalues would decrease in value with frequency (that for F1 being

highest), following the usual spectral tilt of voiced speech. Since formants and F0 are so dynamic, the simpler FT uses undamped harmonically related sinusoids usually with no correlation to F0; as such, the spectral information is widely spread throughout the Fourier coefficients. The KLT, while costly in determining a new set of ϕ_j for each frame, has a much more compact representation. Due to its need for much calculation, it has not had wide application in speech processing [79].

6.7.2 Wavelets

The logarithmic scale seems to play an important role in speech production and especially in perception. The decibel, mel, and semitone scales correlate better with perception than do linear scales for energy and frequency. The ear's resolution decreases as energy and frequency increase. The decibel scale easily handles the nonlinearity for energy, but most spectral displays retain a fixed analysis bandwidth for simplicity. The *wavelet transform* (WT) replaces the fixed bandwidth of the FT with one proportional to frequency (i.e., constant Q), which allows better time resolution at high frequencies than the FT (especially for brief sounds). The resulting loss of frequency resolution as frequency increases is acceptable in most applications. The discrete WT for a speech signal $s(n)$ is

$$WT_n(k) = \sum_{m=-\infty}^{\infty} s(m)\gamma(n, m, k). \tag{6.64}$$

The WT simply replaces the frequency-shifted lowpass filter $e^{-j2\pi km/N}w(n-m)$ of the FT with a wavelet $\gamma(n, m, k)$. Both the FT and WT preserve time shifts (i.e., a delayed speech signal simply delays the spectral representation), but the WT replaces the FT's preservation of frequency shifts with one of time scaling instead. The most common wavelet has the form $\gamma(n, m, k) = \gamma((m-n)k)$; $\gamma(n)$ is usually a bandpass function (often Gaussian-shaped) centered in time around $n = 0$. Since the WT suffers the same basic problem of trading time and frequency as does the FT, its application to speech has been limited [80–82] (see however a recent coder [83]).

6.7.3 Wigner Distribution

While the linear properties of the FT and WT are very useful, their inherent time–frequency trade-off is often a problem. The choice of the length of the FT fixes a constant time and frequency resolution; the WT gives good time resolution at high frequencies and good frequency resolution at low frequencies (which may correspond better to human perception). The basic trade-off nonetheless remains. A class of quadratic TFRs, of which the *Wigner* (or *Wigner–Ville*) *distribution* (WD) is prominent, is able to show fine resolution in time and frequency simultaneously, but at the cost of significant interference terms (ITs) in the representation, as well as negative values, which hinder their interpretation. Linear TFRs (e.g., the FT) have the advantage that the distortion of ITs for multicomponent signals (e.g., speech, with its many harmonics) is limited to the time and frequency ranges where the components overlap. Energy in spectrograms is smeared in time or frequency over a range depending on the analysis bandwidth, but the smearing is local and often easily tolerated in visual or algorithmic interpretation. In quadratic TFRs, ITs go beyond simple smearing to appear at distant time and frequency locations (typically at points corresponding to averages in time or frequency). With *a priori* knowledge about the nature of the components in an input signal (e.g., harmonics), distant ITs may sometimes be attenuated, but in general the interpretation and use of quadratic TFRs are more complicated than for the common linear TFRs.

Given the importance of energy in speech analysis, a quadratic TFR is desirable, but the power or energy spectrum contains cross-terms that do not occur in the linear FT. For a signal with N components $s(n) = \sum_{i=1}^{N} s_i(n)$, the power spectrum has N desired terms (the FT of each $s_i^2(n)$) and $(N^2 - N)/2$ (undesired) cross-terms (the FT of $2s_i(n)s_j(n)$ for each $i \neq j$). The large number of cross-ITs hinders use of quadratic TFRs. There is a general compromise between good time–frequency concentration (e.g., in the Wigner distribution) and small ITs (e.g., in the FT). The WD has many desirable mathematical properties [81], e.g., it is real-valued, preserves time and frequency shifts, and can be viewed as a two-dimensional display of energy over the time–frequency plane:

$$W(t,f) = \int_\tau s(t + \tau/2)s^*(t - \tau/2)\exp(-j2\pi ft)d\tau = \int_v S(f + v/2)S^*(f - v/2)\exp(j2\pi vt)dv.$$

$$(6.65)$$

The ITs of the WD are oscillatory in nature, and thus can be attenuated by smoothing. A smoothed WD trades decreased ITs for some broadening of time–frequency concentration; the Choi–Williams distribution is a popular version. It is doubtful that wavelets or quadratic TFRs will displace the FT [13, 84], which remains the primary basis of speech analysis. A recent application to speech (*minimum cross-entropy time–frequency distribution*) shows promise, but at high cost [85].

6.7.4 Other Recent Techniques

The search for better analysis methods has led to nonlinear techniques [86], which sacrifice simplicity and efficient calculation to obtain more compact or useful representations of speech. One motivation for nonlinear analysis is that, as a random process, speech is not Gaussian, and thus has non-zero third-order (and higher) moments (Gaussians are fully described by their mean and variance). Relatively little speech research has explicitly exploited third- and higher-order statistics ("cumulants") [87]. Linear models cannot handle higher-order statistics of this sort. In particular, apparently random aspects of speech (e.g., in the residuals of LPC) may be due to *chaos* (and hence predictable with nonlinear models) [88]. In most cases, the added cost of nonlinear methods and the small modeling gains (e.g., 2–4 dB in SNR [88]) have limited their application (e.g., nonlinear prediction is much less used than LPC [89]). Recent analysis methods from other domains (e.g., fractals [90]) often do not apply easily to speech, although a recent coder reports good results [91].

6.8 F0 ("PITCH") ESTIMATION

Determining the fundamental frequency (F0) or "pitch" of a signal is important in many speech applications. (Although pitch is perceptual, and what is being measured is actually F0, the estimators are commonly called "pitch detectors.") In voiced speech the vocal cords vibrate; "pitch" refers to the percept of the fundamental frequency of such vibration or the resulting periodicity in the speech signal. It is the primary acoustic cue to intonation and stress in speech, and is crucial to phoneme identification in tone languages. Most low-rate voice coders requires accurate F0 estimation for good reconstructed speech, and some medium-rate coders use F0 to reduce transmission rate while preserving high-quality speech.

F0 patterns are useful in speaker recognition and synthesis (in the latter, natural intonations must be simulated by rule). Real-time F0 displays can also give feedback to the deaf learning to speak.

F0 determination is fairly simple for most speech, but complete accuracy has eluded the many published algorithms, owing to speech's nonstationary nature, irregularities in vocal cord vibration, the wide range of possible F0 values, interaction of F0 with vocal tract shape, and degraded speech in noisy environments [26, 92, 93]. Instrumental methods can estimate F0 using information other than the speech signal, e.g., by measuring the impedance of the larynx as the vocal cords open and close through the use of contact microphones or accelerometers attached to the body, or via ultrasound or actual photography of the vocal cords. Most F0 detectors, however, are algorithms using only the speech signal as input. They often yield a *voicing decision* as part of the process, in which up to four classes of speech can be distinguished; voiced, unvoiced, combined (e.g., /z/), and nonspeech (silence, or background noise). Unlike F0 estimation, voicing determination (involving discrete categories) appears well suited to pattern recognition techniques [94, 95]. Voicing estimates can be accurate to about 95% if SNR exceeds 10 dB, but fail for SNR below 0 dB [96]. While voicing decisions are often a by-product of F0 estimators, better accuracy can result with separate algorithms.

F0 can be determined either from periodicity in time or from regularly spaced harmonics in frequency. Time-domain F0 estimators have three components: a preprocessor (to filter and simplify the signal via data reduction), a basic F0 extractor (to locate pitch epochs in the waveform), and a postprocessor (to correct errors). The algorithms try to locate one or more of the following aspects in the speech signal: the fundamental harmonic, a quasi-periodic time structure, an alternation of high and low amplitudes, or points of discontinuities. Harmonics and periodicities usually provide good results but fail in certain instances. The F0 algorithms trade complexity in one component for that in another; e.g., harmonic extraction requires a complex filter as preprocessor but allows an elementary basic extractor that may simply count zero-crossings of the filtered speech. Nonzero thresholds and hysteresis are used in postprocessing to eliminate irrelevant zero-crossings. The preprocessor is often a simple lowpass filter, but problems in choosing its cutoff frequency arise due to the large range of possible F0 values from different speakers.

Frequency-domain methods for F0 estimation involve correlation, maximum likelihood, and other spectral techniques where speech is examined over a short-term window. Autocorrelation, average magnitude difference, cepstrum, spectral compression, and harmonic matching methods are among the varied spectral approaches [92]. They generally have higher accuracy than time-domain methods, but need more computation.

Real-time F0 estimators must produce values with little delay. Since most frequency-domain methods require a buffer of speech samples prior to the spectral transformation, they are not as fast as those operating directly on the time waveform. Some F0 detectors can be modified for speed, but lose the timing of pitch periods; e.g., periodicity (and the duration of the period) can be evaluated more quickly than finding the actual locations of periods. Such F0 estimators do not output period times (useful for segmentation purposes) but yield period durations suitable for applications such as voice coders.

6.8.1 Time-Domain F0 Techniques

F0 estimation seems simple; humans, especially trained phoenticians, can easily segment most speech into successive pitch periods. Since the major excitation of the vocal tract for a pitch period occurs when the vocal cords close, each period tends to start with high amplitude (referred to as an *epoch*) and then to follow a decaying-amplitude envelope. Since voiced speech is dominated by first-formant energy, the rate of decay is usually inversely proportional to the F1 bandwidth. Except when speech has short periods or a narrow F1, sufficient decay allows epoch location by simple peak-picking, with some basic constraints on how long periods may be. If speakers may range from an infant or soprano singer to a deep baritone, possible pitch periods extend from less than 2 ms to more than 20 ms, i.e., a range >18 ms, although typical ranges are smaller, e.g., about 6 ms for adult males. The rate of F0 change is limited; in a voiced section of speech, F0 usually changes slowly with time, rarely by more than an octave over 100 ms. Before applying such continuity constraints, one must find reliable pitch periods within each voiced section since F0 can change greatly during unvoiced speech (i.e., the resumption of voicing after a silence or obstruent can have F0 very different from that at the end of the previous voiced section).

Most F0 estimation difficulties occur at voiced–unvoiced boundaries, where continuity constraints are less useful and where pitch periods are often irregular. Other problems are due to sudden amplitude and formant changes that may occur at phone boundaries. To aid peak-picking and other methods, the input speech is normally lowpass-filtered in a preprocessing stage to retain only F1 (e.g., the 0–900 Hz range). This removes the influence of other formants (which confound F0 estimation) while still retaining enough strong harmonics to yield a "cleaner" signal for peak-picking. One approach chooses candidates for epochs with a variable-amplitude threshold: since all periods exceed 2 ms, the threshold remains high for 2 ms after each estimated epoch, ignoring all signal excursions right after the start of a period, and then the threshold decays exponentially at a rate typical of pitch periods [97].

A more direct approach filters out all speech energy except the fundamental harmonic and then detects zero crossings (which occur twice every period for a sinusoid such as the fundamental). A major difficulty is determining the cutoff for the lowpass filter: high enough to allow one harmonic from a high-F0 voice yet low enough to reject the second harmonic of a low-F0 voice. Secondly, many applications use bandpass-filtered speech (e.g., telephone speech, which eliminates the 0–300 Hz range), and the fundamental harmonic is often not present. One solution to this latter problem is to reconstruct the fundamental from higher harmonics via a nonlinear distortion, e.g., passing speech through a rectifier, which generates energy at all harmonics.

F0 estimation in the time domain has two advantages: efficient calculation, and specification of times for the pitch epochs. The latter is useful when pitch periods must be manipulated (e.g., for pitch synchronous analysis, or to reconstruct the glottal waveform) [27]. F0 values alone suffice for many analysis applications, e.g., vocoders. However, systems that vary speaking rate (speeding or slowing, depending on preferred listening rates) often delete or duplicate pitch periods, splicing at epoch times to minimize waveform discontinuities. Knowledge of period locations is crucial here, as well as for types of speech synthesis and coding which concatenate periods. Spectral F0 estimators do not provide such information, but normally yield more reliable F0 estimates.

6.8.2 Short-Time Spectral Techniques

The second class of F0 estimators operates on a block (short-time frame) of speech samples, transforming them spectrally to enhance the periodicity information in the signal. Periodicity appears as peaks in the spectrum at the fundamental and its harmonics. While peaks in the time signal are often due to formant (especially F1) interaction with the glottal excitation, spectral peaks are usually easier to relate to F0. In these systems, one can view the spectral transformation as a preprocessor and a spectral peak detector as the basic F0 estimator; a postprocessor then examines estimates from successive frames to correct obvious errors. These errors could be major, e.g., F0 doubling or halving, which result from confusing F0 with its first harmonic. Doubling tends to occur when the energy level in the fundamental is weak compared to adjacent harmonics. (F0 halving is more common in time-domain methods, when two periods are mistaken as one.) Since F0 cannot physically change one octave during a frame (typically 10–30 ms), a postprocessor applies continuity constraints to smooth any estimates out of line with the neighboring F0 contour. *Fine* F0 errors of a few hertz are more difficult to deal with than *coarse*, major errors (e.g., doubling) and tend to arise when analysis frames are too short (not containing enough information to specify F0 accurately) or too long (if F0 changes rapidly within the frame). Since many systems evaluate F0 independently for each frame, fairly simple postprocessing can often significantly improve performance [26].

These examples illustrate the tradeoffs in choosing frame length. As in other windowing applications, the best speech parameters are obtained if the signal is stationary during the frame. Thus the frame must be short, a few pitch periods at most, since F0 may change rapidly. Abrupt spectral changes at phone boundaries can also affect spectral F0 estimators. The frame must nonetheless contain at least two periods to provide periodicity information. The precision of F0 measurement is proportional to the number of samples in the analysis frame; thus short frames inherently are more vulnerable to fine pitch errors. The single F0 estimate from each analyzed frame provides an average F0 value for that frame.

One complication in F0 estimation is caused by phase distortion (found in many transmission media, e.g., telephony) and by phase differences among harmonics. Since speech spectral phase has a shift of 180° near each formant, the harmonics in the 200–900 Hz range of F1 have phase differences that complicate the waveform and can obscure periodicity for time-domain F0 estimators. One solution is to eliminate phase effects by peak-picking, not directly on the filtered speech signal, but on its short-time autocorrelation $\phi(k)$ [98]. Recall that $\phi(k)$ is the inverse Fourier transform of the energy spectrum (i.e., $|X(e^{j\omega})|^2$) and thus sets the phase of each squared harmonic to zero. Although a time-domain signal, $\phi(k)$ cannot locate pitch epochs because of phase loss in the short-time analysis.

Since F0 estimation, and not faithful reproduction of the power spectrum, is the objective here, the speech signal is often distorted during preprocessing before autocorrelation to reduce calculation and to enhance periodicity parameters. *Center clipping s(n)* (Figure 6.20), in which low-amplitude samples are set to zero and the magnitude of high-amplitude samples is reduced, is sometimes used to improve F0 estimation [99]. (Such clipping may, however, hurt F0 detection in noisy speech [100].) A variable clipping threshold, typically 30% of the maximum $|s(n)|$, must be used to adapt to different speech intensities. *Infinite peak clipping*, which reduces $s(n)$ to a zero-crossing signal, also yields good F0 estimation through autocorrelation and significantly reduces calculation, since all multiplications involve only zeros and ones. As an alternative to clipping, the signal can be raised to a high power (while preserving the algebraic sign of each speech sample) in order to highlight peaks in $s(n)$.

Estimating F0 directly by trying to locate the fundamental spectral peak is often unreliable because the speech signal may have been bandpass filtered (e.g., in the telephone network) or the fundamental may have low energy if F1 is high. The harmonic structure (spectral peaks at multiples of F0) is a more reliable indicator of F0; the frequency of the greatest common divisor of the harmonics provides a good F0 estimate. Female speech, with its widely spaced harmonics, often yields more reliable F0 estimates than male speech (sometimes female speech is so dominated by one harmonic as to appear almost sinusoidal).

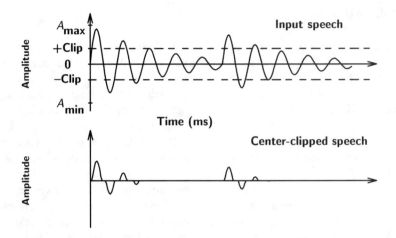

Figure 6.20 An example showing how center clipping affects two pitch periods. (After Sondhi [99] © IEEE.)

One approach measures the separation of adjacent harmonics; an alternative is to compress the spectrum by integer factors (i.e., compress the frequency scale by factors of two, three, four, etc.): a sum of these spectra has its strongest peak at F0 due to reinforcement of harmonics shifted down [26, 101].

Another variation is the *harmonic-sieve* F0 estimator. Rather than shift the speech spectrum, a spectral "sieve" with equally spaced holes is aligned with the spectrum; the frequency spacing at which the most harmonics line up with holes of the sieve is considered to be F0. One implementation [102] processes narrowband DFT spectra to simulate the ear's frequency and temporal resolution in identifying harmonics.

Maximum-likelihood methods provide another F0 estimator, which behaves especially well for noisy speech [103]. One way to determine the period of $s(n)$ in background noise is to add a delayed version, $s(n - D)$, to the original. When $D = 1/F0$, $s(n) + s(n - D)$ is strong, while the noise (out of phase due to the delay) tends to cancel. Finally, a recent F0 estimator with good results (especially for noisy speech) is based on auditory models [104].

Spectral F0 detectors give more accurate estimates than time-domain methods but require about 10 times more calculation due to the spectral transformation. The transformation focuses information about speech periodicity in ways that time-domain analysis cannot. Assuming that voicing determination is part of F0 detection, the performance of different systems can be rated objectively in terms of four types of errors: gross F0 errors (e.g., doubling), fine F0 errors, mistaking a voiced speech frame for unvoiced, and vice versa. No algorithm is superior in all four categories [93]. Alternatively, the detectors can be evaluated perceptually by using them in speech vocoders that represent excitation in terms of F0 and voicing decisions. No one type of objective F0 error correlates well with the subjective quality of coded speech, but voiced-to-unvoiced errors appear to be the most objectionable since they lead to harsh, noisy sounds where periodic sounds are expected [105]. While subjective and objective measures of F0 performance are not well correlated, there does not seem to be a large range of variation in coded speech quality using different major F0 algorithms. A good choice is probably the computationally simple AMDF (see Section 6.3), which ranks high in subjective tests, both for speech coders that crucially rely on voicing decisions and for those more concerned with F0 errors [100].

6.9 ROBUST ANALYSIS

A speech signal contains information from multiple sources: speaker, recording environment, and transmission channel. We are usually interested in extracting information about what is being said (for speech coding or recognition) or who is saying it (for speaker recognition). Most analysis methods, however, cannot easily distinguish the desired speaker signal from the unwanted effects of background noise, competing speakers, and the channel. Many analysis methods degrade as noise increases (e.g., LPC; F0 estimation [98]). Chapter 8 will examine ways to enhance speech signals and Chapter 10 will deal with recognition of noisy signals. Here we briefly discuss some analysis methods to suppress undesired components in speech signals.

Some of the "noise" in speech concerns variability on the speaker's part and must be handled on a stochastic basis, examining much "training" speech to obtain reliable models of speakers' voices (see Chapter 10). Distortions due to the communication channel and recording medium usually vary slowly compared to the dynamics of speech. Background noise (e.g., clicks, pops), on the other hand, often varies more rapidly than vocal tract movements. Suppressing spectral components of a speech signal that vary more quickly or slowing than the desired speech can improve the quality of speech analysis.

Often a mean spectrum or cepstrum is subtracted from that of each speech frame (e.g., blind deconvolution), to eliminate channel effects. The mean may require a long-term average for efficiency, which is difficult for real-time applications. Alternatively, the mean is estimated from a prior section of the input signal thought to be silent; this requires a speech detector and assumes that pauses occur regularly in the speech signal. If the channel changes with time, the mean must be updated periodically.

The RASTA (RelAtive SpecTrAl) method of speech processing has been successfully applied to enhancement and recognition. It bandpasses spectral parameter signals to eliminate steady or slowly varying components (including environmental effects and speaker characteristics) and rapid noise events. The bandpass range is typically 1–10 Hz, with a sharp zero at 0 Hz and a time constant of about 160 ms [57, 106]. Events changing more slowly than once a second (e.g., most channel effects) are thus eliminated by the highpass filtering. The lowpass cutoff is more gradual, smoothing parameter tracks over about 40 ms, to preserve most phonetic events, while suppressing impulse noise. When speech is degraded by convolutional noise, the J-RASTA method replaces the logarithm operation with $Y_i = \log(1 + JX_i)$, where i is a critical band index, J depends on the noise level, and X and Y are the input and output [106].

Another recent analysis method with application to speech recognition is the *dynamic cepstrum* [107], which does a two-dimensional (time–frequency) smoothing to incorporate a forward masking, enhance rapid formant transitions, and suppress slowly varying properties (e.g., channel effects; speaker-dependent global spectral shape). Thus it is similar to RASTA in emphasizing spectral change, but unlike RASTA also includes time–frequency interaction and does not completely eliminate static spectral components. There are other recent time–frequency analysis methods (with application to coding and recognition) [108, 109].

6.10 REDUCTION OF INFORMATION

In both coding and recognition applications, a major objective of speech analysis is to efficiently represent information in the signal while retaining parameters enough to reconstruct or identify the speech. In coding we wish to reduce the storage or transmission rate of speech while maximizing the quality of reconstructed speech in terms of intelligibility, naturalness, and speaker identifiability. Thus an economical representation of the crucial aspects of the speech signal is paramount. In recognitioin systems, the storage question is secondary to recognition accuracy. Nonetheless, recognizers perform faster when the network information or stored templates occupy less memory. Furthermore, small, efficient templates often yield better results, e.g., templates of sampled speech waveforms require much storage but give much worse accuracy than spectral templates.

In analysis, eliminating redundant information in the speech signal is important. Whether information is superfluous depends on the application: speaker-dependent aspects of speech are clearly relevant for speaker identification, but those aspects are often super- fluous for identification of the textual message in automatic speech recognition. It is not always clear which speech aspects can be sacrificed. Acceptable speech can be synthesized with rates under 600 bit/s (100 times lower than that for a simple digital representation). However, as bit rate is reduced, distortion is gradually introduced into the reconstructed speech; e.g., signal aspects relating to speaker identity tend to be lost at low storage rates. Synthesis models emphasize spectral and timing aspects of speech that preserve intelligibility, often at the expense of naturalness.

6.10.1 Taking Advantage of Gradual Vocal Tract Motion

Viewing speech as a sequence of phones linked via intonation patterns, most speech analysis attempts to extract parameters related to the spectral and timing patterns that distinguish individual phonemes. Speech is often transformed into a set of parameter signals that are closely related to movements of the vocal tract articulators. These signals may follow one particular articulator (e.g., the F0 "parameter" follows vocal cord vibration) or may result from several articulators acting together; e.g., the output from a bandpass filter or a DFT spectral sample relates to formant position and amplitude, which in turn are specified by the overall vocal tract configuration.

The vocal tract moves slowly compared to most speech sampling rates; e.g., typical phonetic events last more than 50 ms (although some, like stop bursts, are shorter), while speech may be sampled every 0.1 ms. Thus, speech parameters usually vary slowly and allow decimation; e.g., the short-time DFT (examined at a fixed frequency) is a time signal of bandwidth equal to that of the window used in the spectral analysis. Without loss of information, it may be decimated to a rate of twice the window's bandwidth; e.g., for wideband spectra, the 300 Hz window allows 600 samples/s. Since window bandwidth is not strictly limited in practical applications, small amounts of distortion are introduced in the decimation.

For the vast majority of speech samples, events are slowly varying. Rapid spectral changes are limited to stop onsets and releases or to phone boundaries involving a change in manner of articulation (i.e., when speech switches among the classes of fricatives, nasals, sonorants, and silence). In terms of the total number of analysis frames at a typical 10 ms update rate, only a very small fraction involve sudden changes. Thus, it is inefficient to output spectral parameters at rates up to 600 samples/s. Practical coding and recognition algorithms use parameters at about 25–200 samples/s, depending on the application. This sacrifices accuracy during rapid spectral changes; performance is not greatly degraded (e.g., smoothing rapid changes may not be perceptually noticeable in the reconstructed speech), while parameter storage is greatly reduced.

6.10.2 Smoothing: Linear and Nonlinear

To be able to subsample parameter signals at rates as low as 25/s, the signals should first be lowpass filtered to obey the Nyquist rate. In some cases, an analysis produces an appropriate signal for decimation (e.g., one can choose the window bandwidth in the short-time DFT to match the desired parameter sampling rate P_s). Occasionally, however, a slowly varying parameter is interrupted by rapid fluctuations. In yet other situations, small fine temporal variation may be superimposed on a slowly varying base pattern. Assuming that the slowly varying contour is the desired component for storage, transmission, or further analysis, smoothing is necessary so that subsampling does not give spurious results.

The basic approach is linear lowpass filtering to eliminate energy in the parameter signal above half the desired P_s. This has the advantage of smoothing rapid parameter transitions, e.g., which can be of use in phone segmentation for speech recognizers. If the parameter is simply to be subsampled at a fixed rate, then linear filtering may be best. However, other ways to represent parameter signals in a reduced-data format are often more successful with nonlinear smoothing. Linear filtering is particularly inappropriate for F0 patterns, in which F0 is traditionally considered to be zero during unvoiced sections of speech. Voiced–unvoiced transitions are abrupt, and linear smoothing yields poor F0 values. Linear filters are also suboptimal for signals with discrete values (e.g., unlike continuous parameters such as energy, discrete parameters classify speech into one of a finite set of states, such as phonemes).

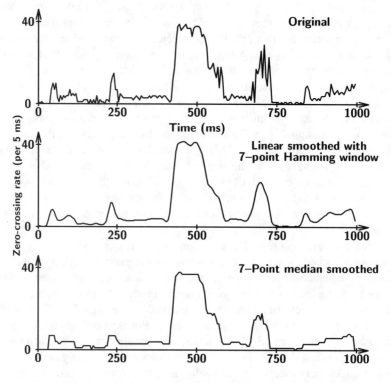

Figure 6.21 Example of smoothing applied to a zero-crossing parameter signal.

Another difficulty with linear filtering is its behavior when mistakes occur in parameter extraction. Formant and F0 estimators are notorious for producing erroneous isolated estimates or *outliers*, deviating from the rest of the parameter contour. Such mistakes should be corrected in postprocessing, but some errors may persist in the output. Linear filters give equal weight to all signal samples, propagating the effect of a mistake into adjacent parts of the smoothed output parameter contour.

One alternative to linear filtering is *median smoothing* [110], which preserves sharp signal discontinuities while eliminating fine irregularities and outliers. Most smoothers operate on a finite time window of the input signal, but linear smoothers linearly combine the windowed samples to produce the smoothed output sample, whereas median smoothing chooses a single value from among the window samples. In each set of windowed data, the samples are ordered in amplitude without regard to timing within the window. The output sample is the median, i.e., the $((N+1)/2)$nd of N ordered samples (for odd N). Sudden discontinuities are preserved because no averaging occurs. Up to $(N-1)/2$ outlier samples, above or below the main contour, do not affect the output (Figure 6.21).

Median smoothers do well in eliminating outliers and in global smoothing, but do not provide very smooth outputs when dealing with noisy signals. Thus they are often combined with elementary linear smoothers to yield a compromise smoothed output, with sharp transitions better preserved than with only linear filtering and with a smoother output signal than would be possible with only median smoothing.

6.11 SUMMARY

This chapter presented an introduction to speech analysis methods, from the viewpoint of transforming the speech signal into a set of parameters that more economically represent its pertinent information. Time-domain analysis yields simple speech parameters, especially suitable for energy and segmentation, whereas spectral analysis provides the more common approach to an efficient representation of speech information.

Since most speech applications use LPC and/or cepstral parameters, let us finish with a summary of the most common steps in speech analysis. After A/D conversion to $s(n)$ with typically 16 bits/sample at F_s samples/s, preemphasis (Equation (6.15)) may be applied (e.g., $x(n) = s(n) - 0.95s(n-1)$). The $x(n)$ samples are then buffered into frames of N samples at a time (e.g., 25 ms units, overlapped and updated every 10 ms) and multiplied by a Hamming window) (Equation (6.2)). For each weighted frame, an autocorrelation matrix is calculated, and then the LPC reflection coefficients are computed (Equation (6.24)). At this point, most coders have the required spectral parameters for their synthesis filters.

For speech recognition, the cepstral coefficients require more computation. They can be obtained directly from the LP parameters, but this way does not include the popular mel-scale mapping. For that, we instead use an FFT on the speech frame (skipping LP analysis), getting $X(k)$ (Eq. (6.14)), then the take the log-magnitude log $X(k)$, multiply by the critical-band triangular filters (Eq. (6.63)), and take the inverse FFT (Eq. (2.17)). The low-order 10–16 parameters are the static mel-scale cepstral coefficients, from which the delta parameters are simply differenced values between two neighboring frames. These cepstral parameters are often weighted by a raised-sine pulse (to de-emphasize low-order values that may relate to channel conditions, as well as high-order values that correspond to less relevant fine spectral detail—see Chapter 10).

PROBLEMS

P6.1.   Consider time windows for speech analysis.
    (a) What are the advantages and disadvantages of short and long windows?
    (b) To what type of filter should the spectrum of a window correspond?
    (c) Explain how the bandwidth of an analysis window affects spectrographic estimation of formants and F0.
    (d) How is placement of a window on the speech signal important?

P6.2.   Consider a pitch detection scheme that lowpass filters the speech to 900 Hz and then calculates an autocorrelation function.
    (a) Why is the speech first lowpass filtered?
    (b) How is the autocorrelation function used to generate a pitch estimate?
    (c) How is an LPC residual useful to find pitch?

P6.3.   Consider a steady vowel with formants at 500, 1500, 2500, ... Hz, lowpass filtered to 4000 Hz, and then sampled at the Nyquist rate.
    (a) Draw a detailed block diagram of a system to generate a good version of this (already sampled) signal at 10,000 sample/s.
    (b) Within the range $|\omega| < \pi$, at which "digital" frequencies ω_k would the formants be for the 10,000 sample/s signal?

P6.4.   "Time windowing" is a basic operation in speech analysis.
    (a) Explain how the durations of the window affects the output of the analysis for the discrete Fourier transform (e.g., spectrograms).
    (b) Instead of multiplying speech by a window, we may convolve the two signals. How is this useful? What features should the window have?

P6.5.   A simple FIR filter has one tap (with multiplier coefficient a).
    (a) For what values of a does the filter act as a simple time window for speech analysis? Explain.
    (b) Is this window useful for wideband or narrowband spectrograms?
    (c) What advantages would there be to use a longer time window?

P6.6.   One measure of a speech signal is its zero-crossing rate. What information about the speech spectrum is available from this measure? Specifically, what information concerning formants and manner of articulation can be found in the zero-crossing rate?

P6.7.   A vowel has formants at 500, 1500, 2,500, ... Hz, etc., and F0 = 200 Hz.
    (a) Which harmonic has the highest amplitude? Explain.
    (b) Suppose the time waveform of the vowel is sharply lowpass filtered so that no energy remains above 4 kHz. Then the waveform is sampled at 6000 sample/s. If the speech is played back now through a digital-to-analog (D/A) converter, how would the signal be different from that before the sampling? Have the formants changed? Explain.
    (c) Suppose instead that the waveform had been properly sampled at the Nyquist rate. Describe in detail a way to change the sampling rate to 6000 sample/s without corrupting the signal.

P6.8.   Consider $x(n) = \sin(\omega n)$, where ω is a fixed frequency, and suppose $x(n)$ is input to a 3-level center clipper whose output is

$$y(n) = \begin{cases} 1 & \text{for } x(n) > C, \\ 0 & \text{for } |x(n)| \leq C, \\ -1 & \text{for } x(n) < -C. \end{cases}$$

    (a) Sketch $y(n)$ for $C = 0.5$ and $C = \sqrt{3}/2$.
    (b) Sketch the autocorrelation function $\phi(k)$ for the two waveforms in part (a).

    (c) How would a simple pitch detector determine an F0 estimate of $x(n)$ based on $\phi(k)$ in part (b)?

P6.9. With all-pole LPC analysis:

    (a) How many poles are needed in the synthesizer to model well speech of 3 kHz bandwidth?

    (b) Why does the analysis window have to be larger when the analysis is done without a pitch detector?

P6.10. In LPC analysis, we can vary the order p of the model (p = number of poles), the length M of the analysis frame window, and the time L between parameter updates.

    (a) If $N = 2$ with LPC coefficients a_1 and a_2, explain how the coefficients would vary for different speech sounds (e.g., a vowel and a fricative).

    (b) Explain the criteria for choosing the window size M; what are the advantages and disadvantages of using a large M?

    (c) Explain the criteria for choosing the update interval L.

    (d) For which set of phonemes is the LPC residual error signal large?

P6.11. Explain the advantages and disadvantages of using wavelets for speech analysis, instead of a Fourier transform.

P6.12. How can pre-emphasis help speech analysis?

7

Coding of Speech Signals

7.1 INTRODUCTION

A major application of speech signal processing is the digital coding (compression) of speech for efficient, secure storage and transmission [1]. From a communications viewpoint (Figure 7.1), speech is transformed by an encoder into a sequence of bits, transmitted over a channel (or temporarily stored), and then converted back into an audible signal. At a receiver, a decoder/synthesizer acts like an inverse of the encoder/analyzer; the inversion is approximate because some information is usually lost during coding due to the conversion of an analog speech signal into a digital bit stream, or during transmission in a noisy channel. Information lost in the A/D (analog-to-digital) conversion can be minimized by an appropriate choice of bit rate and coding scheme. Speech is often coded as parameters that represent the signal economically while still allowing speech reconstruction at the receiver with minimal quality loss. The terms *coding* and *coder* here include both the analysis and synthesis stages of speech processing; whatever is done by the encoder (for efficient transmission) must be undone (or "inverted") by the decoder, to reproduce the output speech.

7.1.1 Coding Noise

Noise often occurs in transmission channels and may distort the bit stream, causing errors in the received bits and degraded output speech; this can be minimized by using *bit protection* during coding, at the cost of a higher bit rate. Both analog and digital transmission suffer from channel noise, but digital coding allows the complete elimination of noise in the output speech. Analog audio tapes corrupt speech signals with tape hiss and other distortions, whereas computers can store speech with only the "distortion" due to the necessary lowpass filtering prior to A/D conversion. To achieve this, however, sufficient bits must be used in the digital representation to reduce the quantization noise introduced in the A/D conversion to

Figure 7.1 Block diagram of digital speech transmission.

below perceptible levels. Analog transmission channels (e.g., radio waves, public telephone networks) always distort audio signals, but digital communication links can eliminate all noise effects if there are sufficient repeater stations along the transmission route (the number depends on the quality of the links). Other advantages of digital speech coding include the relative ease of encrypting digital signals compared to analog signals (for security in certain applications) [2–6] and the ease of multiplexing several signals on one channel.

7.1.2 Applications

Recent advances in computer technology allow a wide variety of applications for speech coding, including digital voice transmission over the general switched telephone network (GSTN; also called POTS—plain old telephone sevice), which is increasingly digital (e.g., the 1.544 Mb/s T1 channel). Transmission can be either on-line (instantaneous or *real time*), as in normal telephone conversations, or off-line, as in storing speech for electronic mail forwarding of voice messages. In either case, the transmission bit rate is crucial to evaluate the practicality of different coding schemes. As for storage, the decreasing cost of computer memory reduces the need for efficient coding. However, wireless transmission (of increasing importance with mobile radio and cellular telephony) requires channel bandwidth, which limits the number of signals carried simultaneously. Since wireless channels are often noisy, efficient speech coders with low bit rates are important to allow room for bit protection. The lower the bit rate for a speech signal, the more efficient the transmission. However, quality normally degrades monotonically (but nonlinearly) with decreasing bit rate.

Coders are evaluated in terms of bit rate, costs of transmission and storage, complexity (realizable on an integrated-circuit chip?), speed (fast enough for real-time applications? perceptible delays?), and output speech quality (intelligible? natural?). Some applications require small coding delays, and delays exceeding 200 ms (e.g., in satellite transmissions) easily impair speech communication [7]; many applications require coding delays of less than 20 ms [8].

7.1.3 Quality

Speech quality is hard to quantify, but the following categorizations are common [9]: (1) *commentary* or *broadcast* quality refers to wide-bandwidth (typically 50–7000 Hz, but 20–20,000 Hz for compact disks) high-quality speech with no perceptible noise; (2) *toll* or *wireline* quality describes speech as heard over the switched telephone network (approximately the 200–3200 Hz range, with signal-to-noise ratio of more than 30 dB and less than 2–3% harmonic distortion); (3) *communications*-quality speech is highly intelligible but has noticeable distortion compared to toll quality; and (4) *synthetic*-quality speech has substantial degradation (sounds "machine-like" and often "buzzy" and suffers from a lack of speaker identifiability [10]) but is about 90% intelligible.

Higher quality is increasingly available at lower rates with continuing advances in speech algorithms. Currently, at least 32–64 kb/s are needed for (wideband) commentary quality (and 96–128 kb/s for very-wideband speech), while (narrowband) toll quality can be found in coders ranging from 64 kb/s (simple coding) to 8 kb/s (complex schemes) (Figure 7.2). Communications-quality applications have bit rates as low as 4 kb/s, and lower rates yield synthetic quality. The former is often found in cellular applications and voice mail (e.g., at 8 kb/s) [11]; mobile radio (e.g., at 4.15 kb/s) and secure voice transmissions can tolerate synthetic quality, allowing lower rates. Toll quality is generally required for public services,

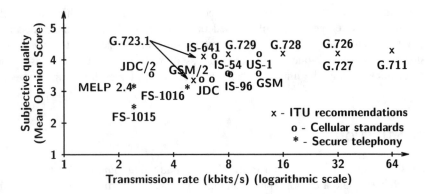

while communications quality can be used in messaging systems, and synthetic quality is mostly limited to toys and to services where bandwidth restrictions are crucial (e.g., military applications).

7.1.4 Classes of Coders

The simplest speech coders are *waveform coders*, which analyze, code, and reconstruct speech sample-by-sample. *Time-domain waveform coders* take advantage of waveform redundancies (e.g., periodicity and slowly varying intensity) to allow data compression; *spectral-domain waveform coders* exploit the nonuniform distribution of speech information across frequencies. More complex systems known as *source coders* or *vocoders* (for "*voice coders*") follow a speech production model, usually separating speech information into that estimating vocal tract shape and that involving vocal tract excitation. To a first-order approximation, excitation and vocal tract filter information can be coded separately, with a large decrease in bit rate.

7.1.5 Chapter Overview

We start with a discussion of the noise introduced by A/D conversion and how it relates to bit rate. The redundant properties of the speech signal that allow preservation of speech quality while bit rate is reduced are noted. The chapter first examines waveform coders, whose objective is the closest possible match to the original signal. Vocoders, on the other hand, recreate crucial speech aspects that emphasize perceptual quality over waveform accuracy. The vocoder's objective is often to match the original spectral magnitude during successive frames of speech data. Waveform coders typically yield superior output speech quality but often operate at bit rates several times those of vocoders. Hybrid vocoders (e.g., CELP), combining aspects of both waveform and source coders, can bridge the gap. *Signal-to-noise ratio* (SNR) is a very useful (though flawed) measure of speech quality for waveform coders only, since vocoders distort the waveform of the original speech sufficiently to render SNR irrelevant as a perceptual measure.

There are several evaluation criteria for speech coders: output speech quality (intelligibility, naturalness, preservation of original speaker features), transmission bit rate, complexity, coding delay, and cost. This chapter examines the tradeoffs for different speech coders.

For time-domain systems, differential coding is explained in which a speech analyzer "predicts" future speech samples based on a linear combination of prior samples. Time-adaptive techniques match predictors and quantization distortion to time-varying speech signals. Very-low-bit-rate coders are discussed, with respect to delayed-decision coding procedures. Finally, the impact of hardware advances on speech coding is noted.

7.2 QUANTIZATION

All digital speech coders use a form of *pulse-code modulation* (PCM) to convert an analog speech signal into a digital representation, which may be further coded to lower the final bit rate (Figure 7.3). Natural speech waveforms are continuous in amplitude and time. Periodically sampling an analog waveform $x_a(t)$ at the Nyquist rate (twice its highest frequency, assuming a lowpass signal) converts it into a discrete-time signal $x(n)$ (where $x(n) = x_a(nT)$ and T is the sampling period). Much digital signal processing theory applies to such discrete-time, yet continuous-amplitude, signals [13]. However, digital applications (e.g., using computers) require number representations with a discrete range, and thus the signal amplitude $x(n)$ at each time instant n must be quantized to be one of a set of L amplitude values (where $B = \log_2 L$ is the number of bits used to digitally code each value). A/D conversion normally involves an instantaneous or memoryless operation, mapping the $x(n)$ amplitude to the nearest available discrete value, which minimizes quantization distortion sample by sample.

   Digital communication of an analog amplitude x (omitting the time index n for simplicity, in memoryless quantization) consists of: A/D conversion, transmission of binary information over a digital channel, and D/A conversion to reconstruct the analog x value. If the channel is noise-free, the output value differs from the input by an amount known as the quantization noise e. Noise e in speech applications is evident as audible distortion impairing the quality of coded speech. This distortion arises from the quantization process and is directly related to design decisions, e.g., the number of bits per sample. Thermal and channel noise found in analog systems, on the other hand, are harder to control. Nonetheless, the distortion effect on the output is similar whether the noise comes from analog channel design or from an economical choice of transmission bit rate. One difference lies in the nature of the noise: analog noise is usually uncorrelated with the transmitted signal, whereas digital noise can be signal-correlated in cases of coarse quantization; this is relevant for perception since white noise is less annoying than bursty noise.

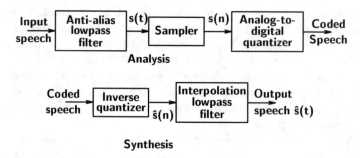

Figure 7.3 Block diagram of a pulse-code modulation (PCM) system.

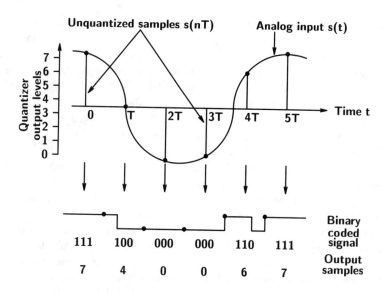

Figure 7.4 Signals in a PCM system.

The A/D process consists of a quantizer mapping function $Q(\cdot)$ and a subsequent encoder that converts a $Q(x)$ discrete amplitude into a digital code word of (typically) binary digits (Figure 7.4). At the decoder, the corresponding D/A process inverts this procedure, grouping the received bits into words (for each $x(n)$ sample) and converting them into output amplitudes for audio playback. The bit rate for a signal is the product of its sampling rate F_s (in samples/second) and the number of bits B used to code each sample.

In most coders, F_s is proportional to the desired speech bandwidth, while the choice of B varies widely depending on the coding scheme. Common values for F_s are 8000/s, 16,000/s and 44,100/s, corresponding to telephone speech (up to 3400 Hz), wideband audio (including music, up to 7 kHz), and the compact-disk standard (of wideband 20 kHz audio). (Sample rates of 10,000/s are also seen in synthesis applications; digital audio tape uses 48,000 samples/s; some applications use up to 96,000/s at 24 b/sample.) In all cases, F_s exceeds the Nyqust rate to minimize aliasing. B ranges from 16 bits in high-quality PCM to a fraction of a bit in very-low-rate coders; 8 or 12 b/sample are often used. While this chapter is dedicated to speech coding, many of the methods here apply to other analog signals, including video [14]. Waveform coding methods described below that do not expressly model vocal tract behavior apply well to many audio signals, if the appropriate bandwidth is chosen (speech is acceptable with a 3 kHz bandwidth, but bandwidths of 7–20 kHz are often preferred for music). (The switched telephone network with carbon microphones severely limits bandwidth, but inexpensive electret microphones can give wideband speech in nontelephone applications.) While video signals are quite different from audio (e.g., TV signals require about 1000 times the rate for speech, using simple coding), they too can use some coders noted below.

7.2.1 Quantization Error or Noise

The simplest quantizer has a uniform mapping or *characteristic*, and minimizes the maximum value of the error e. A graph of the input–output (x vs $y = Q(x)$) mapping of a quantizer resembles a staircase, since digital coding can only support a finite number of output levels (Figure 7.5). The *step size* Δ of this staircase represents the spacing between possible output values; Δ is constant in a *uniform quantizer* but varies with the input x in a nonuniform quantizer. All quantizers assume that the input has a limited range (i.e., $X_{min} \le x \le X_{max}$) so as to assign the output levels efficiently. In practice, many signals (e.g., speech) remain within a certain range virtually all the time but exceed these limits occasionally. These rare input values are ignored when establishing the (X_{min}, X_{max}) range. When the input exceeds this range by more than half a step size (i.e., the normal maximum error), *clipping* occurs where the output reflects the maximum (or minimum) allowed input and can correlate poorly with the input. When evaluating quantizer performance, the percentage of time that clipping occurs (and perhaps typical clipping error values) should be given along with the error statistics in the normal unclipped range, although clipping errors are often ignored in practice [14].

Figure 7.5 shows a typical quantizer with six output levels ($L = 6$). (Such a coarse quantizer is not suitable for directly coding speech waveforms but could be used for speech parameters.) Since $B = \log_2 L$, L is usually chosen to be a power of two to allow an integer number of bits in coding each sample x. Distributing the L output levels symmetrically (since speech samples usually have a symmetric probability distribution, with as many positive amplitudes as negative ones) precludes a level at $y = 0$ if L is even (the *mid-riser* scheme in Figure 7.5a). The alternative *mid-tread* scheme (Figure 7.5b) assigns a level for $y = 0$ because many speech samples are very close to zero (e.g., during silence) and such an assignment reduces quantization error at those times. Having more negative than positive output levels may lead to a slight increase in step size, but this is normally compensated by the decrease in average error for the frequent low-amplitude samples.

The quantizer output follows the 45° line $y = x$ as closely as possible (Figure 7.5) since each deviation is proportional to the quantization error, which is defined as

$$e = y - x = Q(x) - x. \tag{7.1}$$

For uniform quantization, $|e| \le \Delta/2$ when x is within the peak-to-peak range of $X_{max} - X_{min} = L\Delta$ (i.e., the number of levels times the step size). Beyond this range, clipping leads to errors with magnitude exceeding $\Delta/2$. To limit clipping, we examine the statistics of

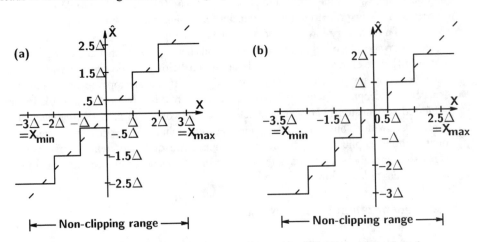

Figure 7.5 Two common uniform quantizer characteristics: (a) mid-riser, (b) mid-tread. The dashed line indicates the ideal curve.

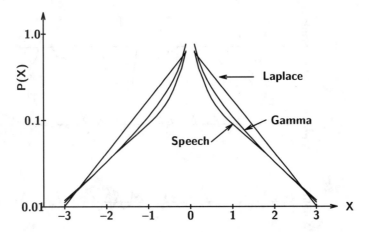

Figure 7.6 Real speech and theoretical gamma and Laplacian probability densities.
(After Paez and Glisson [15] © IEEE.)

typical speech signals. A histogram of typical speech amplitudes approaches a gamma or Laplacian probability distribution (Figure 7.6). If Laplacian, i.e.,

$$p(x) = \frac{1}{\sigma\sqrt{2}} e^{-|x|\sqrt{2}/\sigma}, \tag{7.2}$$

with zero mean and standard deviation σ, a quantizer range of 8σ will limit clipping to one in 300 samples.

The study of quantization is aided by a simple statistical model of the quantization noise $e(n)$. It is often assumed to be stationary white noise, uncorrelated with the input signal, with each error sample uniformly distributed (i.e., equally likely that e takes on any value in the range $[-\Delta/2, \Delta/2]$). Generally, this model increases in validity with the number L of quantization levels. For coarse quantization (e.g., $L = 2$ in Figure 7.7b), the error follows the input signal during periods of slow change; this is perceived as bursty noise or clicks superimposed on the original speech signal, which is less desirable than white noise continuous over all the speech. Fine quantization, as in Figure 7.7(c), leads to greater noise randomness, a better approximation to the assumed noise model, and more perceptually acceptable noise distortion in the output speech. With enough bits (e.g., $B > 6$), the noise can be regarded as white and additive to the speech signal. Coarse quantization produces too much noise–signal correlation to allow such a simplifying view. When coarse quantization is necessary, the input signal may be *dithered* by adding a small pseudo-random sequence prior to quantization [14]. The dither is less than Δ and causes random jumps of ±1 quantizer level when the input is close to a quantizer boundary, effectively whitening the noise at the cost of a slightly increased output noise. If the dither sequence is predictable or known to the decoder, it can be subtracted from the received signal to reduce output noise.

7.2.2 Bit Protection

Figure 7.4 illustrates a bit assignment using 3 bits to code 8 output levels, with the most significant bit coding the polarity of the input. In sending these bits, a channel error in the most significant bit would lead to more serious output degradation than an error in the least

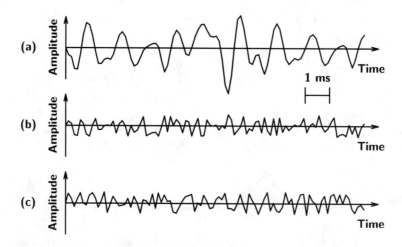

Figure 7.7 (a) Speech waveform; (b) quantization error for 2-bit quantization (same scale
as in part a); (c) quantization error for 10-bit quantization (magnified
$2^8 = 256$ times with respect to part a).

significant bit. In the latter case, the mean output distortion due to a channel error is Δ (since
the decoder assigns a level one distant from the desired one); an error in the most significant
of B bits causes a mean $2^{B-1}\Delta$ error. Such errors add to the quantization error to yield total
output error.

When certain transmitted bits are significantly more important than others, noisy
channels may require *bit protection* [14]. The bit rate is increased slightly by inserting *parity
bits*, whose values are a function of the bits chosen for protection; e.g., to protect N bits, one
parity bit could be assigned a value of 0 or 1, respectively, if an even or odd number of the N
bits have value 1. The received parity bit value is then compared to the values of the N
received bits; if an odd number (e.g., one) of the $N + 1$ bits is received incorrectly, the
decoder detects a problem and can take action, e.g., replacing the erroneous N bits with a
previous set of correctly received bits. Other error-correcting schemes are possible, at the cost
of increased bit rate, by using more parity bits. A difficulty in any coder where the bits have
varying importance is that of frame synchronization; the decoder must know what role each of
the incoming bits plays to interpret them properly.

7.2.3 Signal-to-Noise Ratio (SNR)

In evaluating speech coders, a basic *objective* measure of performance is the SNR of the
average speech energy to the average energy in the error signal, and is usually expressed in
decibels as $10 \log_{10}$ SNR. Maximizing SNR does not guarantee the best perceptual quality,
but it gives an objective measure by which waveform speech coders can be evaluated. A
common alternative to the SNR is the *segmental SNR* (SEGSNR), which is the time average
of SNR (dB) values computed over successive short-time (e.g., 16–20 ms) segments of the
speech. SEGSNR uses the geometric (vs additive) mean since the averaging occurs after the
logarithm operation for decibels, and thus penalizes coders whose performance is more time
variable. SNR is dominated by the intense sections of the speech signal (e.g., vowels), while
SEGSNR averages performance more equally over weak and strong sounds, and correlates

better with perception. Both SNR and SEGSNR are time-domain measures of speech quality. For low-bit-rate coding schemes, frequency-domain measures and, in particular, measures of spectral envelope deviation have better correspondence to perceived quality than do SNRs [16,17]. Close approximations to subjective quality measures require simulations of auditory processing [18].

For a speech signal $x(n)$ and quantization noise $e(n)$, the SNR is

$$\text{SNR} = \frac{\sigma_x^2}{\sigma_e^2} = \frac{E[x^2(n)]}{E[e^2(n)]} = \frac{\sum_n x^2(n)}{\sum_n e^2(n)}, \tag{7.3}$$

where E represents expectation (averaging) over a frame of speech. Assuming a uniform distribution for e over a range Δ, σ_e^2 is easily calculated to be $\Delta^2/12$ [13]. Since $\Delta = 2X_{\max}/2^B$, the SNR in decibels can be expressed as

$$\text{SNR(dB)} = 6.02B + K_1. \tag{7.4}$$

Thus each additional coding bit, which doubles the number of quantizer levels and thus halves Δ, decreases the noise energy and increases SNR by about 6 dB. The K_i factor is a function of the coding block length i (see the later discussion of vector quantization) and of clipping range; assuming "scalar" coding of one sample at a time $(i = 1)$ and that $X_{\max} = 4\sigma_x$, then $K_1 = -7.27$ [1].

This SNR calculation is valid only with a sufficiently large number of quantization levels and with stationary speech of constant σ_x. Signal energy levels can vary up to 40 dB depending on speakers and transmission channels. Moreover, unvoiced sounds have variances (σ_x^2) often 20 dB less than for voiced sounds. If $X_{\max}$ is specified in terms of loud, voiced sounds, the high-order bits will not be utilized during weak, unvoiced sounds. This effectively reduces the quantization range while keeping the step size constant; since the error is proportional to step size, SNR decreases for weaker sounds. While $B = 7$ yields a perceptually acceptable 35 dB SNR by Equation (7.4), in practice 11–12 bits are needed to guarantee this SNR over typical speech ranges (the extra 4–5 bits compensating for 24–30 dB of input dynamic range).

7.2.4 Nonuniform Quantization

Nonuniform quantization can overcome the range problem by making SNR less dependent on signal level. If step size is made proportional to input magnitude, then weaker sounds use a smaller step size than more intense sounds. For a constant percentage of error, the quantization levels are logarithmically spaced (to compensate for the exponential curve of the probability distribution) or, equivalently, the logarithm of the input is coded with a uniform quantizer (Figure 7.8). At the receiver, the sample reconstruction uses the inverse, exponential operation. This *log PCM* process is called *companding*, since the input speech range is effectively *com*pressed at the coder and *expand*ed at the decoder. Viewing quantization as adding noise e and ignoring the sign of x (which is coded in a separate sign bit), the output is $\exp[\log(x) + e] = x \exp(e)$. If $|e| \ll 1$, then $\exp(e) \approx 1 + e$, and the output equals $x + xe$, with the noise term being the product of the quantizer error and the input amplitude. Assuming further that x and e are independent under fine quantization, the SNR will be the inverse of the error energy and hence independent of input energy level.

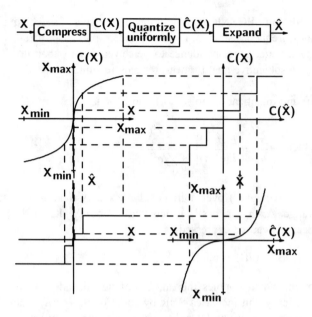

Figure 7.8 Nonuniform quantization with a compression function $c(x)$ resembling a logarithm operation. The equivalent quantizer using nonuniform step sizes is shown in the lower left. (After Jayant and Noll [14].)

A purely logarithmic operation is not practical since $\log(0) = -\infty$, leading to an infinite quantization range. However, two approximations to logarithmic quantization give nearly constant-percentage error and have found wide use in commercial systems (Figure 7.9). In *A-law* quantization, the quantizer characteristic is linear for input magnitudes up to a certain threshold (for $|x| \leq X_{\max}/A$) and logarithmic beyond that. In *μ-law* quantization, the quantizer characteristic is defined with one smooth function as

$$y = X_{\max} \frac{\log[1 + (\mu|x|/X_{\max})]}{\log(1 + \mu)} \, \mathrm{sgn}(x). \tag{7.5}$$

For small input amplitudes ($x \approx 0$) or low values of μ, the numerator log expression can be approximated by a term linear in $|x|$, so that $y \approx \mu[\log(1 + \mu)]x$; thus the quantizer is linear for low input values. For sufficiently large values of x and μ (i.e., for $\mu|x|/X_{\max} \gg 1$), the numerator log expression is approximately of the form $\log(\alpha|x|)$, i.e., y varies directly with the logarithm of $|x|$. The value of μ specifies the relative input amplitude near which the quantizer gradually evolves from a linear to a logarithmic characteristic. Increasing μ makes the quantizer logarithmic over a wider range of input values and therefore increases the input range for which SNR is constant. There is a tradeoff here, however, between dynamic input range and SNR, since SNR decreases slightly with larger values of μ (e.g., increasing μ from 100 to 500 increases dynamic range by a factor of five but lowers SNR by 2.6 dB [19]). A 7-bit μ-law log PCM yields an SNR of about 34 dB and toll-quality speech, over a wide input range (with a standard value for μ of 255). (The much lower SNR than PCM, while retaining equivalent perceptual quality, indicates the limited usefulness of simple SNR in judging speech quality [20].) An 8-bit log PCM (64 kb/s) is a widely accepted transmission standard for speech, with μ-law common in North America and Japan, while Europe uses A-law ($A = 87.56$); the extra eighth bit preserves toll quality while allowing multiple conversions between PCM and analog, which often occur in telephone transmission and slightly degrade the signal. Compared to uniform PCM, log PCM needs about four fewer bits for equivalent quality (Figure 7.10).

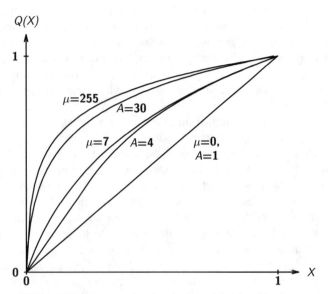

Figure 7.9 Logarithmic compression characteristics: (a) A-law, (b) μ-law.

Instead of trying to maintain a constant SNR over a wide range of input amplitudes, the quantizer could be designed to maximize average SNR. Speech statistics show roughly a Laplacian distribution with decreasing likelihood of samples as amplitude increases. Thus small step sizes (leading to small quantization error) are best allocated to high-probability, small-input amplitudes, with gradually larger values of Δ as input level increases. Simple log PCM only approximately follows the speech density. An *optimal quantizer* would yield

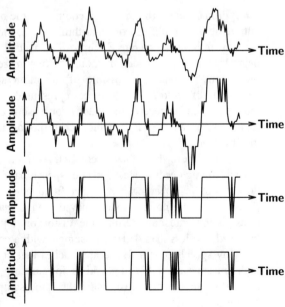

Figure 7.10 Log PCM coding of speech with μ-law quantization ($\mu = 255$). Bit rates are 8, 4, 2, and 1 bit/sample.

higher average SNR than typical logarithmic quantizers [15]. However, since speech is nonstationary, quantizers that are "optimal" on the average do not always yield performance that is superior perceptually. Distribution-matching quantizers are inferior to logarithmic quantizers in terms of dynamic range and idle-channel noise performance. For most coding applications, A-law and μ-law systems are both practical and sufficiently close to optimal. In actual speech systems, the logarithmic curve of the coder and the exponential curve of the receiver are often approximated by piecewise-linear curves to simplify the numerical transformations.

Whenever a nonoptimal quantizer codes a signal, the output levels have nonuniform probability. Coding speech with a uniform quantizer results in a low likelihood for the higher-amplitude levels, whereas a log PCM approach renders each level (and therefore each transmitted bit) more equally likely. One way to compensate for nonoptimal quantization is to employ variable-length Huffman or *entropy* coding, in which signal levels are assigned transmission word lengths in inverse proportion to their likelihood. For example, in order of decreasing probability, the *code words* for a four-level quantizer might be 0, 10, 110, and 111. In standard coding, each word would be two bits; however, if one level occurred more than half the time and another one quarter of the time, the average number of b/word would be less than two in the entropy scheme. The exact design of the entropy code reflects the probabilities of each quantizer level. One difficulty with entropy coding is that some buffering of data is necessary when a series of unlikely samples occurs in succession. On a real-time or synchronous channel, data delays would occur until a set of (likely) samples arrived requiring less than the average number of bits. Entropy coding can be applied to both speech and speech-related signals [21], although it is very sensitive to channel noise.

7.2.5 Relationship of Bandwidth and Noise to Coding Rate

Primary concerns in speech coding are the bandwidth and the perceptual quality of the output signal. In uniform or logarithmic PCM, individual speech samples are quantized and coded with B bits at the rate F_s. Since B is inversely proportional to the quantization noise that degrades the output speech, it should be maximized. It is usually also desirable to recover at the output as much as possible of the input speech bandwidth. With F_s samples/s, a bandwidth of up to $F_s/2$ Hz can be represented. (In practice, imperfect filtering and aliasing reduce the actual speech bandwidth.) For reasons of economy, a third objective is to minimize transmission rate $I = F_s B$, which corresponds to bandwidth reduction in analog speech transmission.

Since these three factors conflict, we look for compromise or alternative approaches. Speech coding needs at least 3 kHz of speech bandwidth to preserve F1–F3, and intelligibility does not suffer greatly when higher frequencies are omitted. For higher quality and more pleasant speech, though, coders may use wider bandwidths. Coder applications also vary in transmission rate and permissible distortion levels. In the following sections, a speech bandwidth of less than 4 kHz is assumed, with a corresponding $F_s = 8000$ samples/s, typical of many speech coders. Basic approaches that code one sample at a time dictate relatively high transmission rates of 88 kb/s for uniform PCM and 56 kb/s for log PCM. Many alternative approaches exist, using the same sampling rate but differing in how the speech samples are coded.

7.2.6 Vector Quantization (VQ)

For simplicity, many coders treat speech samples or parameters one at a time, as independent values to code. Since successive values are usually dependent, however, we can remove further redundancy via *vector quantization* (VQ). VQ considers k samples of a speech signal (or parameter sequence) $v(n)$ together as a block or *vector*, and represents them for transmission as a single vector code, rather than k values independently (*scalar quantization*) [22–25]. The greater the degree of correlation among vector elements, the bigger the advantage for VQ.

7.2.6.1 Codebooks.
VQ renders the analysis stage of a speech coder more complex, and needs extra memory in both analysis and synthesis stages. Starting with a basic analysis yielding k scalar parameters $v(n)$ for each frame, VQ must then determine which k-dimensional vector, among a set of M vectors stored in a *codebook* library or directory, corresponds most closely to the set of $v(n)$. A Voronoi or nearest-neighbor search of the codebook is used, with a chosen distance measure. A $\log_2 M$ bit code (the index of the vector chosen from the codebook) is sent in place of the k scalar parameters. The system's decoder is no more complex than without VQ, but its memory must include a codebook identical to that of the coder. To synthesize the output speech, the decoder uses the parameters listed under the index in the codebook corresponding to the received code.

The key issues in VQ are the design and search of the codebook. In coders with scalar quantization, coding distortion comes from the finite precision for representing each parameter (e.g., 5 b/parameter instead of a precise analog value). VQ distortion comes instead from using synthesis parameters from a codebook entry or *codeword*, which differ from the parameters determined by the speech analyzer. If the codebook were to contain vectors for all distinguishable speech sounds and the optimal vector always chosen, VQ speech would be perceptually the same as scalar-quantized speech. However, practical VQ limits the size M of the codebook, and a reduced (faster) search of the codebook may yield a suboptimal choice, both leading to more speech distortion. M should be large enough that each possible input vector corresponds to a codeword whose substitution for $v(n)$ yields output speech close to the original. However, efficient search procedures usually force M to be 1024 or less.

A distortion measure serves as a performance criterion for the design and search of the codebook. For VQ using vectors of waveform samples (e.g., k consecutive samples of $e(n)$), the most common measure is the Euclidean distance d_E between two vectors $\mathbf{e}_1$ and $\mathbf{e}_2$:

$$d_E(\mathbf{e}_1, \mathbf{e}_2) = \sqrt{\sum_{n=1}^{k} [e_1(n) - e_2(n)]^2}. \tag{7.6}$$

More complicated measures, e.g., the Mahalanobis distance (see Chapter 11), which inversely weights each dimension according to its variance, may not be needed in VQ since they tend to yield similar perceptual results with $k \leq 8$ [26].

When coding vectors of spectral parameters (e.g., LPC), VQ uses distance measures of more perceptual relevance, taking account of the ear's variable sensitivity to different frequencies and intensities. For example, one such measure involves 42 samples of the short-term speech spectral envelope (taken along the mel-scale perceptually weighted frequency axis), where high-energy samples (e.g., formant regions) are given more weight than other samples [27]. Measures which incorporate the perceptual bark scale often correlate better with subjective speech quality [28].

7.2.6.2 Codebook design.

7.2.6.2 Codebook design.   Codebook creation usually requires the analysis of a large training sequence, e.g., of a few minutes (perhaps by several speakers) [26], of varied speech, i.e., containing examples of all phonemes in different phonetic contexts, and of varied conditions (different microphones and background noise). (As an efficient alternative, a 10 s artificial speech signal mimicking average speech statistics across languages was recently proposed for training [29].) Starting from an initial design, an iterative procedure converges on a final codebook that is optimal in minimizing the average distortion measure across the training set. The usual procedure (often called the LBG algorithm [30, 31]) is: (1) Given an initial codebook, calculate the average distortion; if small enough, this codebook suffices. (2) If not, replace each codeword with the "average" of all training vectors which mapped into that codeword (e.g., the *centroid* of those vectors in k-dimensional space for a Euclidean measure). (3) Using the new codebook, repeat steps 1–3. This gradient method usually yields a locally optimum codebook, inferior to the global optimum (only obtainable with a much more expensive, noniterative method); thus the process is often repeated several times with different initial codebooks, to obtain a better final codebook.

The codebook search is aided by a good choice for the initial design. The simplest approach chooses the first M vectors in the training set, or M vectors uniformly spaced in time (to avoid the high degree of correlation between successive vectors in speech). Two other approaches, called *product* and *splitting* codes, typically yield better initial codebooks. A product code assembles a codebook of M vectors of dimension k using smaller codebooks. One can design a scalar quantizer for each dimension, e.g., an L-level quantizer (e.g., in $\log_2 L$-bit uniform PCM, where L is big enough to yield good speech with scalar coding), and generate L^k possible k-dimensional vectors by straightforward concatenation. In the usual case that $L^k > M$, the codebook must be pruned, perhaps by choosing the M vectors that are most utilized by the training set. Besides being useful for initial codebook design, the product-code method often serves for a fast search of the codebook.

The splitting approach designs a codebook of dimension $k = i$ at the ith iteration, starting with a zero-dimension code, i.e., a single codeword equal to the centroid of the entire training set. This point in k-dimensional space is split to yield two codewords, either by a simple perturbation or by choosing a random distant entry in the training set. The general design procedure above finds the "optimum" two-entry codebook (i.e., the training set is partitioned into those vectors closest to each of the two codewords, and then the codewords are replaced by the centroids of the two sets). This one-dimension codebook is then perturbed to yield a four-codeword system, and the process is repeated until a system with $M = 2^k$ codewords is attained.

Since the bits in the VQ codeword (index) usually are unrelated to the actual points in the modeled speech space, channel errors cause serious degradation in the output speech. At the cost of extra computation at the codebook design stage, some VQ systems re-order the codebook ("index assignment") so that similar reference vectors have similar binary indices [32, 33]; in this way, a bit error causes only a small change in the output. Other VQ systems are optimized based on both quantization and channel noise [25]; others use dimensions with only binary values [34] (to limit memory and computation, and increase robustness).

7.2.6.3 Searching the codebook.

7.2.6.3 Searching the codebook.   Compared to scalar speech coding, the major additional complexity for VQ lies in the codebook search for the appropriate codeword to transmit, given a speech vector to code. In a *full codebook search* (needed for unstructured codebooks), the vector for every frame is compared with each of the M codewords, thus requiring M distance calculations (each having k squaring operations and $2k - 1$ additions, for the simple Euclidean distance). The precision of VQ coders (e.g., SNR) grows with increasing dimension k. Ideal coding rates, following rate-distortion theory [35], are approached only with large vectors. To code k speech parameters as a block, using $R = \log_2 M$ b/vector with F_s samples/s and allowing Ik speech samples/vector (I is a decimation factor: in waveform coders $I = 1$, whereas in other systems nonoverlapping frames of N speech samples yield N/I parameters to code), the VQ rate is RF_s/Ik b/s. Thus, for a constant bit rate, R is directly proportional to k, and the size $M = 2^R$ of a VQ codebook rises exponentially with dimension k. Large computation is often acceptable in the off-line design of a codebook. For real-time coder applications, however, the cost of a full codebook search must be balanced against improved speech quality with larger k.

Many practical VQ systems rely on suboptimal search techniques which reduce search time (and sometimes codebook memory), while sacrificing little coder performance. For example, a binary *tree search* replaces 2^R distance calculations and comparisons with only R comparisons of two calculations each. The M codewords form the lowest nodes of a tree, with each higher node being represented by the centroid of all codewords below it in the tree (Figure 7.11). This approach doubles the memory since the centroid vectors must be stored in addition to the actual codeword vectors. The advantage lies in reduced calculation since, at each point in the search, the input vector is compared with only two centroid vectors (which represent a diminishing number of codewords as the search proceeds). Since such a binary tree has R levels, only $2R$ distance calculations are needed. This method assumes that the codebook has a reasonable "geometry" so that in making decisions based on centroid vectors, eventually the optimal vector will be selected. The "splitting" design is an obvious choice for the initial codebook since it produces a codebook in tree form.

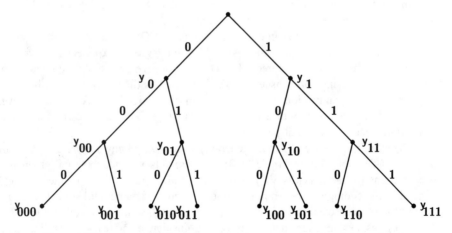

Figure 7.11 Tree-searched VQ. The encoder makes a succession of R minimum distortion choices from binary codebooks, where the available codebook at each level consists of labels of the nodes in the next level. A binary encoder tree is shown for a vector of $R = 3$ speech samples at 1 b/sample. (After Gray [22] © IEEE.)

CODEBOOK

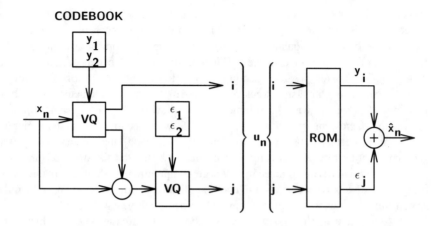

Figure 7.12 Multistage VQ, illustrated with two stages and binary codebooks ($\mathbf{y}_1, \mathbf{y}_2$) and ($\mathbf{z}_1, \mathbf{z}_2$). The channel symbol u_n is composed of 1 bit from each stage ($i, j, \dots$). The decoder fetches from read-only memory the codewords corresponding to u_n and sums them for an output. (After Gray [22] © IEEE.)

Another suboptimal (but efficient) approach is *multistage* VQ, in which a tree search involves small codebooks and successive revisions to the input vector (Figure 7.12) [32]. At the first level ($i = 1$) of the tree, one of a small number M_i of codebook vectors $\mathbf{y}_i$ (two, in the binary tree case) is chosen as the closest to the input vector $\mathbf{x}_n$ (where $M = \prod_{i=1}^{k} M_i$). Then the difference or "error" e between the input and its codeword representation is input to the next level in the tree. The error is simply (1) the distance between the two vectors, in the case of waveform quantization, or (2) the energy of the input speech vector passed through an inverse filter specified by the chosen codeword, in the case of spectral VQ. Each stage successively reduces this error, with the actual codeword index u_n being specified as a product code, 1 bit per stage for a binary tree ($M_i = 2$). The computation load is increased compared with the original tree technique since a new residual vector is calculated at each stage, but the memory is now limited to only $2R$ codewords.

A basic problem with simple "unstructured" VQ is that computation and memory needs are proportional to codebook size M, which grows exponentially with VQ-space dimensions. While "tree-structured" TSVQ does not save on memory, computation goes as $\log_2 M$; this big saving compensates for the loss of a few dB in SNR. While basic multistage VQ uses a finer quantization at later stages, an alternative "fine-coarse" VQ reverses this choice, and leads to a family of decision-tree VQ where trees are "grown" incrementally and then pruned back for optimal performance [36].

VQ is a special case of a more general type of coding known as *tree, trellis, look-ahead,* or *delayed-decision* coding [14, 37–40]. VQ exploits redundancies based on the current speech frame (in memoryless VQ) or on prior frames (in feedback or memory VQ). More general tree encoding delays sending a code for a current frame until some successive frames of input have been examined (in a sense, exploiting the future as well as the past). Such a delay in transmission often makes tree coding unsuitable for real-time coding applications, but reduced storage costs (e.g., 16 kb/s [41]) make it appropriate for voice response and synthesis applications, where short delays are not crucial. In VQ coders, tree-structured codebooks are suitable for variable-rate transmission [42]. Use of backward adaptive prediction can lower delay [43].

7.3 SPEECH REDUNDANCIES (CHARACTERISTICS TO EXPLOIT)

Speech coders attempt to reduce bit rate while preserving output speech quality, by taking advantage of redundancies in the speech signal and of perceptual limitations of the ear. Simple uniform PCM is valid for *any* bandlimited signal; coders that exploit other properties of speech can have lower rates. Log PCM exploits the nonuniform distribution of speech amplitudes, but there are many aspects of speech to distinguish it from other signals. Since natural speech is generated by human vocal tracts, there are distinct limitations on speech signals: (1) in general, vocal tract shape and thus speech spectrum change relatively slowly (although abrupt changes occur at closures of the vocal tract), compared to F_s; (2) the vocal cords vibrate rapidly but change their rate of vibration (i.e., F0) relatively slowly; (3) successive pitch periods are virtually identical much of the time; (4) the vocal tract spectrum varies slowly with frequency, and most speech energy is at low frequency; (5) speech sounds can be modeled as periodic or noisy excitation passing through a vocal tract filter, and each sound can be represented with a few parameters; (6) these parameters have nonuniform probability distributions. All these redundancies in speech production can be exploited to lower the bit rate.

In addition, coders exploit properties of audition: vocoders discard phase information since the ear is relatively phase-insensitive; other systems code more intense parts of the speech spectrum more accurately than low-amplitude frequencies since masking limits the importance of the latter. The following sections show how these properties of speech production and perception are exploited to lower the bit rate while preserving speech quality.

The actual information rate of speech in terms of phonemes is very low: assuming about 12 phonemes/s and 5–6 b/phoneme (given 30–40 phonemes in most languages), about 70 b/s suffice. This calculation ignores other information in the speech signal, e.g., intonation, emotions, and speaker identity, which are difficult to quantify. Nonetheless, certain applications only require communication of phonemes, which allow such low rates, three orders of magnitude below PCM rates.

7.4 MEASURES TO EVALUATE SPEECH QUALITY

Objective speech quality measures (e.g., SNR or SEGSNR), which can be calculated automatically from the speech signal or spectrum, are primarily useful for waveform coders, which reproduce the original speech signal sample-by-sample [44, 45]. These measures are usually simple, but cannot be used for vocoders due to their time-domain evaluation, which requires temporal synchronization (lost in vocoders). Some recent objective measures using spectra and some aspects of auditory modeling (e.g., the Speech Transmission Index) are approaching the utility of *subjective* measures (and at much lower cost) [18]. Subjective quality measures are more costly to obtain but are more relevant since they relate directly to perception. They are usually necessary to evaluate vocoders, but are also used for waveform coders. The primary measure of subjective quality is *intelligibility*, typically defined as the percentage of words (or phonemes) correctly heard, under various recording and coding conditions. All but the lowest-bit-rate coders usually score highly here (since understanding the coded speech is essential in virtually all applications).

Assuming high intelligibility, one can then try to estimate how "good" the speech sounds. Two standard measures used to rate coder performance here are the *mean opinion score* (MOS) and the *opinion-equivalent Q value* (Qop). For synthetic-quality speech, the *articulation equivalent loss* (AEN) can be used [16]. A recent "E-model" attempts to combine many evaluation factors for telephone network applications [46]. Another aspect of speech quality is speaker recognizability (i.e., how well the identity of the speaker is preserved in the coded speech). At very-low bit rates, speech may sound as if spoken by a generic speaker, with few traits other than gender being perceived. Recognizability has only recently been included in coder evaluations.

As a quality measure, the MOS is prevalent. It asks listeners to judge speech as excellent, good, fair, poor, or bad; the score is simply an average, weighting the five categories on a scale from 5 (best—imperceptible impairment) to 1 (very annoying). One point in this scale is roughly equivalent to 6 dB in SNR, with the midpoint of 2.5 MOS corresponding to 0 dB (this does not mean that 15-dB speech has excellent quality as such, but rather that it is highly intelligible). Toll-quality speech often is used for listener calibration (values around 4.0–4.5), whereas communications and synthetic quality have MOS in the 3.5–4.0 and 2.5–3.5 ranges, respectively. MOS tests involve dozens of listeners, hearing phonetically-balanced sentences, and require proper listener training and calibration to yield valid results. A related measure, the degradation MOS (DMOS) [47, 48], can be used for relative judgments, where a superior reference utterance precedes the coded speech and the scale of degradation ranges from inaudible (5) to very annoying (1).

The Qop is an SNR measure, relating speech energy to noise energy where the intentionally added noise is amplitude-modulated by the speech envelope; the SNR level at which a coded speech signal has equivalent perceptual quality to this noisy speech reference is the Qop value. A similar measure, called the *subjective SNR*, measures the SNR of the input speech plus sufficient speech-modulated white noise so that it and the coded speech are equally preferred [49]. The *modulated noise reference unit* (MNRU) has become a standard for noise conditions [50].

For lower-quality synthetic speech, the AEN measure specifies an attenuation loss in decibels; this loss is measured at the 80% articulation level, i.e., at a speech intensity sufficient to have listeners understand 80% of the phonemic information in the signal. The difference in the intensity levels of the original speech signal and of a coded version necessary to attain the 80% score is the AEN measure. The naturalness of coded speech can be measured in terms of the number of bits that log PCM speech would need to attain equivalent quality.

Other common subjective speech measures include the diagnostic rhyme test (DRT) and the diagnostic acceptability measure (DAM) [51]. The DRT tests intelligibility of phonetic features of consonants, while the DAM rates speech naturalness along several perceptual scales. On a scale of 100, the DRT typically ranges from 95 for toll quality to 90 for synthetic quality speech; the range is about 73–54 for the DAM [1].

Another evaluation factor for coders concerns the environment. Listeners can tolerate more distortion in speech over loudspeakers than with headphones, due to room reverberation effects. Using headphones makes users more sensitive to distortion, even compared to telephone handsets [47].

7.5 TIME-DOMAIN WAVEFORM CODING

The basic PCM and log PCM of Section 7.2 used instantaneous quantization; such simple coders ignore most redundancies in speech. This section introduces a family of speech coders which exploit the tendencies of speech to vary slowly in energy and periodicity and to have most energy at low frequencies. Such redundancies are most easily exploited in the time domain. Most speech coders vary in time, adapting their characteristics dynamically to exploit signal changes due to vocal tract movement. This motion is slow compared to the signal sampling rate F_s; so coders here are updated very slowly (typically 20–100/s vs. $F_s \approx 8000/s$). These coding methods are popular for their simplicity, mostly at rates of 24–32 kb/s.

7.5.1 Basic Time-Adaptive Waveform Coding

This section introduces the simplest time-adaptive technique, *adaptive-quantizer pulse-code modulation* (APCM or PCM-AQ), in which the quantizer step size Δ varies in proportion to the short-time average speech amplitude. (Later sections describe how time adaptation can be combined with other coding methods.) In APCM, Δ is minimized to yield little quantization noise but must be large enough (given a fixed number of quantization levels) to handle the input amplitude range with minimal clipping. The solution is to evaluate speech energy over a brief time window and scale Δ accordingly. For intense sounds, Δ is large, while weaker sounds permit smaller values with limited risk of clipping. Thus a constant SNR can be maintained independent of the input variance.

7.5.1.1 Design choices for APCM. The implementation of APCM involves three choices: (1) variable step size or gain, (2) the size of the time window, and (3) feedforward or feedback adaptation. The quantizer adapts either by directly scaling values for Δ in proportion to the estimated signal variance (Figure 7.13a) or by scaling the signal input to the quantizer in inverse proportion (Figure 7.13b). In the latter (variable-gain) approach, a gain factor $G(n)$, inversely proportional to the average $\sigma_x(n)$ of the speech input, multiplies the speech signal, compressing or expanding it to have a uniform range for different inputs. The alternative variable step-size approach requires dynamically changing the quantizer characteristic. The decoder/receiver inverts the adaptation effects of the coder/transmitter by using a variable step size or by dividing the output speech by $G(n)$.

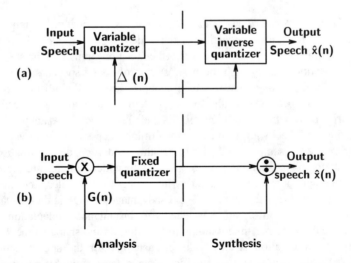

Figure 7.13 Block diagram representation of adaptive quantization: (a) variable–step size version, (b) variable–gain version.

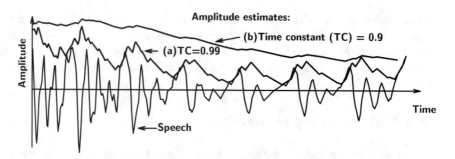

Figure 7.14 Speech variance estimates in (a) instantaneous, (b) syllabic adaptation. For
clarity, values of $\hat{\sigma}_x(n)$ are magnified equally in both plots.

The choice of window size over which to evaluate the speech variance leads to two
classes of APCM coders: *instantaneous* and *syllabic*. Short windows (with durations or time
constants under 2.5 ms) give rapid (so-called "instantaneous") updates for $\sigma_x(n)$ and follow
amplitude variations within individual pitch periods (Figure 7.14a). Syllabic adaptation, on
the other hand, uses longer windows (> 25 ms) and follows slower amplitude variations due to
changes in vocal tract shape or excitation (Figure 7.14b). In terms of optimizing SNR,
instantaneous adaptation is clearly superior but requires frequent updates for the step size;
e.g., one study of APCM speech using a coarse 3 b/sample coding (24 kb/s) found SNR in
the range of 7–10 dB for nonadaptive PCM, about 12 dB for APCM with Δ updated 8
times/s, and about 14 dB when updated 62.5 times/s [14]. While APCM only improves SNR
by a few decibels, SEGSNR can be raised 13 dB (APCM handles a wide dynamic input range
well). The companding techniques of APCM also apply to analog speech processing (e.g.,
single-sideband satellite communication), where automatic gain controls can compress a
60 dB dynamic range for speech into 30 dB, with adaptation times of 5 ms for the *attack*
(when energy increases) and 20 ms for the *decay* (when energy falls off) [52].

7.5.1.2 Feedforward vs feedback adaptation.

Updating Δ requires informing the
decoder of the adaptation occurring at the coder stage. The *feedforward* approach (called
AQF, for adaptive quantization with forward estimation) transmits the step size or gain factor
as *side information*, along with the basic stream of coded speech samples. (The term "side
information" simply notes that this data occupies less bandwidth than the main channel of
information; on a per-bit basis, the former is often more important and can be protected with
fewer parity bits in the case of noisy channels.) The *feedback* approach (AQB—adaptive
quantization with backward estimation) determines step size or gain variation directly from
past *coded* speech samples and eliminates the need for side information (as well as the
opportunity to protect such information). While the coded samples are subject to quantization
noise, signal gain is readily estimated by averaging such samples, and the noise usually has
minimal effect on the gain estimate. The disadvantage of AQF is the increase in transmission
bit rate due to the side information, especially for instantaneous adaptation. $\Delta(n)$ or $G(n)$ must
be sent once or twice per time window (depending on the shape of the window). While the
rate for side information is clearly lower than that for the speech samples (e.g., 8–800
samples/s vs 8000 samples/s), a significant percentage of the bit rate may be used for side
information with frequent updates. With syllabic adaptation, however, the side information is

often less than 1% of the total bit rate (e.g., step size coded with 5–6 bits every 25 ms in 24 kb/s APCM).

A form of instantaneous AQF has been successfully combined with log PCM to yield improved speech quality via *nearly instantaneous companding* [53]. Blocks of typically ten sequential n-bit log PCM speech samples are re-encoded to $(n-1)$-bit uniform PCM, with step size scaled to the maximum speech magnitude within each block, without quality loss. Ease of conversion from PCM and log PCM signals occurring in telephone networks is among the advantages of this method.

A common AQF approach measures speech energy (variance) as

$$\sigma_x^2(n) = \sum_{m=-\infty}^{\infty} x^2(m)w(n-m), \qquad (7.7)$$

where an example time window $w(n)$ is the simple "dying exponential" (a causal version of the signal in Figure 2.3c):

$$w(n) = \begin{cases} \alpha^{n-1} & \text{for } n \geq 1 \text{ (with } 0 < \alpha < 1 \text{ for stability)} \\ 0 & \text{otherwise.} \end{cases} \qquad (7.8)$$

In this case the variance is calculated by passing the squared speech signal through a first-order filter. Quantization of the side information requires the range of $\Delta(n)$ or $G(n)$ to be restricted. To obtain a relatively constant SNR over an input range of 40 dB, the ratio of $\Delta_{\max}/\Delta_{\min}$ should be about 100. If significant time intervals of the input speech are expected to be silent, a small value for $\Delta_{\min}$ will reduce the *idle-channel* noise.

Feedback AQB avoids the need for side information by determining the adaptation factors directly from the output of the quantizer. Because this information is available equally to the coder and decoder (assuming no channel errors), no extra data need be sent. Since the variance estimates are based on quantized (and thus distorted) speech samples, however, they are less reliable than estimates in AQF systems. Channel errors with AQB affect step sizes as well as individual output speech samples and are therefore more serious than sample errors in AQF. Finally, AQF incurs the inherent delay of determining the variance estimate. Normally, a block or frame of N samples is used to estimate the speech gain, and then the corresponding step size is applied to those same samples. In syllabic PCM-AQF, N can correspond to delays in excess of 10–20 ms, which may be too long for some real-time applications. When fast and low-cost operation is paramount, AQB is best.

The variance estimate in AQB can be obtained by windowing the quantizer output (Equation (7.7)), but the filtering must be causal (i.e., $w(n) = 0$ for $n < 0$). No delay or buffering of samples is allowed since the variance estimate for the current sample must be based only on prior quantizer outputs; this restriction also helps the system to run in real time. At 24 kb/s, an SNR of about 12 dB is attainable with a window of only two samples, with little improvement coming from wider windows [14], although longer windows may yield more stable estimates. Alternatively, the step size could be updated in multiplicative fashion by the so-called Jayant quantizer:

$$\Delta(n) = P(n)[\Delta(n-1)]^\beta, \qquad (7.9)$$

where P is proportional to the magnitude of the previous quantizer output [14]. If the prior output utilized one of the extreme quantizer levels, P would exceed unity in order to expand the step size; if one of the interior levels of the quantizer characteristic was used (indicating a small input magnitude), P would be less than unity to decrease the step size. P typically remains in the range (0.6, 3.3). This method leads to about 5 dB SNR improvements compared to μ-law quantization at the same bit rate [14, 54]. β is a constant just less than one, which protects against noisy transmission; any step size error only affects samples over a duration proportional to $1/\beta$.

In summary, APCM improves SNR performance and speech quality when compared to nonadaptive and logarithmic PCM systems. It exploits slow time variations in speech amplitude, which occur over short (instantaneous) and long (syllabic) intervals. The overall amplitude envelope of speech varies with movements of the vocal tract and can be sufficiently sampled at rates of 30–100 samples/s in syllabic APCM. Within individual pitch periods, amplitude slowly declines as a function of the bandwidths of the first two formants; instantaneous APCM takes advantage of these more rapid fluctuations, while still only needing step size updates ten times slower than F_s. Adaptation either uses input or coded speech samples; the former case requires transmission of side information, the latter is more practical for low-cost systems.

7.5.2 Exploiting Properties of the Spectral Envelope

The short-time magnitude spectrum of speech has an envelope, slowly varying in frequency, on which a harmonic line structure is imposed for voiced sounds. The envelope shape is primarily due to the poles and zeros of the vocal tract response. In most cases, the center frequencies and bandwidths of the formants (about 1 per kHz) describe the envelope well, although zeros have effects in nasals and frication. This section deals with a coder called *differential PCM* (DPCM), which exploits this spectral envelope structure.

7.5.2.1 Differential PCM.
Quantization noise follows Δ, which in turn is proportional to σ_x, the standard deviation of the quantizer input (e.g., the input speech). APCM's crude attempt to match Δ to σ_x, using only information about average speech amplitude, yields only a small SNR gain. DPCM achieves larger gains by exploiting time-domain speech behavior (beyond average amplitude) over intervals of only a few samples. Instead of quantizing each speech sample separately, DPCM quantizes the difference between a current sample and a *predicted estimate* of that sample, based on a weighted average of previous samples (i.e., a linear predictor) [55]. If successive samples were uncorrelated, there would be no gain from this procedure, but speech (especially voiced speech) has a high degree of sample-to-sample correlation. Such short-time correlation (over about 1–3 ms) corresponds to the spectral envelope; correlation over longer intervals (e.g., periodicity) relates to spectral fine structure and is discussed later.

The average spectrum for speech in general (Figure 7.15) has most energy below 1 kHz; it peaks near 500 Hz and falls off at about -6 dB/octave with higher frequency, largely due to the mostly smooth shape of voiced glottal pulses. (Voiced speech dominates such statistics because it is strong and occurs more often than unvoiced speech.) High frequencies, though weak in energy, remain very important for intelligibility and naturalness. Coders must sample speech at a rate high enough to preserve bandwidths exceeding 3 kHz, even though energy below 1 kHz generally dominates the speech signal. Due to the dominance of low-frequency energy, sampling voiced speech at a rate designed to model the spectrum up to 3 kHz or more leads to a high degree of correlation among adjacent samples. By formulating a predicted estimate $\tilde{x}(n)$ of each speech sample $x(n)$, DPCM quantizes a difference value $d(n) = \tilde{x}(n) - x(n)$, which has a smaller variance than that of the original speech. Quantization noise is reduced by using smaller step sizes, and SNR improves when speech is reconstructed at the decoder with an operation inverting the differentiation. The difference

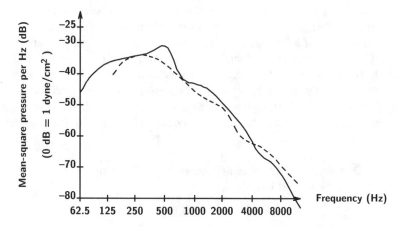

Figure 7.15 Long-time power density spectrum for continuous speech (solid line is male
speech, dashed line is female speech). (After Dunn and White [56].)

signal $d(n)$ is often called a *residual* or *prediction error* (Figure 7.16b) since it is the
waveform remaining after certain predictable aspects of the speech signal have been removed.
This residual is sent at F_s samples/s (but at a lower bit rate than for $x(n)$, by using fewer
b/sample), while parameters of the predictor may be sent at a rate much below F_s; the overall
result is equivalent speech quality at a lower bit rate.

In coding, it is most efficient to transmit signals of maximum entropy, i.e., samples with
minimal correlation. Predictive coders attempt to convert speech into a low-amplitude random
waveform by removing as much redundancy as possible. If the redundancies are estimated

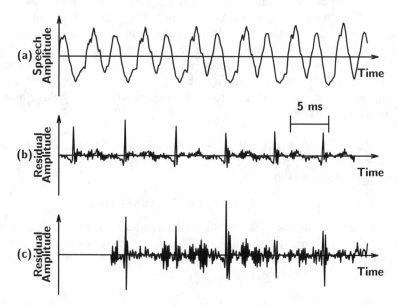

Figure 7.16 Waveforms of (a) original speech and prediction error after (b) spectrum
prediction ($N = 16$) and (c) an additional pitch prediction (of third order).
Waveforms (b) and (c) are magnified by $\sqrt{10}$ and 10, respectively.

efficiently, then model parameters (representing short-time spectra and hence vocal tract shapes) can be transmitted at a low rate, while the remaining less predictable aspects of the speech (in the form of a residual signal) are transmitted at the original sampling rate.

APCM coders remove redundancy from speech in the form of a slowly varying amplitude envelope (in the long-term, over several ms), and log PCM coders exploit the tendency of speech samples to be weak, by compressing amplitude peaks and expanding low-amplitude speech values. Both systems exploit some predictability in the waveform, but ignore the local time structure and frequency content of the speech. Predictive coders exploit this latter area of speech redundancy.

7.5.2.2 A measure of spectral redundancy.
To estimate speech redundancy, the *spectral flatness measure* (SFM)

$$\text{SFM} = \frac{\frac{1}{N}\sum_{k=1}^{N} X_k}{\left(\prod_{k=1}^{N} X_k\right)^{1/N}} \tag{7.10}$$

is often used [9,14], where X_k is the speech energy within a frequency band centered at ω_k, N is the number of frequency bands covering the speech bandwidth, and ω_k typically equals $\pi(k - \frac{1}{2})/N$. The SFM is the ratio of arithmetic mean to geometric mean of the segmented speech spectrum. The numerator is simply the average speech energy, while the denominator reflects the speech's spectral predictability. If the spectrum is flat, SFM equals unity, indicating a random waveform, e.g., white noise. Typically, long-term speech has an SFM of about 8, while short-term values are in the range $2 < \text{SFM} < 500$.

The highest values for SFM are found in vowels with clear line structure in their spectra and narrow formant bandwidths. These yield a high dynamic range for the X_k (especially if $N \cdot \text{F0} > F_s/2$, so that harmonic structure is reflected in the X_k) and thus a low geometric mean. Predictive coders seek to model the variation in X_k with a few parameters that vary slowly in time. Such parameters form the basis of a spectral estimate $\hat{X}(e^{j\omega})$ of the speech (and its synthesizer); the inverted spectrum $1/\hat{X}(e^{j\omega})$ provides the frequency response for an *inverse filter*. DPCM passes speech $x(n)$ through this inverse filter, which yields a residual signal with a flatter spectrum than $X(e^{j\omega})$. This spectral flattening yields a more random and lower-variance waveform to quantize.

7.5.2.3 DPCM details.
Basic short-term DPCM forms an estimate $\tilde{x}(n)$ for each speech sample $x(n)$, based on a linear combination of $x(n - k), k = 1, 2, 3, \ldots, N$, and quantizes the residual $d(n)$ as

$$\hat{d}(n) = Q[d(n)] = Q[x(n) - \tilde{x}(n)] \tag{7.11}$$

(the "hat" notation means "quantized"). At the decoder (assuming no corruption by channel errors), $\hat{d}(n)$ passes through an "integrator" (the inverse of the coder differentiation), yielding the output speech $\hat{x}(n)$. Many DPCM systems do not use this simple approach because the quantization error (at the quantizer output)

$$e(n) = \hat{d}(n) - d(n) \tag{7.12}$$

is subsequently integrated by the decoder and thus propagates to future samples. In PCM and log PCM (coders with no memory), the quantization noise, well modeled as white noise (assuming fine quantization), passes directly through to the output. Integrating the noise instead colors its spectrum, concentrating the distortion at low frequencies. A subsection below shows how noise can be spectrally shaped to perceptual advantage, but for now note that many applications prefer zero-mean, uncorrelated noise with a flat spectrum in the output; e.g., if $e(n)$ does not have zero mean, the error integrated at the decoder grows in size at the output. Even relatively short intervals where the mean error $E(e(n))$ deviates from zero can cause perceptible surges in the output noise.

For these reasons, a structure with the predictor P in a closed-loop feedback around the quantizer Q is more common (Figure 7.17). If P is a linear filter, simple system theory shows that this structure is equivalent to the more direct approach. Treating P as a spectral measure (e.g., $P(z)$), the basic DPCM coder filters the input X with $1 - P$ (the net effect is usually that of a differentiator), while the decoder does inverse filtering with the integrator $1/(1 - P)$. Except for the quantizer, the double feedback system in Figure 7.17 has the same result as a $1 - P$ filter. The advantage of this approach is that the decoder output $\hat{x}(n)$ is also generated at the coder and is used directly in the prediction and quantization; i.e., the estimate $\tilde{x}(n)$ comes from the quantizer output rather than from $x(n)$ directly. Equations (7.11) and (7.12) and the simple algebra of the figure show that $\hat{x}(n) = x(n) + e(n)$, i.e., the output noise is equal to the noise generated at the quantizer. Thus the output noise is memoryless and, given fine enough quantization, approximately white. The improvement in SNR is given by σ_x^2/σ_d^2 since a reduction in input variance to the quantizer is exactly the reduction in the output noise. This SNR change is known as the *prediction gain G* due to predictor P. In practice, the improvement may not be as great because the discussion above assumed that quantizing $d(n)$ was no different from quantizing $x(n)$ except for the size of the variance. The techniques of adaptive step size and/or nonuniform quantization are likely to yield lower SNR gains for $d(n)$ than for $x(n)$ since $d(n)$ has less redundancy. Nonetheless, DPCM is a more powerful technique than APCM or log PCM and usually gives higher output SNR.

7.5.3 Exploiting the Periodicity of Voiced Speech

Besides the formant structure of speech (which appears temporally as a short-term correlation of samples over a few ms), another major redundancy in speech waveforms concerns the short-term periodicity of voiced speech. In principle, the basic DPCM approach can be extended to handle the corresponding fine (harmonic) structure as well as the formants of the spectral envelope. Raising the predictor order p to examine speech over time windows exceeding a pitch period would allow the synthesis spectrum $H(z)$ to have enough detail to model the harmonic lines. (The order p must not be confused with the number of samples M

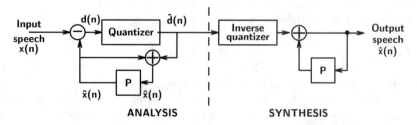

Figure 7.17 General differential PCM: coder on the left, decoder on the right. P is a linear predictor, and the inverse quantizer simply converts transmitted codes back into a single $\hat{d}(n)$ value.

in the time window over which the predictor P is evaluated: $M > p$ (often $M \gg p$), to base the spectral estimation on enough speech signal to reliably determine p predictor coefficients.) However, to model pitch, p would often exceed 100, leading to very complicated evaluations of the predictor coefficients and a complex structure in the predictor filter. This approach is unnecessary since spectral fine structure in voiced speech is highly regular (at least below 3 kHz), with clear harmonics spaced uniformly at multiples of F0.

The short-term *spectral predictor* of DPCM models the speech spectral envelope; to exploit periodicity, we need a long-term *pitch predictor*. (This variance-reducing inverse filter should not be confused with the F0 estimator of Chapter 6, which is used here to specify the parameters for the pitch predictor.) *Long-term prediction* (LTP) can be handled by a filter with only one coefficient, replacing Equation (7.18) with

$$P_d(z) = \beta z^{-M}, \tag{7.13}$$

where β is a scaling factor related to the degree of waveform periodicity and M is the estimated period (in samples). M is often coded with 6–7 bits (e.g., with a range of 20–147 samples at $F_s = 8000/\text{s}$). This predictor has a time response of a single impulse delayed M samples; so the LTP merely estimates that the previous pitch period repeats itself. LTP has no useful effect for unvoiced speech with its flat spectral structure (the unvoiced excitation being random). Thus $\beta = 0$ for a signal with no detectable periodic structure (and M is irrelevant) and $\beta \approx 1$ for steady-state voiced speech.

7.5.3.1 Pitch-adaptive predictive coders (APC).

Coders that employ LTP are often called *adaptive predictive coders* (APC), although that term would logically apply to adaptive DPCM as well. APC often employs forward adaptation, where β, M, and the spectral coefficients are side information. Sometimes a distinction is made between APC and pitch-predictive DPCM (PPDPCM), in that APC uses a 1 bit residual quantizer while PPDPCM uses more than 1 bit [55]. The extra bits and hence better quantization in PPDPCM apparently eliminate echo distortion that is often heard in APC speech.

The synthesis filter $1/(1 - P_d(z))$ corresponding to the pitch predictor has M poles in the z-plane uniformly spaced on a circle of radius $\beta^{1/M}$. The frequency response is a *comb filter* (resembling a picket fence of equally spaced, roughly triangular peaks) and approximates a line spectrum having F0 (in radians) of $2\pi/M$, with the bandwidth of the harmonics shrinking as β approaches unity. Thus different degrees of voicing can be modeled by letting β range from zero to one. In the time domain, the predictor subtracts the speech signal (weighted by β) from itself after a delay equal to the estimated period. This prediction can be extremely effective at reducing quantizer-input variance during steady voiced sounds, but is of little use at times of sudden spectral change. Pitch predictor gain (reduction in variance) for voiced speech averages about 13 dB [9]. A common estimate for β is the ratio of signal autocorrelation at a delay of M samples to signal energy

$$\beta = \frac{\langle x(n)x(n-M) \rangle}{\langle x^2(n-M) \rangle}, \tag{7.14}$$

where $\langle \rangle$ indicates averaging over an appropriate time window.

An F0 estimator must provide a value for the period M so that the residual error is minimized. Unlike in low-rate vocoders (where speech is synthesized at the estimated F0 rate), mistakes here in F0 detection may have mild consequences; e.g., the common error of pitch period doubling is of little significance because what APC seeks is a periodicity estimate over a limited time window. An estimate of twice the actual period suffices but is not as efficient, leading to a decreased β value. When the estimate for M is incorrect, the predictor gain is reduced, increasing the output noise during the frame within which the pitch error occurs. The resulting temporary decrease in SNR depends on how much β (in Equation (7.14)) deviates from the case when pitch is correctly estimated.

When subject to noise, APC speech can also be reverberant due to pitch estimation errors, which propagate for several periods due to the long time response of the corresponding synthesis filter (the sample response has nonzero values every Mth sample, with amplitude $\beta^{n/M}$). F0 estimation errors in vocoders, on the other hand, lead to pitch jumps in the output speech, which are much more annoying than an increase in noise or reverberation with APC coding. Nonetheless, a small amount of noise (e.g., with 30 dB input SNR) may be enough to prevent toll-quality APC output at 16 kb/s due to flaws in pitch prediction [57].

7.5.3.2 Higher-order pitch prediction.
A difficulty with the one-coefficient predictor of Equation (7.13) is that the true pitch period is unlikely to be an exact multiple of $1/F_s$, the sampling period. Thus β cannot be unity since the predictor is only able to align the speech waveform with a delayed version to within the precision of one sample. A common solution is to allow the predictor to be (second or) third order:

$$P_d(z) = \beta_1 z^{-M+1} + \beta_2 z^{-M} + \beta_3 z^{-M-1}. \tag{7.15}$$

This allows interpolation of speech samples in the delayed version to more precisely match the original. The extra degrees of freedom with three coefficients also help to model the bandwidths of the harmonics as a function of frequency. Periodicity is most evident at low frequencies, with the higher harmonics having a less regular structure. By widening the latter's bandwidths, we obtain a better model for the spectrum. Overall, using three coefficients rather than one can increase the predictor gain by about 3 dB [58].

Another way to handle the varying degree of voicing at different frequencies is to divide the spectrum into (typically 2–3) separate bands, performing APC on each band independently, which allows the pitch predictors in different bands to have different β values: high values leading to narrow harmonic bandwidths for low frequencies, lower values for the less periodic higher frequencies. This idea can be extended to dividing up pitch periods into a few time subintervals for more efficient bit allocation since, even after spectral and pitch prediction, there often remains some structure in the residual (see Figure 7.16c). Applying more bits to time subintervals with higher residual energy reduces the average quantization noise. The division into subbands helps, especially at lower bit rates (less than 16 kb/s, or 2 b/sample), where the quantization noise is large enough to cause instabilities in the feedback loop of the decoder. With subbands, each individual loop prediction gain is reduced, thus weakening the noise feedback effect [59].

Whenever a filter has a feedback loop, the potential exists for unstable output if a pole in the z transform of the filter's response is not inside the unit circle. To avoid brief output distortions (e.g., clicks) that are often caused by instabilities, speech coders strive to use only stable filters. With first-order pitch prediction (Equation (7.13)), as long as β is less than unity, stability is guaranteed. Second-order prediction permits a relatively simple stability test, and unstable filters can be easily stabilized [58]. A common approach with third-order systems (Equation (7.15)) uses an empirical test for stability and then first-order prediction instead for frames that would be unstable with a third-order predictor. Such instability occurs in about 8% of speech frames [21].

Optimizing the choice of predictor coefficients takes more computation for three-tap cases, and is often done open-loop. Closed-loop predictors (where reconstructed, output signals are evaluated for each choice of coefficient values) are thus practically often limited to one-tap filters. Closed-loop methods give better speech quality, but so do multiple-tap filters, thus leading to efforts for efficient pitch filters [60].

7.5.3.3 Combining pitch and envelope prediction.

The two types of prediction, pitch (long term) and spectral envelope (short term), can be combined in either order, inside or outside a quantizer feedback loop, with slightly different noise performances. One example is shown in Figure 7.18 (including noise shaping, to be discussed next). The two stages of prediction yield better SNR performance than either one separately, but the gain of the combined system is much less than the sum of the individual gains: one stage of prediction (either short or long term) typically raises SNR by 13–14 dB, while an additional stage adds only about another 3 dB. The first stage removes most of the redundancy from the waveform, leaving a less predictable signal for the second stage; e.g., Figure 7.16 shows how spectral prediction reduces the signal to a noisy version of a periodic impulse train (with less amplitude than the original) and how the second (pitch) prediction stage renders the signal close to white noise, at least for the steady portions of the vowel. The pitch stage modifies only a small portion of the waveform, once per period, and thus has a smaller effect than the first stage of prediction. Thus APC has not been popular, since only small gains occur and the extra computation of a pitch predictor is needed.

7.5.4 Exploiting Auditory Limitations (Noise Shaping)

In waveform coders, output speech fidelity is usually measured by a form of SNR, with the objective of minimizing output noise energy (i.e., the difference between input and output speech). Coders that use log-spectral representations aim for average distortion under 1 dB, which appears to be a JND threshold (assuming no outlier spectral values beyond 4 dB, and $< 2\%$ outliers of 2-4 dB) [62] (distortion under 2 dB is deemed "acceptable"). Since speech is eventually processed by the auditory system, however, a criterion better than SNR would be

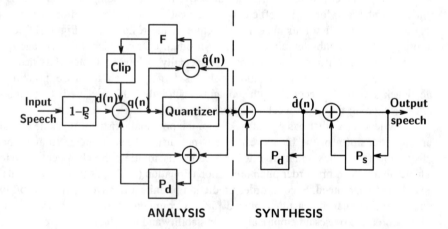

Figure 7.18 APC system with two stages of prediction: a predictor, P_s, based on the short-time spectral envelope and another, P_d, based on pitch structure. The filter F shapes the quantization noise to have less perceptual effect on the output speech. (After Atal and Schroeder [61] © IEEE.)

to minimize the subjective loudness of the noise [63]. Chapter 4 noted that auditory masking has strong effects on the perceptibility of one signal (e.g., noise) in the presence of another (e.g., speech). Noise is less likely to be heard at frequencies of stronger speech energy, e.g., at harmonics of F0, especially in the intense low-frequency formants. (Assuming a JND of 1 dB, a sound will be inaudible at 7 dB (the masking threshold) below a stronger sound of similar duration and spectrum [64].) Hiding quantization noise at frequencies of high speech energy or at times of strong temporal signal (e.g., pitch epochs) [65] can aid coders.

Assuming fine quantization, the basic DPCM coder configuration in Figure 7.17 yields output speech with white noise. Minimizing such noise energy is optimal for SNR but not for perception, since the noise is very noticeable during voiced speech at high frequencies, where speech energy is relatively low (Figure 7.19a) (especially in wideband applications, where the dynamic range is much larger than for telephone-band speech, and thus high-frequency noise is a big problem). The so-called D*PCM system [14], with a prediction filter *preceding* the quantizer, yields output noise with a spectral pattern that follows that of the input speech (Figure 7.19b), since the white quantization noise is so shaped by the synthesis filter. Perceptually, the speech may improve (although the output noise now has memory and risks accumulation of errors) since the noise is partly masked evenly at all frequencies by the speech spectrum. However, the raised noise at low frequencies in sonorants is more noticeable between harmonics. Thus the preferred system is a compromise between DPCM and D*PCM (Figure 7.19c).

In *noise feedback coding* (NFC), the quantization noise is passed through a filter $F(z)$, separate from the predictor $P(z)$ [57, 61]. By adjusting $F(z)$, the output noise may have any spectrum without affecting the speech component of the output. $F(z)$ is typically chosen so that the noise follows the speech spectrum, but with a bias toward less noise at low frequencies, since the ear is more tolerant to noise at high frequencies due to masking by low-frequency energy in speech. A simple approach uses $F(z) = P(\alpha z)$, where $0 \leq \alpha \leq 1$; extreme values for α (0 and 1) yield the D*PCM and DPCM coders, respectively (Figure 7.19a, b). Values for α in the range 0.73–0.9 seem best, causing increases in the bandwidths of the zeros of $1 - F(z)$ so that the noise spectrum is increased in formant regions, but not to the

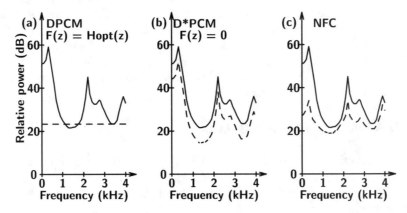

Figure 7.19 Input voiced speech spectra (solid curves) and noise spectra (dashed curves) for (a) ordinary DPCM, (b) D*PCM, and (c) DPCM with noise feedback coding (NFC). $H_{opt}(z)$ is the transfer function for the predictor (i.e., $P(\alpha z)$). (After Atal and Schroeder [61] © IEEE.)

extent of D*PCM [61]. In wideband applications, two noise shaping filters can be used to control the spectral tilt and formant effects independently [20].

One APC implementation (Figure 7.18) shapes the noise to follow the short-term speech spectrum ($F(z) = P_s(\alpha z)$) and relegates the pitch prediction component of the noise to be flat. The noise feedback loop sometimes has a peak limiter to constrain the maximal noise shaping to twice the root-mean-square value of the prediction error; this ensures stability in the presence of quantizer clipping errors, which become important in coarse, two- or three-level quantization. At 19.2 kb/s with a three-level quantizer and side information updated every 10 ms, this system yields an SNR of 21 dB (slightly lower than the 23 dB of DPCM but much better than the 13 dB of D*PCM) [14]. Subjectively, though, the NFC speech is close to 7-bit log PCM (32dB SNR), yielding an effective improvement of 11 dB due to noise-shaped APC. While adaptive DPCM can yield toll quality at 32 kb/s, NFC approaches toll quality at 16 kb/s. At 9.6 kb/s, quality equivalent to 4.5–6 bit log PCM is possible with APC [55]. The US Government standard version of APC transmits speech at 9.6 kb/s but combines a fourth-order spectral predictor with a complex type of APCM coding for the residual signal, instead of using NFC [66].

Another implementation claims toll-quality NFC speech by raising the number of quantization levels to 19 [57]. The side information is updated only every 25 ms and the residual is entropy coded to reduce the actual bit rate to 16 kb/s. A first- or second-order noise-shaping filter $F(z)$, in which the low-order $F(z)$ approximated the eighth-order $P(z)$ via a linear prediction analysis, was found sufficient. The coefficients f_k, $k = 1, \ldots, q$ (where q is 1 or 2) were obtained by solving q linear equations:

$$\sum_{k=1}^{q} f_k \rho_{j-k} = -\rho_j, \qquad \text{with } \rho_j = \sum_{k=0}^{p-|j|} a_k a_{k+|j|}, \qquad \text{for } j = 1, 2, \ldots, q, \qquad (7.16)$$

where ρ is the autocorrelation vector of the p predictor coefficients. Finally, benefits similar to NFC can occur through adaptive "postfiltering" of DPCM speech [48] to compensate for the introduction of noise into the predictor. Postfiltering can be useful for many coders to exploit auditory masking, both in the short term (formants) and long term (F0) [67]. (LTP postfilters often work on the residual, rather than the speech signal, to avoid discontinuities at frame boundaries when F0 changes.) Postfiltering usually attenuates the output speech at frequencies where the speech is weak (vs the quantization noise). Thus spectral valleys between formants and between harmonics are often attenuated, which may lead to a lowpass muffling if too many high frequencies are suppressed [68]. Such spectral attenuation may require gain adjustment, to avoid a fading effect. Postfiltering can also eliminate unwanted frequencies or compensate for unwanted amplification in certain communications equipment. Postfiltering is often found in 4.8–16 kb/s coding standards.

7.6 LINEAR PREDICTIVE CODING (LPC)

Linear prediction is a generalization of the simple DPCM discussed in Section 7.5. In this section, we examine the use of linear prediction in coders, quantizing the difference between actual and predicted speech samples. Virtually all DPCM schemes use a *linear predictor* of the form

$$\tilde{x}(n) = \sum_{k=1}^{p} a_k \hat{x}(n - k), \qquad (7.17)$$

where the estimate $\tilde{x}(n)$ is a linear combination of the p previous inputs to the predictor (see Section 6.5). The predictor P is thus a filter with response

$$P(z) = \sum_{k=1}^{p} a_k z^{-k}. \tag{7.18}$$

The reconstructed speech $\hat{x}(n)$ results from passing $\hat{d}(n)$ through a synthesis (reconstruction) filter of the form (Figure 7.17)

$$H(z) = \frac{1}{A(z)} = \frac{1}{1 - P(z)} = \frac{1}{1 - \sum_{k=1}^{p} a_k z^{-k}}. \tag{7.19}$$

To achieve minimal quantization error, a good predictor/inverse filter $A(z)$ outputs $\hat{d}(n)$ with a flat error spectrum. Thus $P(z)$ is chosen so that $H(z) \approx X(z)$. Determination of the optimal values for the filter coefficients a_k yields an $H(z)$ as close to the speech spectrum $X(z)$ as is possible with p coefficients.

As a simple example, consider first-order prediction ($p = 1$):

$$d(n) = x(n) - a_1 x(n-1). \tag{7.20}$$

(The analysis here ignores quantization noise: the actual feedback predictor input is $\hat{x}(n)$.) By squaring and averaging, the input variance to the quantizer is

$$\sigma_d^2 = (1 + a_1^2 - 2\rho a_1)\sigma_x^2, \tag{7.21}$$

where ρ is the first autocorrelation coefficient (i.e., $\rho = R_x(1)$). If we set $\partial\sigma_d^2/\partial a_1$ equal to zero, the optimal a_1 and minimum input variance result:

$$a_{1,opt} = \rho; \qquad \min(\sigma_d^2) = (1 - \rho^2)\sigma_x^2. \tag{7.22}$$

The corresponding prediction gain G is thus $1/(1 - \rho^2)$.

A prediction gain of 6 dB can be achieved with $p = 1$ (i.e., basing the estimate only on the immediately prior sample) (Figure 7.20) [14]. Such a gain permits speech coding with one fewer bit per sample than for basic PCM. Increasing p to 2 raises the gain about another decibel, but higher-order prediction brings little further improvement with a fixed predictor (i.e., not adaptive in time). The spectral pattern of general speech (Figure 7.15) can be well modeled by $1/(1 - P)$ with only a first- or second-order predictor. For significant further improvements, the predictor must be dynamic. Such adaptive differential PCM (ADPCM) schemes are discussed below.

While DPCM whitens the input to the quantizer and reduces its variance, the signal does not have a uniform distribution but rather a Laplacian (two-sided symmetric exponential) distribution. DPCM often uses adaptive step sizes to compensate for the nonuniform probability, but at low bit rates the coarse quantization is subject to clipping. Use of entropy coding here can yield a 3 dB SEGSNR improvement (e.g., to 13.6 dB with 2 b/sample coding—12.8 kb/s if $F_s = 6400$ samples/s) [69, 70].

DPCM can be applied to other speech-related signals besides speech itself. Whenever a slowly-varying sequence (e.g., step size $\Delta(n)$ in AQF systems) must be coded, it is more efficient to code differences. A fixed second-order predictor, with coefficients based on long-term speech, can increase the input dynamic range of DPCM coders by about 5 dB when an 8 bit residual is sent as side information every 32 ms [71]. DPCM can also be used to code the spectral envelope of speech [72].

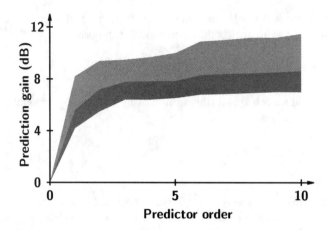

Figure 7.20 Maximum prediction gain versus predictor order for lowpass-filtered speech. The shaded area indicates the range for different speakers, while the middle line shows the average. (After Flanagan *et al.* [9] © IEEE.)

7.6.1 Linear Delta Modulation (LDM)

An important subclass of DPCM systems is *delta modulation* (DM), which uses 1 bit ($B = 1$ in Section 7.2) quantization with first-order prediction ($p = 1$ in Equation (7.18)). The main advantages of DM are simplicity and low cost: the quantizer just follows the input sign bit, and each bit has equal importance, eliminating the need for synchronization in transmission. To compensate for the otherwise large noise arising from a coarse two-level quantizer, the sampling rate must be several times the Nyquist rate: $F_s = 2MF_x$, where $M =$ oversampling ratio and $F_x =$ highest frequency in the input speech $x_a(t)$. This over-sampling may occur in the A/D conversion or in later interpolation, and considerably reduces the input variance to the quantizer due to the high degree of sample-to-sample correlation, which yields very small values for $d(n)$. Transmission rates are similar for DM and DPCM because M is roughly equal to the number of bits in typical DPCM quantizers (e.g., ordinary DPCM might use 5 b/sample with F_s equal to the Nyquist rate—8000 samples/s, with DM using one bit for each of 40,000 samples/s).

Figure 7.21 illustrates the DM operation and its quantizer characteristic. The predictor filter (as in Equation (7.20)) has only one coefficient

$$a_1 = \alpha, \tag{7.23}$$

which is normally chosen to be just less than 1. A value of exactly 1 yields a basic differentiator, and the predictor simply estimates the next input sample as equal to its last output sample. This estimate is justified given the high sampling rate; however, the synthesis filter is then a full integrator, which tends to accumulate errors (including any transmission errors). Hence a "leaky integrator" ($\alpha < 1$) is preferred in which the output eventually decays to near zero in the absence of further input. In DM, the quantized values $\hat{d}(n)$ are $\pm\Delta$, always changing the output by an amount virtually equal to the step size (if $\alpha \approx 1$). An incorrect received bit at time L causes the output to deviate by $(2\Delta)\alpha^{n-L}$ from its desired value at time n. The effects of channel errors thus die out more rapidly for smaller values of α.

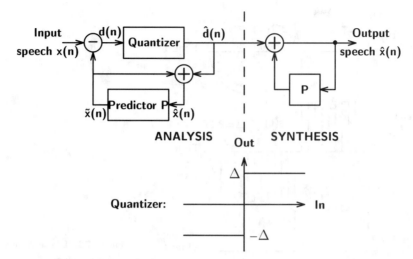

Figure 7.21 Delta modulation system.

The choice of step size Δ is crucial to successful performance in DM. Since the output magnitude can change only by Δ each sample interval T, the Δ must be large enough to accommodate rapid changes:

$$\frac{\Delta}{T} \geq \max\left|\frac{dx_a(t)}{dt}\right| \approx \max\frac{|x(n) - x(n-1)|}{T}. \tag{7.24}$$

Otherwise, a form of clipping called *slope overload* results (Figures 7.22 and 7.23), with the output noise (i.e., the deviation from the desired input speech signal) exceeding the basic limit of $\Delta/2$. Distortions localized to times of rapid signal change occur, as opposed to noise uniformly distributed throughout the signal as in other PCM schemes. On the other hand, if Δ is chosen too large, the usual *granular* noise becomes excessive since this noise is proportional to step size; e.g., when the speech input is silence, the output still oscillates with amplitude Δ.

This fixed-step-size *linear delta modulation* (LDM), so-called because the smoothed output tends to resemble linear ramps as the integrator attempts to follow rapid changes in the input, is not practical for speech because excessive sampling rates are necessary to eliminate slope overload while attaining good SNR over a wide range of input amplitudes. The advantages of LDM include implementations with simple circuits and no need for synchronization of bit patterns (due to its one-bit-per-sample code). Another advantage concerns the D/A conversion that takes place after the reconstruction integrator. Since the original speech is oversampled, it represents a narrowband lowpass signal with nominally all its energy in the range $|\omega| < \pi/M$. The quantization noise affects all frequencies $|\omega| < \pi$ equally, but only $100/M\%$ of the noise is retained in the analog lowpass filtering of the D/A conversion. Since $F_s = 2MF_x$ samples/s, the analog signal has frequencies up to MF_x Hz, but only the range $0\text{–}F_x$ Hz contains speech information. If the analog lowpass filter (required to smooth the piecewise-flat or "staircase" output of a D/A converter, eliminating digital frequencies above π radians) has a cutoff of F_x Hz, only the noise occupying the same frequencies as the speech remains. SNR in LDM is approximately proportional to F_s^3 [9], with one power of F_s due to the noise filtering. This means that a doubling of sampling rate (and hence of bit rate) in LDM

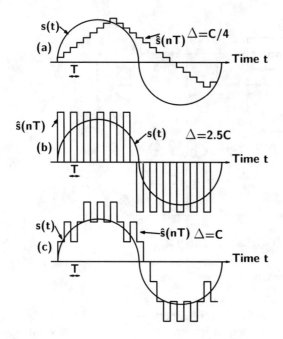

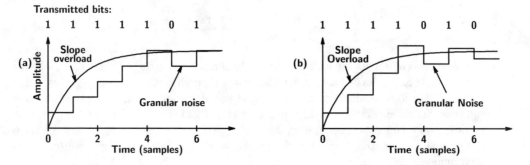

Figure 7.22 DM waveforms when the step size is (a) too small for the input slope, (b) too large for the input slope, and (c) well matched to the input slope. The continuous wave is the input and the staircase curve is the output.

Figure 7.23 Illustration of slope overload and granular noise with (a) fixed step size (LDM) and (b) adaptive step size (ADM).

leads to an incremental gain of only 9 dB in SNR, as opposed to a 6 dB gain *per bit* with normal PCM. LDM with second-order filtering can achieve a 15 dB improvement in SNR over the usual single-order predictor; for example, "double-integration" synthesizers yield 15 dB gain per doubling of F_s by coding speech in terms of its second difference as well as the first difference, where the predictor estimates that the slope of the speech signal stays constant (rather than assuming zero slope).

7.6.2 Adaptive Delta Modulation (ADM)

One obvious way to improve DM is to let the step size change dynamically with the input variance. Such adaptive DM (ADM or DM-AQ) systems are competitive with other waveform coders. The form of adaptation here follows that for APCM. If the AQB approach is used, the simplicity of LDM remains, avoiding frame synchronization of transmitted bits. ADM is superior to log PCM by a few decibels at low bit rates, but it becomes considerably inferior to log PCM as bit rate increases; at 40kb/s, the two systems have equivalent SNRs of about 28 dB [19].

While ADM coders primarily use feedback adaptation of the step size (i.e., DM-AQB), there are many different schemes to implement the adaptation. Most use simple logic, based on the previous 2–4 samples, to raise Δ when the recent transmitted samples have the same algebraic sign and to decrease it when the samples alternate in sign; e.g., constant-factor ADM (CFDM) updates Δ every speech sample,

$$\Delta(n) = \begin{cases} \beta_1\Delta(n-1) & \text{if } c(n) = c(n-1), \\ \beta_2\Delta(n-1) & \text{otherwise,} \end{cases} \tag{7.25}$$

where $\beta_1 > \beta_2$ (with $\beta_1\beta_2 \approx 1$) and $c(n)$ are the transmitted bits. Limits are usually placed on the step size range, $\Delta_{\min} \leq \Delta \leq \Delta_{\max}$, to avoid "overadaptation"; e.g., if Δ were to shrink to near zero during silence, then serious slope overload would occur when speech resumes. Some undesirable output signal oscillation with CFDM can be eliminated by using a 2 bit memory (instead of only $c(n-1)$), at the expense of increased complexity.

Instead of instantaneous adaptation (as in CFDM), some ADM coders "syllabically" adapt step size over time intervals of about 5–20 ms. The adaptation memory (analysis window) is usually only a few samples, but the changes in Δ occur relatively slowly; e.g., in *continuously variable slope DM* (CVSD), the step size can be updated as

$$\Delta(n) = \begin{cases} \beta\Delta(n-1) + D_2 & \text{if } c(n) = c(n-1) = c(n-2), \\ \beta\Delta(n-1) + D_1 & \text{otherwise,} \end{cases} \tag{7.26}$$

where $0 < \beta < 1$ and $D_2 \gg D_1 > 0$. If the output increases or decreases for three consecutive samples, the step size increases; otherwise it decays at a rate specified by β. The CVSD design is flexible enough to allow either syllabic adaptation (when β is near unity and D_2 is small compared to $\Delta_{\max}$) or instantaneous adaptation (when D_2 is large) for step size increases. CVSD is popular in applications with noisy channels (e.g., mobile radio), where β is almost unity to provide slow adaptation, but the prediction coefficient α (in Equation (7.23)) is small, to force the effect of channel errors to die out quickly. At rates under 24 kb/s, CVSD is superior to other ADM schemes because of its better granular noise performance (although slope overload is relatively high) [73].

CVSD can give slightly better SNR performance than CFDM for inputs with narrow dynamic range, but for speech CFDM has constant SNR over a 40 dB input range. Both SNR and dynamic range can be increased a few decibels by using hybrid companding DM, in which both syllabic and instantaneous step size adaptation take place [74]. Yet another 3–4 dB can be gained in SNR by allowing the sampling rate to vary: during inputs with rapid changes, higher rates increase the sample-to-sample correlation, whereas rates can be reduced when the speech signal varies more slowly. Such variable-rate coders, however, have significant implementation difficulties and potential problems regarding buffer delays in synchronous real-time applications. Since bit rate varies directly with sampling rate, samples must be buffered at times of high rates, for transmission later when the sampling rate decreases. This *overflow* condition may require up to 500 ms of delay [70]. Less seriously, an *underflow* condition (when the sampling rate remains below average for significant periods) can be avoided by forcing the sampling rate to match the channel rate when the overflow buffer is empty.

7.6.3 Adaptive Differential Pulse-Code Modulation (ADPCM)

Adaptive differential PCM can refer to DPCM coders that adapt Δ and/or the predictor. Just as PCM and DM benefit from adaptive quantization, SNR can be increased in DPCM if step size may change dynamically. The improvements in SNR are additive: about 6 dB with the differential scheme and another 4–6 dB by adapting the step size to match the quantizer input. The terms DPCM-AQF or DPCM-AQB refer to such systems, to distinguish them from ADPCM systems that adapt the predictor with time (DPCM-AP). Systems which adapt both predictor and quantizer usually do so separately for simplicity, but joint adaptation can yield gains [75].

In general ADPCM, both step size and predictor adapt with time, based on either quantizer inputs (feedforward) or outputs (feedback) (Figure 7.24). As before, the feedforward scheme requires transmission of side information, which is of increased significance for adaptive prediction since p coefficients (Equation (7.18)) are sent (vs the single gain factor in APCM). On the other hand, the feedforward scheme allows bit protection against channel errors for the crucial side information, which uses a small percentage of the bit rate. The data stream in feedback adaptation is homogeneous, so error protection requires modification of the adaptation algorithms themselves. A standard approach there is to restrict the time range over which any predictor parameter can affect the output speech, so that any error leading to an incorrect predictor has limited effect [55]. The feedback approach has been termed a *residual encoder* [54], although that name could apply to all differential speech coders.

With the fixed predictor of DPCM, there was little advantage in a high predictor order ($p > 3$). However, when the predictor can adapt in ADPCM to match the short-time characteristics of a dynamic speech signal, prediction gain increases over a wider range of order; e.g., using predictor updates every 16 ms, prediction gain (compared to nonadaptive

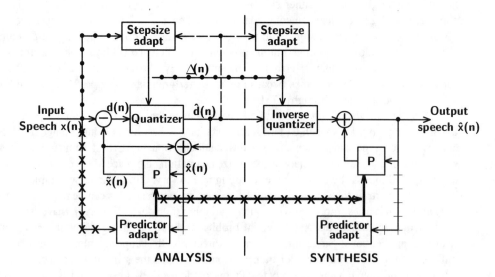

Figure 7.24 ADPCM system with both adaptive quantization and adaptive prediction. Paths are marked for the different options: AQF (dots), AQB (dashes), APF (×), APB (+). Paths drawn with heavy lines indicate vector transmission (e.g., several parameters sent in parallel).

PCM) is about 8 dB for order $p = 1$, 10 dB for $p = 2$, 12 dB for $p = 4$, 14 dB for $p = 10$, and 15 dB for $p = 20$ [14]. Thus, SNR improvement saturates much more slowly with increasing order, although the major gains still occur in the first few orders.

The closer the reconstruction filter $H(z)$ can approximate the speech spectrum, the better the coder performance. For a fixed predictor, $H(z)$ could only match the long-time average speech spectrum. With predictors obtained from windows short enough to consider the speech temporarily stationary, the finer details of individual formants can be modeled in ADPCM. Thus while $p = 1-2$ was sufficient to model the general lowpass characteristic of Figure 7.15, significant SNR gains can be made up to about $p = 12$ for ADPCM (Figures 7.25 and 7.26) (depending on formant separation and bandwidth, typically eight of the filter poles model four formants in 4 kHz bandwidth voiced speech, while additional poles help model the effects of the glottal source and nasality). Further significant gains can be made by modeling the line spectrum of voiced speech rather than just modeling the formant envelope; using the p-sample linear prediction approach of Equation (7.18) would require excessive values for p to model the harmonics (e.g., p must exceed the number of samples in a pitch period), but alternative methods are discussed later.

High-quality speech (not quite toll quality) is feasible with 4-bit ADPCM (i.e., 32 kb/s) [14]. The reduction of 3 b/sample (vs log PCM) is achieved by about 10 dB of prediction gain and 8 dB of noise shaping, which corresponds to the 6 dB/bit SNR effect.

DPCM usually employs an all-pole synthesizer, where the predicted value is a weighted combination of past coder outputs. However, a system using zeros can yield better SNR in ADPCM (e.g., 1–3 dB more for an all-zero filter than for an all-pole filter, for a filter order of eight) [78]. Such a system tracks changes in the speech spectrum better and reduces the sensitivity of the system to channel errors. ADPCM tolerates errors better than PCM,

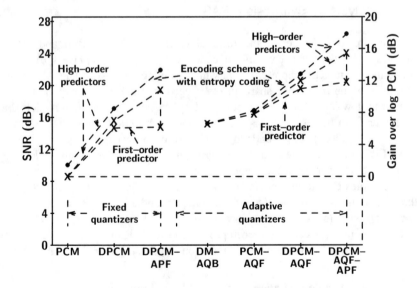

Figure 7.25 Performance of several 24 kb/s PCM coders ($F_s = 8000$ samples/s, $B = 3$). The right vertical axis shows relative SNR gain over 8 bit log PCM. (Reprinted with permission from *The Bell System Technical Journal* [76] © 1975, AT&T.) (By way of comparison, 64 kb/s PCM and 32 kb/s ADPCM yield SNRs of about 37 and 29 dB, respectively [77].)

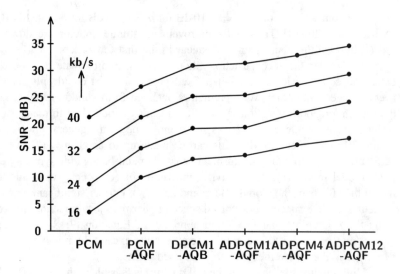

Figure 7.26 SNR for quantization with $16\,kb/s$ ($B = 2$) up to $40\,kb/s$ ($B = 5$). DPCMi
represents DPCM with an ith-order predictor. (Reprinted with permission
from *The Bell System Technical Journal* [76] © 1975, AT&T.)

retaining intelligibility even with 1% errors [79]. Due to its low complexity, ADPCM at
$32\,kb/s$ is widely used in personal communication services (PCS) networks.

7.6.4 Linear Predictive Coders (LPC) vs Linear Predictive Analysis-by-Synthesis (LPAS)

In an ADPCM coder, the residual error $e(n)$ is quantized and transmitted at F_s
samples/s. Unlike such a waveform coder, LPC vocoders replace $e(n)$ by a much more
economical parametric representation, while retaining the basic ADPCM structure. In voiced
speech, $e(n)$ normally has sharp peaks spaced in time by pitch periods, but also has a
significant low-level "noisy" component. The LPC synthesizer often models this $e(n)$ with a
simple uniform train of samples spaced at the pitch period rate (a *buzz source*). Each such
sample (or "pulse") corresponds to the closure of the vocal cords.

LPC and more general *linear prediction-based analysis-by-synthesis* (LPAS) [80]
furnish the best coders in the range 4–16 kb/s. As opposed to the basic LPC, LPAS uses a
more complex excitation specified in an iterative feedback loop (i.e., analysis via synthesis of
the excitation). Most of the recent developments (and all recent standards) in coding involve
LPAS systems. (Most coders below 5 kb/s use a linear predictor to eliminate redundant
information in the speech; further improvements in SNR up to 1.5 dB (and about 0.35 MOS
points) are possible with nonlinear prediction (e.g., using neural networks) [81].)

7.6.4.1 Simple excitation coding in LPC. In unvoiced speech, $e(n)$ resembles white
noise, and LPC synthesizers use a pseudo-random number generator to simulate such an
excitation (a *hiss source*). A feedback shift register of b bits can generate such a sequence of
noise values that repeats only every $2^b - 1$ samples. As long as this cycle exceeds about 4 s,
i.e., $(2^b - 1)/F_s > 4$, the noise periodicity is imperceptible (a 16 bit register suffices for

$F_s \leq 10,000$ samples/s). The autocorrelation function of the noise signal is very small except at time zero and at multiples of the repeat time, which leads to a basically flat spectrum.

For low-bit-rate coding, the error signal $e(n)$ is usually represented by: (a) one bit signifying whether the speech during the frame under analysis is voiced, (b) 5–6 bits (if voiced) for the pitch period duration T_0 (or $F0 = 1/T_0$), (c) 5–6 bits for an energy level or gain factor G, chosen to match the energy of the residual error signal. Since LPC analysis does not guarantee an error spectrum with equal-area harmonics while such a flat excitation spectrum is used in synthesis, specific harmonic energies may not be reproduced exactly (especially in high-F0 voices when a harmonic coincides with a formant peak). Such magnitude discrepancies between the residual and the synthesis excitation can cause spectral distortion in LPC output speech.

7.6.5 Equivalent Forms for LPC Coefficients

LPC analysis produces a set or *vector* of p real-valued predictor coefficients a_k, which represent an optimal estimate to the spectrum of the windowed speech using p poles. Such information can be represented in different formats, some with more use or more ease of physical interpretation than others, depending on desired applications. Quantizing different sets of coefficients has varying effects on important aspects of the LPC filters. The basic LPC representation of a_k ($1 \leq k \leq p$), which directly specifies the unit-sample response of the all-zero $A(z)$ ($= 1 - P(z)$, the inverse filter in the encoder), requires more bits per coefficient than the set of reflection coefficients k_m ($1 \leq m \leq p$) for the same accuracy in the synthesis decoder $H(z) = G/(1 - P(z))$. The difference concerns the synthesis filter structure: a_k are the multiplier parameters in a direct-form digital filter implementation of $H(z)$, whereas k_m are the multipliers in a lattice filter implementation. High-order (e.g., $p \approx 10$) direct-form filters are very sensitive to quantization, particularly in how much the filter poles deviate from their ideal positions in response to multiplier quantization [13]. Cascade or parallel filter structures, using subfilters of first and second order (combining complex-conjugate pairs of poles in second-order subfilters to avoid complex arithmetic), limit the effects of quantization. Lattice filters also have good quantization properties [82] and, in addition, quantization can be partially accounted for within the analysis stage of the lattice method; i.e., in calculating the mth reflection coefficient, quantized versions of the lower-order coefficients can be used so that later calculations partially compensate for the quantization in the first $m - 1$ stages.

Besides the reflection coefficients, equivalent representations for the LPC coefficients include: (a) the impulse response $h(n)$ of the LPC synthesis filter $H(z)$ (the first $p + 1$ values uniquely specify the filter); (b) autocorrelation coefficients for either a_k or $h(n)$ (the first $p + 1$ coefficients again suffice); (c) spectral coefficients from a DFT of either autocorrelation; (d) the cepstrum of a_k or $h(n)$, which can be calculated iteratively, e.g.,

$$\hat{h}(n) = a_n + \sum_{k=1}^{n-1} \left(\frac{k}{n}\right)\hat{h}(k)a_{n-k}, \qquad 1 \leq n \leq p, \qquad (7.27)$$

and (e) the p poles of $H(z)$ or p zeros of $A(z)$.

Two additional forms are popular because of their good quantization properties: the *log-area ratios* and the *inverse sine* functions. While k_m are less spectrally sensitive to quantization than a_k, k_m still cause difficulties when their magnitudes are near unity (i.e., reflection coefficients can be quantization-sensitive when they represent narrow-bandwidth poles). With appropriate nonlinear transformations expanding the region near $|k_m| = 1$, uniform quantization can be used with decreased spectral sensitivity. This is accomplished by both the log-area transformation

$$g_m = \log \frac{1 + k_m}{1 - k_m} = 2 \tanh^{-1} k_m \tag{7.28}$$

or the inverse sine transformation

$$g_m = \sin^{-1} k_m. \tag{7.29}$$

Applying uniform quantization to an LPC parameter minimizes the maximum deviation from the desired parameter value. Alternatively, nonuniform quantization uses parameter statistics (in the form of histograms obtained from much speech) to design optimal quantizers for the individual parameters [83]. This latter approach minimizes average (rather than maximum) parameter deviation. With low-sensitivity parameters such as the inverse sine coefficients, the same average spectral distortion due to quantization can be achieved with 8–10 fewer b/frame by employing nonuniform quantization. A typical 2.4 kb/s coder achieves about 1 dB distortion with either 42 b/frame under uniform quantization or 33 b/frame with optimal quantization [84].

7.6.6 Line Spectrum Pairs/Frequencies

Another representation for the LPC parameters, called the *line spectrum pair/frequency* (LSP or LSF), allows a much lower bit rate than with reflection coefficients, while producing equivalent speech quality. The LSP procedure involves mapping the p zeros of $A(z)$ (or equivalently the poles of the LPC synthesizer) onto the unit circle through two z transforms $P(z)$ and $Q(z)$ of $(p + 1)$th order:

$$P(z) = A(z) + z^{-(p+1)}A(z^{-1}) \tag{7.30}$$

$$Q(z) = A(z) - z^{-(p+1)}A(z^{-1}). \tag{7.31}$$

Thus

$$A(z) = [P(z) + Q(z)]/2. \tag{7.32}$$

If Equations (7.30) and (7.31) are viewed in terms of the LPC equations in Chapter 6, $P(z)$ and $Q(z)$ correspond to a vocal tract model extended by one section to include either a fully closed or open glottis: $A_{p+1}(z)$ with $k_{p+1} = \pm 1$, which guarantees that all zeros are on the unit circle [85]. $P(z)$ and $Q(z)$ correspond to lossless models of the lossy vocal tract response $A(z)$. The zeros of $P(z)$ and $Q(z)$ alternate as ω increases along the circle; the LSP coefficients correspond to the frequencies of these zeros. Since the zeros occur in complex-conjugate pairs, there are only p unique coefficients to find, with $P(z)$ and $Q(z)$ each contributing $p/2$ frequencies. The actual root computation involves $p/2$-order polynomials, and can be done via an iterative search procedure that takes advantage of the interleaving of zeros between the two polynomials $P(z)$ and $Q(z)$. DPCM coding of the frequency differences between successive zeros is efficient, leading to a 30% improvement in bit rate vs using a log-area ratio LPC representation [85, 86]. The LSP coefficients allow interpretation in terms of formant frequencies because each complex zero of $A(z)$ maps into one zero in each of $P(z)$ and $Q(z)$ [87]. If these latter zeros have close frequencies, it is likely that the original $A(z)$ zero corresponds to a formant; otherwise, the zero is likely to be of wide bandwidth and to contribute only to the tilt of the spectrum. While calculation of the LSPs can be complex, recent methods are more efficient, and LSPs have become common spectral parameters [88].

7.6.7 Parameter Updating and Transmission

Typically, finer quantization is used for coefficients that are considered more important to speech quality than others; e.g., if the zeros of $P(z)$ (identified perhaps by factoring the z polynomial) were coded, more bits might be used for the lower-frequency zeros, which correspond to the perceptually important lower formants. With reflection coefficients k_m and their direct transformations (log-area and inverse sine), the number of bits per coefficient varies inversely with m; this is a consequence of the optimality of coefficient k_m as higher-order coefficients are calculated in the Durbin recursion. Given the concave function of prediction error with LPC order, higher-order coefficients contribute to a decreasing degree in spectral estimation. Accurate representation of k_1 and k_2 are of prime importance in modeling speech; e.g., significant quality loss occurs in LPC speech if these two parameters are subject to 1% bit errors during transmission [89].

7.6.8 Variable-Frame-Rate (VFR) Transmission

In basic LP (and other) vocoders, a set of (LP) coefficients is transmitted or stored for every frame of analysis data, with typical update periods of 10–30 ms (while 10 ms frames are common, ones of 22.5 ms are increasingly used for lower bit rates [90]). To economize and to avoid transients in a temporarily unstable synthesis filter, the (LP) vectors are often smoothed (parameters interpolated in time) before use in the synthesizer stage. Speech quality is usually improved if the vocal tract filter $H(z)$ is updated more often than the actual (LP) coefficients are received. Each coefficient can be linearly interpolated across successive (LP) vectors (LSF coefficients yield good results [80, 91, 92]) e.g., if a_k and b_k $(1 \le k \le p)$ represent speech at times 0 and 100 ms, respectively, then $(1 - \alpha)a_k + \alpha b_k$ could be used at times $10, 20, \ldots, 90$ ms with values of $\alpha = 0.1, 0.2, \ldots, 0.9$. This requires a processing delay equal to the interval between transmitted vectors. These intervals could be fixed or variable, corresponding to a synchronous low bit rate or an average low bit rate.

The latter approach, involving a *variable frame rate* (VFR), requires buffering of data if a communications link has bandwidth specified by the average transmission rate [93, 94]. When the speech signal changes rapidly (i.e., due to vocal tract motion), LP vectors might be sent every 10 ms, while during steady vowels (or silence), a much lower rate suffices. Thus, data would be buffered during rapid changes, for later transmission during times of less speech dynamics. VFR vocoders can often reduce bit rate by about 50% without loss of speech quality, but with extra complexity and some delay [93]. Determination of when to transmit a frame of data normally depends on a distance measure comparing the last frame sent with the current analysis frame; when the distance exceeds a threshold (indicating a large enough speech change), 1–2 frames are sent. To avoid the problem of interpolating between two very dissimilar frames of LP coefficients (which may yield LP vectors that poorly represent the intermediate speech frames, since vocal tract movements often do not correspond well with linearly interpolated spectral coefficients), a recent prior frame may be sent along with the current frame if the major spectral change occurred suddenly rather than gradually over the time since the last transmitted frame.

If the LP vector elements are ordered, thus facilitating identification of coefficients that are more vital than others (e.g., the k_m, which decrease in importance as m increases), partial information in the form of subsets of the vectors could be transmitted at a variable frame rate, rather than using a binary decision each frame to send either the entire vector or no information [95]. Since individual parameters usually change slowly over time compared with typical frame rates, they could be transmitted using differential coding or a form of Huffman coding [96].

The ideas in this section can apply easily to other vocoders besides linear prediction. Vocoders analyze speech in blocks of data, send a vector of parameters for each block, and then apply these parameters in resynthesizing the speech for the time block. VFR can apply to any such block approach. Applying VFR to waveform coders, however, which send data and reconstruct sample-by-sample, is difficult.

While many applications cannot tolerate variable rates, the lesser need for channel bandwidth for lower-information sounds (e.g., silence requires very few bits, and the entropy rate for unvoiced sounds is low) allows lower average bit rates for applications where some buffering delay can be tolerated [97, 98]. Recent VFR efforts include an MBE coder (see below) with a 2.8 kb/s average rate, very close in quality to the G.723.1 standard at a fixed 5.3 kb/s [99].

7.6.9 Transmission Details

Linear interpolation is typically done on reflection coefficients before forming the LPC decoder. This guarantees stable synthesis filters if reflection coefficients have magnitude less than unity. LSP coefficients also have good interpolation behavior. Interpolating predictor coefficients a_k, on the other hand, may result in an unstable $H(z)$, even though the transmitted coefficients correspond to stable filters. Whether quantizing or interpolating the a_k, there is no simple test (or remedy) for synthesis filter instability. The F0 and gain parameters, which accompany the LPC vector in vocoder transmission, are usually coded and interpolated logarithmically (e.g., linear interpolation of gain in dB or geometric interpolation of linear gain parameters). This choice reflects perceptual discrimination of loudness and pitch, which follows a log scale more closely than a linear scale.

A typical vector of LPC data for a frame contains about 12 bits for excitation (see above) and an average of 5–6 b/spectral coefficient for 8–12 reflection coefficients or log-area ratios (with the number of coefficients depending on the speech bandwidth). (Coding a_k instead of k_m requires about 8–10 bits each for the same spectral accuracy.) A 2.4 kb/s vocoder might send 60 b/frame every 25 ms. With variable frame rates or differential coding of the parameters (e.g., applying ADPCM to each transmitted parameter as a function of time), equivalent speech quality can be found as low as 1 kb/s. Coding the spectrum of each frame with as few as 10 bits will be discussed in Section 7.9.

7.6.10 Time-Varying LPC Coefficients (‡)

The problem of time-varying spectra can be addressed directly in the formulation of the LPC model. One usually assumes that the input speech signal is stationary during each analysis frame, yielding a set of static LPC coefficients. Alternatively, dynamic speech could be modeled by time-varying LPC coefficients during each frame; e.g., during an N-point analysis frame, the coefficients might be expressed as the sum of r basis functions $b_i(n)$:

$$a_k(n) = \sum_{i=0}^{r-1} a_{ki} b_i(n), \qquad \text{for } 0 \leq n \leq N, \tag{7.33}$$

where $b_i(n)$ could represent eigenfunctions for a simple power series ($b_i(n) = n^i$) or a Fourier series ($b_i(n) = \cos(in\pi/N)$) [100]. Here, longer time windows are possible than with basic LPC, since speech time variation is captured directly in the LPC coefficients. However, the number r of basis functions to adequately model the variation increases with window duration. This method trades off less frequent frame updates for more coefficients per frame. For sufficiently short windows and thus high update rates, basic LPC ($r = 1$) suffices.

Applying the usual minimum mean-square-error criterion leads in general to an autocovariance matrix of size $pr \times pr$ instead of the normal $p \times p$ matrix since the different basis functions must be cross-correlated with the speech signal [100]. Instead of p equations to solve, there are pr equations. Thus, the advantage of accurate time-varying LPC coefficients with long analysis frames must be contrasted against a large increase in computation. There are, of course, exploitable symmetries similar to those found earlier in the original autocorrelation matrix **R**, which had only p unique elements among its p^2 entries. Nonetheless, the number of distinct autocovariance elements to calculate increases significantly with r (roughly pr^2 elements in the autocorrelation method, p^2r in the covariance approach). In practice, the average number of coefficients/s is about half that of basic LPC, i.e., at a rate comparable to VFR systems [100].

Instead of a fixed set of elementary basis functions to encode the LPC coefficients, the set could vary from frame to frame for better adaptation to vocal tract dynamics. If the functions are updated 10–15 times/s (i.e., at about the phoneme rate), a set of about five slowly varying basis functions could be matched to the LPC coefficients and sent as side information in as few as 160 b/s [101]. With another 50 b/s for sending the time boundaries of variable-length coding frames (chosen to be about 100 ms, but specifically located at times of major coefficient change to permit the use of smooth basis functions within each frame), a total bit rate under 1 kb/s yields speech quality equivalent to basic LPC with rates twice as high.

Synthetic LPC speech often suffers from discontinuities in global amplitude patterns, due to quantization in the gain parameter and sudden gain changes at frame boundaries. One recent approach models the dynamic amplitude envelope, ensuring a good match for global amplitude in time (on a scale of phonemes, not pitch periods) and preserving desired, sudden amplitude changes for consonants [102]. At 2.4 kb/s, this speech was preferred over LPC-10e and was comparable to 4.8 kb/s CELP (both recent advanced versions of LPC described below).

7.6.11 Different Excitation Models

The basic LPC vocoder using a periodic excitation source (most commonly, a single sample per period) for voiced speech yields only *synthetic-quality* speech. Slight quality improvements are possible as coding rate increases above 2.4 kb/s, but the limitations inherent in the simplistic LPC model remain, and quantizing the basic LPC parameters more finely does not resolve these difficulties. The major impediment to *toll* or *communications* quality speech with LPC lies in the periodic excitation, which adds a "buzzy" or mechanical aspect to the synthetic speech. Part of the problem lies in the binary decision of whether speech during an analysis frame is voiced. The synthesizer chooses either a periodic waveform or white noise to excite the $H(z)$ filter. Voiced fricatives are thus poorly modeled since they should have a noise excitation with a periodic envelope. More seriously, vowel excitation in natural speech has a noisy component, which is primarily evident above 2–3 kHz. Short-time spectra of vowels show clear harmonic structure in the first few formants, but not a simple line spectrum in the higher formants. Ideally, for the region of each harmonic, one could independently select a voiced or unvoiced excitation [103]. Intelligibility of LPC speech tends to decrease for breathy or nasal speakers where the all-pole, binary-voiced assumptions are less valid [104].

7.6.11.1 Simple mixed-excitation models.
A modified excitation can mix the two sources in different frequency ranges, most often using the sum of a lowpass-filtered periodic waveform and a highpass-filtered noise signal as the input to the LPC synthesis filter. This corresponds to the tendency of periodicity to decrease with frequency, as the plane-wave propagation assumption becomes less valid (see Chapter 3). In one approach, a frequency ω_c marks the boundary between a totally periodic source at low frequencies, a fully random signal at high frequencies, and a brief transition frequency band centered at ω_c in which the excitation is a combination of the two [105]. The variable cutoff frequency reflects how voiced a particular sound is, ω_c being higher for sounds with more harmonics. However, unlike a binary voiced–unvoiced decision, it is difficult to reliably locate ω_c. The LPC normalized error value V_p is a reasonable measure of voicing degree, but it does not specify spectral distribution of periodic vs random energy.

If the LPC residual error is assumed to be a sum of two uncorrelated components, one periodic and one random, the autocorrelation of the error at a lag equal to an estimated pitch period is another voicing measure:

$$\beta = R_e(M) = \langle e(n)e(n-M)\rangle, \tag{7.34}$$

where M is the pitch period. In the case of mostly unvoiced speech, a poor pitch estimate M would lead to a low value for β. Such a measure can specify the proportion of pre-emphasized noise and de-emphasized pulse signal to constitute an LPC excitation [78]. Instead of attempting to find a sharp cutoff frequency ω_c, the transition band is broadened with simple pre-emphasis and de-emphasis giving a good mix of the two types of sources. The normalized error V_p is used as a guideline to ensure an overall flat excitation spectrum, which is required for all LPC excitations. A comb filter $1 - k_3 z^{-M}$ restricts the noise energy at nonharmonic frequencies, where it otherwise would render a voiced phoneme hoarse (noise near the harmonics is more easily masked). Finally, a modified version of the simplified inverse-filtered tracking (SIFT) F0 estimation algorithm [106] can increase pitch period accuracy and reduce perceptual degradations related to small F0 estimation errors (e.g., those due to the finite sampling interval $1/F_s$, which become significant for voices with high F0) [78].

LPC synthetic speech can be made slightly more natural by simply adding jitter to the excitation, randomly varying the pitch pulse positions and amplitudes by small amounts each period. Varying the period length by up to 25% eliminates short tones that can occur in synthesis of female speech. A more effective, but complicated, approach modifies the phase spectrum of the excitation directly [107]. This approach can add natural breathiness to the voice without rendering it hoarse (as occurs with excessive jitter). A new US federal standard [28] achieves 2.4 kb/s (and lower [108, 109]) LPC with quality similar to recent 4.8 kb/s coders. This mixed-excitation LPC (MELP) is distinguished from basic LPC in its (1) excitation (combining noise with time-jittered pulses), (2) post-processing pulse dispersion filter (spreading energy in time, to better model multiple excitations in a glottal cycle), and (3) adaptive spectral enhancement (to better match formant regions).

LPC analysis yields a synthesis filter $H(z)$ that includes glottal and radiation effects as well as the vocal tract response. Since the all-pole assumption is not valid for the glottal and radiation effects, a separate modeling for them might improve LPC speech. The glottal waveform approximately resembles a half-rectified sine wave, but the timing of the opening and closing phases as well as the percentage of time during the pitch period that the vocal cords are open varies considerably for different sounds. By determining glottal pulse parameters to further reduce the LPC error, one can enhance output speech quality at the cost of additional analysis computation and an extra 200–400 b/s (e.g., 3–4 bits each for relative opening and closing vocal cord phases, once per analysis frame) [110].

7.6.11.2 Residual-excited linear predictive (RELP) vocoders (‡).

Between the waveform speech coders that produce toll-quality speech at rates above 8 kb/s and vocoders yielding synthetic quality below 2.4 kb/s lie the communications-quality speech coders. Hybrid speech coders combining LPC spectral modeling and transmission of some aspects of the residual error signal provide coders for the 2.4–8 kb/s range. The major difference between ADPCM and basic LPC is that the former transmits the entire residual error (subject to quantization) while the only excitation parameters the latter sends are voicing, pitch period, and gain. The prime motivation for LPC is to reduce bit rate, but if certain perceptually relevant aspects of the residual can be extracted and coded, then speech quality can be significantly increased without sending the full residual at ADPCM rates.

This approach is taken by several LPC vocoders, most recently CELP systems (see below). To appreciate how these coders developed, earlier hybrid coders are first described, including *residual-excited linear prediction* (RELP) vocoders and *voice-excited vocoders* (VEV). The basic assumption of these latter systems was that the lowest speech frequencies carry the highest perceptual importance. A small *baseband* range (up to typically 1 kHz) was replicated in these coders with an accuracy similar to waveform coders. The baseband provided a major contribution to naturalness and contained most of the energy in voiced sounds (which are the sounds most subject to quality degradations in LPC speech).

In RELP, basic LPC analysis yields the spectral coefficients, transmitted as side information and also used to inverse filter the speech signal to obtain $e(n)$ (Figure 7.27). A baseband $b(n)$ of the residual was extracted by a lowpass filter, decimated (e.g., by a factor of $N = 4-5$), and waveform coded. The F0 and gain parameters for basic LPC are replaced by $b(n)$. Not using a voicing or F0 estimator simplifies the RELP analyzer and avoids the serious consequences of F0 and voicing errors in LPC synthesis.

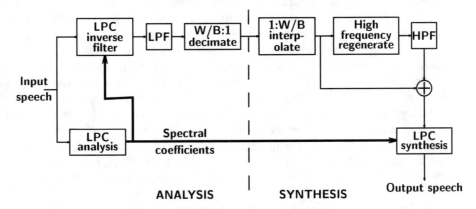

Figure 7.27 Block diagram of a residual-excited linear predictive (RELP) vocoder. LPF and HPF represent lowpass and highpass filters, respectively. *W* and *B* are the bandwidths of the original speech and the decimated residual, respectively. (After Viswanathan *et al.* [111] © IEEE.)

The RELP receiver interpolates $b(n)$ back to the original F_s rate and attempts to reconstruct the fullband residual $e(n)$ through nonlinear distortion. Only the high frequencies need be reconstructed since $b(n)$ is sent intact, so the results of the nonlinear operation are highpass filtered (with the same 800–1000 Hz cutoff as the analysis lowpass filter). The two residual bands are summed and used to excite the LPC synthesizer, which is determined by the spectral coefficients sent as side information.

The two approaches of VEV and RELP differ only in whether to transmit the baseband of speech itself or that of $e(n)$. In VEV, the LPC inverse filter is not used in the analysis stage, and the speech baseband is sent. In this case, the transmitted signal does not have a flat spectrum, and the nonlinear distortion in the receiver creates a signal whose spectrum is less flat than in the RELP case, thus requiring a spectrum flattener before applying the signal as input to the LPC synthesizer. Spectrum flattening can be approximated roughly by waveform clipping, or more precisely by a separate LPC analysis and inverse filtering on the regenerated residual. Since the speech baseband exists intact at the receiver, it can be directly added to a highpass version of the LPC synthesizer output to yield the final speech. Alternative versions of the VEV simply use the LPC synthesis output itself, dispensing with filtering at the receiver, since filtering itself can add distortion.

RELP (dropping the distinction with VEV) has the high quality of waveform coding only in the perceptually important baseband, and suffers in quality elsewhere, typically yielding communications-quality speech. Sending only the baseband requires artificial reconstruction of the higher frequencies, for which the excitation is typically poor, only retaining F0 accuracy, but losing phase information. A simple instantaneous nonlinearity (e.g., squaring or rectification) generates high frequencies from a low-frequency signal but does not yield a flat spectrum. Full-wave rectification, followed by a double-differencing operation, provides a simple method to obtain an essentially flat fullband excitation for the LPC synthesizer [112]. More complex methods include *spectral folding* and *spectral translation*, in which the baseband spectrum is repeatedly copied into the higher-frequency ranges [57].

The objective was to reconstruct the original residual as closely as possible, preserving especially harmonic structure, given only the baseband. A baseband from 0 to 800–1000 Hz is sufficient to retain at least a few harmonics for virtually all voices. RELP at 4.8 kb/s yields communications-quality speech, subjectively comparable to 3–4 bit log PCM [113]. At 13.8 kb/s, RELP is noisier (SNR $\approx$ 17 dB [114]) than APC, but it sounds more natural due to the lack of "hollowness" found in APC [115].

RELP speech quality was limited by speech information lost in the original baseband filtering, i.e., aspects of the residual not well represented in the baseband. One of the major problems of single-pulse basic LPC synthesis is the loss of phase information at low bit rates. Since phase is most important at low frequencies, RELP is adequate. However, merely extending baseband harmonics to the higher frequencies ignores two properties of the residual that are important to achieve naturalness: (1) its spectrum is not exactly flat, and (2) aperiodicity is greater at higher frequencies. Other LPC excitations to be described next do not arbitrarily divide the speech spectrum into a narrow, heavily coded baseband and a poorly represented upperband, and some have found widespread practical applications.

7.6.11.3 Multipulse-excited LPC. An alternative approach to reducing the bit rate for the LPC residual operates in the time domain, while minimizing spectral deviation of the output speech. An LPAS method, *multipulse* LPC (MLPC), represents the residual signal with a small number of pulses per frame of speech data (typically 1 pulse/ms). Decimation factors

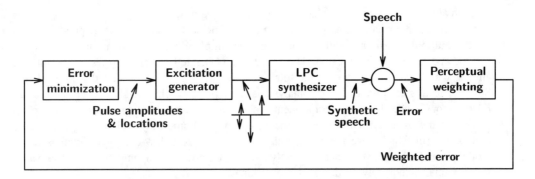

Figure 7.28 An analysis-by-synthesis procedure for determining locations and amplitudes of pulses in MLPC. (After Atal and Remde [116] © IEEE.)

of about 8:1 are common; e.g., a frame of 64 residual samples is reduced to 8 nonzero samples. Rather than use simple decimation, choosing every eighth sample (which would represent only the baseband), a multipulse residual is constructed in which the amplitudes and positions of each pulse are chosen to minimize a perceptually weighted spectral-error criterion [116]. The typical multipulse residual resembles a skeleton of the actual residual signal, in which the major excursions at the start of each pitch period are modeled by several large pulses, and minor excursions are modeled by smaller pulses.

Like RELP, MLPC needs no voicing or F0 detector. As illustrated in Figures 7.28 and 7.29, the procedure can be implemented iteratively. For each frame of speech, the multipulse residual from the prior frame continues to excite an LPC synthesizer to yield the output speech for the current frame, which is then subtracted from the actual speech to give an error signal $E(n)$ for that frame. $E(n)$ is *not* the LPC inverse-filtered residual, which is modeled by the multipulse signal. $E(n)$ is a form of output quantization noise that is minimized after a

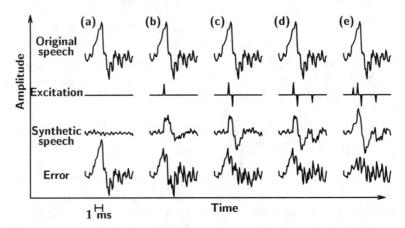

Figure 7.29 Five iterations in the determination of the excitation pulses. In (a), the output is due to the effects of pulses from the previous excitation frame. As each new pulse is added in (b)–(d), the error energy decreases, and the synthetic speech more closely resembles the input. (After Atal and Remde [116] © IEEE.)

perceptual weighting that de-emphasizes the formant regions, since noise at these frequencies is masked by the formant harmonics (similar to APC noise shaping). A sample pulse is added to the multipulse residual, with its position and amplitude chosen to minimize the error energy, and the cycle is repeated. The procedure is iterated as many times as the bit rate allows, with each cycle reducing the total error for the frame and raising the output SNR. Superior results are obtained if the analysis is done pitch-synchronously (which requires an F0 detector), since the major components of the residual occur at the start of each pitch period. In the pitch-*asynchronous* approach, any given frame may include no pitch period boundaries (in which case the SNR will be high because a low-energy residual is being modeled) or perhaps two (where the SNR would be low, since a limited, fixed number of pulses cannot adequately model the large residual).

In terms of the LPC inverse filter $A(z) = 1 - P(z)$, where $P(z) = \sum_{k=1}^{p} a_k z^{-k}$, the weighting filter is

$$W(z) = \frac{1 - P(z)}{1 - P(\gamma^{-1}z)}, \qquad (7.35)$$

where γ is a constant between 0 and 1 that controls noise shaping. A value of 1 gives no shaping (i.e., the mean-square-error energy is minimized), while a value of 0 causes $W(z)$ to equal the LPC inverse filter, which heavily de-emphasizes the formant regions. A precise value (0.8 is typical) is not crucial for output quality.

$H(z) = 1/[1 - P(\gamma^{-1}z)]$ is a bandwidth-expanded synthesis filter, with $h(n)$ as its unit-sample response. The time m and amplitude A_m of the first pulse are then found by minimizing

$$E = \sum_n [d(n) - A_m h(n - m)]^2, \qquad (7.36)$$

where the sum is taken over the frame (in pitch-asynchronous operation, typically 4–5 ms, which is shorter than the LPC analysis frame, to simplify computation), and $d(n)$ is the output of $H(z)$ to the original residual. Setting $\partial E/\partial A_m = 0$ yields the optimal amplitude $A_m = \alpha(m)/\phi(m, m)$, where $\alpha(m)$ is the cross-correlation between $d(n)$ and $h(n)$, and $\phi(i, j)$ is the covariance matrix for $h(n)$. Substituting this amplitude in Equation (7.36):

$$E = \sum_n d^2(n) - \frac{\alpha^2(m)}{\phi(m, m)}. \qquad (7.37)$$

Thus the optimal position $\hat{m}$ can be found by maximizing $\alpha^2(m)/\phi(m, m)$. This process is repeated for L cycles (e.g., $L = 8$). For each iteration, $d(n)$ in Equations (7.36) and (7.37) is updated by subtracting off $A_{\hat{m}} h(n - \hat{m})$ due to the prior cycle; to update $\phi(m)$, it suffices to subtract $A_{\hat{m}} \phi(m, \hat{m})$.

Once all L pulses have been assigned positions m_i within the frame, their amplitudes may be recomputed by minimizing

$$E = \sum_n \left[d(n) - \sum_{i=1}^{L} A_{m_i} h(n - m_i) \right]^2, \qquad (7.38)$$

which leads to a calculation very similar to Lth-order LPC analysis. Ideally, both the positions and the corresponding amplitudes would be determined simultaneously, but the approach above (suboptimal in iteratively choosing the positions) yields good results [58, 80, 117] (Table 7.1). Each pulse needs about 7–8 bits for coding [48]. A 13.2 kb/s MLPC coder is the GSM (Global System Mobile, or Groupe Spéciale Mobile) standard for digital cellular radio

TABLE 7.1   Quality of MLPC speech, in terms of equivalent number of bits in log PCM and the multipulse bit rate.

Bit rate (kb/s)	4.8	9.6	16
Number of pulses per 4 ms	2	4	8
Equivalent number of bits in log PCM	4	5	7

in Europe, where the excitation pulses are selected to be at small, regular intervals (e.g., 0.5 ms) (RPE = regular-pulse excitation) for coding efficiency [117] (2 bits for the local position of the first pulse; 3–4 bits for each amplitude).

While not a good performance measure for narrowband vocoders, SNR is valid for RELP and MLPC because sufficient timing information is preserved in the transmitted residual or multipulse pattern to yield an output signal synchronized to the original speech. SNR for MLPC of a fixed bit rate is usually proportional to pitch period duration because more pulses are available to model longer pitch periods. SNR differences of 6–10 dB occur between male and female voices [118]. To reduce the SNR dependence on F0, a pitch predictor (as in APC) is often used on the multipulse residual before applying it to the synthesizer in the analysis stage. The chosen multipulse residual from earlier coding frames is thus retained in the predictor memory and added (subject to an attenuation factor, which depends on the degree of periodicity) to the multipulse residual of the current frame without requiring the coding of additional pulses. Since the multipulse residual for voiced speech generally has a strong periodic component, only that part of the residual not well modeled by previous multipulse patterns needs to be represented by new pulses in the next coding frame. This is a form of long-term prediction as used in APC. With this method, SNR improvements of 5 dB occur at rates of 1000 pulses/s (yielding an SNR of 17 dB at 10 kb/s) [118].

A mix of voiced and unvoiced excitation automatically occurs in the multipulse determination (unlike with RELP). Single-pulse LPC reproduces the main periodic component of voiced speech but ignores aperiodic components, which are important to good synthetic speech. Since MLPC locates each new pulse where it best contributes to an overall perceptually weighted spectral match, it places the first few pulses to model the periodic component but then is free to handle aperiodic components at whatever frequencies they may occur. Raising the bit rate in single-pulse LPC typically only reduces quantization noise in the LP coefficients or increases the number of poles in the model, resulting in a better model of the vocal tract magnitude spectrum but no improvement in the phase representation. More bits in RELP lead to less quantization noise in the baseband or a wider coded baseband, but the problems of high-frequency regeneration remain. MLPC, on the other hand, approaches ideal output speech more rapidly as bit rate increases, since extra bits are assigned to represent more pulses in the multipulse pattern, which more rapidly approaches the fullband residual.

7.6.12 Waveform Interpolation

We include here another coder which uses a different type of excitation for LP. *Prototype waveform interpolation* (PWI) [119, 120] in the frequency domain and forward–backward waveform prediction in the time domain claim to yield superior speech at rates of 3 kb/s (the latter is efficient as well: 1.3 MIPS vs 10 MIPS for PWI) [121]. In PWI, phase information from prototype speech waveforms (e.g., pitch periods) is implicitly contained in the coded magnitudes of the speech spectrum. Since time-domain interpolation is heuristic and frequency-domain interpolation often has high complexity, a recent compromise (called mixed-domain residual coding) interpolates the LPC residual spectrally, yielding better speech at 3.15 kb/s than other standard coders at rates above 4 kb/s [122]. When combined with a sub-band approach (see below), PWI can be made similar to waveform coding, thus allowing even lower rates with high speech quality [123].

PWI represents speech as an evolving waveform $g(t, \phi)$ in two dimensions, for time t and evolution ϕ. Usually working with an LP residual (instead of speech itself), the signal is decomposed via bandpass filtering into a rapidly evolving waveform (REW), corresponding roughly to unvoiced speech and sampled at a high rate (but with low resolution), and a slowly evolving waveform (SEW), for the voiced portions and sampled at a low rate (but with high resolution). PWI has been slow to be accepted for commercial purposes due to its complexity, but a recent version operates at 2.5 MFLOPS for the decoder (and 7.5 MFLOPS for the coder, which is less crucial commercially, since more customers would buy decoders than coders, at least in broadcast applications) [124].

7.7 SPECTRAL (FREQUENCY-DOMAIN) CODERS

This section deals with waveform coders that make explicit use of the input speech spectrum during coding, either by filtering the speech into separate frequency bands (called *channels* or *sub-bands*) for individual coding or by directly coding a spectral representation of the speech signal. The first two subsections discuss coders of the first type. Within each sub-band, the filtered speech may be waveform-encoded, or relevant measures concerning amplitude and phase may be extracted and coded. The individual coders differ in terms of the number of sub-bands and the detail with which each sub-band is coded. Later subsections discuss coders that dedicate virtually the entire transmitted bit stream directly to spectral information, with only side information to describe other parameters. Since phase information is retained in all such cases, allowing a synchronous comparison between input and output speech signals, SNR remains a viable performance measure. Unlike LPC and other source vocoders (Section 7.8), these spectral coders are waveform coders, despite their use of the spectrum. Of the systems discussed below, sub-band and transform coders exploit both audition and spectral envelope properties; harmonic coders exploit periodicity.

7.7.1 Filter Bank Analysis

The short-time Fourier transform $X_n(e^{j\omega})$ of Chapter 6 suggests the following spectral coder. Speech is input to a bank of bandpass filters covering the range from 0 to $F_s/2$ Hz, and the output signals are waveform encoded. Proper filter design can yield a lossless coder, and the speech waveform is reconstructed by summing the outputs of all channels. Assuming the simplest design, $X_n(e^{j\omega_k})$ are signals in time n for each of N channels centered at frequencies $\omega_k = \pi(k + 1/2)/N$, where $k = 0, 1, 2, \ldots, N - 1$. The time window used in the STFT specifies the shape of the equally spaced bandpass filters (identical except for the shift of their center frequencies). Since the Fourier transform is invertible, the windowed $x(n)$ can be recovered from $X_n(e^{j\omega_k})$ (except for the effects of quantization noise).

$X_n(e^{j\omega_k})$ are lowpass signals that may be decimated to rates as low as F_s/N samples/s, depending on how closely the window filter approximates an ideal lowpass filter. The bandpass signals could be frequency shifted by $\pi k/N$ rad down to low frequency before decimation (Figure 7.30). At the decoder, such signals would be shifted back to their original frequencies before adding all the channel contributions. If the aliasing effects due to nonideal

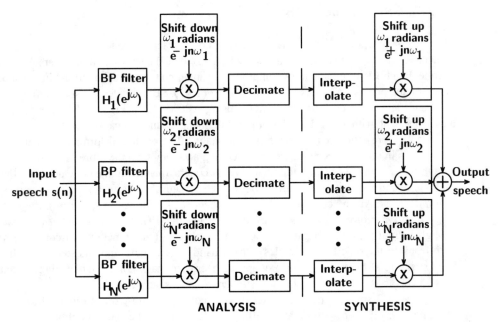

Figure 7.30 Analysis and synthesis operations for a filter bank coder.

filtering are ignored, such frequency shifting is unnecessary when channels of uniform width are centered at multiples of F_s/N: *integer-band sampling* takes advantage of the bandpass version of the Nyquist theorem [13].

Ignoring the frequency shiftings (which have no net effects other than those due to quantizing lowpass rather than bandpass signals), the bandpass coder approach simply passes speech $x(n)$ through a bank of filters $h_k(n)$ to yield outputs $y_k(n)$, which are transmitted and then summed at the decoder to obtain $y(n)$ (which should equal $x(n)$ in the absence of quantization). If the filters have the form $h_k(n) = w(n)e^{j\pi kn/N}$, any time window $w(n)$ of length N samples may be chosen (or any length window, as long as $w(lN) = 0$ for all nonzero integer l). This is made evident by considering the Fourier transform of the overall system

$$H(e^{j\omega}) = \sum_{k=1}^{N} H_k(e^{j\omega}). \tag{7.39}$$

Since $H_k(e^{j\omega})$ are simply versions of $W(e^{j\omega})$ shifted by $\pi k/N$ radians, $H(e^{j\omega})$ can be viewed as the circular convolution of $W(e^{j\omega})$ with an impulse train of period $2\pi/N$. The corresponding impulse response $h(n)$ is thus the product of $w(n)$ with an impulse train in time of period N. Since Equation (7.39) should also equal unity, any $w(n)$ with values of zero at multiples of N suffices.

A finite duration $w(n)$ can be used to reduce implementation complexity. However, longer impulse responses allow narrower bandpass filters, which are useful for decimation. If delay is permitted, linear phase is easily implemented by choosing $w(n)$ symmetric about a time $n = lN$ and ensuring that $w(n) = 0$ at all other multiples of N. The above analysis holds in this case except that the overall system response $h(n)$ is an impulse delayed by lN samples.

7.7.2 Sub-Band Coders (SBC)

The simple filter bank system above is not a practical coder because bit rate is not reduced. Each decimated channel allows at best a $N:1$ rate decrease, but there are N channels to code. Practical systems require nonuniform channel coding, which is found in the subclass of filter bank coders known as *sub-band coding* (SBC). SBC divides the spectrum into about 4–8 bands and codes each bandpass signal using APCM [125] (Figure 7.31). Low-frequency bands are sent with more bits than higher-frequency bands because the former are more important to preserve accurately for speech quality. The pitch and formant structure at low frequencies in voiced speech require more coding accuracy than the more random waveforms at high frequencies. By using individual APCM coders, quantization can be optimized within each band, and the noise in each channel can be isolated from affecting other channels. For example, in the APCM of Section 7.5 (one "channel" for the entire spectrum), the step size adapted to waveform variations of all frequencies. In SBC, the bands are usually narrow enough to limit the dynamic range of spectral amplitudes (as a function of frequency) within each band, so the specific amplitudes of each band directly determine its step size. The sub-band structure also takes advantage of speech energy to mask noise, by matching speech and noise levels in each band in a fashion similar to noise shaping in APC.

In voiced speech, the sub-bands usually contain at most one formant; however, the formants can differ in amplitude by 30–40 dB (F1 having the most amplitude, and higher formants decreasing in intensity). In one-band APCM with syllabic adaptation, step size follows the overall amplitude, which is usually dominated by F1. SBC might use the same step size for the first 1–2 bands but have smaller step sizes for the (lower-energy) upper bands in voiced speech. Quantization noise is reduced in these upper bands because the step size is more directly matched to the individual band energy. Indeed, the output noise is effectively shaped (as in APC systems) to follow the speech spectrum (to the extent that a staircase-like spectrum of 4–8 bands can approximate the formant structure). Furthermore, in reconstructing the speech, the interpolation process uses bandpass filters that eliminate noise from other bands (as DM eliminates noise effects at high frequencies).

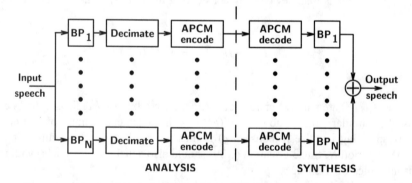

Figure 7.31 Sub-band coder with N bands. The decimators have output sampling rates of $2f_i$, where f_i is the high-frequency cutoff for bandpass filter BP_i. In many systems, the decimation rate can be as low as twice the bandwidth of BP_i. The decoder in each channel includes the interpolator corresponding to the channel's decimator. (After Flanagan *et al.* [9] © IEEE.)

Bandpass filter design is crucial to good performance in SBC. A major potential difficulty with bandpass filtering and subsequent decimation is that of aliasing. Practical filters must have finite-amplitude roll-off with frequencies outside their desired bandwidths, and steeper frequency skirts usually yield more complex filters (i.e., more delay elements, and hence longer coder delay). If the decimation process reduces a band's sampling rate below its corresponding Nyquist rate (twice the entire bandwidth, including the frequency skirts), aliasing corrupts frequencies at the edges of the desired bandwidth. Usually, the rate is chosen high enough to reduce aliasing to acceptable levels, but this requires more samples/s overall than for the original speech signal. (Bit rate reductions come not from fewer samples/s but from fewer b/sample in high-frequency channels.)

***7.7.2.1 Quadrature mirror filters* (‡).** If *quadrature mirror filters* are used to bandpass the speech signal in SBC, aliasing *constructively* minimizes the output speech distortion, with only a few constraints on filter design. Consider the two-band coder in Figure 7.32, with the lower and upper bands having symmetrical frequency responses. In the lower channel, 2:1 decimation imposes a spectral copy at $\omega = \pi$, which aliases the energy near $\omega = \pi/2$. Most of this additional high-frequency copy is filtered out with the decoder lowpass filter, but aliased frequencies remain. A similar situation arises for the other channel. If the filters are mirror images (i.e., identical except for a shift of π rad), the aliasing can be shown to cancel when the two bands are summed for the output [126]. Since the cancellation is not total in the presence of quantization noise, narrow transition bands are still desirable when using

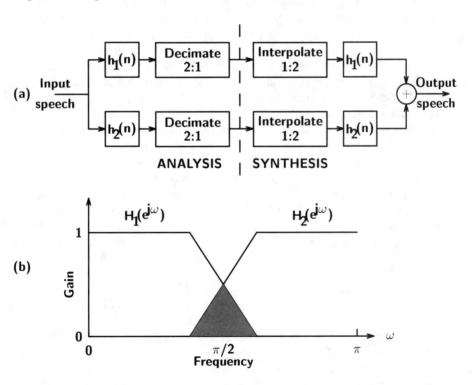

Figure 7.32 Quadrature mirror filtering to split the input spectrum into two equal-width sub-bands (a) implementation and (b) illustration of filter responses to cancel interband aliasing.

mirror filters. On the other hand, short-time filters are also desirable for minimizing delay and echo (e.g., a typical compromise is a 513 tap filter of 689 Hz bandwidth for CD-ROMs [64]).

Although interband aliasing can be eliminated in principle by symmetric design (which simply requires that $h_1(n) = (-1)^n h_2(n)$ in Figure 7.32), amplitude and phase distortion due to the bandpass filters remain problems for SBC [127]. Since in each band the signal is filtered twice (at coder and decoder), before the final summation, the amplitude objective is

$$|H_1(e^{j\omega})|^2 + |H_2(e^{j\omega})|^2 = 1. \qquad (7.40)$$

A 32-tap filter can match this to within ± 0.025 dB, a 16 tap filter to within ± 0.07 dB [126]. Phase control is usually accomplished by using FIR filters with symmetric time responses, which guarantee linear phase. *Polyphase* filters exploit such coefficient symmetry to reduce computation [127], sometimes at the cost of extra latency [128].

For mirror filters, the process of dividing the spectrum in two can be repeated as needed to obtain a larger number of narrower bands; e.g., in octave-band filters, the lower-frequency band continues to be subdivided until the desired number of channels is achieved. Thus, a five-band SBC could use the bands 100–200 Hz, 200–400 Hz, 400–800 Hz, 800–1600 Hz, and 1600–3200 Hz. The first and smallest band would pass through five bandpass filters, each half as wide as the previous one, while the highest band would be filtered only once at the coder. This asymmetry requires delay compensation to synchronize the bands at the decoder.

7.7.2.2 SBC performance.

At 16 kb/s, four- or five-band SBC with octave-band allocations yields speech quality comparable to 24 kb/s DPCM-AQB and typically uses 2 and 4 b/sample, respectively, for the high- and low-frequency channels [14]. At 9.6 kb/s, four-band SBC, with bit allocations of 1.5–3 b/sample, usually resorts to spectral gaps that are not coded, producing reverberation in the output speech. (The alternative of fewer bits per sample yields excessive quantization noise.) If certain bands are not transmitted due to low energy, some aliasing is not canceled with the mirror filters, and a "whisper" quality results from the energy aliased into the spectral gaps. Nonetheless, such SBC yields communications quality (toll-quality SBC requires about 24 kb/s) and is subjectively equivalent to 19.2 kb/s ADM. The gain is due to the variable bit assignment and containment of quantization noise within each band [125]. SBC at a low 4.8 kb/s still yields acceptable speech if the third and fourth bands dynamically follow F2–F3 [129]. This latter case is considerably more complex since accurate formant tracking is required and the speech signal must be dynamically frequency-shifted so that the formants align with fixed-frequency bandpass filters. The benefits lie in the narrower bands permitted for the high frequencies since energy outside the formants can be deleted without seriously degrading quality.

SBC generally uses APCM within each channel to take advantage of the changing amplitude levels as formants move between bands. ADPCM is sometimes used if the number of bands is small (e.g., for wideband audio, as in the G.722 64 kb/s coder [130], where 6 bits code samples in the low-frequency band and 2 bits serve the other band). With many sub-bands (e.g., 32 in Digital Compact Cassette coding), there is a limited degree of spectral redundancy within the narrow bands, for which ADPCM is less useful [131]. Another possibility to improve SBC is to use pitch prediction within each channel in a combined SBC-APC system [59, 132].

Basic audio systems often use 16 b/sample (e.g., compact disk CD-ROMs with 90 dB range require 706 kb/s for wideband speech and 1.4 Mb/s for stereo). Multi-channel audio signals, such as two-channel stereo or 5.1-channel "surround-sound" (3 front speakers, two rear ones and a 0–200 Hz bass boost), do not need full coding for each channel, due to cross-channel correlations. Recent SBC methods preserve high-quality audio at 2–4 b/sample (e.g., MPEG Layer I–III [133, 134]); e.g., Layer III uses 22 sub-bands at 16–32 kb/s [130]. While MPEG-2 BC (backward compatible with MPEG-1 systems) gives good audio quality at 640–896 kb/s for five full channels, newer MPEG-2 AAC (advanced audio coding) provides better quality at half that rate [135, 136].

7.7.2.3 Integer-band sampling ($\ddagger$). To minimize the total bit rate (i.e., the sum of the rates after decimation in each channel), each band could be downshifted in frequency, to lower the highest frequency in the band (which normally specifies the band's sampling rate). Most sub-band coders, however, exploit integer-band sampling to avoid frequency-shifting at the coder and decoder [126]. If the high-frequency cutoff of a bandpass filter is equal to a multiple of its bandwidth, the Nyquist rate is equal to twice the filter's bandwidth rather than twice its highest frequency. This is illustrated in Figure 7.33(b) for a filter of spectral width $\pi/4$ and high cutoff $\pi/2$. After the coder bandpass filter isolates channel 2, the 4:1 decimator retains only every fourth sample, which is equivalent to multiplying the signal by a unit-sample train of period 4 and then compressing the time axis by the same factor. In the frequency domain, four copies of the spectrum are aliased, spaced every $2\pi/4$ rad, and then the frequency axis is expanded by a factor of four. If the filters are appropriately spaced (equal-width bands as shown are just one possibility), no bands overlap in the aliasing process and thus no speech information is corrupted. The decoder can simply interpolate (1:4) the received signal back to the original rate by inserting three zero-valued samples after every sample and then using a bandpass filter identical to the original to yield a smooth output signal. The interpolation corresponds to an expansion of the time axis and therefore a compression of the frequency axis. Thus the range from π to 2π at the bottom of Figure 7.33 winds up in the original location of the second sub-band, and the final filter eliminates undesired frequency components.

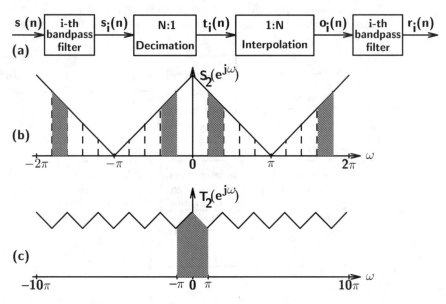

Figure 7.33 Integer-band sampling for equal-width bands: (a) channel i in a four-band coder, and (b) original spectrum and resampled spectrum after decimation, for the second channel and 4:1 decimation. (After Jayant and Noll [14].)

Two major drawbacks to SBC, the complexity and delays (up to 30 ms) inherent in the filtering operations, may be alleviated through a block transformation procedure. Instead of functioning totally in the time domain, as in normal SBC, a block of N speech samples can be frequency-transformed (e.g., using the DFT) and divided into b sub-bands, whose N/b spectral samples could then be inverse-transformed back into one of b slowly varying time signals, subject to the usual APCM coding of SBC. Fast transform algorithms make this an attractive alternative to complicated filtering, especially since the calculation does not increase with the number of bands.

7.7.3 Adaptive Transform Coders (ATC)

In the coders previously discussed (e.g., LPC), the main stream of data involved quantized speech samples in a continuous flow. The speech may be passed through bandpass filters and/or predictors (which change characteristics periodically in adaptive systems), but waveform samples at the original speech sampling rate compose the entire bit stream, except for side information in forward-adaptive coders. In the latter systems, the input speech samples are buffered into analysis frames to allow determination of the adaptation parameters, after which the buffered samples are fed to the updated coder. The samples utilize a predictor or step size that matches their characteristics. The buffer duration (i.e., number of samples divided by F_s) equals the delay inherent in such coders.

In *adaptive transform coding*, speech is not only buffered into frames of N samples but also transformed into a spectral representation. Instead of sending waveform samples, the N transform coefficients are transmitted as a block and inverse-transformed back into the time domain at the decoder (Figure 7.34). The number of parameters sent matches the original sampling rate, so any bit rate improvements must use fewer bits per sample. Bits are dynamically allocated in each frame to every spectral coefficient, usually in rough proportion to its spectral amplitude. This allows the perceptually crucial strong frequencies in low-frequency formants to be well represented with typically 3–5 b/spectral coefficient, while the

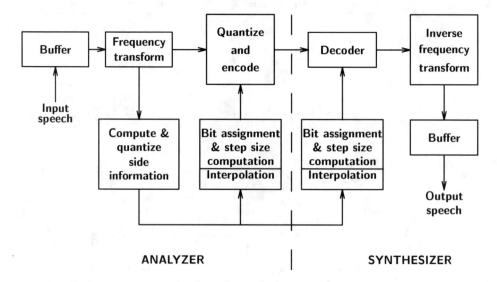

Figure 7.34 Adaptive transform coding. (After Tribolet and Crochiere [137] © IEEE.)

less important high frequencies (and frequencies between formants) are coded with fewer bits. Depending on the overall bit rate, some frequencies with low energy may be assigned zero bits, i.e., their values not transmitted, which leaves spectral gaps in the output speech.

For efficient speech coding in the frequency domain, several possible transforms exist. The Karhunen–Loève transform (KLT) is optimal in producing (independent) orthogonal coefficients, but its operation is complex and requires basis functions that depend on the input data. The familiar DFT is a reasonable alternative, simpler to calculate and with fixed sinusoidal basis functions, but it only approaches KLT's optimality in predictor gain for large transform sizes N [14]. The most popular choice in ATC is the discrete cosine transform (DCT), a relative of the DFT but closer to the KLT in optimality. The DCT of an N-point sequence is

$$X_c(k) = \sum_{n=0}^{N-1} x(n)g(k) \cos\left[\frac{(2n+1)k\pi}{2N}\right] \quad \text{for } k = 0, 1, 2, 3, \ldots, N-1, \quad (7.41)$$

where $g(0) = 1$ and $g(k) = \sqrt{2}$ for $k = 1, 2, 3, \ldots, N-1$. The inverse DCT is

$$x(n) = \frac{1}{N} \sum_{n=0}^{N-1} X_c(k)g(k) \cos\left[\frac{(2n+1)k\pi}{2N}\right] \quad \text{for } k = 0, 1, 2, 3, \ldots, N-1. \quad (7.42)$$

For real-valued speech input, the DCT is also real-valued, and its values as a function of k indicate the speech amplitude at frequencies ω_k equally spaced from 0 to π rad. A modified DCT (MDCT) (also called the time-domain aliasing cancellation filterbank), with 50% overlapping frames (to combat edge effects—see below), is popular in audio coding today [138]. Long blocks can cause "pre-echos", where a loud sound occurring late in a given block propagates its effects back in time in the decoded block [136]; hence block length may vary adaptively with signal power.

7.7.3.1 *Edge effects.*

A problem that arises in *block coders* such as ATC is that of edge discontinuities when blocks of reconstructed speech samples are concatenated in the decoder. Large jumps in the speech waveform at block boundaries every N samples are often heard as "clicks" or "burbles" at the block frequency F_s/N. (Forward-adaptive APCM or DPCM coders can suffer such edge effects when the quantizer or predictor changes characteristics suddenly at frame boundaries, but the problems in these sample-by-sample coders are usually less problematic than with block coders since the residual signal compensates for such jumps.)

The edge problem can be serious if a DFT is used with coarse quantization, as with typical average ATC rates of 1–3 b/sample. Part of the quantization noise can be modeled as multiplicative (in addition to the usual additive noise); after the inverse DFT, this distortion appears as a circular convolution of the noise with the desired speech ($v(n)$ in Figure 7.35a), which causes an exchange of energy between the left and right block edges, or time aliasing (Figure 7.35b). In most cases, the edges do not have similar amplitudes, and such aliasing leads to amplitude bursts that sound like clicks. With the exception of a phase term, the DCT follows the DFT of a $2M$-point sequence $y(n)$ that extends $v(n)$ by using its mirror image to fill out the second M points (Figure 7.35c). When time aliasing occurs here, the edges are symmetric, leading to diminished clicks. In addition, trapezoidal time windows are commonly employed prior to DCT analysis, such that successive frames of data overlap (by less than 10%) and corresponding windows in the reconstruction provide smooth transitions at block edges.

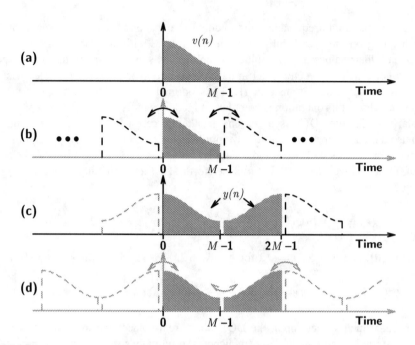

Figure 7.35 Illustration of edge effects: (a) one block of M speech samples $v(n)$, (b) time
aliasing with DFT analysis/synthesis involves abrupt block edges, (c)
equivalent $2M$ samples $y(n)$ in DCT analysis, (d) aliasing with DCT
analysis/synthesis. (After Tribolet and Crochiere [137] © IEEE.)

If output noise with a flat spectrum is desired, the number of quantizer levels for each
spectral coefficient $X_c(k)$ can be set proportional to its variance σ_k^2 (equivalently, the number
of bits is proportional to σ_k in decibels). If the number of bits is limited to integer values, the
bit assignment is determined by thresholds (Figure 7.36), with the levels 6 dB apart (Equation
(7.4)), and the overall level offset is adjusted to match the average number of available bits per
frame. Noise shaping may be used to reduce the perceptibility of noise effects by changing the
shape of the thresholds from horizontal (white noise) to instead follow the speech spectral
shape, as in APC systems.

7.7.3.2 Side information.   Ideally, the number of bits per coefficient would match the
spectrum in each frame of speech, and every coefficient would have its own quantizer with a
step size dependent on the number of bits assigned. To inform the decoder of such a detailed
bit assignment, much side information relating to the spectrum would be sent for each frame,
along with the main data stream of spectral coefficients. Instead, the DCT spectrum is often
divided into 16–24 equal-width bands, and an average spectral value is calculated for each
band (Figure 7.37). These values provide side information, which is expanded into a full
spectrum via geometric interpolation (linear in log amplitudes) of the calculated values. This
averaged *basis spectrum* furnishes both the coder and decoder with information for bit and
step size assignment. With 20 bands covering 4 kHz, one spectral value every 200 Hz yields a
spectrum accurate enough to follow the formant structure, while limiting side information to
about 2 kb/s (40 frames/s, 2.5 b/band).

This approach works well at or above 16 kb/s (about 2 b/spectral coefficient), but at
lower rates the quantization is too coarse to accurately preserve the harmonic structure of

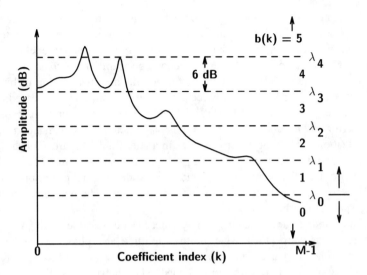

Figure 7.36 Interpretation of bit assignment. Upper curve shows speech spectrum, and lower curve shows error spectrum; dashed lines indicate thresholds λ_k, which determine the number of bits $b(k)$ for coefficient $X_c(k)$. (After Tribolet and Crochiere [137] © IEEE.)

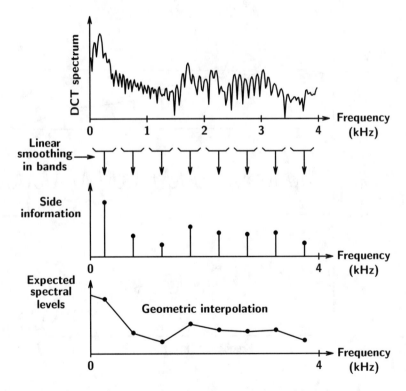

Figure 7.37 Representation of side information as equally spaced samples of the spectral estimate. (After Tribolet and Crochiere [137] © IEEE.)

voiced speech. Thus ATC may also use pitch estimation to exploit not only spectral envelope but also periodicity. If a reliable pitch estimate is sent as side information, the basis spectrum for voiced speech can be the product of a slowly varying formant model (e.g., the interpolated 20 band spectrum above or a linear prediction spectrum) and a *comb* spectrum with spacing equal to F0 (Figure 7.38). This permits the additional concentration of bits for the spectral coefficients at or near harmonics, especially in the formants. The increase in side information is minimal (e.g., 6 bits for F0 → 240 b/s), but this system requires an accurate F0 estimator. A pitch error might lead to a substantial misassignment of bits, with a corresponding increase in quantization noise until the error ceases in a later frame. Figure 7.39 shows a typical DCT spectrum, the bit assignment reflecting pitch and formant structure (2 more bits at the center of harmonics than between them; 2–3 more bits at the formant center than between formants) and the reconstructed spectrum with gaps of no energy where no bits were assigned to low-energy spectral coefficients.

Toll- and communications-quality speech are feasible with ATC at 16 kb/s and 9.6 kb/s, respectively [137]. Since both amplitude and phase information are preserved, ATC is considered a waveform coder and is evaluated using SNR. SEGSNR at these bit rates is usually about 13–18 dB. In noise-shaped ATC, however, SNR decreases while speech quality is enhanced; so the true test for such coders is subjective. Improved speech can be obtained by combining ATC with SBC, i.e., applying ATC techniques within separate frequency sub-bands, to restrict much of the quantization noise to specific spectral ranges. Such hybrid coders can produce speech at 7.2 kb/s subjectively comparable with 19 kb/s CVSD [139].

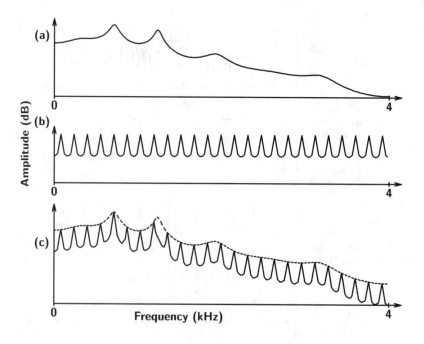

Figure 7.38 Components of the speech spectrum model: (a) formant structure, (b) pitch structure, (c) combined model. (After Tribolet and Crochiere [137] © IEEE.)

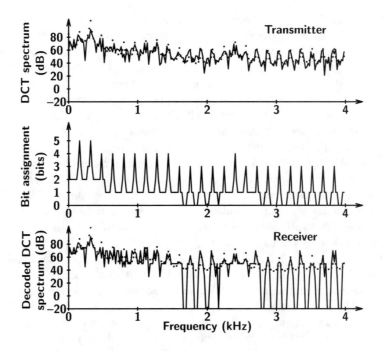

Figure 7.39 Illustration of *speech-specific* or *vocoder-driven* ATC: (a) a 256 point DCT spectrum (solid curve) and spectral estimate (dashed curve), (b) the bit assignment, (c) the synthesized spectrum. (After Tribolet and Crochiere [137] © IEEE.)

Various versions of transform coding have become popular for wideband speech applications [130]. A standard is expected soon for 16 kHz sampled speech at 16–32 kb/s: one candidate runs full-duplex on a 16 bit fixed-point DSP chip in under 15 MIPS (about half the complexity of narrowband coders G.728-729) [140]. Transform coding can help in audio applications where both music and speech are present, since other low-rate coders are often designed just for speech. Good-quality general audio is possible at 1 bit/sample (e.g., 8 kb/s for narrowband speech and 16 kb/s for wideband). One recent method uses multi-stage VQ on MDCT coefficients and on an LPC+pitch representation of the audio spectral envelope [141]; another exploits correlations between the 20 ms frames often used in wideband coders [142].

7.7.4 Harmonic Coding

Since speech quality, especially at low bit rates, depends primarily on accurate representation of the voiced portions of the signal, special attention can be directed toward efficient coding of the strong harmonically spaced peaks in the voiced spectrum. The following sections examine techniques that code the spectrum directly in terms of harmonics. These systems are dependent on accurate F0 estimation, and their performance degrades significantly in the presence of F0 errors. The periodic redundancy of voiced speech was exploited in APC systems via the time domain, using a long-term predictor adaptively tuned to the pitch period. To reduce bit rate, several other coding approaches use the equally spaced fine structure of voiced speech in the spectrum instead.

7.7.4.1 Time-domain harmonic scaling (TDHS). A waveform-coding method called *time-domain harmonic scaling* effectively averages successive pitch periods, allowing the summed signal to be expanded in time (with corresponding reduced bandwidth) to occupy the original signal duration (Figure 7.40) [144]. With 2–3 overlapped periods, decimating the decreased-bandwidth signals by a factor of two or three reduces bit rates in proportion. At the receiver, weighted repetitions of the aliased pitch periods interpolate the speech back to near-original form. The algorithm works well when successive pitch intervals are nearly periodic, but distortion increases during transitional segments.

Although TDHS manipulates time signals, examination of the corresponding spectral effects yields insight. A short-time Fourier transform of 2–3 periods of voiced speech shows a strong harmonic structure. The bandwidths of the harmonics are usually (especially at low frequency) narrow compared to the spacing between harmonics. If the transform is taken pitch-synchronously with a window of exactly two or three periods, deep spectral valleys (exceeding 30–40 dB) are often found between harmonics. If the spectrum around each of these harmonics is shifted down in frequency by a factor of 2–3, without disturbing the detail of the harmonic, very little information is lost since aliasing occurs only in the spectral valleys (Figure 7.41). (Aliasing is substantial but irrelevant for unvoiced speech because fine spectral detail there is much less important than in voiced speech. As in many other coders, the crucial bandwidth–quality tradeoff in TDHS occurs in voiced speech, and unvoiced speech can always be coded at much lower bit rates, if a reliable voicing decision is available. TDHS does not require an accurate voicing detector since an arbitrary time interval suffices as the "period" in unvoiced speech.) The TDHS coder outputs a signal whose bandwidth is compressed by 2–3, allowing decimation and lower bit rates. To reconstruct the speech, the receiver shifts the harmonics back. TDHS requires a pitch estimator to locate precisely the pitch epochs. Any errors would significantly increase speech distortion since the locations of the presumed harmonic valleys would be incorrect and significant aliasing would occur. To avoid this explicit need for pitch detection, a technique related to TDHS, called frequency-domain harmonic scaling (FDHS), can be used with results similar to those of TDHS [145].

ATC could actually shift the harmonics and transmit a compressed spectrum. However, since straightforward correlates for frequency-shifting can be found in the time domain, TDHS usually scales harmonics through time compression/expansion. Simply compressing the time axis over a block of 2–3 pitch periods is inadequate since that affects spectral detail

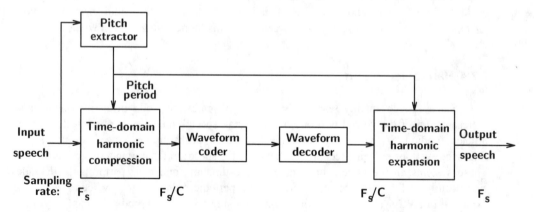

Figure 7.40 Block diagram of a combined TDHS waveform coder. C is the harmonic compression factor. (After Malah *et al.* [143] © IEEE.)

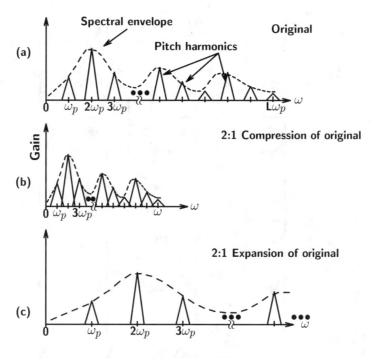

Figure 7.41 Schematic spectral representation of (a) input voiced speech, (b) a frequency-
compressed signal employing pitch harmonic shifting, (c) frequency-
expanded signal. T_p is the pitch period duration and $\Delta\omega_p$ is the width of a
harmonic. (After Malah *et al.* [143] © IEEE.)

in the harmonics. Instead, successive groups of 2–3 periods are multiplied by triangular
windows and then aliased within the group to obtain one "average" period (Figure 7.42). The
purpose of the windows is to make the resultant aliased period evolve throughout its duration
from the characteristics of the first period to the those of the last period. Furthermore,
concatenation of these average periods has no discontinuities at the boundaries. At the
receiver, a similar triangular window interpolates each decoded pitch period back to 2–3
slowly evolving periods (Figure 7.43). In addition to the aliasing distortion (present primarily
during spectral or F0 changes), the triangular window contributes waveform distortion at the
synthesizer. More complex windows can be useful for scaling factors in excess of two.

When combined with other forms of coding, TDHS can give significant reductions in
bit rate with little loss in speech quality. The best results combine TDHS with coders that
exploit different speech redundancies and that have different types of distortion; e.g., TDHS
exploits periodicity and suffers from reverberation in the output speech, while SBC exploits
formant structure and auditory masking across frequencies, with quantization noise being the
major degradation. SBC-HS (sub-band coding with harmonic scaling) at 9.6 kb/s is
comparable to 16 kb/s basic SBC [143]. A saving of 4 kb/s occurs at similar rates for
ATC-HS compared with ATC. ADPCM-HS yields good quality at 4.8–16 kb/s [146]. These
results are based on subjective tests; although TDHS operates in the time domain and the
output speech is reconstructed sample by sample, SNR measures correlate poorly with
perceived speech quality in TDHS due to the windowing distortions.

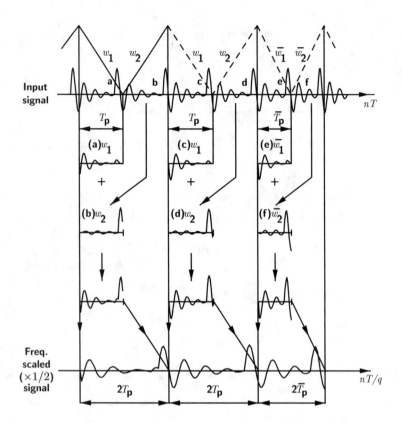

Figure 7.42 Illustration of time-domain operations for 2:1 compression ($q = \frac{1}{2}$) using a triangular window. T_p and $\overline{T_p}$ are two different pitch period durations. (After Malah *et al.* [143] © IEEE.)

TDHS can also be useful in time compression or expansion of speech, e.g., to scan speech rapidly or to slow it down for easier comprehension. (Simply changing F_s seriously distorts the speeded or slowed speech, by scaling linearly F0 and formants, e.g., the "Donald Duck" effect of playing a recording at the wrong speed.) Accelerated speech is normally achieved by periodically deleting (for compressed, faster speech) or repeating (for expanded, slower speech) short signal segments [147]. The best results for voiced speech with this method occur when the segments deleted or repeated are pitch periods since intonation is then preserved, the spectral structure is least disturbed, and discontinuities are minimized. The alternative TDHS method provides smoother speech since periods are not simply deleted or repeated but rather are interpolated. Other, related methods have also been proposed [148]. Methods following natural speaking rate variations seem best; e.g., to accelerate, eliminate pauses and compress consonants and unstressed vowels the most [149].

7.7.4.2 Direct harmonic coding.   An alternative to compressing the harmonics along the frequency axis is to code the amplitudes and phases of each harmonic (e.g., a *sinusoidal transform coder* (STC) [72]), leaving other spectral details to a residual coder. One approach follows a basic ATC coder, except that a residual spectrum is encoded only after subtracting a simplified line spectrum from the full speech spectrum [150, 151]. As in ATC, a block of N

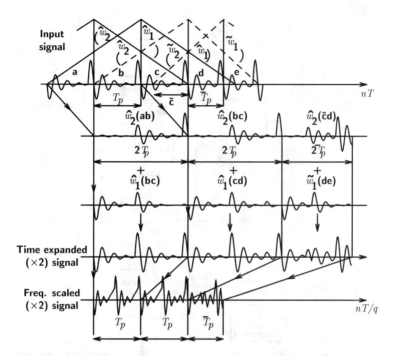

Figure 7.43 Illustration of time-domain operations for $1:2$ expansion using a triangular window. T_p and $\overline{T_p}$ are two different pitch period durations. (After Malah *et al.* [143] © IEEE.)

speech samples is transformed and analyzed with the aid of a pitch estimator to identify the harmonics, which are then modeled as windowed sinusoids (Figure 7.44). Optimal amplitudes and phases for these sinusoids are chosen to minimize the energy in the difference between the spectrum of the original speech and that of the harmonic model. They are then sent, along with the pitch estimate, to the receiver as side information. Using the coded versions of the harmonic amplitudes and phases, an estimate spectrum $\hat{S}$ is created and then subtracted from the original spectrum S to yield a residual spectrum R, which is in turn coded using ATC techniques. The receiver constructs the same $\hat{S}$ from the side information, adds that to the decoded R spectrum, and inverse-transforms the sum back into a block of speech samples.

Bit allocation depends on the voicing decision for each frame, giving most bits to the harmonic model parameters if voicing is strong (where the residual is weak) and to the residual spectrum for unvoiced speech. A binary voiced/unvoiced decision is unnecessary since bits can be assigned to the harmonic model in proportion to the amount of energy it represents in the overall spectrum; e.g., if F0 or the spectrum is rapidly changing within a block of N speech samples, a fixed harmonic model accounts for only a relatively small percentage of the speech energy, and thus the coder assigns more bits to the residual.

The harmonics are subject to many of the same redundancies that speech signals have, leading to coding efficiency. For example, a simplified spectral magnitude estimate (e.g., using geometric interpolation as in ATC) is economical to code and can provide a guideline at the decoder; individual harmonic amplitudes can then be coded relative to their deviations from the model estimate. If the simple model is accurate, fewer bits are needed than for coding the amplitudes directly. The relative continuity of the phases of the harmonics between

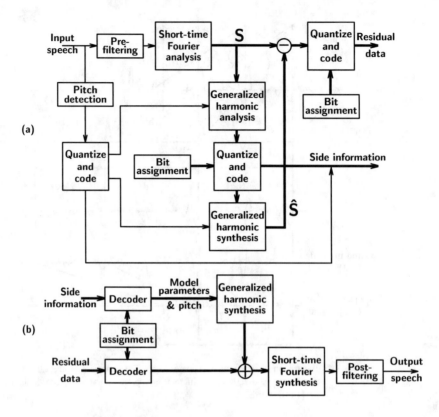

Figure 7.44 Block diagram of a harmonic coder: (a) transmitter, (b) receiver. (After Almeida and Tribolet [150] © IEEE.)

successive frames allows coding deviations from predicted values, as in DPCM. This procedure allows the decoder to generate harmonics whose amplitudes are too weak to justify sending any bits. Since the transmitted F0 estimate tells the receiver where the harmonics should be, the simple spectral model estimates their amplitudes, and the phases of other harmonics (from current and prior frames) can be used to predict their approximate phases. Thus one avoids the perceived "lowpass effect" due to spectral gaps at high frequency in low-bit-rate ATC coders when the weak upper frequencies are assigned no bits and therefore are not present in the reconstructed speech. (The lack of a pitch detector precludes this option in normal ATC.)

Figure 7.45 shows a specific implementation of harmonic coding at 4.8 kb/s, using LPC instead of the DCT for spectral analysis. The residual spectrum is obtained by inverse LPC filtering and a subsequent DFT. The residual harmonics have approximately flat magnitude and thus need few coding bits in this application. Using frame updates every 16 ms (but evaluating the LPC spectrum only every second frame, for economy), each frame of information required 12 bits for F0, 39 bits for the harmonics, and an average 26 bits for the LPC spectral data. Good communications-quality speech resulted, with some tonal change and harshness as well as a slight buzziness for male speech. The harshness disappeared if more bits were assigned to code the harmonic phases. The buzziness seemed due to harmonics receiving no coding bits, of which there were more for male voices since male voices have more harmonics due to their lower F0. At 9.6 kb/s, the harmonic coder sounded

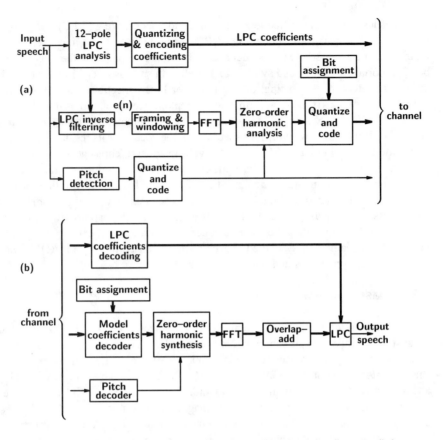

Figure 7.45 Block diagram of a 4.8 kb/s harmonic coder using linear prediction:
(a) transmitter, (b) receiver. (After Almeida and Tribolet [150] © IEEE.)

superior to ATC [150]. Combining harmonic coding for steady-state sounds with waveform coding for transitional speech segments can lead to a superior, hybrid coder as low as 4 kb/s [152].

Given the importance of the spectral envelope for speech perception, harmonic coders must preserve the envelope while modeling harmonics as well. Use of the cepstrum (Chapter 6) is popular for speech recognition, but has only recently been applied to coders, due to its relative inefficiency in accurate envelope representation. To model L harmonic amplitudes a_k at frequencies f_k, if a speech envelope $|S(f)|$ is represented by p cepstral coefficients c_i as $\log |S(f)| = c_0 + \sum_{i=1}^{p} c_i \cos(2\pi f_i)$, and we minimize a squared error, $\varepsilon = \sum_{k=1}^{L}(\log a_k - \log |S(f_k)|)^2$, a simple matrix transformation yields the c_i as a function of the a_k. Because the matrix becomes ill-conditioned as $p \to L$, *regularized* cepstral coefficients have proved useful [153].

7.8 OTHER VOCODERS (NON-LP SOURCE VOICE CODERS) (‡)

The distinction between waveform coders and vocoders has become blurred in recent years by the design of hybrid systems, which code both timing and spectral information. Nonetheless, we distinguish waveform coders that reconstruct speech sample-by-sample (exploiting redundancies in the time or frequency domain) and vocoders (e.g., LPC), that exploit speech-specific models. Waveform coders use SNR as a valid performance measure, while vocoders require subjective measures. Vocoders identify certain aspects of the speech spectrum as being important to model, and synthesize speech with such aspects faithfully reproduced. The usual parameters of F0, voicing, and formants or broad spectral structure involve the same speech redundancies that waveform coders exploit. However, no matter how complex a waveform coder is, requiring side information detailing predictor and step size information, it always sends a detailed waveform or spectrum of the speech or its residual, at the F_s rate. The transmitted residual in ADPCM or APC (waveform coders) represents those aspects of speech that remain poorly understood or are difficult to model. To reduce bit rates, vocoders send data at much lower frame rates (no data at F_s), but suffer in quality. Omitting the residual may be of little importance for intelligibility, but vocoders have been unable to attain the naturalness of toll-quality speech. Hybrid waveform vocoders approach toll or communications quality by augmenting the usual vocoder data with residual coding. The important LPC vocoder has already been described above, since it is based directly on ADPCM techniques. Other vocoder approaches and details are given here.

7.8.1 Phase Vocoder

Although not a practical system, the phase vocoder (PV) [19, 154] is discussed first because it is similar to sub-band and harmonic coders and its technique is instructive. As in SBC, the input speech passes through a bank of bandpass filters; however, the number of channels in PV is greater—about one every 100 Hz. Use of such a narrow channel bandwidth attempts to isolate one harmonic in each band. Rather than use APCM to code the output of each filter as in SBC, the PV estimates the magnitude and phase of each bandpass signal and codes this information instead, much like in the harmonic coder. A major difference is that the phase derivative (not the phase itself) is coded. Taking a derivative sacrifices timing information about the relative phases of the harmonics, which prevents PV speech from replicating the original waveform precisely. Reconstructing the phase of each channel at the decoder requires integration, which is relative to an initial value. This value is not coded and therefore is unknown to the decoder; thus it is set to a constant, which disrupts the relative phases of the harmonics. In compensation for this quality loss, derivative coding permits lower bit rates.

Each phase derivative tracks the frequency of its harmonic rather than phase relationships to other harmonics. In the absence of a pitch detector (which the PV does not need), accurate representation of harmonic frequency is more important than phase relationships. While such frequency information could be obtained from the phase, directly coding the phase to a sufficient accuracy would require higher bit rates.

Instead of direct bandpass filtering, a typical PV channel multiplies the speech $x(n)$ by sinusoids of ω_k rad and lowpass filters (via $w_k(n)$) the frequency-shifted speech to obtain the real and imaginary parts of the short-time Fourier transform $X_n(e^{j\omega_k})$ (Figure 7.46). Appropriate differentiation and squaring yield the magnitude and phase derivative of the speech energy in a band of width δ_k centered at ω_k; δ_k specifies the cutoff frequency of $W_k(e^{j\omega})$ and is usually equal to the frequency spacing of the channels. If δ_k is narrow enough so that the band contains at most one harmonic, the magnitude and phase derivative will vary slowly as the vocal tract shape and excitation, respectively, change from phoneme to phoneme. This allows a low sampling rate for coding the magnitude and phase derivatives in each channel. If, however, F0 falls below $\delta_k/2\pi$, the inclusion of two harmonics in some

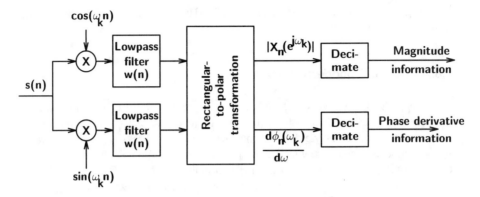

Figure 7.46 Block diagram of one channel in the analyzer of a phase vocoder.

bands disrupts their magnitude and phase estimates, so that the decimation normally used results in aliasing distortion within those bands.

Accommodating typical F0 ranges requires bandwidths of about 100 Hz, which nominally requires channel sampling rates of 200 samples/s. However, due to slow changes in the harmonics (assuming one harmonic/channel), rates of 60 samples/s are feasible. A 7.2 kb/s PV could assign 1–2 bits for each magnitude and 2–3 bits for each phase derivative, with lower-frequency channels getting the extra bit in each case [19]. The PV receiver transforms each channel's magnitude and phase information back into baseband quadrature amplitude signals, which are then modulated to the original ω_k frequencies and summed. For unvoiced speech, the phase derivative is effectively random, and (even at the slow rate of 60 samples/s) the sum of the reconstructed channel signals shows sufficient randomness to be perceived as unvoiced.

Only synthetic-quality speech is possible with vocoders, due to the loss of phase information with the usual source–filter model. It is difficult to compare vocoded speech with waveform-coded speech, since their distortions are different. Waveform coders suffer primarily from additive noise (as measured by SNR); their noise may be shaped for improved perceptual quality and sometimes has clicks and pops. Vocoders instead suffer from other distortions: whistles, burbles, buzziness, harshness, muffled quality; e.g., PV reconstructs the output speech with clean sinusoids (not subject to the quantization noise of waveform coding). The degradation arises instead from the assumed model of the vocoder. The assumption for PV that voiced speech consists solely of clean sinusoids that change slowly with time is only an approximation. Other vocoders often use simplified models of the residual signal, which reduce the bit rate but sacrifice speech quality. Waveform coders and vocoders can be compared perceptually: informal listening tests have established some relationships (e.g., PV quality is equivalent to about 3 bit log PCM speech).

A hybrid vocoder combining SBC at the more perceptually crucial low frequencies with PV at high frequencies can yield higher quality than simple PV, at medium bit rates of 10–20 kb/s. If the low frequencies (e.g., below 1 kHz) are adequately represented through sub-band coding, the upper spectral channels need not be restricted to one harmonic each. Spacing the higher channels following auditory critical bandwidths allows a more economical spectral representation while matching the ear's resolution. One suggested implementation [155] uses two sub-bands of 250–500 Hz and 500–1000 Hz, plus 10 channels of phase vocoding, with

$\frac{1}{6}$-octave channel spacing between 1000 and 3200 Hz; at 3–4 b/parameter, high-quality speech results at rates of 16–20 kb/s.

7.8.2 Channel Vocoders

As with LPC, the vocoders discussed in the remainder of this section typically operate at bit rates under 4.8 kb/s and yield synthetic-quality speech. Simply raising the bit rate further in these systems yields little improvement in quality, due to the limitations of the vocoder models. The phase vocoder (despite its name) eliminates phase relationships among the harmonics but individually codes the harmonic frequencies. The *channel vocoder* (CV) resembles PV but exploits the equal spacing of the harmonics by transmitting the value of the spacing, i.e., a single F0 value, instead of the individual phase derivatives. This requires a binary voicing decision, which is standard in all vocoders except PV. The addition of an F0 estimator adds compexity to these coders (as in APC or harmonic coding) but permits significant reductions in bit rate (since much of the spectral structure in voiced speech is due to F0).

CV usually operates with 14–38 bands, each of about 100–300 Hz bandwidth (Figure 7.47). It shares with PV the transmission of slowly varying spectral magnitudes in each channel, but omits sending detailed phase information. With few bands, severe spectral

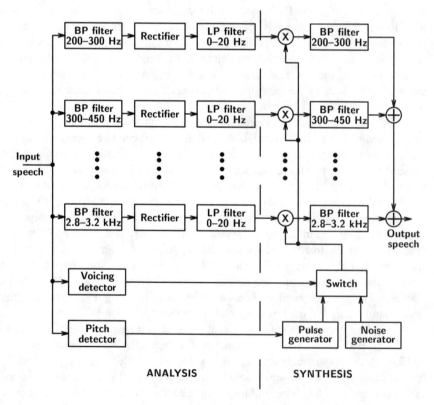

Figure 7.47 Block diagram of a 14-channel vocoder using unequally spaced bands. (After Flanagan *et al.* [9] © IEEE.)

distortion occurs as all harmonics within each band are assigned the identical amplitude during synthesis. The channels may be of nonuniform width to take advantage of the ear's better resolution at low frequencies (although filter bank design is more complex due to unequal filter delays). Since a slowly varying estimate of the signal magnitude in each band is desired, a spectral flattening device (e.g., a rectifier followed by a lowpass filter) is typical in each channel. The bandwidth of the lowpass filter is specified by the desired sampling rate per channel; e.g., 40 samples/s requires a cutoff of 20 Hz. The rate is selected according to the same criteria for updating side information in waveform coders, usually 30–100 samples/s to follow the effects of vocal tract changes.

In CV, the side information for each speech frame has 1 bit for a voiced/unvoiced decision and, for voiced frames, about 5–6 bits to specify F0. At the receiver, each channel is excited by either *pseudo-white noise* (from a random number generator) if unvoiced, or impulses spaced in time every 1/F0 if voiced. (Truly white noise is aperiodic, while most "random number generators" yield only locally random sequences, which are periodic with long cycle times. If the short-time excitation spectrum is flat and the period is long compared with typical pitch periods, such pseudo-white noise suffices.) The excitation is weighted by the channel magnitudes, passed through corresponding bandpass filters, and then all filter outputs are summed. Since channel magnitudes can be adequately coded with less than 5 bits each, channel vocoders can produce intelligible output speech with 2.4 kb/s.

Taking advantage of time and frequency redundancies permits further bit rate reductions—to about 1.2 kb/s [156]. Within a frame, the channel magnitudes can be coded with DPCM in frequency: e.g., a 3 bit log PCM code for the first band and then 2 bit differential coding for other bands, exploiting the correlation between narrowly spaced bands.

CV shares with other filter-bank coders the problems of filter design. Sharp filter cutoffs are desired to minimize spectral distortion (multiple harmonics assigned the same amplitude) and aliasing (overlap between channels) in the decoder, but they result in long time-domain responses. When the speech spectrum changes rapidly, such long responses overlap in time and effectively smear out the desired changes and cause reverberation. Quadrature mirror filters help in SBC but are of little use in CV since residual signals are not transmitted. Second-order Butterworth filters may be suitable for the analysis stage and simple first-order circuits for synthesis, as long as polarities alternate in adjacent bands (i.e., subtract the even-numbered channels from the sum of the odd-numbered ones) [157].

7.8.3 Excitation for Vocoders

Most vocoders have mediocre speech quality due to their simplistic excitation source. They code the spectral envelope in various ways and presume that the excitation has a flat spectrum and contains periodicity information. For voiced speech, an excitation of periodically spaced impulses has the desired flat spectral envelope (i.e., equal harmonic amplitudes). (We ignore deviations from a flat envelope due to changing F0 [158].) However, since no phase information is sent, each harmonic is assigned the same zero phase at the decoder. Phase variations due to the glottal source and to simplicities in vocoder models are ignored. PV is superior to CV in this respect, but only waveform coders retain sufficient phase information (via sending the residual) to render the speech natural-sounding. The latter coders operate at rates above 4.8 kb/s, while most vocoders provide intelligible speech at lower rates.

The basic voiced excitation for vocoders is periodic, often simply one impulse/period, modeling the instant of closure of the vocal cords, when the major excitation of the vocal tract occurs. This basic model ignores other excitations due to complex vocal cord motion. The cords do not close identically each cycle, and closure may not be complete (especially with breathy voices). Concentrating the excitation energy in one impulse/period leads to a more "peaky" waveform than in natural voiced speech. Some vocoders and synthesizers attempt to distribute the excitation in time by repeating a fixed waveshape every period; e.g., a 4 ms chirp of decreasing frequency ($\cos(\pi n^2/62)$, for $n = 0, 1, 2, \ldots, 30$) [159].

For coders that explicitly use F0, the need for precise estimates often exceeds normal sample spacing. Another difficulty arises in voices with high F0, where the sampling interval $1/F_s$ is a significant fraction of the pitch period (e.g., at $F0 = 250$ Hz with $F_s = 8000$ samples/s, one sample in a period means a 3% change). For a 32.5-sample period, a synthesizer could simply use 32- or 33-sample periods (accepting a small unwanted F0 shift) or could alternate 32- and 33-sample periods so that the average F0 is obtained. The latter approach, however, introduces hoarseness into the speech in the form of energy at submultiples of F0 since the true period of the latter excitation is 65 samples. Such problems can be minimized by using high sampling rates when dealing with voiced excitation, leading to *fractional-delay* LTP. At some cost, several commercial systems store their excitation waveforms at a rate higher than the output F_s, allowing accurate selection of pitch period duration, and then decimate the excitation for use in synthesis; e.g., if an impulsive excitation is desired, a 4:1 interpolated version of the unit sample (subject to lowpass filtering with cutoff at $\omega = \pi/4$ at rates of $4F_s$) could serve as the excitation waveform, allowing F0 resolution four times more accurate than without the oversampling. When F0 is not synchronized to $1/F_s$, the excitation distributes the impulse energy over a few samples so that the center of its energy reflects a more accurate F0.

Hybrid vocoders using codebooks of glottal waveforms for excitation are capable of high-quality speech regeneration at medium bit rates [160].

7.8.4 Homomorphic (Cepstral) Vocoder

Vocoders separate excitation and vocal tract shape information. In the usual model of speech $s(n)$, an excitation waveform $e(n)$ rapidly varying in time (e.g., a sharp pulse) excites a vocal tract filter whose time response $h(n)$ is spread over 10–20 ms. Unvoiced excitation uses random noise, with successive samples uncorrelated, while the voiced $e(n)$ often contains periodic impulses separated by long stretches of $e(n) = 0$. In either case, $e(n)$ varies more rapidly than $h(n)$. This property can be exploited via cepstral *deconvolution* of the speech signal into estimates of $e(n)$ and $h(n)$. The cepstrum $\hat{h}(n)$ was shown in Section 6.6 to decay much more rapidly than $h(n)$, which suggests that vocal tract information can be coded using a short duration of $\hat{h}(n)$, with enough information to reconstruct $h(n)$. The alternative of coding part of one pitch period of speech $x(n)$ would not suffice due to the slower decay rate of $h(n)$ and the overlap of copies of $h(n)$ in $x(n)$.

Using $x(n)$ as input, the cepstrum $\hat{x}(n)$ has two additive components, i.e., $\hat{e}(n) + \hat{h}(n)$. Due to the rapid decay of $\hat{h}(n)$, these two components can be separated via a time window. Multiplying $\hat{x}(n)$ by a rectangular $w(n)$ of duration less than the shortest pitch period (e.g., 3 ms) effectively eliminates the F0 contribution to the cepstrum while preserving most of $\hat{h}(n)$. A complementary rectangular window preserving the rest of $\hat{x}(n)$ leaves large samples spaced at the pitch period for voiced speech, allowing F0 estimation.

Coding only the first 2.6 ms of $\hat{x}(n)$ with 6 b/sample (plus side information about voicing and F0, as in LPC) yielded good-quality speech [162] (Figure 7.48). Unvoiced speech may have significant cepstral energy beyond 3 ms, but its elimination has little perceptual

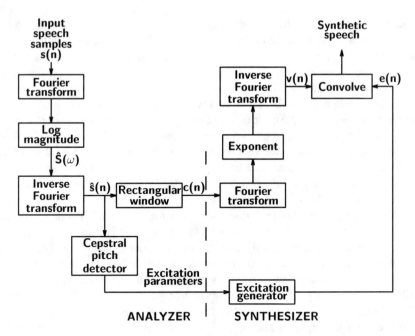

Figure 7.48 Block diagram of a cepstral analysis-synthesis system. (After Weinstein and Oppenheim [161] © IEEE.)

effect in the resynthesized speech. The main drawback to wider use of cepstral vocoders has been the computation: two DFTs each at transmitter and receiver as well as a pitch estimator. Additional difficulties concern, among others [163], (a) the emphasis of low-level, noisy regions of the spectrum due to the logarithm operation, and (b) the need for an F0-adaptive window to isolate the excitation part of the cepstrum, while avoiding elimination of too much spectral information in high-F0 speech.

7.8.5 Other Vocoders

Other speech coders operate at low bit rates and yield synthetic-quality speech. One variation on CV is the *formant vocoder*, which identifies and transmits formant frequencies and bandwidths instead of speech energies in a set of fixed bands [19, 164]. Typical bit rates are under 1 kbit/s, and only the first 3–4 formant frequencies are sent since higher formants can be kept fixed with little perceptual loss. The bandwidths, being less important perceptually, can be coded with few b/frame. When the coder properly identifies the formants, speech quality normally exceeds that of CV (because the spectrum is more realistic; it is not limited to a "staircase" function of piecewise-flat frequency bands). However, the difficulty of accurate formant tracking has hindered the use of formant vocoders, although a recent approach using recognition methods seems promising [165].

In an *articulatory vocoder*, vocal tract parameters are estimated and sent; e.g., about 10 cross-sectional areas, plus a measure of nasal coupling, could describe the vocal tract state, and the excitation could be described through measures of subglottal pressure, glottis area, and vocal cord tension. If analysis-by-synthesis is used to find the parameters, initial estimates (based on a simple spectral analysis) specify a proposed spectrum to compare to the actual speech spectrum [166, 167]; the squared difference of the two spectra is minimized iteratively by subsequent modifications of the parameters until the difference is below a threshold. Such a vocoder is not yet practical, due to our limited understanding of how to accurately model the relationship between vocal tract parameters and the speech spectrum, particularly for excitation within the tract.

For the lowest possible bit rates, vocoders must recognize and transmit phoneme codes along with some prosodic information. Such *phonetic vocoders* can operate at under 100 b/s, corresponding to the rate of phonemic information in speech. Assuming 5–6 bits to represent 32–64 possible phonemes (or allophones) and 12 phonemes/s in typical speech, about 70 b/s suffices to model the vocal tract contributions. If duration and F0 could be coded with 3–4 b/phoneme, a total rate of 100 b/s is feasible. F0 could be coded differentially, with the starting value of F0 assigned about 5 bits once per syllable; a 2-bit DPCM code might allow F0 changes of ±3 or ±6 Hz during each phoneme. Using 2 b/phoneme for duration might allow each phoneme to have a choice of 40, 80, 120, or 160 ms.

Such a system essentially consists of a phoneme recognizer–coder and a phoneme synthesizer–decoder. Since generating synthetic speech from a sequence of phoneme codes is a major aspect of automatic speech synthesis, such decoder details will be examined in Chapter 9. Similarly, obtaining a sequence of phoneme codes from a speech signal is a fundamental part of automatic speech recognition, and such coders will be discussed in Chapter 10. For now, we note that, while such phonetic vocoders can function with fewer than 100 b/s, the speech quality is low and the algorithms are complex. Much speech naturalness is lost at such severe bit rates; e.g., speaker identity characteristics are often ignored and allophonic spectral variation can be handled only very coarsely.

As Chapter 9 notes, concatenating phones without regard to context leads to unintelligible speech. Thus, while phonetic vocoders transmit phoneme codes, the units of analysis and synthesis are typically other phonetic segments, e.g., *diphones*. A diphone consists of the second half of one phone and the first half of the ensuing phone. Since its major spectral variation occurs during the middle of the segment, concatenating diphones usually involves joining speech frames with similar steady-state spectra. Intelligibility in phonetic vocoders apparently increases significantly if diphones replace phones [168]. In theory there are about 1000 diphones (combinations of 32×32 phonemes), but in coding applications diphones can be more generally treated as segments containing one spectral transition, bordered by two steady states. With this simpler definition, a pair of phones with several spectral transitions would be decomposed into more than one diphone. One phonetic vocoder, operating at 231 b/s, uses 13 spectral b/segment (8192 "diphones") and 8 b/segment for prosodic information, with an average of 11 segments/s [168]. Defining diphones based on spectral changes rather than on phonemes is permitted in vocoders. In recognition applications, however, the diphones are usually phoneme-based since the output is text, not speech. As in most speech coders, the transmitted data in phonetic vocoders need not be directly linked to textual or phonemic information, even when an intuitive interpretation involves phonemes.

7.9 VECTOR QUANTIZATION (VQ) CODERS

The speech coders described in Sections 7.5–7.8 use instantaneous coding, where the transmitted values $v(n)$ (either residual $e(n)$, or gain and spectral parameters indexed on time n) are coded individually, without regard for correlation among $v(n)$ values. For simplicity, such coders do not exploit the redundancies remaining in $v(n)$, resulting in a higher bit rate. Buffering samples of $v(n)$ into blocks for simultaneous coding can always reduce bit rate, but with more delay and complexity. Some coders (e.g., LPC) buffer speech samples, but do not code $v(n)$ as a block; e.g., waveform coders often have an implicit memory, via predictive feedback filters that modify the output based on previous speech samples ($x(n - k), k = 1, 2, \ldots, p$ in ADPCM). Vocoders (e.g., LPC) use memory more directly, considering successive frames of N speech samples as data blocks, which yield a small number of $v(n)$ parameters to send (e.g., 10–20 spectral and prosodic parameters for 100–200 speech samples). However, all these $v(n)$ are coded independently.

The greater the degree of correlation among vector elements, the more the bit rate can be lowered. LPC typically sends 50 b/frame (10 coefficients, 5 bits each) with scalar quantization, but VQ succeeds with about 10 bits. A well-chosen set of 1024 spectra (2^{10} for 10 bit VQ) can adequately represent all possible speech sounds. The number of distinct sounds is not large enough to warrant 50 bits, yet coding LPC parameters separately requires about 5 bits each.

In waveform coders, VQ codes short sequences of time samples; blocks of 2–8 samples of $v(n)$ (e.g., an ADPCM residual, or speech itself) at net rates of fewer than 2 b/sample [26]. Compared to simple PCM, SNR increases 8 dB with VQ (e.g., at 2 b/sample, PCM-VQ yields 14 dB SNR, while the best scalar PCM is about 6 dB [15]). PCM-VQ is only about 1–2 dB better than more advanced coders (e.g., DPCM), since the latter coders remove some of the speech waveform redundancy that short-block VQ exploits. However, using no predictor, PCM-VQ has an advantage over DPCM, because channel errors cannot affect the output speech past the block length. In addition, much shorter block lengths (hence smaller delays) are used with waveform VQ than in LPC or ATC. When VQ is combined with DPCM-AQF, the 1–2 dB SNR advantage of VQ remains [169]. If an ADPCM system works on vectors rather than scalars (i.e., using a vector quantizer and a vector linear predictor), good communications quality (20 dB SNR) is feasible at 16 kb/s [170].

7.9.1 Split VQ Coders

A split VQ coder can achieve less than 1 dB spectral distortion (a level which yields perceptual transparency) with 24 b/frame (scalar quantization would require 36 bits), using LSFs with a weighted Euclidean distance measure, where the weights correspond to speech energy at different frequencies [62]. A recent two-stage adaptive VQ coder gets similar quality with 22 b/frame (both require about 40K of memory and about 4 million multiplications/s at 50 frames/s); this coder is also robust to channel errors up to 1 error in 10,000 [171]. Other recent similar methods suggest that 21 b/frame is adequate [172]. These latter methods exploit interframe correlation among successive time frames, whereas most VQ coders only exploit intraframe correlation (for simplicity and real-time applications, e.g., a 29 bit coder in [173]). Interframe or memory VQ systems remove more redundancy from the speech signal, but risk error propagation in noisy transmission channels; in intraframe systems, errors affect only the current frame [174, 175]. (These are the same observations made earlier for non-VQ coders.)

7.9.2 Gain/Shape Vector Quantization

One view of the product-code approach to VQ is in terms of speech features. If the information in each frame can be partitioned into a set of features (e.g., related to formants, periodicity, etc.), the k dimensions of codebook space could be chosen accordingly, allowing faster searches of small codebooks, rather than one costly large search. For example, in APC coding, pitch and gain are treated as side information, while the residual signal is transmitted in the main data stream; segmenting speech into frames of N samples for which one pitch and one gain parameter are sent along with N residual samples, one could code all $N + 2$ parameters as one vector, or treat gain/pitch separately using VQ only on the residual samples.

This section deals with a special case of product-code VQ, where the codebook search is simplified by treating the amplitude (or gain) of each speech frame separately from the rest of its information. This approach is called *gain separation* or *gain/shape* VQ [176, 177] (pitch is usually not considered part of VQ, despite the fact that there is a correlation between F0 and vocal tract shape, that of F0 increasing with more widely spaced formants in shorter vocal tracts). Let the distance between an input vector $\mathbf{x}_n$ (e.g., a frame of speech or residual at time n) and a codeword $\mathbf{y}_i$ be

$$d(\mathbf{x}_n, \mathbf{y}_i) = (\mathbf{x}_n - \mathbf{y}_i)^T \mathbf{W}(\mathbf{x}_n - \mathbf{y}_i), \qquad (7.43)$$

where $\mathbf{W}$ is a positive-definite matrix (for a Euclidean distance, $\mathbf{W} = \mathbf{I}$), which allows more weighting for vector elements that are more perceptually important (e.g., in gain/shape VQ, the single gain factor might carry more weight than the average shape parameter). Expanding the vector product above gives

$$d(\mathbf{x}_n, \mathbf{y}_i) = \mathbf{x}_n^T \mathbf{W} \mathbf{x}_n - 2\mathbf{x}_n^T \mathbf{W} \mathbf{y}_i + \mathbf{y}_i^T \mathbf{W} \mathbf{y}_i. \qquad (7.44)$$

When minimizing d in the design or search of a codebook, the first term in Equation (7.44) is a constant and can be ignored. Each codeword stores the k-dimensional vector $2\mathbf{W}\mathbf{y}_i$ and the scalar $\mathbf{y}_i^T \mathbf{W} \mathbf{y}_i$.

In gain/shape VQ (Figure 7.49), the gain and spectral codebooks are separate, and each entry is $\mathbf{y}_{ij} = \sigma_j \mathbf{a}_i$, a scalar gain times a normalized waveform vector (the $\mathbf{a}_i$ vectors are chosen so that $\mathbf{a}_i^T \mathbf{W} \mathbf{a}_i = 1$). Minimizing the distance in Equation (7.44) reduces to selecting $\mathbf{a}_i$ to maximize $\alpha = \mathbf{x}_n^T \mathbf{W} \mathbf{a}_i$, independent of the average amplitude of the vector. Then a separate gain codebook with scalar entries σ_j (simply a scalar nonuniform quantizer) is scanned to minimize $\sigma_j^2 - 2\alpha\sigma_j$. Tested on vectors of 4–8 speech samples using 1–2 b/sample, the gain/shape approach apparently sacrifices less than 1 dB in SNR performance when compared to VQ using a single vector [177]. Since the gain/shape method allows separate codebook searches, only $2^L + 2^M$ entries must be examined instead of $2^L 2^M$ in the original method, with M shape codewords and L gain possibilities. Furthermore, the gain codebook search is much simpler since it involves scalars, rather than k-dimensional vectors in the shape codebook search. Treating the number of multiplications in the search as a complexity measure, gain/shape VQ yields SNR up to 2 dB higher than normal VQ for equally complex systems [177].

7.9.3 Other Types of Vector Quantization

Another way to reduce coder complexity is through *feedback, memory,* or *finite-state* VQ, which has N small codebooks. The codebook in use depends on past speech frames (Figure 7.50). Rather than always using one large, fixed codebook of M entries, each input vector searches one of N smaller codebooks, and then selects the codebook for the next vector (e.g., codebooks could be designed for different speech energies, with the implicit assumption of a relationship between amplitude and spectrum: the weakest sounds are obstruents, which

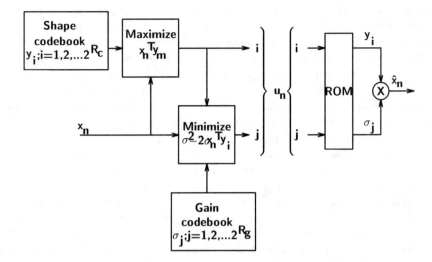

Figure 7.49 Gain/shape VQ. First a spectral vector $\mathbf{y}_i$ is chosen to match the input $\mathbf{x}_n$, by maximizing the inner product over the codewords. A scalar gain codeword σ_j is then selected. The channel symbol u_n is composed of R_c shape bits and R_g gain bits. The decoder fetches from read-only memory the codewords corresponding to u_n and multiplies them for an output. (After Gray [22] © IEEE.)

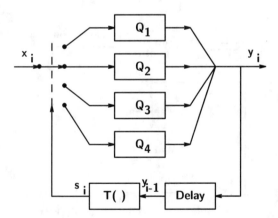

Figure 7.50 Feedback VQ with $N = 4$ codebooks. Codebook choice is based on a transformation T of codewords $\mathbf{y}_i$ from previous frames (for simplicity, the diagram assumes only one stored frame). (After Haoui and Messerschmitt [82] © IEEE.)

have most of their energy at high frequencies; more intense are sonorant consonants, followed by high vowels, and finally the low vowels). By thus partitioning a large codebook into several smaller ones, time/space savings can occur similar to those in product-code VQ. The partition also makes possible the use of different distortion measures for different classes of sounds. Taking advantage of the vocal tract's tendency to move slowly (compared to the analysis frame rate) allows a feedback VQ to search a codebook limited to codewords that could possibly follow the sequence of vectors in the memory. Using waveform VQ with short block lengths (e.g., 3 samples), output speech SNR can be raised by almost 1 dB for each doubling of the number of codebooks in a feedback, predictive VQ coder operating at 2 b/sample [82]. This compares with about 1.7 dB gain with normal VQ when increasing the block length from 3 to 4, which in turn increases calculation time (unlike the feedback approach). In ADPCM-VQ, the degree of voicing in the speech signal is important for the choice of predictor; the first autocorrelation coefficient provides a simple voicing measure, which helps in selecting from a predictor codebook [169].

Due to the exponential increase of memory and search time with block size, VQ has typically been limited to dimensions of $k = 10$–20, which corresponds in waveform coding to frames of less than 2.5 ms. LPC VQ exploits spectral coding redundancies over frames of about 20 ms. VQ can exploit speech correlations over longer periods, e.g., pitch periods separated more than 100 ms can be highly correlated during long vowels. An approach called *hierarchical vector quantization* (HVQ) [178] can be applied to such long durations, while using only codebooks of small dimensions. A three-level HVQ coder (Figure 7.51) could partition a long frame of K samples into L consecutive subvectors, which in turn consist of M consecutive k-dimensional minivectors ($K = kLM$). The minivectors are coded with basic gain/shape VQ, but their gains are normalized by feature vectors based on the full frame. In current systems, only the waveshapes of short blocks of k samples are subject to VQ [178].

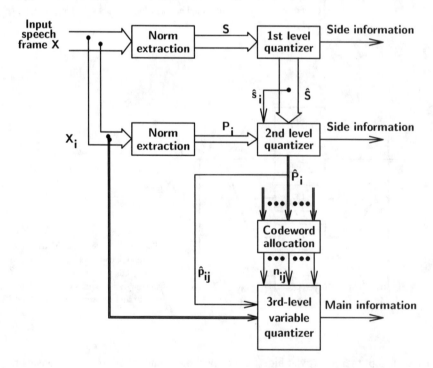

Figure 7.51 Hierarchical VQ. A frame $\mathbf{X}$ is partitioned into consecutive subvectors $\mathbf{X}_i$, which in turn are partitioned into minivectors $\mathbf{X}_{ij}$. Gain features S and P_i are extracted at the top two levels, providing side information through two vector quantizers. Shape VQ is done at the bottom level on $\mathbf{X}_{ij}$ after gain normalization based on the side information $\hat{p}_{ij}$. (After Gersho and Shoham [178] © IEEE.)

(Exploiting waveshape redundancies over long durations such as pitch periods would require an F0 estimator.) As in syllabic APCM, slowly varying amplitude during much of speech can be exploited in vector quantizing the gain at several levels in HVQ. At the first level, the L mean energies of the subvectors form a vector, which is transmitted as side information using basic VQ. Further coding within each subvector uses energy normalized by the mean subvector energy to reduce variance within the subvector. This process can be repeated as needed to minimize the codebook dimension for the gain vectors at each level (e.g., to keep L and M less than 20).

In addition to the application of VQ to blocks of speech samples in PCM or to frames of residual samples in DPCM, VQ can be used in SBC. The output waveforms from a set of bandpass filters may use VQ with codebooks of varying size for different bands, reflecting the assignment of more bits to lower frequencies. Applying gain/shape VQ here also permits the average gains for all bands to be grouped as a vector for each frame, so that, while VQ within each band exploits waveform redundancies, gain VQ exploits redundancies found in a coarse magnitude measure of the full spectrum. VQ can further be used to advantage in APC/ATC/SBC systems. Via SBC, the dynamic range in each band is reduced, alleviating instability problems that can occur in APC. The edge difficulties of ATC reconstruction do not occur with time-domain SBC coding.

7.9.4 Vector Quantization of LPC

For LPC, memoryless VQ involves coding the spectral coefficients for each analysis frame of speech as a block, transmitting a single code rather than a sequence of coded scalar parameters. Since excitation parameters are relatively independent of the spectral parameters, scalar coding is typically used for pitch (including voiced–unvoiced information) and/or gain, while the others are vector quantized. Splitting off the pitch–gain values from the spectral coefficients forms a product-code VQ, which reduces the VQ memory and search requirements, but at the price of suboptimal speech quality since any correlation between the spectrum and its excitation is not exploited. For example, one benchmark system [176] used scalar quantization for pitch (8 b/frame) and gain (5 b/frame) while dedicating up to 10 bits for VQ of 10 LPC coefficients (at 50 frames/s). Measuring speech quality in terms of spectral error (the average deviation of the magnitude spectra between the original and synthesized speech), 10 bit VQ yielded an error of 1.8 dB with a full search procedure and 2.4 dB with a more efficient binary search. These correspond to savings of 27 and 20 b/frame, respectively, over scalar quantization LPC, or roughly half the total bit rate (including pitch and gain). The speech was intelligible but suffered from the usual LPC degradations and had a "warble" or yodel-like quality during long voiced sounds. Including the gain parameter as part of the VQ [179] increased system complexity but also permitted equivalent speech quality with about 3 fewer bits per frame.

The most common distortion measure used in designing and searching an LPC VQ codebook is the modified Itakura–Saito distance [179, 180]. It measures the spectral distance between two LPC vectors in terms of the amount of energy in a residual error signal, obtained by passing one vector through the LPC inverse filter based on the other vector. It follows the same guidelines as in LPC modeling, i.e., minimizing mean-square error over a frame of speech, but permits calculation using LPC coefficients directly instead of time waveforms. This saves memory and computation since ten LPC coefficients can represent a speech frame of 100–200 samples. The distance between an input speech vector $\mathbf{x}_n$ and a codebook vector $\mathbf{y}_i$ is

$$d(\mathbf{x}_n, \mathbf{y}_i) = \frac{\mathbf{a}_i^T \mathbf{R}(\mathbf{x}_n)\mathbf{a}_i}{\sigma_i^2} + \log(\sigma_i^2) - \log(\sigma^2) - 1, \tag{7.45}$$

where $\mathbf{a}_i$ is the augmented LPC inverse vector corresponding to $\mathbf{y}_i$, $\mathbf{R}(\mathbf{x}_n)$ is the $(p+1) \times (p+1)$ autocorrelation matrix of $\mathbf{x}_n$, σ_i is the LPC gain for $\mathbf{y}_i$, and σ is the LPC gain for $\mathbf{x}$. When searching a codebook for the vector $\mathbf{y}_i$ that minimizes this distance, the last two terms in Equation (7.45) are constant and can be ignored. The first term can be rewritten [176] as

$$\sigma_i^{-2}\left[r_x(0)r_i(0) + 2\sum_{m=1}^{p} r_x(m)r_i(m)\right], \tag{7.46}$$

where $\mathbf{r}_x$ is the first column of $\mathbf{R}(\mathbf{x}_n)$ and $r_i(m) = \sum_{k=0}^{p-m} a_i(k)a_i(k+m)$. The r_i values correspond to the autocorrelation of the impulse response of the inverse LPC filter for $\mathbf{y}_i$. Taking the vector product of $\mathbf{r}_x$ and $\mathbf{r}_i$ in Equation (7.46) is equivalent to inverse filtering the input speech with the LPC model for codeword $\mathbf{y}_i$. For efficient computation, each codeword stores $\mathbf{r}_i$ normalized by σ_i^{-2}, and Equation (7.46) requires only $p+1$ multiplications/entry during the codebook search.

In gain-shape VQ, the spectral codeword stores unnormalized $\mathbf{r}_i$, and the search minimizes $\alpha = \mathbf{a}_i^T \mathbf{R}(\mathbf{x}_n)\mathbf{a}_i$ first, determining the best spectral match independent of any gain constraints. Then a separate gain codebook with scalar entries σ_j (i.e., a simple scalar quantizer, nonuniform in general) is scanned to minimize $(\alpha/\sigma_j^2) + \log(\sigma_j^2)$. The gain codebook simply consists of a set of thresholds between pairs of ordered codewords σ_j and σ_{j+1}.

A good distortion criterion for coders is how well the log speech spectrum is preserved by the coding. For simplicity, however, many systems rely on an indirect measure, such as a weighted mean-square error (WMSE) of spectral parameters (e.g., LPC or LSP coefficients). Extending such measures to VQ coders is often done with *ad hoc* weights, assuming that distortions in different dimensions sum simply [62, 176]. For LSP coefficients at rates above 9 b/subvector, at least, this assumption is valid [181]; see also [182].

7.9.5 Code-Excited Linear Prediction (CELP)

The most popular speech coders in the 4–8 kb/s range use CELP, which uses standard LP filters but with a VQ-guided excitation. VQ is applied both to the LPC residual and to the spectral coefficients in such LPAS *stochastic* or *code-excited* coders [183]. At 16 kb/s, CELP is widely used for almost-toll-quality speech. Short sections of the residual waveform (e.g., up to 5 ms or 40 samples) are coded with typically 10 bit codebooks. CELP often uses long-term pitch prediction (LTP), which simplifies the excitation codewords (i.e., no need to model F0 in the codebook, but an F0 estimator is needed). Optional use of an *adaptive codebook* means the excitation is that of the previous period, but at different delays and gains (to accommodate slow changes in F0) [80]. The best CELP needs very precise F0 estimates, often requiring high bit rates and much computation (including a multiple-tap pitch filter) [60].

In CELP, the basic search for an optimal excitation vector c_k among L entries is very similar to finding optimal LP coefficients, i.e., by minimizing a squared error [184]. The calculation reduces to maximization of a fraction where the numerator is the inner product between a residual vector ρ (from the actual speech passed through an inverse filter corresponding to the chosen LPC spectrum) and each codebook entry c_k—thus needing N operations per codeword (where N is the LPC order). The denominator, however, requires NL operations, which has led to many attempts for more efficient search methods (e.g., nonexhaustive searches, exploiting subsampling, interpolation, and hierarchical methods). Instead of a standard time-domain search, computation can be reduced in the frequency domain, e.g., using codebook entries with unity amplitude (thus reducing computation to that of adding phase terms) [185].

7.9.5.1 Faster search.
While the codebook for spectral patterns is usually based on training from much speech, the excitation codebook is often generated independently of speech observations. All excitation vectors are presumed to have a flat spectrum, but differ in phase. In spectral codebooks, a structure is often observed in codewords relating to different vocal tract shapes (and phones), but such a structure is not found for excitations. Thus there is great flexibility in designing excitation codebooks: "sparse" codewords (with many zero-valued samples) are often chosen to reduce computation (most DSP operations are sums of products, and multiplications by zero weights can be omitted). Codeword samples are often limited to values of 0 and ±1 (filtering with such excitations is fast due to the lack of multiplications needed in the codebook search and synthesis). Sometimes the codeword index has a direct relationship with its codeword (e.g., the bits of the index can directly represent the excitation sequence, with perhaps a 0 bit yielding a value of -1 as an excitation sample). Several fast search methods can reduce the large amount of search calculation (which can exceed 300 million instructions/s (MIPS) in basic CELP) [186, 187] (DSP chips can run at 100 MIPS). Sparse and overlapping vectors minimize computation to find the optimal codeword (evaluating each codeword requires a distance calculation, which is simplified if most samples in the codeword are zero). Much of the search computation is due to the perceptual weighting of the error; simplified weighting allows trading speech quality for less computation. Interpolating the filter coefficients (every 5–10 ms—common in basic LPC) within each 20–30 ms frame reduces spectral distortion by about 0.5 dB, but usually increases the CELP excitation search time significantly (but see [91] for a recent way to halve the computation). With sparse excitation patterns of fewer than four nonzero samples per 40 in a sub-frame, quasi-periodic artifacts appear in unvoiced parts of the speech, which require post-processing to ameliorate [188].

While more complex than MLPC, CELP gives higher-quality speech at 4.8 kb/s, where the need for good quality speech led to the US federal standard FS-1016 CELP coder [189]. Such speech is clearly superior to basic LPC speech, but is below communications quality. Achieving superior quality at 4.8 kb/s requires long frames of 30 ms for spectral updating, while using 7.5 ms subframes for the excitation codewords. The 2.4 kb/s LPC-10E coder [190] uses 41 b/frame to achieve a log spectral distortion of 0.5 dB, compared to 1.2 dB for FS-1016 using 34 b/frame; CELP sounds better due to its superior excitation coding.

An 8 kb/s stochastic coder called VSELP (vector-sum-excited linear prediction) is the standard (IS-54) for North American digital cellular speech [11] (analog cellular uses simple frequency-modulation in a 30 kHz bandwidth; digital uses only 10 kHz, including an extra 6 kb/s for error protection). Since a major cost for CELP concerns computation in searching the excitation codebook, VSELP reduces complexity by using highly structured codebooks for fast search: two 7 bit codebooks whose codewords are 40-sample excitations, produced by summing 7 basis functions with binary weights (±1). Since each bit of the codeword controls the sign of a basis vector, channel errors do not seriously degrade the output speech (in other

CELP coders, some bit errors radically change the excitation, but here it only affects one-seventh of the excitation). The input to the synthesizer is the sum of one excitation from each codebook plus a pitch contribution. Since the synthetic output is a linear combination of filtered waveforms, using only 14 basis vectors, the search is rapid. To increase performance, the filtered vectors are orthogonalized as well. A 6.7 kb/s VSELP is the Japanese digital cellular standard [191], and VSELP is a candidate for half-rate standards (i.e., coding two signals in a cellular channel). A disadvantage of VSELP is that it is slightly below toll quality, and a one-way delay of 60 ms (due to 20 ms frames) limits its use for real-time applications. (The idea of orthogonal basis vectors to accelerate construction of the residual was recently extended to eliminate the codebook search via a K–L expansion [192].)

7.9.5.2 Low-delay (LD) CELP.
Typical low-bit-rate coders incur coding delays (not including transmission) of 2–4 frames of input speech data (e.g., about 60 ms), due to buffering and computation at the coder and decoder [67]. Many applications can tolerate such delays (e.g., in video telephony, up to 500 ms). For some real-time applications, however, such delays are unacceptable. Converting a coder to low-delay operation often requires more computation and/or a higher bit rate; e.g., LD-CELP has a standard (G.728) at 16 kb/s for toll quality, while basic CELP can get communications quality at 8 kb/s. To achieve a delay of only 2 ms, the excitation vectors are very short (e.g., 5 samples). In addition, the predictor is backward-adaptive (i.e., no need to invert matrices), which allows a very high-order all-pole model ($p = 50$), which in turn negates the need for LTP (i.e., no pitch estimator). Gain-shape VQ is used for the excitation (3 bit gain, 7 bit shape). LD-CELP yields quality equal to 32 kb/s ADPCM, at half the bit rate (but with more computation). With high model orders, filter complexity and stability becomes an important issue; SNR gains above $p \approx 60$ appear to be minimal [193] and do not justify higher orders. One attempt at 8 kb/s LD-CELP by extending the vector from 5 to 10 samples yielded too noisy speech with a poor spectral match at high frequencies, but using backward adaptation only for low frequencies with a 20-sample vector yielded a fair-to-good MOS of 3.45 and a SEGSNR of 14.2 dB [194].

7.9.5.3 Wideband and multiband CELP.
Wideband CELP or related techniques at 16 kb/s with reduced computation (via use of adaptive codebook preselection and a sparse codebook, or via transform residual coding) is comparable to the 56 kb/s G.722 standard [195, 196]. For wideband speech, CELP often operates on multiple sub-bands to reduce complexity and to allow better control over the noise distribution in frequency [80]. It is possible to have very-low-delay, high-quality CELP of wideband speech (0–7 kHz) at 32 kb/s [130] and very-wideband speech (20 Hz–15 kHz) at 64 kb/s [193]. A recent coder at 16 kb/s, using mel-warping, claims to be better than G.722 at 64 kb/s [197]. In general, for wideband speech below 64 kb/s, the computation in LP-based coders becomes excessive, while quality in transform-based coders is unacceptable [130]. A sub-band analysis-by-synthesis coder combines the advantages of noise-shaping (as in SBC) and VQ (as in CELP) to achieve quality of almost an FS-1016 coder at 8 kb/s [198] with a 25 ms delay.

7.9.5.4 Multiband excitation.
At 8 kb/s, high-quality speech is possible through multiband excitation (MBE) of LPC [199], where the residual is coded in a sub-band fashion. A recent 1.6 kb/s version of MBE uses a two-dimensional (time–frequency) differential coding of LSPs for a low-bit-rate spectral representation, with good intelligibility [200]. Many recent low-rate coders have evolved directly from the MBE concept; e.g., improved MBE (IMBE) is the satellite communication standard (Inmarsat-M) at 4.15 kb/s. In MBE, the sub-

bands vary in width, according to the F0 estimate for each frame, so that a small number of harmonics (often just one) reside in each band. A voiced–unvoiced decision in each band allows good control over the distribution of periodicity in the reconstructed residual used to excite the LP synthesizer. Good speech (MOS of 3.25) is feasible at 2.5 kb/s with only four subbands [201]. Wideband MB-CELP at 24 kb/s outperforms the G.722 coder at 56 kb/s [202].

7.9.5.5 Algebraic CELP methods (ACELP). A very practical development in CELP has been algebraic CELP (ACELP), where the brief vectors of residual samples are no longer stored in a VQ codebook, but rather are directly derived from the transmitted index; i.e., a simple algebraic transformation of the index produces the actual signal used to excite the LP synthesizer. This saves on storage (all pulses typically have a fixed amplitude; only the algebraic sign is stored) and accelerates the search for the optimal excitation, despite the use of about a million vectors.

Conjugate-structure ACELP (CS-ACELP) is now the 8 kb/s ITU-T standard G.729 (Figure 7.52) [12, 204, 205]. It yields toll quality in most cases with a tenth-order LPC, an adaptive perceptual weighting filter, 10 ms frames with 5 ms lookahead (i.e., 15 ms coding delay), an 18-bit LSF spectral representation, and a 17 bit excitation codebook. To allow a fast codebook search, each 40-sample excitation vector is sparse, containing only four nonzero pulses at limited time positions. A recent version (G.729.A) has been implemented on a TMS320C50 fixed-point DSP chip at 12 MIPS, with less than 2K RAM words and 10K ROM [203]. Algebraic codebooks can also apply to wideband CELP [193].

A version of ACELP (IS-461) is now the North American TDMA standard for digital cellular telephony (IS-136); it effectively replaces the previous VSELP standard, lowering the rate for speech from 7.95 kb/s to 7.4 kb/s, thus allowing more bits for error protection in the 13 kb/s total rate [206]. It provided a gain of about 0.5 MOS in noisy cellular conditions, including a respectable MOS above 2.5 at 11 dB SNR.

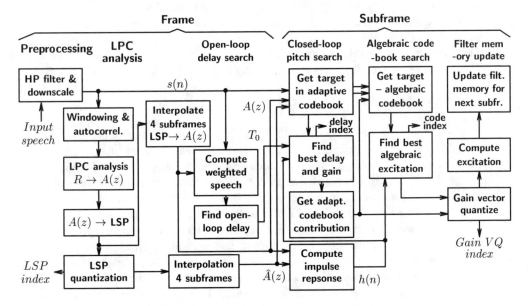

Figure 7.52 CELP G.729 coder. (After Salami *et al* [203] © IEEE.)

In 1997, the European Telecommunications Standards Institute (ETSI) proposed an Adaptive Multi-Rate (AMR) coder for GSM: full rate at 22.8 kb/s and half rate at 11.4 kb/s, adapting both source coding and error protection to the quality of the radio channel. Based on ACELP, the GSM Enhanced full rate and AMR coders provide wireline quality (32 kb/s ADPCM, G.726) for channels better than 10 dB and 7 dB SNR, respectively [207].

7.9.5.6 Other versions of CELP.   To achieve toll quality at rates below 8 kb/s, the frame size in LPAS coders can be increased to 30 ms, at the cost of greater algorithmic delay; e.g., the G.723.1 standard at 5.3–6.3 kb/s [12, 48]. Combining multipulse excitations with an adaptive codebook in CELP (MP-CELP) leads to equivalent quality with a 10 ms frame coder at 6.4 kb/s [208]. For CELP below 4.8 kb/s, quality degrades significantly due to inaccurate modeling of both the excitation (longer excitation vectors lead to reverberation and tonal artifacts) and the spectral envelope (poorer representations of each period, leading to buzzy or noisy speech). Recent extensions of CELP try to retain quality at yet lower rates. One method, based on the estimated F0, classifies each speech frame into one of four categories (voiced, unvoiced, or two transition classes); with four smaller codebooks, the search is faster, even while improving quality [209]. Pitch-synchronous innvovation (PSI)-CELP at 3.6 kb/s (the half-rate standard for cellular transmission in Japan) exploits both fixed and adaptive codebooks to achieve good quality [191].

As noted in Chapter 6, wavelets furnish a new approach for speech analysis. Few coders have so far used wavelets, but recently a hybrid WT (wavelet transform)-CELP coder combined use of 20-coefficient Daubechies wavelets for voiced speech with basic CELP for unvoiced speech to achieve better speech quality than FS-1016 with one-seventh the computation at 4.8 kb/s [210]. Wavelets may also be useful for multiple-sampling-rate applications [211].

Given the current popularity of CELP, it is natural to address issues of how noisy channels affect performance. While the Shannon separation principle [212] says that source and channel codes can be designed independently without performance loss, practical needs to minimize cost and delay usually lead to joint design, seeking source codes that will be robust in noisy channels. Since practical source coders are not ideal (i.e., do not output a stream of equiprobable bits), channel decoders can also be designed to exploit residual redundancy in the CELP bitstream. Using Reed–Solomon and convolutional codes, coding gains of 2–5 dB are feasible in noisy and fading channels [213].

7.9.6 Very-Low-Rate LPC Vocoders

At 800 b/s, an LPC VQ coder [214] can achieve speech quality comparable to that obtained by scalar LPC coding at 2.4 kb/s, with no increase in computation. Using a two-stage 10-bit tree codebook (32 first-level nodes, each representing a further distribution of 32 codewords) reduces the computation needed in a full-search approach (1024 comparisons) to only 64 (finding the closest match among the first 32 "average" nodes and then getting a more precise fit among that node's 32 branches), with minimal quality degradation. (A binary tree search—with 20 comparisons—significantly distorted the output speech and was rejected.) Since the actual LPC coefficients of the input are not needed in the codebook search (only the autocorrelation $\mathbf{R}(\mathbf{x}_n)$ is used in Equation (7.46)), the 64 evaluations each requiring 11 multiplications yielded a computation comparable to the Levinson recursion for scalar LPC. Separate codebooks have been proposed for voiced and unvoiced speech to take advantage of (a) the lesser need for spectral accuracy in unvoiced speech by using a smaller codebook there, and (b) the likelihood of different spectra populating the two codebooks; however, using the voiced codebook for unvoiced speech appeared to have no perceptual effect. Alternatively, a subset of the voiced codebook might be used for unvoiced speech, allowing for decreased computation with little quality loss [214].

Thus memoryless VQ can reduce the bit rate of a standard 2.4 kb/s vocoder to about 800 b/s with little change in output speech quality. Speech degrades rapidly with lower bit rates, however, unless temporal redundancies beyond the range of a 20 ms LPC analysis frame are exploited, in addition to the spectral redundancies in the usual VQ. A type of "matrix quantization" (so-called because the LPC vectors are extended into the time dimension) can exploit temporal redundancies [215, 216]. This approach could combine spectral VQ with variable-frame-rate (VFR) principles. As was the case with scalar-quantized VFR, a bit-rate reduction of up to $3:1$ is possible with little speech degradation, at the cost of greater algorithmic complexity and possible buffer-delay difficulties. The simplest method sends a new LPC vector only when (a) the distance measure between the current frame vector and the last one sent exceeds a threshold, and (b) a closer vector is available for transmission. With an 8 bit codebook and about 45 frames/s, 250 b/s VFR VQ speech has similar quality to fixed-rate 800 b/s VQ [217]. Unfortunately, VFR often requires delays of hundreds of milliseconds, too long for some applications [28].

Selective linear prediction can be combined with VQ to reduce memory and search requirements, at the cost of decreased speech quality [129]. Dividing the speech spectrum into two or more bands, in which LPC analysis of reduced order is done in the higher bands, permits the flexibility to model the lower bands with more poles/Hz. In addition, as in SBC, distortion from one band does not affect other bands. Applying VQ to selective LPC allows a form of product code if the codebook for each band is designed independently. Since there is spectral redundancy between frequency bands, however, such a design likely yields a suboptimal codebook.

7.10 NETWORK AND APPLICATION CONSIDERATIONS

The choice of standard bit rates for speech coders has been motivated primarily by telephone networks. Since many networks attenuate frequencies above 3200 Hz, 8000 samples/s is a standard sampling rate (allowing for imperfect lowpass filtering). Thus, 64 kb/s toll-quality speech, using 8 bit log PCM, is a benchmark to compare with other coders. Designs exist for simple, high-quality coders at 32 kb/s and 16 kb/s to double and quadruple the number of voice signals to be sent on a communications link that handles one 64 kb/s signal. Coding wideband speech at 16,000 samples/s is also being explored for 16, 24, 32 and 64 kb/s links.

In communication networks, transmission bandwidth is a major factor relating to bit rate and the choice of coding approach, whereas the complexity of network switching nodes does not change much for different speech coders. Given the major capital investment in log PCM transmission, however, alternative coding techniques are not likely to be implemented in standard telephone networks until channel capacity becomes scarce. Immediate applications for other coders are found in local area and cellular networks, and in mobile radio [218]. Even with multipath interference causing bit errors over 10% in wireless communication, low-bit-rate coders are proving practical.

Until recently, modem technology could not guarantee digital transmission at rates exceeding 2.4 kb/s over standard telephone lines. (Modem rates up to 56 kb/s and beyond are increasingly common.) Many low-bit-rate vocoders were thus designed for rates at multiples or submultiples of 2.4 kb/s (leading to an integer number of lines per signal or an integer number of signals per line, respectively); e.g., the US secure-voice standard uses 4.8 kb/s.

The recent explosion of applications in cellular telephony and mobile radio has led to several federal and international standards for speech coders. The International Telecommunications Union (ITU; previously known as CCITT) provides many standards, including the recent H.324 for multimedia (including POTS); it uses the G.723.1 audio codec for near-toll-quality speech at 5.3–6.4 kb/s (18–20 MIPS, with an end-to-end delay of 150 ms), or G.729 with 85 ms delay [219]. The US federal standard FS-1015 for LPC-10 at 2.4 kb/s was the first standard [66], but such low-quality speech is not widespread in public networks. A new 2.4 kb/s standard is replacing FS-1015 with quality better than the 4.8 kb/s FS-1016 CELP coder; it uses mixed-excitation LPC (MELP) [220] and combines good quality with real-time performance on a 60 MHz DSP chip (20 MIPS) [28]. At such low rates, voice storage is feasible for message services.

Variable-rate CELP, including QCELP (the IS-95 standard for wideband spread-spectrum digital-cellular mobile radio), can provide communications-quality speech at average rates as low as 2 kb/s [221]. QCELP is an open-loop VBR coder (see below) with potentially four rates from 1 to 8 kb/s, with the update rate of its parameters proportional to the estimated speech energy, although it largely functions in binary (speech vs non-speech) mode [222]. Other similar coders exploit further phonetic classification which allows spectral distortion of 2.4 dB (9–11 b/frame) for unvoiced frames and 1 dB (24–25 b/frame) for voiced speech [222].

7.10.1 Packet Transmission

There is significant recent interest in sending simultaneous voice and data (SVD) over telephone networks, especially with newer higher-rate modems [223] and speech over the Internet. Speech coders often operate in communication networks where many voice signals are simultaneously sent from different origins to various destinations, with different delay requirements. *Packet transmission* systems (e.g., ATM in the ISDN) take advantage of variable speech demand to route blocks of speech data (corresponding to frames of typically 20–50 ms) through different paths in a network, depending on traffic congestion at the nodes of the network [224]. The receiver reconstructs the speech signal from successive packets, which may arrive out of time order if not sharing the same transmission path. For real-time applications (e.g., conversations), the packets must not represent long sections of speech because the system has an inherent delay equal to the packet length plus the (longest) transmission time; e.g., one network sends packets of 1000 bits maximum, where a round trip of almost 10,000 km takes at least 300 ms (compared to 60 ms for the terrestrial telephone network and 600 ms via satellite) [225]. In the case of a "lost" packet (i.e., one delayed beyond the maximum permissible time of about 300 ms [224]), the reconstructed speech must either omit the corresponding section of speech or estimate it from neighboring received packets [226–228]. Often the most recently received packet is repeated (sometimes with decaying amplitude and unvoiced excitation, for vocoders [225]) until a later packet arrives.

To minimize both the effects of a lost packet and the total delay, each packet rarely represents more than 100–200 ms of speech, although efficiency suffers for short packet sizes in integrated networks, where each packet must have a *header* containing a description of its contents and routing information. For speech, this header notes the timing of its data relative to other packets in transmission. Efficiency is poor when narrowband speech is sent via packets, since a 50 ms frame in a 2.4 kb/s coder needs only 120 bits, which is less than the size of the header in many networks [225].

Lost packets are similar to bit errors in other speech transmission systems. Channel errors may occur either randomly for each bit sent or in a "burst" (e.g., fading may cause many errors over brief time intervals of 20–40 ms). (Mobile cellular often suffers 1–2% random Gaussian bit errors, as well as Rayleigh fading, where 5–10% of frames are lost.) The latter are more serious, leading to audible discontinuities, and are harder to compensate for. At the cost of added delay, one can *interleave* data from different frames (e.g., excitation data from one frame sent with spectral data from another). Basic robustness methods use error protection (e.g., parity bits), e.g., adding as much as 60% more bits in cellular standards GSM and IS-54 (which can tolerate 3% error rates, as in car cellular systems). They need more bandwidth, but reduce errors in the protected bits (usually for the more important side information, e.g., F0 and spectra) by about a factor of ten. When a received parity bit signals an error, data from a *bad frame* can be replaced by that of an adjacent frame. With burst errors, replacing multiple frames may require attenuation and spectral flattening of the speech for best perceptual effect, rather than simple interpolation [80].

Telephony over the Internet is increasingly popular due to its low cost; however, given the rates of today's modems, coding speech to 32 kb/s or less is needed, which often requires a fast PC for higher-quality connections [229]. The recent H.323 telephony standard for IP networks allows more conversations among users with different telephony services.

7.10.2 Time Assignment Speech Interpolation (TASI)

Packet systems are often integrated voice/data networks, where speech, signaling tones, and voice-band data are all sent on the same communication path, with either time- or frequency-multiplexing separating different channels of information. Packet speech is used primarily in networks where speech occupies only a small part of the transmission load. These networks have variable demand because of a fluctuating number of users and, for voice, because each speaker is silent about 60% of the time on the average (i.e., when the speaker waits for the other party in a conversation to cease talking).

A system called *time assignment speech interpolation* (TASI) exploits each speaker's underutilization of a network channel by coding speech only while a speaker actually talks [230, 231]. An energy threshold usually separates voice from silence, and transmission becomes *half-duplex*, where simultaneous talking by both parties in a conversation is not allowed. TASI is a form of variable-frame-rate (VFR) coding, where the bit rate is proportional to the amount of speech activity. VFR coders must allow for significant delays (often 300–500 ms), buffering data during periods of high activity. Since such delays are usually unacceptable in real-time speech networks, speech transmission in TASI systems must be shared across several users so that the sum of the activity matches channel capacity. On channels communicating many conversations, while any given speaker may talk at a specific time, the total data rate averages about 40% of the peak of all speakers simultaneously talking. A typical TASI system halves the nominal peak data rate, allowing an extra 10% margin for *hangover time*: e.g., cutting off or *clipping* a speaker's transmission 100–200 ms after talking ceases in typical conversation bursts of 0.3–1.2 s.

This requires a *voice activity detector* to locate speech in noisy backgrounds [232]. Since speech presence is often detected through the high energy of vowels, weak unvoiced sounds adjacent to the vowels are sometimes clipped at the end of a *talkburst* in the absence of this *hangover time*. At the start of a talkburst, clipping can be perceived with as little as the first 15 ms removed, although 50 ms clips are often tolerated. If necessary at times of peak demand, arbitrary clipping of speech in the middle of a burst has little perceptual effect if the clips are smaller than 5 ms and occur less than 1% of the time, but intelligibility suffers with midburst clips greater than 50 ms [77]. Performance is affected by the accuracy of *voice activity detectors*, which often estimate the presence of speech via energy after normalization by an inverse filter (itself due to an estimate of the long-term channel noise). At the receiver, non-speech is often replaced by 'comfort noise' (e.g., coded with 15 b/frame) rather than silence, since listeners prefer a low-level noise to dead silence [232].

When the demand exceeds the available bandwidth, *freeze-out* occurs, in which significant parts of conversations are lost; usually the initiations of speech bursts are cut in as many conversations as necessary. Similar limitations occur in CDMA cellular, where signalling requirements can reduce the bit rate available for speech from 8 kb/s to 4 kb/s (or even to zero) for brief time periods [222]. On digital links, techniques such as *digital speech interpolation* (DSI) permit more acceptable ways to implement TASI [233]. Instead of completely eliminating sections of speech, the number of bits per sample can be reduced at times of high demand. In a typical telephone conversation, both speakers are *simultaneously* active about 5% of the time, but such speech permits coding at reduced accuracy because quantization noise is masked by the dual speech [234]. Furthermore, with some added complexity, DSI can identify which conversations need the most bits at any given time; e.g., during an overload situation, if some speech signals are changing slowly, their last frames could be repeated without transmission, while more rapidly changing signals would have their samples sent. A compression of 2.5:1 is typical for TASI and DSI.

7.10.3 Embedded Coding

Most speech coders are unimodal (i.e., have a fixed algorithm and bit rate). While this approach is simplest, it is wasteful because bit transmission needs vary with the source (the speech) and bit availability varies with the transmission channel. This section discusses multimodal coders, where the bit rate and sometimes the method change to accommodate varying transmission conditions [97]. The VFR systems discussed earlier are examples of open-loop variable-bit-rate (VBR) coders, where bit rate increases during information-intensive voiced speech and falls during weaker sounds (theoretically to zero for silence). Closed-loop VBR coders evaluate several coded versions for the speech before choosing the optimal one for the source+channel conditions [222]; given the increased computation and the lack of consensus on a good speech quality measure, however, most VBR coders use open-loop methods.

An important special case of variable-rate coding is *embedded coding*, where the bit stream for speech can be stripped of less important bits when needed, i.e., a gradual degradation of the output speech as bit rate decreases [235]. PCM and log PCM provide this sort of system; if the M least significant b/sample are omitted from an optimal N b/sample PCM system, the optimal $N - M$ b/sample PCM system results ("optimal" = best SNR). Thus, within an N-bit PCM coder is embedded $N - 1$ other PCM coders, each having one fewer b/sample. Many speech coders, however, do not satisfy this embedded condition. Most DPCM systems, including the standard DPCM of Figure 7.17, are not embedded coders due to the feedback loop in the coder: dropping some bits in transmission affects only the decoder, whereas the coder quantization is based on a predicted estimate using all the bits. An additional decrease in SNR of 3.5–10 dB, beyond the degradation inherent to the lower bit rate (i.e., if an embedded code were to exist), often occurs [236].

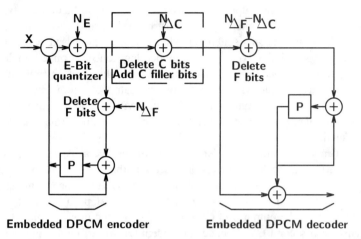

Figure 7.53 Embedded DPCM. Integrators at both coder and decoder use the same signal of $E - F$ bits. When DSI forces the dropping of C bits (assuming $C \leq F$), no additional channel noise appears at the output. The output noise N_D is that of a $D = E - C$ bit DPCM system. (After Goodman [236] © IEEE.)

Figure 7.53 shows one way to obtain embedded DPCM, if the potential number of bits to be dropped is known beforehand. If at most F bits may be omitted during transmission, the coder feedback estimate can take account of this possibility and base the predictor estimate on a worst case assumption. This system is not optimal at normal bit rates because a larger step size than necessary is used when bits are not dropped and the prediction uses a less accurate estimate. On the average, waveform coders sacrifice 0.5–0.8 dB when using this type of technique [236]. ADM and ADPCM can also be embedded (the G.727 standard) [237, 238].

In coders sending side information, DSI drops bits from the main stream since degrading the side information usually has more significant effects. Advanced coders (e.g., SBC, ATC, vocoders) also allow DSI to gradually lower speech quality as bit rate is reduced, but deciding which bits to drop becomes complex. In PCM or DPCM using N b/sample, the bits could be sent in order from most to least significant, allowing (if needed) the removal of the last M out of every N bits. The bit stream in ATC, on the other hand, sends many spectral samples, and dropping bits would require identifying the least significant bits, which occur at different points each frame.

Not all coding schemes scale easily; i.e., the range of rates for which speech quality is proportional to bit rate is often limited. Multistage VQ is especially conducive to embedded coding, since each stage refines the remaining differential residual. For multipulse LPC, the pulses are often located in decreasing order of importance (and hence the final ones could be dropped if channel capacity is reduced) [239]. Sub-band coders provide another good candidate for embedding [240]. Less obviously, embedded CELP is also feasible [241]. Embedded coders can be especially useful to adapt to variable conditions, e.g., in data–voice simultaneous channel (DVSC) cases [242].

7.10.4 Tandeming of Coders (‡)

In certain applications, a communication path may consist of multiple links having different bandwidths. On such a path, it may be necessary to *tandem* or connect two or more speech coders so that the output of one provides the input for another. A typical path may mix digital and analog links, where speech must be A/D- and D/A-converted at several points. For each digital link, a coder suited to the link's bandwidth is used, while analog links directly limit speech bandwidth. *Asynchronous* tandeming concerns mixed analog–digital communication, whereas *synchronous* tandeming is purely digital. Embedded coders permit synchronous tandeming with degradation unrelated to the number of tandems; output speech quality is just a function of the link with the lowest bandwidth. Quality using asynchronous tandems, on the other hand, decreases with the number of links (e.g., about 2–3 dB/tandem).

If identical coders are tandemed, most of the overall speech quality loss (except for initial distortion in the A/D conversion) occurs in the first stage, and subsequent stages have as input a simplified speech signal in which those aspects of the signal that the coder handles poorly were removed at the first stage. For example, slope overload is a major problem in CVSD; however, the output of a CVSD coder is limited in slope and so causes no overload problems for a second CVSD coder in tandem. However, tandeming more than 3–4 stages usually degrades speech significantly more than one stage alone; e.g., −5 dB with three ADPCM coders [243]. Tandem effects are less serious for simpler coders, e.g., log PCM is comparatively robust to repeated encodings [14].

When linking different coders in sequence, serious degradation can occur due to a mismatch in the speech aspects that the individual coders exploit; e.g., one section of a communication network may allow mediumband waveform coding at 16 kb/s, while another section is limited to narrowband coding at 2.4 kb/s (e.g., LPC). Because of substantial differences between coding methods at different rates, especially between waveform coders and vocoders, the output of such a tandem is usually worse than the output of the system with the lower bit rate. For example, LPC often produces a "peaky" signal (a large ratio of peak-to-average amplitude), which can cause slope overload when input to a DCPM coder; similarly, the distortions of waveform coders (quantization noise and slope overload) degrade parameter estimation in vocoders. SBC is superior to DPCM systems when tandemed with LPC vocoders, but serious degradation affecting intelligibility occurs in both cases [17].

7.11 HARDWARE IMPLEMENTATION: INTEGRATED CIRCUITS

The speech coding algorithms described above range from simple PCM or log PCM coders to complex systems such as ATC, APC, or vocoders. All can be implemented in real time hardware if sufficient processing power is available. Most coders are simple enough to permit operation on a single LSI (large-scale integration) chip [244]. The popular DSP chips introduced during the 1980s (e.g., the Texas Instruments TMS320 family) have a reduced instruction set, concentrating on simple arithmetic, which frees chip space for a large register set and an array multiplier. Chips now perform fast double-precision multiplies (e.g., with 16 bits or 24 bits, often with 32 bit accumulation) and have up to 1 Mbit of read-only memory (mask programmable ROM) as well as up to 24 kbytes of data random access memory (RAM), all in a compact dual in-line package. A typical FFT of 256 points can take less than 20 μs. The *Harvard architecture* of separate data and program buses enables fast throughput for many speech applications. They typically use low-power CMOS technology, and cost under $100 in large quantities.

Typical floating-point DSP chips are now capable of 20–30 MIPS. Most state-of-the-art CELP coders need 1–2 such chips for full-duplex real-time operation. Much lower computation is possible for toll quality at 32 kb/s; now applications at 28.8 kb/s are of interest with the ITU-T V.34 modem standard, possibly allowing wideband speech over normal telephone lines [245]. Besides powerful general DSP chips, less costly chips dedicated to specific coding methods are available. On the other hand, more expensive 32-bit floating-point DSP chips are capable of giving very-high-precision arithmetic. Special-purpose chips for speech codecs are relatively inexpensive, and typically use CMOS fabrication (for low power consumption, e.g., 30 mW) and often include a 16 bit A/D converter.

7.12 SUMMARY

This chapter discussed the technical aspects of speech coders (Table 7.2). Waveform coders exploit redundancies in the time or frequency domain to lower the number of bits per second needed to transmit or store speech. They generate output speech that resembles the original waveform sufficiently that signal-to-noise ratios can be used as objective quality measures.

TABLE 7.2 Summary of properties of speech coders (note: G.726 encompasses G.721 and G.723 for ADPCM at 16–40 kb/s; G.727 is the embedded version of G.726).

Category	Type	Quality MOS-DRT-DAM	Bit rate (kb/s)	Complexity (MIPS)	Use	References
Time waveform	PCM	Toll	96	Very low	Common	14
	log PCM (G.711)	4.3 95 73	64	0.01	Common	14
	Wideband (G.722)	High	48–64		Some	195
	APCM/DPCM	Toll	58	Low	Some	14
	ADM/CVSD	Toll	40	Low	Common	73
	ADPCM (G.721)	4.1 94 68	32	2	Some	
	ADPCM (G.726)		16–40	2	Medium	207
	ADPCM-VQ	Communications	16	Medium	Research	26
	APC	Toll	16	High	Research	55
Spectral waveform	SBC	Communications	16	Medium	Some	130
	ATC	Toll	16	High	Research	130
	LD-CELP (G.728)	4--	16	30	Common	67
	RPE-LTP (GSM-FR)	3.5--	13	6	Some	117
	SBC-HS	Communications	9.6	Medium-high	Some	135
	ATC-HS	Toll	9.6	High	Some	137
	Harmonic	Communications	9.6	High	Research	72
Vocoder	VSELP (IS-54)	3.5--	7.95	14	Common	11
	VSELP (GSM-HR)	---	5.6	—	Common	191
	CS-ACELP (G.729)	4--	8	20	Common	204
	CS-ACELP (G.729A)		8	11	Common	203
	MBE-LP	Good	8	—	Some	199
	Multimedia (G.723.1)	3.5--	5.3–6.4	16	—	48
	GSTN visual telephony phase	Synthetic	7.2	High	Little	154
	STC	3.5 93 63	4.8	13	Rare	72
	CELP (FS 1016)	3.2 94 62	4.8	16	Common	189
	QCELP (IS-96)	Communications	0.8–8.5	—	—	222
	Cepstral	Synthetic	4.8	High	Little	161
	STC	3.2 91 56	2.4	13	Rare	246
	Channel	Synthetic	2.4	High	Common	156
	MELP	3.3-	2.4	20.43	—	220
	LPC-10e (FS 1015)	2.3 90 52	2.4	7	Common	190
	Formants	Synthetic	1.2	Very high	Research	165
	LPC-LSP	91	0.8	20	Research	214
	Phonetic	Synthetic	0.2	Very high	Research	168

SNR can be improved over the uniform PCM approach by using average statistics of speech amplitudes to design logarithmic quantizers (log PCM). Slowly varying speech amplitudes allow adaptive adjustment of the quantizer step size to match speech energy (APCM). Slowly changing speech spectra permit differential encoding, where a predictor estimates future speech samples based on previous ones (DPCM). The predictor itself can adapt in time to match the vocal tract frequency response as it changes from one phoneme to the next (ADPCM). In voiced speech, the quasi-periodicity of the signal allows further improvements (APC), either reducing bit rate or raising SNR.

Coders that utilize the speech spectrum directly were divided into waveform coders and vocoders. Fidelity of waveform and SNR are important measures for the former, whereas the latter maximize subjective speech quality at low bit rates. By passing speech through a bank of bandpass filters (SBC) or directly coding the speech spectrum (ATC), bits can be efficiently assigned to the most perceptually important frequencies, such as the harmonics during the first three formants. Indeed, these harmonics can be coded directly (TDHS), if the coder allows the added complexity of a pitch detector.

Vocoders accomplish dramatic bit rate reductions by exploiting the specific model of speech that separates excitation and vocal tract response. Virtually all waveform coders transmit data at the original sampling rate F_s, usually a residual error signal, but possibly spectral data as in ATC. Much of the bit rate primarily concerns the excitation, while the vocal tract spectrum can be efficiently represented in side information, as in ADPCM. Most vocoders lower bit rate and sacrifice speech quality by crudely coding excitation with only three parameters: a voiced/unvoiced bit, F0, and amplitude. The waveform coder's side information effectively becomes the vocoder's main bit stream.

Vector quantization serves to further lower bit rate by grouping blocks of speech or residual samples for simultaneous coding, rather than individual scalar coding. VQ is also useful in vocoders, especially CELP, where all spectral and prosodic parameters from each speech frame are coded as a group, to exploit interparameter redundancies. The chapter ends with a brief discussion of how communication networks can take advantage of certain speech properties and of the integrated circuits that are available for real-time coders.

PROBLEMS

P7.1. (a) In comparing a sub-band coder with a channel vocoder, describe what happens to output speech quality as the number of bands (or channels) is reduced, while keeping overall transmission bit rate constant for each system.

(b) Give a block diagram for the third channel in SBC, where the speech bandwidth of 4 kHz is handled with eight uniformly spaced channels. Show specifically all filtering and describe other mathematical operations necessary in both the transmitter and receiver. (Assume ideal filters are available.)

(c) In quantizing the signal in each channel, certain parameters of the sub-band coder are subject to adaptation in time, with either feedforward or feedback adaptation. What are the advantages of each approach?

P7.2. Noise which has a flat spectrum is usually added to a speech signal as a result of the quantization process.

(a) How can the output noise spectrum be modified, and what would be an ideal noise spectral shape?

(b) What adavantage does a delta modulation system have over standard DPCM in terms of output noise?

P7.3. "Time windowing" is a basic operation in speech analysis. Explain how windows are used in gain-adaptive PCM.

P7.4. In delta modulation systems, two types of noise appear in the output speech. Which is more serious, and why? Note specifically which portions of the spectrum are most affected by each type of noise.

P7.5. Consider the differences between waveform coders (e.g., PCM) and source coders (e.g., channel vocoder).
(a) Describe two techniques to lower bit rate using waveform coders, and note why the rate can be reduced without loss of output speech quality.
(b) Why is speech quality lower with source coders?
(c) How does vector quantization allow lower bit rates without quality loss?

P7.6. (a) How and why can fixed, nonuniform quantization help lower the transmission bit rate of speech (compared to uniform quantization)?
(b) How and why can the rate be lowered by using APCM and DPCM?

P7.7. In low-bit-rate vocoders (e.g., channel or formant vocoders), the tradeoffs include: the number of parameters to transmit, how often to transmit them, and how many bits to assign to each parameter.
(a) Explain the degradations that occur in output speech as each of these is reduced (i.e., fewer parameters, less often, or fewer bits per parameter).
(b) Give examples of reasonable values for each of these three factors. How many bits are used to code intensity and pitch?

P7.8. (a) Why is the predictor in a DPCM scheme often placed in a feedback loop around the quantizer?
(b) Why is a higher-order predictor often used in DPCM with an adaptive scheme than in one without time adaptation?
(c) What limits the utility of very-high-order prediction in speech coding?

P7.9. Speech is input to a digital filter bank vocoder where each filter has an ideal bandwidth of 100 Hz.
(a) Consider one such filter centered at 1050 Hz. At what sampling rate would the vocoder transmit this filter's output to the receiver?
(b) Explain what happens to the output speech (i) if we simply decrease the sampling rate uniformly for each of the filters' outputs; (ii) if we decrease the bandwidths of all the filters uniformly (keeping the center frequencies fixed).

P7.10. Consider a filter bank coding system with M equally spaced filters covering the speech bandwidth from 0 to 4 kHz. The unit-sample response of each bandpass filter is 200 samples in duration.
(a) Making reasonable assumptions about windowing (i.e., rectangular or Hamming windows can be assumed), find the number of filters M.
(b) What is the overall transmission rate in samples/s?

P7.11. (a) In a channel vocoder, what are the advantages and disadvantages of increasing the number of channels?
(b) What are the similarities and differences between channel vocoders and sub-band coders? Which gives better speech quality? What are typical transmission rates for each?
(c) In a sub-band coder with many bands, suppose the times of zero crossings for the signal in each band are calculated. How could one use this information to improve the coding method? How does the number of bands affect the usefulness of the zero crossings?

P7.12. Consider a waveform quantization system, with step size $d(n)$, input $x(n)$, and output $\hat{x}(n)$, where

$$\hat{x}(n) = \begin{cases} 3d(n)/2 & \text{for } d(n) \le x(n), \\ d(n)/2 & \text{for } 0 \le x(n) < d(n), \\ -d(n)/2 & \text{for } -d(n) \le x(n) < 0, \\ -3d(n)/2 & \text{for } x(n) < -d(n), \end{cases}$$

$$d(n) = \begin{cases} Bd(n-1) + D & \text{if } |x(m)| > d(m), \text{ for at least 2 of the 3 times:} \\ & m = n-1, n-2, n-3, \\ Bd(n-1) + E & \text{otherwise} \end{cases}$$

(i.e., D is used if, in two of the last three samples, the input exceeded the step size). Assume that $D > E > 0$, that $d(n) = 0$ for $n \le 0$, and that the sampling rate of $x(n)$ is 10,000 samples/s.
(a) What is the bit rate if this quantizer codes $x(n)$?
(b) Is it necessary to transmit the step size as well as a coded version of $\hat{x}(n)$ each sample instant?
(c) What is the maximum value that $d(n)$ could attain? What sequence of $x(n)$ would lead to such a $d(n)$?
(d) What is the minimum value that $d(n)$ could attain? What sequence of $x(n)$ would lead to such a $d(n)$?
(e) Assume now that $D = 6, E = 0, B = 0.8$ and $x(n) = 20[u(n-3) - u(n-12)]$, where $u(n)$ is the step function. Make a table of values of $x(n)$, $\hat{x}(n)$, and $d(n)$ for $0 \le n \le 23$.
(f) Which well-known system is similar to this waveform quantizer?

P7.13. LPC residual error:
(a) How does an LPC vocoder differ from an adaptive differential PCM (ADPCM) coder as a voice transmission system?
(b) What is the residual error in LPC?
(c) For what type of speech is the residual error large? Explain.
(d) Why is a residual-excited LPC coder considered both a source coder and a waveform coder?
(e) When the error signal is transmitted with limited bandwidth, which frequency range is sent? How is the full signal regenerated at the receiver?
(f) In most LPC systems, the error signal is not transmitted. How is the speech then generated at the receiver?
(g) Is minimizing residual error the best way to get LPC coefficients?

P7.14. For LPC speech:
(a) In spectral modeling of speech, what advantages does LPC have over channel vocoding?
(b) Are typical LPC windows longer or shorter when the analysis is done pitch-asynchronously or when the frames are aligned to pitch periods? Explain.
(c) Why do errors in F0 estimation have more serious effects on LPC synthetic speech than on speech coded by APC?
(d) Why does increasing bit rate in LPC not lead eventually to toll-quality speech?
(e) How can the basic excitation model in LPC be changed to improve quality? What are the costs of such changes?

P7.15. Give examples of some common alternative representations for the LPC coefficients. What advantages does one representation have over another? Compare these to line-spectral frequencies.

8

Speech Enhancement

8.1 INTRODUCTION

People use speech to communicate messages. When speaker and listener are near each other in a quiet environment, communication is generally easy and accurate. However, at a distance or in a noisy background, the listener's ability to understand suffers. Speech can also be sent electrically; the conversion media (microphone, loudspeaker, earphones), as well as the transmission media (telephone, radio), typically introduce distortions, yielding a noisy speech signal. Such degradation can lower the intelligibility and/or quality of speech. This chapter examines speech enhancement (SE), i.e., ways that a speech signal, subject to certain degradations (e.g., additive noise, interfering talkers, bandlimiting), can be processed to increase its intelligibility (the likelihood of being correctly understood) and/or its quality (naturalness and freedom from distortion, as well as ease for listening) (Figure 8.1).

Enhancement of degraded speech is useful in aircraft, mobile, military and commercial communication, and in aids for the handicapped. Applications include speech over noisy transmission channels (e.g., cellular telephony, pagers) and speech produced in noisy environments (e.g., in vehicles or telephone booths). The objectives of SE vary widely:

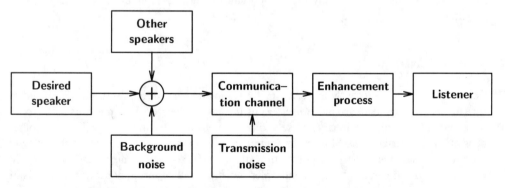

Figure 8.1 Block diagram noting common sources of speech degradation.

reduction of noise level, increased intelligibility, reduction of auditory fatigue, etc. For communication systems, two general objectives depend on the nature of the noise, and often on the signal-to-noise ratio (SNR) of the distorted speech. With medium-to-high SNR (e.g., > 5 dB), reducing the noise level can produce a subjectively natural speech signal at a receiver (e.g., over a telephone line) or can obtain reliable transmission (e.g., in a tandem vocoder application). For low SNR, the objective could be to decrease the noise level, while retaining or increasing the intelligibility and reducing the fatigue caused by heavy noise (e.g., motor or street noise).

The following are often important: (1) the need to detect intervals in a noisy signal where speech is absent (in order to estimate aspects of the noise alone), (2) the difficulty of enhancing weak, unvoiced speech, (3) the difficulty of reducing nonstationary interfering noise, (4) the frequent need to function in real-time, and (5) reducing computation. SE can be used to improve speech signals: (1) for human listening, (2) as a pre- or post-processor in speech coding systems, or (3) as a pre-processor for speech recognizers. The methods can vary depending on the application; for human listening, SE should aim for high quality as well as intelligibility, whereas quality (per se) is largely irrelevant if the enhanced speech serves as input to a recognizer. For coders or recognizers, speech could actually be "enhanced" in such a way as to sound worse, as long as the analysis process eventually yields a high-quality output; i.e., if the "enhanced" input allows more efficient parameter estimation in a coder (or higher accuracy in a recognizer), it serves its overall purpose [1]. For example, pre-emphasizing the speech (to balance relative amplitudes across frequency) in anticipation of broadband channel noise (which may distort many frequencies) does not enhance the speech as such, but allows easier noise removal later (via de-emphasis).

As with synthesizers or low-rate coders, SE often requires costly subjective tests to evaluate performance (i.e., neither quality nor intelligibility can be measured well mathematically), although measuring the effect of SE in recognition of noisy speech is much easier (see Chapter 10). Either objective measures or listening tests can help establish termination criteria in iterative SE methods, where the output speech is refined over several iterations, following a steepest gradient method.

Most SE techniques improve speech "quality" (naturalness and ease of listening) without increasing intelligibility; indeed, some reduce intelligibility [2]. SNR, as an easily computed objective measure of success, is often reported; it reflects quality, not intelligibility. There are many more applications for systems that increase intelligibility than for those that only improve quality. Aspects of quality are of course important in reproducing music and song, and high speech quality is a worthwhile general objective. However, when speech is subject to distortions, it is usually more important to render it intelligible than merely more pleasing.

8.2 BACKGROUND

Considerable research recently has examined ways to enhance speech [3,4], mostly related to speech distorted by background noise (occurring at the source or in transmission)—both wideband (and usually stationary) noise and (less often) narrowband noise, clicks, and other nonstationary interferences. Most cases assume noise whose pertinent features change slowly (i.e., locally stationary over analysis frames of interest), so that it can be characterized in terms of mean and variance (i.e., second-order statistics), either during nonspeech intervals of the input signal [5] or via a second microphone receiving little speech input.

Except when inputs from multiple microphones are available, it has been very difficult for SE systems to improve intelligibility. Thus most SE methods raise quality, while minimizing any loss in intelligibility. As Chapter 5 noted, certain aspects of speech are more perceptually important than others. The auditory system is more sensitive to the presence than absence of energy, and tends to ignore many aspects of phase. Thus speech coding and enhancement algorithms often focus on accurate modeling of peaks in the speech amplitude spectrum, rather than on phase relationships or on energy at weaker frequencies. Voiced speech, with its high amplitude and concentration of energy at low frequency, is more perceptually important than unvoiced speech for preserving quality. Hence, SE usually emphasizes improving the periodic portions of speech. Good representation of spectral amplitudes at harmonic frequencies and especially in the first three formant regions is paramount for high speech quality.

Weaker, unvoiced energy is important for intelligibility, but obstruents are often the first to be lost in noise and the most difficult to recover. Some perceptual studies claim that such sounds are less important than strong voiced sounds (e.g., replacing the former by noise of corresponding levels causes little decrease in intelligibility [6]). In general, however, for good intelligibility, sections of speech (both voiced and unvoiced) undergoing spectral transitions (which correspond to vocal tract movements) are very important.

SE often attempts to take advantage of knowledge beyond simple estimates of SNR in different frequency bands. Some systems combine SE and automatic speech recognition (ASR), and adapt the SE methods to the estimated phonetic segments produced by the ASR component. Since ASR of noisy speech is often less reliable, simpler ASR of broad phonetic classes is more robust, yet allows improved SE [7]. In certain applications (e.g., enhancing emergency calls and black-box recordings), estimates of the corresponding text (based on human listening) can assist SE [8]. Finally, SE is sometimes used to improve the speech of handicapped speakers [9].

8.3 NATURE OF INTERFERING SOUNDS

Different types of interference may need different suppression techniques. Noise may be continuous, impulsive, or periodic, and its amplitude may vary across frequency (occupying broad or narrow spectral ranges); e.g., background or transmission noise is often continuous and broadband (sometimes modeled as "white noise"—uncorrelated time samples, with a flat spectrum). Other distortions may be abrupt and strong, but of very brief duration (e.g., radio static, fading). Hum noise from machinery or from AC power lines may be continuous, but present only at a few frequencies. Noise which is not additive (e.g., multiplicative or convolutional) can be handled by applying a logarithmic transformation to the noisy signal, either in the time domain (for multiplicative noise) or in the frequency domain (for convolutional noise), which converts the distortion to an additive one (allowing basic SE methods to be applied).

Interfering speakers present a different problem for SE. When people hear several sound sources, they can often direct their attention to one specific source and perceptually exclude others. This "cocktail party effect" is facilitated by the stereo reception via a listener's two ears [10,11]. In binaural sound reception, the waves arriving at each ear are slightly different (e.g., in time delays and amplitudes); one can often localize the position of the source and attend to that source, suppressing perception of other sounds. (How the brain suppresses such interference, however, is poorly understood.) Monaural listening (e.g., via a telephone handset) has no directional cues, and the listener must rely on the desired sound source being stronger (or having major energy at different frequencies) than competing sources. When a desired source can be monitored by several microphones, techniques can exploit the distance between microphones [10,12]. However, most practical SE applications involve monaural listening, with input from one microphone. (Directional and head-mounted noise-cancelling microphones can often minimize the effects of echo and background noise.)

The speech of interfering speakers occupies the same overall frequency range as that of a desired speaker, but such voiced speech usually has F0 and harmonics at different frequencies (Figure 8.2). Thus some SE methods attempt to identify the strong frequencies either of the desired speaker or of the unwanted source, and to separate their spectral components to the extent that the components do not overlap. Interfering music has properties similar to speech, allowing the possibility of its suppression via similar methods (except that some musical chords have more than one F0, thus spreading energy to more frequencies than speech does).

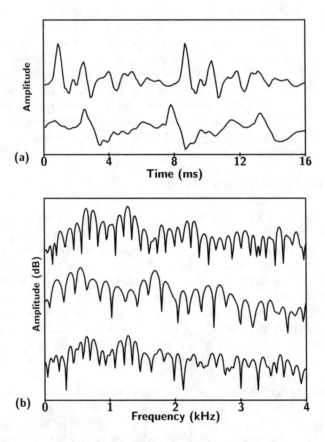

Figure 8.2 (a) Brief portions of voiced speech signals from a male speaker (top) and a female speaker (bottom); (b) corresponding amplitude spectra for the two signals and their sum. Note the simple harmonic structure of the first two spectra (with different fundamentals for the two speakers), compared to the third case where the two speakers interfere.

8.4 SPEECH ENHANCEMENT (SE) TECHNIQUES

There are four classes of SE methods, each with its own advantages and limitations: subtraction of interfering sounds, filtering out such sounds, suppression of nonharmonic frequencies, and resynthesis using a vocoder. The first and most popular method simply estimates either: (1) the important, speech-related components of the distorted input signal (and then retains them, eliminating other components), or (2) the corrupting portions of the signal (and then subtracts them from the input). The suppression of distortion components in the first two methods can be done in the time or frequency domain, and involve filtering or other forms of subtraction. The third method works only for voiced speech, requires an F0 estimate, and suppresses spectral energy between desired harmonics. (The assumption here is that major improvements for noisy speech signals are most feasible on strong periodic sounds, and that unvoiced speech is either irretrievably lost in many noisy environments or is too difficult to enhance.) The fourth method adopts a specific speech production model (e.g., from low-rate coding), and reconstructs a clean speech signal based on the model, using parameter estimates from the noisy speech.

8.4.1 Spectral Subtraction and Filtering

If an interfering sound can also be captured apart from the desired speech (i.e., in multi-microphone applications), the latter is usually enhanced by subtracting out a version of the former. Best results usually require a second microphone placed closer to the noise source than the primary microphone recording the desired speech. The second recording provides a noise reference, which after processing is subtracted from the primary recording.

In single-microphone applications, signal analysis during pauses can furnish an *estimate* of the noise; then an adaptive filter modeling that noise, updated (if feasible) at detected pauses, can suppress the noise (especially periodic noise) [13]. This latter approach usually employs an average spectral model of the noise, and gives much less enhancement than a two-microphone method, because it can only identify the spectral distribution of the noise and not its time variation. Frequencies where noise energy is high can be suppressed in the signal, but this distorts the desired speech at these frequencies. Furthermore, the one-microphone subtraction method is of little use for variable noise, since it assumes that noise during a pause is representative of noise during ensuing speech.

8.4.2 Harmonic Filtering

The harmonic SE method attempts to identify the F0 (and hence harmonics) either of the desired speech or of interfering sources. If the desired sound is the strongest component in the signal, its frequencies can be identified and other frequencies may then be suppressed; otherwise a strong interfering sound's frequencies can be identified and suppressed, with the remaining frequencies presumably retaining some of the desired speech source. Such simple Wiener filtering (suppressing wideband noise between harmonics) improves SNR but has little effect on intelligibility.

8.4.3 Parametric Resynthesis

The last SE method improves speech signals by parametric estimation and speech resynthesis. Speech synthesizers generate noise-free speech from parametric representations of either a vocal tract model or previously analyzed speech. Most synthesizers employ separate representations for vocal tract shape and excitation information, coding the former with about 10 spectral parameters (modeling the equivalent of formant frequencies and bandwidths) and coding the latter with estimates of intensity and periodicity (e.g., F0). Standard methods (e.g., LPC) do not replicate the spectral envelope precisely, but usually preserve enough information to yield good output speech. Such synthesis suffers from the same mechanical quality as found in low-rate speech coding and from degraded parameter estimation (due to the noise), but can be free of direct noise interference, if the parameters model the original speech accurately.

8.5 SPECTRAL SUBTRACTION (SS)

One common and intuitive SE method is applicable to speech with (at least locally) stationary noise. It transforms both a primary signal (the noisy speech $p(n)$) and an estimate of the interference $i(n)$ into Fourier transforms $P(\omega)$ and $I(\omega)$, respectively. Their magnitudes are subtracted, yielding

$$|P(\omega)| - \alpha|I(\omega)|, \qquad (8.1)$$

which is then combined with the original phase of $P(\omega)$, and transformed back into a time signal; the *noise overestimation factor* $\alpha \geq 1$ (typically $\alpha = 1.5$) helps minimize some distortion effects [14] (Figure 8.3). Any negative values in Equation (8.1) are reset to zero, on the assumption that such noisy frequencies cannot be recovered. This basic spectral subtraction (which is linear, except for the floor of zero amplitude) corresponds to maximum likelihood (ML) estimation of the noisy speech signal [15].

In cases of negative signal-to-noise ratio (SNR) (i.e., more energy in the interference than in the desired speech), this method works well for both general noise [16] and interfering speakers [17], although *musical tone* or noise artifacts often occur at frame boundaries in such reconstructed speech. The tones are due to the random appearance of narrowband residual noises at frequencies where the SS method yields a negative spectral amplitude (and the algorithm thus arbitrarily assigns a zero output). Much effort has gone toward reducing the annoying effect of these extraneous tones in the otherwise simple and effective SS technique (e.g., raising α (or allowing it to vary in time or frequency) [18], putting a floor on the filter and smoothing over frequency [19, 20]). Time smoothing helps, but introduces echoes. SS generally reduces noise power (improving quality), but often reduces intelligibility (especially

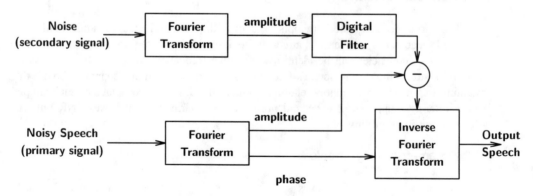

Figure 8.3 Spectral subtraction when two microphones are available.

in low SNR situations), due to suppression of weak portions of speech (e.g., high-frequency formants and unvoiced speech).

There are many variants of the basic SS method [21], often replacing Equation (8.1) with $||P(\omega)|^{\alpha} - |I(\omega)|^{\alpha}|^{1/\alpha}$. Basic SS uses $\alpha = 1$, and power spectral subtraction uses $\alpha = 2$. An advantage of the latter is that time-domain methods involving autocorrelation signals are feasible. Sometimes, the first component in Equation (8.1) (the noisy speech spectrum) is replaced by an average over a few frames (which reinforces the consistent speech components, especially harmonics, at the expense of random noise components); this smooths out speech transitions, however, leading to slurring effects. In all cases, the output phase is that of the input noisy speech, since experiments with other "cleaned" phase estimates have yielded little perceptual improvement [16].

8.6 FILTERING AND ADAPTIVE NOISE CANCELLATION

8.6.1 Filtering

Suppressing unwanted aspects of a distorted speech signal depends largely on either characterizing those undesired components or modeling the desired speech components. Such modeling is often done spectrally, e.g., estimating the spectral amplitude of a section of the noisy input signal which is estimated to be free of speech (and then subtracting this noise spectrum from the whole signal). This requires a *voice-activity detector* to reliably detect speech in a noisy signal, which is increasingly difficult at lower SNR. It also assumes that the noise characteristics stay roughly the same until the next pause (the noise statistics are then re-estimated). (Some recent methods avoid this requirement [22].)

A similar SE method uses orthogonalization to reduce each frame of speech to a small set of parameters, which allows suppression of most dimensions as largely noise components. For example, the KLT (see Chapter 6) characterizes speech efficiently; for a vowel, in a signal vector of high dimension (e.g., a frame of 100 samples), only a few basis signals corresponding to the damped sinusoids of formants will have large eigenvalues. Using a subspace projection onto those dimensions eliminates most noise components in other dimensions, and masking will help reduce the perceptual effect of the remaining noise components. The disadvantage of such a method is the cost of the KLT [23].

The SE methods in this section are mostly variants of classical Wiener filtering, where a simple filter for the noisy speech is designed spectrally via the estimated ratio of the energy in the clean speech to that of the noisy speech. The amount of noise suppression is sometimes controlled by a factor λ ($\lambda = 1$ in the classical case, yielding a linear filter, which is optimal in minimizing mean-square energy). (Thus, spectral subtraction follows maximum likelihood, while Wiener filters use a minimum mean-square-error (MMSE) criterion.) Given a vector **s** of noisy spectral samples, the kth component of the filtered output (i.e., the enhanced speech) is:

$$\hat{s}_k = \frac{P_{sk}}{P_{sk} + \lambda P_{nk}} s_k,$$

where P_{sk} is the kth parameter of the mean power spectrum of **s**, and P_{nk} corresponds to the estimated power spectrum of the noise. (As in SS, phase is not enhanced.) Thus, at any given frequency, if the noise is estimated to be relatively weak, the filter has little effect; however, if the noise dominates, s_k is heavily attenuated. This spectrally varying attenuation accommodates nonwhite noise, and can be updated at any desired frame rate to handle nonstationary noise. A major problem with this approach is estimating P_{nk}, which often needs portions of the input signal estimated not to contain speech.

A Wiener filter with an adjustable input noise level appears optimal for SE [23]. One way is to decompose noisy speech into two subspaces via KLT (using an eigendecomposition of the covariance matrix of the input speech), and do linear estimation after the noise subspace is eliminated. However, the KLT is more costly than the DFT commonly used in SS.

For speech under stationary noise, one successful SE method uses an HMM (see Chapter 10) of clean speech (before the noise degradation) and one of the noise alone (again usually based on analysis of the noisy speech signal at times estimated not to contain speech). The Viterbi path from HMM speech recognition specifies a Wiener filter for each state [24]. This approach can use LPC models [25], filter-bank spectra [26] or cepstra [27].

While Wiener filtering and SS are the most common filtering methods, Kalman filtering has also been used for SE [28], especially when faced with colored noise [29]. Recently, H_∞ filtering has been shown to overcome some of the inappropriate assumptions of the Wiener and Kalman methods (e.g., that the statistics of speech and noise are known in advance) [30].

8.6.2 Multi-Microphone Adaptive Noise Cancellation (ANC)

When more than one microphone is available to furnish pertinent signals, speech degraded by many types of noise can be handled. A processed version of a second "reference" signal $r(n)$ (containing mostly or exclusively interference noise) is directly subtracted in time from the primary noisy speech signal $p(n)$. This ANC method relies on the microphones being sufficiently apart or on having an acoustic barrier between them [31–33]. (ANC is related to, but not the same as, *active noise cancellation*, where noise is fed back acoustically into a limited environment (e.g., a cockpit), to physically cancel the noise waves [34].) For audioconference applications, the ANC method can be extended to an array of microphones (mounted at a convenient location in a room), which electronically focuses on one voice at a time via *beamforming* [35, 36]; in this case, a larger number of microphones limits the need for isolating the desired speech source from other sounds.

While other SE filtering methods get good results with a dynamic filter that adapts over time to estimated changes in the distortion, such adaptation is essential in ANC. Since there will be a delay (perhaps variable) between the times the interference reaches different microphones and since the microphones may pick up different versions of the noise (e.g., the noise at the primary microphone may be subject to echoes and/or spectrally variable attenuation), a secondary signal must be filtered so that it closely resembles the noise present in the primary signal. The ANC method is less successful when the secondary signal contains speech components from the primary source, or when there are several or distributed sources [37]; its performance depends on locations of sound sources and microphones, reverberation, and filter length and updating [38]. ANC does best when the microphones are separated enough so that no speech appears in secondary signals, but close enough so that the noise affecting the main signal is also strong in the secondary signals.

ANC closely resembles echo cancellation in long-distance telephone links. At the hybrid-transformer interface between a two-wire telephone line (local subscriber loop) and a long-distance four-wire trunk line, a version of the original speech is often fed back to the handsets at variable amounts of delay, both near-end echo of very short delay (back to the original speaker), and far-end echo (either to the speaker or listener) (where the delays depend on the length of the four-wire line, or its equivalent in radio links) [39, 40]. For the talker, short delays of a few ms with reasonable attenuation (e.g., 6 dB) are no problem (these correspond to typical small-room echoes, or to the "sideline" found in telephone handsets), but delays over 40 ms can interfere with speech production unless the echo is largely attenuated. For the listener, short delays are annoying; e.g., a 1 ms echo causes nulls in the received speech spectrum every 1 kHz (see Section 8.7).

Both echo cancellation and SE in two-microphone situations involve subtracting out attenuated, delayed versions of one signal from another. There are several ways to obtain the filter coefficients, of which the most attractive is the least-mean-squares (LMS) method via steepest descent [32], due to its simplicity and accuracy (Figure 8.4). More computationally expensive exact least-squares (LS) methods typically yield only marginal gains over the faster stochastic-gradient LMS method; the latter is also useful for enhancement of one-microphone speech degraded by additive noise [41, 42]. In addition to removing noise from degraded speech, the LMS method has been applied to reducing the presence in a signal of an interfering speaker with some success [43].

Filter coefficients are chosen so that the energy in the difference or residual error signal $e(n)$ (i.e., the primary signal $p(n)$ minus a filtered version $v(n)$ of the reference $r(n)$) is minimized. Thus, one selects coefficients $h(k)$ so that the energy in

$$e(n) = p(n) - v(n) = p(n) - \sum_{k=1}^{L} h(k)r(n-k) \qquad (8.2)$$

is minimized; $p(n)$ is the sum of the desired speech signal $s(n)$ and a transformed version of $r(n)$ (or where $p(n)$ is a signal with echo (containing both desired speech $s(n)$ from the far end, plus undesired echo $r(n)$ from the near end) to be processed and $v(n)$ is a filtered version of $r(n)$ (i.e., $r(n)$ is the 4-wire input and $e(n)$ is the output)). As long as the two microphone signals ($r(n)$ and $p(n)$) are uncorrelated, minimizing $e^2(n)$ (a "least mean squares" approach) over time should yield a filter that models the transformed reference, which can thus be subtracted from $p(n)$ to provide enhanced speech, which is actually the minimized residual $e(n)$. Correlation between $r(n)$ and $p(n)$ is undesirable because then the $h(k)$ values are

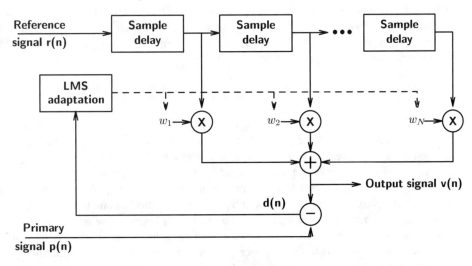

Figure 8.4 Adaptive filtering where the filter coefficients w_i are updated to minimize the least mean square of the difference (error) signal.

affected by the speech and $v(n)$ will partly contain speech rather than only transformed noise, and part of the desired speech will be suppressed. If a correlation does exist, the filter coefficients $h(k)$ should only be updated during pauses in $s(n)$. Solving Equation (8.2) can exploit LS or LPC methods, or simpler LMS techniques which do not require calculating correlation matrices or inverting them. The latter uses a steepest-gradient iteration [44].

Below are details of the two basic methods. The LS approach minimizes the energy in the residual signal $e(n)$. While $e(n)$ contains both the desired (far-end) speech and the echo noise, minimizing its energy is appropriate for choosing the coefficients $h(n)$ of the filter, because the input $r(n)$ to the filter contains none of the speech desired at the output. The FIR filter coefficient vector $\mathbf{h}_n$ (i.e., $h(0)$, $h(1)$, $h(2), \ldots h(L-1)$ (assuming L taps)) is updated with each sample in time n as:

$$\mathbf{h}_{n+1} = \mathbf{h}_n + a\mathbf{r}_n e(n),$$

where the reference signal is $\mathbf{r}_n = [r(n),\ r(n-1),\ r(n-2), \ldots r(n-L+1)]^T$.

In the LS method, the error is attenuated by an exponentially decreasing weight, to fade out the effects of older data and to simplify computation:

$$D(n) = \sum_{k=-\infty}^{n} e^2(k)w(n-k),$$

where weights could be $w(n) = (1-\lambda)^n$, λ controlling the rate of convergence. Taking $\partial D(n)/\partial h(n) = 0$ yields

$$h(n+1) = h(n) + \lambda R^{-1}(n)r(n)e(n) \qquad (8.3)$$

etc. The LS method converges quickly for any input, but needs costly matrix inversion (although fast Kalman methods can simplify this approach) and is sensitive to numerical error accumulation.

The alternative LMS method uses a steepest descent technique to get

$$h_i(n+1) = h_i(n) + 2\mu e(n)r(n-i),$$

where a large value for μ speeds up convergence, but may lead to stability problems. It is much simpler than the LS method (the main difference lies in replacing the covariance matrix R of Equation (8.3) with a simple scalar parameter μ). A modified version with better stability is often used, but may need a pre-whitening filter for fast convergence when faced with nonwhite input such as speech [40]:

$$h_i(n+1) = h_i(n) + ae(n)r(n-i)/\left(\sum_{k=0}^{N-1} r^2(n-k)\right),$$

with control factor $0 < a < 2$.

The order L of the filter is usually a function of the separation of the two sound sources as well as of any offset delay in synchronization between the two (or, equivalently, a function of the echo delay in telephony). In many cases, delays of 10–60 ms lead to fewer than 500 taps (at 8000 samples/s), and an LMS algorithm is feasible on a single chip. Unless the delay is directly estimated, L must be large enough to account for the maximum possible delay, which may lead to as many as 1500 taps when the two microphones are separated by a few meters [45] (or even exceeding 4000 taps in cases of acoustic echo cancellation in rooms). Such long filter responses can lead to convergence problems as well as to reverberation in the output speech [46]. The echo can be minimized by reducing the adaptation step size (a in Equation (8.4), which changes the filter coefficients each iteration), at the cost of increased settling time for the filter. For large delays, versions of ANC operating in the frequency domain may be more efficient [47], e.g., sub-band systems [40].

ANC works for full-duplex data modems (as in CCITT V.32), although the far-end echo can be very long if satellite links occur, thus requiring an echo canceller for each type of echo. One difference between data and speech signals is that small distortions are more tolerable with speech. The use of a linear ANC filter is adequate for speech, even though some distortions (e.g., in A–D and D–A conversions) may be better modeled nonlinearly (which leads to much more complex filters).

In many practical environments where ANC might be useful for hearing aid design, the existence of echo and multiple noise sources significantly reduces the theoretical gains of ANC; e.g., while ANC can completely cancel one noise source in an anechoic situation (and the human binaural system or directional microphones give about 12 dB gains), gains of only 2–3 dB in SNR often occur in practice [48]. A recent nonreal-time system exploiting models of auditory modulation processing reported small increases in intelligibility with a two-channel *modulation spectrogram* [48]. In two-microphone cases where significant crosstalk reduces ANC's utility, a Wiener filtering approach with auditory constraints may be effective [49].

Removal of room reverberation follows similar techniques to those for telephone-line echo, although the former type of echo can be much more variable. Where multiple microphones are available, beamforming methods work well [50, 51]. In teleconferencing applications, stereo sound can give a more realistic presence, but requires more complex echo cancellation [52, 53].

8.7 METHODS INVOLVING FUNDAMENTAL FREQUENCY TRACKING

When a major component of the audio signal to be enhanced is periodic, its harmonic frequencies may be identified for the purposes of either preservation or suppression. *Comb filtering* is a basic method where a dynamic filter is designed to sift or "comb" through the spectrum, modifying energy at equally spaced frequencies: attenuating harmonics (to reject an undesired periodic signal) or amplifying them (to enhance a desired periodic signal) (Figure 8.5) [3]. The frequency response of the filter resembles a comb, i.e., with large values at a specified F0 and its multiples, and low values between these harmonics. The filter is usually implemented in the time domain as

$$y(n) = \sum_{k=-M}^{M} h(k)x(n - kL),$$

(8.5)

where L is the fundamental period (in samples), M is a small number (1, 2, 3), $x(n)$ is the input, and $y(n)$ is the output. The coefficients $h(k)$ are positive and typically vary inversely with $|k|$; they may also vary with the degree of periodicity of the signal being measured (e.g., in cases where the signal is estimated to be unvoiced, comb filtering has no use; setting $h(k) = 0$ (except $h(0) = 1$) causes the filter to have no effect).

$y(n)$ is simply an average of delayed and weighted versions of $x(n)$. If the delay L corresponds to the period of a major component in $x(n)$, then the averaging operation reinforces that component and tends to cancel out other components (those having no period, or a period different from the major component). In this manner, interfering sounds are suppressed. The operation depends crucially on an accurate estimate of the desired signal's period, and its performance is best when this signal is stationary (i.e., its period and spectrum

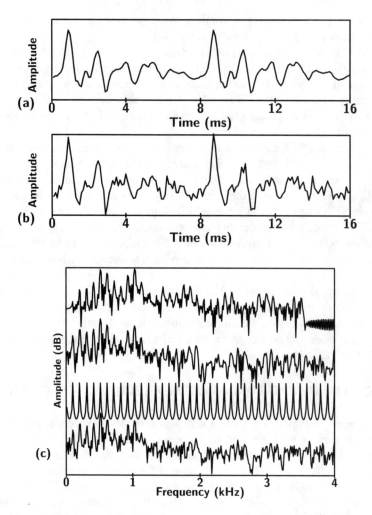

Figure 8.5 (a) Two periods of a typical voiced speech signal; (b) the same signal after adding white noise; (c) amplitude spectra (from top to bottom): of plot (a), of the comb-filtered output speech, of the comb filter, and of plot (b).

not changing over $2LM$ samples). Unfortunately, F0 estimation can be difficult and speech signals can change rapidly, both in harmonics and in spectral envelope. In the case of a spectral change (but constant F0) during the comb filter's window, the filter spreads out the change over the duration of the window; thus a rapid change (e.g., the release of a stop consonant) could be smeared out in time.

A more difficult problem arises when F0 changes during the course of the window [54]. If the durations of successive periods are known, Equation (8.5) can be modified to be

$$y(n) = \sum_{k=-M}^{M} h(k)x(n - kL + C_k), \qquad (8.6)$$

where the C_k are adjustments to properly align periods. In general, however, simplicity would keep $C_k = 0$, and the reinforcement of periods in $y(n)$ may be severely reduced. Thus, most comb filters work best only during sections of speech where F0 is not changing rapidly. This problem can be minimized by choosing $M = 1$ in Equation (8.5) (i.e., averaging only 3 periods); however, the degree of signal reinforcement (thus, SE) is proportional to M. Spectrally, M is inversely proportional to the bandwidth of the comb harmonics. Larger values of M lead to narrow harmonics in the comb filter response, which more effectively suppress energy outside the corresponding harmonics in $x(n)$, but which also smooth desired abrupt phonetic changes more over time.

Instead of direct comb filtering in the time domain, the speech could be Fourier transformed, and harmonically spaced strong frequency components then identified. The spectral components at such frequencies can be extracted, and an inverse Fourier transform can yield enhanced speech [55].

Comb filtering can suppress a wide range of types of noise, but has often been used to suppress an interfering voice [56]. In one experiment, the intelligibility of words in a weak voice under interference of a stronger voice (SNR $= -12$ dB) was raised from 54% to 63% [57]; at -6 dB SNR, the improvement was from 78% to 82%, and comb filtering gave little improvement at positive SNRs. Of course, improvement is most needed at low SNR; intelligibility degrades rapidly below 0 dB SNR [58].

A major problem for comb filtering speech of multiple voices is that tracking one speaker's fundamental in the presence of another is difficult. Speech reconstruction based only on the harmonics of a target speaker which do not overlap those of an interfering speaker leaves too many spectral gaps. One method separates the overlapping harmonics of two speakers by exploiting the shape of harmonic peaks when voicing is both present and mostly uniform over a time window [59]. It works well when speech is voiced, but fails for normal conversation which switches often between voiced and unvoiced speech.

A related F0-based SE method is simple "cut-and-splice" time expansion, where individual pitch periods are duplicated (as in TDHS—see Chapter 7). This is usually done for time expansion/compression (for speech rate modifications), but since listeners often find slowed-down speech more intelligible, it can be viewed as an SE method [60].

An SE method related to comb filtering uses a *dual excitation model*, where a voicing decision separates noisy speech into periodic and aperiodic components, allowing different enhancement techniques (weak harmonic suppression in the voiced portions; standard filtering techniques for the unvoiced parts) [2]. It requires a pitch detector, but claims to reduce slurring and tonal artifacts found in many other SE filtering methods [61]. Another recent method combines MMSE estimation and HMMs with a sinusoidal approach (but without comb filtering) in a way to avoid some difficulties of F0 estimation and also handle nonstationary noise [62]. Such techniques normally do not suffer from the musical tones of SS speech, and can better suppress residual noise between harmonics (especially when widely spaced, as in female voices).

8.8 ENHANCEMENT BY RESYNTHESIS

In some SE cases, low-rate speech coding methods (e.g., LPC) can be directly applied. In the typical low-dimensional production model, speech is assumed to come from passing an excitation signal with a flat spectrum through an all-pole vocal tract model filter, and to have a z-transform response

$$S(z) = G/\left(1 - \sum_{k=1}^{p} a_k z^{-k}\right), \tag{8.7}$$

where G is a gain factor and the LPC (spectral) coefficients a_k are directly related to the pole locations (which are a function primarily of formant frequencies and bandwidths), with $p \approx 10$–12. LPC works best when the coefficients are estimated from noise-free speech, and the system tends to degrade badly on noisy speech [63]. Non-causal Wiener filtering based on the LPC all-pole model attempts to solve for the ML estimate of speech in additive noise; it tends to output speech with overly narrow bandwidths and large frame-to-frame fluctuations (since Wiener filtering treats each frame separately). However, spectral constraints based on redundancies in the human speech production process and on aspects of perception can overcome this flaw and raise speech quality [64, 65], as well as accelerate convergence in iterative Wiener filtering [66].

The LPC synthesis filter (Equation (8.7) is usually excited by either a periodic (typically impulsive) source or a noise source, depending on whether the analyzed speech is estimated to be voiced or not. Speech quality improves if some aspects of phase are preserved in the voiced excitation, rather than being discarded (as is often done in LPC). Phase can be retained by direct modeling of both the amplitude and phase of the original speech harmonics, or by modeling a version of the inverse-filtered speech. The use of direct harmonic modeling in LPC resynthesis of speech degraded by an interfering speaker has not been successful in raising intelligibility, although "quality" may be increased [67]. In general, resynthesis is the least common of the SE techniques, due to the difficulty of estimating model parameters from distorted speech and due to the inherent flaws in most speech models (see Chapter 9 for a discussion of model-based synthesis). It nonetheless has application in certain cases (e.g., improving the speech of some handicapped speakers [68]). Related SE methods can remove impulsive noise (often found in telephony and with analog storage) as well as stationary noise, without degrading speech quality [69].

8.9 SUMMARY

Most SE methods claim to reduce noise or other interfering sounds in a speech signal, thus improving speech quality. However, single-microphone systems rarely succeed in raising the intelligibility of words in the degraded speech signal. Speech intelligibility is a complicated function of many aspects of the speech signal; some aspects (e.g., voicing, pitch, loudness) are robust to interference and likely are in less need of SE techniques, while others (e.g., phonemic place of articulation; rapid spectral transitions at some phoneme boundaries) may be brief or have weak energy and thus be difficult to recover in noisy conditions. SE works best when an interfering sound is sufficiently strong to mask the perception of some key speech aspects, yet can be correctly identified both in time and in frequency to facilitate its removal. Stationary interference is relatively easy to remove, but time-varying interference causes great problems, unless a separate reference is available to permit monitoring the dynamics of the interference.

Significant advances in SE will likely await better understanding of human speech perception and production. The basic SE methods (spectral subtraction, Wiener filtering, comb filtering, resynthesis) have existed for decades. They are largely based on simple ideas such as masking (e.g., suppressing noise at frequencies where the speech harmonics are weak) or on simple speech production models (which lead to cleaner speech, but of still poor quality). Multi-microphone SE using the ANC method performs well where conditions are appropriate (proper separation between microphones, and simple noise sources). Recent system improvements have largely occurred in terms of efficiency (e.g., real-time; faster convergence; less computation).

9

Speech Synthesis

9.1 INTRODUCTION

Text-to-speech synthesis (TTS) is the automatic generation of a speech signal, starting from a normal textual input and using previously analyzed digital speech data [1–6]. Before special-purpose DSP (digital signal processing) chips were introduced in 1978, synthetic speech was generated primarily on large computers, sometimes interfaced with an analog vocal tract model. Such synthesizers have since become widely available for several languages, in forms ranging from inexpensive packages for personal computers to standalone systems. The former produce mostly intelligible (but often highly unnatural) speech, while the latter can yield very intelligible (but still unnatural) speech. We are far from having synthetic speech which listeners cannot distinguish from human speech. Of course, natural speech output is possible if the desired vocabulary is very limited, and the system merely concatenates lengthy stored speech units (i.e., outputs a sequence of previously spoken words or phrases, stored in memory as coded speech). We distinguish here true TTS systems which accept any input text in the chosen language (including new words and typographical errors) versus *voice response systems* of very limited vocabulary, which are essentially voice coders of much simpler complexity, but also inflexible and very limited in applications. The recent increase of commercial synthesizers is due to both advances in computer technology and improvements in the methodology of speech synthesis. This chapter discusses technical aspects of synthetic speech devices, as well as their applications and limitations, and notes where improvements are needed.

The critical issues for current synthesizers concern trade-offs among the conflicting demands of maximizing speech quality, while minimizing memory space, algorithmic complexity, and computational speed. While simple TTS is possible in real time with low-cost hardware, there is a trend toward using more complex programs (tens of thousands of lines of code; megabytes of storage). Special DSP chips are necessary for use with slower computers (under 10 million instructions/s) or for applications that require several output channels. TTS systems constructively synthesize speech from text using linguistic processing and concatenating small speech units (e.g., phonemes). Real-time TTS produces speech that is generally intelligible, but lacks naturalness. Quality inferior to that of human speech is usually due to inadequate modeling of three aspects of human speech production: coarticulation, intonation, and vocal tract excitation.

Most synthesizers reproduce speech either for ranges of 300–3000 Hz (e.g., for telephone applications) or 100–5000 Hz (for higher quality). Omitting frequencies above 3 kHz still allows good vowel perception since vowels are adequately specified by formants F1–F3. The perception of some consonants, however, is slightly impaired if energy in the 3–5 kHz range is omitted. Frequencies above 5 kHz are useful to improve speech clarity and naturalness, but do little to aid speech intelligibility. If we assume that the synthesizer reproduces speech up to 4 kHz, a rate of 8000 samples/s is needed. Since linear PCM requires 12 b/sample for toll-quality speech, storage rates near 100 kb/s result, which are prohibitive except for synthesizers with very small vocabularies.

The memory requirement for a simple synthesizer is often proportional to its vocabulary size. As memory costs continue to decrease with advances in computer technology, it is less imperative to minimize memory than complexity. Nonetheless, storing all possible speech waveforms (even with efficient coding) for synthesis purposes is impractical for TTS. The sacrifices usually made to reduce complexity and memory for large-vocabulary synthesizers involve simplistic modeling of spectral dynamics, vocal tract excitation, and intonation. Such modeling yields quality limitations that are the primary problems for current TTS research.

9.2 PRINCIPLES OF SPEECH SYNTHESIS

Speech synthesis involves the conversion of an input text (consisting of sentences or simply words) into speech waveforms, using algorithms and some form of previously coded speech data. The text might be entered by keyboard or optical character recognition or obtained from a stored database (Figure 9.1). Speech synthesizers can be characterized by the size of the speech units they concatenate to yield the output speech, as well as by the method used to code, store, and synthesize the speech. Using large speech units (e.g., phrases and sentences) can give high-quality output speech but requires much memory. Efficient coding methods reduce memory needs but often degrade speech quality.

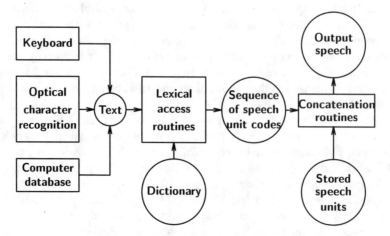

Figure 9.1 Block diagram of the steps in speech synthesis.

Speech synthesizers are available commercially for two different applications, which affect the choices of speech unit size and method of synthesis. Voice-response systems handle input text of limited vocabulary and syntax, while TTS systems accept all input text. TTS systems construct speech from text using small stored speech units and extensive linguistic processing, while voice-response systems reproduce speech directly from large units of coded speech, using signal processing techniques primarily. Voice-response systems are basically speech coders that store their bit streams in computer memory for later playback through a decoder when synthetic speech is needed.

9.2.1 Types of Stored Speech Units to Concatenate

The simplest synthesis concatenates stored phrases (groups of one or more words). This approach can yield high-quality speech but is limited by the need to store in (read-only) memory all the phrases to be synthesized, after they have been spoken either in isolation or in context sentences. For the most natural-sounding synthetic speech, each phrase must originally be pronounced with timing and intonation appropriate for all sentences in which it could be used. Thus if a word could occur in several syntactic contexts, its pronunciation should be recorded and stored using sentences simulating the various contexts. Merely concatenating words originally spoken in isolation usually leads to lower intelligibility and naturalness. The duration and other aspects of stored units must be adjusted during concatenation since such unit features vary in sentential context (especially for units of words or smaller).

For synthesis of unrestricted text, advanced systems generate speech from sequences of basic sounds, which can substantially reduce memory requirements since most languages have only 30–40 phonemes. However, the spectral features of these short concatenated sounds (50–200 ms) must at least be smoothed at their boundaries to avoid jumpy, discontinuous speech. The problem is that the pronunciation of a phoneme in a phrase is heavily dependent on its phonetic context (e.g., on neighboring phonemes, intonation, and speaking rate) via coarticulation. The smoothing and adjustment process, as well as the need to calculate an appropriate intonation for each context, results in complex synthesizers with less natural output speech.

While commercial synthesizers have been primarily based on word or phone concatenation, other possibilities link intermediate-sized units of stored speech such as syllables [7], demisyllables [8, 9], diphones [10, 11], or even subphonemic units [12]. A *syllable* consists of a nucleus (either a vowel or diphthong) plus optional neighboring consonants (sometimes the syllable boundary is uncertain, as in *nesting*, where a linguistic decomposition suggests *nest-ing*, but pronunciation is often *nes-ting*; see Section 3.3). *Demisyllables* are speech units obtained by dividing syllables in half, with the cut in the middle of the vowel, where the effects of coarticulation are minimal (as opposed to the often rapid transitions at phone boundaries) (Figure 9.2). *Diphones* are obtained by dividing a speech waveform into phone-sized units, with a cut in the middle of each phone (thus preserving in each diphone the transition between adjacent phones). When demisyllables or diphones are concatenated in proper sequence (so that spectra on both sides of a boundary match), smooth speech usually results because the adjoining sounds at the boundaries are spectrally similar. For example, to synthesize the word *straight*, the six-diphone sequence /#s-st-tr-re-et-t#/ or two-demisyllable sequence /#stre-et#/ would be used (# denotes silence).

Smoothing of spectral parameters at the boundaries between units is most important for short units (e.g., phones) and decreases in importance as concatenation units increase in size,

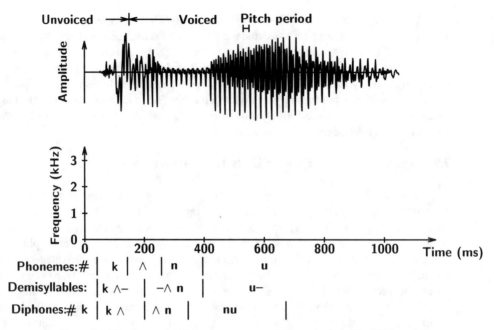

Figure 9.2 Waveform and wideband spectrogram of the word *canoe*. The division of the
word into phones, demisyllables, and diphones is noted.

because of the decrease in frequency of boundaries in the synthesized speech. Smoothing is much simpler when the joined units approximately match spectra at the boundaries. Since diphone boundaries interface spectra from similar sections of two realizations of the same phoneme, their smoothing rules are simple. Systems that link phones, however, must use complex smoothing rules to represent coarticulation in the vocal tract. Not enough is understood about coarticulation to establish a complete set of rules to describe how the spectral parameters for each phone are modified by its neighbors. Diphone synthesizers try to circumvent this problem by storing the parameter transitions from one phone to the next since coarticulation primarily influences the immediately adjacent phones. However, coarticulation often extends over several phones; using only average diphones or those from a neutral context leads to lower-quality synthetic speech [13]. Improved quality is possible by using multiple diphones dependent on context, effectively storing "triphones" of longer duration (which may substantially increase memory requirements); e.g., in the word *strew*, rounded lips necessary for the /u/ cause anticipatory rounding during the preceding three consonants /s/, /t/, and /r/. Some coarticulation effects can be approximated by simple rules, e.g., lowering all resonant frequencies during lip rounding, but others such as the undershoot of phoneme target positions (which occurs in virtually all speech) are much harder to model accurately.

   For concatenative synthesizers employing hundreds or thousands of speech units, it is efficient to have automatic methods of extracting such units from natural speech [14, 15]. Unlike speech recognition, where automatic segmentation of the speech signal into reliable and pertinent units is difficult, TTS often has access to the text of training utterances, and can align the text well with the speech automatically (e.g., boundaries to within 20–30 ms) [16] to locate the desired units. Nonetheless, proper choice of which units to record can be crucial to TTS quality [17].

The modifications needed in concatenating speech units for synthesis are very similar to those found in time expansion/compression, in applications wishing to slow down or accelerate utterances. Such speech-rate modifications are often as simple as "cut-and-splice" methods, where individual pitch periods are duplicated or deleted periodically. For more natural-sounding time- and pitch-scale modifications, more elaborate methods using DFTs or sine-wave models can be employed [18, 19].

9.2.2 Memory Size

A synthesizer consists of (a) a memory storage of speech parameters, obtained from natural speech and organized in terms of speech units, and (b) a program of rules to concatenate these units, smoothing the parameters to create time trajectories where necessary. While it is difficult to quantify program or calculation complexity for different synthesis approaches, the amount of memory needed for the speech units is simpler to determine. The following inventory estimates assume an English TTS system [20]. Since English has more phonemes than most languages and has a wide range of possible syllable structures, the memory required for TTS in other languages is likely to be less. English has 22 consonants and 15 vowels/diphthongs; storing *phone* units would thus require at least 37 parameter vectors (the diphthongs would actually need more than one vector each to describe their transient behavior). Each vector would typically include a spectral representation of the vocal tract (e.g., LPC coefficients, or formants and their bandwidths) and excitation information (amplitude(s) for voicing, aspiration, voiced-unvoiced, etc.). Assuming each vector has 10–20 elements, several hundred stored parameters would suffice to generate all speech. However, such stored vectors represent only target parameter values, derived from pronunciation in isolation or in a neutral context. Phone-concatenation synthesis trades off minimal storage for a complex program to interpolate the target vectors to simulate natural coarticulation.

A way to improve the quality of phone-concatenated speech is to store and use a larger set of context-dependent phones. Such *allophone* synthesis follows phone synthesis methods except that it employs up to perhaps 250 stored variants of phones to reduce the complexity of the interpolation algorithm by trading off increased memory for less program space. (Some recent approaches extend the definition of context to include prosody, thus increasing the number of allophones into the thousands.) The allophones incorporate directly some of the complex phonetic variation and coarticulation due to context which phone synthesis must model explicitly in its smoothing program. The allophones differ according to phonetic context; e.g., /k/ might be represented by two allophones, one corresponding to its pronunciation before a front vowel, the other before a back vowel (*key* vs *coo*) [21, 22]. Allophone synthesis usually represents a compromise between phoneme and diphone synthesis; they concatenate short speech units without yielding jumpy speech, while using a small inventory of units.

Theoretically, English needs $38 \times 38 = 1444$ *diphones* (all pairwise combinations of the 37 phonemes and silence), but some combinations are not used (e.g., /h/+ a consonant). Substantial further reduction is possible by exploiting the symmetry of spectral patterns in many diphones (except for diphones containing stop bursts); e.g., patterns for /ia/ and /ai/ are close to mirror images of each other. Each diphone representation needs at least two vectors, for the two phonemic states at the start and end of the diphone, but many require 3–5 vectors to accurately model the parametric trajectories. Whenever a diphone contains a spectral discontinuity (e.g., at voiced–unvoiced boundaries), simple interpolation of two terminal vectors cannot adequately describe the parametric behavior during the diphone. About 1400–

3000 diphone vectors are needed to generate high-quality synthetic speech in English, French, or German [23]. Diphone synthesis requires more memory and is less flexible in varying speaking rate or speaker style than rule-based synthesis, but tends to yield more natural spectral patterns.

There are more *demisyllables* in English than diphones. Theoretically, each of about 100 initial-consonant clusters could combine with 15 syllabic nuclei (vowels and diphthongs) to yield 1500 initial demisyllables, while about 200 final clusters would generate 3000 final demisyllables. A very large English vocabulary, however, can be produced from fewer than 2000 demisyllables. Unlike diphones, with demisyllables there is a risk that words (e.g., proper names) will be encountered for synthesis for which the corresponding demisyllables did not occur in training (diphone training is often done for all possible legal words, whereas demisyllables are drawn from actual dictionaries, to reduce memory). Since demisyllables consist of 0.5–4.5 phones (half of the syllable's vowel plus up to four adjacent consonants), more vectors must be stored (per speech unit) for demisyllables than for a diphone memory. Perhaps 6000–7000 vectors might be necessary for basic demisyllable synthesis. A more practical system might strip certain consonants from the larger demisyllables for separate storage (e.g., the final /s/ in demisyllables with consonant clusters ending in /s/), assuming that certain consonant sequences tolerate phone concatenation better than sequences involving vowels [7]. Coarticulation needs more modeling precision near the syllabic nuclei than at the ends of the syllable because vowels are more important for high-quality synthesis; e.g., a basic German demisyllable inventory needs about 5400 elements, but exploiting differences in coarticulation importance allowed one system to function well with 1650 elements [9].

If we treat *syllables* as the units of concatenation, about 4400 are sufficient to describe virtually all English words, while the most frequent 1370 syllables are used 93% of the time [20]. If all English words are included, perhaps 20,000 syllables can be found [24]. Assuming 4000 syllables and about six vectors/syllable, on the order of 25,000 vectors would be needed for large-vocabulary syllable synthesis. A method storing all syllables would be tedious for a speaker to utter and require about 10 Mb using a complex waveform technique (e.g., ADPCM) or about 2 Mb using parametric methods (e.g., LPC).

Finally, English has well over 300,000 *words*, although only 50,000 can be considered common [25] (and most people only use about 5000 [6]). These words can be generated more efficiently using about 12,000 *morphemes*, the basic meaningful elements that make up words [3]; e.g., the word *antidisestablishmentarianism* consists of the root morpheme *establish* plus two prefix and four suffix morphemes. Perhaps 80,000 vectors would be needed for a morpheme memory, whereas a word memory could exceed one million entries. Limited-vocabulary synthesizers that concatenate syllables or words would reduce the memory figures above, according to the size of their vocabularies. If the speech unit is smaller than a syllable, however, little memory savings are gained by limiting vocabulary; e.g., 2000 diphones can generate many thousands of words, but a much smaller vocabulary of 1000 words would still require 1000 demisyllables or diphones.

While most synthesizers use concatenative speech units of uniform size, a recent trend uses units of longer length where appropriate [26]. A German synthesizer uses 1086 initial demisyllables, 577 final demisyllables, 88 obstruent suffixes, 234 diphones (across syllable boundaries) and 197 syllables (to handle monosyllabic function words better) [27]. A nonuniform unit selection scheme could automatically choose speech units using objective measures such as a contextual spectral difference, a prototypicality of each segment for its context, the spectral gap between adjacent phonemes, and local spectral discontinuity [28]. At one extreme, we could store more than 100,000 phone units, from many different phonetic contexts, but the uncompressed memory for the spoken speech in one such case was 360 Mbytes [29]. With such large-database synthesis, significant computation is needed to locate the appropriate units for concatenation, to match the desired prosodics needed in the textual context [14].

For large-memory TTS, a serious issue is speaker fatigue, since each speaker whose voice is simulated must utter all speech units as uniformly as possible. Speakers usually find this very arduous for more than a few thousand short phrases at a time, and the longer the time span of recording, the more likely nonuniformity is present. After concatenation, uneven units lead to rough-sounding speech.

9.2.3 Synthesis Method

Synthesizers are classified both by speech unit size and by how they parameterize the speech for storage and synthesis. Very-high-quality synthetic speech requires waveform coders and large memories. More efficient but lower-quality systems use vocoders. Vocoder synthesizers are considered *terminal-analog synthesizers* because they model the speech output of the vocal tract without explicitly accounting for articulator movements. A third way to generate speech is by *articulatory synthesis*, which represents vocal tract shapes directly, using data derived from X-ray or CT analysis of speech production [30–32]. Due to the difficulty of obtaining accurate three-dimensional vocal tract representations and of modeling the system with a small set of parameters, this last method has yielded lower-quality speech and has not had commercial application.

The choice of synthesis method is influenced by the size of the vocabulary. Because they must model all possible utterances, unlimited-text systems are generally more complex and yield lower-quality speech than voice-response systems. Until recently, waveform methods have been used only with small vocabularies (e.g., a few minutes of speech). Advances in memory technology are increasing the vocabulary of low-cost waveform synthesizers, but for greater flexibility, parametric methods are necessary.

Parametric synthesis normally produces only synthetic-quality speech because of inadequate modeling of natural speech production. Unlimited-text parametric synthesizers use small speech units (e.g., phones or diphones) since speech quality does not increase sufficiently with larger units to justify the much larger memory needed. Coding each of about 1200 diphones in English with 2–3 frames of parameters requires storage of about 200 kb. More common are phone synthesizers, which normally store one or two sets of amplitude and spectral parameters for each of the 37 phonemes in as few as 2 kb.

9.2.4 Limited-Text (Voice-Response) Systems

Much synthetic speech (e.g., automatic announcements over the telephone) comes from systems that encode speech (e.g., with an efficient storage method such as LPC) and play back the speech with simple concatenation. The output is limited to combinations of the speech units, usually with their original intonations. This is adequate for many applications such as speaking toys, warning systems, and automatic telephone directory assistance. However, if a standard voice and vocabulary are insufficient for a given application, the synthesis manufacturer must process speech spoken by a user to establish a custom vocabulary. While parts of the analysis procedure are automatic (e.g., the basic LPC algorithm), major additional memory savings come only through human interaction: listening to synthetic speech for sections that can tolerate a more efficient representation than others without perceptual degradation and modifying speech parameters in places where imperfect automatic processing leads to poor synthetic speech. Such manual *ad hoc* processing, which is not possible in real-time vocoders, can give very compact representations.

9.2.5 Unrestricted-Text (TTS) Systems

A significant task for synthesizers that accept general text is the need for a linguistic processor to convert the text into a form suitable for accessing and concatenating the stored speech units (see Figure 9.1). Such processing involves: (1) translating the input sentences into a sequence of linguistic codes to fetch the appropriate stored units, then (2) determining intonation parameters from the text, to vary F0 and duration properly [6]. The first problem can often be handled by a set of language-dependent rules for converting a sequence of letters into one of phonemes [33, 34]. These *letter-to-phoneme* rules (also called letter-to-sound rules) examine the context of each letter to determine how it is pronounced; e.g., the letter *p* in English is pronounced /p/, except before the letter *h* (e.g., *telephone*). English is a Germanic language but has borrowed heavily from Romance languages and needs hundreds of such rules to correctly translate 90% of the words in unlimited text situations [35]. Many frequently used words (e.g., *of, the*) violate basic pronunciation rules and require a list of exceptions. For complex languages such as English, TTS often uses a dictionary or *lexicon* for simple, direct look-up of most pronunciations, with rules as a back-up procedure to handle new words (since even lexicons with many tens of thousands of words cannot anticipate all possible words to synthesize).

Languages where spelling follows phonetics more closely (e.g., Spanish) can be modeled with very few rules since each letter has normally only one pronunciation [36]. Letter-to-phoneme rules developed manually for many languages are capable of very high precision, especially when combined with a dictionary to handle exceptional cases. Errors in phonetic transcription with such advanced systems are almost always due to proper nouns (e.g., names) or foreign words [37, 38]. Such words are often capitalized (or italicized) and may obey nonEnglish letter-to-phoneme rules. They can be analyzed for letter sequences unlikely in English words; then a small set of pronunciation rules (based on an estimate of the identity of the foreign language) could be applied to these words [39, 40].

Letter-to-phoneme rule sets produced via neural networks have been much less successful than rule sets developed by hand [5]. Neural nets have found greater success in speech recognition, where the number of possible utterances and acoustic variation is vast, compared to the number of words in a language (i.e., despite the thousands of words found in most languages, it is still easier and more accurate to develop transcription rules manually than to rely on broad automatic statistical methods).

The pronunciation rules used in the MITalk synthesizer (one of the first complete TTS systems) [3, 41] are preceded by a word decomposition algorithm, which tries to strip prefixes and suffixes from each word. Since there are only a few dozen such affixes in English, and since they can affect pronunciation (e.g., the third vowel in *algebra* vs *algebraic*), the decomposition procedure increases the power of the system at the expense of extra computation. MITalk also has a dictionary of morphemes (the basic lexical units that constitute words), which contains not only phoneme pronunciations but also syntactic "parts of speech." Such syntactic information from a word or morpheme dictionary, combined with a parser to determine linguistic structures in the input text, allows specification of intonation by rule, locating F0 and duration effects to simulate natural intonation. Many synthesizers forgo parsers and large dictionaries as too complex, and rely on simplistic intonation rules or leave F0 for the user to specify directly (e.g., using special symbols inserted manually in the input text). Poor handling of intonation is a major reason why much unlimited text synthesis sounds unnatural [42].

Much of the computation necessary for TTS can be viewed as modular [43], i.e., a series of passes through the text, in which each pass transforms its input into a string of output parameters; e.g., a first pass converts abbreviations, digit sequences, and special punctuation symbols (e.g., $, %, &) into words. This "preprocessor" addresses cases such as "$3.40"→ "three dollars and forty cents," "St. Mark St."→"Saint Mark Street," and "1998"→"nineteen ninety-eight." A second pass would typically output a string of phonemes, punctuation, and word boundaries, with perhaps parts of speech indicated for some or all words. A system such as MITalk also indicates morpheme boundaries for decomposed words. A third pass assigns durations and F0 to each phoneme, using primarily punctuation and syntactic information to estimate an appropriate intonation. Finally, a fourth pass determines the parameter trajectories for the vocal tract model.

Most of the processing in these passes involves applying context-sensitive rules of the *if-then* type, where variables are assigned or modified only if certain phonetic or linguistic conditions are met. Since the conditions can often be expressed in terms of phonetic features, efficient specialized computer languages have been developed. Rule-based systems using these languages can facilitate the linguistic processing of translating an input text into synthesizer parameters [8, 44, 45]. The rules are commonly expressed in the form

$$A \rightarrow B \quad [C \quad \_\_ \quad D],$$

which reads as '*A* is transformed into *B*, if the current input string matches *A* in the sequence *C–A–D*.' For letter-to-phoneme rules, *C–A–D* could be a series of text letters and/or symbols, while *B* could consist of phonemes or phonetic codes; for later stages of synthesis, *A* ... *D* could contain feature information. When many rules have common elements for left context *C* or right context *D*, classes of elements could be defined to simplify the rules and reduce their number; e.g., the English rule for final *s* voicing could be expressed as

$$s \rightarrow /\text{s}/ \quad [\text{U} - \#] \quad (\text{e.g., cats, chiefs})$$
$$s \rightarrow /\text{Iz}/ \quad [\text{F} - \#] \quad (\text{e.g., cashes, buzzes})$$
$$s \rightarrow /\text{z}/ \quad [\text{V} - \#] \quad (\text{e.g., dogs, pies}),$$

where # is a word boundary and three phoneme classes are described by *U*, *F*, and *V*. *U* represents the unvoiced obstruents /f,θ,p,t,k/ and *F* the strident fricatives /s,$\int$,z,$\mathbf{3}$/, while *V* has the remaining voiced phonemes. If the rules are ordered, the third rule need not have a left context test since the union of the three left contexts is the universal set.

Most TTS applications allow any text input and thus require general linguistic processing, which is unnecessary in voice-response systems. Certain interactive human–machine applications, however, may permit an intermediate class of synthesis. In *synthesis from concept*, the synthesizer's input is a concept, not a text [46], that is transformed into words using a limited vocabulary and a restricted syntax. Intonation patterns can be specified in advance in terms of the permitted set of syntactic structures. Phonemic pronunciation and parts of speech are stored in the vocabulary lexicon. In essence, synthesis from concept is a flexible voice-response system that can be useful for interrogating databases. Normally, database information is stored in textual form, but in cases where the information is not simple text but rather involves tables or structures, speech output usually requires a conversion to text before applying a TTS system. If the database uses a restricted vocabulary, the process can be simplified and higher-quality speech obtained by designing a synthesis-from-concept synthesizer to match the database. Instead of converting database information to text, it is transformed into a "concept" suitable to the system. To adapt to other databases, the system's vocabulary and the permitted syntactic output structures would have to be modified.

9.3 SYNTHESIZER METHODS

This section discusses in detail how different synthesis methods function. The four main techniques of articulatory, formant, LPC and waveform synthesis are explained. Two subsections deal with the specification and updating of parameters for these systems. Finally, the problems of generating a natural excitation source, including intonation, are discussed.

9.3.1 Articulatory Synthesis (‡)

Although speech generation via modeling of vocal tract movements has been less successful than terminal-analog synthesis, articulatory synthesis (AS) is discussed first since it is simpler in concept, if not in implementation. In addition, articulatory models are useful to study the physics of speech production. Directly modeling articulatory motion avoids some of the complexities of acoustic–phonetics: acoustic cues for various sounds are complicated functions of phonemic information, speaking rate, prosodics, etc. Coarticulation effects, in particular, must be specified by rule in terminal-analog systems, but follow more directly in AS. AS may be divided into three classes, distinguished by the level at which they receive input in the speech production process: *neuromotor command, articulator*, and *vocal tract shape* [47].

To speak, a person thinks of a message and sends commands to the vocal tract muscles, which cause articulators to move, changing the shape of the vocal tract. The most basic AS transforms an input phoneme sequence into a set of neuromotor muscle commands, following a model based on data from electromyographic studies [48]. It also needs a model relating muscle commands to articulator motion and an algorithm to convert the set of articulator positions into vocal tract shapes or *area functions* (sets of cross-sectional areas A_m (for $m = 1, \ldots, N$) for N short sections constituting the vocal tract) (Figure 9.3a). A sequence of such area functions in time $A_m(n)$ could specify a time-varying lattice filter whose reflection coefficients are determined by the ratios of adjacent areas. Alternatively, formant frequencies and bandwidths could be derived from A_m for use in a formant synthesizer [49].

While neuromotor synthesis is the most theoretically pleasing approach, in that phonemes relate directly to muscle commands, it is also the most complex to implement. Commands for a speech gesture (e.g., tongue-tip raising) tend to be similar across different phonemes that use the same gesture, but the relationships between commands and gestures are complex. A synthesizer that directly maps phonemes into articulator positions and motions avoids this step but must explicitly account for vocal tract behavior that might more easily be described at the muscle level. Since experimental data are more widely available for articulatory movement than for muscle commands, there have been more attempts at articulator synthesis than neuromotor synthesis. Typical systems assume that 7–11 parameters can adequately describe articulatory behavior (Figure 9.4): e.g., one parameter for velum opening, one each for lip protrusion and closure, and two each for the tongue body and tip (each having both vertical and horizontal degrees of freedom) [47, 49]. Other suggested parameters are jaw height, pharynx width, and larynx height [51, 52].

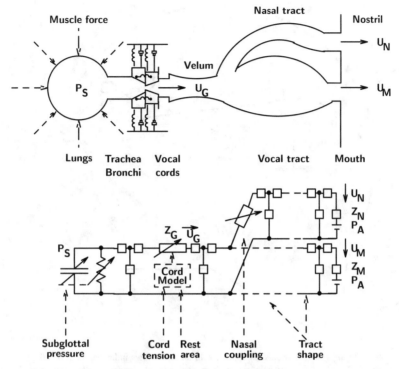

Figure 9.3 An articulatory synthesizer. (a) Schematic diagram of the vocal tract, including a coupled two-mass vocal cord model. Subglottal pressure P_s and volume velocities U are indicated, as well as the glottal waveform of period T. (b) Network representation of the system, with time-varying input parameters indicated. (After Flanagan and Ishizaka [50] © IEEE.)

Target values for these parameters are stored for each phoneme, and the actual time sequence of parameter values is obtained by interpolating between the targets, using coarticulation constraints and different time constants for the various articulators (Figure 9.5); e.g., the small, flexible tongue tip is allowed fast movement, whereas the jaw moves more slowly. Each phoneme can be viewed as having both crucial and unimportant target parameters, where the crucial ones are more resistant to coarticulation; e.g., in producing /p/, lip and velum closures are crucial, while the tongue configuration has little importance.

The model for articulator motion usually is derived from X-ray data of the vocal tract during simple utterances. However, most X-rays show only two dimensions of the three-dimensional vocal tract, and little data are available due to the danger of X-ray exposure. In addition, the actual vocal tract shape is only roughly approximated by the simplified model using 7–11 parameters. Synthetic speech from AS, based on generalizations from limited data, yields lower-quality speech than does terminal-analog synthesis.

Another approach to AS concerns vocal-tract-shape systems, where phonemes are represented by area functions rather than articulator positions. This approach obviates the need to model articulator behavior, but it loses the efficiency of the more compact articulator model (since more than 11 cross-sectional areas are typically used) and it also forfeits an easy description of coarticulation (since the concept of crucial and unimportant parameters is less easily expressed in terms of a set of area values). Coarticulation rules are less precise for vocal

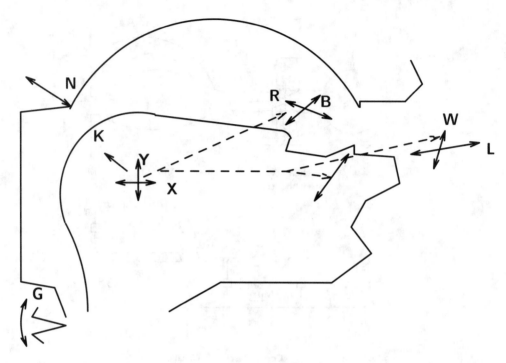

Figure 9.4 An articulatory model, with labeled arrows indicating controllable degrees of freedom and dashed lines showing relationships among parameters. (After Coker *et al.* [53] © IEEE.)

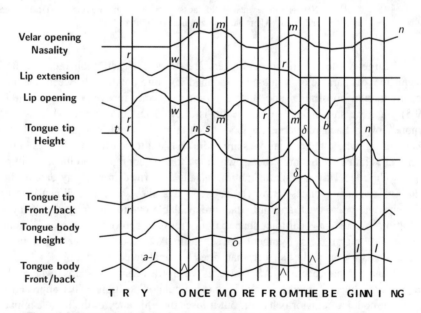

Figure 9.5 Parameter trajectories for the model of Figure 9.4 for the utterance "Try once more from the beginning." Critical points in each contour are labeled with the phonemes causing the relevant articulation. (After Flanagan *et al.* [54] © IEEE.)

tract shapes than for articulators, e.g., an unstressed vowel might use a target shape intermediate between its stressed shape and that of a schwa vowel. Phonemes that involve rapid transitions (e.g., obstruents or nasals) might be assigned linear transitions between target shapes, while slower motion might be exponential in time to reflect gradual articulator movement. One system uses parameter trajectories that follow the first half-period of a cosine wave ($\cos(\pi t/T)$, $0 \le t \le T$, where T is the transition duration) to go from one phoneme's target to the next [51].

One advantage of AS is that vocal tract area models allow accurate modeling of transients due to abrupt area changes, as well as automatically generating turbulence excitation for narrow constrictions, where aerodynamic conditions warrant. In such synthesis, one can observe pressure waves up and down the vocal tract in the time domain, whereas terminal-analog synthesizers model only spectral behavior. Recent research has explored using neural nets for articulatory synthesis [55].

9.3.2 Formant Synthesis

Many synthesizers (both commercial and research) employ formant synthesizers, using a model similar to that shown in Figure 9.6. The system in Figure 9.7 shows a specific implementation that forms the basis of two advanced synthesizers, of cascade and parallel structures. The excitation is generally a periodic train of impulses (for voiced speech), pseudo-random noise (for unvoiced speech), or periodically shaped noise (for voiced fricatives). The vocal tract is usually modeled as a cascade of second-order digital resonators, each representing either a formant or the spectral shape of the excitation source. (Higher-order filters require more bits per coefficient for the same spectral accuracy [56], so second-order filters are computationally efficient and provide good physical models for individual formants.) The cascade filter structure approximates the speech spectrum well for vowels and can be controlled with one amplitude parameter. Advanced synthesizers allow the lowest four formant frequencies and three corresponding bandwidths to vary as a function of time (variation in higher formants has little perceptual effect); e.g., the Klatt synthesizer [57] has 19 control parameters that vary from frame to frame, and the GLOVE synthesizer uses 37 [58]. Simpler systems sacrifice speech quality, varying only F1–F3, with all bandwidths fixed; e.g., one system keeps bandwidths for F1, F2, and F3 at 60, 100, and 120 Hz, respectively,

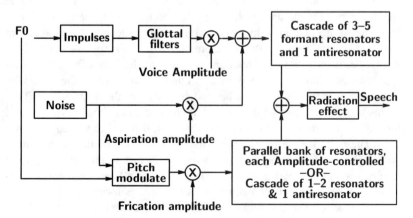

Figure 9.6 Simplified block diagram of a formant synthesizer.

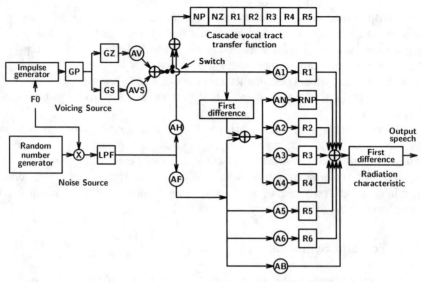

Figure 9.7 Block diagram of a cascade-parallel formant synthesizer. Digital resonators are indicated by the prefix R and amplitude controls by the prefix A. Each resonator R_n has associated resonant frequency and bandwidth control parameters. (After Klatt [57].)

except during nasals where F1's bandwidth increases to 150 Hz [59]. Lack of time variation in the bandwidths yields a degradation that is most noticeable in nasal sounds. Recent research has examined how to control formant synthesis parameters efficiently, primarily for excitation (e.g., parameters to control glottal and constriction areas, and the efficiency of turbulence noise generation) [60, 61].

9.3.2.1 *Simulation of frication* (‡).

Given a vocal tract model providing the envelope of a desired speech spectrum, to simulate natural speech, the noise excitation for unvoiced sounds should have a flat spectrum, and its amplitude distribution should be roughly Gaussian. The output of a pseudo-random number generator has a flat spectrum but a uniform amplitude distribution. Summing several (e.g., 16) of these random numbers approximates a Gaussian (following the central limit theorem of probability, adding independent identical random variables) [57]. Since the signals in most formant synthesizers represent volume velocity, the noise pressure source for fricatives must be converted, which involves estimating the vocal tract impedance at the location of the noise source. A reasonable approximation integrates the pressure signal (most valid at the lips, where the radiation impedance is inductive) and can be modeled by a simple lowpass filter. The -6 dB/oct skirt of this filter cancels the $+6$ dB/oct radiation effect at the lips, leaving a net flat spectral trend for unvoiced sounds, unlike the -6 dB net falloff found in voiced sounds.

The noise source for unvoiced sounds within the mouth cavity excites the vocal tract primarily between the source and the lips. With this shortened acoustic tube, most speech energy is at higher frequency than for the vowels, e.g., very little energy is present in F1–F2. Simulation of obstruents sometimes uses a simple pole-zero network to model the variable cutoff frequency for the highpass frication noise [58]; alternatively, a parallel bank of resonators suffices, so that each filter resonance is individually controlled for amplitude

(Figure 9.7). Recently, use of an inverse-filtered speech waveform as excitation for consonants has increased quality [62]. Hybrid formant/waveform synthesis appears to yield better transitions between voiced and unvoiced sounds [63].

9.3.2.2 Parallel synthesizers.

A parallel bank of filters may be used to generate both vowels and consonants (Figure 9.8), but, compared with the cascade approach, parallel synthesis requires calculation of each formant amplitude as well as an extra amplitude multiplication per formant in the synthesizer [64]. Special attention must be given to modeling the frequency region below F1 in an all-parallel approach because listeners are sensitive to the considerable energy present there in natural speech and because varying formant positions normally changes the gain below F1 in parallel synthesis. An advantage of an all-parallel method is a simpler synthesizer structure, since only one set of resonators suffices for all sounds. Switching between signal paths in the cascade-parallel approach (which occurs at boundaries involving obstruents and vowels) sometimes leads to the perception of separate sound streams; i.e., the output may resemble hissing noises super-imposed on the main voice stream of vowels and sonorants, rather than an integrated single voice [65]. High-quality simulations of singing voices and musical instruments have also been demonstrated using parallel synthesis [66]. Adding the outputs of parallel branches can introduce unwanted spectral zeros and phase effects into the synthetic speech, but recent research has alleviated some of these problems [67]. Whenever formants are added in parallel, they should alternate in sign, i.e., $A1 - A2 + A3 - A4\ldots$, to account for $180°$ phase shifts in the vocal tract transfer function at each formant frequency.

To simulate voiced frication, many formant synthesizers excite a parallel set of resonators with a noise source modulated by a waveform with period 1/F0. While such a noise excitation corresponds well to the pulsating airflow through the oral tract constriction, a simpler mix of periodic and noise excitation suffices perceptually [68]. Typically, F1 has clear harmonic structure in voiced frication, while formants above F2–F3 are fully unvoiced.

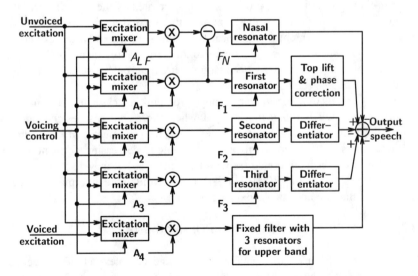

Figure 9.8 Block diagram of an all-parallel formant synthesizer. Variable center frequencies F_i, amplitudes A_i, and voicing mix are specified for each resonator. (After Holmes [64].).

Providing each formant in a parallel synthesizer with its own control for mixing periodic and noise excitation is one approach [64]. Alternatively in cascade-parallel synthesis, noise (perhaps periodically modulated) can excite a parallel set of resonators, while a lowpass-filtered version of the normal glottal signal excites a cascade set of resonators [57].

9.3.2.3 Simulation of nasals (‡). Synthesis of nasals usually requires one more resonator than for vowels because the acoustic path including the nasal cavity is longer than the oral vocal tract, which increases the number of resonances in the speech bandwidth. Frequency spacing between formants decreases about 15%, i.e., one extra formant in a 5 kHz bandwidth. To model the spectral zeros that occur in nasals, a second-order antiresonator is often used for the zero having the lowest frequency (higher-frequency zeros have less perceptual importance). (Obstruents, on the other hand, have more numerous low-frequency zeros due to the large side branch of the vocal tract below the noise source. These zeros are more efficiently modeled via parallel synthesis, where variations in the amplitudes and bandwidths of the resonators can simulate the effects of the zeros.) For efficient implementation of nasals in a cascade synthesizer, the extra resonator and antiresonator can be considered as a complex-conjugate pole-zero pair with equal bandwidths, whose effects cancel except when nasals are to be simulated. A pair could be located at a fixed low value (e.g., 270 Hz), so that F1 combines with the nasal formant and antiformant to yield a broadened-bandwidth region of low-frequency energy typical of nasals [57], although better quality results with two such pairs. In an all-parallel synthesizer, the extra nasal formant is treated like other formants, except that it is excited only during nasals.

9.3.2.4 Implementation aspects (‡). In synthesis implementations using fixed-point arithmetic, e.g., in synthesizer chips and most microprocessors, quantization noise can be a significant problem. When the dynamic range of waveforms varies at different points in the synthesizer, which is especially true in the cascade approach since formant bandwidths are variable, signal levels must be adjusted between filters to fully utilize the available bits in each register. Since dynamic range problems are exacerbated by the -12 dB/oct falloff for voiced glottal waveforms, many synthesizers use the second derivative of the desired glottal waveform instead as input to the vocal tract filters. In this way, the excitation spectrum is relatively flat, which reduces dynamic range. Instead of applying a $+6$ dB/oct radiation effect after the vocal tract filters, an equalization causes the output spectrum to have the desired -6 dB/oct trend.

Another way to reduce dynamic range problems in a cascade of resonators is to position the widest-bandwidth filters first so that when the signal reaches the filters with narrow bandwidths (and hence widest gain range), it has been attenuated at the resonant frequencies of these last filters. A common ordering employs decreasing formant frequencies since formant bandwidths tend to increase with frequency [69]. It may also be desirable to interlace the resonators (e.g., R4, R2, R5, R3, R1) to avoid large intermediate spectral gains at frequencies that are near two proximate formants.

9.3.3 Linear Predictive Coding (LPC) Synthesis

To avoid the need to manually develop the complex set of coarticulation rules for formant synthesis, the automatic method of LPC synthesis has become popular [28, 70]. It has a simpler structure than formant synthesis because all spectral properties of speech (except intensity and periodicity) are included in the LPC coefficients, which are calculated automatically in the analysis of natural speech. A lattice filter is often used for synthesis because the filter coefficients can be linearly interpolated between frames without yielding an unstable filter. The excitation is specified by a gain parameter, a voiced–unvoiced bit, and (if voiced) an F0 value. For simplicity, most LPC systems do not allow mixed excitation for voiced fricatives.

The choice between formant and LPC synthesis is governed by tradeoffs. LPC has a simpler and fully automatic analysis procedure and a simpler synthesis structure than the formant approach. On the other hand, our understanding of formant behavior facilitates parameter interpolation at segment boundaries in formant synthesis, whereas interpolation of LPC reflection coefficients is usually limited because each coefficient affects a wide range of speech frequencies in a complex fashion (LSFs, being related to formants, are easier to interpolate). In addition, formant synthesis is more flexible in allowing simple transformations to simulate several voices. Shifting formant frequencies in formant synthesis can easily alter speaker-related aspects of voice, whereas the LPC reflection coefficients have to be converted into pole locations to allow such modification. Because spectral valleys are modeled more poorly than peaks in LPC analysis, formant bandwidths are often improperly estimated, whereas direct (albeit difficult) bandwidth determination from DFT spectra in the formant approach can yield better estimates. The all-pole assumption of standard LPC leads to less accurate spectral estimation for nasal sounds than for other phones, whereas antiresonators in formant synthesis permit direct modeling of the most important spectral zeros in nasals. In large measure, the LPC vs formant choice trades off the simple, automatic analysis of LPC against the higher speech quality possible with more complex formant synthesis.

9.3.4 Specifying Parameter Trajectories (‡)

Many synthesizers can generate high-quality speech if appropriate input parameters are supplied. Signals indistinguishable from natural human speech can be produced with parallel formant synthesizers that allow time variation of F1–F3 and their bandwidths and that permit mixed excitation for unvoiced fricatives. Parallel-cascade synthesizers can do the same if a nasal antiresonator is included with the formant resonators. With the possible exception of nasals and voiced fricatives, conventional LPC synthesizers can likely also generate such natural speech. The major difficulty in all cases, however, is that such high-quality speech has not been possible automatically by rule, but only semi-automatically if algorithmically selected parameters are modified frame by frame to match human speech patterns ("synthesis by art") [71]. Synthesis models are oversimplified in general, and smoothed parameter tracks obtained from speech analysis (or by rule) must be adjusted to closely match natural speech. The frame-by-frame parameter values that lead to the best speech often exhibit seemingly random discontinuities that are difficult to predict by rule.

The challenge in synthesis research is to accurately model the parameter variations found in natural speech so that they can be generated by rule from an input text. The basic approach in phonemic formant synthesis has been to store target parameters for each phoneme and to interpolate parameter trajectories between target sets simulating coarticulation effects [72]. To avoid contextual effects, the targets for continuant phonemes such as vowels and fricatives are often based on data from isolated utterances of individual phonemes (see tables II and III in [57]). Transient phonemes (e.g., plosives) require adjacent phonemes, and their targets can be derived from utterances with neutral adjacent phonemes (e.g., schwa vowels) or from averaged data using different contexts. Allophonic synthesis involves an extension of this basic approach in which targets are stored for each allophone, directly incorporating contextual effects into the stored parameters.

Linear interpolation provides the simplest way to generate a parameter track using targets from two successive sounds. Linear transitions involving amplitudes (e.g., the intensity of voicing or of frication) are frequently adequate. To model natural formant frequency curves, however, smoother parameter interpolation is often used to avoid slope discontinuities at boundaries or update times. For example, the solution to a critically damped second-degree differential equation yields exponential time curves that provide good fits to the formant motion in natural speech. The motion from an initial parameter value A_i toward a target A_t can be expressed as

$$a(t) = A_t + [V_i t + (A_i - A_t)(1 + t/\tau)]e^{-t/\tau}, \qquad (9.1)$$

where V_i represents the initial parameter velocity (which in general is nonzero if the parameter is not at steady state at the initial time $t = 0$) and τ is a time constant that reflects the duration of the transition [59]. Typically, a function of both phonemes involved in the transition, τ reflects the mass and speed of the articulators employed to produce the phones.

Although natural speech has smooth formant tracks (except at obstruent and nasal boundaries), perceptual experiments have not clearly demonstrated the need to replicate this aspect of natural speech in synthesis. Simplicity often dictates linear interpolation of formant targets [6], which leaves slope discontinuities in the middle of phones [73]. Undershoot of target values can be accomplished either by target modification (based on phoneme context) before interpolation or by updating the interpolation factors (e.g., new values for A_t) before the parameter reaches a steady state. Durations may be specified for each phone, and transition times for each pair of phones or for each diphone [47]. An unstressed vowel may be shorter than the sum of the proposed transition durations (i.e., transition from the prior phone + transition toward the next), in which case the vowel would not attain steady state and the target could be significantly undershot.

In transitions between acoustic segments (e.g., phones or parts of phones), each segment is specified by context-independent targets for spectral parameters that are modified by the context effects of coarticulation. Vowel-to-vowel transitions are good examples where spectral parameters smoothly move from values dominated by the first vowel to values dominated by the second. Whereas the primary cues for vowels are likely to occur in the spectra toward the middle of their durations, plosives rely on parameter transitions near closure onset and release (i.e., at the ends of neighboring phones) to cue place of articulation and voicing. Linear interpolation of targets between segments is generally inappropriate to model sudden acoustic changes such as voiced–unvoiced switches, amplitude changes between obstruents and sonorants, or spectral jumps at nasal or plosive onsets and releases. If, however, parameter values are specified for segment boundaries as a function of the manners of articulation of the phonetic segments involved, piecewise-linear parameter contours (one from the middle of the first segment to the boundary and another from the boundary to the middle of the next segment) may suffice [73]. Phones can be ranked in increasing order of abruptness, e.g., vowels, semivowels, liquids, fricatives, nasals, and plosives, in terms of how important transitions are to their identification. Such a ranking can then specify parameter values at segment boundaries involving different phones, where phones with higher abruptness would dominate the transition.

If the synthesizer concatenates phonetic units whose spectra are very different at the joining boundary, substantial smoothing is necessary to avoid discontinuous speech. Acceptable speech is possible by concatenating large stored units (e.g., words) with a limited amount of smoothing, because most of the phone boundaries are correctly modeled within each word. One approach to word concatenation linearly interpolates stored parameter tracks within a time window of 40–100 ms straddling the boundary between the words. It is inadequate to simply discard the stored parameter trajectories within this smoothing interval and connect the interval endpoints because substantial parameter variation often occurs at the edges of phonetic units [11]. Smoothing over a fixed number of frames at each boundary can lead to overcoarticulated speech (and to perception of two voices) [6].

The parameter interpolation can be weighted in favor of the word with the more rapidly changing parameter, e.g.,

$$a(n) = \frac{b(n)(N - n)B + c(n)nC}{(N - n)B + nC}, \tag{9.2}$$

where $b(n)$ and $c(n)$ are the parameter tracks for the end of the first word and the start of the next word, respectively, $a(n)$ is the smoothed output track, N is the duration of the smoothing interval, and B and C are spectral derivatives of $b(n)$ and $c(n)$ [74]. Rapid spectral change at the beginning or end of a word is often crucial to accurate perception, whereas a steady formant at a word boundary can often be modified over a short time window with little quality loss. By weighting the interpolation spectrally, a rapidly changing formant will dominate the smoothing interval and most of its transition will be preserved.

A more general way to handle coarticulatory influences on parameter targets and their timing is to assign to each target value a weighting function that grows in time, possibly has a steady state, and then finally decays [75]. A parameter's trajectory would be specified by the sum of all phoneme target values, each multiplied by its weighting function, which attains a maximum during the middle of its phone. This allows contextual effects over a broad time domain and thus could be superior to approaches that arbitrarily limit parameter smoothing in time.

9.3.5 Intraframe Parameter Updating (‡)

For terminal-analog synthesis, spectral and excitation parameters are fetched from stored speech units, either periodically (every frame of 10–30 ms) or whenever the synthesis program indicates there should be a significant change in the parameters. (With the latter procedure, a duration must be specified for each stored frame.) Often the parameters are linearly interpolated *during* a frame to allow more frequent updates to the synthesizer; i.e., if $a_i(n)$ and $a_i(n + M)$ (for $1 \leq i \leq N$) represent N synthesis parameters for frames of speech at times n and $n + M$, respectively ($M + 1$ samples/frame), then the parameters used in the synthesis filter at times $n + jL$ would be

$$\frac{(M - jL)a_i(n) + jLa_i(n + M)}{M} \qquad \text{for } 0 \leq j \leq M/L. \tag{9.3}$$

If the update interval L is short (e.g., less than 10 ms), some undesired discontinuities in the speech signal at update times can be avoided, even with long intervals M between frames. The corresponding parameters in natural speech do not in general change linearly over the course of a frame, but, given storage or transmission limitations that often specify a minimum frame duration, linear interpolation is simple and typically improves synthesis quality by helping avoid signal discontinuities inconsistent with the physical articulatory motion. Many synthesizers that interpolate within a frame smooth only parameters that do not change abruptly across frames because large interframe changes often signal abrupt vocal tract motion (e.g., closure–opening of the oral or nasal tract), where the ear expects a sudden acoustic change.

To avoid instabilities, spectral parameters such as formant frequencies or reflection coefficients are interpolated. Since synthesis filters are time varying, keeping their poles inside the unit circle is not always sufficient to avoid instabilities. Even if the spectral poles for both the previous and current frames lay inside the unit circle, instabilities can arise because the contents of the N filter registers (e.g., for an N-pole LPC synthesizer) are based on the prior frame's parameters while the post-update filter coefficients reflect the new parameters. The problem is especially severe when sudden large spectral changes involve narrow-bandwidth formants, e.g., at boundaries involving a nasal and a high vowel, where the bandwidth of F1 is small. Clicks in the speech can be avoided by setting the filter memory to zero when the coefficients are changed, but this leaves unnatural gaps in the output, which appear at the frame rate. One compromise is to clear the filter memory only when large changes between parameters occur, assuming that the large spectral change will mask the brief energy dip. Another possibility is to always use a clear-memory filter on each parameter update and to output the sum of the time responses of all filters, each delayed by the correct number of frames; however, this increases computation by a factor equal to the ratio of the longest impulse response to the frame duration since that number of filters must operate in parallel [76]. More simply, for voiced speech in all types of vocoder synthesis, the parameters of the time-varying vocal tract filter should be updated just before the start of a pitch pulse excitation. At this point the speech signal and synthesis filter registers have decayed to their lowest energy values, and any temporary filter instabilities have limited effects. The problem is much less critical for unvoiced phones since their excitation is more uniform over time, and the excited formants in frication have relatively large bandwidths.

9.3.6 Excitation Modeling (‡)

With either LPC or formant synthesis, many systems use a simple model for most voiced excitation, i.e., waveforms repeated periodically at the F0 rate, often just a unit-sample train. This assumes that the vocal tract is excited once per pitch period and that the filtering action of the vocal cords (to create the puffs of air just above the glottis that resemble a rectified sine wave in time) is stationary throughout the analysis frame and can be well modeled by a few poles or zeros. The effects of glottal zeros in all-pole LPC appear in modifications to the positions of some poles, whereas formant synthesis may directly combine poles and zeros in a specific glottal filter.

Since using a unit-sample train as excitation assigns all harmonics the same zero phase, which leads to a more "peaky" waveform than natural speech, some synthesizers employ excitation signals $e(n)$ more complex than impulses (e.g., approaching a glottal pulse, or the actual LPC residual). Alternative all-pass $e(n)$ have the same flat spectral magnitude envelope as a unit-sample train but allow phase variation that can yield a less peaky speech signal [77, 78].

Since voicing and aspiration originate at the glottis, articulatory synthesizers introduce such excitation at the location in the model representing the vocal cords. Natural frication, on the other hand, is generated just forward of a narrow constriction in the vocal tract, and thus a random noise source can be automatically inserted into the model anterior to the cross-section of minimum area. For typical frication, intensity is inversely proportional to the square of the constriction diameter and can be directly calculated as a function of vocal tract cross-sectional areas; however, the areas are rarely known with sufficient precision to yield accurate models.

Simple periodic waveforms can be used for voiced excitation [52], or laryngeal articulation can be simulated more precisely with the coupled two-mass model of Figure 9.3 [50]. Instead of specifying amplitudes for voicing, aspiration, and frication separately, such a comprehensive model would specify articulatory parameters such as subglottal pressure, vocal cord tension, and a neutral or rest area for the glottis.

9.3.6.1 Filtered excitation for voicing.

The excitation for voiced speech is similar in formant and LPC synthesis. A typical formant approach assumes that the glottal signal $e(n)$ can be modeled as 1 impulse/period exciting 1–3 second-order lowpass filters (where one filter may be an antiresonator). The output of a *critically damped* resonator (one whose bandwidth exceeds its center frequency) closely resembles a time-reversed glottal pulse if the resonator bandwidth is chosen near 50 Hz so that the pulse duration is about 4 ms, which is suitable for F0 near 100 Hz (Figure 9.9). (A wider bandwidth, and hence shorter glottal pulse, is needed for female voices.) The time reversal affects only the spectral phase of the pulse, not its magnitude, and the resulting group delay distortion appears to be perceptually insignificant [64].

To simulate the periodic component in voiced obstruents, a separate excitation can create voice bars, whose energy is at very low frequencies [57]. In addition to the fixed lowpass filter just discussed, a second one with similar bandwidth can be cascaded to create a combined -24 dB/oct falloff above about 100 Hz. After such filtering, only the fundamental and some of the next harmonic remain, which combine to produce the quasi-sinusoidal voice bar.

Normally, synthesis models assume a clear separation between excitation source and vocal tract response, and model each independently. While LPC includes glottal effects in its overall spectral model, the remaining aspects of excitation are still determined separately. Formant synthesis allows the flexibility to inject a certain degree of interaction between excitation and the vocal tract. The quality of formant-based voiced speech can be slightly improved if formant bandwidths are allowed to vary rapidly with vocal cord aperture. When the glottis is open, formant bandwidths (for F1 especially) increase relative to their values with a closed glottis. The losses due to interaction with the subglottal vocal tract primarily affect frequencies below 1 kHz, but their effects can be perceptually significant [71]. Speech

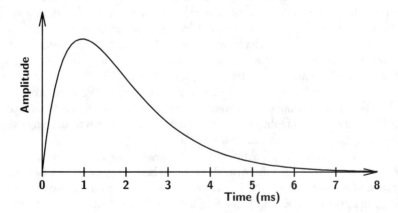

Figure 9.9 Impulse response of a simple second-order lowpass filter, suitable as a glottal waveshape in voiced speech. (After Holmes [64].)

sounds more natural when the bandwidth of F1 oscillates pitch-synchronously between values of about 50 Hz and 200 Hz, corresponding to a closed and open glottis, respectively, than when F1 has a fixed average bandwidth [64]. Compared to vowels, aspiration employs an even wider glottis, with a recommended F1 bandwidth near 300 Hz [57]. Modeling some nonlinear interactions between the glottis and the vocal tract seems to improve synthetic quality [79].

One excitation for formant synthesis is a simple stored $e(n)$ that matches the general time-domain characteristics of a glottal pulse. Here, $e(n)$ may be represented by a small set of parameters determining the relative timing of the rise and fall of the glottal pulse, which can be adjusted for different speech intensities and pitches. Waveforms with discontinuities, such as sawtooth or rectangular pulses, are inappropriate because they have -6 dB/oct decay rates. The desired -12 dB/oct falloff is accomplished through a discontinuity in slope at the time of vocal cord closure, which is abrupt (the gradual opening of the vocal cords, on the other hand, causes no slope discontinuity).

One problem with using a filtered impulse to simulate a glottal pulse is that the filter output achieves a maximum at a fixed time after the impulse input, whereas natural glottal pulses tend to peak at a fixed percentage of the pitch period, reflecting roughly proportional open and closed glottal phases. In practice, the filter characteristics are chosen so that the synthetic and natural glottal signals match for an average value of F0. If F0 deviates significantly from this average, the speech may change quality, corresponding to the differences between soft speech and shouting. Shouting, besides raising speech amplitude, causes the glottal closed phase to be a relatively longer part of the pitch period. The glottal excitation is often described in terms of an open quotient (OQ), i.e., the ratio of the open glottal interval to the closed glottal interval, as a percentage of the fundamental period ($T_0 = 1/F0$). By varying OQ and a skew measure (a measure of the symmetry of the glottal pulse, which tends to rise more slowly than it falls—due to the more rapid closure of the vocal cords), researchers have recently produced more natural-sounding synthetic speech [80–83]. In particular, a 4-parameter ("LF") model is popular [84, 85].

We can also use versions of actual LPC residual waveforms for $e(n)$. Exciting the LPC synthesis filter with its corresponding residual signal (as in ADPCM) reconstructs exactly the original speech (except for quantization noise). RELP exploits this fact by storing a lowpass version of the residual and then using nonlinear techniques to approximate the residual for synthesis. Such bit-saving economy is less important for many synthesis applications. Instead, the problems in synthesis concern how many residual patterns to store and how to modify them under changes in duration and F0; e.g., excellent speech can result if, for each combination of LPC coefficients and desired F0, the corresponding residual excites the appropriate filter. Given thousands of possible LPC vectors (corresponding to perceptually different speech sounds) and perhaps 100 perceivable pitches, the number of residuals to store and then access in real time could lead to memory exceeding 8 Mb, even with an efficient multipulse representation. (This memory estimate ignores the fact that residuals also vary in a complex fashion with amplitude.) Some memory reduction can be done by using a multipulse version of $e(n)$ [86], rather than full residuals.

F0 variation causes some difficulty with these approaches, since the $e(n)$ signal must be truncated, overlapped, or otherwise shortened when the pitch period becomes less than the duration of the stored $e(n)$ [87]. To minimize spectral distortion due to truncation, most of the energy in $e(n)$ should be concentrated in the first 2–3 ms (since virtually all pitch periods are longer), or $e(n)$ could be an "embedded" all-pass signal where truncation does not seriously affect its magnitude spectrum. Unfortunately, exciting the synthesis filter with a fixed waveform $e(n)$ improves speech quality only marginally, compared with speech using a zero-phase impulsive excitation. There is sufficient variability in the natural glottal waveform to make any completely periodic excitation a significant simplification, which is a major cause of the lack of naturalness in speech from parametric synthesis. Fundamentally, we do not understand how to precisely model the excitation to fit different vocal tract responses and pitch periods, and the resulting synthetic speech suffers in naturalness. Another difficulty is that the basic speech production model most commonly used in TTS assumes strict separability and independence of the excitation and vocal tract filter effects; another simplifying assumption is that there is only plane wave acoustic propagation in the vocal tract; neither of these assumptions are completely valid, but removing them renders speech modeling much more complex.

9.3.7 Waveform Concatenation

Many synthesizers have adopted the spectral approach, where the units are described in terms of formants, Fourier amplitudes, or LPC coefficients, due to the more efficient coding of speech spectrally and the flexibility to modify the stored units under changes in prosody or speaker. As an alternative to spectral-based synthesis, waveform synthesis can yield very good synthetic speech, at the cost of increased memory and speaker inflexibility. While concatenating speech units using stored waveforms has been difficult when trying to smooth transitions or to otherwise modify the units depending on context, it can yield good results with appropriate adjustment and smoothing at the unit boundaries.

Recently, very good synthesis quality has been obtained with such a concatentation method called PSOLA (pitch-synchronous overlap-and-add): it overlaps and sums small waveform units, using typically units of two adjacent pitch periods [88]. As in TDHS (Chapter 7), a smooth time window of one period's duration (centered on the maximum amplitude of the period) gradually fades in and out successive pitch periods for concatenation. Like other waveform or diphone synthesis methods, PSOLA cannot be easily modified to simulate voices other than that of the training speaker. As an example of PSOLA, a German system employs 2310 diphones and 440 additional special units containing glottal stops [27]. A French system has 1290 diphones, plus 751 triphones and 288 quadphones (the latter involving sonorant consonants); use of triphones reduces intelligibility errors by 20% [89]. An automatic segmentation using hidden Markov model recognition techniques provided unit boundaries which differed from the phonetician's markings by less than 30 ms in 90% of the cases.

Since one voice suffices for many TTS applications, PSOLA provides a useful alternative to spectral-based TTS. The original time-domain TD-PSOLA suffered from: (1) the need to manually mark pitch periods (for optimal performance) in the original speech analysis, (2) problems in spectral and prosodic smoothing at unit boundaries, and (3) requiring a large memory for the stored units (e.g., 80 kb/s). Recent modifications have lessened some drawbacks, while retaining low computation at synthesis time (7 operations/sample). In particular, the MBROLA (multiband resynthesis) method [6] resynthesizes (once) the entire diphone database at a constant average pitch period, which allows simple linear time interpolation at synthesis time, permitting smooth spectral matching across unit boundaries. It appears that PSOLA can yield quality similar to LPC synthesis using residual excitation (i.e., truncated or expanded residuals of actual pitch periods) [87]. PSOLA speech tends to have a perceived roughness when the prosody is modified significantly [90].

A related method is called analysis-by-synthesis/overlap-add (ABS/OLA) [91, 92]. This hybrid method uses the sinusoidal modeling of Chapter 7 [18] to overlap frames containing a small number of sinusoidal harmonics via inverse FFTs. Being frame-based, it does not require pitch-period markers as in PSOLA. A related hybrid harmonic/stochastic model, mixing Gaussian noise components with harmonics, is superior to basic LPC synthesis in quality and superior to PSOLA methods in simulating different speaking styles, although it appears more breathy than PSOLA in quality [6, 93]. Another hybrid model combines LPC for unvoiced sounds with a sum of sinusoids for voiced speech [94].

9.4 SYNTHESIS OF INTONATION

A major difficulty in synthesizing speech is that of determining a natural intonation corresponding to the input text. When the stored synthesis units are large (e.g., phrases), F0 and intensity are usually stored explicitly with the spectral parameters in LPC and formant synthesizers or implicitly in the residual signals of most waveform synthesizers. When concatenating small units (e.g., words or phones), unnatural speech occurs unless the intonation stored for each unit is adjusted for context (except for word concatenation when generating simple lists of words). Each language has its own intonation rules, and they can be discovered only by comprehensive analysis of much natural speech. While some attempts have been made to automate this analysis, i.e., via statistical methods [43], the discussion below describes traditional methods.

The domain and method of variation are different for the three prosodics: F0, duration, and intensity. (In addition, spectral tilt is sometimes included as a prosodic and affects intensity perception.) The primary variations in intensity are phoneme-dependent, and so intensity parameters are usually stored as part of the synthesis units. Stressed syllables, however, tend to be more intense, and sentence-final syllables less intense, than average. Thus intensity should be modified at the syllable and sentence level when employing smaller synthesis units. For example, in word concatenation, the stored intensity parameters for each word reflect lexical stress, but each word's intensity should be adjusted for sentential stress. In diphone concatenation, intensity should be modified for both lexical and sentential stress.

Duration is usually encoded implicitly in stored speech data. In parametric synthesizers, the parameters are evaluated once per frame. Variable-frame-rate systems take advantage of the tendency for some speech sounds to attain a steady state for several frames; the frame size is adjusted using some measure of spectral continuity between consecutive frames. For diphone and phone concatenation synthesis, however, durations must be determined explicitly (from analyses of the input text) since diphones and phones are stored with arbitrary durations.

It is of little use to store F0 for units smaller than a word, since natural F0 patterns are determined primarily at the level of words and phrases: F0 undergoes major changes on the lexically stressed syllables of emphasized words, with F0 rises and falls marking the starts and ends of syntactic phrases, respectively. Even at the word level, substantially different F0 contours can occur depending on the word's position in a sentence. Thus small-vocabulary synthesizers should record each word or phrase in sentence positions appropriate for all possible output contexts. F0-by-rule algorithms [46, 95–97] often operate on a sentence-by-sentence basis, assigning a basic falling pattern following the declination effect, with superimposed F0 excursions above (and sometimes below) the declination line. F0 may be specified either in terms of explicit contours or simply via targets, whose values then must be interpolated to yield contours. In one approach, two falling declination lines, a high *topline* and a low *baseline* (the latter with less slope), gradually converge toward the end of each sentential utterance [98, 99]. If stressed syllables and major phrasal boundaries can be identified in the input text, F0 can be assigned to follow one of the declination lines except during stressed syllables, where it switches levels, rising at the start of a phrase and falling at its end [100]. This is a reasonable first-order F0 model in many cases, especially for Germanic languages, including English. While the reality of declination lines in conversational speech is still controversial, at least the baseline is found in most F0 algorithms.

An alternative approach, based on models of reaction times for vocal cord muscles that control F0, views an F0 contour as the filtered sum of two components: word-level *accent* commands, and clause-level *utterance* commands (Figure 9.10) [101, 102]. F0 is assumed to be controlled by discrete commands, each of which starts at a certain time, maintains a fixed level for a certain duration, and then switches off. These rectangular command signals excite critically damped, second-order lowpass filters that model the way vocal cord muscles might react to such commands. Good fits to actual F0 contours occur if a step change of amplitude A at time T in the accent command contributes $AW(t-T)$ to the overall log F0 curve (to normalize across male and female F0 ranges, a logarithmic scale for F0 is often used), where

$$W(t) = [1 - (1 + \beta t)e^{-\beta t}]u(t) \tag{9.4}$$

and β is the inverse of a small time constant (about $22\ \text{s}^{-1}$) representing fast F0 changes during stressed syllables. More gradual F0 changes are reflected in the response to the utterance commands, by which a similar step change contributes $AC(t-T)$, where

$$C(t) = \alpha t e^{-\alpha t} u(t) \tag{9.5}$$

and α is the inverse of a large time constant (about $3.3\ \text{s}^{-1}$). The time constants might be expected to vary across speakers, depending on the size and shape of vocal cord muscles. While this model is reasonable, it remains to be seen whether the timing and amplitudes of the F0 commands can be automatically determined from an analysis of the input text.

Another model views the F0 contour as a series of high and low target values connected by transitional functions [103]. To model the tendency of English F0 to fall in a rough exponential fashion after many stressed syllables, this model assumes that F0 "sags" between consecutive high targets (Figure 9.11). If the duration between targets exceeds 800 ms, F0 sags to the baseline; shorter times lead to undershoot. A recent detailed study of one person's

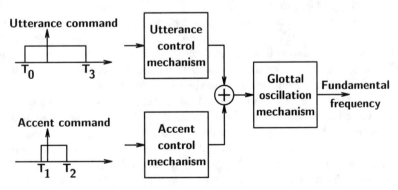

Figure 9.10 Model to generate F0 for a short utterance. (After Fujisaki *et al.* [101] ©
IEEE.)

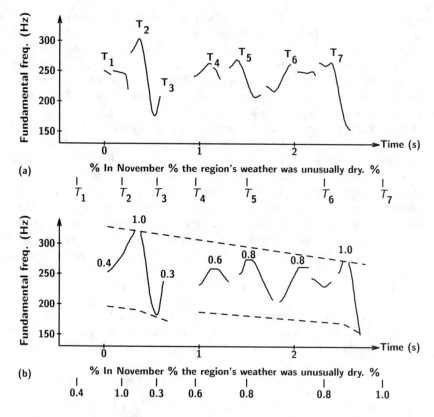

Figure 9.11 F0 contours for the same utterance: (a) natural, (b) synthetic. The T_i indicate
F0 targets located on the stressed syllables of content words and at phrase
boundaries (%). Target values in the range 0–1 specify F0 between the dashed
declination lines. Note the extra dip in the baseline at the end of each phrase,
which models the tendency of F0 to dip low at the ends of major phrases.
Note also the continuation rise at T_3. (After Pierrehumbert [103].)

F0 patterns suggests that a single, underlying contour (modified by segmental effects) can
explain much of F0's variability [104].

Although both accurate duration and F0 modeling are important in synthetic speech
quality, more F0 models have been proposed than have comprehensive duration models.
Compared to F0, duration is more tightly coupled to phonemics and can be roughly specified
by a few simple rules. Vowels are generally longer than consonants, fricatives longer than
stops, unvoiced consonants longer than voiced ones, stressed syllables longer than unstressed
ones, and consonants shorter in clusters [53]. Context affects duration too: vowels are longer
before voiced consonants than before unvoiced ones, syllables lengthen at the end of major
phrases, etc. When speaking rate varies, vowels tend to expand or compress more than
consonants do, leading to the theory that sounds may have a certain minimum duration
beyond which they may not be compressed without loss of speech quality [105]. Given the
multitude of factors (syntactic, semantic, phonetic, phonological) that affect duration, there
has been controversy over the best way to combine effects in calculating durations for speech
synthesis [106, 107]; e.g., the different incremental effects might add to or multiply a base

duration, or they could be modeled as fixed durational increments or percentages of a phoneme's duration.

A major problem for generating natural intonation is the lack of reliable markers in most input text to indicate intonational boundaries, which are usually affiliated with the ends of major syntactical phrases [6]. Sentence- and clause-final punctuation (.?!:;) are reliable places for pauses (lengthening of the final syllables, resetting of the F0 declination lines, F0 rises in yes/no questions, etc.). However, between such punctuation marks in most sentences, we often find a sequence of dozens of words with only (highly unreliable) commas to help locate breaks. For most European languages, a good heuristic places a potential break at the juncture of a content word followed by a function word, because most syntactic phrases start with (low-information-content) function words and end on the more important content words. Highlighting the final word in such sequences (with a durational lengthening and F0 rise) is appropriate in general. (For English, viewing object pronouns as content words and tensed verbs as function words here leads to a better intonation algorithm [38].) A potential break would be typically realized with an actual intonational boundary if the phrase is sufficiently long (perhaps a dozen or so syllables, thus warranting a pause). This could also be a function of speaking rate, since speakers pause more often in slow speech.

9.5 SPEECH SYNTHESIS FOR DIFFERENT SPEAKERS

One view of TTS has been to design a synthesizer capable of producing one good synthetic voice (usually of an adult male), on the assumption that listeners do not need a choice of synthetic voices. However, the ability to modify speech to simulate another voice (*voice conversion*) is useful [108]. Large-memory, waveform-based TTS needs a separate database for each voice. Good quality is achieved at significant cost and time, although ability to vary emotions in such synthetic speech is unclear.

Parametric TTS is more flexible, and recent synthesis products are capable of several voices, male and female, young and old [109]. Since female and child voices are not simply interpolated versions of adult male voices, however, more research is needed to bring the synthetic quality of female and child voices to the level of adult male synthetic speech.

While there is little evidence that human female speech is less intelligible than male speech, coders and synthesizers have not modeled female speech well. The most obvious differences concern the shorter vocal tract and smaller vocal cords of women (with their yet smaller vocal apparatus, children's speech is even more problematic). This leads to fewer resonances in a given bandwidth (e.g., over the telephone) and to more widely spaced harmonics, with correspondingly less clear definition of formants when using traditional spectral analysis methods. Higher F0 causes greater interaction between the glottal source and the vocal tract than for males. Also, the glottal excitation that women use appears to be more symmetric and breathy (the latter causing more randomness in their speech waveforms) than for men [110]. Addressing these differences recently, researchers have obtained a more natural synthesis of female speech [80, 111, 112]. In particular, they adjusted the glottal puff excitation to have a shorter closed phase for female speech and adjusted the positions of vocal tract poles and zeros to better correspond to differences in shorter vocal tracts. Traditionally, researchers have simply doubled the F0 and modeled female vocal tracts as 17 cm male vocal tracts scaled down by 10–15%, which is a reasonable first-order approximation, but ignores the fact that male–female differences do not occur uniformly along the vocal tract; e.g., it is mostly in the lower pharyngeal area that the major difference occurs in length.

When simulating different voices or speaking styles, both intonation and segmentals must be changed. For example, compared to normal speech, a reading style is typically slower (e.g., by 10%) with often much longer pauses and with a lower and less dynamic F0, while an animated speaking style is faster with higher and wide-ranging F0. It is often overlooked that formants also shift with speaking style, by up to 20% [113]. Simulating different emotions synthetically requires many adjustments to prosody and segmentals [114].

In certain applications (e.g., multimedia output from textual databases), synthetic speech can be augmented visually by a computer-graphic version of a 'talking head' [115–117]. Just as lip reading can help speech understanding in noisy conditions, watching a synthetic face in synchrony with a synthetic voice can lead to higher intelligibility.

9.6 SPEECH SYNTHESIS IN OTHER LANGUAGES

Voice-response systems work equally well for all languages since they play back previously stored speech units, which can be of any language. Indeed, if the signals are stored using elementary waveform coders, sounds other than speech can be easily integrated into such systems. PCM, log PCM, APCM, and even DPCM exploit only simple properties of speech signals, which may well apply to other sounds without serious SNR degradation. For TTS synthesis, on the other hand, major portions of the systems are highly language-dependent and must be reprogrammed for each language. Such modifications have been documented for Chinese [118], Dutch [119], French [120–122], Icelandic [123], Gaelic [124], German [27], Hindi [125], Italian [126], Japanese [127], Korean [128], Portuguese [129], Russian [43], Slovenian [130], Spanish [131], Swedish [132], and Welsh [133]. The *front end* of TTS systems, dealing with letter-to-phoneme rules, the relationship between text and intonation, and different sets of phonemes, is language dependent. The *back end*, representing simulation of the vocal tract via digital filters, is relatively invariant across languages. The models in Figures 9.7 and 9.8 are sufficiently general to handle all major languages; even trilled /r/'s (i.e., rapid alternations of brief frication and vowel sounds via vibration of part of the tongue against the roof of the mouth: alveolar in Italian or Spanish, velar in French) are feasible [134]. Languages with sounds (e.g., clicks) other than pulmonic egressives would require some simple modifications to the synthesizer architecture.

The structure of the front end is often flexible enough to support many languages. For example, the rule-based approach to speech synthesis [44] should work well if the actual rules are modified for each language; i.e., each language has its own phonemes, letter-to-phoneme rules, and rules to signal information via intonation, but a general synthesis structure often suffices. Only the detailed rules need to be adapted for each new language [43]. Places of articulation often differ in varying degrees, and some phonemes may be absent in any given language (e.g., the *th* sounds of English are relatively rare in other languages, while English does not have velar fricatives). English does not contrastively utilize nasalization of vowels or rounding of front vowels, unlike French, whereas English has diphthongs and affricates, which are absent in French. Even some detailed rules are often similar across languages; e.g, most languages use the point vowels /i,α,u/ as well as voiced and unvoiced obstruents.

9.7 EVALUATION OF TTS SYSTEMS

Formally evaluating synthetic speech is difficult. Automatic objective measures are desirable for consistent results and for ease of calculation, just as signal-to-noise ratio serves as a reliable and simple measure for wideband speech coders. However, there are many complex factors that enter into the quality of speech signals, dealing with intelligibility and naturalness, as well as flexibility to simulate different voices and rates of speaking. In speech coding, we can compare the output and input speech signals, e.g., sample-by-sample in their waveforms for a signal-to-noise ratio, or frame-by-frame for spectral comparisons (coders are usually evaluated by comparing the input and output speech signals). However, in TTS, we do not have access to ideal speech waveforms or spectra for comparison, in the wide range of possibilities for different utterances and speaking styles. Thus evaluating synthetic speech is almost exclusively a subjective process. However, it is not clear what texts to synthesize, nor what questions to ask listeners. We wish to have highly intelligible speech and a signal that sounds like normal human speech. To evaluate intelligibility, subjects are usually asked to transcribe words or sentences when listening to synthetic speech, either without the aid of a list of choices or from a closed list of textual possibilities. In the past, tests have been designed to evaluate specific phones, often in terms of their phonetic features, to discover how well a synthesizer conveys these features. For example, the Dynamic Rhyme Test examines consonants (e.g., a choice between "foot" and "put" would test how well a synthesizer handles the fricative–stop distinction).

A flaw in such procedures is that they test very selectively only certain phonetic distinctions and in very limited environments, which are not realistic for practical applications. Recently, new evaluation procedures have been proposed [135, 136]. They seek to examine the performance of TTS systems in terms of both the individual components of the systems, as well as their overall synergy. They differ from earlier methods by including the examination of consonant clusters, longer units than words (e.g., sentences and paragraphs), and intonation. Recent work [137] looks at paradigms that detect concatenative speech units that cause the worst synthesizer performance, that judge transcription of proper names, and that use the mean-opinion-score for more global evaluation.

9.8 PRACTICAL SPEECH SYNTHESIS

Commercial synthesizers are widely available for about a dozen of the world's languages, and more are added each year. They generally combine software, memory, and a processing chip, along with a controlling microprocessor, to provide quality ranging from expensive, close-to-natural speech to inexpensive add-ons for personal computers (whose intelligibility is often acceptable, but whose naturalness needs improvement).

General DSP chips are widely used for TTS, but other chips have been dedicated to formant synthesis and other synthesis methods. LPC or formant synthesizers require digital filters of typically 10–12 taps. At sampling rates of 8000 samples/s, this requires about 80,000 multiply-adds/s. Current microprocessors can easily handle such speeds, and indeed synthesizers exist entirely in software. Many systems, however, use DSP chips to simulate the vocal tract, calculate the excitation waveform, and do other repetitive chores, such as interpolating spectral parameters between frame updates.

9.9 CONCLUSION

Speech synthesis is increasingly popular, as the cost and size of computer memory decreases. Limited-vocabulary voice-response systems yield the highest-quality speech and suffice for many applications. Nonetheless, the large number of applications for TTS will lead to quality improvements that will increase its use. These improvements will come from further research into better models of intonation and vocal tract excitation as well as a clearer understanding of the speech production dynamics of the vocal tract and the processes of speech perception.

Recent trends have taken advantage of cheaper memory by using very large inventories of speech units, to overcome some coarticulation and intonation problems. This trend may well be an indication of the immediate future for TTS; indeed it follows closely that of recent automatic speech recognition (ASR) methods. The most widely accepted ASR method is via hidden Markov models (with neural networks becoming the second most used technique). Both of these stochastic methods involve quite simple network models, but require massive amounts of training and memory to accommodate the large amount of variability in the way speakers talk. While TTS need not model such speaker variability (e.g., modeling one speaker well can suffice for many TTS applications), it must handle well the large amount of variability (even within one speaker's voice) across the many different phonetic contexts met in normal speech. Thus we will likely see more TTS research that uses automatic training. Eventually, however, increased understanding of how humans produce and perceive speech will yield more efficient TTS, and some combination of stochastic and knowledge-based methods will approach synthetic speech quite similar to that of humans.

PROBLEMS

P9.1. Consider an unlimited text-to-speech synthesizer that reconstructs speech from a set of diphones.
(a) What is a diphone? What information is stored for each diphone?
(b) What are the advantages of using diphones rather than phones or words as the units of synthesis?

P9.2. Most synthesis-by-rule systems concatenate basic speech units.
(a) Is it feasible to store spoken phones using ADPCM and then concatenate them to produce acceptable synthetic speech? Explain.
(b) Does better-quality speech result when using LPC-coded diphones instead of stored phones in the concatenation procedure? Explain.
(c) What are the major problems with concatenating stored spoken words to form sentences of speech?

P9.3. For text-to-speech synthesis, the input is not a string of phonemes, but an actual text. What information does the text contain (that a string of phonemes would not have) that would be useful in speech synthesis algorithms? Give some examples of how this information would be used.

P9.4. (a) Explain some of the advantages and disadvantages of concatenating small speech units (e.g., phones) instead of large units (e.g., phrases).
(b) If phone concatenation is used, would sub-band coders or channel vocoders provide better speech synthesis? Explain.
(c) If word concatenation with LPC is used instead, note some of the ways the stored units must be modified to create natural-sounding synthetic speech.

P9.5. Give examples of how F0 and duration are used in speech to signal syntactic information, semantic (stress) information, and phonemic features.

P9.6. What are the major differences between articulatory and terminal-analog synthesizers?

P9.7. Why do formant synthesizers often have both a parallel path and a series path of resonators? Why do the parallel resonators alternate in polarity?

P9.8. Why does speech quality improve as the size of the concatenation unit increases? What limits the use of very large units?

10

Automatic Speech Recognition

10.1 INTRODUCTION

Vocal communication between a person and a computer comprises text-to-speech (TTS) synthesis and *automatic speech recognition* (ASR), i.e., understanding speech, or conversion of speech to text. The design of algorithms to perform these two tasks has been more successful for TTS than for ASR due to asymmetries in producing and interpreting speech. It may ultimately prove as difficult to design an unrestricted TTS system whose speech is indistinguishable from that of human speakers as to design a system that approaches human speech recognition performance (humans have error rates currently about 2–10 times lower than ASR [1]). However, among current commercial speech products, we find acceptable (albeit unnatural-sounding) unrestricted synthesizers, while recognition products suffer from significant limitations (e.g., number of speakers allowed, what words can be used, whether a pause is required after each word, and how much training is needed). This chapter examines the methods of converting speech into text, based on the input speech and on prior acoustic and textual analyses. We usually assume a unimodal input of one (sometimes noisy) speech channel, although some applications may allow multiple microphones or exploit visual information (e.g., lipreading [2]).

10.1.1 ASR Search: Vast and Expensive

In theory, ASR could be as simple as a large dictionary where each entry (e.g., word or sentence utterance) is a digitized stored waveform labeled with a text *pronunciation*. Given an input utterance, the system would just search the dictionary for the closest match (using some distance or correlation metric) and find the corresponding text from a look-up table. An inverted version of such a memory would suffice for TTS as well, where text is input and the waveform is output. Indeed, simple voice response systems are often so organized, using efficient speech coding to save space.

For ASR, however, this approach is utterly impractical because of the immense memory, training, and search calculation required for even the simplest applications. As an example, consider brief one-syllable utterances of about 0.5 s (e.g., the words *yes* vs *no*), coded at a low 2 kb/s (e.g., with LPC), which yields theoretically 2^{1000} patterns to consider—an immense number. If longer utterances are allowed, the computation and memory increase exponentially (and more efficient coding, e.g., VQ, is not much help here). Even for a simple task of distinguishing between *yes* and *no*, the number of waveforms that could be produced (even by a single speaker) is enormous. While the two words in this small vocabulary only correspond to a very small portion of the 2^{1000} patterns, there is no clear way to partition these patterns into separate word classes, without applying more complex pattern recognition methods as noted below. Indeed it is hard to identify which patterns would sound like legitimate speech (vs nonspeech sounds). Thus much more efficient procedures are necessary.

Another way of viewing the ASR task is in terms of a large acoustic space of N dimensions, where each utterance corresponds to a point in the space with N parameters (or features) in the speech spectral representation. Even for short words, N can easily exceed 100 (e.g., 8 spectral coefficients every 10 ms frame). If the parameters are well chosen, contiguous regions in the space would correspond to different words (or sentences), and the ASR problem would reduce to partitioning the space appropriately, so that each unknown input utterance would be labeled with the text corresponding to the region in which its spectral representation fell. While this approach is closer to the actual methods used for ASR, there are major problems with this simple technique: (1) how to determine the decision boundaries between regions (as vocabulary grows, the boundaries are very complex), and (2) how to handle larger values of N for longer utterances.

Properly characterizing the regions in an ASR acoustic space requires much training data (i.e., utterances), usually corresponding to possible texts to be recognized. While it is impossible to have a table for all possible utterances (even for small sets of words), one can hope to model the space well (given enough training data). Even for large-vocabulary recognition (LVR) applications (where the space becomes more densely packed, with similar words near each other), we could expect clear boundaries between the regions for different words. However, different pronunciations of words can lead to ambiguous boundaries. Indeed, many utterances do not have clear textual interpretations.

A common problem is insufficient training data to characterize the regions adequately (current databases can train models having up to about 10^7 parameters [3]). Given the variability of speakers and a finite amount of training, a probabilistic approach is usually adopted. The two most common ways to do this are: averaging representations of repetitions of the same text, or estimating a probability density function (PDF) for each text based on the repetitions. In the first case, training yields representative average points in N-dimensional space for each text; during recognition, the space is searched for the closest match (taking into account contributions of differing weights in different dimensions) among these reference points to the point corresponding to the input utterance. In the second case, each PDF is evaluated using the input point to find the PDF yielding the highest likelihood.

How to optimize the ASR representation and memory and to search for the best match or highest likelihood are major topics of this chapter. One simplification is to restrict the vocabulary a speaker may use, which limits the search. Second, in speaker-dependent ASR, the search is limited to patterns for a single speaker. Third, ASR normally uses efficient spectral representations of speech units, rather than waveform samples. Later sections discuss in detail how the theoretically infinite ASR search space is reduced to practical applications.

10.1.2 Variability in Speech Signals

There are so many possibilities to examine in an ASR search because of the many sources of variability in speech. A major difference between TTS and ASR concerns *adaptation* to such variability. When hearing synthetic speech, human listeners modify their expectations and usually accept it as they do speech from a strange dialect or with a foreign accent. In ASR, however, the computer must adapt to the different voices used as input. Producing one synthetic voice to which human listeners adapt is easier than designing ASR that can accept the many ways different speakers pronounce the same sentence or can interpret the variations that a single speaker uses in pronouncing the same sentence at different times. Human listeners are more flexible in adapting to a machine's accent than a computer is in deciphering human accents.

Most commercial ASR is *speaker-dependent* (SD), accepting only speakers who have previously trained the system. Such systems "adapt" to new users by requiring them to enter their speech patterns into the ASR memory. Since memory and training time in such systems grow linearly with the number of speakers, less accurate *speaker-independent* (SI) recognizers are useful if a large population must be served. Among the billions of speakers in the world each has a different vocal tract and a different style of speaking (independent of choice of language). This creates *inter-speaker* variability, a major cause of complexity for SI systems. Such systems are trained on the speech of many speakers, in an attempt to examine as many contexts (speakers, texts, styles, etc.) for speech as possible. Many systems adapt in time via learning procedures as speakers enter speech; the input speech modifies patterns stored in memory, refining SD models or instead allowing SI models to evolve into *speaker-adaptive* (SA) models.

SI systems often have different models for certain groups of speakers, e.g., male and female models, if identifiable groups have significantly different acoustics. In particular, children's speech has often been poorly recognized when using only adult models [4]. An ASR system could use 2–3 models in parallel, choosing the best output.

Differences among speakers is just one source of speech variation. *Intra-speaker variability* refers to differences within each speaker's utterances, i.e., humans never say exactly the same thing twice. Recording and transmission conditions also significantly affect the quality of speech input to ASR systems. Inter- and intra-speaker variability, along with background and channel distortions, massively increases the number of possible utterances an ASR system must handle, quite apart from issues of size of allowed vocabulary. Understanding such variability is key to solving the search problem in ASR.

10.1.3 Segmenting Speech into Smaller Units

The complexity of the search task increases with utterance length; so ASR cannot accept arbitrarily long utterances as input. In practice, to simplify the search, many systems require speakers to modify their speech, e.g., by pausing after each word or by speaking clearly and slowly. To illustrate one of the major difficulties of ASR, consider the problem of *segmentation*. For both synthesis and recognition, input is often divided up for efficient processing, typically into segments of some linguistic relevance. In TTS, the input text (symbols or ASCII characters) is easily automatically separated into words and letters.

For ASR, however, it is very hard to segment the speech input reliably into useful smaller units, e.g., phones. Sudden large changes in speech spectrum or amplitude help to estimate unit boundaries, but these cues are often unreliable due to coarticulation [5]. Syllable units can often be located roughly via intensity changes, but exact boundary positions are elusive in many languages which allow successive vowels or consonants (e.g., English). Word boundaries are even harder to find than phone or syllable boundaries (in languages having polysyllabic words). Essentially, finding boundaries for units bigger than phones combines the difficulties of detecting phone edges and of deciding which phones group to form the bigger units. Segmenting utterances into smaller units for ASR simplifies computation and often aids accuracy by reducing the search space, but only if the partitioning is correct.

Pauses play an important role in segmenting speech, but silence periods in natural speech are unreliable cues. Short silences often correspond to stop closures, but not all silences under 100 ms represent phonemes. Speakers normally pause only after several words, and sometimes pause within words.

Many commercial recognizers require speakers to adopt an artificial style of talking, pausing briefly after each word, to facilitate segmentation. In order of increasing ASR difficulty, four *styles* of speech can be distinguished: *isolated-word* or *discrete-utterance* speech, *connected-word* speech, *continuously read* speech, and *spontaneous* (normal conversational) speech. Requiring a pause for at least 100–250 ms between words in isolated-word recognition (IWR) is unnatural for speakers and forces a slower rate of speech (e.g., 20–100 words/min), but it simplifies locating words in the input speech [6]. Such pauses between words are long enough to avoid being confused with long plosives and to allow the recognizer to compare words rather than longer utterances; this reduces computation and memory, and raises accuracy. Some systems accept very brief 20–30 ms pauses, but then special allowances must be made for words with plosives.

The other three speaking styles comprise continuous speech recognition (CSR) [7], which requires little or no imposition of an artificial speaking style on system users. CSR allows more rapid input (e.g., 150–250 words/min), but is more difficult to recognize. Connected-word speech represents a compromise between awkward isolated-word speech and (often rapid) spontaneous speech; the speaker need not pause, but must pronounce and stress each word clearly (e.g., for a series of digits or letters, as in postal codes, telephone numbers, or spelled-out words). Clear pronunciation of each word reduces some effects of coarticulation, and renders each word in a test utterance closer in form to word utterances in reference patterns.

10.1.4 Performance Evaluation

Most ASR systems use accuracy or *error rates* (e.g., the percentage of words not correctly recognized of those spoken) to measure performance. Cost, speed, and the likelihood of an input being rejected are other important factors. These measures vary with applications and depend on (a) recording environment (e.g., head-mounted, noise-canceling microphone in a quiet room vs a noisy telephone booth); (b) the number and confusability of words the system accepts (i.e., its *vocabulary*); (c) speaker dependence; and (d) the style of speech (e.g., IWR or CSR).

Because performance is so dependent on the choice of vocabulary, several word sets are commonly used as standards, e.g., the *digit vocabulary* of the first ten digits (*zero* or *oh, one, two,...*, *nine*) and the *A–Z alphabet vocabulary* of the 26 letters (*ay, bee, see,...*, *zee**) [8]. The 36-word combined *alphadigit* vocabulary contains highly confusable subsets which share a vowel: e.g., the *E-set* (B-C-D-E-G-P-T-V-Z-3), the *A-set* (A-H-J-K-8), and the *Eh-set* (F-L-M-N-S-X). The best accuracy for ASR on separately spoken letters is about 95% [1]. For

---

* z is pronounced 'zed' in some countries.

connected speech, a 91% accuracy is typical [9], although continuously spoken digits well exceed 99% [1]. For large vocabularies (> 1000 words), accuracy often exceeds 99% for SD IWR, but falls to 90–95% for SI CSR. (As a minimal baseline performance, simply guessing among N vocabulary words in IWR would yield $100/N$% accuracy.) Alternative performance measures (besides error rate) have been proposed to directly account for vocabulary complexity [10] (e.g., one measure employs statistics of confusions in human speech perception [11]), but simple error rate continues to be the most widely used.

While most ASR uses word or sentence error rate to evaluate performance, *speech understanding* systems [12, 13] measure comprehension of aspects of the speech message. The mean *word-error rate* (WER) does not reflect the varying communicative importance of words in an utterance. If ASR replaces keyboards for input of text to computers (to enter data, ASR is faster than typing), then WER is a good performance measure. However, for performing actions (e.g., control a wheelchair; get information from a database), errors can be tolerated if they do not cause a misunderstanding. In applications where sentences are subject to strong syntactic constraints, poor recognition of function words (e.g., mistaking *a* for *the*) might be irrelevant to message comprehension; e.g., in one study, only 63% of sentences were error-free, but 78% were nonetheless understood correctly [14]. Some systems use *word-spotting*: the user may say anything, but only key words recognized as part of the system vocabulary cause action to be taken.

The performance error rate measures the likelihood of misinterpreting a word, but not the rate at which *rejections* are made; such *no-decision* outputs are not strictly errors but degrade performance. The additional problem of *false acceptances* is often overlooked: recognizers may incorrectly respond to coughs and other extraneous noises, interpreting them as words. A simple error figure does not account for the differing costs of erroneous substitutions, deletions, and insertions of words, rejections, and false acceptances, and it may not provide information on the distribution of errors (e.g., if certain words are more likely than others to be input, errors on those words are more problematic). To simplify matters in the face of different evaluation criteria, we will mostly employ WER, because it is a simple measure and is the one most often cited.

10.1.5 Databases for Speech Recognition

Evaluation of ASR performance requires databases of speech labelled with textual transcriptions. Ideally, databases would align each speech signal with its words and phones, so that word-based and phone-based models could be trained automatically. Unfortunately, few databases are so labelled. The TIMIT database of 630 speakers, each uttering ten sentences, is one of the few noting the timing of each phone. Most speech databases simply give the corresponding text with no time alignment (or only word boundaries).

Databases used in many ASR studies include: Resource Management, Wall Street Journal (WSJ) (and its extension, North American Business news), Air Travel Information System (ATIS), Radio Broadcast News (BN), and Switchboard (SWB) [15, 16]. The first three contain read speech, and the others have a spontaneous style. (Read speech normally has fewer disfluencies than spontaneous speech.) SWB was recorded over telephone lines, while the others used microphones (BN, so-called 'found speech' in commercial broadcasts, has both styles). Both style and channel heavily affect ASR accuracy. The SWB and CallHome databases are currently the most difficult recognition tasks, with WERs of 40–50%. (Read versions of the texts of SWB conversations are easier: 29% WER [1].) Other typical WERs are: 2% for the 2000 word ATIS task, 8% for 64,000 word WSJ and 27% for BN.

The late 1980s saw a major effort to develop ASR for conversational speech. In Europe, the Esprit SUNDIAL (Speech UNderstanding and DIALog) project examined database access for train and air travel in English, French, German and Italian [17]. A German version is available to the public via telephone [18]. The US DARPA project attained 91% understanding of ATIS inquiries (with 2.3% word error rates) [14]. Other recent dialog systems handle requests for Swedish ferries [19], California restaurants [20], and Massachusetts tours [14]. MIT has developed several dialog systems, including a real implementation of ATIS, an Internet (WWW) interface for accessing yellow-page information, and a telephone-only access to weather forecasts (using TTS) [14].

10.2 BASIC PATTERN RECOGNITION APPROACH

ASR is a pattern recognition task, for which standard techniques are often employed, as in robotics (image identification) or data communications (converting analog signals to digital information at a receiving modem). Ignoring speech understanding for now, ASR requires a mapping between speech and text so that each possible input signal is identified with (an estimate of) its corresponding text. Like all pattern recognition tasks, ASR has two phases: *training* and *recognition* (testing). The training phase establishes a *reference memory* or *model*, in the form of a dictionary of speech patterns or a network of information, where the patterns, states, or network outputs are assigned text labels. In SI systems, training is performed *offline* (i.e., nonreal-time) during system development and may combine manual and automatic methods, whereas commercial SD recognizers are trained online by customers. The automatic (and often real-time) recognition phase assigns each input speech signal a text label.

10.2.1 Pattern Recognition Methods

In general, ASR involves several steps: normalization, parameterization and feature estimation, a similarity evaluation, and a decision (Figure 10.1). The first two steps constitute the ASR *front end* (speech analysis) [21]: information reduction or elimination of redundancies in the input data sequence, as done for lower bit rates for speech coders. Since the ASR goal is to get a text message (and not to preserve sufficient information to reproduce the speech), data reduction can eliminate many speech aspects that affect naturalness but not intelligibility. Speech coders try to preserve both aspects, but ASR needs only speech traits that aid in sound discrimination; e.g., low-bit-rate coding via LPC (omitting the residual signal) is practical for ASR, because it reduces memory usage while preserving virtually all of the speech information dealing with the text message. (What is primarily lost in discarding the LPC residual is the speech naturalness.)

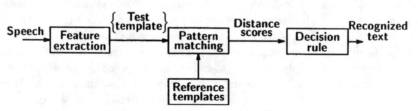

Figure 10.1 Traditional pattern recognition model for speech recognition.

Data reduction is essential to make the ASR task computationally feasible. The objective is to find a proper compromise between the conflicting constraints of minimizing cost and assuring that the reduction omits little useful information.

The initial normalization step tries to reduce variability in the input speech due to environment (e.g., background noise, recording level, communication channel). Variability due to the speaker (e.g., changes in speaker, or in speaking rate and intensity) may be handled by a later *speaker normalization* step or by incorporating speaker characteristics directly into the ASR models. (This normalization step is not needed for coders.) ASR requires a comparison between test and reference patterns, for which the evaluation should concentrate on the relevant aspects of speech to distinguish vocal tract shapes. Eliminating variability between patterns due to factors other than vocal tract shape (or its acoustic correlate—spectral envelope) increases ASR accuracy. In coding however, the objective is to reproduce the speech faithfully; thus normalization is unnecessary.

Most data reduction occurs in converting speech into parameters and features. Acoustic *parameters* for ASR are mostly those of standard analysis (e.g., LPC coefficients, amplitudes of filter bank outputs, cepstra), while *features* denote the outputs of further data reduction. Thus parameterization closely follows speech coding methods. Feature estimation is not found in coders and is optional for ASR (e.g., commercial systems rarely use features), due to its complexity and lower reliability.

The focus of ASR and the major concentration of this chapter (indeed most current ASR research) concerns how to compare *templates* (patterns) or models based on parametric (or feature) representations of both *test* (unknown) and *reference* (training) speech. The comparison or evaluation involves finding the best match in terms of a weighted distance (or a correlation) between templates or deciding which reference model is the most likely. The reference templates or stochastic models are derived during a training phase prior to any actual recognition. At recognition time, the test template or model $\mathbf{T}$ (a parametric representation derived from the test speech) is compared with some or all of the stored reference templates or models $\mathbf{R}_i$. The memory may be partitioned for an efficient search (e.g., in SD ASR, only the models for one speaker are examined). The evaluation determines how similar $\mathbf{T}$ and $\mathbf{R}_i$ are, or how well $\mathbf{R}_i$ models $\mathbf{T}$. Based on $\mathbf{T}$ and the trained models, the most likely $\mathbf{R}_i$ is chosen, i.e., the $\mathbf{R}_i$ best modeling or matching $\mathbf{T}$, yielding a text output corresponding to that reference. However, if the best match is nonetheless poor or if other $\mathbf{R}_i$ provide similar matches, ASR may postpone a decision and ask the speaker to repeat the utterance.

10.2.2 Different Viewpoints Toward ASR

One can view ASR from either a *cognitive* or an *information-theoretic* perspective [22]. In the cognitive, *knowledge* or *expert system* view, phoneticians, linguists, and engineers observe the relationships between speech signals and their corresponding text messages, and postulate phonetic rules to explain the phenomena [23]. Aspects of human speech production and spectrograms are typically examined to develop techniques (including feature extraction) to segment and label speech. Capturing the complex interrelationships of speech redundancies manually in one comprehensive model, however, is very difficult [24].

The information-theoretic approach (preferred by mathematicians and computer scientists) views speech as a signal about which information is derived through statistical analysis. Speech properties are exploited as part of a general framework (often using networks). Spectral parameters (e.g., cepstral coefficients) derived from the input speech are used in a statistical model that maximizes the likelihood (or minimizes the average cost) of choosing the correct symbols (e.g., text) corresponding to the input. The models are trained on many speech signals, and may use general comparison techniques involving templates and standard distance measures. They also use *language models*, which contain statistics of word sequences in relevant texts. This information-theoretic approach has dominated commercial applications, using either a parametric method (e.g., *Markov models*) that yields relatively fast recognition at the cost of lengthy training, or a nonparametric method (e.g., *dynamic time warping*) which is easy to train but is computationally expensive in the recognition phase.

Another major choice in ASR approach concerns whether recognition is best served starting from the speech signal or from the possible text outputs. Speech comprises a linguistic hierarchy of units (in order of decreasing size): sentences, words, syllables, phones, and acoustic segments. Following this structure, ASR uses two basic approaches: *bottom-up* and *top-down*. This distinction was noted in Chapter 5 for human speech perception, where humans analyze speech via perceptual features (bottom-up) that can be interpreted by higher-level cognitive processes suggesting possible meanings (top-down). Data reduction, converting a waveform to parameters, (possibly) features, and eventually words and sentences, follows the bottom-up approach (Figure 10.1), where decisions are made going up the hierarchy. Such a simple approach works best for small-vocabulary IWR applications. The increasing difficulty as vocabulary grows and pauses are eliminated between words requires a more complex approach to ASR in general, including feedback for low-level acoustic decisions using high-level linguistic information. The top-down method is more generative than analytical and attempts recognition through analysis-by-synthesis. In its simplest form, all possible sentences following a system's grammar and vocabulary are generated, synthesized (in some sense), and compared against each input utterance. Many systems employ both approaches (Figure 10.2): bottom-up analysis to obtain reduced data representations, and top-down methods to generate hypotheses for evaluation. Verification of hypotheses is simpler and less prone to error (but usually takes more computation) than bottom-up methods. A hybrid system may be best: applying acoustic analysis as far as reliable decisions can be made (e.g., to cepstral parameters) and then evaluating the analysis output with top-down hypotheses. The following sections explore the ASR process in more detail.

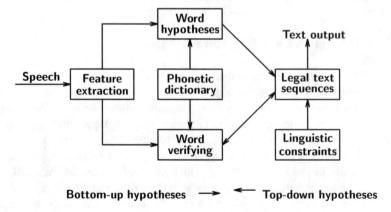

Figure 10.2 Typical model for continuous speech recognition, employing both top-down and bottom-up methods. (After Smith and Sambur [25].)

10.3 PREPROCESSING

Aspects of the input speech that reflect the recording environment and communications channel (as well as variations in speaking style) normally hinder the ASR task of identifying the spoken text. The signal may be partly *cleaned up* or normalized in a preprocessing stage prior to parameterization, to reduce extraneous factors that may distort ensuing ASR processing. If the environmental conditions are stationary or their variations can be determined, such effects may be removable from the signal. The simplest normalization adjusts maximum signal amplitude to a standard level to account for variations in recording level, distance from the microphone [26], original speech intensity, and loss in transmission. Such variations are assumed to be constant or slowly changing, which permits updating the amplitude scaling factor (by which the received signal is multiplied) at long intervals, corresponding typically to utterances bounded by easily identifiable pauses.

Automatic gain control (AGC), as in radio receivers, may be used with a long time constant so that gain is not adjusted too rapidly; rapid AGC might obscure prosodic information (i.e., amplitude variations relevant to discriminating phonemes) [27, 28]. Amplitude is often normalized separately for each short *analysis frame* (5–20 ms); e.g., the fullband average speech energy is subtracted from each of the outputs of bandpass filters, LPC coefficients are used without the LPC gain factor, or the first cepstral coefficient is ignored. Such local normalization preserves the relative spectral differences within each frame but destroys interframe amplitude information [29]. The difference in energy between successive frames (*delta energy*) is used for ASR more often than energy itself.

Analyzing the speech signal during presumed pauses (where the amplitude is weak) can yield a spectral estimate of the combined background and transmission noise. With a corresponding inverse filter, the stationary portion of such noise can be reduced in the received speech. Since noise is random, however, the benefits of this approach are limited, unless a separate measurement can be taken of the noise simultaneously with the speech (or multiple microphones are used to record the speech [30]).

Similarly, if the transmission medium between speaker and recognizer acts as a filter (e.g., a bandpass filter in dialed-up telephone lines), the received signal can be compensated by raising amplitudes at frequencies where the signal has been attenuated (Chapter 8). Yet other speech variations are due to different styles among speakers and changes in speaking rate [31]. Normalization for these variations is best handled after parameterization; it may involve questions of SD templates and nonlinear time warping.

10.4 PARAMETRIC REPRESENTATION

To parameterize speech for efficient data reduction without losing information relevant for ASR, most recognizers follow the speech model exploited in vocoding (Chapters 6 and 7), which separates excitation and vocal tract response. Despite clear correlations between successive speech frames, virtually all ASR systems parameterize each frame separately, to simplify computation (i.e., prefer to examine separate *vectors* of frame-based spectral parameters, vs a larger evolving matrix of parameters indexed on both time and frequency). Dynamic (*delta*) parameters (i.e., the differences between parameter values over successive frames) are often included in each frame's vector to accommodate some temporal information.

In a speech frame, excitation is typically represented for vocoders by a voicing decision, amplitude, and an F0 estimate. These excitation parameters are usually ignored (and therefore not computed) in ASR, on the assumption that enough information for ASR resides in the spectral envelope. The voicing and F0 features, which require extra calculation beyond basic LPC or DFT analysis, are subject to error and are often difficult to interpret for phonetic decisions. Amplitude and F0 are more influenced by higher-level linguistic phenomena (e.g., syntax and semantic structure) than by phonemics (e.g., F0 is only weakly related to phonemic identity). As in coding, spectral phase is rarely used for ASR because of its relative paucity of phonemic information.

Thus, the spectral envelope provides the primary ASR parameters. Most recognizers calculate about 8–14 coefficients, derived from a Fourier transform, LPC analysis, or bank of bandpass filters. (Some recognizers use as few as 5 or as many as 80 parameters/frame [32].) The most common ASR parameters are *mel-based cepstral coefficients*, but LPC coefficients a_k, LSFs, energies from a channel vocoder, reduced forms of DFT, and zero-crossing rates in bandpass channels are other examples (Figure 10.3). They all attempt to capture in about 10 parameters enough spectral information to identify spoken phones.

To model the short-time spectral envelope (including the first 3–4 formants) for ASR, 8–14 coefficients are considered sufficient and efficient. While spectral detail at frequencies above F4 contains phonemic information (e.g., high energy there suggests frication, and its distribution helps identify place of articulation), it is often efficient to restrict the analyzed speech bandwidth to about 4 kHz. If wider bandwidth is available (not true for telephone speech), using frequencies up to about 6.4 kHz can improve consonant recognition. Extra bandwidth, however, may actually deteriorate ASR performance [33]; e.g., LPC parameters weight spectral peaks equally across frequency, whereas most acoustic detail useful for ASR is below 4 kHz. To benefit, higher-frequency information is better in a form more suited to its importance (e.g., using the mel scale) than simply extending analysis bandwidth.

The advantages of sub-band coding (Chapter 7) are starting to be applied in ASR. Multi-band ASR can be more accurate in noise than other methods, by combining likelihoods from different frequency bands [34]. Partitioning the speech spectrum into separate bands does not seem to lose phonetic information, and can exploit differences in timing across bands [35].

The ease with which vocal tract parameters can be converted into a frequency response and then a synthetic speech signal (e.g., in an articulatory synthesizer) suggests looking for an

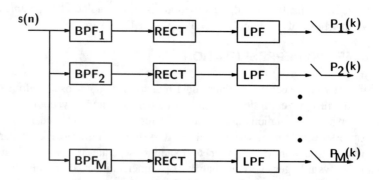

Figure 10.3 Filter bank (channel vocoder) model for parameterization. M bandpass filters BPF$_i$ ($i = 1, 2, \ldots, M$) cover the input speech bandwidth range. Their outputs are usually converted to slowly varying estimates of channel energies via a nonlinear distortion (e.g., rectification), lowpass filtering, and decimation.

acoustic-to-articulatory inversion mapping, whereby speech would be directly converted to a set of vocal tract area functions, from which corresponding phonemes could be identified. If energy loss were localized to one part of the vocal tract, such a mapping would be possible [36]. This has been very difficult in practice [37], but recent speech production experiments with electromagnetics and small coils placed on the tongue suggest better success in the future [38].

10.4.1 Parameters Used in Recognition

The most widely used parameters are the MFCCs (mel-frequency cepstral coefficients) (see Chapter 6), obtained from DFT or LPC spectra. LPC coefficients and their transformations (e.g., reflection coefficients, LSFs) model the spectral envelope well and are widely used in ASR [39]. Since questions of LPC synthesis filter stability under parameter quantization or interpolation are irrelevant for ASR purposes (unlike in coding or synthesis applications), the direct a_k coefficients can be used, rather than reflection coefficients or log area ratios.

As with MFCCs, ASR using bandpass filter-bank output energies usually approximates the auditory system by spacing the filters linearly until about 1 kHz and then logarithmically above 1 kHz, i.e., filter bandwidths of about 100 Hz in the F1 region and up to 500–1000 Hz at high frequencies [21]. This mel-scale frequency-warping improves performance vs ASR that linearly weights contributions from all frequencies [40–42], and reflects the nonuniform distribution in frequency of phonemic information. The bandpass filters can be as simple as two-pole Butterworth filters or as complex as FIR filters with several hundred taps [43]. As in channel vocoders, the filter outputs are rectified and lowpass filtered before decimation.

Typical rates for parameters are 40–60 samples/s (i.e., lowpass filter cutoffs of 20–30 Hz). Higher rates can better analyze speech transients (e.g., stop releases), but may lead to pitch interference in (vocal tract) parameter tracks (e.g., filter cutoffs above 100 Hz allow the fundamental in male voices to introduce oscillation into the tracks, mixing undesired F0 with vocal tract information); 3–4 bits/filter output seem to be adequate for recognition [44].

ASR may pre-emphasize the speech signal (i.e., raise the generally weaker amplitude of high frequencies) before parameterization, so that high and low frequencies receive more equal weight. This follows human perceptual emphasis of the 1–3 kHz range, and is especially useful for accurate consonant recognition [43], where most of the spectral detail distinguishing place of articulation occurs above 1 kHz. Pre-emphasis can result in slightly poorer accuracy for vowels, however [45].

ASR rarely models the nonlinear dynamics of the inner ear that affect human speech perception. Efforts that have applied such effects in calculating parameters for ASR have demonstrated only limited success in improving recognition accuracy [46–48], although interest continues in exploring auditory models for ASR [49–51]. One popular method is *perceptual linear prediction* (PLP) that combines LPC with several aspects of auditory models [52]. To accommodate noisy channels, RASTA (from 'RelAtive SpecTrA') methods can filter time trajectories of speech parameters [53]. Its very broad bandpass filtering eliminates very-slowly-varying distortions (much like cepstral mean subtraction—see below).

10.4.2 Feature Extraction

Most recognizers pass directly from parameterization to evaluation, without further data reduction or phonetic interpretation. Some, however, prefer to reduce a parametric representation to features. Such features may be subdivided into acoustic and phonetic features, depending on the degree of data reduction. *Phonetic features* have a discrete range and assign sounds to linguistic categories, e.g., *voiced* or *fricative*; they represent major data reduction toward a phonemic decision. *Acoustic features* (e.g., formants, F0) [54, 55] represent an intermediate step between parameters and phonetic features (and phonemes). Features are fewer in number than parameters and therefore potentially more efficient for ASR; they are speech-specific and require classifications that can be erroneous. Feature extraction is most common in expert systems.

Parameterization is straightforward, whereas the choice and estimation of features are highly dependent on the approach followed in the remaining ASR steps. For example, estimating most spectral parameters (e.g., LPC coefficients) is automatic, and errors are usually limited to the precision of the model used (e.g., the degree to which the LPC spectrum matches the original speech spectrum), whereas relying on formant tracking for ASR can lead to serious errors when a formant is missed [56]. While ASR rarely uses features today, LVR systems may well use them in the future to get higher ASR accuracy [54].

10.5 EVALUATING THE SIMILARITY OF SPEECH PATTERNS

At the heart of ASR lies the measurement of similarity between two localized (windowed) speech patterns, i.e., the representation of a frame of the input speech and one from a set of reference patterns or models (obtained during training). Each parametric (or feature) pattern for a frame of speech can be viewed as an N-dimensional vector (or point in N-dimensional space, or N-space for short), having N parameters/frame (Figure 10.4). (Features are often associated with groups of frames, but this section will ignore timing considerations, and thus parameters will not need to be distinguished from features here). If the parameters are well chosen (i.e., have similar values for different renditions of the same phonetic segment and have distinct values for segments differing phonetically), then separate regions can be established in the N-space for each segment. (As a simple example, using F1 and F2 as features could partition vowels along the vowel triangle in two dimensions.)

A memory of reference models, each characterized by an N-dimensional feature vector, is established during training in which a speaker (or several) usually utters a controlled vocabulary, and acoustic segments are parameterized and automatically labeled with phonetic codes corresponding to the training texts. For segments corresponding to short speech frames,

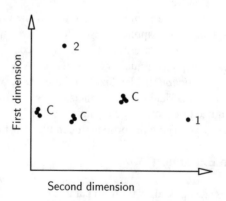

Figure 10.4 Illustration of clustering of tokens in two dimensions. Three multitoken
clusters C are shown, along with two unitoken clusters 1 and 2 (*outliers*).

the codes involve phonetic segments (e.g., phonemes). Generalizing to longer speech segments (syllables, words, or even phrases) requires expanding N to include several frames and thus time variation in the parameters. For word-based ASR, templates of words are M-dimensional vectors or $L \times N$ matrices, where $M = LN$ and the L vectors of dimension N are extracted at uniformly spaced intervals for each word in the system vocabulary. A fixed value of L for all words is assumed here, which implies linear time normalization. (The problems of time normalization and aligning models are examined later.) In discussing evaluation measures, this section assumes that a single N- or M-dimensional vector adequately describes an utterance. Later sections deal with the unequal distribution of speech information over time and frequency.

10.5.1 Frame-Based Distance Measures

The similarity between two patterns is often expressed via a distance or *distortion*, measuring how close the patterns are in N-space (possibly accounting for correlations among dimensions and unequal weighting of dimensions) [57]. Sometimes a correlation between patterns replaces this distance measure. Another popular method is statistical, where the reference models store PDFs and similarity is judged in terms of the likelihood of the test pattern for each PDF. To handle multiframe utterances (i.e., all practical cases), local (frame) distance measures typically sum to yield a global (utterance) distance, or probabilities are multiplied to yield a joint likelihood (assuming independence between frames). The reference pattern yielding the smallest distance or highest probability is usually chosen for the ASR output.

The patterns used for ASR are typically vectors representing the spectral envelope of speech frames. Since the distortion measure should represent perceptual similarity (to exploit information that speakers implicitly use in speech production), some aspects of the envelope should be emphasized and others ignored; e.g., a good ASR measure focuses on similarities in formant positions (primarily) and bandwidths (secondarily), largely ignores spectral tilt, deemphasizes the higher frequencies (e.g., uses the bark scale), and ignores low-amplitude details (often noisy).

10.5.1.1 Euclidean and Mahalanobis distances. In ASR involving templates, each unknown test utterance is converted to an N-parameter test template, to be compared against reference templates to find the closest match. (For an L-frame utterance, this process is usually repeated periodically L times, summing local distances, but one could envision a single match with templates of NL dimensions.) The similarity of two templates is inversely proportional to the distance in N-space between points corresponding to the templates. A distance measure $d(\mathbf{x}, \mathbf{y})$ between templates $\mathbf{x}$ and $\mathbf{y}$ is called a *metric* if it satisfies three conditions: positive definiteness ($d \geq 0$, and $d = 0$ only when $\mathbf{x} = \mathbf{y}$), symmetry ($d(\mathbf{x}, \mathbf{y}) = d(\mathbf{y}, \mathbf{x})$), and triangle inequality ($d(\mathbf{x}, \mathbf{z}) \leq d(\mathbf{x}, \mathbf{y}) + d(\mathbf{y}, \mathbf{z})$). For ASR the two most important aspects of a distance measure are its subjective significance (following perceptual similarity) and mathematical tractability. Metrics ensure tractability, but several common ASR distance measures are not metrics; those satisfying only the first condition above are *distortion measures*.

The most common metric is the Euclidean distance (or *L2*-norm),

$$d_2(\mathbf{x}, \mathbf{y}) = \sqrt{(\mathbf{x} - \mathbf{y})^{\mathrm{T}}(\mathbf{x} - \mathbf{y})} = \sqrt{\sum_{i=1}^{N}(x_i - y_i)^2}, \qquad (10.1)$$

which is the normal interpretation of distance between two points in *N*-space. In the family of distances called L_p norms,

$$d_p(\mathbf{x}, \mathbf{y}) = \left(\sum_{i=1}^{N} |x_i - y_i|^p \right)^{1/p}, \qquad (10.2)$$

d_2 is the most popular, but d_1 (the *Chebyshev* or *city-block* distance) is simpler to compute. The latter trades decreased recognition performance for fast (no multiply) computation: one sums separately the distances along each dimension: $D_C(\mathbf{x}, \mathbf{y}) = \sum_{n=1}^{N} |x_n - y_n|$. As p increases, d_p increasingly concentrates on peak distortion (rather than average distortion across all parameters), i.e., it emphasizes dimensions with the largest distortions. Such a weighting can often be justified perceptually; e.g., listeners tend to focus on differences in the strongest formant peaks.

Another common speech metric is the Mahalanobis or *covariance-weighted* distance, which for two templates $\mathbf{x}$ and $\mathbf{y}$ is

$$d(\mathbf{x}, \mathbf{y}) = \sqrt{(\mathbf{x} - \mathbf{y})^T \mathbf{W}^{-1}(\mathbf{x} - \mathbf{y})}, \qquad (10.3)$$

where $\mathbf{W}$ is a positive-definite matrix that allows different weighting for individual parameters depending on their utility in identifying the speech segments in *N*-space. The Euclidean distance sets $\mathbf{W}$ (and $\mathbf{W}^{-1}$) to be the identity matrix $\mathbf{I}$, whereas the more general Mahalanobis distance sets $\mathbf{W}$ to be the autocovariance matrix corresponding to the reference vector.

For the Mahalanobis distance, the elements along the main diagonal of $\mathbf{W}$ reflect the intra-parameter variances, with small $\mathbf{W}$ values for more useful ASR parameters. For less useful parameters (i.e., those having highly variable patterns for the same phone or word), large matrix values discount their weighting in calculating an overall distance. Calculation is simplified considerably if the features are orthogonal (allowing a diagonal $\mathbf{W}^{-1}$) or orthonormal (allowing $\mathbf{W}^{-1} = \mathbf{I}$). However, a *principal components* or Karhunen–Loève transformation on the parameters (to achieve orthogonality) significantly increases calculation in forming the test template. Nonetheless, as the numbers of models and parameters grow in many ASR applications, distance or likelihood computations dominate computation, which suggests the utility of reducing templates to a small set of independent features.

Despite the advantages of the Mahalanobis distance in weighting properly, ASR often uses the Euclidean distance (e.g., with cepstral parameters) or an LPC distance, because: (1) it is difficult to reliably estimate $\mathbf{W}$ from limited training data, and (2) the latter two distances require only *N* multiplications for an *N*-dimensional parameter vector vs N^2 multiplications with the Mahalanobis distance.

Representation of parameter vectors whose elements are highly correlated is a problem for many pattern recognizers. Full covariance matrices are needed to account for cross-parameter correlation, which leads to a large number of parameters to estimate. In the common case of many parameters and limited training data (called *undertraining*), robust estimation is difficult. Hence, diagonal covariance matrices are often assumed, which trades the poor assumption of independence across dimensions (e.g., ignoring the obvious correlation between static and delta parameters) for faster computation.

10.5.1.2 Stochastic similarity measures. The Mahalanobis distance has origins in statistical decision theory. If each utterance of a word (or other unit) represents a point in N-space, the many possible pronunciations of that word describe a multivariate PDF in N-space. Assuming ASR among equally likely words and *maximum likelihood* (ML) as the decision criterion, Bayes' rule specifies choosing the word whose PDF is most likely to match the test utterance. Because of the difficulty of estimating accurate PDFs from a small amount of training data, many systems assume a parametric form of PDF, e.g., a Gaussian, which can be simply and fully described by a mean vector μ and a covariance matrix $\mathbf{W}$. Since ASR parameters often have unimodal distributions resembling Gaussians, the assumption can be reasonable. A simpler alternative, the Laplacian or symmetric exponential, can also be used [58]; it corresponds to the city-block distance (i.e., Gaussians use d^2 distance measures, emphasizing the importance of large distance components, while Laplacians use d). Laplacians are sometimes better at approximating the tails of speech PDFs.

The Gaussian PDF of an N-dimensional parameter vector $\mathbf{x}$ for word i is

$$P_i(\mathbf{x}) = (2\pi)^{-N/2} |\mathbf{W}_i|^{-1/2} \exp\left[-\frac{(\mathbf{x} - \mu_i)^T \mathbf{W}_i^{-1} (\mathbf{x} - \mu_i)}{2} \right], \qquad (10.4)$$

where $|\mathbf{W}_i|$ is the determinant of $\mathbf{W}_i$ and μ_i is the mean vector for word i. Most ASR systems use a fixed $\mathbf{W}$ matrix (vs a different $\mathbf{W}_i$ for each word) because (a) it is difficult to obtain accurate estimates for many $\mathbf{W}_i$ from limited training data, (b) using one $\mathbf{W}$ matrix saves memory, and (c) $\mathbf{W}_i$ matrices are often similar for different words. (The use of individual $\mathbf{W}_i$ also causes the Mahalanobis distance not to be a metric.) Given a test vector $\mathbf{x}$ for recognition, word j is selected if

$$P_j(\mathbf{x}) \geq P_i(\mathbf{x}) \qquad \text{for all words } i \text{ in the vocabulary.} \qquad (10.5)$$

Applying a (monotonic) logarithmic transformation and eliminating terms that are constant across words (i.e., a common $|\mathbf{W}|$), Equations (10.4) and (10.5) reduce to minimizing the Mahalanobis distance of Equation (10.3), using μ_i in place of $\mathbf{y}$. The simpler Euclidean distance, setting $\mathbf{W}^{-1} = \mathbf{I}$, trades ASR accuracy for fewer calculations; it is optimal only in the unusual case that the N parameters are mutually independent and have equal variances (i.e., contribute equally to the distortion). A better alternative could be an approximate full matrix, split into two elements, one full and one diagonal, tied at separate levels (see discussion on tying later). Typically the full elements are extensively tied, resulting in only a small increase in the number of parameters compared to the diagonal case [59].

Ideally, repetitions of the same speech segment (e.g., pronunciations of a phoneme at different times, by different speakers or in different linguistic contexts) would yield consistent parameter values and therefore small *clusters* or regions in the N-space. In addition, different speech segments would provide distinct measurements and hence widely separated points in the space (Figure 10.4). The best parameters would show little intrasegment variance and large intersegment variances, and they would be independent of each other and with equal importance. In practice, however, ASR parameters share speech information and some are much more relevant than others. Not accounting for their interdependence and their unequal importance lowers ASR accuracy.

The reliability of the training data is often an issue, especially with unsupervised training or with poorly segmented or transcribed data. With standard averaging, outliers can drastically affect models. If reliable, such outliers (Figure 10.4) can be exploited in discriminatve training; otherwise, selective training could deemphasize their use [60].

10.5.1.3 LPC distance measures (‡). The measures in the previous sections are general and can be used with many sets of parameters. Given that the focus in ASR is the speech spectral envelope and that LPC parameterizes that envelope efficiently, distances exist that exploit aspects of LPC for efficiency and ASR accuracy. Two such related distance measures are the *Itakura–Saito* (IS) distance and the *log-likelihood ratio* (LLR) [61, 62]. They exploit the mathematics of LPC modeling to weight the effects of the different coefficients without requiring orthogonalization. In its simplest and most common form, the IS distance between two templates represented by a test LPC vector $\mathbf{a}_T$ and one of L reference vectors $\mathbf{a}_i$ $(i = 1, 2, \ldots, L)$ is

$$d_{IS_i} = d_{IS}(\mathbf{a}_i, \ \mathbf{a}_T) = \frac{\sigma_i^2}{\sigma_T^2} \frac{\mathbf{a}_i^T \mathbf{V}_T \mathbf{a}_i}{\mathbf{a}_T^T \mathbf{V}_T \mathbf{a}_T} + \log\left(\frac{\sigma_T^2}{\sigma_i^2}\right) - 1, \tag{10.6}$$

where $\mathbf{V}_T$ is the autocorrelation matrix of the test utterance, and σ_T and σ_i are the LPC gain parameters for the test and reference templates, respectively. The LLR is a gain-normalized version of the IS distance:

$$d_{LLR_i} = d_{LLR}(\mathbf{a}_i, \ \mathbf{a}_T) = \log\left[\frac{\mathbf{a}_i^T \mathbf{V}_T \mathbf{a}_i}{\mathbf{a}_T^T \mathbf{V}_T \mathbf{a}_T}\right]. \tag{10.7}$$

Just as cepstral c_0 is often ignored, the LLR assumes that amplitude is irrelevant for ASR (e.g., the same word may be uttered loudly or softly; speaker distance from the microphone and the transmission channel also affect amplitude). Temporal amplitude variations are useful to distinguish utterances longer than a single word, but gain normalization is common for templates of words or smaller units.

In computing these LPC distances, the test frame of speech is in effect passed through the inverse LPC filter for each reference template to yield a scalar residual error energy $(\mathbf{a}_i^T \mathbf{V}_T \mathbf{a}_i)$. This error is normalized by the actual residual error for the test template $(\mathbf{a}_T^T \mathbf{V}_T \mathbf{a}_T)$. In the case where the two templates correspond to similar acoustic segments, the inverse filter provides a good match to the test speech, and the two errors are small and similar. With a perfect match, the errors are identical and Equation (10.7) appropriately yields a zero distance. (The IS distance is based on the error ratio and the ratio of the gains of the individual LPC vectors.) For mismatched templates, the residual (resulting from inverse filtering the test speech by a different LPC analysis filter) is large, and the distances in Equations (10.6) and (10.7) become large.

Expanding vector operations in Equation (10.7), we obtain for the LLR distance [60]

$$d_{LLR_i} = \log\left[\sum_{k=0}^{N} \hat{\mathbf{V}}_T(k) R_a(k)\right], \tag{10.8}$$

where N is the vector dimension and LPC model order, $\hat{\mathbf{V}}_T$ is the autocorrelation vector of the test utterance normalized by its LPC error (i.e., the first $N + 1$ values of the autocorrelation function, starting with the test utterance energy as the first element, divided by the LPC error; all values are obtained during LPC analysis of the test utterance), and $\mathbf{R}_a$ is the autocorrelation vector of the extended LPC coefficient vector $(1, -a_1, -a_2, \ldots, -a_N)^T$. Equation (10.8) requires only $N + 1$ multiplications per reference template, making the LPC distances comparable in computation to the Euclidean distance.

The LPC distances are asymmetric (i.e., not metrics): filtering the test utterance by a reference inverse LPC filter is not the same as passing a reference utterance through the test inverse filter, although similar values usually occur. The asymmetry is often largest for large distortions, and may be justified on perceptual terms (e.g., it is easier to perceive noise in a masking tone, than to hear a tone in noise) [63]. Equations (10.6) and (10.7) yield high ASR performance while minimizing both distance calculation and memory for the reference templates. LPC analysis must be performed on each test utterance, yielding the autocorrelation vector and LPC error, although the test LPC coefficients as such are not needed. For each reference template, only the autocorrelation vector based on the LPC coefficients of the reference utterances need be stored ($N + 1$ values/template).

While it is difficult to compare ASR experiments under different conditions, the LLR distance seems superior when using LPC-based templates [64], but see 65], but the Euclidean distance with MFCCs is generally preferred over LPC measures [40, 66]. Mel-scale frequency warping appears to raise ASR performance for cepstra but not for LPC recognizers.

The LLR distance applies in non-LPC ASR as well, where $LR = P(O|A)/P(O|B)$ compares two stochastic models A and B to see which better models a speech observation vector O. Here the LLR can be defined as

$$\text{LLR} = [\log P(O|A) - \log P(O|B)]/d,$$

where d is the duration (in frames) of O. For *utterance verification* or *keyword spotting* (i.e., estimating whether key speech has been properly identified), where discrimination of similar words is important, A could be a keyword model and B an *anti*-model from clustering of highly confusing alternative words (units smaller than words can also be used) [67].

10.5.1.4 Cepstral distance measure.
When comparing speech frames using cepstral parameters c_n, a simple Euclidean distance is common, which reflects the uncorrelated nature of c_n. Since the logarithmic power spectrum $\log S(\omega)$ of speech is the Fourier transform of its cepstrum, Parseval's theorem can be used to equate a Euclidean cepstral distance to the RMS log-spectral distance:

$$d_{cep}^2 = \sum_{n=-\infty}^{\infty} (r_n - t_n)^2 = (2\pi)^{-1} \int_{\omega=-\pi}^{\pi} |\log R(\omega) - \log T(\omega)|^2 \, d\omega, \qquad (10.9)$$

where r_n and t_n are the c_n for reference and test utterances, respectively. Under certain regular conditions [66], c_n (except for energy c_0) have zero means and have variances that vary approximately as the inverse of n^2. (c_n generally decays in amplitude with n, and so the number of terms in the summation above can be truncated, to about 10–30 [63].) If we normalize the cepstral distance to account for the decreasing spread of higher order coefficients (i.e., $d_{ncep}^2 = \sum_{n=-\infty}^{\infty} (nr_n - nt_n)^2$), this distance compares the spectral slopes of the speech power spectra (since multiplying in the time domain by n corresponds to a derivative in the frequency domain). This deemphasis of low-order coefficients has some foundation in speech production, where the broadest spectral effects (those changing slowly with frequency) are more due to excitation factors (e.g., spectral tilt) than to vocal tract factors (the latter being more important for ASR). They are also deemphasized because they vary significantly with transmission factors (e.g., bandpass filtering in telephone channels) and speaker characteristics, which are irrelevant for phonetic decisions.

Cepstral analysis is often done on the smooth LPC spectrum rather than on the DFT, to eliminate aspects of the DFT in the c_n that are irrelevant to ASR (e.g., excitation effects, such as F0). Weighting this *LPC cepstrum* by n yields the sum of the roots of the LPC polynomial $A(z)$ with increasing powers [63]: $nc_n = \sum_{k=1}^{p} z_k^n$. (The LPC cepstrum is a flawed spectral measure, however, known to model sounds like nasals and obstruents less well [9].) d_{ncep} is called the *root-power sum (RPS) distance*; it emphasizes movements of sharp spectral peaks (e.g., formants) more than other LPC measures. Using the fact that perceived loudness follows the cube root of speech power, a method called *root spectral compression* improves modeling of spectral zeros [3].

A more common procedure is to weight c_n with a raised cosine function $1 + (L/2)\sin(n\pi/L)$ (a finite-length window for $n = 1, 2, \ldots, L$). A distance with this weighting deemphasizes both low- and high-order c_n, on the assumption that, as n increases, LPC-based c_n are more influenced by artifacts of the LPC analysis [63]. Comparing both regions of deemphasis, attenuating the low-order c_n seems more useful for ASR [68].

10.5.1.5 Other distance measures. In the case of noisy speech, ASR accuracy can be improved by weighting more heavily the components of the distance measure that correspond to frequencies of higher energy (e.g., during vowels, the first 2–3 formants) [69]. The diversity of distance measures used in ASR reflects the difficulty of finding one that is sensitive to fine phonetic distinctions, yet insensitive to irrelevant spectral variation; e.g., most measures are not invariant to F0 changes, even though F0 has little effect on segmentals [70]. Other distance measures are discussed in [63, 64, 71, 72].

10.5.2 Making ASR Decisions

Given a speech input s (i.e., a set of samples from a speech signal), the objective of ASR is usually to output the most likely estimated text $\hat{t}$ from the set of all texts t (often constrained by the choice of language, vocabulary, and sometimes syntax). This *maximum likelihood* (ML) estimation approach is used for most ASR tasks. Stochastic methods of ASR (e.g., Markov models) explicitly address this probabilistic approach. For deterministic ASR methods using template-matching, however, there is an implicit assumption that different versions of utterances are equally likely. Typically, representations of repeated utterances for training reference templates are simply averaged. More realistic (non-uniform) PDFs are hard to use with templates.

In a scheme where each possible text corresponds to many points in N-space and where ASR searches for the closest match, we first assume that the set of points for each text describes a uniform PDF. In this case, the best match is equivalent to a maximum *a posteriori* (MAP) probability (i.e., the conditional probability $P(t|s)$). Since factors other than a spectral distance measure (e.g., language models) are often used in ASR, since all such factors can often be modelled stochastically, and since template matching methods can also be interpreted stochastically, we will unify our discussion here in terms of maximizing probability.

We have no direct way of estimating *posterior probabilities* $P(t|s)$, since it is impossible to examine all possible speech signals s (or even a reasonable subset) during training. Using Bayes' rule, we thus choose $\hat{t}$ so that

$$P(\hat{t}|s) = \max_t P(t|s) = \max_t \frac{P(t)P(s|t)}{P(s)}; \qquad (10.10)$$

i.e., the conditional probability for a given s is maximized over all t. Since the denominator $P(s)$ does not depend on the chosen t in the maximization operation, the recognition problem reduces to choosing $\hat{t}$ so that $P(t)P(s|t)$ is maximized. In some ASR systems, either all texts t are equally likely or their *a priori* (prior) probabilities $P(t)$ are unknown (i.e., no language model is used); then the problem further reduces to maximizing *likelihood* $P(s|t)$, i.e., choosing the text for which the input speech signal is most likely. Thus Bayes' rule converts the ASR problem from the very difficult one of estimating posterior probabilities ($P(t|s)$) into the computationally easier task of estimating separate prior likelihoods for acoustics ($P(s|t)$) and text ($P(t)$).

While the denominator $P(s)$ in Equation (10.10) can be ignored at recognition time, it affects training methods. The standard ML training method is poor at discriminating similar acoustic classes because it does not take account of alternative hypotheses in adjusting model parameters.

Many speech phenomena are more accurately modeled on time spans much larger than frames, e.g., intonation, choice of speaker, transmission channel, and noise effects. While many recognizers use delta coefficients to account for some dynamic effects, their range is typically 3–5 frames, much less than one's short-term memory (ranges of 160–200 ms have been suggested for optimal processing [3]). All these important issues are discussed later, in the context of handling timing variability.

10.5.2.1 Alternative success criteria.
Other performance measures are possible (e.g., if costs can be associated with different types of ASR errors, we could minimize average cost). Basic ML estimation is used for most ASR tasks, but is often inadequate for confusable vocabularies (e.g., the alphabet: A, B, ..., Z). Training ASR systems to directly minimize error rates (*minimum classification error*—MCE) instead has been often difficult [42, 73, 74], in part because we have no metric to measure the ordering of output hypotheses [75]. A criterion emphasizing model discrimination (e.g., *maximum mutual information estimation*) can raise accuracy, but with increased cost [76, 77] and some convergence problems [60]. Discrimination can also be improved via *divergence measures* (see Chapter 11) [78].

Many alternative methods rely on gradient descent optimization, which often find local minima. *Deterministic annealing* is a method that minimizes a randomized MCE cost subject to a constraint of a gradually relaxing entropy. It recognizes spoken letters well in background noise [79].

Linear discriminant analysis (LDA) is a common method for pattern recognition to improve the discrimination between classes (e.g., spoken digits) in a high-dimensional vector space [80]. The original parameter space is linearly transformed by an eigenvector decomposition of the product of two covariance matrices, an interclass matrix and the inverse of an average intraclass one. Thus it emphasizes dimensions which spread out different sound classes, while minimizing the divergence within each class. Applying LDA to acoustic states of an ASR model with a single transformation (once per speech frame), rather than individual state mappings (applied to each of many models), minimizes computation [58]. Such methods are robust in noise, but need knowledge of SNR for good results [81].

10.5.2.2 Multiple outputs (nearest neighbors).
The desired output for ASR is usually the single best text corresponding to the input speech; e.g., $\hat{i}$ corresponds to the reference template with the closest match to, or smallest distance from, the test template. Following this *nearest-neighbor* (NN) rule, ASR calculates distances d_i for $i = 1, 2, \ldots, L$ (for L models in the system) and returns index $\hat{i}$ for $d_{\min}$, the minimum d_i (or equivalently the MAP likelihood). If there are several models for each text (corresponding to pronunciations of the text by several speakers, or several repetitions of the word by one speaker), a version of the *K-nearest neighbor* (KNN) rule may be applied. The original KNN rule finds the nearest K neighbors (among all models) to the unknown and chooses the text with the maximum number of entries among the K best matches (the NN rule breaks ties) [82]. In an alternative KNN rule (which requires more computation for a given K) [83], the selected output corresponds to the text that minimizes the average distance between the test template and

the best K matches for each vocabulary word; i.e., ASR finds the K reference templates closest to the test template among the P templates representing each word and chooses the word with the smallest average distance. When enough models represent each word (e.g., $P \geq 6$), as in many SI systems, improved ASR accuracy results with the KNN rule for $K = 2$–3, compared with the NN rule [83]. For systems having over 100 templates/word, accuracy improves with even higher values of K (e.g., 7 in [82]), but computation increases as well.

10.5.2.3 Decision thresholds.   *Thresholds* may be used as part of a decision rule to reduce ASR errors, at the cost of delaying the output response. If the smallest distance between the test template and all reference templates exceeds a chosen threshold (or the best MAP probability across reference models is too low), the speaker can be asked to repeat an utterance because the best text candidate for the first utterance is nonetheless a poor match. Such a *rejection* is feasible only for interactive ASR, where the speaker expects immediate feedback. Based on experiments, the *rejection threshold* can be set to balance the ASR error rate and the *false rejection* rate: a high (or no) threshold leads to few (or no) rejections but risks more wrong identifications, while a low threshold minimizes incorrect recognitions but increases the likelihood of a rejection when the best match is indeed correct. A second threshold may further reduce errors: a decision can be refused if the two best matches have very similar distances (or probabilities), because an error is more likely if one candidate must be selected from a set of similar matches than if one candidate is clearly superior [84]. The balance points are specified by the relative costs of ASR errors and rejections [85]. Rejection delays can frustrate system users, but errors can have a highly variable cost.

In cases where a final decision is delayed, a preliminary ordered set of candidates may be output consisting of the most likely matches, e.g., the best M matches in order. *Certainty factors* (derived from the evaluation measures) may be linked to each candidate, indicating its likelihood of being correct; e.g., if two reference templates had similar small distances from the test template, they would be assigned similar high factors.

10.6 ACCOMMODATING BOTH SPECTRAL AND TEMPORAL VARIABILITY

Most of our discussion so far has assumed a comparison of individual sounds, where a single representation of each utterance (e.g., from an average of all frames) suffices. This evaluation procedure suffices only in the very limited circumstances of stationary speech (i.e., where the vocal tract is kept constant). In virtually all ASR, however, vocabulary entries (i.e., output texts) involve sequences of acoustic events. Even in simple cases (e.g., digit or A–Z vocabularies), almost all words contain multiple sounds (e.g., among the letters, only *A*, *E*, *I* and *O* involve single phonemes). A single average spectral feature set would suffice only for very restricted vocabularies, where the words are short and have very distinct sounds; e.g., for *yes*/*no* (a two-word vocabulary), energy in *yes* is concentrated at higher frequencies than for *no*, so the frequency of the mean spectral peak (averaged over each word) could distinguish these two words.

In almost all practical situations, utterances are subdivided in time, yielding sequences of parameter vectors. As in speech coders, speech is divided into equal-duration frames of 10–30 ms, each producing a parameter vector. (The frames are often overlapping in time by a fixed percentage, to account for nonuniform weighting via windows; e.g., 25 ms Hamming-weighted frames, evaluated every 10 ms.) Speech could be segmented into longer multiframe sections (homogeneous in some sense) (e.g., syllables [86, 87]) before parameterization, but here we will assume that each utterance is transformed into a parameter matrix $\mathbf{M}$ or pattern of parameter vectors. A parameter (or feature) vector $F(i)$ for frame i consists of Q parameters $f_1(i)$, $f_2(i)$, ..., $f_Q(i)$ ($Q \approx 8$–30 typically, e.g., including static and delta cepstral coefficients). For a total of L frames in an utterance, the pattern $\mathbf{M}$ consists of

$$F(1), \; F(2), \; \ldots, \; F(L). \tag{10.11}$$

Ideally, if a segmenter could reliably divide each utterance into acoustic units (e.g., phones or words), the frame size could be variable and correspond to each unit (hence L such units per utterance). This would minimize storage and comparison computation, and guarantee that when a test pattern is compared to a reference pattern for the same "word," corresponding acoustic segments would align properly, yielding a good match.

Since reliable segmentation is difficult, most ASR compares templates (or evaluates probabilities) frame-by-frame instead, which leads to alignment problems. Utterances are spoken at different speaking rates, even for individual speakers repeating a single word; thus, test and reference utterances usually have different durations (i.e., an unequal number of frames). One (suboptimal) way to facilitate frame-by-frame comparison is to normalize frame lengths so that all templates share a common number of frames; e.g., if a typical word lasts 400 ms and a sampling of 20 frames/word is estimated to be needed for accurate ASR, the frame intervals would exceed 20 ms for words longer than 400 ms and be proportionately less for shorter words. Such *linear time normalization* or *warping* can be done either through frame adjustment before parameterization or through decimation/interpolation of the parameter sequence.

Accurate time alignment of templates is crucial for ASR performance. Linear warping is rarely sufficient to align all speech events properly because the effects of speaking-rate change are nonlinear and widespread; e.g., vowels and stressed syllables tend to expand and contract more than consonants and unstressed syllables. Thus linear warping of two utterances of the same text often aligns frames from different phones. For example, the main difference between long and short versions of the word *sues* usually occurs in the /u/ duration; linearly compressing the long version to the same number of frames as the short one would align some frames at the start and end of /u/ in the long version with frames from /s/ and /z/ in the short version; a large distance in comparing these two versions of the same word then would result for these frames, since vowels and fricatives are very different spectrally. If enough frames are misaligned, the overall ASR distance is often large enough to cause a rejection or to output a different word. (For simple monosyllabic words, ASR improves with a procedure that appends silence to the ends of the shorter of the test and reference templates, and aligns energy peaks so that the vowels are correctly compared [40, 88].)

By its very nature, any time warping will hinder the exploitation of durational information in ASR. Duration helps cue phonemes in speech perception, e.g., long vowels suggest an ensuing voiced consonant, and frication duration helps distinguish stops and fricatives. Time warping obscures many of these cues. Few current ASR systems directly exploit durational cues, but future systems will.

10.6.1 Segmenting Speech into Smaller Units

Determining time boundaries for acoustic segments in a test utterance is a significant problem for all ASR tasks. (For training, segmenting reference utterances may be assisted manually, which is tedious but straightforward—except for ASR products that need automatic SD training.) In most ASR, either acoustic unit boundaries are found implicitly as part of the model evaluation or the problem is bypassed. For expert-system ASR, however, segmenting speech is a major explicit task, and for most ASR, at least the start and end (*endpoints*) of each utterance must be found. For IWR, this estimation is needed for each word.

10.6.1.1 Endpoint detection. Proper estimation of the start and end of speech (vs silence or background noise) leads to efficient computation (i.e., not wasting ASR evaluations on preceding or ensuing silence) and, more importantly, to accurate recognition. Misplaced endpoints cause poor alignment for template comparison; e.g., weak speech (stops or /f,θ/) at misaligned boundaries may be incorrectly compared to background noise. In one isolated-digit experiment [61], the ASR error rate was 7% with correct endpoints; small endpoint errors ($\pm$60 ms) led to 10% ASR errors, and larger endpoint deviations caused severe degradation (e.g., missing the first 130 ms led to 30% errors).

In a signal free of noise, finding where speech starts and ends is simple: speech vs zero-valued silence samples. Noise comes from speakers (lip smacks, heavy breaths, mouth clicks), environment (stationary: fans, machines, traffic, wind, rain; nonstationary: music, shuffling paper, door slams), and transmission (channel noise, crosstalk). The variability of durations and amplitudes for different sounds makes reliable speech detection difficult; strong vowels are easy to find, but boundaries between weak obstruents and background noise are often poorly estimated.

Most endpoint detectors rely on functions of signal amplitude or energy to separate nonspeech from speech [89]. The method shown in Figure 10.5 locates *energy pulses* (typically syllables or words), by comparing energy in decibels against four thresholds k_1, k_2, k_3, k_4 [90, 91]. Time A_1 notes when energy exceeds the lowest threshold k_1 (3 dB above background noise). If it rises above k_2 (10 dB) before falling below k_1, a pulse is considered detected starting at A_1 (unless duration $A_2 - A_1$ exceeds 75 ms, where A_2 is then viewed as the start time and the signal preceding A_2 as breath noise). The end time is similarly found using thresholds k_2 and k_3 (5 dB) (A_4 is the end time unless $A_4 - A_3 > 75$ ms). Such a pulse is rejected, however, if it is too short (e.g., < 75 ms) or too weak (its peak lies below k_4). Successive energy pulses may be considered part of one unit if the delay between pulses is less than 150 ms (the longest possible stop closure).

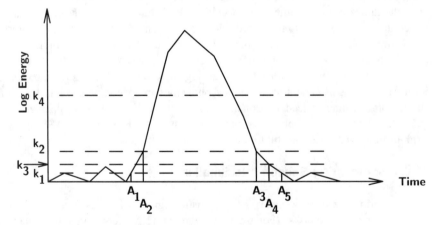

Figure 10.5 Example illustrating the use of energy thresholds to find start and end frames of possible speech units. (After Lamel *et al.* [90] © IEEE.)

When the available speech bandwidth exceeds 3 kHz (e.g., nontelephone speech), spectral information at high frequencies is sufficient to refine energy-determined boundaries with simple spectral measures [92]; e.g., zero-crossing rate (ZCR) provides a basic estimate of the frequency of major energy concentration. Background noise often has a flat or broad lowpass spectrum, and thus its ZCR corresponds roughly to a frequency in the middle-to-low range of the signal bandwidth. For speech obstruents, on the other hand, the ZCR is either high (corresponding to the high-frequency concentration of energy in fricatives and stop bursts) or very low (if a voicebar dominates). Weak fricatives, which cause the most detection difficulties, have high ZCRs.

The endpoint detection problem can be viewed as a subset of the problem of voiced/unvoiced/silence classification of speech, discussed briefly in Chapter 6 for pitch detectors. Endpoint detection can be done by combining a silence detector [93] with a postprocessor that heuristically eliminates short "silences" (i.e., stop closures) amid longer nonsilences.

10.6.1.2 Segmentation of speech into words (‡). While endpoint detection (speech–nonspeech discrimination) often allows a straightforward solution, finding relevant unit boundaries *within* speech segments is much more difficult. It is often implicitly and incorrectly assumed that speech is linear (a 1:1 correspondence between phonemes and nonoverlapping acoustic segments) and invariant (a 1:1 mapping between phonemes and acoustic features) [94]. In IWR, the use of word models avoids accounting for the effects of coarticulation, which obviates these assumptions. When segmenting continuous speech, however, coarticulation cannot be ignored. Direct segmentation of normal speech into words is in general very difficult.

Segmentation is simplified if each word is clearly spoken and the vocabulary is severely limited (e.g., connected-word speech). For example, an SI statistical approach can be applied to word strings of arbitrary length. Successful word segmentation can then be followed by IWR on the separated words. A linear or quadratic estimator (Figure 10.6) is designed via training on all pairs of words that may occur in a test utterance [95]. Frames of energy features (e.g., outputs of a bank of bandpass filters), orthogonalized into principal components via a Karhunen–Loève process to minimize the number of dimensions, provide a parameter vector $\mathbf{x}$ for every analysis window. The window is about 450 ms long to ensure that at most one word boundary may lie within it. Defining a target value z equal to 1 if the window contains a boundary and zero otherwise, a linear estimator $d = E(\mathbf{x}) = \mathbf{a} \cdot \mathbf{x}$ minimizes the mean value of $(z - d)^2$. From the Wiener–Hopf equation, the estimator vector is

$$\mathbf{a} = \langle \mathbf{x}\mathbf{x}^T \rangle^{-1} \cdot \langle z \cdot \mathbf{x} \rangle. \qquad (10.12)$$

Using a 26-component $\mathbf{x}$, word boundaries in sequences of digits were located with an average 32 ms error [95].

10.6.2 Dynamic Time Warping

This section deals with a major method for comparing two speech template patterns, which was very popular in the 1980s and is still used today. It specifically addresses the problem of time alignment, by nonlinearly stretching (*warping*) one template in an attempt to synchronize similar acoustic segments in the test and reference templates. This *dynamic time warping* (DTW) procedure combines alignment and distance computation in one dynamic programming procedure [60, 96–98]. DTW finds an optimal *path* through a network of

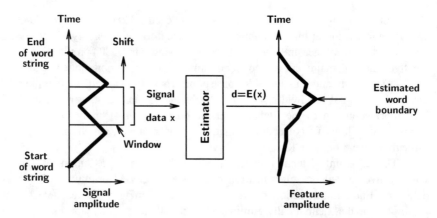

Figure 10.6 Example of segment boundary estimation: (a) a window is periodically shifted
along the time axis of a speech parameter, (b) an estimator calculates a value
d, whose maximum indicates the chosen boundary time. (After Zelinski and
Class [95] © IEEE.)

possibilities in comparing two multiframe templates, using the Bellman optimality principle
[99]. Linear time alignment is a special case of DTW, where only a single path comparing
synchronous frames between templates is considered. In DTW, small deviations from this
linear frame-by-frame comparison are allowed if the distance for a frame pair slightly off the
main path is smaller than other local frame comparisons. Phonetic segmentation (other than
endpointing) is not usually done on the test template (cf. segmentation difficulty above). Thus
DTW aligns it as a whole with each reference template by finding a time warping that
minimizes the total distance measure, which sums the individual *frame distances* in the
template comparison, i.e., sums the measures of successive frame-to-frame matchings.

Basic DTW assumes that (1) global variations in speaking rate for a person uttering the
same word at different times can be handled by linear time normalization; (2) local rate
variations within each utterance (which make linear normalization inadequate) are small and
can be handled using distance penalties called *local continuity constraints*; (3) each frame of
the test utterance contributes equally to ASR; and (4) a single distance measure applied
uniformly across all frames is adequate. The first two assumptions seem reasonable, but the
latter two are less so and have led to refinements of the basic DTW method. With many
vocabularies, ASR decisions can be based on specific parts of words (e.g., in the *E*-set,
examination of the vowels is irrelevant), which invalidates the third assumption above. As for
the fourth assumption, a single spectral measure (e.g., an LPC distance) may be efficient for
comparing vowels, but not for analyzing speech transients [100]. Despite these flaws, DTW is
an efficient method for some ASR. DTW has few advantages for monosyllabic utterances
(where linear normalization often suffices), but substantial increases in accuracy occur for
DTW in matching polysyllabic utterances [101].

DTW finds use also in training recognizers. Extracting training data or reference
templates for short acoustic segments reliably from continuous or connected speech can
require tedious hand segmenting and labeling. By relaxing local continuity constraints, DTW
has been used to align phones in unlabeled natural utterances with both synthetic and
previously labeled natural utterances [102]. Labeled utterances permit automatic extraction of
phone models from continuous speech.

10.6.2.1 Details of DTW operation.   Consider two patterns **R** and **T** (as in Equation (10.11)) of R and T frames each, corresponding to the reference template and test template, respectively. DTW finds a warping function $m = w(n)$, which maps the principal time axis n of **T** into the time axis m of **R** (Figure 10.7). Frame-by-frame through **T**, DTW searches for the best frame in **R** (subject to certain constraints) against which to compare each test frame. Since **T** is compared against many reference templates, the test axis is usually treated as the domain and the reference axis as the range. (Switching the two axes degrades ASR performance only slightly [103], even though w may not be invertible. If the templates under comparison are unequal in duration, it may be better to use the longer one on the horizontal axis, i.e., warp the shorter to the longer [28].) The warping curve derives from the solution of an optimization problem

$$D = \min_{w(n)} \left[\sum_{n=1}^{T} d(T(n), R(w(n))) \right], \qquad (10.13)$$

where each d term is a frame distance between the nth test frame and the $w(n)$th reference frame. D is the minimum distance measure corresponding to the *best path* $w(n)$ through a grid of $T \times R$ points (Figure 10.8a).

In theory, TR frame distances must be calculated for each template comparison, matching each test frame against every reference frame. In practice, continuity constraints restrict the search space, so that typically only about 30% of the matches are performed. Nonetheless, computation increases significantly: a linear frame-by-frame comparison for a typical 25 frame template requires only 25 distance calculations, while DTW needs about 150–200 distances ($\approx 0.3 \times 25^2$). Since DTW calculation usually increases as T^2 (vs T for a linear path), computation is heavy for long templates involving several words at a time. Computation may be limited by restricting the warp path to stay within a *window* of $\pm W$ frames of the linear path, which leads to about $2WT$ distance calculations (see Figure 10.9b). However, W must often be expanded for good recognition of longer utterances.

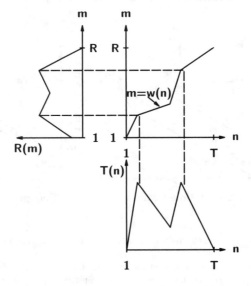

Figure 10.7 Example of nonlinear time alignment of a test $T(n)$ pattern and reference $R(m)$ pattern. (After Rabiner *et al.* [104] © IEEE.)

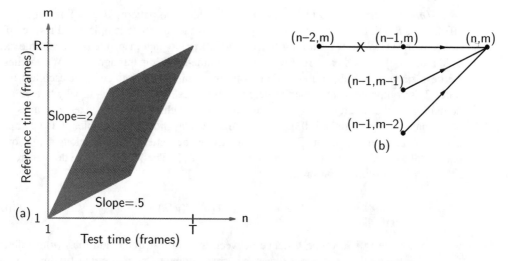

Figure 10.8 (a) Typical DTW plot, illustrating the optimal warp path $w(n)$ mapping the test time axis n into the reference time axis m. If the template endpoints are forced to match and the warping is restricted to lie within slopes of $\frac{1}{2}$ and 2, the shaded area shows the subset of points that is considered. (b) Permitted transitions to the grid point (n, m). Since two horizontal transitions are not allowed, the step marked $\times$ is illegal.

One way to decrease computation, at the cost of a small decrease in ASR accuracy, is to determine the warp path before calculating distances. Normally, the path is simultaneously specified as the local distances are computed, with the minimum accumulated distance determining the path. Few differences, however, exist among paths using distance measures of varying complexity (e.g., paths determined from Euclidean distances involving 1, 2, 4, 8, or 16 mel-cepstral coefficients are quite similar [105]). Rather than using costly distance

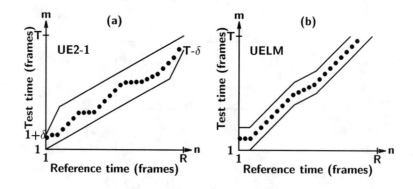

Figure 10.9 Variants on the DTW algorithm: (a) the UE2-1 (unconstrained endpoints, 2:1 slope constraints) method allows the omission from consideration of up to δ frames at the start and end of the reference template (similar allowance could also be made for the test template), and (b) the UELM (unconstrained endpoints, local minimum) method restricts the search area to a limited range around the locally optimum path. (After Rabiner *et al.* [104] © IEEE.)

measures just to find the warp path, intricate distances need be applied only after a path is found via simple measures. (The computational savings apply mostly to general-purpose hardware, e.g., microprocessors, where multiplications cost more than logical operations such as comparisons. With advances in computer technology, however, mathematical operations approach the speed of logical operations, raising the utility of mathematically intensive methods and eliminating the need for such shortcuts.)

10.6.2.2 Efficiency via search space reduction (‡).

For a point (n, m) in the grid, the minimum accumulated distance $D_a(n, m)$ from the start point $(1, 1)$ can be recursively defined:

$$D_a(n, m) = d(T(n), R(m)) + \min_{k \leq m} [D_a(n - 1, k)p(n - 1, k)], \qquad (10.14)$$

where p represents a penalty for deviating from the linear path or for violating continuity constraints, and d is the frame distance at point (n, m). Some systems use a binary penalty function (e.g., $p = 1$ for an acceptable path or $p = \infty$ for an unacceptable one [106]), while others allow p to follow the deviation of the path from the linear ideal [40]. Limiting the search to the range $k \leq m$ reflects the reasonable assumption that the warp path should be monotonic (i.e., no temporal backtracking). DTW limits the range further by continuity constraints, e.g., those in Figure 10.8(b), which require the reference index m to advance at least one frame for every two test frames and to skip no more than one reference frame for each test frame. This effectively makes the reasonable assumption that speaking rate changes by no more than 2:1 within a template utterance. Extrapolating these local slope constraints to the global grid in Figure 10.8(a), minimum and maximum slopes of $\frac{1}{2}$ and 2, respectively, restrict the set of grid points to be examined. Since these standard constraints lead to an asymmetric distance, symmetric versions have been proposed [88, 96]. Overall ASR performance, however, seems to vary little whether the standard constraints or other possibilities are used [103].

Figure 10.8(a) illustrates the *constrained endpoints* (CE) DTW algorithm. In the original approach, ASR accuracy is highly dependent on good endpoint detection of each unit (e.g., word) in the input test utterance, because no freedom is permitted in matching the first and last template frames. The two alternatives of Figure 10.9 are used in cases where endpoints are unreliable. A UE2-1 variant (unconstrained endpoints, 2:1 slope constraints) of DTW permits relaxing the local constraints by up to δ frames, but only for the first and last test frames. A similar procedure could eliminate the first or last few test frames from the total distance measure, relaxing the test axis as well as (or instead of) relaxing the reference axis at the endpoints. In either case, when comparing templates corresponding to the same "word" but with misaligned endpoints, the total distance remains low, unlike in the CE case. A further variant to UE2-1 extends each pattern with a few frames from a silence template [107].

One way to relax the endpoints (to raise ASR accuracy) yet reduce the search space (and hence calculation) is the *unconstrained endpoints, local minimum* (UELM) method of Figure 10.9(b). UELM follows the locally optimum path at time n, discarding paths that deviate more than a few reference frames from the best path up to that time. The CE method discards a path only if D_a exceeds a threshold, indicating that even if the remaining match were perfect, the total distance would be unacceptable (Figure 10.10). UELM allows more paths at the start (not rejecting a possibly good match due to poor alignment), but prunes other paths that the CE method would evaluate (thus a smaller search space). As Figure 10.9(b) shows, the final endpoint constraint is also dropped, which makes UELM especially suitable to applications where the final endpoint is unknown, e.g., in continuous speech

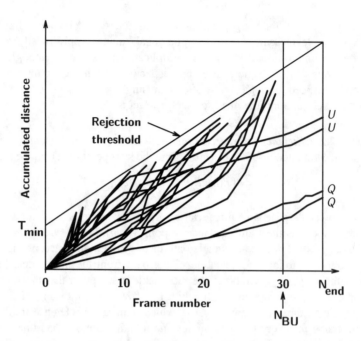

Figure 10.10 Plots of accumulated distance D_a as a function of frame number in the test template, corresponding to the letter Q in the A–Z vocabulary. Comparing the test Q against two reference templates each for all 26 letter utterances yields 52 paths. Only the letters Q and U have DTW paths that remain under the "discard" (rejection) threshold throughout the utterance duration. A typical threshold is specified by a slope (0.7 here) and a starting offset T_{min}. Some systems specify a number of "backup frames" N_{BU} at the end of the test template, which may be discarded if D_a rises suddenly at word's end, on the assumption that breath noise may be included via poor endpoint detection. (After Rabiner *et al.* [83] © IEEE.)

recognition or when searching for a keyword in continuous speech (*word spotting*). In one test on an alphadigit vocabulary, the CE method was superior for most utterances, but UELM performed best on words that were unusually long or short [83].

10.6.2.3 Problems with DTW. Apart from the major difficulty of adequately representing each speech unit with just one (averaged) reference template, DTW has some specific drawbacks, including: (1) still heavy computational load (vs a linear template match), and (2) treatment of durational variations as noise to be eliminated via time normalization. Furthermore, basic DTW does not allow weighting different parts of an utterance by their information contribution to ASR. For example, in the A–Z vocabulary, recognizing consonants is much more important than vowel identification in determining which of 26 letters was spoken; nonetheless, all frames of the test template contribute equally in basic DTW, and most frames pertain to vowels since they tend to be longer than consonants [108].

Some of these difficulties can be overcome by modifications to DTW: (a) nonlinear sampling in time, where frame intervals in both test and reference templates are nonuniform, can allow more speech representation during transients than during steady states (cf. variable-frame-rate speech coding [109]); (b) omitting highly correlated frames when producing templates (e.g., keeping only every second or third frame during the middle of continuant phones) apparently causes little loss in ASR accuracy, with reductions of up to 50% in memory (and hence of 75% in distance calculations) [110]. These modifications have drawbacks: the added complexity of aligning such warped templates and the extra computation to determine which frames to delete (both for the reference templates and for each test template). One (less effective) alternative uses longer (and fewer) frames, interpolating extra template frames (from neighboring frames) only during speech transients where the interframe distance exceeds a threshold [28].

A related approach [111] emphasizes spectral transients: the spectral distances between successive pairs of equal-length frames in a template are summed to obtain a measure of how much total spectral change occurs during the template, and the template utterance is reanalyzed at unequal time intervals so that the spectral change is uniformly distributed among the frames. Compared with standard DTW, error rate and computation decrease for this *trace segmentation* approach, but the savings depend on many factors such as vocabulary composition, distance measures, and hardware implementation. One difficulty with this technique is that steady-state segments may be compressed so much that some sounds are missed (e.g., the stop closure in X /ɛks/, which distinguishes it from S /ɛs/).

Basic DTW compensates for time variability in utterances. DTW can also use *frequency warping* so that small spectral deviations are allowed while using a simple distance measure [112]. Accommodating slight deviations in formant positions could be done by designing better distance measures, but it is easier to modify the calculation of Equation (10.14) to include a simple frequency deviation measure in addition to the usual spectral distance.

10.6.2.4 Applying DTW to continuous speech (‡).

Basic DTW succeeds best for relatively short utterances, e.g., words of a few syllables. Performance decreases with template length, due to computation (increasing as the square of utterance duration) and poorer ASR accuracy. In long utterances, speaking rate changes tend to affect word components differently, and simple local continuity DTW constraints become less valid. As template length increases, there is more chance that the optimal grid path may be discarded due to a locally large distance early in the warp. These mistakes can be avoided by relaxing the discard threshold or the continuity constraints, but only at the cost of increased computation due to more and longer paths examined.

With small vocabularies (e.g., < 100 words) in IWR, the task is small enough to permit an exhaustive search, i.e., one simply compares each test template against all reference models. Also, with corresponding small memory size, it is unnecessary to heavily compress frame representations to save space. However, if CSR is desired and if vocabulary increases to the thousands of words needed to handle general conversation, both memory and the time needed to search it become large enough to warrant more efficient procedures than exhaustive model evaluations. This section examines ways to reduce memory and search time while preserving ASR accuracy.

In CSR, reference templates corresponding to words are concatenated to form utterance-length templates, which are then compared with the test template (Figure 10.11). Word endpoints are not known within the test utterance, and so constrained-endpoint DTW can be used only for the start of the first word and the end of the last word. Elsewhere a form of UELM is applied, allowing utterance-internal word boundaries freedom, subject to the global constraints of the DTW search space. The simplest procedure does DTW for all possible combinations of words in the vocabulary. In the absence of linguistic restrictions (i.e., without a language model), a V-word vocabulary allowing utterances of up to W words in

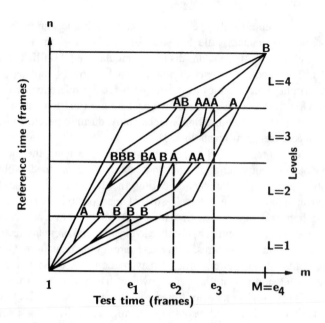

Figure 10.11 DTW plot applying a test template on the horizontal axis against a series of word reference templates on the vertical axis. This example assumes that the test utterance consists of four words. For a vocabulary of [A, B] and a test utterance BAAB, the local word paths ending at different times for each reference level are labeled A or B, depending on which reference template gave the smallest word distance. The ending times of the path with the least total accumulated distance to each reference level are noted as e_i. (After Myers and Rabiner [113] © IEEE.)

sequence has more than V^W word combinations, each requiring a template comparison. Language constraints for a given application reduce the number of comparisons (e.g., in spelled-out words, certain letter sequences are illegal in English). However, the large number of possibilities, combined with the fact that DTW calculation increases as the square of template duration, makes this exhaustive approach impractical for utterances of more than a few words.

A major problem for most CSR systems is the lack of adequate coarticulation modeling. Applying DTW to concatenated templates of isolated words works well at slow speaking rates for connected words, i.e., about 100–130 (usually monosyllabic) words/min. However, the use of polysyllabic words and more typical conversational rates (180–300 words/min) causes substantial accuracy loss.

10.6.2.5 Level building (‡). Several methods have been proposed to reduce the calculation of DTW for CSR. One is the *two-level* approach, which compares templates in two steps, one for individual words and one for the entire phrase [114]. An alternative method called *level building* (LB), however, is significantly more efficient [113]. Recognition is performed level by level, where each word reference template $\mathbf{R}_i$ represents a level. At the first level, the LB method applies DTW to compare $\mathbf{R}_i$ for each word that may appear in initial position in a test utterance against the initial portion of the test template $\mathbf{T}$. For each comparison, distance scores are stored for all allowed endpoints in $\mathbf{T}$, subject to the normal continuity constraints. At level 2, $\mathbf{R}_i$ for all possible second-position words are compared against $\mathbf{T}$, with paths starting from the endpoints of the previous level and proceeding to allowed endpoints for the second word. This procedure continues until all levels have been processed.

If we know the number of words in the test utterance (i.e., the number of levels), we may normalize $\mathbf{T}$ to match the number of frames in $\mathbf{R}_i$ (i.e., if each $\mathbf{R}_i$ has L frames and the test utterance has W words, $\mathbf{T}$ could be adjusted to LW frames for good DTW results). If, however, we only know the maximum test utterance length (e.g., less than 8 words), the local continuity constraints must be relaxed and normalization of $\mathbf{T}$ is less feasible; more comparisons must be made on the grid since each $\mathbf{R}_i$ could correspond either to all or part of $\mathbf{T}$.

While the number of local distance calculations is much less for LB than for the exhaustive approach, more information must be passed from level to level and fewer paths may be discarded than in standard DTW. In the example above, the number of local distances needed for LB DTW is proportional to V (or approximately $2V$, if continuity constraints are heavily relaxed), compared with V^W in the exhaustive case. However, at each level boundary, the distances for each $\mathbf{R}_i$ and for each allowed endpoint must be linked with the path distances for the next level to determine the minimal distances (and the identity of the best matching $\mathbf{R}_i$) to pass on to the next level. In addition to the usual template storage of IWR systems, *backtracking* information must be stored to determine the sequence of words in the test utterance. At each of W levels, LB employs three backtracking arrays of length T (if $\mathbf{T}$ has T frames): minimum accumulated distance, best template, and starting time in $\mathbf{T}$ from the previous level, all for each test frame (three $W \times T$ matrices). After the time warp, the output text is found by backtracking through the third (start time) matrix, picking up the text codes in the second matrix in backward order. The average number of local distance comparisons is about $VRWT/3$, where the factor $\frac{1}{3}$ represents the savings by applying local continuity constraints and R is the average number of frames in each reference template. The test template of T frames could be viewed as being warped against a composite reference template of WR frames, V times corresponding to each word in the vocabulary. In practice, the warping is performed level by level against reference templates of R frames each, with the same amount of calculation.

ASR accuracy can be increased at the cost of more complexity by allowing endpoint freedom at level boundaries, as illustrated in Figure 10.12. For each word reference template, the first δ_{R_1} frames and last δ_{R_2} frames can be treated as optional, i.e., the local word paths need not include them in their distance calculation. No frames in the test template may be skipped (as usual in DTW), but allowance is made at level boundaries to compare a test frame against either a final reference frame from the previous level or an initial frame in the current level. Calculation may be limited, with little risk of decreased accuracy, by constraining both M_T, a multiplier restricting the range of possible starting frames at each level, and ε, the UELM width [106].

Approaches to CSR that require prior segmentation suffer from inevitable errors in boundary placement, whereas nonsegmenting DTW methods (e.g., LB) insert short, spurious words into the output transcription. One hybrid approach, using the best of both methods, raises ASR performance by first dividing test utterances into segments approximating syllables and then allowing a UELM-type DTW to modify boundary locations to match the best warp paths [116]. Insertion of spurious segments is minimized by applying quadratic penalties to paths with high slope compression (i.e., big deviation from the linear warp path) or with large values for the average distance per frame.

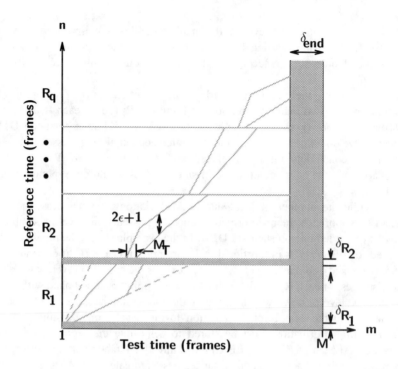

Figure 10.12 Illustration of level-building parameters δ_{R_1}, δ_{R_2}, δ_{end}, M_T, and ε. A test template of M frames is compared with up to $L_{\max}$ word reference templates. Typical values are $\varepsilon = 15$, $\delta_{\text{end}} = 4$, $\delta_{R_1} = 0\text{–}4$, $\delta_{R_2} = 3\text{–}6$, $M_T = 1.4$ [113,115]. (After Myers and Rabiner [113] © IEEE.)

10.6.2.6 The one-stage approach (‡). A method related to LB, called the *one-stage* approach, requires much less warping memory and, for long utterances (12 or so words), significantly less computation than the LB approach [117, 118]. The three LB backtracking matrices are replaced by two smaller $(V \times R)$ matrices and two T-dimensional arrays. For the minimum accumulated distance matrix $D(k, m, n)$, which notes the best distance up to time n in the test template for frame m in the kth reference template, the LB method stores values for all test frames and all levels. The new approach stores the values of D for all frames of all reference templates and updates this matrix for each test frame. Since T averages about WR frames, the new D storage is less if $W^2 > V$ (i.e., if the square of the maximum number of words in an utterance exceeds the vocabulary size). Similar arguments hold for the back-pointer matrices. The "best template" matrix of the LB method is replaced with two arrays indexed along the test template time axis, one keeping track of potential word boundaries and the other following recognition decisions. Memory savings for this last matrix replacement occur for utterance lengths of more than two words.

The one-stage method evaluates local distance measures once for each test frame against each reference frame in memory and applies continuity constraints only in summing up the distances; i.e., the one-stage dynamic programming does not limit which distances are to be calculated in the search space as standard DTW does. Thus VRT distances are needed. Dynamic programming is used to find the optimal path through the search space *after* having computed all local distances. If $W/3 > 1$ (the $\frac{1}{3}$ continuity factor again), fewer distances are needed in the one-stage approach than in level-building. Using a *reduced* LB approach, which limits the search space to deviations of only $\pm R$ frames from the linear warp path, can make the distance calculations of the two methods comparable. Since the best path may deviate beyond R frames, the reduced LB method cannot guarantee the optimal path that the one-stage method does.

10.6.2.7 Hybrid segmentation-DTW recognition (‡). A comparison of DTW with an alternative approach of segmenting speech into small acoustic units and then labeling them shows that DTW has the advantage of better accuracy for IWR at the cost of higher computation. To exploit the efficiency of the segment/label approach over DTW, while avoiding accuracy loss due to the former's segmentation errors, a hybrid segmentation-DTW technique may be fruitful. The typical *segmenting recognizer* often misses short acoustic segments and subdivides homogeneous segments, but DTW can (to a limited degree) bypass short spurious segments, overlook missing segments, and merge successive similar segments. In hybrid recognizers, the segmenter may propose either many segment boundaries, including many spurious ones (i.e., not phone boundaries), or just a few very reliable boundaries, e.g., voicing transitions. In the first approach, the number of template frames is reduced by merging frames between boundaries to yield average frames. If the number of proposed segments is significantly fewer than the original number of frames, computation and memory are decreased [119]. As in the trace segmentation method, however, this approach may overemphasize speech transients at the expense of the longer continuant phones.

The second hybrid method of few reliable boundaries allows restricting the scope of DTW to within major segments (thus shortening the durations of templates involved) or, in the case of certain vocabularies, even eliminating DTW for some segments [120]. Consider the A–Z vocabulary, where each word (except W) consists of a vowel, preceded or followed by 0–2 consonants. Comparing low-frequency energy in the 100–800 Hz region against total energy provides a reliable segmenter to isolate the vocalic portion of each word since consonants usually have most energy at higher frequencies. By partitioning the vocabulary into subclasses (*cohorts*) depending on whether the words have initial or final consonants, only a fraction of the reference templates must be examined for any test utterance [120].

10.6.3 Applying Vector Quantization to ASR

Vector quantization (VQ) is often applied to ASR for the same reason it was useful for speech coders, i.e., efficient data reduction. Since transmission rate is not a major issue for ASR, the utility of VQ here lies in the efficiency of using compact codebooks for reference models and codebook searches in place of more costly evaluation methods. For IWR, each vocabulary word gets its own VQ codebook, based on a training sequence of several repetitions of the word. The test speech is evaluated by all codebooks, and ASR chooses the word whose codebook yields the lowest distance measure (the sum of the frame distances). In basic VQ, codebooks have no explicit time information (e.g., the temporal order of phonetic segments in each word and their relative durations are ignored), since codebook entries are not ordered and can come from any part of the training words. However, some indirect durational cues are preserved because the codebook entries are chosen to minimize average distance across all training frames, and frames corresponding to longer acoustic segments (e.g., vowels) are more frequent in the training data. Such segments are thus more likely to specify codewords than less frequent consonant frames, especially with small codebooks. Codewords nonetheless exist for consonant frames because such frames would otherwise contribute large frame distances to the codebook. Often a few codewords suffice to represent many frames during relatively steady sections of vowels, thus allowing more codewords to represent short, dynamic portions of the words. This relative emphasis that VQ puts on speech transients can be an advantage over other ASR comparison methods for vocabularies of similar words.

10.6.3.1 Incorporating timing information into VQ ASR (‡).

VQ's major weakness for ASR is its poor use of timing information. One way to directly incorporate temporal cues into VQ ASR uses multiple codebooks for each word, dividing it into equal-duration segments (usually eight or fewer), with separate codebooks for each segment [121]. Ideally, each word would be divided into distinct acoustic segments (e.g., phones), where very small codebooks would suffice to accurately describe each segment. Even when using equal-length segments (which avoids difficult phone segmentation), small codebooks suffice because each section has only a fraction of the acoustic variation during the word. Template memory is larger for multiple (vs single) codebooks because similar codewords are repeated in codebooks for adjacent word segments. The advantage of this approach lies in its direct (albeit coarse) utilization of timing information.

An alternative procedure exploits timing detail more precisely by using likelihood functions for each codeword [122]. Assuming I frames in each word template, a probability function $p_k(i)$ specifies how often the kth codeword appears at frame i ($1 \leq i \leq I$) in the training data. During ASR, each local distance measure sums the usual "spectral" distance (which can also include other information, e.g., energy) and a "temporal" distance ($-\log[p_k(i)]$). Roughly equal weighting between the two gives the best results. One drawback here is a large increase in memory to store the $p_k(i)$: typical codewords have about 8–10 parameters (e.g., LPC coefficients), compared to I probability values (e.g., $I = 40$ frames/word). On the other hand, ASR performance for the VQ approach is comparable to that of DTW, with less computation compared to DTW with multiple templates per word (e.g., speaker-independent systems). DTW with Q reference templates/word requires about $QI^2/3$ frame distances/word, compared to LI VQ distances/word if each codebook has L entries. VQ recognition can be up to 20 times more efficient in cases where small codebooks suffice (e.g., $Q = 12$ and $L = 8$ [122]).

10.6.3.2 VQ codebook and search techniques (‡).

VQ can also be used to reduce distance computation in the case of LVR systems. Assume that a large codebook can handle all speech sounds for a given speaker (in SD systems) or all speakers (for SI ASR). Such codebooks of about 1024 entries are typical in speech coding and can also be applied to ASR, which may not need as much representation accuracy as coding does. So most VQ ASR uses 64-, 128-, or 256-entry codebooks, i.e., 6–8 b/codeword (Figure 10.13). Smaller codebooks for specific words could be subsets of a large universal codebook; however, some optimality might be sacrificed this way, rather than locating codewords independently for each vocabulary word. Since each test frame need be compared only once against each codeword in the universal set, ASR using a universal codebook eliminates duplicating distance calculations for the same codewords in separate codebooks. If the ASR vocabulary has sufficiently diverse sounds, which is typical for vocabularies of more than 20 words, a universal codebook often yields performance comparable to systems using separate codebooks.

Most VQ ASR has used full-search algorithms to find the optimal codeword. Computation could be reduced by applying a binary tree search and/or using a table lookup for the distances. In the latter approach, all possible N^2 distances between codewords in a codebook of N entries would be stored in a table, and the only distance computations during

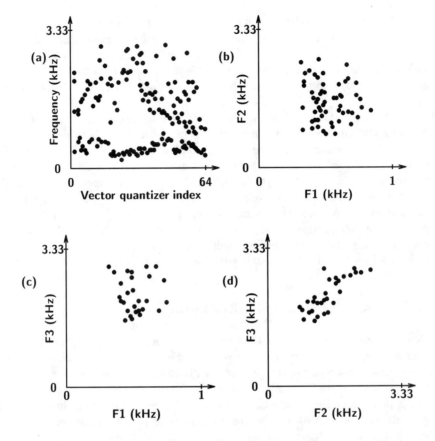

Figure 10.13 Plots of locations of the first three resonances (formants) of 64 codebook vectors: (a) as a function of codebook index, (b) in the F1–F2 plane (as in the vowel triangle), (c) in the F1–F3 plane, (d) in the F2–F3 plane. (After Rabiner *et al.* [123]. Reprinted with permission from the *Bell System Technical Journal* © 1983, AT&T.)

ASR would be those of the codebook searches of the test frames. The disadvantage is that the stored distances include two distortions rather than one: the use of a codebook for the reference frames introduces the first distortion, and quantizing the test frame before distance evaluation introduces the second. ASR accuracy usually suffers from the extra distortion. Thus it is preferable not to vector-quantize the test frame unless accuracy must be sacrificed for decreased computation.

10.6.3.3 Levenshtein distance. Limiting the representation for speech frames to a small set of possible spectra, as VQ does, allows the use of an efficient alternative to standard DTW called the *Levenshtein distance* (LD) [124]. Comparing two strings of textual ASR output (or templates as symbol strings of feature vectors, each represented by a VQ index), the LD is the minimum number of symbols needed to convert one string to the other, via deletion, insertion, or substitution (e.g., the string ABBC can be changed into ABCCC by substituting a C for one B and inserting another C; hence LD = 2). Most ASR systems try to minimize the word error rate, often using the LD as an error measure, which is not the same as maximizing $P(t|s)$.

By weighting insertions and deletions equally (for symmetry) and heavily (vs substitutions), a *weighted* LD (WLD) can be efficiently implemented through dynamic programming as an alternative to DTW (e.g., 95% accuracy for isolated digits with 16 codewords [124]). If one string is L symbols longer than the other, time normalization is accomplished by subtracting from the WLD a weight equal to L times the weight of a deletion.

The application of VQ to ASR is an example of clustering. Designing a codebook by choosing codeword vectors so that the average distance of all templates to their nearest codewords is minimized can be time-consuming in the training phase but yield good performance in the recognition phase. Normally, an initial codebook estimate is refined iteratively, e.g., via the splitting techniques of Chapter 7, until the mean distance falls below a threshold or remains stable for two iterations. Simpler codebook generation appears to suffice for ASR applications, however. In the *covering* approach [125], the first frame of training data provides the initial codeword, and each subsequent training frame is added to the codebook only if its distance to all previous codeword vectors exceeds a threshold. The resulting codebook may be pruned, without apparent loss of accuracy, by discarding up to about 30% of the least-used codewords.

10.7 NETWORKS FOR SPEECH RECOGNITION

Networks are used in many ASR systems to represent information about acoustic events in speech [126, 127]. For example, knowledge about syntactic and semantic constraints on allowable sequences of words may be efficiently coded in terms of a network whose states are the vocabulary words. Transitions between states are allowed only if the resulting string of words produces a legal sentence following the system's grammar. Such networks can be generalized to other ASR applications if the states represent acoustic segments or frames of speech data.

Networks in ASR employ a statistical, rather than rule-based, representation of acoustic information. Let's first apply networks to IWR: model each word with a succession of phonetic states i (corresponding roughly to phones), linked by transitions specified by likelihoods a_{ij}. This probability of a phonetic segment j following segment i governs the transition between the states representing those two sounds. Consider *pass* as an example word, where states for /p/ closure (silence), /p/ burst, /pæ/ aspiration, /æ/, and /s/ might be chosen via coarse segmentation, VQ, or some other technique. To allow for the chance that the /p/ burst and/or aspiration may be missing (or overlooked in the analysis of some training samples), the a_{ij} may vary considerably; they typically correspond to the frequency of actual transitions in the training data.

For IWR, each input word utterance is evaluated by each word network, to find the network most likely to have generated the word. Instead of searching a DTW space for a path of minimal distance, each network is searched for the path maximizing the product of all transition probabilities between states corresponding to the test utterance. In practice, log likelihoods are used so that probability values may be summed, instead of multiplied, for faster computation.

10.7.1 Hidden Markov Models (HMMs)

The most common network for ASR is the *first-order Markov process* or *chain*, where the likelihood of being in a given state depends only on the immediately prior state (and not on earlier states) [128–131] (Figure 10.14). To exploit the temporal order of events in speech, only left-to-right transitions are allowed. Thus the model states are ordered, with initial, middle and final states, respectively, corresponding to the beginning, middle and end of an utterance being modeled. The networks are often called *hidden Markov models* (HMMs) [132] because the models must be inferred through observations of speech outputs, not from any internal representation of speech production. States may be viewed as corresponding roughly to acoustic events; in a word model, the first few states represent word-initial phones and the last states model the final phones. Thus, unlike normal Markov models, the underlying speech production of HMMs is not directly observable. However, we can align observed speech frames and the states of an HMM probabilistically.

To better understand Markov models, consider a simple *nonhidden* case of two people A and B alternating turns according to some probabilistic event (e.g., tossing a 6-sided die) every cycle (corresponding to a time frame). When A tosses the die, suppose A retains it if the result is 1, 2, 3 or 4; if B has the die, it is passed back to A if 6 is thrown. In this case, the transition probabilities are thus: $a_{11} = 2/3$, $a_{12} = 1/3$, $a_{21} = 1/6$, $a_{22} = 5/6$. An *observation sequence* here is just a listing of the turns, e.g., AABBAB... if A held the die two turns then passed it to B, etc. Someone analyzing a long enough sequence would easily be able to estimate the a_{ij} from simple statistics, if it was known to be a first-order model. (If the passing rule were more complex, involving past history (e.g., A passes if a 6 is thrown *and* A has kept it for 3 cycles), higher-order Markov models would be needed, requiring more analysis.) The observations are usually associated with states (i.e., they appear on each cycle depending on the state used); this is called a *Moore* finite-state machine. (We will ignore the alternative Mealy machine, which associates an observation to each *transition* [99].)

For HMMs, each state k is also characterized by a probabilistic event b_k, e.g., flipping a coin. Suppose person A in state 1 flips a dime weighted so that a head occurs 70% of the time, while B flips a normal penny (50% heads, 50% tails, i.e., $b_2 = 1/2$ each for H and T). Every cycle, either A or B flips their coin and records the result (heads H or tails T) with an observer (e.g., a listener). From the observation sequence (e.g., HHTTHTTHHH), an analysis may

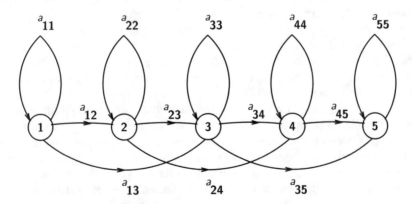

Figure 10.14 Five-state Markov model with Bakis restrictions on transitions. With each state j is associated an observation vector $\mathbf{b}_j$, whose elements indicate the likelihood of observing different speech spectra in that state and a set of transitions, each denoted by an arc with probability a_{ij} of arriving in that state from state i. (After Rabiner *et al.* [133]. Reprinted with permission from the *AT&T Bell Laboratories Technical Journal* © 1984, AT&T.)

estimate both the state and transition probabilities. There is no single solution for HMMs, but ML or MAP methods described later make reasonable estimates.

10.7.1.1 Speech HMMs.

Generalizing now to speech HMMs, the number of states for an HMM modeling a phone, word, or larger speech unit is usually more than two (roughly corresponding to the number of distinct acoustic segments in a typical utterance being modeled). The outputs are not just H or T, but come from a much larger alphabet (e.g., a VQ codebook with hundreds of speech spectra).

A phone HMM might use three states to represent, in order, an initial transition spectrum from a prior phone, a spectrum from the phone's presumed steady state, and a final transition spectrum to an ensuing phone. To account for variability (from coarticulation, speaking rate, different speakers, etc.), each state is represented by a PDF of spectra rather than a fixed spectrum; e.g., the middle state of a model for /u/ would have high state probabilities b for spectra with F1 near 300 Hz and F2 near 900 Hz. In comparing an unknown phone to this HMM, the likelihood of a match is reflected in the b values. Formally, the correspondence between model states and acoustic segments is described by an observation probability matrix $\mathbf{B}$ whose elements $b_j(k)$ are the likelihoods of observing symbol k (columns) in state j (rows). Symbols normally correspond to spectra of acoustic segments, represented by 8–14 parameters; thus $\mathbf{B}$ is a matrix of multivariate probability distributions. These column distributions are often discrete, e.g., 64–256 spectra chosen by VQ. Continuous $\mathbf{B}$ functions, e.g., a weighted sum of five Gaussian densities [61], however, provide better ASR performance than discrete functions [123]. Many ASR systems model each state PDF as a sum or weighted *mixture* (combination) of several Gaussian PDFs, because: (1) PDF's modeling variability across different speakers and phonetic contexts often have complex shapes, and (2) Gaussian PDF's are simple to model. (One ASR system uses the maximum of a set of Gaussian PDF's, rather than a weighted sum, to save computation [58].)

In the *Bakis model* of Markov chains [134] (Figure 10.14), three transitions are allowed from each state: (1) a *self-loop* transition back to the same state i (representing the *insertion* or continuation of an acoustic segment), (2) a transition to the next state $i + 1$ (a *substitution* or new segment), and (3) a *skip* transition to the following state $i + 2$ (corresponding to the *deletion* of the acoustic segment for the skipped state). More general HMMs allowing transitions to any succeeding state $j > i$ (rather than only states i, $i + 1$, $i + 2$) increase computation but not ASR accuracy. The *state transition* matrix $\mathbf{A}$ of probabilities a_{ij} is zero below the main diagonal for the standard left-to-right case. For the Bakis model, only three diagonals of $\mathbf{A}$ are nonzero. (A simplified Bakis model allowing only single jumps has just two nonzero diagonals.)

The time-ordered association of each state with successive acoustic segments is only an approximation that depends on how many states are used to model each word or phoneme. Since efficiency suggests minimizing the number of states, some cases may not use enough states to permit clear sound-state association. The utility of timing information is reflected in the number of states needed to handle different vocabularies. For example, the 0–9 vocabulary in English can almost be discriminated based on just the vowels of the digits (only *five* and *nine* present a possible confusion); beyond three states per model, there is only a weak relationship between ASR accuracy and an increasing number of states [123]. A more confusable vocabulary involving longer words having similar vowels exhibits the more expected relationship of increasing accuracy with more states [133]. The type of errors that an HMM sometimes allows (e.g., between *in* and *evening*) suggests that the Markov structure may not fully exploit temporal cues unless sufficient states are employed.

10.7.1.2 Training Markov models. We now turn to the major tasks for speech HMMs: their training and evaluation. The *training* of the parameters in each HMM involves an initial estimation of the **A** and **B** matrices and then their iterative *reestimation*. A standard method is the *expectation-maximization* (E-M) algorithm [135], a procedure similar to that of designing VQ codebooks, where a good initial guess both accelerates the codebook evolution and raises the likelihood of achieving a good model. As in VQ design, the training iterations using a gradient or hill-climbing method guarantee only a locally optimum model. If training is not done in real time, several HMMs could be developed for each word, starting from different initial estimates [123]. Training can accomplish speaker adaptation and can be modified to handle noisy or stressed speech conditions [136].

Some systems rely on random initial parameter estimates, although performance can vary significantly for HMMs based on different initial values (e.g., ±1% variations on an average 4% error rate [123]). More realistic starting values can be obtained by examining repeated training utterances to yield many redundant states (those with similar spectra) for each acoustic segment. Merging such states (or averaging all frames within segments identified by coarse segmentation) yields a more efficient initial HMM. Among the training *tokens* (utterances) examined, the network with the most states (after merging) can be selected as the prototype. States corresponding to many mergers (and thus to long acoustic segments) may be split into two successive states to ensure that phones are not skipped by deletion transitions (of the Bakis model) during recognition.

In reestimation, the initial prototype acoustic vector for each state (however obtained) evolves iteratively to a full PDF, through an averaging or clustering procedure involving the rest of the training data. Typically the initial vector provides the first estimate of the mean of the PDF. Similarly, each transition probability, possibly assigned an initial likelihood of $1/L$ (where L is the number of transitions from each state), evolves in response to how often that transition appears in the training set. The most common averaging procedures are variations of the *Viterbi algorithm* [134, 137, 138] (e.g., the gradient method), the *Baum–Welch algorithm* [139], or the *forward–backward* (F–B) algorithm [32, 140].

Consider an observation matrix **O** of spectral vectors from T training utterances; the elements O_{kj} could be pth-order vectors of LPC coefficients, where $k = 1, 2, \ldots, F$ (F frames/utterance) and $j = 1, 2, \ldots, T$. The probability of **O** being generated by an N-state HMM with parameter matrices **A** and **B** is

$$P = \prod_{j=1}^{T} \sum_{i_1, i_2, \ldots, i_F} b_{i_1}(O_{1j}) a_{i_1 i_2} b_{i_2}(O_{2j}) \cdots a_{i_{(F-1)} i_F} b_{i_F}(O_{Fj}), \qquad (10.15)$$

i.e., the joint probability (over T training tokens) of the sum of the path probabilities for all possible paths through the model (each index i ranges over all N states). Each path probability is the product of F probabilities b (functions of the observation **O** and corresponding to the F frames of each token) and F-1 transition probabilities a (representing the F-1 transitions among states for F frames). The objective of HMM training is to choose the **A** and **B** matrix parameters to maximize P, a classical problem in constrained optimization ("constrained" because each matrix row or column is a set of probabilities and must sum to 1).

In the F–B method, a forward joint probability $\alpha_t(i)$ for each N-state HMM is defined for being in state j ($1 \leq j \leq N$) and observing the data up to time t (i.e., $O_1, O_2, \ldots, O_t$). The final probability for each model over T frames is $P = \sum_{i=1}^{N} \alpha_T(i)$, calculated inductively starting initially as $\alpha_1(j) = \pi_j b_j(O_1)$, with induction step $\alpha_{t+1}(j) = (\sum_{i=1}^{N} \alpha_t(i) a_{ij}) b_j(O_{t+1})$. While theoretically N^T paths must be examined, this method notes that, in calculating P, the local probability $\alpha_t(i)$ at each state i needs no more than the product of the next observation likelihood $b_j(O_{t+1})$ and the N weighted likelihoods from the previous time t (from the previous N $\alpha_t(i)$). A similar backward probability $\beta_t(i)$ for the remaining speech data (from t to T frames), starting from state i, is also used. The total calculation is reduced from $2TN^T$ calculations to N^2T.

In the popular Baum–Welch approach [140], each parameter is reestimated as follows (with a_{ij} as an example):

$$a'_{ij} = \frac{a_{ij}\partial P/\partial a_{ij}}{\sum_{k=1}^{N} a_{ik}\partial P/\partial a_{ik}}. \qquad (10.16)$$

In terms of the forward and backward probabilities,

$$a'_{ij} = \frac{\sum_{t=1}^{T}\alpha_{t-1}(i)a_{ij}b_j(O_t)\beta_t(j)}{\sum_{t=1}^{T}\alpha_{t-1}(i)\beta_t(i)}.$$

The reestimation cycle continues until P no longer increases between two iterations (or, to minimize computation, the iteration can be truncated after a few cycles). (The algorithm is robust but slow [141]). Initial parameter estimates should not be zero (other than structurally constrained elements of matrix $\mathbf{A}$) because any parameter initially estimated as zero remains so during reestimation. If, after reestimation completes, some $b_j(k)$ values are zero (because the kth spectrum was not observed during the jth state in the training data), they should either be interpolated from neighboring values [32] or be assigned an arbitrary small probability (and the other values rescaled) [123]. Assuming L training frames for the model, one often assigns a minimum probability of approximately $1/L$ to each b parameter (for a VQ codebook with $M \ll L$ entries), on the assumption that a further training token might have exhibited the missing spectrum.

One of the problems for HMM ASR is the considerable training needed to reasonably specify a large number of model parameters. For a typical 5-state, 64-spectrum VQ HMM (Figure 10.15), the $\mathbf{A}$ matrix does not present any difficulty because it has only $5^2 = 25$ entries, many of which are null by definition (i.e., the Bakis model). The $\mathbf{B}$ matrix, however, has $5 \times 64 = 320$ parameters to estimate. Assuming a typical 40 frames/word utterance, even 100 training tokens for each vocabulary word are barely adequate to estimate the b values. Many systems assume a multivariate Gaussian PDF for the $\mathbf{b}$ vector in each HMM state [61]; e.g., instead of a 64-element discrete PDF for VQ with 64 codewords, training results in a smooth PDF in L dimensions for frames of $L \approx 10$ spectral parameters. Since accurately determining the mean vector and covariance matrix for a general ten-dimension Gaussian requires much training data, the covariance matrix is often assumed to be diagonal, reducing the number of parameters per frame to 20.

The $\mathbf{b}$ vectors can be taken to be nonparametric instead of Gaussian, where the number of elements in each $\mathbf{b}$ vector corresponds to the spectral sampling resolution. VQ is popular for HMMs because it clusters the training spectra into a relatively small number of possibilities. (When VQ is used, one might think that training tokens yielding large distortion measures should be discarded when estimating the HMM parameters, but such tokens are useful [123].) While codebooks of 64 entries provide adequate spectral resolution in many cases, ASR performance improves with well-trained, larger codebooks. To accurately estimate

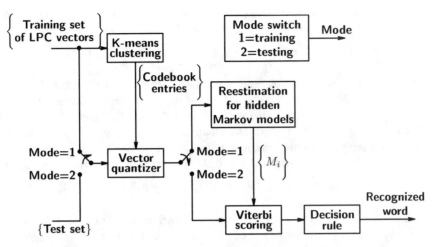

Figure 10.15 Block diagram of HMM–VQ recognition. (Reprinted with permission from the *Bell System Technical Journal*. © 1983, AT&T [123].)

the **B** matrix for large codebooks presents a significant training problem, especially for SD systems, where each user may be asked to utter thousands of training words. Although more training is required for SI than for SD applications, the task of SI training can be spread among many speakers.

Given an HMM structure and a choice of acoustic parameters, training methods such as the Baum–Welch algorithm estimate appropriate values for the models. However, the structure and parameters must be chosen *a priori*, and so far their selection has been suboptimal, since we do not know what model is best.

10.7.1.3 Classification via HMMs.   After training, the major ASR task for HMMs is evaluation or classification of test utterances. Equations (10.15) and (10.16) can be used, by calculating P for the corresponding test observation $\mathbf{O}$ with all trained HMMs. The ASR output corresponds to the model yielding the highest P. (Since each time there is only a single test observation matrix $\mathbf{O}$, as opposed to multiple training tokens, the second subscript for $\mathbf{O}$ in Equation (10.15) is dropped here.) A version of the Viterbi algorithm [123, 133] yields similar results while considerably reducing calculation. This method defines frame probabilities $f_j(i)$, for $i = 1, 2, \ldots, N$; $j = 1, 2, \ldots, F$, as the likelihood that the jth test frame is in state i for each of the N HMM states. To minimize further computation, logarithms of probabilities are used. Assuming a left-to-right HMM, the first frame must be in state 1 (more general cases allow an initial probability vector noting explicitly the likelihoods for each state at the start); thus

$$f_1(i) = \log[0] = -\infty, \qquad \text{for } i \neq 1,$$
$$f_1(1) = \log[b_1(O_1)]$$

(10.17)

notes the likelihood that the first test frame O_1 could have come only from the first state of the HMM under examination. The algorithm then proceeds recursively ($j = 1, 2, \ldots, F$)

through the F frames, maximizing frame values, which at each frame involve the prior frame's value, the transition probabilities, and the observation probabilities:

$$f_j(k) = \max_i \{f_{j-1}(i) + \log[a_{ik}] + \log[b_k(O_j)]\} \qquad \text{for } 1 \le k \le N, \qquad (10.18)$$

where the maximization is over states i that have transitions into state k. The final probability P for the HMM is $\exp f_F(N)$, that of the last frame that must represent the final state.

This simpler Viterbi search is much faster than the F–B method because it locates only the one best path in the HMM, rather than calculating the sum of probabilities of all paths. When log probabilities are used, no multiplications are needed; e.g., if $d(t, i)$ is the minimum "distance" (in terms of summed log likelihoods) to state i at time t, then in a recursion

$$d(t, i) = \min_j \{d(t-1, j) - \log[a_{ji}] - \log[b_i(O_i)]\},$$

where $d(1, i) = -\log[\pi_i] - \log[b_i(O_1)]$. For backtracking to know the states along the optimal path, we define the best last state ending at state i at time t as $s(t, i) = \min_j \{d(t-1, j) - \log[a_{ji}]\}$, where $s(1, i) = 0$, all for $1 \le (i, j) \le N$. The Viterbi search is especially useful in training because the best path provides a direct segmentation of each utterance, specifying which frames correspond to each of the states of the HMM, via use of a backpointer during the search. There is no explicit segmentation in the F–B method since all paths are examined and contribute equally.

10.7.1.4 Sub-word models.
The crucial question of what speech unit size is best for ASR leads us to explore units smaller than the word, and bigger than phones, to capture coarticulation effects well. We saw the same tradeoffs in speech synthesis, where voice response systems had more vocabulary flexibility and smaller memory requirements for smaller stored speech units. However, for much the same reasons as in synthesis, ASR accuracy deteriorates with shorter units. For LVR, diphone or tied-phone models represent a reasonable compromise, avoiding both huge memories for word models and poor ASR accuracy with CI phone models. If the input speech contains unstressed syllables (i.e., any application except monosyllabic IWR), accuracy improves significantly when reference models are stored for both stressed and unstressed versions of the sub-word units employed [108].

Assuming that about 1000 diphones suffice to represent a language and that each model has about 20 frames, such a sub-syllable template memory could handle unlimited vocabulary and still only require memory comparable to that of 500 word templates at 40 frames/word [142]. When using sub-word speech units, the reference memory must also contain a dictionary mapping each word into its sequence of these units, e.g., the sequence of diphones constituting each vocabulary word. This additional dictionary is nonetheless small compared with the template memory, e.g., needing only about 10 b/diphone for an average of 6 diphones/word [142]. Diphone ASR often requires a hand-segmented database, however.

Replacing word models with sub-word models reduces ASR accuracy [142]. The major difficulties are that (1) coarticulation and stress effects extend beyond immediately adjacent phones, and (2) constructing word models by concatenating smaller units requires significant modifications to the merged units (e.g., at each unit boundary, smoothing template frames or merging HMM states). In addition to spectral smoothing at boundaries, some units should be shortened when forming polysyllabic models, because word duration does not increase linearly with the number of syllables in a word.

Because constructing sub-word dictionaries (for either ASR or TTS applications) can be tedious, automatic procedures have been developed [143]. If a phonetician establishes a set of sub-word reference models for one speaker, sets for other speakers may be automatically obtained by applying DTW between the speech of new speakers and reference templates of the original set. Sub-word models can be applied to CSR in different ways. The complexities of combining short models to form word models can be avoided if speech is first segmented into sub-word units; e.g., date–time sentences (e.g., "September third at 3 p.m.") of 4–16 syllables were recognized with 94% accuracy in a SD task using DTW on syllable templates [88].

10.7.1.5 Context-dependent acoustic models.

To simplify the ASR search, many systems use *context-independent* (CI) acoustic models, where each model unit (e.g., word or phone) is trained independently of its neighbors, ignoring their coarticulation effects. With small amounts of training data, this minimizes *undertraining* problems, where model parameters are often poorly estimated (for lack of enough data) when using more numerous *context-dependent* (CD) models.

CD models are typically *triphone* HMMs representing N phonemes each with N^2 models; e.g., /p/ has a separate model for each combination of all possible left and right neighbors (/ipi,ipu,upa . . . /). CD models capture most coarticulatory effects, but at the cost of developing and searching N^3 models (e.g., with $N \approx 30$–40 phones). In many cases, there are insufficient resources (e.g., memory and training data) to support a full set of such models. Undertrained CD models have low ASR accuracy. Sometimes N^2 *biphone* models are used, conditioned on either right or left context, as a compromise between undertraining and memory. Similarly, diphone models, modeling phone-to-phone transitions (as in TTS), can also be used.

10.7.1.6 Tying sub-word speech models.

One important way to reduce undertraining is to *share* or *tie* parameters across models, using the same values in all models pertinent to a given context. Having separate triphone CD models for all sequences of three phones is inefficient, since many phone contexts have similar coarticulatory effects; e.g., the effects of labial /f,v,p,b,m/ on an adjacent vowel are very similar. *Tied* models share the same parameter values to reduce the total number of parameters to train; CD models are tied where their contexts are viewed to have similar phonetic effects (Figure 10.16). Tying can be automatic (e.g., with unsupervised, data-driven decision trees [144]), or guided by linguistic properties (e.g., grouping contexts with labels such as labial, velar, fricative, etc.). When tying involves Gaussian PDFs, the models are called *semi-continuous* HMMs. Related *allophone clustering* also reduces the number of models, while retaining the power of CD models and improving their accuracy [145]; e.g., one study raised keyword accuracy by 15% while reducing model memory by 40% [146].

When two or more word-network models share sub-word sections (or when their parameters are tied), memory for the reference models and ASR computation are both reduced. Sharing can be applied at many levels: word, syllable, diphone, phone, frame (*fenonic*) [147, 148] or parameter.

Even with tied states, use of continuous Gaussian mixtures in HMMs is expensive in computation and memory [149]. Some ASR ties parameters, e.g., using a single set of Gaussian PDFs; then, each HMM state is characterized just by its mixture weights. We assume that a few hundred PDFs suffice to model all acoustic space (much like a 10 b VQ dictionary works for speech coders). The training problem for each state then reduces to estimating these weights, rather than finding all parameters for mixtures of Gaussian PDFs separately (especially expensive if each frame vector has dozens of parameters and a full covariance is used).

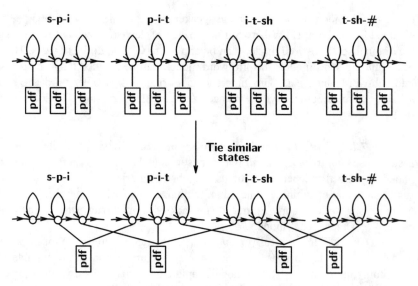

Figure 10.16 View of state tying for HMMs.

10.7.1.7 Comparing HMMs and DTW.   As in DTW, HMMs use a form of dynamic programming to find the best match between a test utterance and different reference models. Viterbi HMM determines the sequence of states i_1, i_2, ..., i_F that maximizes P, while DTW finds a warp path to minimize an accumulated distance (Figure 10.17). Unlike most DTW methods, no multiplications are required for Viterbi HMM. Furthermore, in IWR, the number of HMM states to examine is usually much less than the number of frames in DTW (e.g., 3–8 states vs 25–40 frames). One major advantage of HMM over DTW is reduced calculation in the recognition phase. DTW is a nonparametric speech model, which codes temporal and

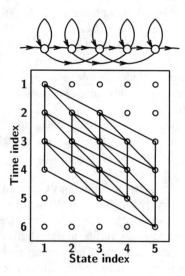

Figure 10.17 Interpretation of an HMM as a trellis.

speaker variability in a brute-force approach of storing many templates, each having many frames of data. The distance measure and warping constraints attempt to account for some variability, but at the cost of much computation for each reference template.

HMMs, on the other hand, incorporate more structure than DTW and capture much speaking variability in the matrices **A** and **B** during the (often off-line) training phase. The recognition phase is relatively rapid, needing no expensive distance calculations and only summing path probabilities for a network whose size is usually less than the number of frames in templates. Where DTW applies a fixed penalty to temporal distortions (e.g., the 2:1 assumption), HMMs are more flexible in modeling temporal and spectral variability. In addition to the vast decrease in computation for HMMs compared with DTW, HMM–VQ requires about ten times fewer storage locations than standard DTW.

10.7.1.8 Modeling durations in HMMs.

Merging successive, acoustically similar utterance frames for a phone into 1–2 HMM states decreases memory and computation, but yields an inaccurate model of temporal information. The objective of both DTW and HMM is efficient frame comparison, with sufficient temporal flexibility to normalize the different ways a word may be pronounced. DTW constrains the temporal freedom via local and global continuity constraints. Durational information for a first-order HMM lies in the probability of a loop transition a_{ii} for state i. The likelihood of remaining in state i for n frames is $a_{ii}^{n-1}(1 - a_{ii})$. This *geometric* (exponential) distribution is a poor model for speech durations, which follow Poisson distributions more closely (a most likely state exit after only one frame $(n = 1)$ is, in particular, a bad assumption). Thus, generalizing the basic HMM to allow nongeometric models for duration [150, 151] raises ASR accuracy, but at the cost of added complexity [61, 152]. Most systems concentrate instead on modeling the state probabilities, which in practice dominate ASR decisions [3].

HMMs have been applied to CSR, where the models can be both fewer and smaller in size than for large-vocabulary IWR with word HMMs [153]. HMMs to model phones appear to need only about three states (corresponding to the initial transition, steady state, and final transition of the phone), and about 30–40 such CI HMMs suffice for all words in a given language. This represents a significant memory and computation saving when compared with IWR using a 5–8-state HMM for each vocabulary word. One added complication, of course, for continuous speech is that of segmentation, determining when to start and stop applying each HMM to the long sequence of test frames. A simple, but expensive, way to avoid the segmentation problem is to build large HMM networks, stringing together word HMMs for all possible word sequences, with one-state HMMs representing silence as options between words (in case the speaker pauses between words) [113].

HMMs require much data to obtain robust parameters and are inflexible in terms of exploiting some acoustic–phonetic cues useful in ASR (e.g., durational and spectral transient cues). DTW works better with little training data, but is poor at modeling spectral variability. The current techniques of DTW and HMMs, while yielding good performance in limited applications, are both too rigidly formulated with structures that exclude many acoustic factors known to affect human speech perception. By themselves, neither DTW nor HMMs are likely to solve the general problem of CSR. Improved accuracy will derive from efforts combining the best aspects of different ASR methods.

10.7.1.9 Improving HMMs.

A major difficulty with HMMs is the frame-independence assumption from the use of first-order Markov models. ASR usually processes speech in frames of 10 ms, and assumes independence of successive HMM states. The use of delta coefficients to include timing information over several frames (e.g., 50 ms) is helpful but inefficient. Future ASR must exploit timing better. One recent method identifies local spectral peaks in each frame, and groups neighboring peaks into dynamic trajectories [154]. Other recent attempts to better model speech include *stochastic trajectory models* [155]. Smoother trajectories have been found when using formants (vs cepstra), although ASR accuracy has not improved much so far [156]. *Trended* HMMs [157, 158] and *linear trajectory* HMMs [159] are other examples.

Generalizing the basic HMM to allow Markov models of order higher than one raises ASR accuracy (by exploiting restrictions on how speech frames occur in sequence). However, the computational complexity of such models has hindered their application in ASR, but limited ways of exploiting interframe dependence have been recently explored [158, 160].

We must find ways to incorporate into the HMM architecture more information about speech production and perception, i.e., the sort of *knowledge* that expert systems exploit. One preliminary example is a *phonetic property HMM* [161]; another possibility is integrating articulatory features directly into HMMs [162].

10.8 ADAPTING TO VARIABILITY IN SPEECH

The ASR methods discussed above all try to accommodate aspects of the variability in speech. In this section, we examine in more detail the sources of this variability (intraspeaker, interspeaker, and environment) and how major methods (e.g., HMMs) explicitly handle them.

10.8.1 Intraspeaker Variability (Speaker Freedom)

People cannot repeat utterances exactly. Even the same speaker saying the same words will exhibit at least small differences. Very often, large variations appear due to speaking rate [163] and emotional changes. As part of their basic models, most ASR techniques handle well some of the ways each individual varies pronunciations; e.g., Gaussian PDFs in HMMs are good models for many inherent intraspeaker variations, and DTW is specifically designed to handle speaking rate changes. Intraspeaker variability is usually less than that across speakers (this is a basis of speaker identification—Chapter 11). Some of the larger variations within a speaker's voice however are similar to interspeaker variations.

10.8.2 Interspeaker Variability (Everybody's Different)

ASR requires a training phase before actual recognition may occur. In speaker-dependent (SD) systems, each user trains the system to "learn" that voice, and only reference models for that speaker are examined at recognition time. The simplest SD DTW systems employ *casual training*, in which each speaker utters every vocabulary word one or more times, and a reference model R_i is stored for each token (word utterance). To handle intraspeaker variability, training often uses many repeated tokens; this increases the likelihood that each test token will match one of the training utterances. Since both memory for the R_i and the number of distance computations for recognition are proportional to the number of templates, however, efficiency decreases with more R_i per word. Trading off accuracy and efficiency, most SD systems use 1–3 templates/word, while SI ASR often uses 10–12 [83]. Accuracy is higher in SD systems because fewer templates need be examined than in SI systems (i.e., fewer potential confusions) and because the templates match the user's voice.

The lesser variability in a small set of speaker-specific templates (vs a large set of multiple-speaker templates) leads to better separability among templates of different words.

10.8.2.1 *Clustering of reference templates.*

Storing a template for each training utterance to account for speaking variation is simple but inefficient. Furthermore, casual tokens may not be *robust* (reliable), which can be judged only through ASR experiments. Efficiency increases when the number of templates per lexical item is reduced by clustering (e.g., averaging) them into a smaller set. If done properly, ASR accuracy need not suffer. Simply averaging all tokens for a word into one reference model risks creating an unrepresentative pattern if the tokens differ substantially, which can occur both in SD systems and (especially) when averaging across speakers for SI ASR.

A practical compromise for SD systems, which combines limited training with better ASR accuracy than casual training: (1) has each speaker repeating every word (suitably separated in time, to generate independent tokens) until a pair of the tokens for each word is sufficiently similar (i.e., the distance between their templates falls below a threshold), and then (2) averages the two templates along a warp path specified via DTW (since the distance measure may be asymmetric and there is no reason to distinguish among the pair, the average of two DTWs is used, reversing the axes of the DTW each time) [164]. ASR accuracy on an alphadigit task was comparable between this one-template/word approach and a casually trained system with two templates/word. Thus, using an averaged template halves memory and computation, but needs more training (typically four word repetitions vs two in the casual method).

For good ASR accuracy in SI systems, at least 100 speakers must provide multiple training tokens for each word; thus efficiency requires substantial clustering to merge the tokens into a representative set of typically 10–12 templates. The two most common clustering techniques for SI ASR are the *k-means* [165] and *unsupervised without averaging* (UWA) [166] methods. The k-means approach iteratively merges N templates into M clusters: (1) M training templates chosen randomly act as the initial *cluster centers*; (2) using the nearest-neighbor rule, the other templates are assigned to the M clusters; (3) within each cluster, a new center is chosen to be the *minimax center* token, such that the maximum distance between that token and all tokens in that cluster is minimized; and (4) steps 2 and 3 are iterated until the cluster centers converge to a stable set.

The UWA method specifies one cluster at a time, employing a distance threshold T as the maximal "radius" of each cluster, until all tokens are assigned to clusters (T is adjusted to obtain the desired number M of clusters). The original formulation of UWA [166] was: (1) specify a minimax center for all unclustered tokens; (2) create a new cluster having all tokens within T of the center; (3) calculate a new minimax center for these tokens; (4) iterate steps 2 and 3 until convergence; (5) repeat steps 1–4 to generate other clusters until all tokens are clustered; and (6) replace each minimax cluster center by a template of parameters averaged over the tokens of that cluster. An improved version of UWA [167] modifies step 1 so that a cluster center is the unclustered token with the *maximum number* of unclustered tokens within distance T; this guarantees clusters of decreasing size as the iteration proceeds and improves performance. A third method called *complete-link clustering*, based on a graph coloring problem, gives yet better recognition accuracy than UWA [167].

10.8.2.2 *Speaker accommodation in HMMs.*

Accommodating different speakers is more economical with HMMs. Rather than have large numbers of models, many systems simply have one model per speech unit (e.g., phone or word), trained on multiple speakers. It is assumed that the PDFs properly incorporate interspeaker variability directly. In practice, the state PDFs broaden significantly when including multiple speakers in one model, causing reduced discrimination between unit classes. The only clear way to avoid this loss of discrimination is to have several models for different groups of speakers. Often, such models are developed for clearly-identifiable classes of speakers (e.g., men vs women, different dialects). Numerous systems have reported better ASR by testing on separate male and female models. Usually this doubles computation, since all speech is run through both models in parallel, where the final output is chosen from the model with the best match (since automatic gender estimation from speech is not 100% accurate). This approach can extend to background environments and transmission channels. One current ASR task (BN) consists of music, speech, and other sounds on commercial radio (sometimes with telephone quality); a common approach is to classify the sound input first and then apply the appropriate model [168].

10.8.2.3 Speaker-adaptive systems. A common approach to ASR starts with an SI system, trained on large amounts of data from many speakers, and then adapts the HMM parameters to each new individual user's voice [169–171]. This works best when the system is informed when the speaker changes (thus not as useful in audioconferences). Such *speaker-adaptive* (SA) systems can achieve the accuracy of SD systems with about six times as much training data (not counting the original SI data); e.g., 400 s of data can reduce word errors by 7%. Indeed, even short amounts of adaptation data are useful (e.g., 9% improvement with a single 3 s utterance [172]). This adaptation is especially useful for foreign speakers (whose error rates with SI ASR are up to three times as high as for native speakers) (e.g., improvements up to 50% [173]).

If an initial SI system has models for different cohorts or classes of speakers, SA may identify (from limited speech of each new speaker) which cohort is most appropriate, and then modify or transform that cohort model for use with the new speech [174].

MAP adaptation [175, 176] often requires much training data (e.g., several minutes) to have significantly better accuracy, because only those models corresponding to sounds in the adaptation speech are modified. A related method for inputs with widely varying speakers, channels and background conditions is Maximum Likelihood Linear Regression (MLLR) [177, 178], which calculates transforms of speaker space using unsupervised adaptation data, grouped automatically into similar data sets.

Vector-field smoothing adapts parameters across models incrementally and therefore rapidly, achieving good results with only a few words of adaptation [179]. Tree-structure speaker clustering can improve accuracy with as little as 5 s of adaptation [180]. Principal components analysis of SD model parameter sets can extract a small number $K \approx 5$ of "eigenvoices," which then allows modeling each new speaker in the spanning K space, lowering error rates with as few as four brief words of adaptation speech [181].

Inverse transform speaker-adaptive training is based on removing the differences between speakers before training, rather than modeling them during training. This method uses a linear transformation of model parameter means, is faster, requires less disk space, and is more accurate than other adaptation methods [182]. Commercial systems often do speaker adaptation on-line during use, assuming that any output text left uncorrected by each user is correct.

One method for SA is via vocal-tract-length normalization (VTLN), where one estimates each speaker's tract length from the current input speech (e.g., by estimating an average F3 [183]) and then transforms SI models accordingly [184]. Some approaches use frequency warping via a *scale-cepstrum*, that provides better separability between vowels and is robust to noise [185, 186]. Exploiting approximate formant positions can raise accuracy and lower computation in such warping [187]. Another way is via a *scale transform* [188].

Generally, SI ASR accuracy is proportional to the amount of training data and to the complexity of the algorithm. However, this rule does not apply to performance on foreign speakers, when the SI system is largely trained on native voices; indeed, more compact models allow faster adaptation in SA systems [173].

10.8.3 Environmental Variability (Noise Robustness)

The last (and perhaps most difficult) variability that ASR must handle is that due to background and channel noise and other distortions that may appear in a speech signal [189]. While variation due to speakers can be modeled reasonably by appropriate prior training, it is difficult to anticipate many signal distortions, which by their nature are often beyond speaker control. Environmental noise enters the speech signal additively at the microphone, and transmission channels often have convolutional noise. Basic spectral subtraction techniques (Chapter 8) help with additive noise, while cepstral methods (which convert multiplication in the spectral domain to cepstral addition) help suppress convolutional noise.

Many speech enhancement methods in Chapter 8 are used as preprocessors for recognition of noisy speech. The focus should be on highlighting the high-amplitude parts of the input signal spectrum, on the reasonable assumption that such frequencies have mostly strong speech formants, are the most relevant for speech perception, and are relatively less corrupted by noise [41]. The analysis methods for ASR are similar to those for low-rate coding, and they give less accurate parameters as distortion in the input speech signal increases. Unlike in high-rate coding (where performance gradually degrades with more noise), ASR accuracy can fall abruptly once input SNR decreases below a certain level, due to a breakdown in the analysis model's reliability in adverse conditions. To handle distorted speech, two methods are normally used: *robust parameterization* or *model transformation*. The former seeks analysis parameters that are resistant to noise, or employs speech enhancement methods. The latter adapts the ASR models to accommodate the distortion.

As with speech coders, acoustic noise and other speech distortions (e.g., Lombard effect [190]) reduce performance in ASR [81, 191–194], and much more so for machines than for humans. One study showed error rate increasing from 7% to 13% as SNR dropped to 10 dB even with noise compensation (without compensation, it was 40%), while humans maintained a 1% rate [1]. While random omission of spectral channels in ASR does not always hurt ASR rates [195], the type of loss of information found with typical noise often has serious effects on ASR (e.g., in automobiles, motor and road surface noise is dominant below 500 Hz, with wind noise above 1 kHz). While an array of microphones can compensate for noise and echo when speakers are distant [195–198], most ASR uses a single microphone input.

The cepstrum is often viewed as being a robust parameterization (e.g., more resistant to noise than DFT analysis) [199], although the low-order MFCCs are often de-weighted as being too linked to channel conditions. Similarly, pre-emphasis (sometimes used in ASR) hinders accuracy in noisy speech since it boosts the noise at high frequencies where speech is weak [199]. Thus a cepstral *lifter* emphasizing the mid-range MFCCs is best. A cepstral projection distance appears better than the Euclidean distance for noisy ASR [200].

Transitional information, in the form of delta coefficients over a 50–100 ms window, usually increases accuracy, especially in cases of channel mismatch between testing and training. *Cepstral mean subtraction* (CMS), like RASTA processing [53], eliminates very slowly varying signal aspects (presumed to be mostly from channel distortion). The mean value for each parameter over time (typically for periods exceeding 250 ms) is subtracted from each frame's parameter, thus minimizing environmental and intraspeaker effects. Other *blind equalization* ways of removing channel effects include *signal bias removal* [201]. Channel noise is often assumed to be constant over an utterance, but portable telephones suffer fading channel effects which require more frequent estimations [202].

CMS removes not only convolutional channel effects, but also some speaker-dependent aspects, and does not help with additive channel noise and nonlinearities. Long-term average subtraction is inappropriate for short utterances, where much speaker-dependent information would be removed. More general filtering of parameter sequences has found it best to emphasize speech modulations around 3 Hz (i.e., the syllable rate of speech) [203].

We saw in Chapter 8 that comb filtering was too complex for practical enhancement, but the idea of exploiting speech periodicity (vs incoherent noise) is used in ASR methods that do all-pole modeling of the autocorrelation of speech (rather than of the speech itself, as in normal LPC) [204].

Some robust ASR systems use a spectral mapping between a noisy speech space and a set of VQ codebooks trained on clean speech; e.g., the mapping could involve fuzzy clustering and piecewise-linear transformations [205]. Another example of a model transformation to improve ASR accuracy in conditions of either additive or convolutional noise is *Parallel Model Combination* (PMC) [206] (Figure 10.18). First, HMMs are built for both clean speech and noise, using standard cepstral methods, then state parameters are converted back into linear spectra and added for different levels of noise; finally, the summed parameters are converted back to the cepstral domain. For stationary noise, a simple one-state HMM suffices as a noise model; nonstationary noise requires more complex models. Since, in practice, input speech may have any noise level, such PMC systems must try various combinations of noise modeling to find appropriate matches, which increases computation.

Different handsets (especially the difference between carbon-button and electret microphones) are a major source of training mismatch over the telephone, leading to major

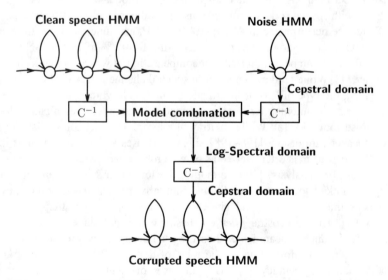

Figure 10.18 Operation of parallel model combination.

increases in error rates. One ASR study had 6.6% errors with a close-talking microphone and 23.9% errors with an electret one (while humans had only 0.4–0.8% errors) [1]. Commercial ASR often uses headset-mounted, pressure-gradient microphones to isolate the speech of a user (vs background noise), thus maximizing input SNR.

10.9 LANGUAGE MODELS (LMs)

Early ASR systems only used acoustic information to evaluate text hypotheses. The speech signal was assumed to have all information needed to convert speech to text. In the early 1980s, incorporating knowledge about the text being spoken was found to significantly raise ASR accuracy, by exploiting textual redundancies. Most speech corresponds to texts which follow linguistic rules (e.g., syntax and semantics). Exploiting these rules is as crucial for ASR performance as exploiting periodicity and slow-moving vocal tracts is for speech coding [207, 208].

Sometimes people utter (apparently) random sequences of words (e.g., digits in a telephone number). Such cases have no text redundancies; each word in the small vocabulary may follow any other. Normally, however, given a history of prior (recognized) words in an utterance, the number of words P that one (either a listener or ASR) must consider as possibly coming next is much smaller than the vocabulary size V. (For simple digit sequences, however, $V = P = 10$.) P is called the *perplexity* or *average branching factor* (ABF) of a language model (LM). LMs are stochastic descriptions of text, usually involving the likelihoods of local sequences of N consecutive words in training texts (typically $N = 1, 2, 3$). Integrating a LM with the normal acoustic HMMs is now common in most ASR systems.

10.9.1 Grammars in ASR

Without a LM, ASR usually outputs a sequence of symbols representing phonemes or phonetic segments, corresponding to the proposed recognized text. The sequence may involve sets of possibilities, e.g., a weighted list of boundary locations and phone candidates for each segment, often in the form of a *lattice*. Due to the difficulty of locating word (or even syllable) boundaries, segmenting the sequence into words can be left to a postprocessor that compares the symbol string or lattice against the set of vocabulary words to optimally partition the sequence into words for the output text [209]. The *grammar* or structure of permitted phoneme sequences raises ASR accuracy by eliminating candidate phone sequences not legal under the grammar [210].

Grammars can be applied equally well to sequences of words from the output of an IWR system and to phone sequences from CSR analysis [22]. Traditionally, grammars refer to syntactic rules through which sentences are parsed into component words and phrases [211]. Since natural language (e.g., unrestricted English) has a very complex grammar, some CSR systems impose restrictions on users so that test utterances follow simpler grammars. Usually, the grammar rules pertain to how words from different syntax classes (e.g., nouns, verbs, prepositions) may combine to form legal sentences. Some systems use a *slot–frame* grammar, where slots in frame sentences may be filled from sets of words; e.g., a date–time grammar might have the frame ⟨month-date-*at*-hour-minutes-*p.m.* or *a.m.*⟩, where the *month* slot can be filled by one of 12 words, the *date* slot by one of 31 numbers, etc. Such methods fit well with keyword spotting [212].

Markov models are a form of *finite-state* grammar, which is not powerful enough to generate all and only legal English sentences [94]. *Context-free* and *context-sensitive* grammars have also been used in ASR and have been generalized to include other aspects of speech communication that have regular structure, e.g., semantics and phonetics. Some systems even employ a *pragmatic* component, which aids ASR by keeping track of discourse structure [213]: since words tend to repeat in discourse, previously recognized words (via a cache memory) should have their prior probabilities raised when evaluating ensuing words [214].

The use of HMMs to describe the sequence of acoustic segments in words from a vocabulary is an example of a phonetic grammar. Grammars for ASR are often efficiently represented by networks, where each network state represents an acoustic event (e.g., phone or word) and transitions between states denote the permitted order of events according to the vocabulary and grammar. Sentence networks can handle semantic and syntactic constraints through an *augmented transition network* (ATN), which modifies the standard Markov model to allow linguistic information to be popped and pushed to and from stacks on each transition [12, 215]. In word networks, states commonly represent short acoustic segments, and transitions are usually weighted by probabilities determined from training data. Similar transition probabilities could be specified for sentence networks where states represent "words"; e.g., in an IWR application for spelled-out words using an alphadigit vocabulary, the likelihood of one letter following another can be determined by a statistical evaluation of the vocabulary of words (e.g., the sequence *K-X* is rare in English words).

Some ASR tasks have no grammar at certain levels; e.g., the connected-digit task has no sentence-level grammar. The same is true in general for certain languages such as Russian, where word inflection instead cues syntactic structure. Since the phonemic composition of words in most languages is highly restricted (e.g., the sequences /tz/ and /sd/ are illegal in English syllables), each language has a word-level grammar, which can often be simplified for applications whose vocabulary is a small subset of the language's words. ABF or perplexity P is one measure of a grammar's restrictiveness, that specifies how many possibilities may follow a current element of the grammar in an average utterance. In terms of networks, P is the mean number of transitions leaving a node. Typically, $P \ll V$ (number of vocabulary words)—often an order of magnitude smaller due to the constraints of syntax alone, and another factor of 10–30 for semantics [12]. P rarely exceeds 200 for most common databases having V in the tens of thousands [16]. As a measure of the difficulty of a particular ASR task, P is better than the more commonly noted V. Perplexity can be related to the concept of *entropy* to characterize task difficulty [32, 216]. Given a PDF $p(t)$ for a text t of n words from a vocabulary of V words, the entropy per word is

$$H = \lim_{n \to \infty} - (1/n) \sum_t p(t) \log_2 p(t).$$

Thus $H \leq \log_2 V$ (reaching maximum for texts where the word sequence is fully random). Not using a grammar in ASR is like using nonsense utterances, where any word may follow another; using a vocabulary of 1000 words with no grammar, one study showed 17% ASR errors and 2% human perception errors [1]. This shows the importance of LMs, as well as the continuing gap between human and machine performance.

10.9.2 Integrating Language Models into ASR

Most LVR uses Markov models to represent both language statistics and speech acoustics [217]. Acoustically, HMMs account for speech signal variability. For text, simpler LMs capture the redundancy of sequences of words, in terms of the probabilities of occurrence for each word in the ASR vocabulary. Typically, *N-gram* models estimate the likelihood of each word, given the context of the preceding *N*-1 words, e.g., *bigram* models use statistics of word pairs and *trigrams* model word triplets [216, 218]. *Unigrams* are simply prior likelihoods for each word, independent of context. These probabilities are determined by analysis of much text, and are incorporated into a Markov language model. LMs capture both syntactic and semantic redundancies in text. They are not HMMs because each text word is directly observable, and not modeled by a PDF.

As vocabulary (*V* words) increases for practical ASR, the size of an LM (V^N) grows exponentially with *V*. This problem is most serious for highly-inflected languages (e.g., Estonian, Finnish), where each lexical word (i.e., basic dictionary entry) has many forms with different suffixes. (In English, a lexical entry such as *cat* has only *cats* as an inflected form, and *eat* has only *eats, ate, eaten* and *eating*; on the other hand, French has typically 39 different words for each lexical verb.) Large lexicons lead to seriously undertrained LMs, inadequate appropriate texts for training, increased memory needs, and lack of enough computation power to search all textual possibilities.

In practice, most ASR has employed unigram, bigram and trigram statistics. Current text databases are adequate for such modeling for up to 60,000 words [3]. *N*-grams for $N > 3$ (when used) are highly selective. Since many longer word sequences are rarely found (if at all) in the available training texts (e.g., 60% of trigrams found in Switchboard test data do not occur in 2 million training words—150 h of speech), some way must be found to estimate their likelihood. *Back-off* methods fall back on lower-order statistics when higher *N*-grams are not found [219]. Usually, the LM contributes the following likelihood to the ASR evaluation:

$$\alpha_1 P(W_1) + \alpha_2 P(W_1|W_2) + \alpha_3 P(W_1|W_2, \ W_3),$$

where α_i are *i*-gram weights for the likelihood of current word W_1, given preceding words $W_2, \ \ldots, \ W_i$. When the trigram $W_3 W_2 W_1$ has not occurred in training, $\alpha_3 = 0$ and the other weights are raised to compensate (similarly, if no $W_2 W_1$, then $\alpha_2 = 0$). Finally, if W_1 has not been seen either, it is an *out-of-vocabulary* (OOV) word. Instead of simple back-off methods, some systems smooth the statistics after training, to give small, nonzero probabilities to unseen *N*-grams. *Deleted interpolation* is one such method [220].

How to combine LMs with acoustic HMMs is not clear. HMMs operate on 10 ms speech frames, while the domain of LMs is the word. To date, most ASR simply adds the two log likelihoods from the numerator of Equation (10.10) to obtain a total probability:

$$\beta \log P(t) + \log P(s|t),$$

where β is an empirical weighting factor to balance the two contributions. This factor is needed due to the imbalance between the low values for the acoustical joint probability of many frames and the higher values for word sequences in LMs.

The most successful ASR uses domain-specific LMs, i.e., ones trained specifically for an immediate task at hand, rather than a general LM to handle all speech. Thus we see LMs designed for doctors, lawyers, business, etc., each trained on restricted databases of texts for these applications. It is becoming common to train acoustic HMMs broadly across many speakers, but to specialize LMs. As increasing amounts of on-line texts become available (e.g., transcribed television scripts, web-based sources), LMs for many specific ASR tasks are feasible. Combining such LMs for more general applications usually involves back-off methods as above [221].

LMs as noted work well for English, but often need modifications to handle other languages [222] (e.g., the many compound words of German or the many homophones of

French [223]). Text normalization and proper handling of capital letters is critical for many cases [224].

In an attempt to increase the power of N-gram LMs, one can use classes of words (rather than individual words) as lexical units. Training and using statistics of L classes (e.g., nouns, verbs) is much easier than for $V \gg L$ words. The classes can be partly semantic as well as syntactic, and can be automatically determined via *clustering* (rather than follow traditional linguistic guidelines) [225]. While more efficient than normal N-gram LMs however, class-based LMs give lower performance [222].

LMs are intended to exploit various constraints that are present in texts. Local constraints are captured well via N-gram language modeling, but global constraints are much more difficult to capture efficiently [226]. Future LMs must remain efficient while integrating global contexts, e.g., phrase-based LMs [227] and latent semantic analysis [228]. Languages such as German with agreement between widely spaced verbs in a sentence need wide-range LMs.

10.10 SEARCH DESIGN

It is clear that current ASR methods are suboptimal, given the variance between human and ASR performance. Many compromises have been made to accommodate computational efficiency, including limiting LMs to trigrams and using first-order HMMs with tied states and diagonal covariances. Earlier ASR methods used the expert-system approach, but had great difficulty integrating the many *knowledge sources* (KSs) that humans exploit in speech perception. One early form of CSR (e.g., Harpy [12]) integrated all speech knowledge in the form of a large network of acoustic segment states, which resulted from replacing word states in a sentence network (incorporating syntax and semantic constraints) by word networks of phone states. Coarticulation and phonological effects were handled within and between word networks (Figure 10.19). As networks grew with vocabulary size, computational efficiency suffered (due to exponential growth) in much the same way as occurs when matching templates of many frames.

Efficient dynamic programming procedures can combine two sources of information for ASR grammar networks and phone or word lattices from the acoustic analysis stage of ASR [106]. One powerful control structure to handle information relevant to ASR from different KSs employs a *blackboard* (Figure 10.20). An acoustic analyzer "writes" its output (a segment string) on the blackboard, which then is available to other KSs (word hypothesizer, intonation analyzer, syntax and semantic modules, etc.), each of which refines the string until a text sentence is ready as output. Future ASR systems are likely to incorporate different aspects from several ASR approaches [229]; e.g., the proposed system in Figure 10.21 exploits networks, hypothesis verification, phonological rules, and diphone templates.

10.10.1 Efficient Searches

The Viterbi method (a *breadth-first* approach) is efficient in searching a network for the best path, but large ASR networks still need much calculation. A *best-first* or *depth-first* approach follows the most likely transitions from state to state (e.g., a *stack* or A^* search), and backtracks to examine a number of alternative paths once a path spanning the sentence network has been found. A *beam-search* approach [230] comes closest to DTW, in examining

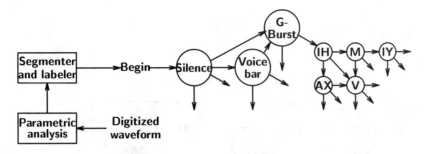

Figure 10.19 Block diagram of the Harpy CSR system, showing a small (hypothetical) fragment of the state transition network, including paths accepted for sentences starting with "Give me …." To handle the 1011 word vocabulary, many paths may leave each of the 15,000 nodes. (After Klatt [12].)

a narrow *beam* of likely alternatives around the locally best path through the network [231]. Assuming a *beam width* δ around the likelihood L of the current most likely partial hypothesis in a network, one removes (i.e., *prunes*) all hypotheses whose probability is below $L - \delta$ [232]. Beam searches have been successfully applied to phoneme-level networks (e.g., Harpy) and syllable-level networks [88] for CSR, as well as word-level networks in DTW-based IWR systems [119]. Search strategies may include *fuzzy* approaches [215, 233].

Phone *look-ahead* is a common method to prune hypotheses, thus reducing computation. Each time a hypothesis crosses a phone boundary, the model is examined to see if the

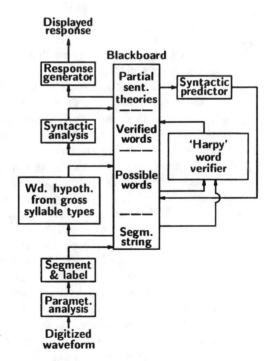

Figure 10.20 Block diagram of the Hearsay-II CSR system. (After Klatt [12].)

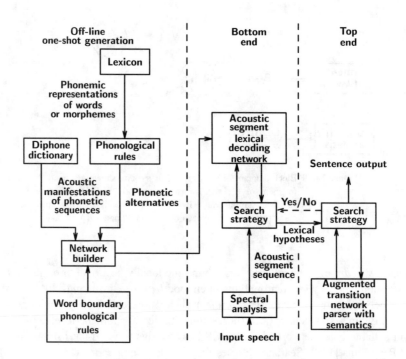

Figure 10.21 A proposed future speech recognition system, with both bottom-up analysis and top-down hypotheses. The ASR memory combines diphone templates with phonological rules. Networks are used as models for high-level hypothesis generation and for low-level acoustic segment analysis. (After Klatt [12].)

ensuing few frames reasonably match it; if not, that hypothesis is abandoned in favor of other more promising paths.

Examining the search space for LVR often needs large computational resources, in both time and memory. Some systems employ a multi-pass strategy for efficiency. A first pass uses simpler models (less expensive in memory and computation) to do a coarse recognition, pruning away unlikely hypotheses. With simple acoustic and language models (or using coarse segmentation and labeling via robust features), the number of word candidates to consider during a more detailed second analysis pass is reduced [234]. A second pass then examines the remaining possibilities, often in the form of a word-lattice or a word- or transcription-graph [235]. As long as few correct hypotheses are incorrectly discarded early (i.e., a high *first-pass inclusion rate* is maintained), this method eliminates detailed examination of many useless paths [236]. The second pass may compare the test data only against reference models in the subset or cohort specified by the first pass; e.g., for the A–Z vocabulary, first-pass recognition of a test letter as containing /i/ would allow the second-pass search to be limited to the initial portions of models for the E set [237]. The second-pass measure could also be weighted for each reference frame according to its importance in discriminating words within the subclass; e.g., heavier weights for the louder frames [105] or for the initial consonant frames in the E set [238]. The second pass is often viewed as a *re-scoring* of N hypotheses furnished by the first pass (e.g., finding which of the initial N-best hypotheses should be the final output).

10.10.2 Allowing Vocabulary Freedom

Some applications do not require recognition of all words uttered, but of only a few *keywords*; e.g., searching for a few words of interest (as one locates a word in a text-processing editor) [239]. When asked to utter one of a small set of keywords in telephone-answering services, users often (about a third of the time) respond with extraneous words (e.g., *make it collect please*, rather than just *collect*) [240]. *Word spotting* ASR allows speakers unrestricted use of words and phrasing, while the system tries to recognize only certain keywords from a limited vocabulary, assuming that the spoken message can be deciphered based on ASR of these keywords. This approach avoids a major difficulty of most systems, which try to recognize every spoken word; if a spoken word is not in their vocabulary (OOV), either they request that the speaker repeat or they erroneously output a word from the vocabulary. By allowing any words between crucial words, word-spotting ASR allows great flexibility while retaining good accuracy (e.g., 95% for five keywords [240]).

10.10.2.1 Word spotting. Basic word spotting applies word models or templates for each keyword to the entire test utterance, effectively shifting the test time axis a few frames at a time for each new analysis [240, 241]. If the match for a keyword at any start frame exceeds a threshold (or a total distance is small enough), that word is deemed to have been spotted there. Dynamic programming may be used in a second stage of processing to eliminate poor-scoring matches, using models of both keywords and nonkeyword speech. Sub-word models (i.e., units smaller than words) can be efficient here [193]. Computation can be minimized by using larger frame shifts, but this could require a higher distance threshold before abandoning an unlikely comparison. Short words with voiced obstruents are the most difficult words to spot, especially if they are phonologically reduced in continuous speech [94].

Keyword ASR can be incorporated into CSR by designing *filler* or *garbage* models to handle the non-keyword speech [242]; e.g., short words (such as *the, of, for, at, to,* and *from*) commonly used in speech could function as filler models, e.g., along with a set of syllable models obtained by vector quantization on syllables from a wide range of speech. More commonly, the filler models are less complex than keyword models (e.g., fewer HMM states); how many models and how they are chosen are empirical issues [193]. Accuracy usually increases in proportion to the detail of filler models. At one extreme, full LVR can be used, recognizing all words, with a final lexical search among the output word list to locate the keywords; this method yields the highest keyword performance, but at high cost. Phone-based phonetic filler models, along with word models for all keywords, can yield similar performance, with much less computation [243].

Keyword spotting can require almost as much computation as full CSR. For faster performance, at some loss of accuracy, a phone lattice can be obtained from the speech, to which many keywords could be examined with a fast lexical search [244]. For audio indexing or document retrieval, such a fast spotter, missing a few keywords, would be preferred over a more precise but slower system. A simple word-pair language model can also help in keyword spotting [146]. Word spotting with HMM methods requires significant amounts of training data, which is sometimes difficult for small sets of keywords. Thus, DTW is still useful, especially for SD applications [193].

Good keyword ASR means locating as many keywords as possible, while minimizing *false alarms* (i.e., speech incorrectly identified as keywords). One performance measure is the keyword detection rate for a given false alarm rate (e.g., typically 10 false alarms/h). A *figure-of-merit* (FOM) can be calculated as the average score of p_i, where p_i is the percentage of keywords found before the ith false alarm [193]. The FOM is more stable than most other measures.

10.10.3 Out-of-Vocabulary Words

Extending keyword spotting to longer phrases refers to *utterance verification*, accepting keyword strings and rejecting *out-of-vocabulary* (OOV) words as irrelevant [66, 245]. *Confidence measures* can be associated with the likelihood that a word is OOV [213]. The usage of words beyond a known vocabulary is a major problem for many ASR systems. Unlike TTS synthesis (which is often truly unlimited in vocabulary in the sense that it accepts any textual input), ASR has no easy response to spoken words not in its active vocabulary. Such OOV words (i.e., those not occurring in the training data) appear often because users rarely limit themselves to restrictive lists of words. Even in simple applications requesting just a yes-or-no answer or a list of digits, many users insert extraneous words (e.g., *OK, sure, uh*). For vocabularies beyond a few dozen words, many utterances contain illegal words.

Many limited-domain ASR applications (e.g., ATIS) have vocabularies of about 1000 words. If such systems are trained on only 10,000 words, OOV rates exceed 10% (i.e., more than one word in every ten is not found in the dictionary) [14]. OOV rates typically fall in proportion to training size. A 20,000 word WSJ dictionary may require tens of millions of training words to achieve OOV rates below 1% (the WSJ database has over 200 million words).

In one sense, OOV words present a converse task to keyword spotting. In a keyword application, most words are OOV and the system searches for occurrences of a few keywords. In normal ASR, most words are in the legal vocabulary, and only a few are OOV. Keyword ASR simply ignores the OOV words as irrelevant, but normal ASR must explicitly handle OOV words. If no allowance is made for OOV words, ASR will incorrectly output a word from its dictionary for each OOV occurrence.

Some ASR systems use *generic* or *trash* word models as fillers to locate OOV words, while others simply accept lower accuracy rates when OOV words occur. Yet others attempt to detect such words, notifying the user that specific sections of speech are unidentifiable. If the ASR is interactive, users could then be asked to augment the dictionary by perhaps spelling out and defining each new word. This is especially useful for proper names, since few training databases are exhaustive with names.

10.11 ARTIFICIAL NEURAL NETWORKS

In the late 1980s, a new ASR paradigm appeared, using *artificial neural networks* (ANNs), based on simple simulations of groups of nerve cells in the human central nervous system. Each real *biological neuron* has many protrusions (dendrites) which receive inputs from nearby neurons. If a weighted sum of a neuron's inputs exceeds a threshold, its axon emits an electrical firing (see Chapter 4), sending its output to other neurons. In humans, billions of neurons are interconnected in a highly complex network.

Simulating simple versions of such a network, ANNs can accomplish useful pattern recognition tasks, including aspects of ASR. An individual *node* simulating a neuron can make a binary classification (via the presence or absence of a firing), based on a set (frame) of M input data samples (e.g., M spectral parameters from a frame of speech). A group of N such nodes all receiving the same M inputs can thus classify speech frames into one of $L \leq 2^N$ classes. Usually, such a basic ANN is configured so that only one of the N nodes should emit a firing for each frame (i.e., $L = N$). Such a *single-layer* ANN or *perceptron* (one set of nodes, all receiving the same inputs) is a linear classifier that partitions an acoustic space of M dimensions into N hyperellipsoids or classes.

Such simple classifiers do not solve most ASR problems; e.g., deciding to which of N phonemes an M-dimensional speech frame belongs. In the M-space for most speech parameters (e.g., LPC, cepstra), phonemes often have very complex shapes, requiring complicated decision surfaces (and not the simple hyperplanes of perceptrons). Allowing one layer of M_1 neurons to feed into a second layer of M_2 neurons creates a two-layer *connectionist* ANN, capable of distinguishing among many convex surfaces in acoustic space. In practice, ASR often uses a third layer, so that the original set of M_1 speech parameters feeds into a *hidden layer* of M_2 nodes, in turn feeding another hidden layer of M_3 nodes, finally yielding a set of N outputs (Figure 10.22). While M_1 and N correspond to the number of parameters in each input frame and the number of output classes (e.g., phonemes), respectively, the sizes of the hidden layers (M_2 and M_3) are empirically chosen in a compromise between complexity and classification accuracy.

Each node in an ANN emits a value of 1 (i.e., a neural firing) when a weighted sum of its inputs x_i exceeds a threshold Θ, i.e., when

$$\sum_{i=1}^{M} w_i x_i > \Theta. \tag{10.19}$$

Many ANNs go beyond the original biological idea of a binary output, and allow a *sigmoid* output, which monotonically ranges from 0 to 1 as the sum in Equation (10.19) increases.

10.11.1 Training ANNs

The power of an ANN lies in its weights w_i, which must be chosen to perform proper classification, often based on a labelled corpus of speech data (*supervised training*). The renaissance of ANNs began with the discovery of an efficient method to estimate these ANN weights. The *back propagation learning* (BPL) algorithm [246] is a stochastic gradient-descent method. We view the difference between the desired and actual ANN outputs (weighted in some fashion) as an error measure of an ANN. The error, as a function of all $K = M_1 + M_2 + M_3$ weights, describes an *error surface* in K dimensions. By iteratively modifying the w_i values, starting from initial estimates, the BPL method descends along the surface, to create an ANN where error is small. Like any gradient method, BPL risks finding a

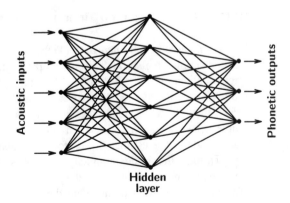

Figure 10.22 Example of a three-level ANN.

local minimum if the initial point is poorly chosen or the surface is complex (the latter is often true due to simplistic choices of input parameters). Another problem is determining a *stopping criterion*; normally, we continue until the error changes little between iterations (or reaches a computation threshold), but this may overtrain the ANN to fit the training data too closely. Some *cross-validation* measure is needed to avoid this [247].

Consider an *L*-layer ANN with N_k nodes at the *k*th layer. The *activation value* (or output) of the *i*th node in that layer is

$$x_i(k+1) = f\left[\sum_{j=1}^{N_k} w_{ij}(k)x_j(k) - \theta_i(k)\right],$$

where $f(u)$ is a monotonic mapping, with output ranging from 0 to 1 as *u* increases. The original ANNs used a simple (binary) step function for

$$f(u) = \begin{cases} 0 & \text{for } u < 0 \\ 1 & \text{for } u \geq 0 \end{cases},$$

following the example of natural neurons which *fire* once the threshold $\theta_i(k)$ is exceeded. Experiments have since shown that a smooth sigmoid function (e.g., $f(u) = 1/(1 + e^{-u})$) gives better ASR results. The value of an ANN lies primarily in its weights $w_{ij}(k)$, which are obtained by a BPL algorithm that iteratively modifies them to minimize the mean-squared error (MSE) (as in LPC modeling) between the desired outputs and the actual outputs of the ANN:

$$w_{jk} \leftarrow w_{ij}(k) - \eta \frac{\partial R}{\partial w_{ij}(k)},$$

where η controls the learning rate of the network. This procedure is sometimes modified for *radial basis functions*, which are faster to train [248]. Sometimes relative entropy replaces the MSE in training.

For simple ASR tasks, ANNs can provide high accuracy, even for difficult vocabularies, e.g., 75% accuracy for phonemes in TIMIT [249]. Due to their difficulties handling timing issues, ANNs have not replaced HMMs as the standard ASR method. However, ANNs are increasingly used in efficient training of HMM probabilites [232]. Such hybrid ANN/HMM systems keep the basic HMM structure and recognition process, but estimate their PDF's via ANNs in training, where timing issues are of lesser importance. For this application, the final ANN layer outputs nonbinary probability estimates [247, 248].

10.11.2 Accommodating Timing in ANNs

Time-delay neural networks (TDNN) [250] have been proposed to accommodate the fact that simple time shifts severely hamper basic ANN ASR, but have little effect on speech perception and other methods of ASR (e.g., DTW was designed to handle timing variations, and HMMs explicitly model state transitions). By feeding back information from each current speech frame to ANN input nodes corresponding to earlier frames, TDNNs can better handle simple delays and speaking rate variations. However, such *recurrent* networks require many more weights to be estimated (i.e., for all feedback paths), rendering such systems complex.

Despite the basic simplicity of ANNs, they have several advantages over HMM methods: (1) no need for detailed assumptions about the underlying stochastic distributions of speech, (2) easily accommodate discriminative training, (3) including several frames as inputs to an ANN automatically handles context dependence across frames, and (4) modeling boundaries between speech classes (rather than class distributions) is more efficient. For LVR, hybrid ANN/HMM systems often have far fewer parameters than standard HMM recognizers [3]. Recursive estimation MAP methods (REMAP) for smoothing transition probabilities have shown promise in discriminant HMMs [3].

10.12 EXPERT-SYSTEM APPROACH TO ASR

Until the late 1970s, ASR was dominated by the expert-system (ES) approach. Generally using a bottom-up method, speech was reduced to parameters (usually a DFT) and then features (usually formant-based). Complex sets of phonetic rules, designed by phoneticians looking at spectrograms, then made phonemic decisions. Since statistics were not employed well (if at all), decision surfaces in acoustic space were often arbitrarily defined, based on limited information, and often did not generalize well to SI applications. However, this method was neither suitable for SD cases because of the manual nature of the training procedure. We nonetheless review below some of the major issues for this approach, highlighting its strengths and weaknesses. Given different weaknesses in the HMM approach, optimal ASR may well need to integrate ideas from both approaches.

10.12.1 Segmenting Speech into Syllables

Unlike stochastic ASR methods, expert-system ASR cannot easily postpone segmentation decisions until all speech information is considered. ES basically has a choice: segment each test utterance into small units, and then label them phonetically, or label each frame first, then group similar frames together. We describe here the difficulties of reliable speech segmentation into small units. For languages with few syllables (e.g., 131 in Japanese, 408 in Chinese), an accurate division into syllables can be a major ASR step.

In general, segmenting continuous speech into words, based on acoustic analysis alone, is impossible. There are few reliable acoustic cues to distinguish word boundaries without using linguistic information, e.g., a dictionary and a language model. Acoustically segmenting speech into syllable-sized units, however, is feasible, independent of the vocabulary, since each syllable has a strong vowel center, usually easily distinguished from its weaker consonant neighbors (especially in the many languages with a strict consonant+vowel structure for each syllable). There is however a problem of context dependence: the significance of an energy dip for segmentation depends on the energy in surrounding segments.

The *convex hull* method provides one simple segmentation approach [251]. After isolating speech segments between pauses (here defined as silences > 200 ms), a convex hull is determined from the speech *loudness function* (a perceptually weighted energy vs time plot, lowpassed to eliminate pitch period effects) (Figure 10.23). This hull exhibits minimal magnitude, monotonically nondecreasing until the loudness peak, and monotonically nonincreasing thereafter. The depth of each loudness valley under the hull indicates the likelihood of a boundary there. If the maximum depth exceeds 2 dB, a boundary is declared and the process repeated with new hulls on both sides of the boundary. Since loudness change is more abrupt at syllable onset than offset, syllable-initial boundaries are more accurately located than syllable-final ones. Located boundaries do not always correspond to standard syllable units because intervocalic consonants may be assigned to the "wrong" vowel (e.g., to which syllable does the /t/ in *beating* belong?). Some postprocessing is also necessary to merge short

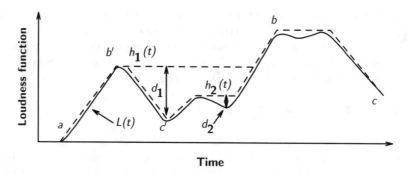

Figure 10.23 Example of segmenting a speech loudness function into syllables: $h_1(t)$ is
the first convex hull for the full speech segment $a - b - c$; if the valley
depth d_1 exceeds a threshold, c' is marked as a boundary; the new convex
hull $h_2(t)$ for segment $c' - b - c$ leads only to small valleys such as d_2, so
no further boundaries are marked. (After Mermelstein [251].)

segments with their neighbors, since fricatives are often separated from the vowels of their
syllables by weaker obstruents (e.g., the word *stops* may produce three segments corresponding to /s/-/tɑp/-/s/). Durational constraints could also help merge short segments with their
longer neighbors if intervening valleys are short enough.

A segmentation method similar to the convex hull approach has been applied to large-
vocabulary IWR using demisyllable templates [252]. Unlike the demisyllable method
described earlier, where short templates were merged to form word templates, each isolated
word here was segmented into syllables and then each syllable was further divided, so that
demisyllables were directly compared. For vocabularies of more than 500 words, the
demisyllable+segmentation approach showed better ASR accuracy than systems using
isolated-word templates.

10.12.2 Segmentation of Continuous Speech into Phones

While segmenting speech into approximate syllable units is often easy and sometimes
useful, reliably locating phones in continuous speech is one of the most desired but difficult
tasks in ASR. Most systems avoid such explicit segmentation, doing simultaneous phone
boundary location and labeling in one process. In this section, we nonetheless examine the
problem and propose solutions (e.g., for expert systems) to appreciate its difficulty. Explicitly
segmenting and labeling continuous speech is closely linked to artificial intelligence [253].
The procedures described below were derived by analyzing the ways speech experts "read"
spectrograms [23].

A good phone segmentation facilitates an ensuing ASR step of labelling phone units.
Typical speech parameters and features are useful both for segmenting speech and for labeling
acoustic segments. The sequence of segmenting and labeling is a controversial issue;
segmenting first is more efficient because typical phone units contain several frames and
labeling a phone often requires examination of dynamic spectral behavior over the course of
the phone's frames. Many approaches nonetheless label each frame independently before
segmentation, despite the higher computation load [254, 255]. More often, a coarse
segmentation is provided first and then boundary positions are refined during the labeling
phase. The preliminary segmentation usually goes beyond the syllable division described

above to smaller units (e.g., fricatives, stops, and vowels) that can be reliably located with robust and simple tests involving bandpass energies, zero-crossing rates, and durations. Dynamic programming can be used to overcome label/segment errors by aligning phonetic labels with estimated boundaries.

Even though expert-system ASR has typically used formants for labeling, coarse segmentation employs more reliable features [256–258]. The speech spectrum may be divided into four regions, some of which correspond roughly to formant ranges, but errors such as missed formants are avoided by using broad energy measures in each frequency range: (a) a *voice* range of about 80–250 Hz (used to identify voiced sounds, for speech not subject to telephone bandpassing); (b) a *low* range of 300–1000 Hz (noting the presence of F1); (c) a *middle* range of 700–2500 Hz (for F2); and (d) a *high* range above 2500 Hz. (These ranges are typical, but values differ considerably among systems.) Recognizers may employ zero-crossing rates within some bands as crude formant detectors to help segmentation. Others use coarse spectral measures, e.g., the first autocorrelation coefficient or normalized LPC error (which helps separate vowels from frication) and/or parameters of a one-formant approximation to the speech spectrum (obtained using centroids, moments, or a two-pole LPC analysis).

Several systems use a four-category initial segmentation: vowels, silences, fricatives, and dips (the following rules are from one such system [256]). *Silences* can be identified by segments longer than 10 ms whose energy above 300 Hz falls below a threshold (typically about 3 dB above background noise level); if the voice range is excluded, obstruents with voice bars are included in this category. The *vowel* category includes sonorant consonants and identifies voiced segments (using a voicing detector or simply high energy in the voice range) longer than 25 ms with more energy at low than at high frequencies. The frames after a silence can be examined to detect a possible stop burst, looking for very brief energy in the high range: such an unvoiced segment exceeding 70 ms would be called a fricative, one less than 25 ms would be a stop burst, otherwise it would be stop aspiration. Voiced energy *dips* (drops of more than 60% relative to adjacent energy peaks) between vowels often indicate obstruents, as long as such a segmentation does not propose adjacent vowels of less than 25 ms. Nasals, in particular, are well identified by dips in the mid-range. Since phones are rarely shorter than 40 ms, *dip detectors* usually smooth the energy parameters over a few frames before attempting segmentation.

These four broad categories are further subdivided during segmentation by some systems [258, 259]; e.g., the *silence* category is easily split into voiced and unvoiced versions (to distinguish stop voicing via voicebar detection); frication may be subdivided to include fricatives and aspiration (using duration and energy tests); sonorant consonants may be separated from vowels. Such systems typically report 4–7% of actual boundaries missed and 5–10% extraneous boundaries proposed. Systems attempting (more ambitious) segmentation into actual phones tend to have more errors (e.g., 22% extra segments in [255]).

Recognizers often utilize *spectral derivatives* to propose boundary locations (*landmarks*), due to a high correlation between sudden acoustic change and segment edges [257, 260]. Sudden changes in speech amplitude or voiced–unvoiced changes are often the most reliable phone boundary cues, but many such boundaries exhibit neither. Sudden spectral changes (e.g., formant jumps) can help divide long sections of voiced speech involving sonorants. A spectral derivative can be defined as the sum of changes in a set of outputs from bandpass filters or as the average absolute value of changes at sampled frequencies in the speech spectrum between adjacent frames. A one-frame peak in a spectral derivative could indicate a nasal boundary or a boundary in a sequence of fricatives. More difficult to segment are sequences involving vowels, glides, and liquids, where the spectral derivatives often exhibit broad peaks over several frames, corresponding to large but smooth spectral changes. Coarticulation and undershoot effects in speech [261] often cause segmenters to miss boundaries or to propose extraneous ones.

10.12.3 Labeling Phones

Identifying an acoustic segment with one or more possible corresponding phoneme labels can be accomplished by applying distance measure techniques (described above for IWR) to phone templates. For CSR, however, methods using formant trajectories are more common, in part because durational considerations are more easily integrated into the labeling procedure. Most segmenting ASR tries to label acoustic segments corresponding to phonemes [262, 263], but some do diphone segments using synthesized templates (a form of analysis by synthesis) [258]. Diphone and statistical ASR approaches appear to yield only about 63% correct phoneme identification [255], although accuracy is usually improved by postprocessing a set of candidates (rather than forcing a decision to one candidate on acoustic information only). The following discussion describes how the best acoustic–phonetic analyzer of the ARPA speech understanding project (a major CSR effort during the early 1970s [12, 264]) handled labeling [256].

After coarse segmentation, vowel-like segments are often CVC (consonant–vowel–consonant) syllables because initial and final sonorant consonants are difficult to separate from the vowel via simple tests. In particular, prevocalic /r/ may be very short, causing no peak in the spectral derivative; it can be identified by a rising F3 close to F2 for more than 35 ms. (Postvocalic /r/ in American English is often manifest only by a shift in the vowel spectrum.) Nasals can be identified by a low F1 and a low ratio of F2 amplitude to F1 amplitude [265], although postvocalic nasals are often missed because they may be evident only through nasalization of the vowel [266]; /l/ and /w/ are associated with low F2 and a large separation between F2 and F3. The diphthongs /ɑj/ and /ɔj/ must have initial formant positions close to those for /ɑ/ and /ɔ/, respectively, and either be longer than 250 ms or have large rises in F2 (300 Hz rise for /ɑj/, 750 Hz for /ɔj/). The requirements for the diphthong /ju/ are a low F1, an initial high falling F2, F2 and F3 close in the middle of the segment, and initial falling F3.

For the remaining vocalic segments, weak unstressed or reduced vowels are identified by comparing peak amplitudes with those of adjacent syllables. For segments of sufficient amplitude whose spectrum is relatively stable, specific vowels are identified by comparing average values of F1 and F2 (and F3, if low enough to indicate a retroflex vowel) in the test segment to speaker-normalized values for all English vowels. Normalization is typically a linear scaling of formant values based on how the point vowels /i,ɑ,u/ for the speech under test deviate from a standard set [267], although more complex forms of normalization exist [36, 268].

In analyzing the *dip* category, sonorant consonants are identified via tests as described above, with some modifications to isolate obstruents. Sonorant dips must exceed 25 ms; otherwise a flapped /t/ is output. A dip must have significant F3 energy to be a nasal; otherwise a voicebar is assumed. Fricatives are classified according to energy, voicing, and the frequency of major energy concentration. High-frequency fricatives (energy center above about 3500 Hz) are considered either /s/ or /z/ (depending on the voicing decision); /ʃ/ and /ʒ/ are separated from the other (weak) fricatives by an energy threshold.

Identifying stop place of articulation is a very difficult task because of the variety of acoustic cues and large coarticulation effects [269]. Complex analyses of burst spectra (for

CV transitions) and of formant transitions (for CV and VC cases) have led to accuracies nearing 95%, but only for systems with very complex rules [270].

A better method for detecting nasals in continuous speech than the simple approach above applies speech energies in three frequency ranges plus a frequency centroid of the 0–500 Hz range to a multivariate statistical decision method [271]. Sampling the parameters every 12.8 ms, this method correctly located 91% of the nasal boundaries. Once located, intervocalic nasals can be partitioned into /m/ and /n/ categories with 94% accuracy [272]. Segment-and-label approaches are not unique to CSR applications; 95% accuracy was achieved for a 20-word vocabulary in speaker-independent IWR, using simple energy and zero-crossing rate measurements in four frequency bands [273].

10.12.4 Phonological Rules

Some effects of coarticulation in continuous speech can be accounted for via *phonological rules*, which note how the standard phone composition of words can change due to the context of adjacent words [274, 275]. While phone deletion (i.e., speakers omitting phones normally uttered) rarely occurs in words pronounced in isolation, acoustic segments are commonly deleted, inserted, or substituted during conversational speech. English, with its levels of stress (stressed, unstressed, and reduced syllables), causes more difficult CSR problems than most other languages (e.g., Italian [276]). Many vowels in unstressed syllables tend to have spectra closer to the middle of the vowel triangle than respective versions in stressed syllables.

As one speaks more rapidly, many unstressed English vowels are either reduced to forms of schwa or disappear completely (e.g., the /I/ in *multiply* may be evident only in the unvoiced /t/ burst). Such *vowel reduction/deletion* also is manifest in word-final unstressed syllables containing schwa plus a nasal or /l/, which often delete the schwa to form syllabic sonorants (e.g., *bottle*). A similar form of reduction occurs in syllables having /r/ plus an unstressed vowel, which revert to syllabic /ɝ/ (*introduction*). Few languages have as much vowel reduction as English and Portuguese.

Stops are often shortened or deleted as well: intervocalic /t,d/ often reduces to a 10–30 ms flap before unstressed vowels, and few people articulate the /t/ in *mostly* (a case of *homorganic stop deletion*: when the stop is between two consonants of similar place of articulation, or preceding an unstressed vowel, it tends to disappear). On the other hand, an acoustic analyzer might detect a stop after /n/ in *prince,* due to an energy dip before the /s/ (*homorganic stop insertion*). English, which has no nasal vowel phonemes, tends to nasalize vowels before nasal consonants to such an extent that a separate nasal consonant is often hard to detect.

Some phonological rules apply across word boundaries: *geminate reduction* shortens the duration of successive identical phones ("some meat"); *palatalization* renders alveolar consonants palatal when followed by another palatal ("did you" → /dIʃu/); and *devoicing* frequently deletes voicing from final voiced consonants when preceding an unvoiced one ("his shoe" → /hIsʃu/). ASR performance can be significantly improved if such phonological rules appropriate for the language (e.g., English) are incorporated into hypothesis generation. In the *generative* form of the rules (as above), they can expand the number of phonemic sequences assigned to each vocabulary word to handle pronunciation variants; e.g., each word could have several network models. In an *analytic* form, the rules could be applied directly to the output sequence of proposed phones to suggest alternative phone possibilities.

In an attempt to better recognize unstressed words, some systems treat short sequences of common words (especially unstressed words) as lexical units, e.g., *let me*, *you know*, *going to*. Such expressions are often highly reduced in articulation (e.g., /lɛmi/, /yno/, /gʌnʌ/) and are poorly recognized using standard techniques.

10.12.5 Using Prosodics to Aid Recognition

Despite the evidence in Chapters 3 and 5 that F0, duration, and energy convey information in human speech communication, intonation is rarely used in ASR. Other than including energy as a supplementary parameter to LPC coefficients in template comparisons [122], most systems assume that spectral cues contain sufficient information for recognition and that prosodic cues are unreliable. Nonetheless, there is clear evidence that accuracy can be improved by properly exploiting prosodics. Segments of speech corresponding roughly to syllables are more accurately identified if they have the acoustic correlates of stress (longer durations, higher or changing F0, and higher amplitude) [277]. If such stressed syllables can be detected, they provide *islands of reliability* in the speech signal, where segmentation and labeling decisions are likely to be more accurate. While most ASR analyzes speech in sequential (left-to-right) order, a hybrid *middle-out* approach can yield superior results at the cost of extra computation: basically proceeding left to right but delaying analysis of unstressed syllables until the next stressed one is found [12, 278, 279]. A simple form of stress detector involving only energy can improve CSR accuracy in DTW and HMM methods by effectively highlighting stressed syllables [29].

Prosodics can also aid in phone identification and in providing syntactic information useful for linguistic postprocessing. Tone languages (e.g., Chinese, Thai) require F0 to distinguish the use of tones phonemically [280, 281]. The presence and/or identity of consonants is sometimes cued by intonation [278]: (a) voiced consonants usually cause a dip in F0 of more than 10%; (b) a 10–20% fall in F0 at the start of a stressed syllable usually indicates the presence of a preceding unvoiced consonant; and (c) relatively long vowels indicate ensuing voiced consonants, etc. Syntactically, an utterance-final F0 rise or a relatively low falloff rate for F0 during the utterance can cue a yes/no question. A syllable identified as stressed is almost always part of a *content word* (e.g., noun, verb, adjective). Thus stress identification can rule out certain hypotheses based on spectral analysis; e.g., "Give me fish" and "Have you fished?" have similar spectral patterns, but an initial unstressed syllable and rising F0 in the second sentence would rule out confusion with the first sentence.

The primary benefit of intonation, however, appears to lie in identifying major syntactic boundaries: 90% of such boundaries in English are preceded by F0 falls of more than 7% and are followed by rises exceeding 7% [278]. Parenthetical clauses have even more pronounced (20%) F0 dips. Besides F0, the duration between centers of successive stressed syllables, called an *interstress interval*, is useful in locating major boundaries; 95% of perceived boundaries can be detected by a simple test on interstress intervals. Since intervals in uninterrupted speech average 0.3–0.4 s, a threshold of 0.5 s separates them from typical 1 s intervals including clause boundaries and 1.5 s intervals for sentence boundaries [278]. However, 23% of the intervals exceeding 0.5 s are not perceived boundaries, although most of these are syntactic boundaries useful for segmenting an input speech signal.

10.13 COMMERCIAL SYSTEMS

The last few years have seen rapid progress in providing advanced ASR systems at decreasing cost. Besides improvements in ASR algorithms, the cost of computation and memory has declined rapidly. The need for special-purpose hardware (application-specific integrated circuit chips) has declined as personal computers have become more powerful. Several software-only products now exist (e.g., from Dragon Systems, IBM, Philips, and Lernout & Hauspie). In the 1980s, products were limited to IWR. Since then, CSR has been gradually gaining accuracy and therefore user acceptance. Dictation systems are available for several major languages (e.g., French, German, Swedish, Italian, Spanish, Arabic, as well as both American and British English). There is now even a service for ASR via the telephone, where the output text is sent to the customer via the Internet [276]. Active vocabularies range up to 60,000 words, with back-up dictionaries to 200,000 words. Virtually all manufacturers quote well in excess of 90% ASR accuracy, but impartial comparative tests are rarely done [259]. Several companies manufacture ASR boards for use with personal computers [58].

10.14 SUMMARY OF CURRENT ASR DESIGN

To summarize the steps used in a typical design of current ASR systems, there is a development or training step (taking many hours of computation) and then the actual recognition or testing step (which may be real-time). Training involves automatic analysis of successive frames of speech (e.g., every 10 ms, using 25 ms windows), each yielding a parameter vector (e.g., 10–16 mel-cepstral coefficients, augmented by their delta values). Phone HMMs (usually context-dependent) are developed via the Baum–Welch algorithm, using mixtures of Gaussian densities to model each state's PDF. The models are often bootstrapped from initial coarse models from other speakers or from context-independent models. Phonetically labeled corpora (e.g., TIMIT) allow such automatic initial model generation. Later, finer training often involves using a preliminary, coarse recognizer to determine which models and states are to be updated for each speech frame, thus using estimates (of phones and boundaries) which are not fully reliable. Iterative training is intended to refine the estimates.

   During recognition, the same speech analysis is done, frame by frame, as for training. The Viterbi algorithm finds the most likely path through the HMM states, obeying the left-to-right sequence within each phone model and requiring proper sequencing for successive triphone models (e.g., a /ibu/ model for /b/ could be followed by an /but/ model, but not a /gut/ one). An empirical weighting combines the acoustic score with a trigram language model score, to determine the likeliest word sequence, for which the word transcriptions match the phone sequence.

10.15 CONCLUSION

Speech recognition can provide a practical way to control machines or to input data such as text to a computer. Even using words separated by pauses, most people can enter data via speech faster than by typing (up to 150 words/min via speech vs 50 words/min for good typists and 15 for poor ones) [282]. The fact that error rate increases with vocabulary size need not be a major difficulty because small vocabularies (e.g., 50 words) are sufficient for many ASR applications.

   Most ASR uses statistical pattern recognition, applying general models (e.g., networks) as structures to incorporate knowledge about speech in terms of reference models. The parameters of the models are estimated during a training procedure in which speakers utter words or sentences, which may be repeated later during actual ASR. Employed primarily in CSR, the alternative cognitive approach to pattern recognition analyzes speech from the production point of view [283]. Research on cognitive methods examines speech-specific models, rather than general Markov networks, which lead to a better understanding of how humans generate speech. While such approaches should be more efficient than template-matching schemes, to date they have been less successful than statistical methods because of our inadequate knowledge of speech production. (Similar comments would apply when comparing terminal-analog and articulatory speech synthesizers.)

In one view of artificial intelligence, better simulations of human processes are found in better models of how humans function. Thus, improved automatic speech synthesis and recognition should derive from better understanding of human speech production and perception, respectively [284]. However, since synthetic speech is intended to be processed by human ears, it is more likely that improved naturalness in synthetic speech will come from better models of how the ear transforms the speech signal than from modeling perturbations in vocal tract motion. Similarly, while parameter transformations following ear nonlinearities have had some (limited) success in ASR, a better model of how humans produce the speech that recognizers must process is likely the key to improved recognition performance.

As hardware costs decrease, ASR with vocabularies of thousands of words will become commonly used. However, practical systems to recognize spontaneous speech will require more significant progress in natural language understanding. Such future ASR will combine today's statistical techniques with more advanced expert systems exploiting phonetic feature extraction [285, 286], rather than simple template matching [3]. In addition to fluent dialog with machines, advances in ASR and TTS will eventually allow automatic translation programs allowing two humans to converse, each using one's own language [286].

PROBLEMS

P10.1. Consider a system that attempts to recognize a sequence of five letters (from the set A, B, C, ..., Y, Z), spoken without intervening pauses by anyone in your town. The system uses stored templates for each of the 26 letters in the recognition process.
   (a) Divide the set of letters into several classes, within which there would be the most recognition errors (i.e., the most confusions).
   (b) How many templates would there be for each letter? What information would each template contain? Explain.
   (c) What are the advantages and disadvantages of using templates of letters rather than of "words" (of five letters each)?

P10.2. (a) Discuss some of the extra problems that arise when doing continuous speech recognition that do not occur with discrete word recognition.
   (b) Discuss some of the differences found between speaker-dependent and speaker-independent recognition systems.
   (c) Recognition systems may use either syllables or phonemes as the units of recognition. What are some of the advantages and disadvantages of each?

P10.3. In an isolated-word recognition system, an input test word must be preprocessed or "normalized" before its features can be compared with those of the stored templates. Describe two such normalizations. Why are they useful?

P10.4. (a) Why is a vocabulary of the 26 alphabet letters harder to recognize than a vocabulary of the names of the 26 largest cities in America?
   (b) Besides the problem of locating word boundaries, why is continuous speech more difficult to recognize than isolated words?

P10.5. Consider a word recognizer with the following vocabulary: *bid, did, bad, dad, bud, dud, bead, deed.*

(a) What would be the most frequent word confusions with a dynamic programming-based similarity function?

(b) Suggest methods to reduce these confusions.

(c) What minimal temporal and spectral resolution would be needed to achieve minimal success? Explain the limitations.

(d) If the vocabulary is reduced to words with initial b, how would your answer to part (c) change?

P10.6. Why do some recognizers use a Euclidean distance? Give an example of speech parameters for which such a distance is appropriate, and one where it is not.

P10.7. How does a recognizer based on hidden Markov models handle timing and spectral variability in speech? How is segmentation effectively accomplished with HMMs?

P10.8. How can recognizers accommodate variability across speakers?

P10.9. Segmenting and labeling are two major tasks for recognition. Give advantages for doing one and then the other, versus a simultaneous approach.

P10.10. Give examples of two different vocabularies (with the same size) that could appear in a practical recognition system, and explain why one may be much easier to recognize.

P10.11. How does dynamic time warping help in recognition? What are its disadvantages?

11

Speaker Recognition

11.1 INTRODUCTION

Computer analysis of speech has many purposes. Chapters 7 and 10 examined coding and recognition, the major applications for speech analysis. Other uses include real-time displays of speech spectra and F0 (Chapter 6), which are useful as aids for the handicapped, e.g., in teaching the deaf to speak. This chapter deals with a final important application of speech analysis: automatic speaker or voice recognition. In speech recognition (ASR), variation due to different speakers in speech signals corresponding to the same spoken text was viewed as "noise" to be either eliminated by speaker normalization or (more commonly) accommodated through reference models drawn from a large number of speakers. When the task is to identify *who* is talking rather than *what* is said, speech must be processed to extract measures of speaker variability instead of segmental features [1].

Compared to ASR, there has been less speaker recognition research because fewer applications exist and less is understood about which speech aspects identify a speaker than about segmental acoustic–phonetics. There are two main speaker recognition applications: (1) verifying a person's identity prior to admission to a secure facility or to a transaction over the telephone, and (2) associating a person with a voice in police work [2] or in audioconferences. Other applications include identifying the gender [3] or the accent of a speaker [4], and the language being spoken [5]. While fingerprints or retinal scans are usually more reliable ways to verify a claimant, voice identification has the convenience of easy data collection over the telephone. Many companies furnishing limited access to computer databases would like to provide automatic customer service by telephone. Since personal number codes (typed on a keypad) or physical keys can be lost, stolen, or forgotten, speaker recognition provides a viable alternative.

For ASR, much is known about the speech production process linking a text and its phonemes to the spectra and prosodics of a corresponding speech signal. Phonemes have specific articulatory targets, and the corresponding acoustic events have been well studied (but remain not fully understood). For speaker recognition, however, the acoustic aspects of what characterizes the differences between voices are obscure and difficult to separate from signal aspects that reflect segment recognition. There are three sources of variation among speakers: differences in vocal cords and vocal tract shape, differences in speaking style (including variations in both target positions for phonemes and dynamic aspects of coarticulation such as speaking rate), and differences in what speakers choose to say. Automatic speaker recognizers exploit only the first two variation sources examining low-level acoustic features of speech [6] since a speaker's tendency to use certain word and syntactic structures (the third source) is difficult to quantify and too easy to mimic.

Unlike the clear correlation between phonemes and spectral resonances, there are no acoustic cues specifically or exclusively related to speaker identity. Most of the parameters and features in speech analysis (Chapter 6) contain information useful for the identification of both the speaker and the spoken message. The two types of information, however, are coded very differently. Unlike ASR, where decisions are made for every phone or word, speaker recognition usually requires only one decision, based on an entire test utterance (exception: identifying speakers in a conversation [7, 8]). There is no simple set of acoustic cues that reliably distinguishes speakers. Speaker recognizers can utilize long-term statistics averaged over entire utterances or exploit analyses of specific sounds. The latter approach is common in *text-dependent* (TD) applications where utterances of the same text are used for training and testing; statistical average methods are often used in *text-independent* (TI) cases where training and testing employ different phrases. While only one decision is made in speaker recognition, the set of choices can vary. Most practical applications need only a binary decision (i.e., is the claimant correct?), but some ask which of N stored voices matches a test input.

11.2 VERIFICATION VS RECOGNITION

There are two related but different types of voice recognition: *automatic speaker verification* (ASV) or authentication [9] and *automatic speaker identification* (ASI) [10]. (For discussions applying to both ASV and ASI, the abbreviation ASV/I will be used, reserving ASR as a common abbreviation for automatic speech recognition.) Both use a stored database of reference models for N known speakers, and similar analysis and decision techniques are employed. ASV is the simpler task since it requires only evaluating the test pattern with one reference model and a binary decision whether the test speech matches the model of the claimant. In ASV, speakers known to the system are *customers*, while unregistered speakers are *impostors*. ASI, on the other hand, requires choosing which of N known voices best matches a test voice. Since N comparisons and decisions are often necessary, the error rate rises with N for ASI, while ASV can have rates independent of N [6] (Figure 11.1).

We distinguish *closed-set* and *open-set* experiments; in the first, only customers are considered; in the second, the voice of the test speaker (*claimant*) may not be among the N stored patterns, in which case a "no match" decision should be made. Since most practical cases require real-time response, another option for both ASI and ASV is to delay a decision in the case of uncertainty and ask the speaker to furnish more speech. While ASV is much more common than ASI, ASI is useful in audioconferencing, if registered users in a room move around, using several microphones (e.g., determining who is talking would allow use of speaker-dependent speech recognition) [11]. Segmenting conversational speech into speaker turns is also useful [7]. For reasons of cost, however, most ASV/I uses single-microphone input.

While the worst performance for both ASI and ASV is 0% correct, simple guessing yields 50% for ASV (assuming equal numbers of customers and impostors), but only $100/N\%$ for closed-set ASI (assuming the test speaker is known to the system and each speaker is equally likely). There are two classes of errors: *false acceptances* (FA or Type I

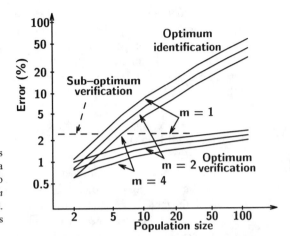

Figure 11.1 Expected error rate in simulations of speaker identification and verification as a function of the number of speakers known to the system. The recognition process used m features, assumed to be Gaussian-distributed. Performance curves for $m = 1, 2,$ and 4 features are shown. (After Doddington [6].)

error) and *false rejections* (FR or Type II error). In FA, the system incorrectly accepts an impostor during ASV or identifies a wrong person during ASI. In FR, the system rejects a true claimant in ASV or incorrectly finds "no match" in ASI. The decision to accept or reject usually depends on a threshold: if the distance between a test and a reference template exceeds the threshold (or a model likelihood is too low), the system rejects a match.

Depending on the costs of each type of error, systems can be designed to minimize an overall cost by biasing the decisions in favor of less costly errors. Low thresholds are generally preferred because FAs are usually more expensive (e.g., admitting an impostor to a secure facility might be disastrous, while excluding some authorized personnel is usually only annoying). (In financial transactions authorized by telephone voice, the allowed amount of the transaction could be set inversely proportional to the likelihood of error.) Many researchers adjust system parameters so that the two types of error occur equally often (*equal error rate (EER) condition*) [12]). Plots of FR vs FA are called *receiver operating curves* (ROC) and resemble hyperbolas (since we can trade off FR and FA). On a log FA vs log FR plot, the ROC approaches a straight line perpendicular to the 45° EER line, with lower ROCs corresponding to better systems.

Informally, speakers whose speech is easy to recognize (or to code with high quality) have been called *sheep*, vs more difficult speakers (*goats*). In ASI/V this "animal" classification extends to: goats with high FR rates (sheep have low rates), *lambs* easy to impersonate (*rams* are hard), and *wolves* with high FA rates (and *badgers* low) [13]. How such classes of speakers are distinguished acoustically is far from clear.

11.3 RECOGNITION TECHNIQUES

Analysis techniques are similar for speech and speaker recognition since both involve pattern recognition of speech signals. Data reduction via parameterization and feature extraction are important in ASI/V for the same reasons of efficiency as in ASR. While template matching, distance measures, and stochastic models are common to both applications, the templates/models may employ different information for speech and speaker recognition; ASI/V models emphasize speaker characteristics rather than word information. Just as model memory grows linearly with vocabulary size in ASR, ASI/V memory expands similarly with the number of speakers. Memory grows with both vocabulary and population size, but ASI/V employs much smaller vocabularies (e.g., ten digits) than most ASR systems. Thus the problem of memory expansion is much more serious for speaker-dependent word-based ASR than for ASI/V Feature-based ASI/V has small memory requirements with no correspondence to vocabulary, but is usually more difficult to implement than template- or model-based ASI/V.

11.3.1 Model Evaluation

Since typical speech parameters and features contain information about both phone segments and the speaker, some ASI/V systems use methods identical to those for ASR, except that the models are created for speakers rather than for words. In general, such systems store information for every speaker's utterances, each typically of one or more isolated words. To minimize memory and computation, simple systems use one model per speaker, clustered from repetitions of one word during a training period. At increased cost, performance can be improved by storing models for several words and/or several repetitions of the same word without clustering.

As in Chapter 10, dynamic time warping can compare test and reference templates, and a nearest-neighbor (NN) rule (or a KNN rule for multiple templates) [14, 15] can select the closest reference template, outputting the speaker's identity corresponding to that template in the case of ASI. For ASV, the test template is compared only against the reference template(s) for the claimed speaker; if the distance (of the best match, in the case of multiple templates) falls below a threshold, the speaker is accepted (Figure 11.2). (Thresholds can also be applied in ASI, if "no match" is an acceptable output.) Similar comments hold for the use of HMMs in ASI/V, where thresholds would apply to likelihoods rather than distances.

11.3.2 Text Dependence

Evaluating test utterances for speaker identity is much simpler when the underlying text matches that of a training utterance. The straightforward application of ASR methods to ASI/V is possible only for cooperative speakers, who train the system and later test it with the same word(s). This text-dependent (TD) case, using the same text for training and testing, permits the simple comparison of word models and occurs frequently in ASV applications but rarely for ASI. In forensic work, speakers are often uncooperative, training may be done surreptitiously, and the test and training texts are rarely the same. Having different texts for training and testing, the text-independent (TI) case can still use model matching, but much different information must be stored in the models than when test and reference utterances are simply repetitions of the same word. Error rates for TI recognition are higher than for comparable TD cases [16]. To achieve good results for TI ASI/V, much more speech data are usually needed for both training and testing than for TD ASI/V (Figure 11.3); training often exceeds 30 s per speaker and test utterances are usually longer than 5 s. On the other hand, the performance of TD systems is highly correlated with the vocabulary that is chosen. Furthermore, TD ASI/V may have more security problems than TI ASI/V: stolen recordings of stored models could be used to fool TD systems, whereas a TI system could request different words on each recognition test (stolen tapes could still fool TI systems that employ average statistics, but they would be less successful with those examining dynamic features).

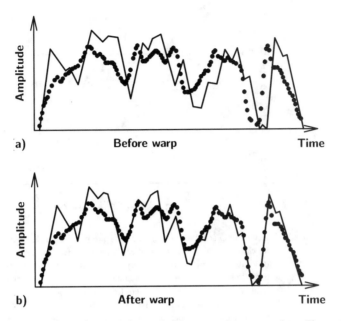

Figure 11.2 Time alignment of the amplitude contours for two templates. The contour
from the test utterance (solid curve) is aligned to that of the reference
utterance (dotted curve). (a) The curves after linear warping to align
endpoints; (b) the curves after nonlinear alignment using an amplitude
distance. After alignment, the utterance is divided into 20 equal sections,
where each section contributes to an overall distance measure in proportion to
its usefulness. (After Rosenberg [9] © IEEE.)

11.3.3 Statistical vs Dynamic Features

Since acoustic cues to a speaker's identity occur throughout each utterance, some
systems utilize models of averaged parameters rather than exploit the full-time sequence of
parameters as in ASR. This global approach is most useful in TI cases since the time
sequences of training and test utterances do not correspond. The simplest approach
conceptually (although not computationally) takes long-term averages of speech parameters
over all available data from each speaker to yield one mean vector template. Long-term
spectra can yield good recognition accuracy for normal speech and even for speech spoken
under stress, but not for disguised (impersonation) speech [18]. For example, one study of 17
speakers used a 22-dimensional vector containing the means and standard deviations of F0
and the reflection coefficients in a tenth-order LPC analysis [19]: averaging over 1000 speech
frames or about 39 s/speaker, error rates were 2% for ASI and 4% for (equal error condition)
ASV. With this method, template matching is a simple comparison of two 22-element vectors,
but much calculation is necessary to estimate F0 and ten LPC coefficients for 1000 frames. In
place of F0 and LPC coefficients, another study used long-term (30 s) averages of spectral
correlations between adjacent frequencies [20]. The long test utterances needed to obtain
long-term averages in these studies usually preclude real-time applications. Furthermore,
long-term spectra are sensitive to speaker effort and to variations in transmission channels
(e.g., the telephone) [6]; they also ignore much speaker-dependent information in the speech
signal.

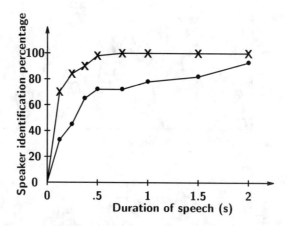

Figure 11.3 Recognition accuracy as a function of speech duration. Duration refers to how much of the training/test utterance "May we all learn a yellow lion roar" was used in the template matching. Ten female speakers uttered this sentence six times, yielding five training utterances and one test utterance each. The templates stored cepstra derived from a 12th order LPC analysis at 40 uniformly spaced frames in the 1.8–2.8 s utterances. Recognition was based on a single distance measure, the average of 1–40 frame distances (depending on the duration used). The upper and lower curves correspond to the TD and independent cases, respectively. "Text independence" was achieved artificially by randomly ordering the 40 frames, destroying the template synchronization. (After Atal [17].)

Statistical averaging has successfully been applied in TD cases also, to reduce run-time computation by using templates of few dimensions. Dynamic time warping (DTW) has seen less use recently in ASR (displaced largely by HMMs), but it is still often used for ASV [21]. In cases where training data are sparse, DTW outperforms both VQ and HMMs [16]. DTW computation increases as the square of template duration, whereas computation of statistics (e.g., moments, covariances) typically increases only linearly with utterance length. Furthermore, after determining the spectral parameters, calculation of statistical means requires no multiplications. Using 40-frame words, one study found similar recognition results with either DTW template matching or a single distance measure involving a 20-dimension statistical vector [22]. Among the 20 features were the means of F0 and 12 LPC log-area ratios, plus a group of seven second-order statistics of these F0 and LPC parameters.

Since recognition via long-term statistics is often impractical for real-time TI applications, another approach in such cases involves identifying specific sounds in the test speech and comparing them with stored sounds for each speaker. Specific phones drawn from each speaker's training data (segmented manually, if necessary) are stored in reference memory. At recognition time, each utterance of unknown text and speaker is scanned (*phone spotting*) to locate phones corresponding to those in memory. Distance measures between spectral patterns of each test phone and its corresponding reference are averaged over all the located phones in the test utterance to yield an overall measure. This measure is then compared against a threshold in ASV applications; or the minimal measure over all speakers is sought for ASI [6].

11.3.4 Stochastic Models

Stochastic approaches have largely replaced the use of templates and long-term averages in recent ASI/V. The HMM method for ASR has been applied directly to ASI/V, replacing Markov models for words or phonemes with those for speakers [23]. Instead of training HMMs for specific linguistic units and across many speakers, we develop a set of HMMs for each speaker. The set may use word-based HMMs, if the ASI/V system is text-dependent, or phone-based otherwise. Tied-mixture (semi-continuous) HMMs usually give better results than discrete HMMs; with enough training, 1% EER is possible for 7-digit tests [24].

Recently, single-state stochastic models have become popular for ASI/V. *Gaussian mixture models* (GMMs) retain the common mixture approach to HMM-based ASR, but omit the timing information implicit in HMMs. Since ASI/V makes only a single speaker decision, no distinction is needed across the many frames of each input utterance. In this way, the GMM method resembles a VQ approach to ASI/V (see next section). Typically, 16 mixtures using diagonal covariances provide good performance; training on a minute of speech and testing with 5 s utterances gave good results [25].

11.3.5 Vector Quantization

Since automatic segmentation of continuous speech into phones is difficult, ASV based on analysis of specific phones is not common. Alternative techniques for TI applications attempt to compare corresponding test and reference phones without explicitly locating them in a test utterance. Vector quantization (VQ) is one such technique successfully applied to both ASR and ASI/V, in similar ways and for similar reasons, e.g., to avoid the segmentation problem. The data-reduction efficiency of VQ in parameterizing speech was paramount for speech coding applications and is useful in ASI/V to minimize memory. As for ASR, the primary advantage of VQ for ASI/V lies in the codebook approach to determining the similarity between utterances. VQ may also be more robust with one-session training data than other methods [24].

Chapter 7 noted that codebooks of about 1000 entries appear necessary for good speech coding, while Chapter 10 said that smaller codebooks suffice for ASR. One ASI/V study designed a 1000-entry codebook so that a speech space using 12 LPC coefficient dimensions was fully "covered" with relatively fixed separation ("radius") between entries [26]. To simplify computation, only the most frequently occuring 400 entries, which included 90% of the training speech frames within a radius of an entry, were used to represent the speaker templates. Training samples 100 s long from each of 11 speakers were used to select 40 of the 400 entries that best represented each speaker. An entry was selected if its average percentage occurrence in the speaker's training data exceeded the mean appearance in the training data for all other speakers and if the entry's percentages were stable with increasing amounts of training data. The basic idea is to find spectra used in the general speech of each speaker and distinctive to each speaker's voice. The 40 entries for each speaker covered 25–40% of his or her training data, but only 7–12% of the data for other speakers. During recognition, the unknown speech was vector quantized with the 400 entries, and the speaker model whose 40 entries most overlapped with the set of entries for the unknown was selected. VQ does no direct phone comparisons and thus needs no segmentation, but by comparing the 40 distinctive spectra for each speaker with the spectra found in the test utterance, a rough phone comparison implicitly occurs. Recognition accuracy with test utterances of 10, 5, and

3 s was 96, 87, and 79%, respectively, which showed that high performance is possible with short test utterances in TI applications.

Besides avoiding segmentation and allowing short test utterances, VQ is computationally efficient compared with storing and comparing large amounts of template data in the form of individual spectra. Thus VQ can be useful for TD as well as TI recognition. One experiment employed isolated digits (0–9) both for training and testing of 100 speakers with one codebook per speaker [27]; each test utterance was identified with the speaker whose codebook yielded the lowest coding distortion. Recognition error decreased substantially as a function of both codebook size and test utterance duration, with errors below 2% for 10-digit tests and 64-word codebooks (Figure 11.4). Increasing codebook size raises computation but decreases errors by reducing the standard deviations of the distortions (Figure 11.5). The performance increase with duration depends on the degree of correlation among words in the test utterance: when the test utterance of 10 different digits was replaced by a single digit repeated 10 times, error increased dramatically. While this study was partially TI (i.e., the speakers were free to say the digits in any order), true TD recognition allows incorporation of timing information into the distance measures to reduce errors.

One way to improve word recognition is to use different codebooks for instantaneous and transitional spectral information [28]. Exploiting timing information via *matrix quantization* (as in Chapter 7) is also useful [29]. Another approach uses multistage codebooks that compare equal-duration subword templates. Applied to ASI/V, one study designed *NW* multistage tenth-order LPC codebooks for each of *N* speakers saying *W* different isolated digits [30]. A classification (reject or accept for ASV; identify for ASI) was based on a plurality of decisions for all words in the test utterance. Using 8-entry codebooks for each 8-frame section of every word, test utterances of 10 different digits led to 0.8% false rejections and 1.8% false acceptances with 16 speakers and 111 impostors.

In summary, ASI/V via VQ can yield high accuracy in both TD and independent cases, with relatively short test utterances. As in speech recognition, VQ often has the advantage of

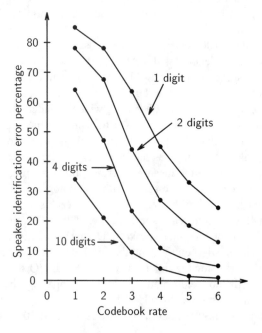

Figure 11.4 Recognition error percentage as a function of codebook rate R for test utterances of 1, 2, 4, and 10 different digits. The test used telephone speech of 200 isolated digit utterances and codebooks containing 2^R entries of eighth-order LPC spectra. (After Soong *et al* [27] © IEEE.)

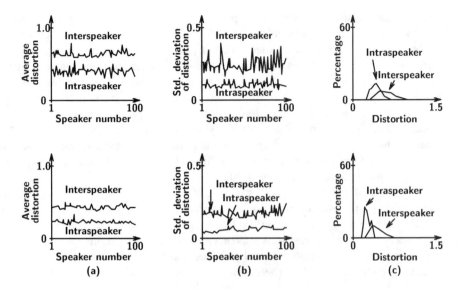

Figure 11.5 Distortion measures during recognition with 1-digit tests for codebooks of 8 entries (top row) and 32 entries (bottom row). (a) The average distance or distortion when coding each of the 100 speakers' test data with that speaker's codebook ("intraspeaker") and all the other codebooks ("interspeaker"). (b) The respective standard deviations of the distortions. (c) Histograms of the distortions, where the likelihood of error is indicated by the overlap of the two curves. (After Soong *et al.* [27] © IEEE.)

smaller reference memory than word templates in the DTW approach. For example, in the first study described above, 400 LPC vectors covering all speakers are stored, and each speaker needs storage of only 40 indexes. The second study requires 64 vectors per speaker. The third, multistage study needs the most storage, about 400 vectors per speaker (10 digits × 8 entries/codebook × about 5 stages/word), which is comparable with the storage for DTW (25–40 frames/word × 10 digits).

A comparison of VQ and HMM methods for ASV/I noted that HMMs were superior except when few data are available, and that HMMs with continuous distributions outperformed discrete HMMs [16, 31]. Within the HMMs, the state transitions provided little information for TI applications.

11.3.6 Similarity and Distance Measures

To match templates or calculate VQ distortions, the same distance measures tend to be used for both speech and speaker recognition [32]. For LPC coefficients, the Itakura distances described in Chapter 10 are common. When other parameters and features are involved, Euclidean and Mahalanobis distances have often yielded good results. Other measures such as correlations [20] and city-block distances are sometimes used but may give inferior results. Recall that the Mahalanobis distance between two M-dimensional vectors $\mathbf{x}$ and $\mathbf{y}$ is

$$d(\mathbf{x}, \mathbf{y}) = \sqrt{(\mathbf{x} - \mathbf{y})^T \mathbf{W}^{-1} (\mathbf{x} - \mathbf{y})}. \tag{11.1}$$

The **W** matrix allows different weighting for the M vector parameters depending on their utility in yielding small distances for vectors from the same speaker. (The process of choosing the parameters is the subject of a later section.) The off-diagonal matrix elements represent correlations between parameters, while the diagonal elements represent the intraspeaker parameter variances (variability within one speaker's speech). This distance has origins in statistical decision theory; each utterance may be viewed as a point in M-dimensional space and the utterances for each speaker describe a multivariate probability density function in that space. Assuming ASI among equally likely speakers, Bayes' rule specifies choosing the speaker whose density is most likely to have generated the test utterance. Points of equal Mahalanobis distance from **y** form a hyperellipsoid centered at **y**, whose principal axes and lengths are the eigenvectors and eigenvalues, respectively, of $\mathbf{W}^{-1}$ [14].

Because of the difficulty of estimating density functions from a limited amount of training data [33], most recognizers assume a parametric form of density such as a Gaussian, which can be simply and fully described by a mean vector μ and a covariance matrix **W**. Since many speech parameters used in ASI/V have unimodal distributions resembling Gaussians, the assumption is reasonable. (It will be noted later how **W** may be used to help select parameters to use for ASI/V.) The density of a feature vector **x** for speaker i would be

$$P_i(\mathbf{x}) = (2\pi)^{-M/2}|\mathbf{W}_i|^{-1/2}\exp[-\tfrac{1}{2}(\mathbf{x} - \mu_i)^T\mathbf{W}_i^{-1}(\mathbf{x} - \mu_i)], \qquad (11.2)$$

where $|\mathbf{W}_i|$ is the determinant of $\mathbf{W}_i$. Most systems use a fixed **W** matrix averaged over all speakers, instead of individual $\mathbf{W}_i$ because (a) it is difficult to obtain accurate estimates for $\mathbf{W}_i$ from the limited training data of individual speakers, (b) using one **W** matrix saves memory, and (c) $\mathbf{W}_i$ matrices are similar for different speakers. While recognition accuracy may increase in some systems by using individual $\mathbf{W}_i$ when examining each speaker's density [19], the improvement must be weighed against increased memory and computation.

Given a test vector **x** for ASI, speaker j is selected if

$$P_j(\mathbf{x}) > P_i(\mathbf{x}) \qquad \text{for all speakers } i \neq j. \qquad (11.3)$$

Applying a (monotonic) logarithm transformation and eliminating terms constant across speakers (i.e., a common $|\mathbf{W}|$), Equations (11.2) and (11.3) reduce to minimizing the Mahalanobis distance of Equation (11.1), using μ_i in place of **y**. The simpler Euclidean distance, which sets $\mathbf{W} = \mathbf{I}$ trades optimal recognition accuracy for fewer calculations, and is popular for recognizing speakers [3]. The Euclidean distance is optimal only if the M parameters are mutually independent and have equal variances (i.e., contribute equally to the distance measure). One advantage of the Mahalanobis distance is its invariance to nonsingular linear transformations such as the Fourier transform [10]. Suitable transformations (i.e., rotation and scaling) of the M dimensions can render the parameters orthogonal, allowing the use of a Euclidean distance without loss of optimality. Since orthogonalizing typical speech parameters usually requires more calculations than is saved with the Euclidean distance, the Mahalanobis distance is preferred for most ASI/V.

Another distance measure used for ASV is the Bhattacharyya distance [34, 35]. For two speakers i and j, modeled by feature distributions whose means are μ_i and μ_j and whose covariance matrices are $\mathbf{W}_i$ and $\mathbf{W}_j$, this distance has two terms:

$$d_B^2 = \frac{1}{2}\log\left(\frac{|(\mathbf{W}_i + \mathbf{W}_j)/2|}{\sqrt{|\mathbf{W}_i||\mathbf{W}_j|}}\right) + \frac{1}{8}(\mu_i - \mu_j)^T\left(\frac{(\mathbf{W}_i + \mathbf{W}_j)}{2}\right)^{-1}(\mu_i - \mu_j).$$

The first term depends only on the **W** matrices (i.e., the average *shape* of the distributions), while the second resembles a Mahalanobis distance [36].

11.3.7 Cepstral Analysis

Among transformations of LPC parameters (e.g., reflection coefficients, log-area ratios), the cepstral representation appears to be superior for ASI/V [17] Besides being invariant to fixed spectral distortions from recording and transmission (e.g., telephone) environments, cepstral coefficients yield high recognition accuracy. Excellent results have been demonstrated through template matching patterns of 18-dimensional cepstral vectors [37]. As an example, the process shown in Figure 11.6 inputs all-voiced sentences of 6–7 short words and calculates ten cepstral coefficients every 10 ms via LPC. (Performance was similar whether the cepstra were calculated directly with Fourier transforms or with LPC, but the LPC method was twice as fast.) The mean value for each coefficient over time is subtracted from each coefficient function (cepstral mean subtraction—CMS), which yields a signal that minimizes environmental and intraspeaker effects. The coefficients in each 90 ms section of the utterance are then expanded into orthogonal polynomials so that each coefficient is represented by the slope of its function, in addition to the coefficient itself. An 18-element feature vector for each 10 ms frame consists of the 10 cepstral coefficients plus 8 of the 10 polynomial coefficients (inclusion of the extra 8 coefficients cuts error rates by two-thirds). This study found a weighted city-block distance to be sufficient for good performance, although other studies prefer the more complex measures noted above. Cepstra based on LPC and LSPs, combined with a Bhattacharyya distance, are also useful [36].

Transitional information, in the form of delta coefficients over a 50–100 ms window, usually increase accuracy, especially in cases of channel mismatch between testing and training [28]. CMS, like RASTA processing [38], eliminates very slowly varying signal aspects, on the assumption that channel behavior is such (except for portable telephones). It removes not only convolutional channel effects, but also some speaker-dependent aspects, and does not help with additive channel noise and nonlinearities. Long-term average subtraction is inappropriate for short utterances, where much speaker-dependent information would be removed [23].

ACW (adaptive component weighting) of the cepstrum emphasizes formant structure, while attenuating broad-bandwidth spectral components of speech [39, 40]. ACW resembles pre-emphasis in that it increases the amplitude of weak resonances. Pre-emphasis changes the slope of the spectral envelope, on the assumption that most speech has spectra falling off with frequency. ACW, on the other hand, makes no such assumptions, and adjusts the level of each resonance to be roughly equal. By emphasizing formant peaks, other frequency ranges contribute less to the speaker identification decisions.

11.3.8 Orthogonal LPC Parameters (‡)

In the search to isolate speaker-dependent features from speech parameters that also carry segmental information, LPC coefficients are frequently examined because they are convenient to calculate and usually model speech spectra well. Besides the standard ASI/V methods utilizing direct LPC coefficients or cepstral features, another LPC transformation known as *orthogonal linear prediction* has demonstrated some success [41, 42]. Orthogonal transformations are usually intended to concentrate information from a set of p parameters into a smaller set by rotating and scaling p-dimensional space so that the revised parameters

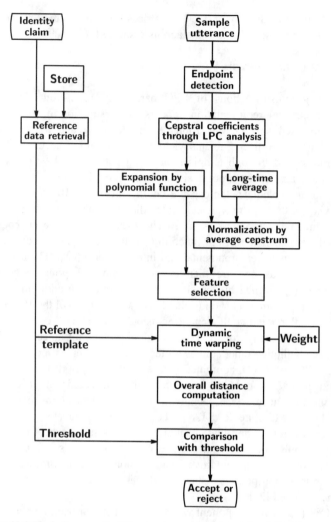

Figure 11.6 Block diagram of a TD recognizer using orthogonal polynomials based on tenth-order LPC cepstra. (After Furui [37] © IEEE.)

become independent and most of the variance (i.e., information) rests in a low-order subset of the revised parameters. Except for the increase in computation, such an approach can be useful for speech coding or recognition. For ASI/V, however, it was proposed that, while the low-order high-variance orthogonal LPC coefficients would reflect phonemic information, the high-order low-variance ones might contain cues dependent on speakers and on the recording environment [41]. Using 12th-order LPC on 4 kHz speech, the variances of the last seven orthogonal coefficients were very small compared with those of the first five, indicating that the latter reflected segmental information (e.g., voicing and the first three formants) that varied throughout an utterance, whereas the high-order coefficients contained information that did not change during the utterance. Since the latter parameters were different between speakers uttering the same sentence, they proved useful for ASI/V.

The procedure was as follows [41]. Given a sequence of J LPC vectors $\mathbf{x}$ of p coefficients each from an utterance of J frames, form a $p \times p$ covariance matrix $\mathbf{R}$ whose elements are

$$r_{ik} = \frac{1}{J-1} \sum_{j=1}^{J} (x_{ij} - x_i)(x_{kj} - x_k), \tag{11.4}$$

where x_i is the average value for the ith LPC coefficient over the J frames. The variances or *eigenvalues* λ_i of the orthogonal parameters ϕ_i are found by solving p simultaneous equations specified by $|\mathbf{R} - \lambda\mathbf{I}| = 0$, where $\mathbf{I}$ is the identity matrix and the p solutions for λ are the λ_i. Solving the equations

$$\lambda_i \mathbf{b}_i = \mathbf{R}\mathbf{b}_i, \qquad 1 \leq i \leq p, \tag{11.5}$$

yields *eigenvectors* $\mathbf{b}_i$. Finally, the ith orthogonal parameter in the jth frame is

$$\phi_{ij} = \sum_{k=1}^{p} b_{ik} x_{kj} = \mathbf{x}_j^T \mathbf{b}_i. \tag{11.6}$$

(A covariance matrix using ϕ_{ij} as input would be diagonal, with the diagonal elements being the λ_i values.)

In this case, the Mahalanobis distance reduces (because the parameters are orthogonal) to

$$\sum_{i=p_1}^{p_2} \frac{(\theta_i - \phi_i)^2}{\lambda_i}, \tag{11.7}$$

where ϕ_i is the ith orthogonal coefficient for a given speaker (averaged over all the speaker's training frames) and θ_i is the ith test coefficient from the vector $\mathbf{y}^T\mathbf{b}_i$, where $\mathbf{y}$ is the test LPC vector averaged over all test frames. In practice, p was raised to 14 to allow two extra LPC poles to model recording and telephone transmission effects, and the four highest-order ϕ_i were assumed to represent such effects. Using only the middle six coefficients (ϕ_i, $5 \leq i \leq 10$), recognition of 21 speakers was 94.4% [41]. An increase to 96% was obtained, at the cost of extra computation, by treating the variances λ_i as speaker-dependent parameters in addition to the ϕ_i. When the system was trained and tested using different utterances (i.e., the TI case), accuracy dropped only to 94%. Subsequent experiments [42] showed that variations in transmission conditions affected performance, despite the elimination of the highest four coefficients. Since other recognizers using LPC coefficients have demonstrated higher accuracy without the need for orthogonal calculations, the orthogonal approach has not been used recently.

11.3.9 Neural Network Approaches

Neural network (NN) methods have had some success in ASI/V [43]. Instead of simply training NNs for each speaker (like NN models for words in ASR), the NNs are often discriminative, trained to model differences among known speakers, which allows a smaller number of parameters (more efficient to train and test). NN methods are comparable in complexity and performance to VQ recognizers. The main disadvantage is the need to retrain the entire network for each new speaker.

11.4 FEATURES THAT DISTINGUISH SPEAKERS

For simplicity, most ASI/V systems use standard speech parameters, e.g., 8–12 LPC coefficients or 17–20 bandpass filter bank energies [10, 32]. Viewing ASI/V as a problem of separating probability densities in M-dimensional space, however, we can obtain better results and lower computation by more careful selection of the parameters or features that make up the space. Ideally, the space should use a few independent features that have similar small intraspeaker variances and large interspeaker variances, which lead to compact widely separated clusters for individual speakers [44]. Independent features eliminate calculations for the off-diagonal elements of **W** in Equation (11.1), and features of equal weight permit a Euclidean distance. In practical terms, the features should also be easy to measure, be stable over time, change little in different environments, and not be susceptible to mimicry [45]. Most systems find it useful to use a *parametric* speech model (e.g., LPC, HMMs), assuming some structure or model of speech production, rather than treat acoustic space in an unstructured fashion. A parametric approach has the advantage of being easier to understand and of reducing the size of the model (thus minimizing *undertraining* problems when faced with limited training and testing data).

One way to select acoustic features for ASI/V is to examine which features correlate with human perceptions of voice similarity. When multidimensional scaling analysis is applied to such judgments, the following account for most of the speaker variance: F0, formants F1–F3 [46], word duration, speaker sex and age [47]. Since sex and age are not acoustic features, it appears that F0, timing cues, and spectral cues are the most likely candidates for ASI/V. Voice individuality is lost if F1–F3 are shifted by 5%, but much larger variations are tolerated in F0 and formant bandwidths [48].

The two sources of speaker variation, physiological and behavioral differences, lead to two types of useful features. *Inherent* features are relatively fixed for a speaker and depend on the anatomy of the speaker's vocal tract. While they can be affected by health conditions (e.g., colds that congest the nasal passages), inherent features are less susceptible to the mimicry of impostors than *learned* features. The latter refer to the dynamics of vocal tract movement, i.e., the way a speaker talks. While learned features can be used to distinguish people with similar vocal tracts, impostors usually find it easier to fool recognizers that are based on learned features than those using inherent features [9]. Mimics usually imitate F0 (both mean and variance) and global speaking rate well, but not fine spectral detail. Statistical features based on long-term averages reflect inherent features more than learned ones and are suitable for TI recognition [49].

11.4.1 Measures of the Effectiveness of Features for Recognition

One measure of effectiveness for individual features is called the *F-ratio* [45, 50], which compares inter- and intraspeaker variances:

$$F = \frac{\text{variance of speaker means}}{\text{mean intraspeaker variance}}, \tag{11.8}$$

where the numerator is large when values for the speaker-averaged feature are widely spread for different speakers, and the denominator is small when feature values in utterance repetitions by the same speaker vary little (the denominator averages intraspeaker variances over all speakers). The F ratio has been successfully used in the design of ASI/ASV systems. Although features with higher F ratios do not guarantee fewer errors, the F ratio tends to be high for features for which one or two speakers are very different from the rest, which suggests that F ratios are most useful in eliminating poor features rather than choosing the best [51].

Generalizing the F ratio to M features and including effects of feature interdependence, we define a *divergence* measure as

$$D = \langle [\mu_i - \mu_j]\mathbf{W}^{-1}[\mu_i - \mu_j]^T \rangle_{i,j}, \tag{11.9}$$

where $\langle\ \rangle_{i,j}$ represents averaging over all speakers, $1 \leq i, j \leq N$; μ_i is the mean feature vector for speaker i (averaged over all the speaker's training data); and $\mathbf{W}$ is the intraspeaker covariance matrix. Equation (11.9) can be expressed using the trace function, where Tr is the sum of the elements along the main diagonal [10], as

$$D = Tr(\mathbf{W}^{-1}\mathbf{B}), \tag{11.10}$$

using the interspeaker covariance matrix $\mathbf{B}$ (with μ representing $\langle\mu_i\rangle_i$):

$$\mathbf{B} = \langle (\mu_i - \mu)(\mu_i - \mu)^T \rangle_i. \tag{11.11}$$

The F ratio is a flawed measure, however, because many speaker distributions have similar means. As a simple example, a feature might give a tight distribution for one speaker and a wide one for another, but have the same mean. Despite the speaker-discriminating power of these features, the F ratio would call them useless; similar comments hold for (common) multimodal distributions. Thus, measures other than the F ratio are preferred [36].

11.4.2 Techniques to Choose Features

A direct way to evaluate the utility of features for ASI/V involves *probability-of-error* criteria in a *knock-out* procedure [50]. Starting with a set of L features, all L possible subsets of $L - 1$ features are used in a recognition system to determine which subset yields lowest error. The feature not used in this best subset is viewed as the least useful feature and is "knocked out" of consideration. The process is repeated with $L - 1$ subsets of $L - 2$ features, etc., leading to a ranking from worst to best features, with the single feature in the last round being the "best." One study examined a total of 92 features, including formant frequencies and bandwidths for vowels, resonances during nasals and fricatives, F0 statistics and dynamics, and some timing measurements (e.g., formant trajectory slopes in diphthongs, voice-onset time for stops) [50]. Among the most useful features were F2 (near 1 kHz) in /n/, F3 or F4 (1700–2200 Hz) in /m/, F2–F4 in vowels, and mean F0. A small test applying the five best features to recognition of 11 speakers led to only one recognition error in 320 trials.

For TI applications employing long-term feature averages, a dynamic programming evaluation procedure [52] can find a set of features having better recognition accuracy than either a knock-out feature set or a set of LPC reflection or cepstral coefficients (for the same number of features). A more efficient way to select a set of features than the knock-out method is the *add-on* procedure. Initial recognition tests are done with each of L features, one at a time, selecting the best single feature. Then tests with two features, including the best one, select the second-best feature. The cycle repeats until the desired number of features has been chosen or until the recognition error falls below a threshold. Using this procedure, one study [51] found the following features most useful: minimal F2 and maximal F1 in an /ar/ trajectory, minimal F2 during /o/ and / ɔ j/ and minimal F3 in /ɝ/.

11.4.3 Spectral Features

Spectral features (e.g., formant center frequencies and bandwidths) in specific sounds tend to be very useful for ASI/V [3, 44, 53]. In addition to the features noted in the last section, formants in retroflex vowels [54] and nasals [16, 20] are said to yield good recognition performance. Vowels, nasals, and fricatives (in decreasing preference) are often recommended for ASI/V because they are relatively easy to identify in speech signals and their spectra contain features that reliably distinguish speakers. Nasals have been of particular interest because the nasal cavities of different speakers are distinctive and are not easily modified (except by colds). The difficulty of locating poles and zeros during nasals has hindered their application to ASI/V, but one study found nasal coarticulation between /m/ and an ensuing vowel to be more useful than spectra during nasals themselves [55]. During /m/, the tongue moves in anticipation of the ensuing vowel and makes a rapid movement that is difficult for speakers to consciously modify. The difficulties of phone segmentation in TD cases and of phone identification in TI applications have led many recognizers to avoid examining specific sounds and to use log-term spectral averages or general spectral distance measures during template matching.

The high-frequency end of speech spectra (3–8 kHz) has been suggested as robust for ASI/V: less dependent on phonetic information than the lower F1–F3 range, more robust against echoes, and hard to mimic [56]. However, this range is not preserved over the telephone and is not robust to noise, due to weaker speech energy at high frequencies. For telephone speech, including *fine structure* features of formant amplitude modulation and glottal pulses appears to help, but requires a formant estimator [57].

11.4.4 Prosodic Features

Both speech and speaker recognition rely primarily on spectral features, but ASI/V has made more use of prosodics (F0 in particular) than ASR has. Mean F0 averaged over all test data from an unknown speaker is often used as a simple feature to classify speakers into broad groups (e.g., male adults, female adults, children). The dynamics of F0 as measured in a contour over time, however, may be a more powerful feature in TD recognition [45, 58, 59], although some measures of F0 appear to be highly variable over different recording sessions [50].

One study sampled F0 at 40 equal intervals in an all-voiced utterance averaging 2 s (Figure 11.7) and then compressed those 40 features via a Karhunen-Loève transformation

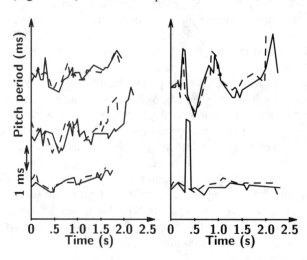

Figure 11.7 Pairs of pitch period contours (one solid, one dashed) for five speakers saying "May we all learn a yellow lion roar." Pairs are offset from each other for ease of viewing. The intraspeaker difference between each pair is generally small, whereas the differences across speakers are great. (After Atal [60].)

(KLT) into 20, which accounted for 99.5% of the variance [60]. With these 20 features, the Mahalanobis distance attained 97% recognition for ten speakers, while Euclidean and correlation measures gave only 68–70%. Using instead the first four moments of the F0 values (statistical, not dynamic, measures) yielded 78% recognition. These results exhibit the utility of both dynamic F0 data and the Mahalanobis distance. To put the utility of F0 in perspective, however, a feature set of 12 cepstral parameters needed only 0.5 s of these 2 s utterances to achieve 98% accuracy [17]. Thus, use of a set of spectral features is more powerful than prosodic methods for ASI/V. While F0 dynamics should be useful, some studies have found only mean F0 to be a reliable speaker cue over time [50]. The use above of the KLT is not typical for ASI/V, both in terms of expense and performance (the KLT is optimal for representing classes with the same mean, but not for class discrimination) [36].

F0 and energy provide two TD ASI/V features that are partly independent and simpler to obtain than spectral features [9]. Recognition rarely exploits the third prosodic, duration, even though phone durations and speaking rate are distinctive aspects of speakers. Lack of knowledge of how speakers use durations is evident in poor durational models for speech synthesis, and it is not surprising that duration is little used in ASI/V. One study showed good recognition by avoiding having to model phone durations, instead simply calculating 40 statistical timing measures dealing with "speech bursts" (times when energy exceeds a threshold) [61]; for a fixed text, the pattern of such bursts reflects speaking style in terms of rate and segment durations. Other studies have shown the usefulness of word durations, voice onset time [45], and formant slope in diphthongs [50] to ASI/V.

11.5 SYSTEM DESIGN

In ASR, task difficulty is measured in terms of vocabulary size, perplexity, and confusability of words based on phonemic similarity. For ASI/V, however, the "vocabulary" is a set of speakers, whose characteristics are much more difficult to describe than the phonemic compositions of words. A vocabulary of *yes–no* is clearly easier to recognize that one of *B–P*, but only unreliable human perceptions of voice similarity can provide a measure of the inherent difficulty of discriminating two voices. Comparing ASI/V experiments using different sets of speakers is difficult, since one study may use a homogeneous set of speakers (e.g., one sex, narrow age range, raised in a small geographical area) while another uses a heterogeneous set (e.g., males and females of varying ages and dialects); the latter yields much higher recognition accuracy. Another factor limiting the utility of many ASI/V studies is that many employ less than 100 speakers [9, 62].

11.5.1 Data Collection

Besides speaker selection, the time span over which training speech is collected is of crucial importance to ASI/V performance. Speaking style often changes substantially over the course of a day, from day to day, and over longer periods of time. Experiments using reference and test data from the same recording session usually yield high recognition accuracy (e.g., using the TIMIT database), which is misleading since practical applications often compare test data with reference data that were obtained much earlier. Performance usually decreases (often dramatically) as the interval between training and testing increases [22]. Reference data must be updated periodically for best results [37]. Some systems consider each recognized utterance as new training data, revising the reference templates to reflect changes in a person's speaking style over time. For people who use an ASV system infrequently, each test utterance should revise the reference models, whereas with frequent users computational constraints might dictate less frequent updating (e.g., once a week). In one adaptive system, customer rejection is 10% in the first few trials after initial training, but then quickly drops to 1%, and gradually declines to 0.25% after 10,000 trials [6].

In any pattern recognition task, training and test data should be kept separate. If the same utterances are used to train and test a recognizer, artificially high accuracy results [63]. With common training and test data, it is difficult to know whether the system has been designed to take advantage of specific speaker characteristics that may not be reliable for new data. Given K utterances per speaker as data, a common procedure trains the system using $K - 1$ as data and one as test, but repeats the process K times treating each utterance as test once. Technically, this *leave-one-out* method designs K different systems, but it verifies whether the system design is good using a limited amount of data, while avoiding the problems of common train and test data.

11.5.2 Sequential Decision Strategy

Most ASV applications require real-time processing, where the system responds immediately to accept or reject a speaker. Many systems employ a sequential decision procedure in which borderline decisions are postponed pending further test input. Rather than use a single threshold to accept or reject, two thresholds divide the distance range into three choices: accept if the distance falls below the lower threshold, reject if it's above the higher threshold, but ask for more input otherwise. Such an approach allows shorter initial test utterances and faster response time, while avoiding errors in close cases. One study found 30% and 73% improvement in error rates by delaying decisions in 5% and 10% of the test trials, respectively [37].

For example, the TI system samples utterances of four monosyllables every 10 ms with 14 bandpass filters uniformly spaced from 300 to 3000 Hz [6]. Templates consist of 24 14-dimensional spectral vectors (10.8 kbit/speaker): six from each syllable, spaced at 20 ms intervals centered around the time of maximum energy in each syllable. In one evaluation of this system using 50 speakers and 70 impostors, the error rate was 1.6% with one test phrase, but it dropped to 0.42% and 0.23% with two and three phrases, respectively [9]. A sequential decision method averages 1.6 phrases per test; customers are rejected and impostors accepted with rates under 1% [6].

11.5.3 Multiple-stage Recognition

In ASI, computation and response time usually increase linearly with population size (i.e., the number of speakers whose models are stored) because each speaker's model must be examined. One way to minimize computation is to set up a hierarchy of reference patterns so that speakers are clustered into groups [64, 65] that can be rapidly identified from a test utterance; e.g., speakers could be classified according to mean F0 so that only a relatively small subset of speakers whose F0 is close to that of the test need be examined further. The concept is very similar to the idea of *cohorts* in speech recognition, where reliable coarse segmentation and feature extraction eliminate most of the vocabulary from consideration and where finer spectral analyses choose the response from among the remaining alternatives. For ASI/V, cohorts often contain both similar and dissimilar impostors, using groups well spread out in acoustic space, to reduce redundancy in the background speaker set. Pooled models based on speaker similarity seem to be better than individual cohort models [66].

One ASI study used a two-stage approach where partitioning via mean F0 was followed by a more computationally intensive analysis involving autocorrelation coefficients, without significant increase in error rate [67]. The multistage method may also help in recognizing speakers with varying dialects. If speakers can be partitioned by dialect, mean F2 and certain prosodic features have been shown to be effective in distinguishing accented voices [68].

One method judges speaker similarity by a log likelihood distance

$$d(\lambda_A, \lambda_B) = \log\left(\frac{p(X_A|\lambda_A)}{p(X_A|\lambda_B)}\frac{p(X_B|\lambda_B)}{p(X_b|\lambda_A)}\right),$$

where X_A and X_B are feature vectors from two speakers A and B, respectively, and λ_A and λ_B are their speaker models [69]. Using a universal background model, trained once for customers, and 2048 Gaussian mixtures (vs 128 in individual speaker models), this study found that only the top five mixture components were needed to model each frame.

11.5.4 Effects of Different Communication Channels (‡)

Since many ASI/V applications involve telephone speech or speech subject to other environmental distortions, the effects on recognition accuracy due to environment must be examined. We noted earlier that cepstral representations have the advantage of being invariant under linear distortions, suggesting that variation in cepstral coefficients about their means might be good ASI/V features. Among the distortions that a telephone link introduces is bandpass filtering, preserving speech only in the 300–3200 Hz range. Successful ASI/V on such limited-spectrum speech has been demonstrated using *filtered logarithmic spectra*: the differences of log spectra between successive time frames, smoothed by a lowpass filter to eliminate the effects of pitch period excitation [42].

Telephone distortions, however, are not limited to bandlimiting, and subsequent studies using real telephone speech indicate difficulties for ASI/V. A large percentage of calls for customer service contain competing speech, music, or traffic noise [70]. Typical long-distance telephone links have signal-to-noise ratios in the range of 19–33 dB (with an average of 27 dB) [14]. A major cause of mismatch is the type of handset, especially carbon vs electret microphone; one study found large performance gain with a handset normalization procedure [69].

Because different links demonstrate large variability in quality compared with that during transmission over one link, it is important for telephone ASI/V to train and test using different links [63]. One TI study, using ten speakers and cepstral features, found the error rate increasing from 17% to 56% when test data were drawn from a different link than the training data [14]. Normalizing each feature over a recording session (by subtracting off its mean) to yield channel-invariant features reduced this degradation but also decreased net performance because useful speaker information was also eliminated. Multichannel error rate was reduced to 32% by incorporating a Gaussian model to account for transmission effects.

In addition to handling telephone speech, ASI/V has been attempted on digitally coded speech, which is becoming popular for voice transmission. One TI study tested several types of coded 4 kHz speech using 20 speakers and 20-dimensional LPC feature vectors consisting of 10 reflection coefficients and 10 cepstral coefficients [71]. Compared with a 95% accuracy for uncoded speech, performance generally fell with bit rate, with 2.4 kbit/s LPC-coded speech yielding 80%. These results are comparable to human recognition of coded voices [72]. Waveform-coded speech gave relatively poor results (16 kbit/s CVSD: 80%; 9.6 kbit/s APC: 75%) because the quantization noise degradation led to poor LPC modeling. A recognition method using features based on parameters other than LPC might do better on such speech; e.g., ASV performance using only F0 and gain features appears to be unaffected by either telephone or coding (LPC or ADPCM) distortions [73], which suggests the utility of prosodics as robust recognition features.

11.6 LANGUAGE AND ACCENT IDENTIFICATION

In addition to recognizing what is being said and who is talking, another application for speech processing is language identification (LI) [5]. Telephone operators receiving an emergency call are sometimes confronted with a caller speaking an unknown language. Finding people knowledgeable in different languages to understand such a speaker is awkward; hence an automatic estimation of the language, based on several seconds of speech, can be very useful. Like ASI/V, LI exploits different aspects of speech, including broad and narrow phonetic and prosodic features, and uses methods ranging from HMMs and ANNs to expert systems. The OGI telephone corpus is a popular database of more than 11 languages [74]. As a baseline, limited perceptual experiments of humans identifying ten languages from 6 s excerpts found performance around 70%, but still improving with experience [74].

LI typically uses HMMs with units of phones or broad phonetic classes (e.g., stop, nasal), and uses language models based on *bigram* sequences of such units (*phonotactics*) (and not with text-based language models, which are hard to develop for text-independent LI). Since languages differ in which phonemes they use, parallel use of phone-based HMMs for several languages, feeding into phoneme-unit language models for 11 languages had 11% errors, using 45 s utterances [5]. With shorter utterances, error rates increase (e.g., 51% with 2 s, 40% with 10 s), although bilingual distinctions (e.g., French vs English) are feasible with only 2 s (76%) [75]. In addition to phonotactics, use of acoustic–phonetic and prosodic cues increases accuracy, especially for short utterances [76].

Another application concerns ASR in multilingual countries, where speakers are free to choose one of two or more languages. Rather than design a universal ASR system to handle several languages at a time, it may be more efficient to first identify the language being spoken, and then to apply a language-specific ASR system. However, some systems do the inverse, i.e., employ language-dependent, phone-based speech recognizers as a first step to LI [77].

Better ASR accuracy occurs with more specific (e.g., speaker-dependent) models. For speaker-independent applications, however, it is impossible to precede ASR with ASI (to permit use of speaker-dependent models). Nonetheless, automatic identification of some speaker characteristics, e.g., gender [75, 78], accent, and language, that may be reliably estimated from their speech allow the use of more specific models in ASR (e.g., many ASR systems use two sets of models trained exclusively by male and female talkers). Using phone-based likelihoods, 97% gender identification is possible with one word of speech (e.g., 400 ms) [75].

One study using strings of 7–8 words classified four different accents of English at 93% accuracy, allowing use of accent-specific models in ASR, which improved accuracy substantially [4]. This study also noted that the 1500–2500 Hz range (F2–F3) was most important, and suggested a non-mel-scale frequency mapping. (In general, the mel-scale is used less often in ASI/V than ASR.) Accent-estimation algorithms often have accuracy close to that for humans [79].

11.7 SPEAKER RECOGNITION BY HUMANS

People can reliably identify familiar voices, although error rates often exceed 20% for brief utterances [80]. About 2–3 s of speech is sufficient to identify a voice, although performance decreases for unfamiliar voices. Speaker recognition is one area of artificial intelligence where machine performance can exceed human performance: using short test utterances and a large number of speakers, ASI/V accuracy often exceeds that of humans. This is especially true for unfamiliar speakers, where the *training time* for humans to learn a new voice well is very long compared with that for machines [81]. Constraints on how many unfamiliar voices a person can retain in short-term memory usually limit studies of speaker recognition by humans to about 5–10 speakers. Such small speaker sets lead to large statistical variation from one set to another because distinctiveness and degree of familiarity of voices often vary widely across speakers. While perceptually rated scales of *distinctiveness* (i.e., whether a voice stands out) appear to have little correlation with ability to recognize a voice, recognition performance using both uncoded and LPC-coded speech increases dramatically with more familiarity between listener and speaker [72, 82].

One review of speaker recognition by humans [83] notes that many studies of 8–10 speakers (work colleagues of the listening subjects) yield in excess of 97% accuracy if a sentence or more of the test speech is heard. Performance falls to about 54% (but still significantly above chance levels) when duration is short (e.g., less than 1 s) and/or distorted (e.g., severely highpass or lowpass filtered). One study of 29 familiar speakers had 31%, 66%, and 83% recognition with one word, one sentence, and 30 s of speech, respectively [84]. Performance also falls significantly if training and test utterances are processed through different transmission systems [73]. A study using voices of 45 famous people in 2 s test utterances found only 27% recognition in an open-choice test, but 70% recognition if listeners could select from six choices [83]; if the utterances were increased to 4 s, but played *backward* (which distorts timing and articulatory cues), 57.5% accuracy resulted. Widely varying performance on this backward task suggested that cues to voice recognition vary from voice to voice and that voice patterns may consist of a set of acoustic cues from which listeners select a subset to use in identifying individual voices.

Recognition often falls sharply when speakers attempt to disguise their voices [82] (e.g., 59–81% accuracy depending on the disguise vs 92% for normal voices in one study [85]). This is reflected in ASI/V, where accuracy decreases when mimics act as impostors [59]. Humans appear to handle mimics better than machines do, easily perceiving when a voice is being mimicked (e.g. 90% accuracy [86]). If the target (intended) voice is familiar to the listener, he often *associates* the mimic voice with it but does not *confuse* them. Certain voices are more easily mimicked than others, which lends further evidence to the theory that different acoustic cues are used to distinguish different voices [83].

The ability to identify speakers via *voiceprints* (spectrograms of their voices) has been of legal interest [2]. However, voiceprints cannot reliably identify speakers [6, 87]. Experts may be able to match reference spectrograms to test spectrograms by the same speaker to a certain degree, but performance often degrades substantially if speakers use disguise. For example, one study of 15 speakers used spectrograms of nine different monosyllabic words excerpted from different sentences: with normal voices, experts achieved 57% accuracy;

when speakers spoke very slowly, accuracy fell to 43%; when they used free disguise, recognition was only 22% [88]. Furthermore, certain speakers were considerably more difficult to identify than others.

11.8 CONCLUSION

It is useful to examine the lack of commercial applications (until very recently) for ASI/V compared with the greater success for ASR. Both speech and speaker recognition analyze speech signals to extract F0 and spectral parameters such as LPC or cepstral coefficients. Furthermore, both often employ similar evaluation methods, distance measures, and decision procedures. Speech and speaker recognition, however, have different objectives, e.g., selecting which of M words was spoken or which of N speakers spoke. Speech analysis techniques have primarily been developed for phonemic analysis, e.g., to preserve phonemic content during speech coding or to aid phoneme identification in ASR. Our understanding of how listeners exploit spectral cues to identify human sounds far exceeds our knowledge of how we distinguish speakers. For TD ASI/V, using template matching methods borrowed directly from ASR yields good results in limited tests, but performance decreases under adverse conditions that might be found in practical applications. For example, telephone distortions, uncooperative speakers, and speaker variability over time often lead to accuracy levels unacceptable for many applications.

Studies that have suggested phonetic features useful for ASI/V, e.g., specific formants in certain phones, may eventually result in improved ASI/V, but the problems of phone spotting have led to few studies exploiting such specific features. As ASR techniques improve, perhaps ASI/V will adopt them to yield parallel improvements. Even more than in ASR, statistical methods have dominated ASI/V research. High recognition accuracy (e.g., 1.1% error in ASI [36]) comes from gathering a large number of speech features and evaluating their utility in ASI/V via the weighting matrix in a Bhattacharyya or Mahalanobis distance. These methods yield no insight into the speaker recognition process, but they serve ASI/V objectives to a certain extent.

Practical recognition applications for ASV now use TD techniques. The more difficult task of ASI is often impractical because of the tendency of increasing error probability as population size increases. Even for large populations, current ASV techniques appear to yield sufficient accuracy for practical applications where high-quality speech is available. For further reading, there are several good reviews of the ASI/V field [6, 9, 10, 32, 89, 90]. In particular, see Table 2 in [36] showing progress over 25 years.

PROBLEMS

P11.1. (a) How do recognition methods differ between speech and speaker identification?
(b) Why is recognition using statistical features difficult for real-time applications?
(c) Why is the use of the Mahalanobis distance more common in speaker recognition than in speech recognition?
(d) What advantages do vector quantization methods have for real-time speaker recognition?

P11.2. Why is speaker recognition easier when the same text is used for training and testing?

P11.3. (a) Why is speaker identification more difficult than speaker verification?

(b) For both identification and verification, explain how different types of errors might be reflected in system performance measures.

P11.4. (a) Explain the advantages and disadvantages of exploiting either physiological or behavioral differences between speakers for recognition.

(b) Which acoustic features give the best speaker recognition performance?

P11.5. Why is it important not to use the same data for training and testing recognizers?

P11.6. If a recognizer cannot make a reliable decision based on a test utterance, what procedures may be followed?

Appendix: Computer Sites for Help on Speech Communication

The list below notes many internet sites (WWW—World Wide Web) providing information (and occasionally software) on topics found in this book. This list will be updated periodically on the site affiliated with this book (`www.inrs-telecom.uquebec.ca/users/spchww/English/persons/dougo/book.html`). Grateful acknowledgment is given to Dr. Philip Rubin (Haskins Laboratories, New Haven, CT) for the original compilation of much of this list (presented at the 136th Meeting of the Acoustical Society of America, Norfolk, VA, Oct. 1998). Listings with multiple entries per site are abbreviated (e.g., `www.x-/y-/z` means URLs `www.x/y` and `www.x/z`).

A1 RESEARCH ORGANIZATIONS

`www.haskins.yale.edu/haskins`
- `-/asaper98.htm`: Haskins Laboratories (the source of much of this list)
- `-/heads.html`: Talking Heads synthesis

`www.speech.cs.cmu.edu`
- `-/comp.speech`: Carnegie Mellon University: very useful site for speech information
- `-/cgi-bin/cmudict`: CMU dictionary on the WWW

`c.gp.cs.cmu.edu: 5103/prog/webster`: Webster's dictionary online

`www.dcs.shef.ac.uk`
- `-/research/ilash`: University of Sheffield (UK) speech projects and lexical databases
- `-/research/groups/spandh/pr/ShATR/ShATR.html`: Simultaneous-speaker corpus
- `-/~martin`: auditory modelling and ASR in noise (Martin Cooke)

`www.icp.inpg.fr`: Institut de la Communication Parée (Grenoble)

`ophale.icp.inpg.fr`

`-/ex.html`: ICP Museum of Speech Synthesis

`-/esca/esca.html`: European Speech Communication Association (ESCA)

`-/esca/labos.html`: ESCA list of research sites

`cristal.icp.grenet.fr/Relator/homepage.html`: RELATOR project: linguistic resources

`www.cse.ogi.edu/CSLU`: Center for Spoken Language Understanding (Oregon)

`-/research/TTS/research/sing.html`: Lyricos singing speech synthesis

`-/HLTsurvey/HLTsurvey.html`

`speech.cse.ogi.edu/pub/releases`: speech database

`-/tools`: OGI (Oregon Graduate Institute) Speech Tools

`www.limsi.fr/Recherche/TLP`: LIMSI ASR(France)

`www.tue.nl/ipo`

`-/sli.html`: IPO (Institute for Perception Research—Netherlands)

`-/hearing/webspeak.htm`: very useful site

`mambo.ucsc.edu/psl`: UCSC Perceptual Science Laboratory (PSL)

`-/smus/smus.html`: UCSC PSL Museum of Speech

`-/dwm/da.html`: McGurk Effect Demo (UCSC PSL)

`-/fan.html`: UCSC PSL Facial Animation

`-/psl/speech.html`: list of web sites for speech

`www.sls.lcs.mit.edu`: Spoken Language Systems Group at MIT

`www.hip.atr.co.jp`: ATR (Japan) human information processing

`www-csli.stanford.edu/csli/index.shtml`: speech and language at Stanford University

`www.cstr.ed.ac.uk`: Center for Speech Technology Research (Edinburgh)

`www.speech.kth.se`: KTH Department of Speech (Stockholm)

`www.media.mit.edu`: MIT MediaLab

`rleweb.mit.edu/groups/g-spe.htm`: MIT RLE Speech Communications Group

`cuneus.ai.mit.edu`: 8000`/research/miketalk/miketalk.html`: Mike Talk

`natsci.ucsc.edu/acad/scicom/SciNotes/9601/Speech/00Intro.html`

`www.itl.atr.co.jp/chatr`: ATR CHATR Speech Synthesis

`www.uni-koeln.de/phil-fak/phonetik/synthese/index_e.html`: Articulatory Synthesis

`www.cs.bham.ac.uk/~jpi/museum.html`: John Iles' overview of TTS

`ncvs.shc.uiowa.edu`: National Center for Voice and Speech

`www.psy.uwa.edu.au/uwa_mrc.htm`: MRC Psycholinguistic Database

`www.fb9-ti.uni-duisburg.de/demos/speech.html`: Multi-Lingual

`wwwtios.cs.utwente.nl/say`: Web-based TTS

`www-gth.die.upm.es/research/synthesis/synth-form-concat.html`: Spanish TTS

`www.tik.ee.ethz.ch/cgi-bin/w3svox`: German TTS

`www.icsl.ucla.edu/~spapl/projects/mri.html`: UCLA speech analysis

`www.york.ac.uk/~rpf1/yorktalk.html`: YorkTalk (University of York)

`www-dsp.rice.edu/software`: programs for Digital Signal Processing (Rice University)

`spib.rice.edu/spib/select_noise.html`: NOISEX-92 database

`www.isip.msstate.edu`

`-/software`: Discrete HMM demonstration software

`-/publications/1996/speech_recognition_short_course`:   Speech

Recognition Course Notes

`www.cstr.ed.ac.uk`: Centre for Speech Technology Research, Edinburgh University

`theory.lcs.mit.edu/~fftw`: free FFT software

`www.cs.tu-berlin.de/~jutta/toast.html`: GSM 06.10 Compression

`asl1.ikp.uni-bonn.de/~tpo/Hadifix.en.html`: Hadifix German speech synthesis

`www.speech.kth.se/NICO/index.html`: NICO Artificial Neural Network Toolkit for ASR

A2 RESEARCH ASSOCIATIONS

`www.ldc.upenn.edu`: Linguistic Data Consortium (source of many databases)

`www.esca-speech.org`: ESCA—Speech Communication Association (sponsor of the biannual Eurospeech conference)

`www.humnet.ucla.edu/humnet/linguistics/faciliti/phonlab.htm`: UCLA Phonetics Lab

`www.icp.grenet.fr/ELRA/home/html`: European Language Resources Association

`www.avios.com`: American Voice Input/Output Society (AVIOS)

`www.cs.columbia.edu`: 80/~acl: Association for Computational Linguistics (ACL)

`cslab.anu.edu.au/~bruce/assta`: ASSTA: Australian Speech Science and Technology

`www.nist.gov`: National Institute of Standards and Technology (NIST).

A3 JOURNALS DEALING WITH SPEECH COMMUNICATION

`ojps.aip.org/journals/doc/JASMAN-home/top.html`: Journal of the Acoustical Society of America

`www.elsevier.com/locate/specom`: Elsevier Science: Speech Communication journal

`www.apnet.com`: Academic Press Limited: Computer Speech and Language Journal

`www.yahoo.com/Science/Computer_Science/Artificial_Intelligence/Natural_Language_Processing/Speech`: Yahoo's speech site

A4 COMMERCIAL SYNTHESIS AND RECOGNITION

`www.att.com/aspg`: AT&T Advanced Speech Products Group

`www.bell-abs.com/project/tts/voices.html`: Bell Labs Text-to-Speech Synthesis

`www.entropic.com`: Entropic (truetalk and esps/waves)

`www.kayelemetrics.com`: Kay Elemetrics (Computerized Speech Lab)

`www.apple.com/macos/speech`: Apple's TTS and ASR

`www.sens.com`: Sensimetrics TTS

`www.voicerecognition.com`: 21st Century Eloquence: ASR

`www.acuvoice.com`: Acuvoice, Inc. TTS

`www.artcomp.com/speak.htm`: Advanced Recognition Technologies, Inc: smARTspeak

`www.altech.com`: Applied Language Technologies, Inc.: SpeechWorks

`www.artcomp.com`: ART: Advanced Recognition Technologies, Inc `www.artsys.com`: Articulate Systems PowerSecretary speech recognition

`www.crl.research.digital.com/projects/speech/plan.html`: Cambridge Research Lab.

`www.interval.com/~malcolm/pubs.html`: Auditory and signal processing (Malcolm Slaney)

`www.bbn.com/products/speech/recog.htm`: BBN (ASR)

`www.brite.com`: Brite: Computer Telephony Integration & Interactive Voice Response

`www.ptt-telecom.nl/cave`: CAVE: Caller Verification

`www.bestspeech.com/index.html`: Berkeley Speech Technologies TTS

`wwwtios.cs.utwente.nl/say`: TTS

`www.surftalk.com`: Digital Dreams ASR

`www.dragonsys.com`: Dragon Systems (ASR)

`www.cis.rl.ac.uk/proj/psych/eat/eat`: Edinburgh Associative Thesaurus

`www.elan.fr`: Elan Informatique: ProVerbe Speech Synthesis Engine

`www.eloq.com`: Eloquent Technology (TTS)

`www.entropic.com/htk.html`: Entropic's KTK (Hidden-Markov Model Toolkit)

`www.elis.rug.ac.be`
  `~/t&i`: ELIS (Belgium) US
  `~/ELISgroups/speech/research/eurovocsold.html`: Eurovocs speech samples

`www.software.ibm.com/speech`: IBM ASR (ViaVoice)

`www.hijinx.com.au`: InterFACE from Hijinx

`www.icsi.berkeley.edu`: International Computer Science Institute in Berkeley, CA

`www.vocaltec.com`: Internet Phone from VocalTec

`www.keywareusa.com`: Keyware Technologies Speaker Verification

`www.labs.bt.com/innovate/speech/laureate`: TTS

`www.lhs.com`: Lernout and Hauspie (Belgium: TTS, ASR)

`www.islandnet.com/jts/listen2.htm`: Listen2 TTS

`www.bell-labs.com/project/tts`: Lucent Technologies multilingual TTS

`www.lowtek.com/macyack`: MacYack Pro TTS

`www.mathworks.com`: Matlab plus Signal Processing Toolbox

`tcts.fpms.ac.be/synthesis/mbrola.html`: MBROLA speech synthesis

`www.research.microsoft.com/research/srg`: Microsoft TTS and ASR

`www.firstbyte.davd.com`: First Byte ASR

`www.nortelnetworks.com/products/dirasst`: Nortel's ASR for telephone directory assistance

`www.nuance.com`: Nuance Communications ASR

`www.bellcore.com/ORATOR`: Orator from Bellcore: TTS

`www.speech.be.philips.com`: Philips ASR

`www.quadravox.com`: Quadravox Speech Processing Products

`www.promotor.telia.se/infovox/product.htm`: Infovox multilingual TTS

`www.voiceautomated.com`: SCI VoiceAutomated ASR

`www.sensoryinc.com`: Sensory Circuits: ICs for TTS and ASR

`agoralang.com/signalyze.html`: Signalyze speech analysis from InfoSignal

`www.sunlabs.com/research/speech`: Speech Applications at Sun Microsystems Labs

`www.speechtech.com/home/speechtech`: Speech Technology Research Ltd.

`www.voicecontrol.com/speechid.html`: Voice Control Systems, Inc.

`www.srapi.com`: SRAPI: Speech Recognition API

`tcts.fpms.ac.be`: TCTS: MBROLA TTS and SPRACH ASR

`www.t-netix.com`: T-Netix speaker verification for cellular communications

`www.dspg.com`: TrueSpeech capability for WWW pages

`www.verbex.com`: Verbex: Listen for Windows speech recognition

`www.dfki.uni-sb.de/verbmobil`: Verbmobil project home page

`www.ti.com`: Texas Instruments

`www.wildfire.com`: Wildfire—an Electronic Assistant

`www.pcww.com/index.html`: WinSpeech text-to-speech application

`www.cogsci.princeton.edu/~wn`: WordNet home page

A5 SPEECH CODERS

`www.sipro.com`
  `-/acelp.html`: ACELP Codecs from Sipro Lab Telecom Inc.
  `-/g729a.html`: G.729 Annex A from Sipro Lab Telecom Inc

`www.arl.wustl.edu/~jaf/lpc`: LPC- 10 speech coding software

`www.itu.ch/itudoc/itu-t/rec/g/g700-799.html`: ITU standards for speech coders (G ...)

`admii.arl.mil/~fsbrn/phamdo/speech_demo.html`: Speech Coding Demonstration

A6 WWW SITES OFFERING SPEECH INFORMATION, DATA AND PROGRAMS VIA FTP (FILE TRANSFER PROTOCOL)

File downloading is done without WWW access, usually by typing *ftp X*, where *X* is an address below (e.g., as a UNIX command). For logging in, type *anonymous* as the username and then one's e-mail address as an informal password.

`svr-ftp.eng.cam.ac.uk/pub/comp.speech`
  `-/recognition/AbbotDemo`: ASR software
  `-/recognition/hmm-1.03.tar.gz`: Hidden Markov Model software
  `-/recognition/recnet-1.3.tar.Z`: recurrent neural network ASR software
  `-/dictionaries/beep.tar.gz`: BEEP pronunciation dictionary
  `-/dictionaries/homophones-1.01.txt`: Homophone list
  `-/analysis/fft-stuff.tar.gz`: FFT Software
  `-/coding/G711_G721_G723.tar.Z`: G711, G721, G723 speech coding software
  `-/coding/celp_3.2a.tar.gz`: CELP speech coding software
  `-/coding/shorten.tar.gz`: shorten audio-file compression software
  `-/synthesis/klatt.3.04.tar.gz`: Klatt speech synthesis software
  `-/synthesis/rsynth-2.0.tar.gz`: rsynth: speech synthesis software
  `-/synthesis/english2phoneme.tar.gz`: Text to phoneme program
  `-/info/DIY_SpeechRecognition`: Do-it-yourself speech recognition
  `-/info/SpeechRecognitionProducts`: Lists of speech recognition products

`wocket.vantage.gtc.com/pub/standard_dictionary`: comprehensive list of American words

`www.cwi.nl/ftp/audio/adpcm.shar`: 32 kbps ADPCM

`ftp.cwi.nl/pub/audio/ccitt-adpcm.tar.Z`: G.723, G.721, *A*-law, μ-law and linear PCM `ftp.apple.com/pub/malcolm`: Auditory Toolbox for Matlab

`ftp.cs.jhu.edu/pub/brill`: Brill part-of-speech tagger

`ftp.super.org/pub/speech/celp_3.2a.tar.Z`: CELP 3.2a and LEC-10 speech
    coders

`ftp.cs.cmu.edu/project/fgdata/dict`: CMU dictionary

`magenta.com/pub/cyberphone`: CyberPhone internet voice communication

`sunsite.unc.edu/pub/Linux/apps/sound/speech/ears-0.26.tar.gz`:
    EARS ASR software

`ftp.elan.fr/Voice_products`: Elan Informatique (TTS—France)

`ftp.cstr.ed.ac.uk/pub/festival`: Festival Speech Synthesis System

`ftp.coast.net/simtel/msdos/c/mixfft03.zip`: FFT Software

`dspsun.eas.asu.edu/pub/speech/ldcelp.tgz`: G.728 CELP Compression

`ftp.cs.tu-berlin.de/pub/local/kbs/tubmik/gsm/gsm-1.0.7.tar.gz`:
    GSM 06.10 Compression

`ftp.mv.com/pub/ddj/1994.12/gsm-105.zip`: GSM 06.10 Compression

`asl1.ikp.uni-bonn.de/pub/hadifix/hadidemo.zip`: Hadifix speech synthesis
    demo software

`ftp.vocaltec.com/pub/phone09.exe`: Internet Phone from VocalTec

`ftp.informatik.uni-ulm.de/pub/NI/jialong/spkrtool.zip`: Speaker
    Recognition

`ftp.mrc-apu.cam.ac.uk/pub/aim`: John Holdsworth's Auditory Modeller

`pitch.phon.ucl.ac.uk/pub/kpe80.src.tar.Z`: Klatt Synthesis and Parameter
    Editor

`ftp.sanpo.t.u-tokyo.ac.jp/pub/nigel/lotec/lotec.tar.Z`: Lotec ASR
    software

`suna.lut.ac.uk/public/hulpo/lutear`: Lowel O'Mard's Auditory Modeller

`ftp.super.org/pub/speech/lpc10-1.0.tar.gz`: LPC-10 speech coding soft-
    ware

`flp.dcs.shef.ac.uk/share`
    `-/ilash/Moby`: Moby lexical resources
    `-/spandh/ShATR`: ShATR: A Mulfi-simultaneous-speaker corpus

`ftp.tnt.uni-hannover.de/pub/MPEG/audio`: MPEG-1 and MPEG-2 audio soft-
    ware

`ftp.ccett.fr/pub/mpeg`
    `-/mpeg2`: MPEG-2 audio encoder and decoder at CCETT
    `-/audio_new`: MPEG-1 audio layer 1 and 2 decoder and verifier

`ftp.iuma.com/audio_utils/converters/source`: MPEG-1 audio Layer 1 and
    2 encoder–decoder

`ota.ox.ac.uk/pub/ota/public/dicts/info`: MRC Psycholinguistic Database
    and Dictionary

`crlftp.nmsu.edu/pub/non-lexical/NL_Software_Registry`: Natural
    Language Software Registry

`usc.edu/pub/C-numanal`: Numerical analysis software: including FFT

`ota.ox.ac.uk/pub/ota/public/dicts/710`:   Oxford Advanced Learner's
    Dictionary

`ftp.islandnet.comm/jts/pam_en3c.zip`: talking personal assistant

`ptolemy.berkeley.edu/pub`: Ptolemy signal processing software

`ftp.isip.msstate.edu/pub/software/signal_detector/`
`sigd_v2.2.tar.gz`: End-Point Detection
`ftp.coast.net/SimTel/msdos/voice`: SIMTEL speech software
`evans.ee.adfa.oz.au/mirrors/tibbs/applications/spchsyn.exe`:
Speech synthesis
`wilma.cs.brown.edu/pub/speak.tar.Z`: TTS
`shark.cse.fau.edu/pub/src/phon.tar.Z`: Text-to-phoneme program
`ftp.doc.ic.ac.uk/packages/unix-c/utils/phoneme.c.gz`: Text-to-phoneme software
`ftp.cs.keio.ac/jp/pub/NeXT/source/TheBigMouth1.0.tar.Z`:   NeXT speech synthesizer
`ftp.netcom.com/pub/eb/ebohlman`: Tinytalk shareware screen reader
`ftp.coast.net/SimTel/msdos/voice/vm110.zip`: Voicemaker speech synthesis

A7 OTHER USEFUL LISTS OF SPEECH SITES

`www.aist-nara.ac.jp/IS/Shikano-lab/database/internet-resource/`
`e-www-site.html`: Shikano's extensive list of WWW sites on speech and acoustics
`fonsg3.let.uva.nl`
   `-/Welcome.html`: Institute of Phonetic Sciences (Amsterdam)
   `-/IFA-Features.html`
   `-/Other_pages.html`
`www.linguistlist.org/associations.html`
`www.tiac.net/users/rwilcox/speech.html`: Russ Wilcox's list of Commercial Speech Recognition

References

References noted with an asterisk are those of significant tutorial interest.

CHAPTER 1—INTRODUCTION

1. P. Denes & E. Pinson (1963) *The Speech Chain* (Bell Telephone Labs: Murray Hill, NJ).
*2. G. Fant (1960) *Acoustic Theory of Speech Production* (Mouton: The Hague).
*3. D. Klatt (1977) "Review of the ARPA speech understanding project," *J. Acoust. Soc. Am.* **62**, 1345–1366.
4. A. Oppenheim & R. Schafer (1975) *Digital Signal Processing* (Prentice-Hall: Englewood Cliffs, NJ).
5. W. Zemlin (1981) *Speech and Hearing Science: Anatomy and Physiology,* 2nd ed. (Prentice-Hall: Englewood Cliffs, NJ).
6. R. Stark (1981) *Language Behavior in Infancy and Early Childhood* (North-Holland: New York).
7. G. Yeni-Konshima, J. Kavanaugh & C. Ferguson (1980) *Child Phonology* (Academic: New York).
8. H. Levitt, J. Pickett & R. Houde (1980) *Sensory Aids for the Hearing Impaired* (IEEE: New York).

CHAPTER 2—MATH REVIEW

1. A. Oppenheim & R. Schafer (1989) *Discrete-time Signal Processing* (Prentice-Hall: Englewood Cliffs, NJ).
2. L. Rabiner & B. Gold (1975) *Theory and Application of Digital Signal Processing* (Prentice-Hall: Englewood Cliffs, NJ).
3. C. Helstrom (1984) *Probability and Stochastic Processes for Engineers* (Macmillan: New York).
4. A. Papoulis (1965) *The Fourier Integral and Its Application* (McGraw-Hill: New York).
5. T. Kailath (1980) *Linear Systems* (Prentice-Hall: Englewood Cliffs, NJ).

CHAPTER 3—SPEECH PRODUCTION AND ACOUSTIC-PHONETICS

The following are abbreviated in the reference list:

RAP   I. Lehiste (1967) *Readings in Acoustic Phonetics* (MIT: Cambridge, MA).
PSP   P. Eimas & J. Miller (1981) *Perspectives on the Study of Speech* (Erlbaum: Hillsdale, NJ).

PS   P. MacNeilage (1983) *The Production of Speech* (Springer-Verlag: New York).

SL   N. Lass (1984) *Speech and Language: Advances in Basic Research and Practice* (Academic Press: New York).

1. J. Ohala (1983) "The origin of sound patterns in vocal tract constraints," in PS, pp. 189–216.

2. G. Fant (1993) "Some problems in voice source analysis," *Speech Comm.* **13**, 7–22.

3. B. Sonesson (1968) "The functional anatomy of the speech organs," in *Manual of Phonetics* B. Malmberg (ed.), (North-Holland: Amsterdam), pp. 45–75.

*4. G. Borden & K. Harris (1980) *Speech Science Primer: Physiology, Acoustics, and Perception of Speech* (Williams & Wilkins: Baltimore, MD).

*5. R. Daniloff, G. Shuckers & L. Feth (1980) *The Physiology of Speech and Hearing* (Prentice-Hall: Englewood Cliffs, NJ).

*6. W. Zemlin (1968) *Speech and Hearing Science, Anatomy and Physiology* (Prentice-Hall: Englewood Cliffs, NJ).

7. B. Lindblom (1983) "Economy of speech gestures," in PS, pp. 217–245.

8. R. Orlikoff, R. Baken & D. Kraus (1997) "Acoustic and physiological characteristics of inspiratory phonation," *J. Acoust. Soc. Am.* **102**, 1838–1845.

*9. P. Ladefoged (1982) *A Course in Phonetics*, 2nd ed. (Harcourt Brace Jovanovich: New York).

10. K. Thomas (1997) "EPG and aerodynamic evidence for the coproduction and coarticulation of clicks in Isizulu," *Proc. Europ. Conf. Speech Comm. & Tech.*, pp. 379–382.

11. N. Warner (1996) "Acoustic characteristics of ejectives in Inguish," *Proc. Int. Conf. on Spoken Lang. Proc.*, pp. 1525–1528.

12. A. Winkworth, P. Davis, R. Adams & E. Ellis (1995) "Emotions and speech: some acoustical correlates," *J. Speech Hear. Res.* **38**, 124–144.

13. I. Titze & J. Sundberg (1992) "Vocal intensity in speakers and singers," *J. Acoust. Soc. Am.* **91**, 2936–2946.

14. H. Hanson (1997) "Vowel amplitude variation during sentence production," *Proc. IEEE Int. Conf. ASSP*, pp. 1627–1630.

*15. I. Titze (1994) *Principles of Voice Production* (Prentice-Hall: Englewood Cliffs, NJ).

16. J. van der Berg, J. Zantema & P. Doornenbal (1957) "On the air resistance and the Bernoulli effect of the human larynx," *J. Acoust. Soc. Am.* **29**, 626–631.

17. K. Stevens (1971) "Airflow and turbulence noise for fricative and stop consonants: Static considerations," *J. Acoust. Soc. Am.* **50**, 1180–1192.

18. W. Vennard (1967) *Singing: the Mechanism and the Technic* (Fischer: New York).

19. K. Stevens & C. Bickley (1986) "Effect of vocal tract constriction on the glottal source," *J. Phonetics* **14**, 373–382.

20. B. Story & I. Titze (1995) "Voice simulation with a body-cover model of the vocal folds," *J. Acoust. Soc. Am.* **97**, 1249–1260.

21. J. Liljencrants (1996) "Experiments with analysis by synthesis of glottal airflow," *Proc. Int. Conf. on Spoken Lang. Proc.*, pp. 1289–1292.

22. I. Titze (1984) "Parameterization of the glottal area, glottal flow, and vocal fold contact area," *J. Acoust. Soc. Am.* **75**, 570–580.

23. I. Titze (1989) "A four parameter model of the glottis and vocal fold contact area," *Speech Comm.* **8**, 191–201.

24. L. Mongeau, N. Franchek, C. Coker & R. Kubli (1997) "Characteristics of a pulsating jet through a small modulated orifice, with application to voice production," *J. Acoust. Soc. Am.* **102**, 1121–1133.

25. C. Coker, M. Krane, B. Reis & R. Kubli (1996) "Search for unexplored effects in speech production," *Proc. Int. Conf. on Speech Lang. Proc.*, pp. 1121–1124.

26. J. Flanagan & K. Ishizaka (1978) "Computer model to characterize the air volume displaced by the vibrating vocal cords," *J. Acoust. Soc. Am.* **63**, 1559–1565.

27. A. Löfqvist, N. McGarr & K. Honda (1984) "Laryngeal muscles and articulatory control," *J. Acoust. Soc. Am.* **76**, 951–954.

28. R. Collier (1975) "Physiological correlates of intonation patterns," *J. Acoust. Soc. Am.* **58**, 249–255.

29. C. Shadle (1985) "Intrinsic fundamental frequency of vowels in sentence context," *J. Acoust. Soc. Am.* **78**, 1562–1567.

30. G. Farley (1994) "A quantitative model of voice F0 control," *J. Acoust. Soc. Am.* **95**, 1017–1029.

31. G. Peterson & H. Barney (1952) "Control methods used in a study of vowels," *J. Acoust. Soc. Am.* **24**, 175–184; also in RAP, pp. 188–127.

32. J. Sundberg (1979) "Maximum speed of pitch changes in singers and untrained subjects," *J. Phonetics* **7**, 71–79.

33. J. Atkinson (1978) "Correlation analysis of the physiological factors controlling fundamental voice frequency," *J. Acoust Soc. Am.* **63**, 211–222.

34. J. Pind (1998) "Auditory and linguistic factors in the perception of voice offset time as a cue for preaspiration," *J. Acoust. Soc. Am.* **103**, 2117–2127.

35. A. Behrman & R. Baken (1997) "Correlation dimension of electroglottographic data from healthy and pathologic subjects," *J. Acoust. Soc. Am.* **102**, 2371–2379.

36. R. Whitehead, D. Metz & B. Whitehead (1984) "Vibratory patterns of the vocal folds during pulse register phonation, *J. Acoust. Soc. Am.* **75**, 1293–1297.

37. V. Heiberger & Y. Horii (1982) "Jitter and shimmer in sustained phonation," in SL **7**, pp. 299–332.

38. R. Orlikoff (1990) "Vowel amplitude variation associated with the heart cycle," *J. Acoust. Soc. Am.* **88**, 2091–2098.

39. E. Yumoto, W. Gould & T. Baer (1982) "Harmonics-to-noise ratio as an index of the degree of hoarseness," *J. Acoust. Soc. Am.* **71**, 1544–1550.

40. N. Hiraoka, Y. Kitazoe, H. Ueta, S. Tanaka & M. Tanabe (1984) "Harmonic intensity analysis of normal and hoarse voices," *J. Acoust. Soc. Am.* **76**, 1648–1651.

41. Y. Qi & T. Shipp (1992) "An adaptive method for tracking voicing irregularities," *J. Acoust. Soc. Am.* **91**, 3471–3477.

42. J. Kreiman, B. Gerratt & G. Berke (1994) "The multidimensional nature of pathological vocal quality," *J. Acoust. Soc. Am.* **96**, 1291–1302.

43. H. Hanson (1997) "Glottal characteristics of female speakers: Acoustic correlates," *J. Acoust. Soc. Am.* **101**, 466–481.

44. S. Hamlet, H. Bunnell & B. Struntz (1986) "Articulatory asymmetries," *J. Acoust. Soc. Am.* **79**, 1164–1169.

45. G. Feng & E. Castelli (1996) "Some acoustic features of nasal and nasalized vowels: A target for vowel nasalization," *J. Acoust. Soc. Am.* **99**, 3694–3706.

46. M. Stone & A. Lundberg (1996) "Three-dimensional tongue surface shapes of English consonants and vowels," *J. Acoust. Soc. Am.* **99**, 3728–3737.

47. J. Perkell (1969) *Physiology of Speech Production: Results and Implications of a Quantitative Cineradiographic Study* (MIT Press: Cambridge, MA).

48. H. Hertrich & H. Ackermann (1997) "Articulatory control of phonological vowel contrasts: Kinematic analysis of labial gestures," *J. Acoust. Soc. Am.* **102**, 523–536.

49. K. Munhall, E. Vatikiotis-Bateson & Y. Tohkura (1995) "X-ray film database for speech research," *J. Acoust. Soc. Am.* **98**, 1222–1224.

50. J. Perkell *et al* (1992) "Electromagnetic midsagittal articulometer systems for transducing speech articulatory movements," *J. Acoust. Soc. Am.* **92**, 3078–3096.

51. T. Kaburagi & M. Honda (1994) "Determination of sagittal tongue shape from the positions of points on the tongue surface," *J. Acoust. Soc. Am.* **96**, 1356–1366.

52. B. Story, I. Titze & B. Hoffman (1996) "Vocal tract area functions from magnetic resonance imaging," *J. Acoust. Soc. Am.* **100**, 537–554.

53. S. Narayanan, A. Alwan & K. Haker (1997) "Toward articulatory-acoustic models for liquid at proximants based on MRI and EPG data," *J. Acoust. Soc. Am.* **101**, 1064–1089.

54. K. Stevens & S. Keyser (1989) "Primary features and their enhancement in consonants," *Language* **65**, 81–106.

55. R. Mowrey & I. MacKay (1990) "Phonological primitives: Electromyographic speech error evidence," *J. Acoust. Soc. Am.* **88**, 1299–1312.

56. S. Shattuck-Hufnagel (1983) "Sublexical units and suprasegmental structure in speech production planning," in PS, pp. 109–136.

57. O. Bloodstein (1995) *A Handbook on Stuttering* (National Easter Seal Society: Chicago), pp. 327–357.

58. V. Zue & M. Laferriere (1979) "Acoustic study of medial /t,d/ in American English," *J. Acoust. Soc. Am.* **66**, 1039–1050.

59. P. Zawadzki & D. Kuehn (1980) "A cineradiographic study of static and dynamic aspects of American English /r/," *Phonetica* **37**, 253–266.

60. S. Boyce & C. Espy-Wilson (1997) "Coarticulatory stability in American English /r/," *J. Acoust Soc. Am.* **101**, 3741–3753.

61. K. Stevens (1993) "Modelling affricate consonants," *Speech Comm.* **13**, 33–43.

*62. J. Flanagan (1972) *Speech Analysis, Synthesis and Perception*, 2nd ed. (Springer-Verlag: New York).

63. K. Stevens, S. Blumstein, L. Glicksman, M. Burton & K. Kurowski (1997) "Acoustic and perceptual characteristics of voicing in fricatives and fricative clusters," *J. Acoust. Soc. Am.* **91**, 2979–3000.

64. K. Pirello, S. Blumstein & K. Kurowski (1997) "The characteristics of voicing in syllable-initial fricatives in American English," *J. Acoust. Soc. Am.* **101**, 3754–3765.

65. F. Bell-Berti (1975) "Control of pharyngeal cavity size for English voiced and voiceless stops," *J. Acoust. Soc. Am.* **57**, 456–461.

66. J. Westbury (1983) "Enlargement of the supraglottal cavity and its relation to stop consonant voicing," *J. Acoust. Soc. Am.* **73**, 1322–1336.

*67. P. Ladefoged & I. Maddieson (1990) "Vowels of the world's languages," *J. Phonetics* **18**, 93–122.

68. S. Wood (1979) "A radiographic analysis of constriction locations for vowels," *J. Phonetics* **7**, 25–43.

69. F. Bell-Berti, T. Baer, K. Harris & S. Niimi (1979) "Coarticulatory effects of vowel quality on velar function," *Phonetica* **36**, 187–193.

70. R. McGowan (1992) "Tongue tip trills and vocal-tract wall compliance," *J. Acoust. Soc. Am.* **91**, 2903–2910.

71. R. Wilhelms-Tricarico (1996) "A biomechanical and physiologically-based vocal tract model and its control," *J. Phonetics* **24**, 23–28.

72. V. Sanguineti, R. Laboissière & D. Ostry (1997) "An integrated model of the biomechanics and neural control of the tongue, jaw, hyoid and larynx system," *Proc. Europ. Conf. Speech Comm. & Tech.*, pp. 2023–2026.

*73. R. Potter, G. Kopp & H. Green (1947) *Visible Speech* (Van Nostrand: New York; republished by Dover, 1966).

74. J. Hillenbrand, L. Getty, M. Clark & K. Wheeler (1995) "Acoustic characteristics of American English vowels," *J. Acoust. Soc. Am.* **97**, 3099–3111.

75. D. Kewley-Port (1982) "Measurement of formant transitions in naturally produced stop consonant-vowel syllables," *J. Acoust. Soc. Am.* **72**, 379–389.

76. R. Hagiwara (1997) "Dialect variation and formant frequency: The American English vowels revisited," *J. Soc. Am.* **102**, 655–658.

77. I. Lehiste & G. Peterson (1961) "Transitions, glides, and diphthongs," *J. Acoust. Soc. Am.* **33**, 268–277.

78. A. Holbrook & G. Fairbanks (1962) "Diphthong formants and their movements," *J. Speech Hear. Res.* **5**, 38–58; also in RAP, pp. 249–269.

79. C. Espy-Wilson (1992) "Acoustic measures for linguistic features distinguishing the semivowels /wjrl/ in American English," *J. Acoust. Soc. Am.* **92**, 736–757.

*80. G. Fant (1968) "Analysis and synthesis of speech processes," in *Manual of Phonetics* B. Malmberg (ed.) (North-Holland: Amsterdam), pp. 173–277.

81. O. Fujimura (1962) "Analysis of nasal consonants," *J. Acoust. Soc. Am.* **34**, 1865–1875; also in RAP, pp. 238–248.

82. M. Chen (1997) "Acoustic correlates of English and French nasalized vowels," *J. Acoust. Soc. Am.* **102**, 2360–2370.

83. J. Fletcher & D. Newman (1991) "[s] and [ʃ] as a function of linguapalatal contact place and sibilant groove width," *J. Acoust. Soc. Am.* **89**, 850–858.

84. V. Zue (1976) "Acoustic characteristics of stop consonants: A controlled study," Indiana U. Linguistics Club paper.

85. D. Rostolland (1982) "Phonetic structure of shouted voice," *Acustica* **51**, 80–89.

86. A. Andersson, A. Eriksson & H. Traunmüller (1996) "Cries and whispers: Acoustic effects of variations in vocal effort," *Royal Institute of Technology, TMH-QPSR*, vol. 2, pp. 127–130.

87. D. Michael, G. Siegel & H. Pick (1995) "Effects of distance on vocal intensity," *J. Acoust. Soc. Am.* **38**, 1176–1183.

88. V. Tartter, H. Gomes & E. Litwin (1993) "Some acoustic effects of listening to noise on speech production," *J. Acoust. Soc. Am.* **94**, 2437–2440.

89. J-C. Junqua (1996) "The influence of acoustics on speech production: A noise-induced stress phemonenon known as the Lombard reflex," *Speech Comm.* **20**, 13–22.

90. K. Cummings & M. Clements (1995) "Analysis of the glottal excitation of emotionally styled and stressed speech," *J. Acoust. Soc. Am.* **98**, 88–98.

91. G. Bloothooft & R. Plomp (1985) "Spectral analysis of sung vowels. II. The effect of fundamental frequency on vowel spectra," *J. Acoust. Soc. Am.* **77**, 1580–1588.

92. J. Sundberg (1987) *The Science of the Singing Voice* (No. Illinois U.: De Kalb, IL).

93. I. Titze & B. Story (1997) "Acoustic interactions of the vocal source with the lower vocal tract," *J. Acoust Soc. Am.* **101**, 2234–2243.

94. C. Nakatani & J. Hirschberg (1994) "A corpus-based study of repair cues in spontaneous speech," *J. Acoust. Soc. Am.* **95**, 1603–1616.

95. S. Oviatt, G-A. Levow, M. MacEachern & K. Kuhn (1996) "Modeling hyperarticulate speech during human-computer error resolution," *Proc. Int. Conf. on Spoken Lang. Proc.*, pp. 801–804.

96. E. Nwokah, P. Davies, A. Islam, H-C. Hsu & A. Fogel (1993) "Vocal affect in 3-year-olds: A quantitative acoustic analysis of child laughter," *J. Acoust. Soc. Am.* **94**, 3076–3090.

97. R. Hillman & B. Weinberg (1981) "Estimation of glottal volume velocity waveform properties," in SL **6**, pp. 411–473.

98. M. Sondhi & J. Resnick (1983) "The inverse problem for the vocal tract: Numerical methods, acoustical experiments & speech synthesis," *J. Acoust Soc. Am.* **73**, 985–1002.

99. T. Uzzle (1996) "The propagation of sound," *Sound & Video Contractor* **14**, no. 1, 18–22.

100. M. Sondhi (1986) "Resonances of a bent vocal tract," *J. Acoust. Soc. Am.* **79**, 1113–1116.

101. R. Kent & A. Murray (1982) "Acoustic features of infant vocalic utterances at 3, 6, and 9 months," *J. Acoust. Soc. Am.* **72**, 353–365.

*102. G. Fant (1973) *Speech Sounds and Features* (MIT Press: Cambridge, MA).

103. R. Adler, L. Chu & R. Fano (1960) *Electromagnetic Energy Transmission and Radiation* (John Wiley & Sons: New York).

104. K. Stevens (1972) "The quantal nature of speech: Evidence from articulatory-acoustic data," in *Human Communication: A Unified View*, E. David Jr. & P. Denes (eds.) (McGraw-Hill: New York), pp. 51–66.

105. M. Sondhi & J. Schroeter (1986) "A nonlinear articulatory speech synthesizer using both time- and frequency-domain elements," *IEEE Int. Conf. ASSP*, pp. 1999–2002.

106. J. Heinz & K. Stevens (1961) "On the properties of voiceless fricative consonants," *J. Acoust. Soc. Am.* **33**, 589–596; also in RAP, pp. 220–227.

107. S. Maeda (1982) "The role of the sinus cavities in the production of nasal vowels," *Proc. IEEE Int. Conf. ASSP*, pp. 911–914.

108. J. Dang & K. Honda (1997) "Acoustic characteristics of the piriform fossa in models and humans," *J. Acoust. Soc. Am.* **101**, 456–465.

*109. G. Fant (1960) *Acoustic Theory of Speech Production* (Mouton: The Hague).

110. K. Stevens, S. Kasowski & G. Fant (1953) "An electrical analog of the vocal tract," *J. Acoust. Soc. Am.* **25**, 734–742; also in FR, pp. 108–116.

111. P. Badin & G. Fant (1984) "Notes on vocal tract computation," *STL-QPSR, Royal Institute of Technology, Stockholm*, **2–3**, 53–108.

112. D. Chalker & D. Mackerras (1986) "Models for representing the acoustic radiation impedance of the mouth," *IEEE Trans. ASSP*, **ASSP-33**, 1606–1609.

113. L. Nord, T. Ananthapadmanabha & G. Fant (1984) "Signal analysis and perceptual tests of vowel responses with an interactive source filter model," *STL-QPSR, Royal Institute of Technology, Stockholm*, **2–3**, 25–52.

114. D. Allen & W. Strong (1985) "A model for the synthesis of natural sounding vowels," *J. Acoust. Soc. Am.* **78**, 58–69.

115. P. Meyer & H. Strube (1984) "Calculations on the time varying vocal tract," *Speech Comm.* **3**, 109–122.

116. K. Stevens (1989) "On the quantal nature of speech," *J. Phonetics* **17**, 3–45.

117. J. Perkell & W. Nelson (1985) "Variability in production of the vowels /i/ and /a/," *J. Acoust. Soc. Am.* **77**, 1889–1895.

118. J. Perkell (1996) "Properties of the tongue help to define vowel categories: Hypotheses based on physiologically-oriented modeling," *J. Phonetics* **24**, 3–22.

*119. L. Rabiner & R. Schafer (1979) *Digital Processing of Speech Signals* (Prentice-Hall: Englewood Cliffs, NJ).

120. B. Atal, J. Chang, M. Mathews & J. Tukey (1978) "Inversion of articulatory to acoustic transformation in the vocal tract by a computer sorting technique," *J. Acoust. Soc. Am.* **63**, 1535–1555.

121. K. Honda (1994) "Organization of tongue articulation for vowels," *J. Phonetics* **24**, 39–52.

122. F. Bell-Berti & K. Harris (1981) "A temporal model of speech production," *Phonetica* **38**, 9–20.

123. H. Sussman & J. Westbury (1981) "The effects of antagonistic gestures on temporal and amplitude parameters of anticipatory labial coarticulation," *J. Speech Hear. Res.* **46**, 16–24.

References   **475**

124. B. Tuller & J. Kelso (1984) "The timing of articulatory gestures: Evidence for relational invariants," *J. Acoust. Soc. Am.* **76**, 1030–1036.

125. D. Sharf & R. Ohde (1981) "Physiologic, acoustic & perceptual aspects of coarticulation: Implications for the remediation of articulatory disorders," in SL **5**, pp. 153–245.

126. W. Nelson, J. Perkell & J. Westbury (1984) "Mandible movements during increasingly rapid articulations of single syllables," *J. Acoust. Soc. Am.* **75**, 945–951.

127. K. Munhall, A. Löfqvist & J. Kelso (1994) "Lip-larynx coordination in speech: Effects of mechanical perturbations to the lower lip," *J. Acoust. Soc. Am.* **95**, 3605–3616.

128. R. Kent (1983) "The segmental organization of speech," in PS, pp. 57–89.

129. H. Loevenbruck & P. Perrier (1997) "Motor control information recovering from the dynamics with the EP Hypothesis," *Proc. Europ. Conf. Speech Comm. & Tech.*, pp. 2035–2038.

130. S-J. Moon & B. Lindblom (1994) "Interaction between duration, context, and speaking style in English stressed vowels," *J. Acoust. Soc. Am.* **96**, 40–55.

131. K. Stevens & A. House (1963) "Perturbation of vowel articulations by consonantal context: An acoustical study," *J. Speech Hear. Res.* **6**, 111–128.

132. Y. Xu (1994) "Production and perception of coarticulated tones," *J. Acoust. Soc. Am.* **95**, 2240–2253.

133. D. O'Shaughnessy (1974) "Consonant durations in clusters," *IEEE Trans. ASSP*, **ASSP-22**, 282–295.

134. S. Blumstein & K. Stevens (1979) "Acoustic invariance in speech production: Evidence from measurements of the spectral characteristics of stop consonants," *J. Acoust. Soc. Am.* **66**, 1001–1017.

135. D. Recasens (1997) "A model of lingual coarticulation based on articulatory constraints," *J. Acoust. Soc. Am.* **102**, 544–561.

136. D. van Bergem (1994) "A model of coarticulatory effects on the schwa," *Speech Comm.* **14**, 143–162.

137. T. Edwards (1981) "Multiple features analysis of intervocalic English plosives," *J. Acoust. Soc. Am.* **69**, 535–547.

138. M. Mack & S. Blumstein (1983) "Further evidence of acoustic invariance in speech production: The stop-glide contrast," *J. Acoust. Soc. Am.* **73**, 1739–1750.

139. J. Perkell & D. Klatt (1986) *Invariance and Variability in Speech Processes* (Erlbaum: Hillsdale, NY).

140. K. Stevens & S. Blumstein (1981) "Acoustic correlates of phonetic features," in PSP, pp. 1–38.

141. P. Delattre, A. Liberman & F. Cooper (1955) "Acoustic loci and transitional cues for consonants," *J. Acoust. Soc. Am.* **27**, 769–773.

142. P. Perrier & D. Ostry (1994) "Dynamic modeling and control of speech articulators," in *Fundamentals of Speech Synthesis and Recognition*, E. Keller (ed.) (John Wiley & Sons: Chichester) pp. 231–251.

143. G. Peterson & I. Lehiste (1960) "Duration of syllable nuclei in English," *J. Acoust. Soc. Am.* **32**, also in RAP, pp. 191–201.

144. S. Ohman (1967) "Numerical model of coarticulation," *J. Acoust. Soc. Am.* **41**, 310–328.

145. V. Kozhevnikov & L. Chistovich (1965) *Speech: Articulation and Perception* US Department of Commerce Joint Publication Research Services, **30**, 543.

146. C. Fowler (1980) "Coarticulation & theories of extrinsic timing," *J. Phonetics* **8**, 113–133.

147. J. Kelso, B. Tuller, E. Vatikiotis-Bateson & C. Fowler (1984) "Functionally specific articulatory cooperation following jaw perturbations during speech: Evidence for coordinative structures," *J. Exp. Psych. Human Percep. & Perf.* **10**, 812–832.

148. H. Sussman, N. Bessell, E. Dalston & T. Majors (1997) "An investigation of stop place of articulation as a function of syllable position: A locus equation perspective" *J. Acoust. Soc. Am.* **101**, 2826–2838.

149. C. Fowler (1994) "Invariants, specifiers, cues: An investigation of locus equations as information for place of articulation," *Percept. & Psychoph.* **55**, 597–610.

150. B. Lindblom (1990) "Explaining phonetic variation: A sketch of the H and H theory," in *Speech Production and Speech Modeling*, W. Hardcastle & A. Marchal (eds.) (Kluwer: Netherlands), pp. 403–439.

151. H. Lane & J. Webster (1991) "Speech deterioration in postlingually deafened adults," *J. Acoust. Soc. Am.* **89**, 859–866.

152. C. Browman & L. Goldstein (1990) "Gestural specification using dynamically defined articulatory structures," *J. Phonetics* **18**, 299–320.

153. J. Kelso, E. Saltzman & B. Tuller (1986) "The dynamical theory of speech production: Data and theory," *J. Phonetics* **14**, 29–60.

154. C. Savariaux, P. Perrier & J-P. Orliaguet (1995) "Compensation strategies for the perturbation of the rounded vowel [u] using a lip tube," *J. Acoust. Soc. Am.* **98**, 2528–2442.

155. E. Saltzman & K. Muinhall (1989) "A dynamical approach to gesture patterning in speech production," *Ecol. Psychol.*, **1**, 1615–1623.

156. R. McGowan & M. Lee (1996) "Task dynamic and articulatory recovery of lip and velar approximations under model mismatch conditions," *J. Acoust. Soc. Am.* **99**, 595–608.

157. K. Johnson, P. Ladefoged & M. Lindau (1993) "Individual differences in vowel production," *J. Acoust. Soc. Am.* **94**, 701–714.

158. T. Kaburagi & M. Honda (1996) "A model of articulatory trajectory formation based on the motor tasks of vocal-tract shapes," *J. Acoust. Soc. Am.* **99**, 3154–3170.

159. D. Byrd (1992) "Preliminary results on speaker-dependent variation in the TIMIT database," *J. Acoust. Soc. Am.* **92**, 593–596.

160. C. Williams & K. Stevens (1972) "Emotions and speech: Some acoustical correlates," *J. Acoust. Soc. Am.* **52**, 1238–1250.

161. I. Murray & J. Arnott (1993) "Toward the simulation of emotion in synthetic speech: A review of the literature on human vocal emotion," *J. Acoust. Soc. Am.* **93**, 1097–1108.

162. L. Leinonen, T. Hiltunen, I. Linnankoski & M-L. Laakso (1997) "Expression of emotional-motivational connotations with a one-word utterance," *J. Acoust. Soc. Am.* **102**, 1853–1863.

163. H. Lane *et al* (1997) "Changes in sound pressure and fundamental frequency contours following changes in hearing status," *J. Acoust Soc. Am.* **101**, 2244–2252.

164. L. Arslan & J. Hansen (1997) "A study of temporal features and frequency characteristics in American English foreign accent," *J. Acoust. Soc. Am.* **102**, 28–40.

165. T. Crystal & A. House (1988) "Segmental durations in connected speech signals," *J. Acoust Soc. Am.* **83**, 1553–1585.

166. G. Allen (1975) "Speech rhythm: Its relation to performance universals and articulatory timing," *J. Phonetics* **3**, 75–86.

167. W. Summers, D. Pisoni, R. Bernacki, R. Pedlow & M. Stokes (1988) "Effects of noise on speech production: Acoustic and perceptual analyses," *J. Acoust. Soc. Am.* **84**, 917–928.

168. M. Picheny, N. Durlach & L. Braida (1989) "Speaking clearly for the hard of hearing: An attempt to determine the contribution of speaking rate to differences in intelligibility between clear and conversational speech," *J. Speech Hear. Res.* **32**, 600–603.

169. G. Fant, A. Kruckenberg & L. Nord (1991) "Durational correlates of stress in Swedish, French and English," *J. Phonetics* **19**, 351–365.

170. T. Crystal & A. House (1990) "Articulation rate and the duration of syllables and stress groups in connected speech," *J. Acoust. Soc. Am.* **88**, 101–112.

171. D. Klatt (1976) "Linguistic uses of segmental duration in English: Acoustic and perceptual evidence," *J. Acoust. Soc. Am.* **59**, 1208–1221.

172. N. Umeda (1977) "Consonant duration in American English," *J. Acoust. Soc. Am.* **61**, 846–858.

173. P. Luce & J. Charles-Luce (1985) "Contextual effects on vowel duration, closure duration and the consonant/vowel ratio in speech production," *J. Acoust. Soc. Am.* **78**, 1949–1957.

174. G. Fant & A. Kruckenberg (1996) "On the quantal nature of speech timing," *J. Phonetics* **19**, 351–365.

175. T. Arai & S. Greenberg (1997) "The temporal properties of spoken Japanese are similar to those of English," *Proc. Europ. Conf. Speech & Tech.*, pp. 1011–1014.

176. G. Weismer & A. Fennell (1985) "Constancy of (acoustic) relative timing measures in phrase-level utterances," *J. Acoust. Soc. Am.* **78**, 49–57.

177. J. Miller (1981) "Effects of speaking rate on segmental distinctions," in PSP, pp. 39–74.

178. B. Tuller, K. Harris & J. Kelso (1982) "Stress and rate: Differential transformations of articulation," *J. Acoust. Soc. Am.* **71**, 1534–1543.

179. R. Port (1981) "Linguistic timing factors in combination," *J. Acoust Soc. Am.* **69**, 262–274.

180. J. Miller & T. Baer (1983) "Some effects of speaking rate on the production of /b/ and /w/," *J. Acoust. Soc. Am.* **73**, 1751–1755.

181. M. Fourakis (1991) "Tempo, stress and vowel reduction in American English," *J. Acoust. Soc. Am.* **90**, 1816–1827.

182. T. Gay (1978) "Effect of speaking rate on vowel formant movements," *J. Acoust. Soc. Am.* **63**, 223–230.

183. D. Ostry & K. Munhall (1985) "Control of rate and duration of speech movements," *J. Acoust. Soc. Am.* **77**, 640–648.

184. S. Eady (1982) "Differences in the F0 patterns of speech: Tone language versus stress language," *Lang. & Speech* **25**, 29–42.

185. D. Hirst & A. di Cristo (1994) *Intonation Systems: A Survey of 20 Languages* (Cambridge University Press: Cambridge).

186. D. O'Shaughnessy & J. Allen (1983) "Linguistic modality effects on fundamental frequency in speech," *J. Acoust, Soc. Am.* **74**, 1155–1171.

187. D. R. Ladd (1984) "Declination: A review and some hypotheses," *Phonology Yearbook* **1**, 53–74.

188. S. Eady & W. Cooper (1986) "Speech intonation and focus location in matched statements and questions," *J. Acoust. Soc. Am.* **80**, 402–415

189. R. Ohde (1984) "Fundamental frequency as an acoustic correlate of stop consonant voicing," *J. Acoust. Soc. Am.* **75**, 224–230.

190. P. Price, M. Ostendorf, S. Shattuck-Hufnagel & C. Fong (1991) "The use of prosody in syntactic disambiguation," *J. Acoust. Soc. Am.* **90**, 2956–2970.

191. A. Cutler, D. Dahan & W. van Donselaar (1997) "Prosody in the comprehension of spoken language," *Lang. & Speech* **40**, 141–201.

192. S. Lee, A. Potamianos & S. Narayanan (1997) "Analysis of children's speech: Duration, pitch and formants," *Proc. European Conf. Speech Comm. & Tech.*, 473–476.

193. E. Slawinski (1994) "Acoustic correlates of [b] and [w] produced by normal young to elderly adults," *J. Acoust. Soc. Am.* **95**, 2221–2230.

194. J. Deller, M. Liu, L. Ferrier & P Robichaud (1993) "The Whitaker database of dysarthic (cerebral palsy) speech," *J. Acoust. Soc. Am.* **93**, 3516–3518.

CHAPTER 4—HEARING

The following is abbreviated in the reference list:

CG   R. Carlson & B. Granstrom (eds.) (1982) *The Representation of Speech in the Peripheral Auditory System* (Elsevier Biomedical Press: Amsterdam).

1. D. Van Tassel (1993) "Hearing loss, speech, and hearing aids," *J. Speech Hear. Res.* **36**, 228–244.
2. R. Tyles *et al* (1997) "Performance over time of adult patients using the Ineraid or Nucleus cochlear implant," *J. Acoust. Soc. Am.* **102**, 508–522.
3. E. Yund & K. Buckles (1995) "Enhanced speech perception at low signal-to-noise ratios with multichannel compression hearing aids," *J. Acoust. Soc. Am.* **97**, 1224–1240.
4. L. Chen, P. Trautwein, N. Powers & R. Salvi (1997) "Two-tone rate suppression boundaries of cochlear ganglion neurons in chickens following acoustic trauma," *J. Acoust. Soc. Am.* **102**, 2245–2254.
*5. B. Moore (1982) *An Introduction to the Psychology of Hearing* (Academic: London).
*6. J. Pickles (1982) *An Introduction to the Physiology of Hearing* (Academic: London).
*7. D. Green (1976) *An Introduction to Hearing* (Erlbaum: Hillsdale, NJ).
*8. J. Flanagan (1972) *Speech Analysis, Synthesis and Perception*, 2nd ed. (Springer-Verlag: New York).
9. T. Glattke (1973) "Elements of auditory physiology," in *Normal Aspects of Speech, Hearing, and Language*, F. Minifie, T. Hixon & F. Williams (eds.) (Prentice-Hall: Englewood Cliffs, NJ), pp. 285–341.
*10. J. Allen (1985) "Cochlear modeling," *IEEE ASSP Magazine* **2**, no. 1, 3–29.
*11. D. Gelfand (1998) *Hearing: An Introduction to Psychological and Physiological Acoustics* (Marcel Dekker: New York).
12. J-C. Lafon (1968) "Auditory basis of phonetics," in *Manual of Phonetics*, B. Malmberg (ed.) (North-Holland: Amsterdam), pp. 76–104.
13. F. Wightman & D. Kistler (1997) "Monaural localization revisited," *J. Acoust. Soc. Am.* **101**, 1050–1063.
14. C. Giguère & P Woodland (1994) "A computational model of the auditory periphery for speech and hearing research," *J. Acoust. Soc. Am.* **95**, 331–349.
15. C. Shera & G. Zweig (1992) "Middle ear phenomenology: The view from the three windows," *J. Acoust. Soc. Am.* **92**, 1356–1370.
16. S. Puria, W. Peake & J. Rosowski (1997) "Sound pressure measurements in the cochlear vestibule of human-cadaver ears," *J. Acoust. Soc. Am.* **101**, 2754–2770.
17. G. Stevin (1984) "A computational model of the acoustic reflex," *Acustica* **55**, 277–284.
18. I. Russell & P. Sellick (1981) "The responses of hair cells to low frequency tones & their relationship to the extracelluar receptor potentials & sound pressure level in the guinea pig cochlea," in *Neuronal Mechanisms of Hearing* J. Syka & L. Aitkin (eds.) (Plenum: New York) pp. 3–15.
19. M. Hewitt & R. Meddis (1991) "An evaluation of eight computer models of mammalian inner hair-cell function," *J. Acoust. Soc. Am.* **90**, 904–917.
20. E. de Boer (1993) "The sulcus connection. On a mode of participation of outer hair cells in cochlear mechanics," *J. Acoust. Soc. Am.* **93**, 2845–2859.
21. A. Hudspeth & V. Markin (1994) "The ear's gears: Mechanoelectrical transduction by hair cells," *Physics Today* **47**, no. 2, 22–28.
22. D. Webster (1992) "An overview of mammalian auditory pathways with an emphasis on humans," in *Mammalian Auditory Pathway: Neuroanatomy* D. Webster, A. Popper & R. Fay (eds.) (Springer-Verlag: New York) pp. 1–22.

23. W. Ainsworth & G. Meyer (1993) "Speech analysis by means of a physiologically-based model of the cochlear nerve and cochlear nucleus," in *Visual Representations of Speech Signals*, M. Cooke *et al* (eds.) (John Wiley & Sons: Chichester) pp. 119–126.

24. G. von Békésy (1960) *Experiments in Hearing* E. Wever (ed.) (McGraw-Hill: New York), pp.

25. H. Strube (1985) "A computationally efficient basilar-membrane model," *Acustica* **58**, 207–214.

26. F. Rattay, I. Gebeshuber & A. Gitter (1998) "The mammalian auditory hair cell: A simple electric circuit model," *J. Acoust. Soc. Am.* **103**, 1558–1565.

*27. R. Daniloff, G. Schuckers & L. Feth (1980) *The Physiology of Speech and Hearing: An Introduction* (Prentice-Hall: Englewood Cliffs, NJ).

28. J. Allen & S. Neely (1992) "Micromechanical models of the cochlea," *Physics Today* **45**, no. 7, 40–47.

29. L. Carney (1993) "A model for the responses of low-frequency auditory-nerve fibers in cat," *J. Acoust. Soc. Am.* **93**, 401–417.

30. L. Deng & I. Kheirallah (1993) "Dynamic formant tracking of noisy speech using temporal analysis on outputs from a nonlinear cochlear model," *IEEE Trans. Biomed. Eng.* **40**, 456–467.

31. T. Dau, D. Püschel & A. Kohlrausch (1996) "A quantitative model of the 'effective' signal processing in the auditory system," *J. Acoust. Soc. Am.* **99**, 3615–3631.

32. R. Patterson, M. Allerhand & C. Giguère (1995) "Time-domain modeling of peripheral auditory processing: A modular architecture and a software platform," *J. Acoust. Soc. Am.* **98**, 1890–1894.

33. E. Evans (1975) "The sharpening of cochlear frequency selectivity in the normal and abnormal cochlea," *Audiology* **14**, 419–442.

34. P. Dallos (1992) "The active cochlea," *J. Neurosci.* **12**, 4575–4585.

35. C. Köppl (1995) "Otoacoustic emissions as an indicator for active cochlear mechanics: A primitive property of vertebrate hearing organs," in *Advances in Hearing Research* G. Maley *et al* (eds.) (World Scientific: Singapore), pp. 207–218.

36. M. Hicks & S. Bacon (1999) "Psychophysical measures of auditory nonlinearities as a function of frequency in individuals with normal hearing," *J. Acoust. Soc. Am.* **105**, 326–338.

37. D. Mills (1997) "Interpretation of distortion product otoacoustic emission measurements," *J. Acoust. Soc. Am.* **102**, 413–429.

38. N. Kiang (1975) "Stimulus representation in the discharge patterns of auditory neurons," in *The Nervous System: III. Human Communications and Its Disorders* D. Tower (ed.) (Raven: New York) pp. 81–96.

39. A. Palmer & E. Evans (1981) "On the peripheral coding of the level of individual frequency components of complex sounds at high sound levels," *Exp. Brain Res., Suppl. II*, 19–26.

40. R. Carlyon & B. Moore (1984) "Intensity discrimination: A severe departure from Weber's law," *J. Acoust. Soc. Am.* **76**, 1369–1376.

41. S. Greenberg, C. Geisler & L. Deng (1986) "Frequency selectivity of single cochlear-nerve fibers based on the temporal response pattern to two-tone signals," *J. Acoust. Soc. Am.* **79**, 1010–1019.

42. B. Delgutte (1996) "Physiological models for basic auditory percepts," in *Auditory Computation* H. Hawkins *et al* (eds.) (Springer-Verlag: New York), pp. 157–220.

43. J. Rose, J. Hind, D. Anderson & J. Brugge (1971) "Some effects of stimulus intensity on response of auditory nerve fibers in the squirrel monkey," *J. Neurophysiol.* **34**, 685–699.

44. B. Delgutte (1982) "Some correlates of phonetic distinctions at the level of the auditory nerve," in CG, pp. 131–149.

45. R. Smith, M. Brachman & R. Frisina (1985) "Sensitivity of auditory nerve fibers to changes in intensity: A dichotomy between decrements & increments," *J. Acoust. Soc. Am.* **78**, 1310–1316.

46. E. Relkin & J. Doucet (1991) "Recovery from forward masking in the auditory nerve depends on spontaneous firing rate," *Hear Res.* **55**, 215–222.

*47. A. Small (1973) "Psychoacoustics," in *Normal Aspects of Speech, Hearing, and Language*. F. Minifie, T. Hixon & F. Williams (eds.) (Prentice-Hall: Englewood Cliffs, NJ), pp. 343–420.

48. F. Winckel (1968) "Acoustical foundations of phonetics," in *Manual of Phonetics* B. Malmberg (ed.) (North-Holland: Amsterdam), pp. 17–44.

49. M.J. Collins & J. Cullen, Jr. (1984) "Effects of background noise level on detection of tone glides," *J. Acoust. Soc. Am.* **76**, 1696–1698.

50. J. Madden & K. Fire (1996) "Detection and discrimination of gliding tones as a function of frequency transition and center frequency," *J. Acoust. Soc. Am.* **100**, 3754–3760.

51. W. Hartmann, B. Rakerd & T. Packard (1985) "On measuring the frequency-difference limen for short tones," *Perc. & Psychophys.* **38**, 199–207.

52. E. Ozimek & J. Zwislocki (1996) "Relationships of intensity discrimination to sensation and loudness levels: Dependence on sound frequency," *J. Acoust. Soc. Am.* **100**, 3304–3320.

53. S. Stevens (1938) *Handbook of Experimental Psychology* (John Wiley & Sons: New York).

54. D. Robinson & R. Dadson (1956) "A redetermination of the equal-loudness relations for pure tones," *Br. J. Appl. Phys.* **7**, 166–181.

55. W. Hartmann (1996) "Pitch, periodicity, and auditory organization," *J. Acoust. Soc. Am.* **100**, 3491–3502.

56. G. Miller (1951) *Language and Communication* (McGraw-Hill: New York).

57. K. Miyazaki (1993) "Absolute pitch as an inability: Identification of musical intervals in a tonal context," *Music Perception* **11**, 55–72.

58. E. Zwicker & H. Fastl (1990) *Psychoacoustics* (Springer-Verlag: Berlin).

59. S. Handel (1989) *Listening: An Introduction to the Perception of Auditory Events* (MIT Press: Cambridge, MA).

60. R. Meddis & L. O'Mard (1997) "A unitary model of pitch perception," *J. Acoust. Soc. Am.* **102**, 1811–1820.

61. E. Zwicker & E. Terhardt (1974) *Facts and Models in Hearing* (Springer-Verlag: Berlin).

62. C. Darwin & R. Gardner (1986) "Mistuning a harmonic of a vowel: Grouping and phase effects on vowel quality," *J. Acoust. Soc. Am.* **79**, 838–845.

63. F. Wightman (1973) "The pattern-transformation model of pitch," *J. Acoust. Soc. Am.* **54**, 407–416.

64. R. Remex & P. Rubin (1984) "On the perception of intonation from sinusoidal sentences," *Perc. & Psychophys.* **35**, 429–440.

65. B. Moore & B. Glasberg (1989) "Difference limens for phase in normal and hearing-impaired subjects," *J. Acoust. Soc. Am.* **86**, 1351–1365.

66. R. M. Warren & J. Wrightson (1981) "Stimuli producing temporal and spectral cues to frequency," *J. Acoust. Soc. Am.* **70**, 1020–1024.

67. R. Carlyon (1997) "The effects of two temporal cues on pitch judgments," *J. Acoust. Soc. Am.* **102**, 1097–1105.

68. P. Srulovicz & S. Goldstein (1983) "A central spectrum model: A synthesis of auditory-nerve timing and place cues in monaural communication of frequency spectrum," *J. Acoust. Soc. Am.* **73**, 1266–1276.

*69. A. Møller (1983) *Auditory Physiology* (Academic: New York).

70. A. de Cheveigné (1998) "Cancellation model of pitch perception," *J. Acoust. Soc. Am.* **103**, 1261–1271.

71. J. Egan & H. Hake (1950) "On the masking pattern of a simple auditory stimulus," *J. Acoust Soc. Am.* **22**, 622–630.

72. P. Stelmachowicz & W. Jesteadt (1984) "Psychophysical tuning curves in normal-hearing listeners: Test reliability and probe level effects," *J. Speech Hear. Res.* **27**, 396–402.

73. C. Geisler & A. Nuttall (1997) "Two-tone suppression of basilar membrane vibrations in the base of the guinea pig cochlea using 'low-side' suppressors," *J. Acoust. Soc. Am.* **102**, 430–440.

74. H. Fletcher (1929) *Speech and Hearing* (Van Nostrand: New York).

75. G. Ruske (1982) "Auditory perception and its application to computer analysis of speech" in *Computer Analysis and Perception: II. Auditory Signals*, C. Suen & R. de Mori (eds.) (CRC Press: Boca Raton, FL) pp.

76. E. Zwicker & A. Jaroszewski (1982) "Inverse frequency dependence of simultaneous tone-on-tone masking patterns at low levels," *J. Acoust. Soc. Am.* **71**, 1508–1512.

77. M. Schroeder, B. Atal & J. Hall (1979) "Objective measure of certain signal degradations based on masking properties of human auditory perception," in *Frontiers of Speech Communication Research*, B. Lindblom & S. Ohman (eds.) (Academic: London), pp. 217–229.

78. J. Hall (1997) "Asymmetry of masking revisited: Generalization of masker and probe bandwidth," *J. Acoust. Soc. Am.* **101**, 1023–1033.

79. R. Pastore (1981) "Possible psychoacoustic factors in speech perception," in *Perspectives on the Study of Speech*, P. Eimas & J. Miller (eds.) (Erlbaum: Hillsdale, NJ), pp. 165–205.

80. S. Buus (1985) "Release from masking caused by envelope fluctuations," *J. Acoust. Soc. Am.* **78**, 1958–1965.

81. R. Patterson & D. Green (1978) "Auditory masking," in *Handbook of Perception, IV*, E. Carterette & M. Friedman (eds.) (Academic: New York), pp. 337–361.

82. P. Joris & T. Yin (1992) "Responses to amplitude-modulated tones in the auditory nerve of the cat," *J. Acoust. Soc. Am.* **91**, 215–232.

83. E. Zwicker & E. Terhardt (1980) "Analytical expressions for critical-band rate and critical bandwidth as a function of frequency," *J. Acoust Soc. Am.* **68**, 1523–1525.

84. S. Umesh, L. Cohen & D. Nelson (1999) "Fitting the mel scale," *Proc. IEEE Int. Conf. ASSP*, pp. 217–220.

85. B. Glasberg & B. Moore (1990) "Derivation of auditory filter shape from notched-noise data," *Hear Res.* **47**, 103–138.

86. R. Lutfi (1985) "A power-law transformation predicting masking by sounds with complex spectra," *J. Acoust Soc. Am.* **77**, 2128–2136.

87. L. Humes, L. Lee & W. Jesteadt (1992) "Two experiments on the spectral boundary conditions for nonlinear additivity of simultaneous masking," *J. Acoust. Soc. Am.* **92**, 2598–2606.

88. D. Klatt (1982) "Speech processing strategies based on auditory models," in CG, pp. 181–196.

89. H. Duifhuis (1973) "Consequences of peripheral frequency selectivity for nonsimultaneous masking, *J. Acoust Soc. Am.* **54**, 1471–1488.

90. E. Zwicker (1984) "Dependence of post-masking on masker duration and its relation to temporal effects in loudness," *J. Acoust. Soc. Am.* **75**, 219–223.

91. D. Eddins & D. Green (1995) "Temporal integration and temporal resolution," in *Hearing*, B. Moore (ed.) (Academic: San Diego, CA) pp.

92. S. Buus, M. Florentine & T. Poulsen (1997) "Temporal integration of loudness, loudness discrimination, and the form of the loudness function," *J. Acoust. Soc. Am.* **101**, 669–680.

93. T. Dolan & A. Small Jr. (1984) "Frequency effects in backward masking," *J. Acoust. Soc. Am.* **75**, 932–936.

94. A. Gilbert & J. Pickles (1980) "Responses of auditory nerve fibers in the guinea pig to noise bands of different widths," *Hearing Res.* **2**, 327–333.

95. H. Fastl & M. Bechly (1983) "Suppression in simultaneous masking," *J. Acoust. Soc. Am.* **74**, 754–757.

96. D. Weber & B. Moore (1981) "Forward masking by sinusoidal and noise maskers," *J. Acoust. Soc. Am.* **69**, 1402–1409.

97. Viemeister & S. Bacon (1982) "Forward masking by enhanced components in harmonic complexes," *J. Acoust. Soc. Am.* **71**, 1502–1507.

98. B. Moore & B. Glasberg (1985) "The danger of using narrow-band noise maskers to measure 'suppression,'" *J. Acoust. Soc. Am.* **77**, 2137–2141.

99. W. Jesteadt & S. Norton (1985) "The role of suppression in psychophysical measures of frequency selectivity," *J. Acoust. Soc. Am.* **78**, 365–374.

100. B. Moore, B. Glasberg & B. Roberts (1984) "Refining the measurement of psychophysical tuning curves," *J. Acoust. Soc. Am.* **76**, 1057–1066.

101. E. Javel (1981) "Suppression of auditory nerve responses," *J. Acoust. Soc. Am.* **69**, 1735–1745.

*102. M. Schroeder (1975) "Models of hearing," *Proc. IEEE* **63**, 1332–1350.

103. L. Mendoza, J. Hall & J. Grose (1995) "Within- and across-channel processes in modulation detection interference," *J. Acoust. Soc. Am.* **97**, 3072–3079.

104. P. Kim & E. Young (1994) "Comparative analysis of spectro-temporal receptive fields, reverse correlation functions, and frequency tuning curves of auditory-nerve fibers," *J. Acoust. Soc. Am.* **95**, 410–422.

105. J. Hall & J. Grose (1990) "Comodulation masking release and auditory grouping," *J. Acoust. Soc. Am.* **88**, 119–125.

106. P. Gordon (1997) "Coherence masking protection in brief noise complexes: Effects of temporal patterns," *J. Acoust Soc. Am.* **102**, 2276–2283.

107. B. Wright (1996) "Correlated individual differences in conditions used to measure psychophysical suppression and signal enhancement," *J. Acoust. Soc. Am.* **100**, 3295–3303.

108. H. Gustafsson & S. Arlinger (1994) "Masking of speech by amplitude-modulated noise," *J. Acoust. Soc. Am.* **95**, 518–529.

109. P. Howard-Jones & S. Rosen (1983) "Uncomodulated glimpsing in 'checkerboard' noise," *J. Acoust. Soc. Am.* **93**, 2915–2922.

110. S. Carlile & D. Wardman (1996) "Masking produced by broadband noise presented in virtual auditory space," *J. Acoust. Soc. Am.* **100**, 3761–3768.

111. W. Hartmann & A. Wittenberg (1996) "On the externalization of sound images," *J. Acoust. Soc. Am.* **99**, 3678–3688.

112. M. Sachs, R. Winslow & C. Blackburn (1988) "Representation of speech in the auditory periphery" in *Auditory Function*, G. Edelman, W. Gall & W. Cowan (eds.) (John Wiley & Sons: New York), pp. 747–774.

113. B. Delgutte & N. Kiang (1984) "Speech coding in the auditory nerve," *J. Acoust Soc. Am.* **75**, 866–918.

114. E. Young & P. Barta (1986) "Rate responses of auditory nerve fibers to tones in noise near masked threshold," *J. Acoust. Soc. Am.* **79**, 426–442.

115. M. Sachs, R. Winslow & C. Blackburn (1988) "Representation of speech in the auditory periphery" in *Auditory Function*, G. Edelman, W. Gall & W. Cowan (eds.) (John Wiley & Sons: New York), 747–774.

116. T. Moore & J. Cashin (1976) "Response of cochlear-nucleus neurons to synthetic speech," *J. Acoust. Soc. Am.* **59**, 1443–1449.

117. T. McGee *et al* (1996) "Acoustic elements of speechlike stimuli are reflected in surface recorded responses over the guinea pig temporal lobe," *J. Acoust. Soc. Am.* **99**, 3606–3614.

118. D. Sinex & C. Geisler (1984) "Comparison of the responses of auditory nerve fibers to consonant-vowel syllables with predictions from linear models," *J. Acoust. Soc. Am.* **76**, 116–121.

119. M. Miller & M. Sachs (1983) "Representation of stop consonants in the discharge patterns of auditory-nerve fibers," *J. Acoust. Soc. Am.* **74**, 502–517.

120. N. Kiang (1980) "Processing of speech by the auditory nervous system," *J. Acoust. Soc. Am.* **68**, 830–835.

121. A. Palmer, I. Winter & C. Darwin (1986) "The representation of steady-state vowel sounds in the temporal discharge patterns of the guinea pig cochlear nerve," *J. Acoust. Soc. Am.* **79**, 100–113.

122. R. Conley & S. Keilson (1995) "Rate representation and discriminability of second formant frequencies for /ɛ/-like steady-state vowels in cat auditory nerve," *J. Acoust. Soc. Am.* **98**, 3223–3234.

123. B. Moore & B. Glasberg (1983) "Masking patterns for synthetic vowels in simultaneous and forward masking," *J. Acoust. Soc. Am.* **73**, 906–917.

124. V. Summers & M. Leek (1997) "Intraspeech spread of masking in normal-hearing and hearing-impaired listeners," *J. Acoust. Soc. Am.* **101**, 2866–2876.

125. B. Moore & B. Glasberg (1983) "Forward masking patterns for harmonic complex tones," *J. Acoust. Soc. Am.* **73**, 1682–1685.

126. S. Resnick, M. Weiss & J. Heinz (1979) "Masking of filtered noise bursts by synthetic vowels," *J. Acoust. Soc. Am.* **66**, 674–677.

127. Q. Summerfield, M. Haggard, J. Foster & S. Gray (1984) "Perceiving vowels from uniform spectra: Phonetic exploration of an auditory aftereffect," *Perc. & Psych.* **35**, 203–213.

128. D. Kewley-Port (1998) "Auditory models of formant frequency discrimination for isolated vowels," *J. Acoust. Soc. Am.* **103**, 1654–1666.

129. P. Mermelstein (1978) "Difference limens for formant frequencies of steady-state and consonant-bound vowels," *J. Acoust. Soc. Am.* **63**, 572–580.

130. J. Hawks (1994) "Difference limens for formant patterns of vowel sounds," *J. Acoust. Soc. Am.* **95**, 1074–1084.

131. J. Lyzenga & J. Horst (1997) "Frequency discrimination of stylized synthetic vowels with a single formant," *J. Acoust. Soc. Am.* **102**, 1755–1767.

132. B. Moore, B. Glasberg & M. Shailer (1984) "Frequency and intensity difference limens for harmonics within complex tones," *J. Acoust. Soc. Am.* **75**, 550–561.

133. R. Carlson, G. Fant & B. Granstrom (1974) "Vowel perception and auditory theory," *Acustica* **31**.

134. J. Sundberg & J. Gauffin (1982) "Amplitude of the voice source fundamental and the intelligibility of super pitch vowels," in CG, pp. 223–228.

135. M. Sommers & D. Kewley-Port (1997) "Modeling formant frequency discrimination of female vowels," *J. Acoust. Soc. Am.* **99**, 3770–3781.

136. J. Alcántara & B. Moore (1995) "The identification of vowel-like harmonic complexes," *J. Acoust. Soc. Am.* **97**, 3813–3824.

137. I. Lehiste (1970) *Suprasegmentals* (MIT Press: Cambridge, MA).

138. D. Klatt (1973) "Discrimination of fundamental frequency contours in synthetic speech: implications for models of pitch perception," *J. Acoust. Soc. Am.* **53**, 8–16.

139. M. Scheffers (1984) "Discrimination of fundamental frequency of synthesized vowel sounds in a noise background," *J. Acoust. Soc. Am.* **76**, 428–434.

140. L. Pols & M. Schouten (1982) "Perceptual relevance of coarticulation," in CG, pp. 203–208.

141. C. Witting (1962) "A method of evaluating listeners' transcriptions of intonation on the basis of instrumental data," *Lang. & Speech* **5**, 138–150.

142. J. 't Hart (1981) "Differential sensitivity to pitch distance, particularly in speech," *J. Acoust. Soc. Am.* **69**, 811–821.

143. M. van der Broecke & V. van Heuven (1983) "Effect and artifact in the auditory discrimination of rise & decay time: Speech & nonspeech," *Perc. & Psychophys.* **33**, 305–313.

144. P. Howell & S. Rosen (1983) "Production and perception of rise time in the voiceless affricate/fricative distinction," *J. Acoust. Soc. Am.* **73**, 976–984.

145. R. Carlson, B. Granstrom & D. Klatt (1979) "Vowel perception: the relative perceptual salience of selected acoustic manipulations," *KTH-STL-QPSR* **3–4**, 73–83.

146. R. Bladon & B. Lindblom (1981) "Modeling the judgment of vowel quality differences," *J. Acoust. Soc. Am.* **69**, 1414–1422.

147. J. Bernstein (1981) "Formant-based representation of auditory similarity among vowel-like sounds," *J. Acoust. Soc. Am.* **69**, 1132–1144.

148. M. Nilsson, S. Soli & J. Sullivan (1994) "Development of the Hearing In Noise Test for the measurement of speech reception thresholds in quiet and in noise," *J. Acoust. Soc. Am.* **95**, 1085–1099.

149. R. Pastore, L. Harris & J. Kaplan (1982) "Temporal order identification: Some parameter dependencies," *J. Acoust. Soc. Am.* **71**, 430–436.

150. M. Shailer & B. Moore (1985) "Detection of temporal gaps in bandlimited noise: Effects of variations in bandwidth and signal-to-masker ratio," *J. Acoust. Soc. Am.* **77**, 635–639.

151. J. Madden (1994) "The role of frequency resolution and temporal resolution in the detection frequency modulation," *J. Acoust. Soc. Am.* **95**, 454–462.

152. J. Cutting & B. Rosner (1974) "Categories and boundaries in speech and music," *Perc. & Psychophys.* **16**, 564–570.

153. M. Penner (1978) "A power law transformation resulting in a class of short-term integrators that produce time-intensity trades for noise bursts," *J. Acoust. Soc. Am.* **63**, 195–201.

154. R. M. Warren & R. P. Warren (1970) "Auditory illusions and confusions," *Sci. Am.* **223**, 30–36.

155. E. Foulke & T. Sticht (1969) "Review of research on the intelligibility and comprehension of accelerated speech," *Psych. Bull.* **72**, 50–62.

156. P. Divenyi (1979) "Some psychoacoustic factors in phonetic analysis," *Proc. 9th Int. Cong. Phonetic Sciences*, pp. 445–452.

157. B. Espinoza-Varas & D. Jamieson (1984) "Integration of spectral and temporal cues separated in time and frequency," *J. Acoust. Soc. Am.* **76**, 732–738.

158. A. Huggins (1972) "Just noticeable differences for segment duration in natural speech," *J. Acoust. Soc. Am.* **51**, 1270–1278.

159. A. Huggins (1972) "On the perception of temporal phenomena in speech," *J. Acoust. Soc. Am.* **51**, 1279–1290.

160. H. Ruhm, E. Mencke, B. Milburn, W. Cooper Jr. & D. Rose (1966) "Differential sensitivity to duration of acoustic signals," *J. Speech Hear. Res.* **9**, 371–384.

161. S. Nooteboom & G. Doodeman (1983) "Production and perception of vowel length in spoken sentences," *J. Acoust. Soc. Am.* **67**, 276–287.

162. D. Klatt & W. Cooper (1975) "Perception of segment duration in sentence contexts," in *Structure and Process in Speech Perception*, A. Cohen & S. Nooteboom (eds.) (Springer-Verlag: New York), pp. 69–89.

163. A. Bregman (1990) *Auditory Scene Analysis: The Perceptual Organization of Sound* (MIT Press: Cambridge, MA).

164. P. Singh & A. Bregman (1997) "The influence of different timbre attributes on the perceptual segregation of complex-tone sequences," *J. Acoust. Soc. Am.* **102**, 1943–1952.

165. M. Cooke & G. Brown (1994) "Separating simultaneous sound sources: Issues, challenges and models," in *Fundamentals of Speech Synthesis and Recognition*, E. Keller (ed.) (John Wiley & Sons: Chichester) pp. 295–312.

166. Q. Summerfeld & J. Culling (1994) "Auditory computations that separate speech from competing sounds," in *Fundamentals of Speech Synthesis and Recognition*, E. Keller (ed.) (John Wiley & Sons: Chichester) pp. 313–338.

CHAPTER 5—SPEECH PERCEPTION

The following volume is abbreviated as CG in the reference list:

R. Carlson & B. Granstrom (eds.) (1982) *The Representation of Speech in the Peripheral Auditory System* (Elsevier Biomedical Press: Amsterdam).

1. J. Allen (1994) "How do humans process and recognize speech?" *IEEE Trans. Speech Audio Proc.* **2**, 567–577.

2. C. Pavlovic & G. Studebaker (1984) "An evaluation of some assumptions underlying the articulation index," *J. Acoust. Soc. Am.* **75**, 1606–1612.

3. M. Power & L. Braida (1996) "Consistency among speech parameter vectors: Application to predicting speech intelligibility," *J. Acoust. Soc. Am.* **100**, 3882–3898.

4. G. Miller & P. Nicely (1955) "An analysis of perceptual confusions among some English consonants," *J. Acoust. Soc. Am.* **27**, 338–352 (reprinted in *Readings in Acoustic Phonetics*, I. Lehiste (ed.) (MIT Press: Cambridge, MA), 1960.

5. S. Gelfand & S. Silman (1979) "Effects of small room reverberation upon the recognition of some consonant features," *J. Acoust. Soc. Am.* **66**, 22–29.

6. D. Massaro, M. Cohen & P. Smeele (1996) "Perception of asynchronous and conflicting visual and auditory speech," *J. Acoust. Soc. Am.* **100**, 1777–1786.

7. P. Delattre, A. Liberman & F. Cooper (1955) "Acoustic loci and transitional cues for consonants," *J. Acoust. Soc. Am.* **27**, 769–773.

8. F. Cooper, P. Delattre, A. Liberman, J. Borst & L. Gerstman (1952) "Some experiments on the perception of synthetic speech sounds," *J. Acoust. Soc. Am.* **24**, 597–606 (reprinted in *Readings in Acoustic Phonetics*, I. Lehiste (ed.) (MIT Press: Cambridge, MA), 1960.

9. B. Moore (1982) *An Introduction to the Psychology of Hearing* (Academic: London).

10. J. Miller, K. Green & T. Shermer (1984) "A distinction between the effects of sentential speaking rate and semantic congruity on word identification," *Perc. & Psychophys.* **36**, 329–337.

11. K. Payton, R. Uchanski & L. Braida (1994) "Intelligibility of conversational and clear speech in noise and reverberation for listeners with normal and impaired hearing," *J. Acoust. Soc. Am.* **95**, 1581–1592.

12. M. Studdert-Kennedy, A. Liberman, K. Harris & F. Cooper (1970) "The motor theory of speech perception: A reply to Lane's critical review," *Psych. Rev.* **77**, 234–249.

13. D. Massaro & M. Cohen (1983) "Categorical or continuous speech perception: A new test," *Speech Comm.* **2**, 15–35.

14. R. Pastore (1981) "Possible psychoacoustic factors in speech perception," in *Perspectives on the Study of Speech* P. Eimas & J. Miller (eds.) (Erlbaum: Hillsdale, NJ), pp. 165–205.

15. M. Schouten & A. van Hessen (1992) "Modeling phoneme perception. I: Categorical perception," *J. Acoust. Soc. Am.* **92**, 1841–1855.

16. R. Jakobson, G. Fant & M. Halle (1961) *Preliminaries to Speech Analysis: The Distinctive Features and Their Correlates* (MIT Press: Cambridge, MA).

17. N. Chomsky & M. Halle (1968) *The Sound Pattern of English* (Harper & Row: New York).

18. S. McCandless (1974) "An algorithm for automatic formant extraction using linear prediction spectra," *IEEE Trans. ASSP*, **ASSP-22**, 135–141.

19. A. Bladon (1982) "Arguments against formants in the auditory representation of speech," in *The Representation of Speech in the Peripheral Auditory System* R. Carlson & B. Granstrom (eds.) (Elsevier Biomedical: Amsterdam), pp. 95–102.

20. W. Cooper (1978) *Speech Perception and Production: Selected Studies on Adaptation* (Cambridge University Press: Cambridge).

21. D. Massaro & M. Cohen (1976) "The contribution of fundamental frequency and voice onset time to the /zi/ - /si/ distinction," *J. Acoust. Soc. Am.* **60**, 704–717.

22. K. Stevens & S. Blumstein (1978) "Invariant cues for place of articulation in stop consonants," *J. Acoust. Soc. Am.* **64**, 1358–1368.

23. K. Stevens & S. Blumstein (1981) "The search for invariant acoustic correlates of phonetic features," in *Perspectives on the Study of Speech* P. Eimas & J. Miller (eds.) (Erlbaum: Hillsdale, NJ), pp. 1–38.

24. R. Remez (1979) "Adaptation of the category boundary between speech and nonspeech: A case against feature detectors," *Cognitive Psych.* **11**, 38–57.

25. S. Shattuck-Hufnagel & D. Klatt (1979) "The limited use of distinctive features and markedness in speech production: Evidence from speech error data," *J. Verbal Learning & Verbal Behavior* **18**, 41–56.

*26. K. Stevens (1975) "Speech perception," in *The Nervous System: III, Human Communications and Its Disorders* D. Tower (ed.) (Raven: New York), pp. 163–171.

27. C. Fowler (1986) "An event approach to the study of speech perception from a direct-realist perspective," *J. Phonetics* **14**, 3–28.

28. C. Fowler (1996) "Listeners do hear sounds, not tongues," *J. Acoust. Soc. Am.* **99**, 1730–1741.

*29. A. Liberman, F. Cooper, D. Shankweiler & M. Studdert-Kennedy (1967) "Perception of the speech code," *Psych. Rev.* **74**, 431–461.

30. M. Schouten (1980) "The case against a speech mode of perception," *Acta Psychologica* **44**, 71–98.

31. B. Repp (1983) "Trading relations among acoustic cues in speech perception are largely a result of phonetic categorization," *Speech Comm.* **2**, 341–361.

32. J. Cutting & B. Rosner (1974) "Categories and boundaries in speech and music," *Perc. & Psychophys.* **16**, 564–570.

33. B. Repp (1983) "Categorical perception: Issues, methods, findings," in *Speech and Language: Advances in Basic Research and Practice* **10** N. Lass (ed.) (Academic: New York), pp.

34. B. Rosner (1984) "Perception of voice-onset-time continua: A signal detection analysis," *J. Acoust. Soc. Am.* **75**, 1231–1242.

35. P. Kuhl (1993) "Psychoacoustics and speech perception: Internal standards, perceptual anchors and prototypes," in *Developmental Psychoacoustics* L. Werner & E. Rubel (eds.) (Academic: San Francisco), pp. 293–332.

36. Working Group on Speech Understanding and Aging (1988) "Speech understanding and aging," *J. Acoust. Soc. Am.* **83**, 859–894.

37. L. Lotto, K. Kluender & L. Holt (1998) "Depolarizing the perceptual magnet effect," *J. Acoust. Soc. Am.* **103**, 3648–3655.

38. J. McClelland & J. Elman (1986) "The TRACE model of speech perception," *Cogn. Psych.* **18**, 1–86.

39. D. Massaro (1975) "Backward recognition masking," *J. Acoust. Soc. Am.* **58**, 1059–1065.

40. R. Crowder (1981) "The role of auditory memory in speech perception and discrimination," in *The Cognitive Representation of Speech*, T. Myers, J. Laver & J. Anderson (eds.) (North-Holland: Amsterdam) pp.

41. V. Kozhevnikov & L. Chistovich (1965) *Speech: Articulation and Perception* US Dept. of Commerce Joint Publication Research Services **30**, 543.

42. W. Marslen-Wilson & A. Welsh (1978) "Processing interactions and lexical access during word recognition and continuous speech," *Cognitive Psych.* **10**, 29–63.

43. L. Nakatani & K. Dukes (1977) "Locus of segmental cues for word juncture," *J. Acoust. Soc. Am.* **62**, 714–719.

44. J. Fodor, T. Bever & M. Garrett (1974) *The Psychology of Language* (McGraw-Hill: New York).

45. P. Luce, D. Pisoni & S. Goldinger (1990) "Similarity neighborhoods of spoken words" in *Cognitive Models of Speech Processing* (MIT Press: Cambridge, MA), pp. 122–147.

46. G. Fant (1967) "Auditory patterns of speech," in *Models for the Perception of Speech and Visual Form* W. Wathen-Dunn (ed.) (MIT Press: Cambridge, MA), pp. 111–125.

47. D. Klatt (1980) "Speech perception: A model of acoustic-phonetic analysis and lexical access," in *Perception & Production of Fluent Speech* R. Cole (ed.) (Erlbaum: Hillsdale, NJ), pp. 243–288.

48. D. Klatt (1979) "Speech perception: A model of acoustic-phonetic analysis and lexical access," *J. Phonetics* **7**, 279–312.

49. W. Wickelgren (1976) "Phonetic coding and serial order," in *Handbook of Perception*, VII (Academic: New York), pp.

50. J. Kingston & R. Diehl (1995) "Intermediate properties in the perception of distinctive feature values," in *Phonology and Phonetic Evidence: Papers in Laboratory Phonology IV*, B. Connell & A. Arvanti (eds.) (Cambridge University Press: Cambridge), pp. 7–27.

51. T. Nearey (1997) "Speech perception as pattern recognition," *J. Acoust. Soc. Am.* **101**, 3241–3254.

52. J. Hillenbrand & R. Gayvert (1993) "Identification of steady-state vowels synthesized from the Peterson and Barney measurements," *J. Acoust. Soc. Am.* **94**, 668–674.

53. A. Bladon (1985) "Diphthongs: A case study of dynamic auditory processing," *Speech Comm.* **4**, 145–154.

54. W. Klein, R. Plomp & L. Pols (1970) "Vowel spectra, vowel spaces, and vowel identification," *J. Acoust. Soc. Am.* **48**, 999–1009.

55. A. Syrdal & H. Gopal (1986) "A perceptual model of vowel recognition based on the auditory representation of American English vowels," *J. Acoust. Soc. Am.* **79**, 1086–1100.

56. L. Chistovich (1985) "Central auditory processing of peripheral vowel spectra," *J. Acoust. Soc. Am.* **77**, 789–805.

57. A. Bladon (1983) "Two formant models of vowel perception: Shortcomings and enhancements," *Speech Comm.* **2**, 305–313.

58. K. Johnson (1990) "The role of perceived speaker identity in F0 normalization of vowels," *J. Acoust. Soc. Am.* **88**, 642–654.

59. A. de Cheveigné, S. McAdams & C. Marin (1997) "Concurrent vowel identification. II. Effects of phase, harmonicity, and task," *J. Acoust. Soc. Am.* **101**, 2848–2865.

60. A. Watkins & S. Makin (1996) "Effects of spectral contrast on perceptual compensation for spectral-envelope distortion," *J. Acoust. Soc. Am.* **99**, 3749–3757.

61. J. Kreiman & C. Papçun (1991) "Comparing discrimination and recognition of unfamiliar voices," *Speech Comm.* **10**, 265–275.

62. J. Mullennix, K. Johnson, M. Topcu-Durgin & L. Farnsworth (1995) "The perceptual representation of voice gender," *J. Acoust. Soc. Am.* **98**, 3080–3095.

63. D. Pisoni (1997) "Some thoughts on 'normalization' in speech perception," in *Talker Variability in Speech Processing,* K. Johnson & J. Mullennix (eds.) (Academic: San Diego, CA), pp. 9–32.

64. H. Fujisaki & T. Kawashima (1968) "The roles of pitch and higher formants in the perception of vowels," *IEEE Trans. Audio & Electroac.* **AU-16**, 73–77.

65. J. Holmes (1986) "Normalization in vowel perception," in *Invariance & Variability in Speech Processes*, J. Perkell & D. Klatt (eds.) (Erlbaum: Hillsdale, NJ), pp. 346–357.

66. K. Suomi (1984) "On talker and phoneme information conveyed by vowels: A whole spectrum approach to the normalization problem," *Speech Comm.* **3**, 199–209.

67. W. Strange, J. Jenkins, and T. Johnson (1983) "Dynamic specification of coarticulated vowels," *J. Acoust. Soc. Am.* **74**, 695–705.

68. E. Parker & R. Diehl (1984) "Identifying vowels in CVC syllables: Effects of inserting silence and noise," *Perc. & Psychophys.* **36**, 369–380.

69. J. Jenkins, W. Strange & S. Miranda (1994) "Vowel identification in mixed-speaker silent-center syllables," *J. Acoust. Soc. Am.* **95**, 1030–1041.

70. A. Nábalek & A. Ovchinnikov (1997) "Perception of nonlinear and linear formant trajectories," *J. Acoust. Soc. Am.* **101**, 488–497.

71. R. Diehl, S. McCusker & L. Chapman (1981) "Perceiving vowels in isolation and in consonantal context," *J. Acoust. Soc. Am.* **69**, 239–248.

72. T. Gottfried & W. Strange (1980) "Identification of coarticulated vowels," *J. Acoust. Soc. Am.* **68**, 1626–1635.

73. R. Shannon, F-C. Zeng, V. Kamath, J. Wygonski & M. Ekelid (1995) "Speech recognition with primarily temporal cues," *Science*, **270**, 303–304.

*74. R. Cole & B. Scott (1974) "Toward a theory of speech perception," *Psych. Rev.* **81**, 348–374.

75. A. Liberman, P. Delattre, L. Gerstman & F. Cooper (1956) "Tempo of frequency change as a cue for distinguishing classes of speech sounds," *J. Exp. Psychol.* **52**, 127–137.

76. P. Shinn & S. Blumstein (1984) "On the role of the amplitude envelope for the perception of [b] and [w]," *J. Acoust. Soc. Am.* **75**, 1243–1252.

77. S. Hawkins & K. Stevens (1985) "Acoustic and perceptual correlates of the nonnasal–nasal distinction for vowels," *J. Acoust. Soc. Am.* **77**, 1560–1575.

78. E. Bogner & H. Fujisaki (1986) "Analysis, synthesis, and perception of the French nasal vowels," *Proc. IEEE Int. Conf. ASSP*, pp. 1601–1604.

79. A. Abramson, P. Nye, J. Henderson & C. Marshall (1982) "Vowel height and the perception of consonantal nasality," *J. Acoust. Soc. Am.* **70**, 329–339.

80. P. Beddor & W. Strange (1982) "Cross-language study of perception of the oral–nasal distinction," *J. Acoust. Soc. Am.* **71**, 1551–1561.

81. M. Hedrick & R. Ohde (1993) "Effect of relative amplitude of frication on perception of place of articulation," *J. Acoust. Soc. Am.* **94**, 2005–2026.

82. D. Sharf & R. Ohde (1984) "Effect of formant frequency onset variation on the differentiation of synthesized /w/ and /r/ sounds," *J. Speech Hear. Res.* **27**, 475–479.

83. D. Recasens (1983) "Place cues for nasal consonants with special reference to Catalan," *J. Acoust. Soc. Am.* **73**, 1346–1353.

84. R. Smits, L. ten Bosch & R. Collier (1996) "Evaluation of various sets of acoustic cues for the perception of prevocalic stop consonants," *J. Acoust. Soc. Am.* **100**, 3852–3881.

85. R. Ohde (1994) "The development of the perception of cues to the [m]-[n] distinction in CV syllables," *J. Acoust. Soc. Am.* **96**, 675–686.

86. L. Polka & W. Strange (1985) "Perceptual equivalence of acoustic cues that differentiate /r/ and /l/," *J. Acoust. Soc. Am.* **78**, 1187–1197.

87. L. Christensen & L. Humes (1997) "Identification of multidimensional stimuli containing speech cues and the effects of training," *J. Acoust. Soc. Am.* **102**, 2297–2310.

88. M. Dorman, M. Studdert-Kennedy & L. Raphael (1977) "Stop-consonant recognition: Release bursts and formant transitions as functionally equivalent, context-dependent cues," *Perc. & Psychophys.* **22**, 109–122.

89. O. Fujimura, M. Macchi & L. Streeter (1978) "Perception of stop consonants with conflicting transitional cues: A cross-linguistic study," *Lang. & Speech* **21**, 337–346.

90. D. Massaro & G. Oden (1980) "Evaluation and integration of acoustic features in speech perception," *J. Acoust. Soc. Am.* **67**, 996–1013.

91. R. Ohde & K. Stevens (1983) "Effect of burst amplitude on the perception of stop consonant place of articulation," *J. Acoust. Soc. Am.* **74**, 706–714.

92. B. Repp (1984) "Closure duration and release burst amplitude cues to stop consonant manner and place of articulation," *Lang. & Speech* **27**, 245–254.

93. S. Blumstein & K. Stevens (1980) "Perceptual invariance and onset spectra for stop consonants in different vowel environments," *J. Acoust. Soc. Am.* **67**, 648–662.

94. S. Blumstein (1986) "On acoustic invariance in speech," in *Invariance & Variability in Speech Processes*, J. Perkell & D. Klatt (eds.) (Erlbaum: Hillsdale, NJ), pp. 178–193.

95. A. Walley & T. Carrell (1983) "Onset spectra and formant transitions in the adult's and child's perception of place of articulation in stop consonants," *J. Acoust. Soc. Am.* **73**, 1011–1022.

96. D. Kewley-Port, D. Pisoni & M. Studdert-Kennedy (1983) "Perception of static and dynamic acoustic cues to place of articulation in initial stop consonants," *J. Acoust. Soc. Am.* **73**, 1779–1793.

97. D. Kewley-Port & P. Luce (1984) "Time-varying features of initial stop consonants in auditory running spectra: A first report," *Perc. & Psychophys.* **35**, 353–360.

98. A. Lahiri, L. Gewirth & S. Blumstein (1984) "A reconsideration of acoustic invariance for place of articulation in diffuse stop consonants: Evidence from a cross-language study," *J. Acoust. Soc. Am.* **76**, 391–404.

99. M. Dorman & P. Loizou (1996) "Relative spectral change and formant transitions as cues to labial and alveolar place of articulation," *J. Acoust. Soc. Am.* **100**, 3825–3830.

100. H. Sussman, H. McCaffrey & S. Matthews (1991) "An investigation of locus equations as a source of relational invariance for stop place categorization," *J. Acoust. Soc. Am.* **90**, 1309–1325.

101. J. Miller (1977) "Nonindependence of feature processing in initial consonants," *J. Speech Hear. Res.* **20**, 510–518.

102. P. Eimas, V. Tartter, J. Miller & D. Marcus (1978) "Asymmetric dependencies in processing phonetic features," *Perc. & Psychophys.* **23**, 12–20.

103. G. Carden, A. Levitt, P. Jusczyk & A. Walley (1981) "Evidence for phonetic processing of cues to place of articulation: Perceived manner affects perceived place," *Perc. & Psychophys.* **29**, 26–36.

104. V. Mann & B. Repp (1980) "Influence of vocalic context on perception of the [SH]-[s] distinction," *Perc. & Psychophys.* **28**, 213–228.

105. B. Repp & V. Mann (1981) "Perceptual assessment of fricative-stop coarticulation," *J. Acoust. Soc. Am.* **69**, 1154–1163.

106. V. Mann (1980) "Influence of preceding liquid on stop-consonant perception," *Perc. & Psychophys.* **28**, 407–412.

107. R. Cole & W. Cooper (1975) "The perception of voicing in English affricates and fricatives," *J. Acoust. Soc. Am.* **58**, 1280–1287.

108. S. Soli (1982) "Structure and duration of vowels together specify fricative voicing," *J. Acoust. Soc. Am.* **72**, 366–378.

109. D. Massaro & M. Cohen (1983) "Phonological context in speech perception," *Perc. & Psychophys.* **34**, 338–348.

110. I. Lehiste (1976) "Influence of fundamental frequency pattern on the perception of duration," *J. Phonetics* **4**, 113–117.

111. T. Gruenenfelder & D. Pisoni (1980) "Fundamental frequency as a cue to postvocalic consonant voicing: Some data from speech perception and production," *Perc. & Psychophys.* **28**, 514–520.

112. W. van Dommelen (1983) "Parameter interaction in the perception of French plosives," *Phonetica* **40**, 32–62.

113. J. Hillenbrand, D. Ingrisano, B. Smith & J. Flege (1984) "Perception of the voiced–voiceless contrast in syllable-final stops," *J. Acoust. Soc. Am.* **76**, 18–26.

114. L. Lisker (1975) "Is it VOT or a first-formant transition detector?" *J. Acoust. Soc. Am.* **57**, 1547–1551.

115. A. Liberman, P. Delattre & F. Cooper (1958) "Some cues for the distinction between voiced and voiceless stops in initial position," *Lang. & Speech* **1**, 153–167.

116. L. Lisker, A. Liberman, D. Erickson, D. Dechovitz & R. Mandler (1978) "On pushing the voicing-onset-time (VOT) boundary about," *Lang. & Speech* **20**, 209–216.

117. C. Darwin & J. Seton (1983) "Perceptual cues to the onset of voiced excitation in aspirated initial stops," *J. Acoust. Soc. Am.* **74**, 1126–1135.

118. M. Haggard, S. Ambler & M. Callow (1970) "Pitch as a voicing cue," *J. Acoust. Soc. Am.* **47**, 613–617.

119. Q. Summerfield & M. Haggard (1977) "On the dissociation of spectral and temporal cues to the voicing distinction in initial stop consonants," *J. Acoust. Soc. Am.* **62**, 435–448.

120. B. Repp (1979) "Relative amplitude of aspiration noise as a voicing cue for syllable-initial stop consonants," *Lang. & Speech* **27**, 173–189.

121. B. Espinoza-Varas (1983) "Integration of spectral and temporal cues in discrimination of nonspeech sounds: A psychoacoustic analysis," *J. Acoust. Soc. Am.* **74**, 1687–1694.

122. M. Tekieli & W. Cullinan (1979) "The perception of temporally segmented vowels and consonant-vowel syllables," *J. Speech & Hear. Res.* **22**, 103–121.

123. H. Kato, M. Tsuzaki & Y. Sagisaka (1997) "Acceptability for temporal modification of consecutive segments in isolated words," *J. Acoust. Soc. Am.* **101**, 2311–2322.

124. R. Port & J. Dalby (1984) "Consonant/vowel ratio as a cue for voicing in English," *Perc. & Psychophys.* **32**, 141–152.

125. H. Fitch, T. Halwes, D. Erickson & A. Liberman (1980) "Perceptual equivalence of two acoustic cues for stop-consonant manner," *Perc. & Psychophys.* **27**, 343–350.

126. B. Repp (1984) "The role of release bursts in the perception of [s]-stop clusters," *J. Acoust. Soc. Am.* **75**, 1219–1230.

127. E. Parker, R. Diehl & K. Kluender (1986) "Trading relations in speech and nonspeech," *Perc. & Psychophys.* **30**, 129–142.

128. B. Repp (1983) "Bidirectional contrast effects in the perception of VC-CV sequences," *Perc. & Psychophys.* **33**, 147–155.

129. V. Tartter, D. Kat, A. Samuel & B. Repp (1983) "Perception of intervocalic stop consonants: The contributions of closure duration and formant transitions," *J. Acoust. Soc. Am.* **74**, 715–725.

130. S. Wayland, J. Miller & L. Volaitis (1994) "Influence of sentential speaking rate on the internal structure of phonetic categories," *J. Acoust. Soc. Am.* **95**, 2694–2701.

131. S. Nooteboom & C. Doodeman (1983) "Production and perception of vowel length in spoken sentences," *J. Acoust. Soc. Am.* **67**, 276–287.

132. J. Miller (1981) "Effects of speaking rate on segmental distinctions," in *Perspectives on the Study of Speech*, P. Eimas & S. Miller (eds.) (Erlbaum: Hillsdale, NJ), pp. 39–74.

133. B. Repp (1984) "Effects of temporal stimulus properties on the perception of the [sl]-[spl] distinction," *Phonetica* **41**, 117–124.

134. P. Shinn, S. Blumstein & A. Jongman (1985) "Limitations of context conditioned effects in the perception of [b] and [w]," *Perc. & Psychophys.* **38**, 397–407.

135. R. Verbrugge, W. Strange, D. Shankweiler & T. Edman (1976) "What information enables a listener to map a talker's vowel space?" *J. Acoust. Soc. Am.* **60**, 198–212.

136. W. Ainsworth (1974) "The influence of precursive sequences on the perception of synthesized vowels," *Lang. & Speech* **17**, 103–109.

137. J. Pickett & L. Decker (1960) "Time factors in perception of a double consonant," *Lang. & Speech* **3**, 1–17.

138. Q. Summerfield (1975) "How a full account of segmental perception depends on prosody and vice versa," in *Structure and Process in Speech Perception*, A. Cohen & S. Nooteboom (eds.) (Springer-Verlag: New York) pp.

139. W. Ainsworth (1973) "Durational cues in the perception of certain consonants," *Proc. Br. Acoust. Soc.* **2**, 1–4.

140. B. Repp, A. Liberman, T. Eccardt & D. Pesetsky (1978) "Perceptual integration of acoustic cues for stop, fricative, and affricate manner," *J. Exp. Psych. Human Perc. & Perf.* **4**, 621–636.

141. J. Brockx & S. Nooteboom (1982) "Intonation and the perceptual separation of simultaneous voices," *J. Phonetics* **10**, 23–36.

142. P. Lieberman & S. Michaels (1962) "Some aspects of fundamental frequency and envelope amplitude as related to the emotional content of speech," *J. Acoust. Soc. Am.* **34**, 922–927.

143. L. Streeter, N. Macdonald, W. Apple, R. Krauss & K. Galotti (1983) "Acoustic and perceptual indicators of emotional stress," *J. Acoust. Soc. Am.* **73**, 1354–1360.

144. D. R. Ladd, K. Silverman, F. Tolkmitt, G. Bergmann & K. Scherer (1985) "Evidence for the independent function of intonation contour type, voice quality, and F0 range in signaling speaker affect," *J. Acoust. Soc. Am.* **78**, 435–444.

145. B. Brown, W. Strong & A. Rencher (1973) "Perceptions of personality from speech: Effects of manipulations of acoustical parameters," *J. Acoust. Soc. Am.* **54**, 29–35.

146. C. Williams & K. Stevens (1972) "Emotions and speech: Some acoustical correlates," *J. Acoust. Soc. Am.* **52**, 1238–1250.

147. V. Tartter & D. Brown (1994) "Hearing smiles and frowns in normal and whisper registers," *J. Acoust. Soc. Am.* **96**, 2101–2107.

148. B. Blesser (1972) "Speech perception under conditions of spectral transformation: I. Phonetic characteristics," *J. Speech Hear. Res.* **15**, 4–41.

149. A. Sluijter, V. van Heuven & J. Pacilly (1997) "Spectral balance as a cue in the perception of linguistic stress," *J. Acoust. Soc. Am.* **101**, 503–513.

150. G. Stoll (1984) "Pitch of vowels: Experimental and theoretical investigation of its dependence on vowel quality," *Speech Comm.* **3**, 137–150.

*151. I. Lehiste (1970) *Suprasegmentals* (MIT Press: Cambridge, MA).

152. O. Ghitza (1992) "Auditory nerve representation as a basis for speech processing," in *Advances in Speech Signal Processing*, S. Furui & M. Sondhi (eds.) (Marcel Dekker: New York), pp. 453–485.

153. D. Fry (1955) "Duration and intensity as physical correlates of linguistic stress," *J. Acoust. Soc. Am.* **27**, 765–768.

154. D. Fry (1958) "Experiments in the perception of stress," *Lang. & Speech* **1**, 126–152.

155. D. Bolinger (1958) "A theory of pitch accent in English," *Word* **14**, 109–149.

156. H. Mol & E. Uhlenbeck (1956) "The linguistic relevance of intensity in stress," *Lingua* **5**, 205–213.

157. P. Lieberman (1960) "Some acoustic correlates of word stress in American English," *J. Acoust. Soc. Am.* **32**, 451–454.

158. P. Howell (1993) "Cue trading in the production and perception of vowel stress," *J. Acoust. Soc. Am.* **94**, 2063–2073.

159. J. Morton & W. Jassem (1965) "Acoustic correlates of stress," *Lang. & Speech* **8**, 159–181.

160. I. Fónagy (1962) "Electrophysiological and acoustic correlates of stress and stress perception," *J. Speech Hear. Res.* **9**, 231–244.

161. C. Adams & R. Munro (1978) "In search of the acoustic correlates of stress," *Phonetica* **35**, 125–156.

162. J. Gaitenby (1965) "Stress and the elastic syllable," *Haskins Labs.* **SR-41**, 137–152.

163. N. Thorsen (1982) "On the variability in F0 patterning and the function of F0 timing in languages where pitch cues stress," *Phonetica* **39**, 302–316.

164. V. van Heuven & L. Menert (1996) "Why stress position bias?" *J. Acoust. Soc Am.* **100**, 2439–2451.

165. D. Hermes (1997) "Timing of pitch movements and accentuation of syllables in Dutch," *J. Acoust. Soc. Am.* **102**, 2390–2402.

166. I. Lehiste & G. Peterson (1959) "Vowel amplitude and phonemic stress in American English," *J. Acoust. Soc. Am.* **31**, 428–435 (reprinted in *Readings in Acoustic Phonetics*, I. Lehiste (ed.) (MIT Press: Cambridge, MA, 1960), pp.).

167. J. Pierrehumbert (1979) "The perception of fundamental frequency declination," *J. Acoust. Soc. Am.* **60**, 363–369.

168. D. O'Shaughnessy (1974) "Consonant durations in clusters," *IEEE Trans. ASSP*, **ASSP-22**, 282–295.

169. C. Sorin (1981) "Functions, roles and treatments of intensity in speech," *J. Phonetics* **9**, 359–374.

170. L. Nakatani & J. Schaffer (1977) "Hearing 'words' without words: Prosodic cues for word perception," *J. Acoust. Soc. Am.* **63**, 234–245.

171. L. Larkey (1983) "Reiterant speech: An acoustic and perceptual validation," *J. Acoust. Soc. Am.* **73**, 1337–1345.

172. I. Lehiste (1977) "Isochrony reconsidered," *J. Phonetics* **5**, 253–263.

173. D. Klatt (1975) "Vowel lengthening is syntactically determined in a connected discourse," *J. Phonetics* **3**, 129–140.

174. P. Delattre (1970) "Syntax and intonation, a study in disagreement," *Modern Lang. J.* **54**, 3–9.

175. J. 't Hart, R. Collier & A. Cohen (1990) *A Perceptual Study of Intonation: An Experimental-phonetic Approach to Speech Melody* (Cambridge University Press: Cambridge).

176. M. Studdert-Kennedy & K. Hadding (1973) "Auditory and linguistic processes in the perception of intonation contours," *Lang. & Speech* **16**, 293–313.

177. K. Hadding & M. Studdert-Kennedy (1974) "Are you asking me, telling me, or talking to yourself?" *J. Phonetics* **2**, 7–14.

178. J. Kooij (1971) *Ambiguity in Natural Language* (North-Holland: Amsterdam).

179. L. Streeter (1978) "Acoustic determinants of phrase boundary perception," *J. Acoust. Soc. Am.* **64**, 1582–1592.

180. N. Macdonald (1976) "Duration as a syntactic boundary cue in ambiguous sentences," *Proc. IEEE Int. Conf. ASSP*, pp. 569–572.

181. I. Lehiste, J. Olive & L. Streeter (1974) "The role of duration in disambiguating syntactically ambiguous sentences," *J. Acoust. Soc. Am.* **60**, 119–1202.

182. D. Scott (1982) "Duration as a cue to the perception of a phrase boundary," *J. Acoust. Soc. Am.* **71**, 996–1007.

183. I. Lehiste (1960) "An acoustic-phonetic study of internal open juncture," *Phonetica* **5** Suppl., 1–54.

184. R. Nash (1970) "John likes Mary more than Bill," *Phonetica* **22**, 170–188.

185. A. Rosenberg, R. Schafer & L. Rabiner (1971) "Effects of smoothing and quantizing the parameters of formant-coded voiced speech," *J. Acoust. Soc. Am.* **50**, 1532–1538.

186. J. 't Hart (1974) "Discriminability of the size of pitch movements in speech," *IPO Annual Prog. Rep.* **9**, 56–63.

187. D. Klatt (1973) "Discrimination of fundamental frequency contours in synthetic speech: Implications for models of pitch perception," *J. Acoust. Soc. Am.* **53**, 8–16.

188. P. Léon & P. Martin (1972) "Machines and measurements," in *Intonation*, D. Bolinger (ed.) (Penguin: Harmondsworth), pp. 30–47.

189. M. Studdert-Kennedy (1980) "Perceiving phonetic segments," *Status Rep. on Speech Res.*, Haskins Labs., SR-61, pp. 123–134; also in *The Cognitive Representation of Speech*, T. Myers, J. Laver & J. Anderson (eds.) (North-Holland: Amsterdam).

190. R. Fox (1985) "Within- and between-series contrast in vowel identification: Full-vowel versus single-formant anchors," *Perc. & Psychophys.* **38**, 223–226.

191. D. Pisoni, J. Logan & S. Lively (1994) "Perceptual learning of non-native speech contrasts: Implications for theories of speech perception," in *Development of Speech Perception*, H. Nusbaum & J. Goodman (eds.) (MIT Press: Cambridge, MA), pp. 121–166.

192. J. Lauter (1983) "Stimulus characteristics and relative ear advantages: A new look at old data," *J. Acoust. Soc. Am.* **74**, 1–17.

193. H. Nusbaum (1984) "Possible mechanisms of duplex perception: Chirp identification versus dichotic fusion," *Perc. & Psychophys.* **35**, 94–101.

194. M. Schroeder (1975) "Models of hearing," *Proc. IEEE* **63**, 1332–1350.

195. A. Oppenheim & J. Lim (1981) "The importance of phase in signals," *IEEE Proc.* **69**, 529–541.

196. B. Scott (1976) "Temporal factors in vowel perception," *J. Acoust. Soc. Am.* **60**, 1354–1365.

197. M. Schroeder & H. Strube (1986) "Flat-spectrum speech," *J. Acoust. Soc. Am.* **79**, 1580–1583.

198. I. Pollack & J. Pickett (1963) "Intelligibility of excerpts from conversational speech," *Lang. & Speech* **6**, 165–171.

199. R. Reddy (1976) "Speech recognition by machine: A review," *Proc. IEEE*, **64**, 501–531.

200. G. Miller & S. Isard (1963) "Some perceptual consequences of linguistic rules," *J. Verbal Learning & Verbal Behavior* **2**, 217–228.

201. A. Bronkhorst, A. Bosman & C. Smoorenburg (1993) "A model for context effects in speech recognition," *J. Acoust. Soc. Am.* **93**, 499–509.

202. R. Warren (1970) "Perceptual restoration of missing speech sounds," *Science* **167**, 393–395.

203. A. Samuel (1981) "Phonemic restoration: Insights from a new methodology," *J. Exp. Psych. Genl.* **110**, 474–494.

204. R. Warren, K. Reiner, J. Bashford & B. Brubaker (1995) "Spectral redundancy: Intelligibility of sentences heard through narrow spectral slits," *Perc. & Psychophys.* **57**, 175–182.

205. P. Eimas, C. Tajchman, L. Nygaard & N. Keuthen (1996) "Phonemic restoration and integration during dichotic listening," *J. Acoust. Soc. Am.* **99**, 1141–1147.

206. A. Cutler & D. Foss (1977) "On the role of sentence stress in sentence processing," *Lang. & Speech* **20**, 1–10.

207. J. Martin (1972) "Rhythmic (hierarchical) versus serial structure in speech and other behavior," *Psych. Rev.* **79**, 487–509.

*208. R. Cole & J. Jakimik (1980) "A model of speech perception," in *Perception & Production of Fluent Speech*, R. Cole (ed.) (Erlbaum: Hillsdale, NJ), pp. 133–163.

209. W. Marslen-Wilson (1985) "Speech shadowing and speech comprehension," *Speech Comm.*, **4**, 55–73.

210. R. Wilson, J. Arcos & H. Jones (1984) "Word recognition with segmented-alternated CVC words: A preliminary report on listeners with normal hearing," *J. Speech Hear. Res.* **27**, 378–386.

211. F. Grosjean (1985) "The recognition of words after their acoustic offset: Evidence and implications," *Perc. & Psychophys.* **38**, 299–310.

212. B. Berglund, K. Harder & A. Preiss (1994) "Annoyance perception of sound and information extraction," *J. Acoust. Soc. Am.* **95**, 1501–1509.

213. J. Kreiman, B. Gerratt, G. Kempster, A. Erman & G. Berke (1993) "Perceptual evaluation of voice quality: Review, tutorial and a framework for future research," *J. Speech Hear. Res.* **30**, 21–40.

214. I. Noordhoek & R. Drullman (1997) "Effect of reducing temporal intensity modulations on sentence intelligibility," *J. Acoust. Soc. Am.* **101**, 498–502.

215. A. Boothroyd, B. Mulhearn, J. Gong & J. Ostroff (1996) "Effects of spectral smearing on phoneme and word recognition," *J. Acoust Soc. Am.* **100**, 1807–1818.

216. T. Baer & B. Moore (1994) "Effects of spectral smearing on the intelligibility of sentences in the presence of interfering speech," *J. Acoust. Soc. Am.* **95**, 2277–2280.

217. D. Rostolland (1985) "Intelligibility of shouted voice," *Acustica*, **57**, 103–121.

218. D. Beasley & J. Maki (1976) "Time- and frequency-altered speech," in *Contemporary Issues in Experimental Phonetics*, N. Lass (ed.) (Academic: New York), pp. 419–458.

219. C. Sherrick (1984) "Basic and applied research on tactile aids for deaf people: Progress and prospects," *J. Acoust. Soc. Am.* **75**, 1325–1342.

220. J. Pickett (1982) "Hearing through sight and feeling," *IEEE Spectrum* **19**, no. 4, 37–41.

221. C. Reed, W. Rabinowitz, N. Durlach, L. Braida, S. Conway-Fithian & M. Schultz (1985) "Research on the Tadoma method of speech communication," *J. Acoust. Soc. Am.* **77**, 247–257.

CHAPTER 6—ANALYSIS

1. B. Kingsbury, N. Morgan & S. Greenberg (1998) "Robust speech recognition using the modulation spectrogram," *Speech Comm.* **25**, 117–132.

2. R. Reininger & J. Gibson (1985) "Backward adaptive lattice and transversal predictors in ADPCM," *IEEE Trans. Comm.*, **COM-33**, 74–82.

3. A. Nuttall (1981) "Some windows with very good sidelobe behavior," *IEEE Trans. ASSP*, **ASSP-29**, 84–91.

4. M. Ross, H. Schafer, A. Cohen, R. Freuberg & H. Manley (1974) "Average magnitude difference function pitch extractor," *IEEE Trans. ASSP*, **ASSP-22**, 353–362.

5. H. Strube, D. Helling, A. Krause & M. Schroeder (1985) "Word and speaker recognition based on entire words without framewise analysis," in *Speech and Speaker Recognition*, M. Schroeder (ed.) (Karger: Basel), pp. 80–114.

6. A. Oppenheim & R. Schafer (1975) *Digital Signal Processing* (Prentice-Hall: Englewood Cliffs, NJ).

*7. J. Flanagan (1972) *Speech Analysis, Synthesis and Perception* (Springer-Verlag: New York).

8. S. McCandless (1974) "An algorithm for automatic formant extraction using linear prediction spectra," *IEEE Trans. ASSP*, **ASSP-22**, 135–141.

9. R. Schwartz & S. Roucos (1983) "A comparison of methods for 300–400 b/s vocoders," *Proc. IEEE Int. Conf. ASSP*, pp. 69–72.

10. G. Kopec (1986) "A family of formant trackers based on hidden Markov models," *Proc. IEEE Int. Conf. ASSP*, pp. 1225–1228.

11. M. Paraskevas & J. Mourjopoulos (1995) "A differential perceptual audio coding method with reduced bitrate requirements," *IEEE Trans. Speech & Audio Proc.*, **3**, 490–503.

12. R. Monsen & A.M. Engebretson (1983) "The accuracy of formant frequency measurements: A comparison of spectrographic analysis & linear prediction," *J. Speech Hear. Res.* **26**, 89–97.

13. R. Smits (1994) "Accuracy of quasistationary analysis of highly dynamic speech signals," *J. Acoust. Soc. Am.* **96**, 3401–3415.

14. R. Snell & F. Milinazzo (1993) "Formant location from LPC analysis data," *IEEE Trans. Speech & Audio Proc.*, **1**, 129–134.

15. B. Yegnanarayana (1978) "Formant extraction from linear-prediction phase spectra," *J. Acoust. Soc. Am.* **63**, 1638–1640.

16. N. S. Reddy & M. Swamy (1984) "High-resolution formant extraction from linear prediction phase spectra," *IEEE Trans. ASSP*, **ASSP-32**, 1136–1144.

17. N. Mikami & R. Ohba (1984) "Pole-zero analysis of voiced speech using group delay characteristics," *IEEE Trans. ASSP*, **ASSP-32**, 1095–1097.

18. A. Rosenberg, R. Schafer & L. Rabiner (1971) "Effects of smoothing & quantizing the parameters of formant-coded voiced speech," *J. Acoust. Soc. Am.* **50**, 1532–1538.

19. S. Palethorpe, R. Wales, J. Clark & T. Sanserrick (1996) "Vowel classification in children," *J. Acoust. Soc. Am.* **100**, 3843–3851.

20. S. Kajita & F. Itakura (1995) "Robust speech feature extraction using SBCOR analysis," *Proc. IEEE Int. Conf. ASSP*, pp. 421–424.

21. M. Bakkum, R. Plomp & L. Pols (1995) "Objective analysis versus subjective assessment of vowels pronounced by deaf and normal-hearing children," *J. Acoust. Soc. Am.* **98**, 745–762.

22. P. Maragos, J. Kaiser & T. Quatieri (1993) "Energy separation in signal modulations with application to speech analysis," *IEEE Trans. Signal Proc.*, **41**, 3024–3051.

23. H. Hanson, P. Maragos & A. Potamianos (1994) "A system for finding speech formants and modulations via energy separation," *IEEE Trans. Speech & Audio Proc.*, **2**, 436–443.

24. J. Markel & A. Gray (1976) *Linear Prediction of Speech* (Springer-Verlag: New York).

25. J. Makhoul (1975) "Linear prediction: A tutorial review," *Proc. IEEE*, **63**, 561–580.

26. D. Hermes (1993) "Pitch analysis," in *Visual Representations of Speech Signals*, M. Cooke *et al* (eds.) (John Wiley & Sons: Chichester), pp. 3–24.

27. D. Childers & C. Lee (1987) "Co-channel speech separation," *Proc. IEEE Int. Conf. ASSP*, pp. 181–184.

28. A. Isaksson & M. Millnert (1989) "Inverse glottal filtering using a parameterized input model," *Signal Proc.*, **18**, 435–445.

29. L. Vanhove (1983) "An algorithm for LPC gain matching," *IEEE Trans. ASSP*, **ASSP-31**, 1566–1569.

30. J. LeRoux & C. Gueguen (1977) "A fixed point computation of partial correlation coefficients," *IEEE Trans. ASSP*, **ASSP-25**, 257–259.

31. G. Saleh, M. Niranjan & W. Fitzgerald (1995) "The use of maximum a posteriori parameters in linear prediction of speech," *Proc. Europ. Conf. Speech Comm. & Tech.*, pp. 263–266.

32. M. Morf, B. Dickinson, T. Kailath & A. Vieira (1977) "Efficient solution of covariance equations for linear prediction," *IEEE Trans. ASSP*, **ASSP-25**, 429–433.

33. L. Rabiner & R. Schafer (1979) *Digital Processing of Speech Signals* (Prentice-Hall: Englewood Cliffs, NJ).

34. S. Jean & L. Lee (1983) "An efficient low bit rate speech coder with simplified algorithms for digital speech communications," *Proc. IEEE Globecom*, pp. 799–803.

35. K. Assaleh & R. Mammone (1994) "New Lp-derived features for speaker identification," *IEEE Trans. Speech & Audio Proc.*, **2**, 630–638.

36. D. Wong, C. Hsiao & J. Markel (1980) "Spectral mismatch due to preemphasis in LPC analysis/synthesis," *IEEE Trans. ASSP*, **ASSP-28**, 263–264.

37. J. Campbell & T. Tremain (1986) "Voiced/unvoiced classification of speech with applications to the U.S. government LPC-10E algorithm," *Proc. IEEE Int. Conf. ASSP*, pp. 473–476.

38. J. Deller (1983) "On the time domain properties of the two-pole model of the glottal waveform and implications for LPC," *Speech Comm.*, **2**, 57–63.

39. Atlas, L. & Hengky, L. (1985) "Cross-channel correlation for the enhancement of noisy speech," *Proc. IEEE Int. Conf. ASSP*, pp. 724–727.

40. E. Schichor & H. Silverman (1984) "An improved LPC algorithm for voiced-speech synthesis," *IEEE Trans. ASSP*, **ASSP-32**, 180–183.

41. D. Messerschmitt (1984) "Echo cancellation in speech and data transmission," *IEEE J. Selected Areas in Comm.* **SAC-2**, 283–297.

42. C. Xydeas, C. Evci & R. Steele (1982) "Sequential adaptive predictors for ADPCM speech encoders," *IEEE Trans. Comm.*, **COM-30**, 1942–1954.

43. J. Turner (1985) "Recursive least-squares estimation and lattice filters," in *Adaptive Filters*, Cowan & Grant (eds.) (Prentice-Hall: Englewood Cliffs, NJ), pp. 91–134.

44. H. Wakita (1979) "Estimation of vocal-tract shapes from acoustical analysis of the speech wave: The state of the art," *IEEE Trans. ASSP*, **ASSP-27**, 281–285.

45. P. Milenkovic (1984) "Vocal tract area functions from 2-point acoustic measurements with formant frequency constraints," *IEEE Trans. ASSP*, **ASSP-32**, 1122–1135.

46. J. Makhoul (1977) "Stable and efficient lattice methods for linear prediction," *IEEE Trans. ASSP*, **ASSP-25**, 423–428.

47. J. Makhoul & L. Cosell (1981) "Adaptive lattice analysis of speech," *IEEE Trans. ASSP*, **ASSP-29**, 654–659.

48. M. Honig & D. Messerschmidt (1982) "Comparison of adaptive linear prediction algorithms in PCM," *IEEE Trans. Comm.*, **COM-30**, 1775–1785.

49. S. Sihghal & B. Atal (1984) "Improving performance of multi-pulse LPC coders at low bit rates," *Proc. IEEE Int. Conf. ASSP*, pp. 1.3.1–4.

50. Y. Miyoshi, K. Yamato, M. Yanagida & O. Kakusho (1986) "Analysis of speech signals of short pitch period by the sample-selective linear prediction," *Proc. IEEE Int. Conf. ASSP*, pp. 1245–1248.

51. W. Harrison, J. Lim & E. Singer (1986) "A new application of adaptive noise cancellation," *IEEE Trans. ASSP*, **ASSP-34**, 21–27.

52. K. Paliwal & P. Rao (1982) "On the performance of Burg's method of maximum entropy spectral analysis when applied to voiced speech," *Signal Proc.* **4**, 59–63.

53. K. Paliwal (1984) "Performance of the weighted Burg methods of AR spectral estimation for pitch-synchronous analysis of voiced speech," *Speech Comm.* **3**, 221–231.

54. C-H. Lee (1988) "On robust linear prediction of speech," *IEEE Trans. ASSP*, **ASSP-36**, 642–650.

55. H. Hermansky, B. Hanson, H. Wakita & H. Fujisaki (1985) "Linear predictive modeling of speech in modified spectral domains," *Digital Proc. on Signals in Comm., IERE Conf.*, pp. 55–62.

56. H. Hermansky (1990) "Perceptual linear prediction (PLP) analysis of speech," *J. Acoust. Soc. Am.* **87**, 1738–1752.

57. H. Hermansky (1998) "Should recognizers have ears?," *Speech Comm.* **25**, 3–27.

58. M. Slaney & R. Lyon (1993) "On the importance of time—a temporal representation of sound," in *Visual Representations of Speech Signals*, M. Cooke *et al* (eds.) (John Wiley & Sons: Chichester), pp. 95–116.

59. O. Ghitza (1994) "Auditory models and human performance in tasks related to speech coding and speech recognition," *IEEE Trans. Speech & Audio Proc.* **2**, 115–132.

60. J. Hernando & C. Nadeu (1994) "Speech recognition in noisy car environment based on OSALPC representation and robust similarity measuring techniques," *Proc. IEEE Int. Conf. ASSP* vol. II, pp. 69–72.

61. D. Mansour & B-H. Juang (1989) "The short-term modified coherence representation and its application for noisy speech recognition," *IEEE Trans. ASSP* **ASSP-37**, 795–804.

62. P. Chu & D. Messerschmitt (1982) "A frequency weighted Itakura–Saito spectral distance measure," *IEEE Trans. ASSP* **ASSP-30**, 545–560.

63. H. W. Strube (1980) "Linear prediction on a warped frequency scale," *J. Acoust. Soc. Am.* **68**, 1071–1076.

64. Y. Miyanaga, N. Miki & N. Nagai (1986) "Adaptive identification of a time-varying ARMA speech model," *IEEE Trans. ASSP* **ASSP-34**, 423–433.

65. H. Morikawa & H. Fujisaki (1986) "A speech analysis-synthesis system based on the ARMA model and its evaluation," *Proc. IEEE Int. Conf. ASSP* pp. 1253–1256.

66. D. Childers, J. Principe & Y. Ting (1995) "Adaptive WRLS-VFF for speech analysis," *IEEE Trans. Speech & Audio Proc.* **3**, 209–213.

67. I-T. Lim & B. Lee (1996) "Lossy pole-zero modeling for speech signals," *IEEE Trans. Speech & Audio Proc.* **4**, 81–88.

68. S. Boll & D. Pulsipher (1980) "Suppression of acoustic noise in speech using two microphone adaptive noise cancellation," *IEEE Trans. ASSP* **ASSP-28**, 752–753.

69. W. Gardner & B. Rao (1997) "Non-causal all-pole modeling of voiced speech," *IEEE Trans. Speech & Audio Proc.* **5**, 1–10.

70. B. Friedlander (1983) "Efficient algorithm for ARMA spectral estimation," *IEE Proc.* **130**, Part F, 195–201.

71. H. Morikawa & H. Fujisaki (1984) "System identification of the speech production process based on a state-space representation," *IEEE Trans. ASSP* **ASSP-32**, 252–262.

72. H. Morikawa & H. Fujisaki (1982) "Adaptive analysis of speech based on a pole-zero representation," *IEEE Trans. ASSP* **ASSP-30**, 77–88.

73. K. Song & C. Un (1982) "Pole-zero modeling of noisy speech and its application to vocoding," *Proc. IEEE Int. Conf. ASSP* pp. 1581–1584.

74. W. Verhelst & O. Steenhaut (1986) "A new model for the short-time complex cepstrum of voiced speech," *IEEE Trans. ASSP* **ASSP-34**, 43–51.

75. A. Noll (1967) "Cepstrum pitch determination," *J. Acoust. Soc. Am.* **41**, 293–309.

76. K. Tokuda, T. Kobayashi, T. Masuko & S. Imai (1994) "Mel-generalized cepstral analysis – a unified view to speech spectral estimation," *Int. Conf. On Spoken Lang. Proc.*, pp. 1043–1046.

77. P. Alexandre & P. Lockwood (1993) "Root cepstral analysis: A unified view," *Speech Comm.*, **12**, 277–288.

78. D. Duttweiler & D. Messerschmitt (1976) "Nearly instantaneous companding for nonuniformly quantized PCM," *IEEE Trans. Comm.*, **COM-24**, 864–873.

79. V. Algazi, K. Brown, M. Ready, D. Irvine, C. Cadwell & S. Chung (1993) "Transform representation of the spectra of acoustic speech segments with applications," *IEEE Trans. Speech & Audio Proc.* **1**, 180–195; 277–286.

80. G. Evangelista (1993) "Pitch-synchronous wavelet representations of speech and music signals," *IEEE Trans. Signal Proc.*, **41**, 3313–3330.

81. F. Hlawatsch & G. Boudreaux-Bartels (1992) "Linear and quadratic time-frequency signal representations," *IEEE Signal Proc. Mag.*, **9**, no. 2, 21–67.

82. I. Pintér (1996) "Perceptual wavelet-representation of speech signals and its application to speech enhancement," *Comp., Speech & Lang.*, **10**, 1–22.

83. D. Stefaniou, R. Kastantin & G. Feng (1995) "Speech coding based on the discrete-time wavelet transform and human auditory system properties," *Proc. Europ. Conf. Speech Comm. & Tech.*, pp. 661–664.

84. M. Rangoussi & F. Pedersen (1995) "Second- and third-order Wigner distributions in hierarchical recognition of speech phonemes," *Proc. Europ. Conf. Speech Comm. & Tech.*, pp. 259–262.

85. J. Pitton, L. Atlas & P. Loughlin (1994) "Applications of time-frequency distributions to speech processing," *IEEE Trans. Speech & Audio Proc.*, **22**, 554–566.

86. G. Kubin (1995) "Nonlinear processing of speech," in *Speech Coding and Synthesis*, W. Kleijn & K. Paliwal (eds.) (Elsevier: Amsterdam), pp. 557–610.

87. M. Nakatsui & P. Mermelstein (1982) "Subjective speech-to-noise ratio as a measure of speech quality for digital waveform coders," *J. Acoust. Soc. Am.* **72**, 1136–1144.

88. A. Kumar & S. Mullick (1996) "Nonlinear dynamical analysis of speech," *J. Acoust. Soc. Am.* **100**, 615–629.

89. B. Townshend (1991) "Nonlinear prediction of speech," *Proc. IEEE Int. Conf. ASSP*, pp. 425–428.

90. P. Maragos (1991) "Fractal aspects of speech signals: Dimension and interpolation," *Proc. IEEE Int. Conf. ASSP*, pp. 417–420.

91. Z. Wang (1996) "Predictive fractal interpolation mapping: Differential speech coding at low bit rates," *Proc. IEEE Int. Conf. ASSP*, pp. 251–254.

92. W. Hess (1992) "Pitch and voicing determination," in *Advances in Speech Signal Processing*, S. Furui & M. Sondhi (eds.) (Marcel Dekker: New York), pp. 3–48.

93. L. Rabiner, M. Cheng, A. Rosenberg & C. McGonegal (1976) "A comparative performance study of several pitch detection algorithms," *IEEE Trans. ASSP*, **ASSP-24**, 399–418.

94. B. Atal & L. Rabiner (1976) "A pattern recognition approach to voiced-unvoiced-silence classification with applications to speech recognition," *IEEE Trans. ASSP*, **ASSP-24**, 201–212.

95. L. Siegel & A. Bessey (1982) "Voiced/unvoiced/mixed excitation classification of speech," *IEEE Trans. ASSP*, **ASSP-30**, 451–460.

96. Y. Qi & B. Hunt (1993) "Voiced-unvoiced-silence classifications of speech using hybrid features and a network classifier," *IEEE Trans. Speech & Audio Proc.* **1**, 250–255.

97. B. Gold & L. Rabiner (1969) "Parallel processing techniques for estimating pitch periods of speech in the time domain," *J. Acoust. Soc. Am.* **46**, 442–448.

98. D. Krubsack & R. Niederjohn (1991) "An autocorrelation pitch detector and voicing decision with confidence measures developed for noise-corrupted speech," *IEEE Trans. ASSP* **ASSP-39**, 319–329.

99. M. Sondhi (1968) "New methods of pitch extraction," *IEEE Trans. Audio and Electroac.* **AU-16**, 262–266.

100. K. Paliwal & B. Atal (1993) "Efficient vector quantization of LPC parameters at 24 bits/frame," *IEEE Trans. Speech & Audio Proc.* **1**, 3–14.

101. M. Schroeder (1968) "Period histogram and product spectrum: New methods for fundamental frequency measurement," *J. Acoust. Soc. Am.* **43**, 829–834.

102. H. Duifhuis, L. Willems & R. Sluyter (1982) "Measurement of pitch in speech: An implementation of Goldstein's theory of pitch perception," *J. Acoust. Soc. Am.* **71**, 1568–1580.

103. D. Friedman (1978) "Multidimensional pseudo-maximum-likelihood pitch estimation," *IEEE Trans. ASSP* **ASSP-26**, 185–196.

104. L. van Immerseel & J-P. Martens (1992) "Pitch and voiced/unvoiced determination with an auditory model," *J. Acoust. Soc. Am.* **91**, 3511–3526.

105. C. McGonegal, L. Rabiner & A. Rosenberg (1977) "A subjective evaluation of pitch detection methods using LPC synthesized speech," *IEEE Trans. ASSP* **ASSP-25**, 221–229.

106. H. Hermansky & N. Morgan (1994) "RASTA processing of speech," *IEEE Trans. Speech & Audio Proc.* **2**, 578–589.

107. K. Aikawa, H. Singer, H. Kawahara & Y. Tokhura (1996) "Cepstral representation of speech motivated by time-frequency masking: An application to speech recognition," *J. Acoust Soc. Am.* **100**, 603–614.

108. H. Kawahara (1997) "Speech representation and transformation using adaptive interpolation of weighted spectrum: Vocoder revisited," *Proc. IEEE Int. Conf. ASSP*, pp. 1303–1306.

109. D. Macho & C. Nadeu (1998) "On the interaction between time and frequency filtering of speech parameters for robust speech recognition," *Int. Conf. on Spoken Lang. Proc.*, pp. 1487–1490.

110. L. Rabiner, M. Sambur & C. Schmidt (1975) "Applications of a non-linear smoothing algorithm to speech processing," *IEEE Trans. ASSP*, **ASSP-23**, 552–557.

CHAPTER 7—CODING

*1. A. Spanias (1994) "Speech coding: A tutorial review," *Proc. IEEE* **82**, 1541–1582.

*2. A. Gersho & R. Steele (1984) "Encryption of analog signals: A perspective," *IEEE J. Selected Areas in Comm.* **SAC-2**, 423–425.

3. H. Beker & F. Piper (1985) *Secure Speech Communications* (Academic: London).

4. L.-S. Lee & G.-C. Chou (1986) "A general theory for asynchronous speech encryption techniques," *IEEE J. on Selected Areas in Comm.* **SAC-4**, 280–287.

5. D. Hiotakakos, C. Xydeas & C. Boyd (1994) "A new approach for scrambling speech signals prior to analysis-by-synthesis LPC coding," *Proc. Europ. Signal Proc. Conf.*, pp. 987–990.

6. V. Senk, V. Delić & V. Milosević (1997) "A new speech scrambling concept based on Hadamard matrices," *IEEE Signal Proc. Lett.* **4**, 161–163.

7. S. Dimolitsas & J. Phipps (1995) "Experimental quantification of voice transmission quality of mobile-satellite personal communications systems," *IEEE Trans. Selected Areas in Comm.*, **13**, 458–464.

8. V. Cuperman & A. Gersho (1993) "Low delay speech coding," *Speech Comm.* **12**, 193–204.

*9. J. Flanagan, M. Schroeder, B. Atal, R. Crochiere, N. Jayant & J. Tribolet (1979) "Speech coding," *IEEE Trans. Comm.* **COM-27**, 710–736.

10. P. Papamichalis & G. Doddington (1984) "A speaker recognizability test," *Proc. IEEE Int. Conf. ASSP* pp. 18B.6.1–4.

11. I. Gerson & M. Jasiuk (1991) "Vector sum excited linear prediction (VSELP)," in *Advances in Speech Coding*, B. Atal, V. Cuperman & A. Gersho (eds.) (Kluwer: Norwell, MA), pp. 69–79.

12. R. Cox (1997) "Three new speech coders from the ITU cover a range of applications," *IEEE Comm. Mag.* **35**, no. 9, 40–47.

13. A. Oppenheim & R. Schafer (1975) *Digital Signal Processing* (Prentice-Hall: Englewood Cliffs, NJ).

14. N. Jayant & P. Noll (1984) *Digital Coding of Waveforms* (Prentice-Hall: Englewood Cliffs, NJ).

15. M. Paez & T. Glisson (1972) "Minimum mean squared error quantization in speech," *IEEE Trans. Comm.*, **COM-20**, 225–230.

16. N. Kitawaki (1992) "Quality assessment of coded speech," in *Advances in Speech Signal Processing*, S. Furui & M. Sondhi (eds.) (Marcel Dekker: New York), pp. 357–385.

17. D. Goodman, C. Scagliola, R. Crochiere, L. Rabiner & J. Goodman (1979) "Objective and subjective performance of tandem connections of waveform coders with an LPC vocoder," *Bell Syst. Tech. J.* **58**, 601–629.

18. S. Voran (1998) "A simplified version of the ITU algorithm for objective measurement of speech codec quality," *Proc. IEEE Int. Conf. ASSP* pp. 537–540.

19. L. Rabiner & R. Schafer (1979) *Digital Processing of Speech Signals* (Prentice-Hall: Englewood Cliffs, NJ).

20. N. Jayant, J. Johnston & R. Safranek (1993) "Signal compression based on models of human perception," *Proc. IEEE* **81**, 1385–1422.

21. V. Viswanathan, J. Makhoul & R. Schwartz (1982) "Medium and low bit rate speech transmission," in *Automatic Speech Analysis and Recognition*, J.-P. Haton (ed.) (Reidel: Dordrecht), pp. 21–48.

22. R. Gray (1984) "Vector quantization," *IEEE ASSP Mag.* **1**, 4–29.

23. W-Y. Chan & A. Gersho (1994) "Generalized product code vector quantization: A family of efficient techniques for signal compression," *Digital Signal Proc.* **4**, 95–126.

*24. A. Gersho & R. Gray (1991) *Vector Quantization and Signal Compression* (Kluwer: Norwell, MA).

25. P. Hedelin, P. Knagenhjelm & M. Skoglund (1995) "Vector quantization for speech transmission," in *Speech Coding and Synthesis*, W. Kleijn & K. Paliwal (eds.) (Elsevier: New York), pp. 311–345.

26. H. Abut, R. Gray & G. Rebolledo (1982) "Vector quantization of speech," *IEEE Trans. ASSP* **ASSP-30**, 423–435.

27. D. Paul (1982) "A 500–800 bps adaptive vector quantization vocoder using a perceptually motivated distance measure," *Globecom Conf.*, pp. 1079–1082.

28. A. McCree, K. Truong, E. George, T. Barnwell & V. Viswanathan (1996) "A 2.4 kbit/s coder candidate for the new U.S. Federal standard," *Proc. IEEE Int. Conf. ASSP*, pp. 200–203.

29. K. Itoh, N. Kitawaki, H. Irii & H. Nagabuchi (1994) "A new artificial speech signal for objective quality evaluation of speech coding systems," *IEEE Trans. Comm.*, **COM-42**, 664–672.

30. Y. Linde, A. Buzo & R. Gray (1980) "An algorithm for vector quantizer design," *IEEE Trans. Comm.* **COM-28**, 84–95.

31. X. Wu & L. Guan (1994) "Acceleration of the LBG algorithm," *IEEE Trans. Comm.* **COM-42**, 1518–1523.

32. N. Phamdo, N. Farvardin & T. Moriya (1993) "A unified approach to tree-structured and multistage vector quantization for noisy channels," *IEEE Trans. Info. Thy.* **IT-39**, 835–851.

33. R. Hagen (1996) "Robust LPC spectrum quantization—vector quantization by a linear mapping of a block code," *IEEE Trans. Speech & Audio Proc.*, **4**, 266–280.

34. Z-X. Yuan, B-L. Xu & C-Z. Yu (1999) "Binary quantization of feature vectors for robust text-independent speaker identification," *IEEE Trans. Speech & Audio Proc.*, **7**, 70–78.

35. T. Berger (1971) *Rate Distortion Theory* (Prentice-Hall: Englewood Cliffs, NJ).

36. N. Moayeri & D. Neuhoff (1994) "Time-memory tradeoffs in vector quantizer codebook searching based on decision trees," *IEEE Trans. Speech & Audio Proc.* **2**, 490–506.

37. H. Fehn & P. Noll (1982) "Multipath search coding of stationary signals with applications to speech," *IEEE Trans. Comm.* **COM-30**, 687–701.

38. B-H. Juang (1986) "Design and performance of trellis vector quantizers for speech signals," *Proc. IEEE Int. Conf. ASSP*, pp. 437–440.

39. C-D. Bei & R. Gray (1986) "Simulation of vector trellis encoding systems," *IEEE Trans. Comm.* **COM-34**, 214–218.

40. M. Soleymani (1994) "A new tandem source-channel trellis coding scheme," *IEEE Trans. Speech & Audio Proc.* **2**, 24–28.

41. T. Svendsen (1986) "Multi-dimensional quantization applied to predictive coding of speech," *Proc. IEEE Int. Conf. ASSP*, pp. 3063–3066.

42. A. Haoui & D. Messerschmitt (1985) "Embedded coding of speech: A vector quantization approach," *Proc. IEEE Int. Conf. ASSP*, pp. 1703–1706.

43. P. Sriram & M. Marcellin (1994) "Performance of adaptive predictive algorithms for trellis coded quantization of speech," *IEEE Trans. Comm.*, **COM-42**, 1512–1517.

44. S. Quackenbush, T. Barnwell & M. Clements (1988) *Objective Measures for Speech Quality* (Prentice-Hall: Englewood Cliffs, NJ).

45. S. Wang, A. Sekey & A. Gersho (1992) "An objective measure for predicting subjective quality of speech coders," *IEEE Trans. Selected Areas in Comm.*, **10**, 819–829.

46. N. Johannesson (1997) "The ETSI computation model: A tool for transmission planning of telephone networks," *IEEE Comm. Mag.*, **35**, no. 1, 71–79.

47. S. Dimolitsas, F. Corcoran & C. Ravishankar (1995) "Dependence of opinion scores on listening sets used in degradation category rating assessments," *IEEE Trans. Speech & Audio Proc.*, **3**, 421–424.

48. R. Cox & P. Kroon (1996) "Low bit-rate speech coders for multimedia communication," *IEEE Comm. Mag.*, **34**, no. 12, 34–41.

49. M. Nakatsui & P. Mermelstein (1982) "Subjective speech-to-noise ratio as a measure of speech quality for digital waveform coders," *J. Acoust. Soc. Am.* **72**, 1136–1144.

50. M. Perkins, K. Evans, D. Pascal & L. Thorpe (1997) "Characterizing the subjective performance of the ITU 8 kb/s speech coding algorithm—ITU G.729," *IEEE Comm. Mag.*, **35**, no. 9, 71–79.

51. W. Voiers (1977) "Diagnostic acceptability measure for speech communication systems," *Proc. IEEE Int. Conf. ASSP*, pp. 204–207.

52. K. Jonnalagadda & L. Schiff (1984) "Improvements in capacity of analog voice multiplex systems carried by satellite," *Proc. IEEE* **72**, 1537–1547.

53. D. Duttweiler & D. Messerschmitt (1976) "Nearly instantaneous companding for nonuniformly quantized PCM," *IEEE Trans. Comm.* **COM-24**, 864–873.

54. P. Chu & D. Messerschmitt (1982) "A frequency weighted Itakura-Saito spectral distance measure," *IEEE Trans. ASSP* **ASSP-30**, 545–560.

*55. J. Gibson (1982) "Adaptive prediction in speech differential encoding systems," *Proc. IEEE* **68**, 488–525.

56. H. Dunn & S. White (1940) "Statistical measurements on conversational speech," *J. Acoust. Soc. Am.* **11**, 278–288.

57. J. Makhoul & M. Berouti (1979) "Adaptive noise spectral shaping and entropy coding in predictive coding of speech," *IEEE Trans. ASSP* **ASSP-27**, 63–73.

58. R. Ramachandran (1995) "The use of pitch prediction in speech coding," in *Modern Methods of Speech Processing*, R. Ramachandran & R. Mammone (eds.) (Kluwer: Norwell, MA), pp. 3–22.

59. M. Honda & F. Itakura (1979) "Bit allocation in time and frequency domains for predictive coding of speech," *IEEE Trans. ASSP* **ASSP-32**, 465–473.

60. S. McClellan & J. Gibson (1999) "Efficient pitch filter encoding for variable speech processing," *IEEE Trans. Speech & Audio Proc.* **7**, 18–29.

*61. B. Atal & M. Schroeder (1979) "Predictive coding of speech signals and subjective error criteria," *IEEE Trans. ASSP* **ASSP-27**, 247–254.

62. K. Paliwal & B. Atal (1993) "Efficient vector quantization of LPC parameters at 24 bits/frame," *IEEE Trans. Selected Areas in Comm.*, **11**, 3–14.

63. M. Schroeder, B. Atal & J. Hall (1979) "Optimizing digital speech coders by exploiting masking properties of the human ear," *J. Acoust. Soc. Am.* **66**, 1647–1652.

64. R. Veldhuis & A. Kohlrausch (1995) "Waveform coding and auditory masking," in *Speech Coding and Synthesis*, W. Kleijn & K. Paliwal (eds.) (Elsevier: New York), pp. 397–431.

65. J. Skoglund & W. Kleijn (1998) "On the significance of temporal masking in speech coding," *Int. Conf. on Spoken Lang. Proc.* pp. 1791–1794.

66. T. Tremain (1985) "The government standard adaptive predictive coding algorithm: APC-04," *Speech Tech.* Feb./Mar., 52–62.

67. J-H. Chen, R. Cox, Y-C. Lin, N. Jayant & M. Melchner (1992) "A low-delay CELP coder for the CCITT 16 kb/s speech coding standard," *IEEE Trans. Selected Areas in Comm.*, **10**, 830–849.

68. J-H. Chen & A. Gersho (1995) "Adaptive postfiltering for quality enhancement of coded speech," *IEEE Trans. Speech & Audio Proc.*, **3**, 59–71.

69. S. Hrvatin & J. Mark (1984) "Predictive entropy coding for speech analysis," *IEE Proc.* part F, **131**, 537–541.

70. P. Bocci & J. LoCicero (1982) "Bit rate reduction of digitized speech using entropy techniques," *IEEE Trans. Comm.*, **COM-31**, 424–430.

71. K. Wong & R. Steele (1985) "ADPCM using vector predictor and forward adaptive quantiser with step-size prediction," *Electron. Lett.* **21**, 74–75.

72. R. McAulay & T. Quatieri (1992) "Low-rate speech coding based on the sinusoidal model," in *Advances in Speech Signal Processing*, S. Furui & M. Sondhi (eds.) (Marcel Dekker: New York), pp. 165–208.

73. J. Makhoul (1985) "Speech coding and processing," in *Modern Signal Processing*, T. Kailath (ed.) (Hemisphere: New York), pp. 211–247.

74. C. Un & D. Cho (1982) "Hybrid companding delta modulation with variable-rate sampling," *IEEE Trans. Comm.*, **COM-30**, 593–599.

75. S. Crisafulli, G. Rey, C. Johnson & R. Kennedy (1994) "A coupled approach to ADPCM adaptation," *IEEE Trans. Speech & Audio Proc.* **2**, 90–93.

76. P. Noll (1975) "A comparative study of various quantization schemes for speech encoding" *Bell Syst. Tech. J.* **54**, 1597–1614.

77. J. Gruber & N. Le (1983) "Performance requirements for integrated voice/data networks," *IEEE J. on Selected Areas in Comm.* **SAC-1**, 981–1005.

78. S. Kwon & A. Goldberg (1984) "An enhanced LPC vocoder with no voiced/unvoiced switch," *IEEE Trans. ASSP* **ASSP-32**, 851–858.

79. N. Jayant (1992) "Signal compression: Technology targets and research directions," *IEEE Trans. Selected Areas in Comm.* **10**, 796–818.

80. P. Kroon & W. Kleijn (1995) "Linear predictive analysis by synthesis coding," in *Modern Methods of Speech Processing*, R. Ramachandran & R. Mammone (eds.) (Kluwer: Norwell, MA), pp. 51–74.

81. L. Wu, M. Niranjan & F. Fallside (1994) "Fully vector-quantized neural network-based code-excited nonlinear predictive speech coding," *IEEE Trans. Speech & Audio Proc.* **2**, 482–489.

82. M. Honig & D. Messerschmidt (1984) *Adaptive Filters: Structures, Algorithms, and Applications* (Kluwer Academic: Boston).

83. A. Erell, Y. Orgad & J. Goldstein (1991) "JND's in the LPC poles of speech and their application to quantization of the LPC filter," *IEEE Trans. ASSP*, **ASSP-39**, 308–318.

84. J. Markel & A. Gray (1980) "Implementation & comparison of two transformed reflection coefficient scalar quantization methods," *IEEE Trans. ASSP*, **ASSP-28**, 575–583.

85. F. Soong & B-H. Juang (1984) "Line spectrum pair (LSP) and speech data compression," *Proc. IEEE Int. Conf. ASSP*, pp. 1.10.1–4.

86. F. Soong & B-H. Juang (1988) "Optimal quantization of LSP parameters," *Proc. IEEE Int. Conf. ASSP*, pp. 394–397.

87. H. Kim & H. Lee (1999) "Interlacing properties of line spectrum pair frequencies," *IEEE Trans. Speech & Audio Proc.* **7**, 87–91.

88. C-H. Wu & J-H. Chen (1997) "A novel two-level method for the computation of the LSP frequencies using a decimation-in-degree algorithm," *IEEE Trans. Speech & Audio Proc.* **5**, 106–115.

89. C. Un & J. Lee (1983) "Effect of channel errors on the performance of LPC vocoders," *IEEE Trans. ASSP*, **ASSP–31**, 234–237.

90. C. Laflamme, R. Salami, R. Matmti & J-P. Adoul (1996) "Harmonic-stochastic excitation (HSX) speech coding below 4 kbit/s," *Proc. IEEE Int. Conf. ASSP*, pp. 204–207.

91. M. Yong (1995) "A new LPC interpolation technique for CELP coders," *IEEE Trans. Comm.* **COM–42**, 34–38.

92. J. Erkelens & P. Broersen (1998) "LPC interpolation by approximation of the sample autocorrelation function," *IEEE Trans. Speech & Audio Proc.* **6**, 569–573.

*93. V. Viswanathan, J. Makhoul, R. Schwartz & A. Huggins (1982) "Variable frame rate transmission: A review of methodology and application to narrow-band LPC speech coding," *IEEE Trans. Comm.* **COM–30**, 674–686.

94. E. George, A. McCree & V. Viswanathan (1996) "Variable frame rate parameter encoding via adaptive frame selection using dynamic programming," *Proc. IEEE Int. Conf. ASSP*, pp. 271–274.

95. P. Papamichalis & T. Barnwell (1983) "Variable rate speech compression by encoding subsets of the PARCOR coefficients," *IEEE Trans. ASSP* **ASSP–31**, 706–713.

96. P. Papamichalis (1985) "Markov-Huffman coding of LPC parameters," *IEEE Trans. ASSP* **ASSP-33**, 451–453.

*97. A. Gersho & E. Paksoy (1995) "Multimode and variable-rate coding of speech," in *Speech Coding and Synthesis*, W. Kleijn & K. Paliwal (eds.) (Elsevier: New York), pp. 257–288.

98. V. Cuperman & P. Lupini (1995) "Variable rate speech coding," in *Modern Methods of Speech Processing*, R. Ramachandran & R. Mammone (eds.) (Kluwer: Norwell, MA), pp. 101–120.

99. E. Erzin, A. Kumar & A. Gersho (1997) "Natural quality variable-rate spectral speech coding below 3.0 kbps," *Proc. IEEE Int. Conf. ASSP*, pp. 1579–1582.

100. M. Hall, A. Oppenheim & A. Willsky (1984) "Time-varying parametric modeling of speech," *Signal Proc.*, **5**, 267–285.

101. B. Atal (1983) "Efficient coding of LPC parameters by temporal decomposition," *Proc. IEEE Int. Conf. ASSP*, pp. 81–84.

102. I. Atkinson, A. Kondoz & B. Evans (1995) "Time envelope vocoder, a new LP based coding strategy for use at bit rates of 2.4 kb/s and below," *IEEE Trans. Selected Areas in Comm.* **13**, 449–457.

103. D. Griffin & J. Lim (1984) "A new pitch detection algorithm," in *Digital Signal Processing-84*, V. Cappellini & A. Constantinides (eds.) (Elsevier Science: Amsterdam), pp. 395–399.

104. M. Kahn & P. Garst (1983) "The effects of five voice characteristics on LPC quality," *Proc. IEEE Int. Conf. ASSP*, pp. 531–534.

105. J. Makhoul, V. Viswanathan, R. Schwartz & A. Huggins (1978) "A mixed-source model for speech compression and synthesis," *IEEE Int. Conf. ASSP*, pp. 163–166.

106. J. Markel & A. Gray (1976) *Linear Prediction of Speech* (Springer-Verlag: New York).

107. G. Kang & S. Everett (1985) "Improvement of the excitation source in the narrow-band linear prediction vocoder," *IEEE Trans. ASSP* **ASSP-33**, 377–386.

108. A. McCree & J. de Martin (1998) "A 1.7 kb/s MELP coder with improved analysis and quantization," *Proc. IEEE Int. Conf. ASSP*, pp. 593–596.

109. T. Unno, T. Barnwell & K. Truong (1999) "An improved mixed excitation linear prediction (MELP) vocoder," *Proc. IEEE Int. Conf ASSP*, pp. 245–248.

110. P. Hedelin (1986) "High quality glottal LPC-vocoding," *Proc. IEEE Int. Conf. ASSP*, pp. 465–468.

111. V. Viswanathan, A. Huggins, W. Russell & J. Makhoul (1980) "Baseband LPC coders for speech transmission over 9.6 kb/s noisy channels," *Proc. IEEE Int. Conf. ASSP*, pp. 348–351.

112. C. Un & J. Lee (1982) "On spectral flattening techniques in residual-excited linear prediction vocoding," *Proc. IEEE Int. Conf. ASSP*, pp. 216–219.

113. M. Nakatsui, D. Stevenson & P. Mermelstein (1981) "Subjective evaluation of a 4.8 kbit/s residual-excited linear prediction coder," *IEEE Trans. Comm.* **COM-29**, 1389–1393.

114. L. Stewart, R. Gray & Y. Linde (1982) "The design of trellis waveform coders," *IEEE Trans. Comm.* **COM-30**, 702–710.

115. G. Rebolledo, R. Gray & J. Burg (1982) "A multirate voice digitizer based upon vector quantization," *IEEE Trans. Comm.* **COM-30**, 721–727.

116. B. Atal & J. Remde (1982) "A new model of LPC excitation for producing natural-sounding speech at low bit rates," *Proc. IEEE Int. Conf. ASSP*, pp. 614–617.

117. P. Kroon, E. Deprettere & R. Sluyter (1986) "Regular-pulse excitation—a novel approach to effective and efficient multipulse coding of speech," *IEEE Trans. ASSP* **ASSP-34**, 1054–1063.

118. S. Singhal & B. Atal (1984) "Improving performance of multi-pulse LPC coders at low bit rates," *Proc. IEEE Int. Conf. ASSP*, pp. 1.3.1–4.

119. W. Kleijn & J. Haagen (1995) "Waveform interpolation for speech coding and synthesis," in *Speech Coding and Synthesis*, W. Kleijn & K. Paliwal (eds.) (Elsevier: New York), pp. 175–208.

120. J. Thyssen, W. Kleijn & R. Hagen (1997) "Using a perception-based frequency scale in waveform interpolation," *Proc. IEEE Int. Conf. ASSP*, pp. 1595–1598.

121. G. Yang, H. Leich & R. Boite (1995) "Voiced speech coding at very low bit rates based on forward-backward waveform prediction," *IEEE Trans. Speech & Audio Proc.* **3**, 40–47.

122. J. de Martin & A. Gersho (1996) "Mixed domain coding of speech at 3 kb/s," *Proc. IEEE Int. Conf. ASSP*, pp. 216–219.

123. W. Kleijn, H. Yang & E. Deprettere (1998) "Waveform interpolation coding with pitch-spaced subbands," *Int. Conf. on Spoken Lang. Proc.*, pp. 1795–1798.

124. Y. Shoham (1997) "Very low complexity interpolative speech coding at 1.2 to 2.4 kbps," *Proc. IEEE Int. Conf. ASSP*, pp. 1599–1602.

125. R. Crochiere (1977) "On the design of sub-band coders for low bit rate speech communication," *Bell Syst. Tech. J.* **56**, 747–770.

126. H. Crochiere & L. Rabiner (1983) *Multirate Digital Signal Processing* (Prentice-Hall: Englewood Cliffs, NJ).

127. M. Smith & T. Barnwell (1986) "Exact reconstruction techniques for tree structured subband coders," *IEEE Trans. ASSP*, **ASSP-34**, 434–441.

128. C. Creusere & S. Mitra (1996) "Efficient audio coding using perfect reconstruction noncausal IIR filter banks," *IEEE Trans. Speech & Audio Proc.* **4**, 115–123.

129. M. Copperi & D. Sereno (1984) "9.6 kbit/s piecewise LPC coder using multiple-stage vector quantization," *Proc. IEEE Int. Conf. ASSP*, pp. 10.5.1–4.

130. J-P. Adoul & R. Lefebvre (1995) "Wideband speech coding," in *Speech Coding and Synthesis*, W. Kleijn & K. Paliwal (eds.) (Elsevier: New York), chapter 8.

131. T. Barnwell (1982) "Subband coder design incorporating recursive quadrature filters and optimum ADPCM coders," *IEEE Trans. ASSP*, **ASSP-30**, 751–765.

132. R. Crochiere (1979) "A novel approach for implementing pitch prediction in subband coding," *Proc. IEEE Int. Conf. ASSP*, pp. 526–529.

133. J. Johnston & K. Brandenburg (1992) "Wideband coding—perceptual considerations for speech and music," in *Advances in Speech Signal Processing*, S. Furui & M. Sondhi (eds.) (Marcel Dekker: New York), pp. 109–140.

134. D. Sinha & J. Johnston (1996) "Audio compression at low bit rates using a signal adaptive switched filterbank," *Proc. IEEE Int. Conf. ASSP*, pp. 1053–1056.

135. M. Bosi (1997) "Perceptual audio coding," *IEEE Signal Proc. Mag.* **14**, no. 5, 43–49.

136. P. Noll (1997) "MPEG digital audio coding," *IEEE Signal Proc. Mag.* **14**, no. 5, 59–81.

137. J. Tribolet & R. Crochiere (1979) "Frequency domain coding of speech," *IEEE Trans. ASSP* **ASSP-27**, 512–530.

138. A. Ferreira (1996) "Convolutional effects in transform coding with TDAC: An optimal window," *IEEE Trans. Speech & Audio Proc.* **4**, 104–114.

139. S. Foo & L. Turner (1983) "Hybrid frequency-domain coding of speech signals," *IEE Proc.*, part F, **130**, 459–467.

140. J-H. Chen (1997) "A candidate coder for the ITU-T's new wideband speech coding standard," *Proc. IEEE Int. Conf. ASSP*, pp. 1359–1362.

141. T. Moriya, N. Iwakami, A. Jin, K. Ikeda & S. Miki (1997) "A design of transform coder for both speech and audio signals at 1 bit/sample," *Proc. IEEE Int. Conf. ASSP*, pp. 1371–1374.

142. M. Paraskevas & J. Mourjopoulos (1995) "A differential perceptual audio coding method with reduced bitrate requirements," *IEEE Trans. Speech & Audio Proc.* **3**, 490–503.

143. D. Malah, R. Crochiere & R. Cox (1981) "Performance of transform and subband coding systems combined with harmonic scaling of speech," *IEEE Trans. ASSP*, **ASSP-29**, 273–283.

144. D. Malah (1979) "Time-domain algorithms for harmonic bandwidth reduction and time scaling of speech signals," *IEEE Trans. ASSP*, **ASSP-27**, 121–133.

145. D. Malah & J. Flanagan (1981) "Frequency scaling of speech signals by transform techniques," *Bell Syst. Tech. J.* **60**, 2107–2156.

146. J. Melsa & A. Pande (1981) "Mediumband speech encoding using time domain harmonic scaling & adaptive residual encoding," *IEEE Int. Conf. ASSP*, pp. 603–606.

147. S. Duker (1974) *Time-Compressed Speech* (Scarecrow: Metuchen, NJ).

148. H. Reininger & D. Wolf (1983) "Adaptive filtering of binary quantized speech," in *Signal Processing II: Theories and Applications*, H. Schüssler (ed.) (Elsevier Science: Amsterdam), pp. 379–381.

149. M. Covell, M. Withgott & M. Slaney (1998) "MACH1: Nonuniform time-scale modification of speech," *Proc. IEEE Int. Conf. ASSP*, pp. 349–352.

150. L. Almeida & J. Tribolet (1983) "Nonstationary spectral modeling of voiced speech," *IEEE Trans. ASSP*, **ASSP-31**, 664–678.

151. J. Marques & L. Almeida (1986) "A background for sinusoid based representation of voiced speech," *Proc. IEEE Int. Conf. ASSP*, pp. 1233–1236.

152. E. Shlomot, V. Cuperman & A. Gersho (1998) "Combined harmonic and waveform coding of speech at low bit rates," *Proc. IEEE Int. Conf. ASSP*, pp. 585–588.

153. T. Eriksson, H-G. Kang & Y. Stylianou (1998) "Quantization of the spectral envelope for sinusoidal coders," *Proc. IEEE Int. Conf. ASSP*, pp. 37–40.

154. J. Flanagan (1980) "Parametric coding of speech spectra," *J. Acoust. Soc. Am.* **68**, 412–419.

155. J. Flanagan & S. Christensen (1980) "Computer studies on parametric coding of speech spectra," *J. Acoust. Soc. Am.* **68**, 420–430.

156. B. Gold, P. Blankenship & R. McAulay (1981) "New applications of channel vocoders," *IEEE Trans. ASSP*, **ASSP-29**, 13–23.

157. J. Holmes (1980) "The JSRU channel vocoder," *IEE Proc.* part F, **127**, 53–60.

158. B. Gold & C. Rader (1967) "The channel vocoder," *IEEE Trans. Audio & Electroac.* **AU-15**, 148–161.

159. B. Babu (1983) "Performance of an FFT-based voice coding system in quiet and noisy environments," *IEEE Trans. ASSP*, **ASSP-31**, 1323–1327.

160. D. Childers & H. Hu (1994) "Speech synthesis by glottal excited linear prediction," *J. Acoust. Soc. Am.* **96**, 2026–2036.

161. C. Weinstein & A. Oppenheim (1971) "Predictive coding in a homomorphic vocoder," *IEEE Trans. Audio & Electroac.* **AU-19**, 243–248.

162. A. Oppenheim (1969) "Speech analysis-synthesis system based on homomorphic filtering," *J. Acoust. Soc. Am.* **45**, 459–462.

163. K. Paliwal (1982) "On the performance of the quefrency-weighted cepstral coefficients in vowel recognition," *Speech Comm.* **1**, 151–154.

164. A. Rosenberg, R. Schafer & L. Rabiner (1971) "Effects of smoothing & quantizing the parameters of formant-coded voiced speech," *J. Acoust. Soc. Am.* **50**, 1532–1538.

165. W. Holmes (1998) "Towards a unified model for low bit-rate speech coding using a recognition-synthesis approach," *Proc. IEEE Int. Conf. ASSP*, pp. 1787–1790.

166. J. Flanagan, K. Ishizaka & K. Shipley (1980) "Signal models for low bit-rate coding of speech," *J. Acoust. Soc. Am.* **68**, 780–791.

167. S. Gupta & J. Schroeter (1993) "Pitch-synchronous frame-by-frame and segment-based articulatory analysis by synthesis," *J. Acoust Soc. Am.* **94**, 2517–2530.

168. S. Roucos, R. Schwartz & J. Makhoul (1983) "A segment vocoder at 150 b/s," *Proc. IEEE Int. Conf. ASSP*, pp. 61–64.

169. C. Xydeas, C. Evci & R. Steele (1982) "Sequential adaptive predictors for ADPCM speech encoders," *IEEE Trans. Comm.* **COM-30**, 1942–1954.

170. V. Cuperman & A. Gersho (1985) "Vector predictive coding of speech at 16 kb/s," *IEEE Trans. Comm.* **COM-33**, 685–696.

171. M. Ferrer-Ballester & A. Figueiras-Vidal (1995) "Efficient adaptive vector quantization of LPC parameters," *IEEE Trans. Speech & Audio Proc.* **3**, 314–317.

172. J. Loo, W-Y. Chan & P. Kabal (1996) "Classified nonlinear predictive vector quantization of speech spectral parameters," *Proc. IEEE Int. Conf. ASSP*, pp. 761–764.

173. R. Ramachandran, M. Sondhi, N. Seshadri & B. Atal (1995) "A two codebook format for robust quantization of line spectral frequencies," *IEEE Trans. Speech & Audio Proc.* **3**, 157–168.

174. T. Eriksson, J. Lindén & J. Skoglund (1996) "Exploiting interframe correlation in spectral quantization," *Proc. IEEE Int. Conf. ASSP*, pp. 765–768.

175. R. Laroia, N. Phamdo & N. Farvardin (1991) "Robust and efficient quantization of speech LSP parameters using structured vector quantizers," *Proc. IEEE Int. Conf. ASSP*, pp. 641–644.

176. A. Buzo, A. Gray, R. Gray & J. Markel (1980) "Speech coding based upon vector quantization," *IEEE Trans. ASSP*, **ASSP-28**, 562–574.

177. M. Sabin & R. Gray (1984) Product code vector quantizers for waveform and voice coding," *IEEE Trans. ASSP*, **ASSP-32**, 474–488.

178. A. Gersho & Y. Shoham (1984) "Hierarchical vector quantization of speech with dynamic codebook allocation," *Proc. IEEE Int. Conf. ASSP*, pp. 10.9.1–4.

179. R. Gray, A. Gray, G. Rebolledo & J. Markel (1981) "Rate-distortion speech coding with a minimum discrimination information distortion measure," *IEEE Trans. Info. Theory* **IT-27**, 708–721.

180. R. Gray, A. Buzo, A. Gray & Y. Matsuyama (1980) "Distortion measures for speech processing," *IEEE Trans. ASSP*, **ASSP-28**, 367–376.

*181. W. Gardner & B. Rao (1995) "Theoretical analysis of the high-rate vector quantization of LPC parameters," *IEEE Trans. Speech & Audio Proc.* **3**, 367–381.

182. J. Pan (1996) "Two-stage vector quantization-pyramidal lattice vector quantization and application to speech LSP coding," *Proc. IEEE Int. Conf. ASSP*, pp. 737–740.

183. N. Moreau & P. Dymarski (1994) "Selection of excitation vectors for the CELP coders," *IEEE Trans. Speech & Audio Proc.* **2**, 29–41.

184. J. Campbell, T. Tremain & V. Welch (1991) "The federal standard 1016 4800 bps CELP voice coder," *Digital Signal Proc.* **1**, no. 3, 145–155.

185. J. Trancoso (1995) "An overview of different trends on CELP coding," in *Speech Recognition and Coding: New Advances and Trends*, pp. 351–368.

186. W. Kleijn, D. Krasinski & R. Ketchum (1990) "Fast methods for the CELP speech coding algorithm," *IEEE Trans. ASSP*, **ASSP-38**, 1330–1342.

187. J. Trancoso & B. Atal (1990) "Efficient search procedures for selecting the optimum innovations in stochastic coders," *IEEE Trans. ASSP*, **ASSP-38**, 385–396.

188. R. Hagen, E. Ekudden, B. Johansson & W. Kleijn (1998) "Removal of sparse-excitation artifacts in CELP," *Proc. IEEE Int. Conf. ASSP*, pp. 145–148.

189. J. Campbell, T. Tremain & V. Welch (1991) "The DOD 4.8 KBPS standard (proposed federal standard 1016)," in *Advances in Speech Coding*, B. Atal, V. Cuperman & A. Gersho (eds.) (Kluwer: Norwell, MA), pp. 121–133.

190. J. Campbell & T. Tremain (1986) "Voiced/unvoiced classification of speech with applications to the U.S. Government LPC-10E algorithm," *Proc. IEEE Int. Conf. ASSP*, pp. 473–476.

191. K. Mano *et al* (1995) "Design of a pitch-synchronous innovation CELP coder for mobile communications," *IEEE Trans. Selected Areas in Comm.* **13**, 31–41.

192. J. Choi (1995) "A fast determination of stochastic excitation without codebook search in CELP coder," *IEEE Trans. Speech & Audio Proc.* **3**, 473–480.

193. C. Murgia, G. Feng, A. Le Guyader & C. Quinquis (1996) "Very low delay and high-quality coding of 20 Hz–15 kHz speech signals at 64 kbit/s," *Int. Conf. on Spoken Lang. Proc.*, pp. 302–305.

194. S. Chui & C. Chan (1996) "A hybrid input/output spectrum adaptation scheme for LD-CELP coding of speech," *Proc. IEEE Int. Conf. ASSP*, pp. 773–776.

195. S. Sasaki, A. Kataoka & T. Moriya (1995) "Wideband CELP coder at 16 kbit/s with 10-ms frame," *Proc. Europ. Conf. Speech Comm. & Tech.*, pp. 41–44.

196. J-H. Chen & D. Wang (1996) "Transform predictive coding of wideband speech signals," *Proc. IEEE Int. Conf. ASSP*, pp. 275–278.

197. K. Koishida, G. Hirabayashi, K. Tokuda & T. Kobayashi (1998) "A wideband CELP speech coder at 16 kbit/s based on mel-generated cepstral analysis," *Proc. IEEE Int. Conf. ASSP*, pp. 161–164.

198. A. Popescu & N. Moreau (1995) "Subband analysis-by-synthesis coding," *Proc. Europ. Conf. Speech Comm. & Tech.*, pp. 673–676.

199. D. Griffin & J. Lim (1988) "Multiband excitation vocoder," *IEEE Trans. ASSP*, **ASSP-36**, 1223–1235.

200. W. Yu & C-F. Chan (1995) "Efficient multiband excitation linear predictive coding of speech at 1.6 kbps," *Proc. Europ. Conf. Speech Comm. & Tech.*, pp. 685–688.

201. K. Chui & P. Ching (1996) "Quad-band excitation for low bit rate speech coding," *J. Acoust. Soc. Am.* **99**, 2365–2369.

202. A. Ubale & A. Gersho (1998) "A low-delay wideband speech coder at 24 kbps," *Proc. IEEE Int. Conf. ASSP*, pp. 165–168.

203. R. Salami, C. Laflamme, B. Bessette & J-P. Adoul (1997) "ITU-T G.729 Annex A: Reduced complexity 8 kbit/s CS-ACELP codec for digital simultaneous voice and data," *IEEE Comm. Mag.* **35**, no. 9, 56–63.

204. R. Salami *et al* (1995) "Description of the proposed ITU-T 8 kb/s speech coding standard," *IEEE Workshop on Speech Coding for Telecommunications*, pp. 3–4.

205. A. Kataoka, T. Moriya & S. Hayashi (1996) "An 8-kb/s conjugate structure CELP (CS-CELP) speech coder," *IEEE Trans. Speech & Audio Proc.* **4**, 401–411.

206. T. Honkanen, J. Vainio, K. Järvinen, P. Haavisto, R. Salami, C. Laflamme & J-P. Adoul (1997) "Enhanced full-rate speech codec for IS-136 digital cellular system," *Proc. IEEE Int. Conf. ASSP*, pp. 731–734.

207. J. Vainio, H. Mikkola, K. Järvinen & P. Haavisto (1998) "OSM EFR based multi-rate codec family," *Proc. IEEE Int. Conf. ASSP*, pp. 141–144.

208. K. Ozawa & M. Serizawa (1998) "High quality multipulse based CELP speech coding at 6.4 kb/s and its subjective evaluation," *Proc. IEEE Int. Conf. ASSP*, pp. 153–156.

209. C-C. Kuo, J. Jean & H-C. Wang (1995) "Speech classification embedded in adaptive codebook search for low bit-rate CELP coding," *IEEE Trans. Speech & Audio Proc.* **3**, 94–98.

210. J. Ooi & V. Viswanathan (1995) "Applications of wavelets to speech processing: A case study of a CELP coder," in *Modern Methods of Speech Processing*, R. Ramachandran & R. Mammone (eds.) (Kluwer: Norwell, MA), pp. 449–464.

211. W. Dobson, J. Yang, K. Smart & F. Guo (1997) "High quality low complexity scalable wavelet audio coding," *Proc. IEEE Int. Conf. ASSP*, pp. 327–330.

212. C. Shannon (1948) "A mathematical theory of communication," *Bell Syst. Tech. J.* **27**, 379–423.

213. J. Alajaji, N. Phamdo & T. Fuja (1996) "Channel codes that exploit the residual redundancy in CELP-encoded speech," *IEEE Trans. Speech & Audio Proc.* **4**, 325–336.

214. D. Wong, B-H. Juang & A. Gray (1982) "An 800 bit/s vector quantization LPC vocoder," *IEEE Trans. ASSP*, **ASSP-30**, 770–779.

215. C. Tsao & R. Gray (1985) "Matrix quantizer design for LPC speech using the generalized Lloyd algorithm," *IEEE Trans. ASSP*, **ASSP-33**, 537–545.

216. M. Honda & Y. Shirakai (1992) "Very low-bit-rate speech coding," in *Speech Signal Processing*, S. Furui & M. Sondhi (eds.) (Marcel Dekker: New York), pp. 209–230.

217. D. Wong, B-H. Juang & D. Cheng (1983) "Very low data rate speech compression with LPC vector and matrix quantization," *IEEE Int. Conf. ASSP*, pp. 65–68.

218. M. McLaughlin, D. Linder & S. Carney (1984) "Design and test of a spectrally efficient land mobile communications system using LPC speech," *IEEE J. Selected Areas in Comm.* **SAC-2**, 611–620.

219. D. Lindbergh (1996) "The H.324 multimedia standard," *IEEE Comm. Mag.* **34**, no. 12, 46–51.

220. L. Supplee, R. Cohn, J. Collura & A. McCree (1997) "MELP: The new federal standard at 2400 bps," *Proc. IEEE Int. Conf. ASSP*, pp. 1591–1594.

221. S. McClellan & J. Gibson (1997) "Variable-rate CELP based on subband flatness," *IEEE Trans. Speech & Audio Proc.* **5**, 120–130.

222. A. Das, E. Paksoy & A. Gersho (1995) "Multimode and variable-rate coding of speech," in *Speech Coding and Synthesis*, W. Kleijn & K. Paliwal (eds.) (Elsevier: New York), pp. 257–288.

223. G. Bremer & K. Ko (1996) "Simultaneous voice and data on the general switched telephone network using framed QADM," *IEEE Comm. Mag.* **34**, no. 12, 58–63.

*224. B. Gold (1977) "Digital speech networks," *Proc. IEEE* **65**, 1636–1658.

225. C. Weinstein & J. Forgie (1983) "Experience with speech communication in packet networks," *IEEE J. on Selected Areas in Comm.* **SAC-1**, 963–980.

226. D. Goodman, G. Lockhart, O. Wasem & W. Wong (1986) "Waveform substitution techniques for recovering missing speech segments in packet voice communications," *IEEE Trans. ASSP*, **ASSP-34**, 1440–1448.

227. K. Matsumoto (1996) "Real-time high accurate cell loss recovery technique for speech over ATM networks," *Proc. IEEE Int. Conf. ASSP*, pp. 248–250.

228. J-L. Chen & B-S. Chen (1997) "Model-based multirate representation of speech signals and its application to recovery of missing speech packets," *IEEE Trans. Speech & Audio Proc.* **5**, 220–231.

229. R. Grigonis (1997) "Audio, video and data conferencing over the internet," *Comp. Telephony*, March, 192–236.

230. R. Cox & R. Crochiere (1980) "Multiple user variable rate coding for TASI and packet transmission systems," *IEEE Trans. Comm.* **COM-28**, 334–344.

231. G. Langenbucher (1982) "Efficient coding and speech interpolation: Principles and performance characterization," *IEEE Trans. Comm.* **COM-30**, 769–779.

232. A. Benyassine, E. Shlomot, H-Y. Su, D. Massaloux, C. Lamblin & J-P. Petit (1997) "ITU recommendation G. 729 Annex B: A silence compression scheme," *IEEE Comm. Mag.* **35**, no. 9, 64–73.

233. K. Kou, J. O'Neal & A. Nilsson (1985) "Digital speech interpolation for variable rate coders with applications to subband coding," *IEEE Trans. Comm.* **COM-33**, 1100–1108.

234. L. Paratz & E. Jones (1985) "Speech transmission using an adaptive burst mode technique," *IEEE Trans. Comm.*, **COM-33**, 588–591.

235. E. Singer, R. McAulay, R. Dunn & T. Quatieri (1996) "Low rate coding of the spectral envelope using channel gains," *Proc. IEEE Int. Conf. ASSP*, pp. 769–772.

236. D. Goodman (1980) "Embedded DPCM for variable bit rate transmission," *IEEE Trans. Comm.* **COM-28**, 1040–1046.

237. I. Wassell, D. Goodman & R. Steele (1988) "Embedded delta modulation," *IEEE Trans. ASSP*, **ASSP-36**, 1236–1243.

238. M. Sherif, D. Bowker, G. Bertocci, B. Orford & G. Mariano (1993) "Overview and performance of CCITT/ANSI embedded ADPCM algorithms," *IEEE Trans. Comm.*, **COM-41**, 391–399.

239. S. Zhang & G. Lockhart (1997) "Embedded RPE based on multistage coding," *IEEE Trans. Speech & Audio Proc.* **5**, 367–371.

240. B. Tang, A. Shen, A. Alwan & G. Pottie (1997) "A perceptually based embedded subband speech coder," *IEEE Trans. Speech & Audio Proc.* **5**, 131–140.

241. A. Le Guyader, C. Lamblin & E. Boursicaut (1995) "Embedded algebraic CELP/VSELP coders for wideband speech coding," *Speech Comm.* **16**, 319–328.

242. T. Unno, T. Barnwell & M. Clements (1997) "The multimodal multipulse excitation vocoder," *Proc. IEEE Int. Conf. ASSP*, pp. 1683–1686.

243. R. Reininger & J. Gibson (1985) "Backward adaptive lattice and transversal predictors in ADPCM," *IEEE Trans. Comm.* **COM-33**, 74–82.

244. J. Allen (1985) "Computer architecture for digital signal processing," *Proc. IEEE* **73**, 852–873.

245. J-H. Chen (1995) "Low-complexity wideband speech coding," *Proc. IEEE Workshop on Speech Coding for Telecom.*, pp. 27–28.

246. S. Ahmadi & A. Spanias (1998) "A new phase model for sinusoidal transform coding of speech," *IEEE Trans. Speech & Audio Proc.* **6**, 495–501.

CHAPTER 8—ENHANCEMENT

1. G. Kang & L. Fransen (1989) "Quality improvement of LPC processed noisy speech by using spectral subtraction," *IEEE Trans. ASSP*, **ASSP-37**, 939–942.

2. J. Hardwick, C. Yoo & J. Lim (1993) "Speech enhancement using the dual excitation model," *IEEE Trans. ASSP*, **ASSP-28**, 137–145.

3. J. Lim (1983) *Speech Enhancement* (Prentice-Hall: Englewood Cliffs, NJ).

4. S. Boll (1992) "Speech enhancement in the 1980s: Noise suppression with pattern matching," in *Advances in Speech Signal Processing*, S. Furui & M. Sondhi (eds.) (Marcel Dekker: New York). pp. 309–325.

5. D. Krubsack & R. Niederjohn (1994) "Estimation of noise corrupting speech using extracted speech parameters and averaging of logarithmic modified periodograms," *Digital Signal Proc.* **4**, 154–172.

6. C. Cherry & R. Wiley (1967) "Speech communication in very noisy environments," *Nature* **214**, 1184.

7. J. Hansen & L. Arslan (1995) "Markov model-based phoneme class partitioning for improved constrained iterative speech enhancement," *IEEE Trans. Speech & Audio Proc.* **3**, 98–104.

8. B. Pellom & J. Hansen (1996) "Text-directed speech enhancement using phoneme classification and feature map constrained vector quantization," *Proc. IEEE Int. Conf. ASSP*, pp. 645–648.

9. N. Bi & Y. Qi (1997) "Application of speech conversion to alaryngeal speech enhancement," *IEEE Trans. Speech & Audio Proc.* **5**, 97–105.

10. H. Strube (1981) "Separation of several speakers recorded by two microphones (cocktail-party processing)," *Signal Processing* **3**, 355–364.

11. D. Chan, P. Rayner & S. Godsill (1996) "Multi-channel signal separation," *Proc. IEEE Int. Conf. ASSP*, pp. 649–652.

12. W. Mikhael & P. Hill (1988) "Performance evaluation of a real-time TMS32010-based adaptive noise canceller (ANC)," *IEEE Trans. ASSP* **ASSP-36**, 411–412.

13. M. Sambur (1979) "A preprocessing filter for enhancing LPC analysis/synthesis of speech," *IEEE Int Conf. ASSP*, pp. 971–974.

14. S. Boll (1979) "Suppression of acoustic noise in acoustic noise speech using spectral subtraction," *IEEE Trans. ASSP*, **ASSP-37**, 113–120.

15. R. McAulay & M. Malpass (1980) "Speech enhancement using a soft-decision noise suppression filter," *IEEE Trans. ASSP*, **ASSP-28**, 137–145.

16. D. Wang & J. Lim (1985) "The unimportance of phase in speech enhancement," *IEEE Trans. ASSP*, **ASSP-30**, 679–681.

17. D. Childers & C. Lee (1987) "Co-channel speech separation," *Proc. IEEE Int. Conf. ASSP*, pp. 181–184.

18. R. Le Bouquin (1996) "Enhancement of noisy speech signals: Application to mobile radio communications," *Speech Comm.* **18**, 3–19.

19. M. Berouti, R. Schwartz & J. Makhoul (1979) "Enhancement of speech corrupted by acoustic noise," *Proc. IEEE Int. Conf. ASSP*, pp. 208–211.

20. L. Arslan, A. McCree & V. Viswanthan (1995) "New methods for adaptive noise suppression," *Proc. IEEE Int. Conf. ASSP*, pp. 812–815.

21. P. Lockwood & J. Boudy (1992) "Experiments with a nonlinear spectral subtractor (NSS), Hidden Markov Models and the projection, for robust speech recognition in cars," *Speech Comm.* **11**, 215–228.

22. H. Hirsch & C. Ehrlicher (1995) "Noise estimation techniques for robust speech recognition," *Proc. IEEE Int. Conf. ASSP*, pp. 153–156.

23. Y. Ephraim & H. van Trees (1995) "A signal subspace approach for speech enhancement," *IEEE Trans. Speech & Audio Proc.* **3**, 251–266.

24. Y. Ephraim (1992) "Statistical-model-based speech enhancement systems," *Proc. IEEE* **80**, 1526–1555.

25. Y. Ephraim (1992) "A Bayesian estimation approach for speech enhancement using hidden Markov models," *IEEE Trans. ASSP*, **ASSP-40**, 725–735.

26. L. Gagnon (1993) "A state-based noise reduction approach for non-stationary additive interference," *Speech Comm.* **12**, 213–219.

27. C. Seymour & M. Niranjan (1994) "An HMM-based cepstral domain speech enhancement system," *Int. Conf. on Spoken Lang. Proc.*, pp. 1595–1598.

28. J. Gibson, B. Koo & S. Gray (1991) "Filtering of colored noise for speech enhancement and coding," *IEEE Trans ASSP*, **ASSP-39**, 1732–1742.

29. K. Lee & K. Shirai (1996) "Efficient recursive estimation for speech enhancement in colored noise," *IEEE Signal Proc. Lett.* **3**, 196–199.

30. X. Shen, L. Deng & A. Yasmin (1996) "H_∞ filtering for speech enhancement," *Int. Conf. on Spoken Lang. Proc.*, pp. 873–876.

31. W. Harrison, J. Lim & E. Singer (1986) "A new application of adaptive noise cancellation," *IEEE Trans. ASSP*, **ASSP-34**, 21–27.

32. B. Widrow *et al* (1975) "Adaptive noise cancelling: Principles and applications," *Proc. IEEE* **63**, 1692–1716.

33. D. van Compernolle (1992) "DSP techniques for speech enhancement," *Proc. ESCA Workshop in Speech Proc. in Adverse Conditions*, pp. 21–30.

34. K. Zangi (1993) "A new two-sensor active noise cancellation algorithm," *Proc. IEEE Int. Conf. ASSP*, vol. II, 351–354.

35. K. Farrell, R. Mammone & J. Flanagan (1992) "Beamforming microphone arrays for speech enhancement," *Proc. IEEE Int. Conf. ASSP*, pp. 285–288.

36. S. Affes & Y. Grenier (1997) "A signal subspace tracking algorithm for microphone array processing of speech," *IEEE Trans. Speech & Audio Proc.* **5**, 425–437.

37. B. Widrow & S. Stearns (1985) *Adoptive Signal Processing* (Prentice Hall: Englewood Cliffs, NJ).

38. M-H. Lu & P. Clarkson (1993) "The performance of adaptive noise cancellation systems in reverberant rooms," *J. Acoust. Soc. Am.* **93**, 1112–1135.

39. C. Gritton & D. Lin (1984) "Echo cancellation algorithms," *IEEE ASSP Mag.* **1**, no. 2, 30–38.

40. K. Murano, S. Unagami & F. Amano (1990) "Echo cancellation and applications," *IEEE Comm. Mag.* **28**, no. 1, 49–55.

41. J. Kim & C. Un (1986) "Enhancement of noisy speech by forward/backward adaptive digital filtering," *Proc. IEEE Int. Conf. ASSP*, pp. 89–92.

42. M. Sambur (1978) "Adaptive noise cancelling for speech signals," *IEEE Trans. ASSP*, **ASSP-26**, 419–423.

43. S. Alexander (1985) "Adaptive reduction of interfering speaker noise using the least mean squares algorithm," *Proc. IEEE Int. Conf. ASSP*, pp. 728–731.

44. J. Proakis *et al* (1992) *Advanced Topics in Signal Processing* (Macmillan: New York).

45. S. Boll & D. Pulsipher (1980) "Suppression of acoustic noise in speech using two microphone adaptive noise cancellation," *IEEE Trans. ASSP*, **ASSP-28**, 752–753.

46. B. Farhang-Boroujeny (1997) "Fast LMS/Newton algorithms based on autoregressive modeling and their application to acoustic echo cancellation," *IEEE Trans. Signal Proc.* **SP-45**, 1987–2000.

47. F. Reed & P. Feintuch (1981) "A comparison of LMS adaptive cancellers implemented in the frequency domain and the time domain," *IEEE Trans. ASSP*, **ASSP-29**, 770–775.

48. B. Kollmeier & R. Koch (1994) "Speech enhancement based on physiological and psychoacoustical models of modulation perception and binaural interaction," *J. Acoust. Soc. Am.* **95**, 1593–1602.

49. S. Nandkumar & J. Hansen (1995) "Dual-channel iterative speech enhancement with constraints on an auditory-based spectrum," *IEEE Trans. Speech & Audio Proc.* **3**, 22–34.

50. J. Allen, D. Berkely & V. J. Blauert (1977) "Multimicrophone signal-processing technique to remove room reverberation of speech signals," *J. Acoust. Soc. Am.* **62**, 912–915.

51. H. Wang & F. Itakura (1991) "An approach of dereverberation using multi-microphone subband envelope estimation," *Proc. IEEE Int. Conf. ASSP*, pp. 953–956.

52. J. Benesty, D. Morgan & M. Sondhi (1997) "A better understanding and an improved solution to the problems of stereophonic acoustic echo cancellation," *Proc. IEEE Int. Cont ASSP*, pp. 303–306.

53. S. Makino (1997) "Acoustic echo cancellation," *IEEE Signal Proc. Mag.* **14**, no. 5, 39–41.

54. J. Graf & N. Hubing (1993) "Dynamic time warping comb filter for the enhancement of speech degraded by white Gaussian noise," *Proc. IEEE Int. Conf. ASSP*, vol. II, pp. 339–342.

55. M. Weiss, E. Aschkenasy & T. Parsons (1974) "Processing speech signals to attenuate interference," *IEEE Symp. on Speech Recognition*, pp. 292–295.

56. D. Morgan, E. George, L. Lea & S. Kay (1997) "Co-channel speaker separation by harmonic enhancement and suppression," *IEEE Trans. Speech & Audio Proc.* **5**, 407–424.

57. B. Hanson & D. Wong (1984) "The harmonic magnitude suppression (HMS) technique for intelligibility enhancement in the presence of interfering speech," *Proc. IEEE Int. Conf. ASSP*, pp. 18A.5.1–4.

58. Y. Perlmutter, L. Braida, R. Frazier & A. Oppenheim (1977) "Evaluation of a speech enhancement system," *Proc. IEEE Int. Conf. ASSP*, pp. 212–215.

59. T. Parsons (1976) "Separation of speech from interfering speech by means of harmonic selection," *J. Acoust. Soc. Am.* **60**, 911–918.

60. S. Wenndt, J. Burleigh & M. Thompson (1996) "Pitch-adaptive time-rate expansion for enhancing speech intelligibility," *J. Acoust. Soc. Am.* **99**, 3853–3856.

61. C. Yoo & J. Lim (1995) "Speech enhancement based on the generalized dual excitation model with adaptive analysis window" *Proc. IEEE Int. Conf. ASSP*, **3**, pp. 832–835.

62. M. Deisher & A. Spanias (1997) "Speech enhancement using state-based estimation and sinusoidal modeling," *J. Acoust. Soc. Am.* **102**, 1141–1148.

63. J. Lim & A. Oppenheim (1979) "Enhancement and bandwidth compression of noisy speech," *Proc. IEEE* **67**, 1586–1604.

64. J. Hansen & M. Clements (1991) "Constrained iterative speech enhancement with applications to speech recognition," *IEEE Trans. ASSP*, **ASSP-39**, 795–805.

65. J. Hansen & S. Nandkumar (1995) "Robust estimation of speech in noisy backgrounds based on aspects of the auditory process," *J. Acoust. Soc. Am.* **97**, 3833–3849.

66. T. Sreenivas & P. Kirnapure (1996) "Codebook constrained Wiener filtering for speech enhancement," *IEEE Trans. Speech & Audio Proc.* **4**, 383–389.

67. B. Hanson, D. Wong & B. Juang (1983) "Speech enhancement with harmonic synthesis," *Proc. IEEE Int. Conf. ASSP*, pp. 1122–1125.

68. Y. Qi, B. Weinberg & N. Bi (1995) "Enhancement of female esophageal and tracheoesophageal speech," *J. Acoust. Soc. Am.* **98**, 2461–2465.

69. S. Godsill & P. Rayner (1996) "Robust noise reduction for speech and audio signals," *Proc. IEEE Int. Conf. ASSP*, pp. 625–628.

CHAPTER 9—SYNTHESIS

1. Y. Sagisaka (1990) "Speech synthesis from text," *IEEE Comm. Mag.* **28**, no. 1, 35–41, 55.

2. H. Sato (1992) "Speech synthesis for text-to-speech systems," in *Advances in Speech Signal Processing*, S. Furui & M. Sondhi (eds.) (Marcel Dekker: New York), pp. 833–853.

*3. J. Allen (1992) "Overview of text-to-speech systems," in *Advances in Speech Signal Processing*, S. Furui & M. Sondhi, (eds.) (Marcel Dekker: New York), pp. 741–790.

4. S. Hertz (1991) "Streams, phones, and transitions: Toward a phonological and phonetic model of formant timing," *J. Phonetics* **19**, 91–109.

*5. D. Klatt (1987) "Review of text-to-speech conversion for English," *J. Acoust. Soc. Am.* **82**, 737–793.

*6. T. Dutoit (1997) *From Text to Speech: A Concatenative Approach* (Kluwer: Amsterdam).

7. O. Fujimura & J. Lovins (1978) "Syllables as concatenative phonetic units," in *Syllables and Segments*, A. Bell & J. Hooper (eds.) (North-Holland: Amsterdam), pp. 107–120.

8. C. Browman (1980) "Rules for demisyllable synthesis using LINGUA, a language interpreter," *Proc. IEEE Int. Conf. ASSP*, pp. 561–564.

9. H. Dettweiler & W. Hess (1985) "Concatenation rules for demisyllable speech synthesis," *Acustica* **57**, 268–283.

10. C. Shadle & B. Atal (1979) "Speech synthesis by linear interpolation of spectral parameters between dyad boundaries," *J. Acoust. Soc. Am.* **66**, 1325–1332.

11. R. Schwartz, J. Klovstad, J. Makhoul, D. Klatt & V. Zue (1979) "Diphone synthesis for phonetic vocoding," *Proc. IEEE Int. Conf. ASSP*, pp. 891–894.

12. S. Werner & E. Keller (1994) "Subphonemic segment inventories for concatenative speech synthesis," in *Fundamentals of Speech Synthesis and Recognition*, E. Keller (ed.) (John Wiley & Sons: Chichester), pp. 69–85.

13. H. Kaeslin (1986) "A systematic approach to the extraction of diphone elements from natural speech," *IEEE Trans. ASSP*, **ASSP-34**, 264–271.

14. A. Hunt & W. Black (1996) "Unit selection in a concatenative speech synthesis system using a large speech database," *Proc. IEEE Int. Conf. ASSP*, pp. 373–376.

15. W. Ding & N. Campbell (1997) "Optimizing unit selection with voice source and formants in the CHATR speech synthesis system," *Proc. Eurospeech*, pp. 537–540.

16. A. Ljolje, J. Hirschberg & J. van Santen (1994) "Automatic speech segmentation for concatenative inventory selection," *Proc. 2nd ESCA/IEEE Workshop on Speech Synthesis*, pp. 93–96.

17. H. Hon, A. Acero, X. Huang, J. Liu & M. Plumpe (1998) "Automatic generation of synthesis units for trainable text-to-speech systems," *Proc. IEEE Int. Conf. ASSP*, pp. 273–276.

18. T. Quatieri & R. McAulay (1992) "Shape invariant time-scale and pitch modification of speech," *IEEE Trans. ASSP*, **ASSP-40**, 497–510.

19. M. Pollard, B. Cheetham, C. Goodyear & M. Edgington (1997) "Shape-invariant pitch and time-scale modification of speech by variable order phase interpolation," *Proc. IEEE Int. Conf. ASSP*, pp. 919–922.

20. E. Sivertsen (1961) "Segment inventories for speech synthesis," *Lang. & Speech* **4**, 27–89.

21. K-S. Lin, K. Goudie, G. Prantz & G. Brantingham (1981) "Text-to-speech using LPC allophone stringing," *IEEE Trans. Cons. Elec.* **CE-27**, 144–150.

22. W. Ainsworth (1976) "Allophonic variations of stop consonants in a speech synthesis-by-rule program," *Int. J. Man-Machine Studies* **8**, 159–168.

23. E. Moulines & F. Charpentier (1990) "Pitch synchronous waveform processing techniques for text-to-speech synthesis using diphones," *Speech Comm.* **9**, 453–467.

24. D. Lee & F. Lochovsky (1983) "Voice response systems," *ACM Comp. Surv.* **15**, 351–374.

25. H. Kucera & W. Francis (1967) *Computational Analysis of Present-Day American English* (Brown University Press: Providence, RI).

26. T. Hirokawa & K. Hakoda (1994) "Segment selection and pitch modification for high-quality speech synthesis using waveform segments," *Proc. Int. Conf. Spoken Lang. Proc.*, pp. 337–340.

27. T. Portele, F. Höfer & W. Hess (1994) "Structure and representation of an inventory for German speech synthesis," *Proc. Int. Conf. Spoken Lang. Proc.*, pp. 1759–1762.

28. Y. Sagisaka, N. Kaiki, N. Iwahashi & K. Mimura (1992) "ATR v-Talk speech synthesis system," *Proc. Int. Conf. Spoken Lang. Proc.*, pp. 483–486.

29. A. Hauptmann (1993) "SpeakEZ: A first experiment in concatenation synthesis from a large corpus," *Proc. Eurospeech*, pp. 1701–1704.

30. S. Gupta & J. Schroeter (1993) "Pitch-synchronous frame-by-frame and segment-based articulatory analysis by synthesis," *J. Acoust. Soc. Am.* **94**, 2517–2530.

31. S. Parthasarathy & C. Coker (1992) "On automatic estimation of articulatory parameters in a text-to-speech system," *Comp. Speech & Lang.* **6**, 37–76.

32. B. Gabioud (1994) "Articulatory models in speech synthesis," in *Fundamentals of Speech Synthesis and Recognition*, E. Keller (ed.) (John Wiley & Sons: Chichester), pp. 215–230.

33. L. R. Morris (1979) "A fast Fortran implementation of the U.S. Naval Research Laboratory algorithm for automatic translation of English text to Votrax parameters," *Proc. IEEE Int. Conf. ASSP*, pp. 907–913.

34. S. Hunnicutt (1980) "Grapheme-to-phoneme rules: A review," *Royal Institute of Technology, Stockholm* STL-QPR, no. 2–3, pp. 38–60.

35. H. S. Elovitz, R. Johnson, A. McHugh & J. E. Shore (1976) "Letter-to-sound rules for automatic translation of English text to phonetics," *IEEE Trans. ASSP*, **ASSP-24**, 446–459.

36. B. Sherwood (1978) "Fast text-to-speech algorithms for Esperanto, Spanish, Italian, Russian & English," *Int. J. Man-Machine Studies* **10**, 669–692.

37. K. Church (1986) "Stress assignment in letter-to-sound rules for speech synthesis," *Proc. IEEE Int. Conf. ASSP*, pp. 2423–2426.

38. M. Liberman & K. Church (1992) "Text analysis and word pronunciation in text-to-speech synthesis," in *Advances in Speech Signal Processing*, S. Furui & M. Sondhi (eds.) (Marcel Dekker: New York), pp. 791–831.

39. T. Vitale (1991) "An algorithm for high accuracy name pronunciation by parametric speech synthesizer," *Comp. Linguistics* **16**, 257–276.

40. K. Belhoula (1993) "Rule-based grapheme-to-phoneme conversion of names," *Proc. Eurospeech*, pp. 881–884.

41. J. Allen, S. Hunnicutt, R. Carlson & B. Granstrom (1979) "MITalk-79: the 1979 MIT text-to-speech system," *ASA-50 Speech Communication Papers*, J. Wolf & D. Klatt (eds.) (Acoustical Society of America: New York), pp. 507–510.

42. G. Akers & M. Lennig (1985) "Intonation in text-to-speech synthesis: Evaluation of algorithms," *J. Acoust. Soc. Am.* **77**, 2157–2165.

43. E. Pavlova, Y. Pavlov, R. Sproat, C. Shih & P. van Santen (1997) "Bell Laboratories Russian text-to-speech system," *Comp. Speech & Lang.* **6**, 37–76.

44. S. Hertz, J. Kadin & K. Karplus (1985) "The Delta rule development system for speech synthesis from text," *Proc. IEEE* **73**, 1589–1601.

45. S. Hertz & M. Huffman (1992) "A nucleus-based timing model applied to multi-dialect speech synthesis by rule," *Proc. Int. Conf. Spoken Lang. Proc.*, pp. 1171–1174.

46. S. Young & F. Fallside (1980) "Synthesis by rule of prosodic features in Word Concatenation Synthesis," *Int. J. Man-Machine Studies* **12**, 241–258.

47. I. Mattingly (1970) "Speech synthesis for phonetic and phonological models," *Haskins Lab. Stat. Rep. Speech* **SR-23**, 117–149; also in *Current Trends in Linguistics XII*, T. Sebeok (ed.) (Mouton: The Hague), pp.

48. S. Hiki (1970) "Control rule of the tongue movement for dynamic analog speech synthesis," *J. Acoust. Soc. Am.* **47**, 85.

49. C. Coker (1976) "A model of articulatory dynamics and control," *Proc. IEEE* **64**, 452–460.

50. J. Flanagan & K. Ishizaka (1976) "Automatic generation of voiceless excitation in a vocal cord-vocal tract speech synthesizer," *IEEE Trans. ASSP*, **ASSP-24**, 163–170.

51. P. Mermelstein (1973) "Articulatory model for the study of speech production," *J. Acoust. Soc. Am.* **53**, 1070–1082.

52. P. Rubin, T. Baer & P. Mermelstein (1981) "An articulatory synthesizer for perceptual research," *J. Acoust. Soc. Am.* **70**, 321–328.

53. C. Coker, N. Umeda & C. Browman (1973) "Automatic synthesis from ordinary English text," *IEEE Trans. Aud. Electr.* **AU-21**, 293–298; also in FR, pp. 400–411.

54. J. Flanagan, C. Coker, L. Rabiner, R. Schafer & N. Umeda (1970) "Synthetic voices for computers," *IEEE Spectrum* **7**, no. 10, 22–45; also in FR, pp. 432–455.

55. M. Rahim, C. Goodyear, B. Kleijn, J. Schroeter & M. Sondhi (1993) "Intonation in text-to-speech synthesis: Evaluation of algorithms," *J. Acoust. Soc. Am.* **93**, 1109–1121.

56. A. Oppenheim & R. Schafer (1989) *Discrete-Time Signal Processing* (Prentice-Hall: Englewood Cliffs, NJ).

*57. D. Klatt (1980) "Software for a cascade/parallel formant synthesizer," *J. Acoust. Soc. Am.* **67**, 971–995.

58. R. Carlson, B. Granstrom & I. Karlsson (1991) "Experiments with voice modeling in speech synthesis," *Speech Comm.* **10**, 481–489.

59. L. Rabiner (1968) "Speech synthesis by rule: An acoustic domain approach," *Bell Syst. Tech. J.* **47**, 17–37; also in FR, pp. 368–388.

60. D. Williams, C. Bickley & K. Stevens (1992) "Inventory of phonetic contrasts generated by high-level control of a formant synthesizer," *Proc. Int. Conf. Spoken Lang. Proc.*, pp. 571–574.

61. N. Pinto, D. Childers & A. Lalwani (1989) "Formant speech synthesis: Improving production quality," *IEEE Trans. ASSP*, **ASSP-37**, 1870–1887.

62. S. Pearson, H. Moran, K. Hata & F. Holm (1994) "Combining concatenation and formant synthesis for improved intelligibility and naturalness in text-to-speech systems," *Proc. 2nd ESCA/IEEE Workshop on Speech Synthesis*, pp. 69–72.

63. G. Fries (1994) "Hybrid time- and frequency-domain speech synthesis with extended glottal source generation," *Proc. IEEE Int. Conf. ASSP*, pp. I-581–584.

64. J. Holmes (1983) "Formant synthesizers—cascade or parallel?" *Speech Comm.* **2**, 251–273.

65. J. Kerkhoff & L. Boves (1993) "Designing control rules for a serial pole-zero vocal tract model," *Proc. Eurospeech*, pp. 893–896.

66. X. Rodet (1980) "Time-domain formant-wave-function synthesis," in *Spoken Language Generation and Understanding*, J. Simon (ed.) (Reidel: Dordrecht), pp. 429–441.

67. S. Grau, C. d'Alessandro & G. Richard (1993) "A speech formant synthesizer based on harmonic+random formant-waveforms representations," *Proc. Eurospeech*, pp. 1697–1700.

68. J. Holmes (1973) "The influence of glottal waveform on the naturalness of speech from a parallel formant synthesizer," *IEEE Trans. Aud. Electr.* **AU-21**, 298–305.

69. B. Gold & L. Rabiner (1968) "Analysis of digital and analog formant synthesizers," *IEEE Trans. Aud. Electr.* **AU-16**, 81–94.

70. J. Olive (1990) "A new algorithm for a concatenative speech synthesis system using an augmented acoustic inventory of speech sounds," *Proc. ESCA Workshop on Speech Synthesis*, Autrans, France.

71. D. Childers & K. Wu (1990) "Quality of speech produced by analysis/synthesis," *Speech Comm.* **9**, 97–117.

72. A. Liberman, F. Ingemann, L. Lisker, P. Delattre & F. Cooper (1959) "Minimal rules for synthesizing speech," *J. Acoust. Soc. Am.* **31**, 1490–1499; also in FR, pp. 330–339.

73. J. Holmes, I. Mattingly & J. Shearme (1964) "Speech synthesis by rule," *Lang. & Speech* **7**, 127–143; also in FR, pp. 351–367.

74. L. Rabiner, R. Schafer & J. Flanagan (1971) "Computer synthesis of speech by concatenation of formant-coded words," *Bell Syst. Tech. J.* **50**, 1541–1558; also in FR, pp. 479–496.

75. I. Mattingly (1980) "Phonetic representation & speech synthesis by rule," *Haskins Lab. Status Rep. Speech* **SR-61**, 15–21; also in *The Cognitive Representation of Speech*, T. Myers, J. Laver & J. Anderson (eds.) (North-Holland: Amsterdam), pp. 145–419, 1981.

76. W. Verhelst & P. Nilens (1986) "A modified-superposition speech synthesizer and its applications," *Proc. IEEE Int. Conf. ASSP*, pp. 2007–2010.

77. A. Rosenberg (1971) "Effect of glottal pulse shape on the quality of natural vowels," *J. Acoust. Soc. Am.* **49**, 583–590.

78. B. Guérin, M. Mrayati & R. Carré (1976) "A voice source taking account of coupling with the supraglottal cavities," *Proc. IEEE Int. Conf. ASSP*, pp. 47–50.

79. H. Ohmura & K. Tanaka (1997) "Evaluation of a speech synthesis method for nonlinear modeling of vocal folds vibration effect," *Proc. IEEE Int. Conf. ASSP*, pp. 935–938.

80. I. Karlsson (1992) "Consonants for female speech synthesis," *Proc. Int. Conf. Spoken Lang. Proc.*, pp. 491–494.

81. I. Karlsson & L. Neovius (1993) "Speech synthesis experiments with the GLOVE synthesizer," *Proc. Eurospeech*, pp. 925–928.

82. J. Koreman, L. Boves & B. Cranen (1992) "The influence of linguistic variations on the voice source characteristics," *Proc. Int. Conf. Spoken Lang. Proc.*, pp. 125–128.

83. S. Palmer & J. House (1992) "Dynamic voice source changes in natural and synthetic speech," *Proc. Int. Conf. Spoken Lang. Proc.*, pp. 129–132.

84. G. Fant, J. Liljencrants & Q. Lin (1985) "A four-parameter model of glottal flow," *Speech Transmission Lab. Q. Prog. Rep.* **4**, 1–12.

85. Y. Qi & N. Bi (1994) "A simplified approximation of the four-parameter LF model of voice source," *J. Acoust. Soc. Am.* **96**, 1182–1185.

86. B. Caspers & B. Atal (1983) "Changing pitch and duration in LPC synthesized speech using multi-pulse excitation," *J. Acoust. Soc. Am.* **73**, S1, S5.

87. M. Macchi, M. Altom, D. Kahn, S. Singhal & M. Spiegel (1993) "Intelligibility as a function of speech coding method for template-based speech synthesis," *Proc. Eurospeech*, pp. 893–896.

88. E. Moulines & J. Laroche (1995) "Non-parametric techniques for pitch-scale and time-scale modification of speech," *Speech Comm.* **16**, 175–205.

89. D. Bigorgne *et al* (1993) "Multilingual PSOLA text-to-speech system," *Proc. IEEE Int. Conf. ASSP*, pp. II-187–190.

90. R. Kortekaas & A. Kohlrausch (1999) "Psychoacoustical evaluation of PSOLA. II. Double-formant-stimuli and the role of vocal perturbation," *J. Acoust. Soc. Am.* **105**, 522–535.

91. M. Macon & M. Clements (1996) "Speech concatenation and synthesis using an overlap-add sinusoidal model," *Proc. IEEE Int. Conf. ASSP*, pp. 361–364.

92. E. George & M. Smith (1997) "Speech analysis/synthesis and modification using an analysis-by-synthesis/overlap-add sinusoidal model," *IEEE Trans. Speech & Audio Proc.* **5**, 389–406.

93. A. Syrdal, Y. Stylianou, A. Conkie & J. Schroeter (1998) "TD-PSOLA versus harmonic plus noise model in diphone based speech synthesis," *Proc. IEEE Int. Conf. ASSP*, pp. 273–276.

94. F. Violaro & O. Böeffard (1999) "A hybrid model for text-to-speech synthesis," *IEEE Trans. Speech & Audio Proc.* **6**, 426–434.

95. J. Olive (1975) "Fundamental frequency rules for the synthesis of simple English sentences," *J. Acoust. Soc. Am.* **57**, 476–482.

96. D. O'Shaughnessy (1977) "Fundamental frequency by rule for a text-to-speech system," *Proc. IEEE Int. Conf. ASSP*, pp. 571–574.

97. J. Véronis, P. di Cristo, F. Courtois & C. Chaumette (1998) "A stochastic model of intonation for text-to-speech synthesis," *Speech Comm.* **26**, 233–244.

98. W. Cooper & J. Sorenson (1981) *Fundamental Frequency in Sentence Production* (Springer-Verlag: New York).

99. S. Werner & E. Keller (1994) "Prosodic aspects of speech," in *Fundamentals of Speech Synthesis and Recognition*, E. Keller (ed.) (John Wiley & Sons: Chichester), pp. 23–40.

100. J. 't Hart & A. Cohen (1973) "Intonation by rule: a perceptual quest," *J. Phonetics* **1**, 309–327.

101. H. Fujisaki, M. Ljungqvist & H. Murata (1993) "Analysis and modeling of word accent and sentence intonation in Swedish," *Proc. IEEE Int. Conf. ASSP*, pp. II-211–214.

102. S. Ohman (1967) "Word and sentence intonation: A quantitative model," *Royal Institute of Technology, Stockholm* STL-QPR, no. 2–3, 320–354.

103. J. Pierrehumbert (1981) "Synthesizing intonation," *J. Acoust. Soc. Am.* **70**, 985–995.

104. J. van Santen & J. Hirschberg (1994) "Segmental effects on timing and height of pitch contours," *Proc. Int. Conf. Spoken Lang. Proc.*, pp. 719–722.

105. D. Klatt (1976) "Linguistic uses of segmental duration in English: Acoustic and perceptual evidence," *J. Acoust. Soc. Am.* **59**, 1208–1221.

106. R. Port (1981) "Linguistic timing factors in combination," *J. Acoust. Soc. Am.* **69**, 262–274.

107. J. van Santen (1993) "Timing in text-to-speech systems," *Proc. Eurospeech*, pp. 1397–1404.

108. Y. Stylianou & O. Cappé (1998) "A system for voice conversion based on probabilistic classification and a harmonic plus noise model," *Proc. Int. Conf. ASSP*, pp. 281–284.

109. I. Karlsson & L. Neovius (1994) "Rule-based female speech synthesis—segmental level improvements," *Proc. 2nd ESCA/IEEE Workshop on Speech Synthesis*, pp. 123–126.

110. D. Childers & C. Lee (1991) "Voice quality factors: Analysis, synthesis & perception," *J. Acoust. Soc. Am.* **90**, 2394–2410.

111. D. Klatt & L. Klatt (1990) "Analysis, synthesis, and perception of voice quality variations among female and male talkers," *J. Acoust. Soc. Am.* **87**, 820–857.

112. D. Hermes (1991) "Synthesis of breathy vowels: Some research methods," *Speech Comm.* **10**, 497–502.

113. M. Abe & H. Mizuno (1994) "A strategy for changing speaking styles in text-to-speech systems," *Proc. 2nd ESCA/IEEE Workshop on Speech Synthesis*, pp. 41–44.

114. I. Murray & J. Arnott (1993) "Toward the simulation of emotion in synthetic speech: A review of the literature on human vocal emotion," *J. Acoust. Soc. Am.* **93**, 1097–1108.

115. B. Le Goff, T. Guiard-Mariguy, M. Cohen & C. Benoit (1994) "Real-time analysis-synthesis and intelligibility of talking faces," *Proc. 2nd ESCA/IEEE Workshop on Speech Synthesis*, pp. 53–56.

116. D. Massaro (1997) *Perceiving Talking Faces* (MIT Press: Cambridge, MA).

117. J. Robert-Ribes, J-L. Schwartz, T. Lallouache & P. Escudier (1998) "Complementarity and synergy in bimodal speech: Auditory, visual, and audio-visual identification of French oral vowels in noise," *J. Acoust. Soc. Am.* **103**, 3677–3689.

118. J. Zhang (1997) "National assessment of speech synthesis systems for Chinese," *Proc. Int. Conf. Speech Proc.*, pp. 35–42.

119. T. Rietveld *et al* (1997) "Evaluation of speech synthesis systems for Dutch in telecommunication applications in GSM and PSTN networks," *Proc. Eurospeech*, pp. 577–580.

120. E. Tzoukermann (1994) "Text-to-speech for French," *Proc. 2nd ESCA/IEEE Workshop on Speech Synthesis*, pp. 179–182.

121. M. Divay & G. Guyomard (1977) "Grapheme-to-phoneme transcription for French," *Proc. IEEE Int. Conf. ASSP*, pp. 575–578.

122. D. O'Shaughnessy (1984) "Design of a real-time French text-to-speech system," *Speech Comm.* **3**, 233–243.

123. B. Granstrom, P. Helgason & H. Thráinsson (1992) "The interaction of phonetics, phonology and morphology in an Icelandic text-to-speech system," *Proc. Int. Conf. Spoken Lang. Proc.*, pp. 185–188.

124. I. Murray & M. Black (1993) "A prototype text-to-speech system for Scottish Gaelic," *Proc. Eurospeech*, pp. 885–887.

125. S. Agrawal & K. Stevens (1992) "Towards synthesis of Hindi consonants using Klsyn88," *Proc. Int. Conf. Spoken Lang. Proc.*, pp. 177–180.

126. B. Angelini, C. Barolo, D. Falavigna, M. Omologo & S. Sandri (1997) "Automatic diphone extraction for an Italian text-to-speech synthesis system," *Proc. Eurospeech*, pp. 581–584.

127. Y. Ooyama, H. Asano & K. Matsuoka (1996) "Spoken style explanation generator for Japanese Kanji using a text-to-speech system," *Proc. Int. Conf. Spoken Lang. Proc.*, pp. 1369–1372.

128. S-H. Kim & J-Y. Kim (1997) "Efficient method of establishing words tone dictionary for Korean TTS system," *Proc. Eurospeech*, pp. 247–250.

129. E. Albano & A. Moreira (1996) "Archisegment-based letter-to-phone conversion for concatenative speech synthesis in Portuguese," *Proc Int. Conf. Spoken Lang. Proc.*, pp. 1708–1711.

130. J. Gros, N. Pavesik & F. Mihelic (1997) "Speech timing in Slovenian TTS," *Proc. Eurospeech*, pp. 323–326.

131. L. Aguilar *et al* (1994) "Evaluation of a Spanish text-to-speech system," *Proc. 2nd ESCA/IEEE Workshop on Speech Synthesis*, pp. 207–210.

132. M. Ljungqvist, A. Lindström & K. Gustafson (1994) "A new system for text-to-speech conversion, and its application to Swedish," *Proc. Int. Conf. Spoken Lang. Proc.*, pp. 1779–1782.

133. B. Williams (1994) "Diphone synthesis for the Welsh language," *Proc. Int. Conf. Spoken Lang. Proc.*, pp. 739–742.

134. C. Shih (1996) "Synthesis of trill," *Proc. Int. Conf. Spoken Lang. Proc.*, pp. 2223–2226.

135. L. Pols (1992) "Quality assessment of text-to-speech synthesis by rule," in *Advances in Speech Signal Processing*, S. Furui & M. Sondhi (eds.) (Marcel Dekker: New York), pp. 387–416.

136. R. van Bezooijen & L. Pols (1990) "Evaluating text-to-speech systems: Some methodological aspects," *Speech Comm.* **9**, 263–270.

137. J. van Santen (1993) "Perceptual experiments for diagnostic testing of text-to-speech systems," *Comp. Speech and Lang.* **7**, 49–100.

CHAPTER 10—RECOGNITION

The following are abbreviated in the reference list:

DM N. Dixon & T. Martin (1979) *Automatic Speech and Speaker Recognition* (IEEE: New York),

L W. Lea (1980) *Trends in Speech Recognition* (Prentice-Hall: Englewood Cliffs, NJ).

1. R. Lippmann (1997) "Speech recognition by humans and machines," *Speech Comm.* **22**, 1–15.

2. P. Silsbee & A. Bovik (1996) "Computer lipreading for improved accuracy in automatic speech recognition," *IEEE Trans. Speech & Audio Proc.* **4**, 337–351.

3. H. Bourlard, H. Hermansky & N. Morgan (1996) "Towards increasing speech recognition error rates," *Speech Comm.* **18**, 205–231.

4. S. Das, D. Nix & M. Picheny (1998) "Improvements in children's speech recognition performance," *Proc. IEEE Int. Conf. ASSP*, pp. 433–436.

5. J. van Hemert (1991) "Automatic segmentation of speech," *IEEE Trans. ASSP*, **ASSP-39**, 1008–1012.

6. A. Biermann, R. Rodman, D. Rubin & J. Heidlage (1985) "Natural language with discrete speech as a mode for human-to-machine communication," *Comm. ACM* **28**, 628–636.

7. K-F. Lee & F. Alleva (1992) "Continuous speech recognition," in *Advances in Speech Signal Processing*, S. Furui & M. Sondhi (eds.) (Marcel Dekker: New York), pp. 623–650.

8. P. Loizou & A. Spanias (1996) "High-performance alphabet recognition," *IEEE Trans. Speech & Audio Proc.* **4**, 430–445.

9. D. Masaho, Y. Gotoh & H. Silverman (1996) "Analysis of LPC/DFT features for an HMM-based alphadigit recognizer," *IEEE Signal Proc. Lett.* **3**, 103–106.

10. R. J. Andrews (1984) "Beyond accuracy: Tools for evaluating performance of speech recognition systems," *Speech Tech.* Aug./Sept., 84–88.

11. R. Moore (1977) "Evaluating speech recognizers," *IEEE Trans. ASSP*, **ASSP-25**, 178–183.

*12. D. Klatt (1977) "Review of the ARPA speech understanding project," *J. Acoust. Soc. Am.* **62**, 1345–1366; also in DM, pp. 114–135.

13. R. Cole *et al* (1995) "The challenge of spoken language systems: Research directions for the nineties," *IEEE Trans. Speech & Audio Proc.* **3**, 1–21.

14. V. Zue (1997) "Conversational interfaces: Advances and challenges," *Proc. Europ. Conf. Speech Comm. & Tech.* pp. KN-9–18.

15. J. Godfrey, E. Holliman & J. McDaniel (1992) "Switchboard: Telephone speech corpus for research and development," *Proc. IEEE Int. Conf. ASSP*, pp. I:517–520.

16. S. Young & L. Chase (1998) "Speech recognition evaluation: A review of the U.S. CSR and LVCSR programmes," *Comp. Speech & Lang.* **12**, 263–279.

17. J. Mariani (1997) "Spoken language processing in multimodal communication" *Proc. Int. Conf. Speech Proc. (Korea)*, pp. 3–12.

18. W. Eckert, T. Kuhn, H. Niemann, S. Rieck, S. Scheuer & E. Schukat-Talmazzini (1993) "Spoken dialogue system for German intercity train timetable enquiries," *Proc. Europ. Conf. Speech Comm. & Tech.* pp. 1871–1874.

19. R. Carlson & S. Hunnicutt (1996) "Generic and domain-specific aspects of the Waxholm NLP and dialogue modules," *Proc. Int. Conf. Spoken Lang. Proc.*, pp. 667–680.

20. D. Jurafsky, C. Wooters, G. Tajchman, J. Segal, A. Stolcke, E. Fosler & N. Morgan (1994) "The Berkeley restaurant project," *Proc. Int. Conf. Spoken Lang. Proc.*, pp. 2139–2142.

21. C. Jankowski, H-D. Vo & R. Lippmann (1995) "A comparison of signal processing front ends for automatic word recognition," *IEEE Trans. Speech & Audio Proc.* **3**, 286–293.

22. S. Levinson (1985) "Structural methods in automatic speech recognition," *Proc. IEEE* **73**, 1625–1650.

*23. V. Zue (1985) "The use of speech knowledge in automatic speech recognition," *Proc. IEEE* **73**, 1602–1615.

24. D. Fohr, J-P. Haton & Y. Laprie (1994) "Knowledge-based techniques in acoustic-phonetic decoding of speech: Interest and limitations," *Int. J. Pattern Rec. & Artif. Intell.* **8**, 133–153.

25. A. R. Smith & M. Sambur (1980) "Hypothesizing and verifying words for speech recognition," in L, pp. 139–165.

26. J. Smolders, T. Claes, G. Sablon & D. van Campernolle (1994) "On the importance of the microphone position for speech recognition in the car," *Proc. IEEE Int. Conf. ASSP*, vol. I, pp. 429–432.

27. G. Kang & M. Lidd (1984) "Automatic gain control," *Proc. IEEE Int Conf. ASSP*, pp. 19.6.1–4.

28. S. Das (1982) "Some experiments in discrete utterance recognition," *IEEE Trans. ASSP*, **ASSP-30**, 766–770.

29. L. Rabiner (1984) "On the application of energy contours to the recognition of connected word sequences," *AT&T Bell Labs Tech. J.* **63**, 1981–1995.

30. T. Sullivan & R. Stern (1993) "Multi-microphone correlation-based processing for robust speech recognition," *Proc. IEEE Int. Conf. ASSP*, II, pp. 91–94.

31. N. Morgan, E. Fosler & N. Mirghafori (1997) "Speech recognition using on-line estimation of speaking rate," *Proc. Europ. Conf. Speech Comm. & Tech.* 2079–2082.

32. L. Bahl, F. Jelinek & R. Mercer (1983) "A maximum likelihood approach to continuous speech recognition," *IEEE Trans. Pattern Anal. Machine Intell.* **PAMI-5**, 179–190.

33. G. Kopec & M. Bush (1985) "Network-based isolated digit recognition using vector quantization," *IEEE Trans. ASSP*, **ASSP-33**, 850–867.

34. S. Okawa, E. Bocchieri & A. Potamianos (1998) "Multi-band speech recognition in noisy environments," *Proc. IEEE Int. Conf. ASSP*, pp. 641–644.

35. N. Mirghafori & N. Morgan (1998) "Transmissions and transitions: Study of two common assumptions in multi-band ASR," *Proc. IEEE Int. Conf. ASSP*, pp. 713–716.

36. H. Wakita (1977) "Normalization of vowels by vocal-tract length and its application to vowel identification," *IEEE Trans. ASSP*, **ASSP-25**, 183–192.

37. J. Schroeter & M. Sondhi (1994) "Techniques for estimating vocal tract shapes from the speech signal," *IEEE Trans. Speech & Audio Proc.* **2**, 1819–1834.

38. J. Hogden *et al* (1996) "Accurate recovery of articulatory positions from acoustics: New conclusions based on human data," *J. Acoust. Soc. Am.* **100**, 1819–1834.

39. J. Picone (1993) "Signal modeling techniques in speech recognition," *Proc. IEEE* **81**, 1215–1247.

40. S. Davis & P. Mermelstein (1980) "Comparison of parametric representations for monosyllabic word recognition in continuously spoken sentences," *IEEE Trans. ASSP*, **ASSP-28**, 357–366.

41. R. Lippmann & B. Carlson (1997) "A robust speech recognition with time-varying filtering, interruptions, and noise," *IEEE Workshop on Speech Recognition*, pp. 365–372.

42. R. Chengalvarayan & L. Deng (1997) "HMM-based speech recognition using state-dependent, discriminatively derived transforms on mel-warped DFT features," *IEEE Trans. Speech & Audio Proc.* **5**, 243–256.

43. B. Dautrich, L. Rabiner & T. Martin (1983) "On the effects of varying filter bank parameters on isolated word recognition," *IEEE Trans. ASSP*, **ASSP-31**, 793–807.

44. E. Zwicker (1986) "Peripheral preprocessing in hearing and psychoacoustics as guidelines for speech recognition," *Proc. Montreal Symp. Speech Recog.*, pp. 1–4.

45. K. Paliwal (1984) "Effect of preemphasis on vowel recognition performance," *Speech Comm.* **3**, 101–106.

46. E. Zwicker, E. Terhardt & E. Paulus (1979) "Automatic speech recognition using psychoacoustic models," *J. Acoust. Soc. Am.* **65**, 487–498.

47. O. Ghitza (1992) "Auditory nerve representation as a basis for speech processing," in *Advances in Speech Signal Processing*, S. Furui & M. Sondhi (eds.) (Marcel Dekker: New York), pp. 453–485.

48. Y. Gao & J-P. Haton (1993) "Noise reduction and speech recognition in noise conditions tested on LPNN-based continuous speech recognition system," *Proc. Europ. Conf. Speech Comm. & Tech.*, pp. 1035–1038.

49. B. Strope & A. Alwan (1997) "A model of dynamic auditory perception and its application to robust word recognition," *IEEE Trans. Speech & Audio Proc.* **5**, 451–464.

50. K. Aikawa, H. Singer, H. Kawahara & Y. Tokhura (1996) "Cepstral representation of speech motivated by time-frequency masking: An application to speech recognition," *J. Acoust. Soc. Am.* **100**, 603–614.

51. S. Sandhu & O. Ghitza (1995) "A comparative study of mel cepstra and EIH for phone classification under adverse conditions," *Proc. IEEE Int. Conf. ASSP*, pp. 409–412.

52. J-C. Junqua, H. Wakita & H. Hermansky (1993) "Evaluation and optimization of perceptually-based ASR front end," *IEEE Trans. Speech & Audio Proc.* **1**, 39–48.

53. H. Hermansky & N. Morgan (1994) "RASTA processing of speech," *Trans. Speech & Audio Proc.* **2**, 578–589.

54. P. Garner & W. Holmes (1998) "On the robust incorporation of formant features into hidden Markov models for automatic speech recognition," *Proc. IEEE Int. Conf. ASSP*, pp. 1–4.

55. K. Paliwal (1997) "Spectral subband centroids as features for speech recognition," *IEEE Workshop on Speech Recognition*, pp. 124–131.

56. L. Welling & H. Ney (1998) "Formant estimation for speech recognition," *IEEE Trans. Speech & Audio Proc.* **6**, 36–48.

57. K. Shikano & F. Itakura (1992) "Spectrum distance measures for speech recognition," in *Advances in Speech Signal Processing*, S. Furui & M. Sondhi (eds.) (Marcel Dekker: New York), pp. 419–452.

58. V. Steinbiss *et al* (1995) "Continuous speech dictation—from theory to practice," *Speech Comm.* **17**, 19–38.

59. M. Gales (1998) "Semi-tied covariance Matrices," *Proc. IEEE Int. Conf. ASSP*, pp. 657–660.

60. L. Arslan & J. Hansen (1999) "Selective training for hidden Markov models with applications to speech coding," *IEEE Trans Speech & Audio Proc.* **7**, 46–54.

61. F. Itakura (1975) "Minimum prediction residual principle applied to speech recognition," *IEEE Trans. ASSP*, **ASSP-23**, 67–72; also in DM, pp. 145–150.

62. B-H. Juang & L. Rabiner (1985) "Mixture autoregressive hidden Markov models for speech signals," *IEEE Trans. ASSP*, **ASSP-33**, 1404–1413.

*63. L. Rabiner & B. Juang (1993) *Fundamentals of Speech Recognition* (Prentice-Hall: Englewood Cliffs, NJ).

64. N. Nocerino, F. Soong, L. Rabiner & D. Klatt (1985) "Comparative study of several distortion measures for speech recognition," *IEEE Int. Cont ASSP*, pp. 25–28.

65. K. Paliwal (1982) "On the performance of the frequency-weighted cepstral coefficients in vowel recognition," *Speech Comm.* **1**, 151–154.

66. B. Juang, L. Rabiner & J. Wilpon (1986) "On the use of bandpass filtering in speech recognition," *Proc. IEEE Int. Conf. ASSP*, pp. 765–768.

67. R. Sukkar & C-H. Lee (1996) "Vocabulary-independent discriminative utterance verification for nonkeyword rejection in subword based speech recognition," *IEEE Trans. Speech & Audio Proc.* **4**, 420–429.

68. Y. Tohkura (1984) "A weighted cepstral distance measure for speech recognition," *IEEE Trans. ASSP*, **ASSP-35**, 1414–1422.

69. B. Yegnanarayana, S. Chandran & A. Agarwal (1984) "On improvement of performance of isolated word recognition for degraded speech," *Signal Processing* **7**, 175–183.

70. D. Klatt (1986) "Representation of the first formant in speech recognition and in models of the auditory periphery," *Proc. Montreal Symp. Speech Recog.*, pp. 5–7.

71. R. Gray, A. Buzo, A. Gray Jr. & Y. Matsuyama (1980) "Distortion measures for speech processing," *IEEE Trans. ASSP*, **ASSP-28**, 367–376.

72. Y. Kobayashi, Y. Ohmori & Y. Niimi (1986) "Recognition of vowels in continuous speech based on the dynamic characteristics of WLR distance trajectories," *J. Acoust. Soc. Japan* **7**, 29–38.

73. W. Chou, C-H. Lee, B-H. Juang & F. Soong (1994) "A minimum error rate pattern recognition approach to speech recognition," *Int. J. Pattern Rec. & Artif. Intell.* **8**, 5–31.

74. B-H. Juang, W. Chou & C-H. Lee (1997) "Minimum classification error rate methods for speech recognition," *IEEE Trans. Speech & Audio Proc.* **5**, 257–265.

75. K-Y. Su & C-H. Lee (1994) "Speech recognition using weighted HMM and subspace projection approaches," *IEEE Trans. Speech & Audio Proc.* **2**, 69–79.

76. Y. Normandin, R. Cardin & R. de Mori (1994) "High-performance connected digit recognition using maximum mutual information estimation," *IEEE Trans. Speech & Audio Proc.* **2**, 299–311.

77. H. Cung & Y. Normandin (1997) "MMIE training of large vocabulary recognition systems," *Speech Comm.* **22**, 303–314.

78. P. Loizou & A. Spanias (1997) "Improving discrimination of confusable words using the divergence measure," *J. Acoust. Soc. Am.* **101**, 1100–1111.

79. A. Rao, K. Rose & A. Gersho (1998) "Deterministically annnealed design of speech recognizers and its performance on isolated letters," *Proc. IEEE Int. Conf. ASSP*, pp. 461–464.

80. M. Hunt & C. Lefèbvre (1989) "A comparison of several acoustic representations for speech recognition with degraded and undegraded speech," *Proc. IEEE Int. Conf. ASSP*, pp. 262–265.

81. Y. Gong (1995) "Speech recognition in noisy environments," *Speech Comm.* **16**, 261–291.

82. V. Gupta, M. Lennig & P. Mermelstein (1984) "Decision rules for speaker-independent isolated word recognition," *Proc. IEEE Int. Conf. ASSP*, pp. 9.2.1–4.

83. L. Rabiner, S. Levinson, A. Rosenberg & J. Wilpon (1979) "Speaker-independent recognition of isolated words using clustering techniques," *IEEE Trans. ASSP*, **ASSP-27**, 336–349.

84. B. Aldefeld, L. Rabiner, A. Rosenberg & J. Wilpon (1980) "Automated directory listing retrieval system based on isolated word recognition," *Proc. IEEE* **68**, 1364–1379.

85. J. Holtzman (1984) "Automatic speech recognition error/no decision tradeoff curves," *IEEE Trans. ASSP*, **ASSP-32**, 1232–1235.

86. S. Wu, B. Kingsbury, N. Morgan & S. Greenberg (1998) "Incorporating information from syllable-length time scales into automatic speech recognition," *Proc. IEEE Int. Conf. ASSP*, pp. 721–724.

87. A. Ganapathiraju *et al* (1997) "Syllable—a promising recognition unit for LVCSR," *IEEE Workshop on Speech Recognition*, pp. 207–213.

88. M. Hunt, M. Lennig & P. Mermelstein (1983) "Use of dynamic programming in a syllable-based continuous speech recognition system," in *Time Warps, String Edits, and Macromolecules: The*

Theory and Practice of Sequence Comparison, D. Sankoff & J. Kruskall (eds.) (Addison-Wesley: Reading, MA), pp. 163–187.

89. J-C. Junqua, B. Mak & B. Reaves (1994) "A robust algorithm for word boundary detection in the presence of noise," *IEEE Trans. Speech & Audio Proc.* **2**, 406–412.

90. L. Lamel, L. Rabiner, A. Rosenberg & J. Wilpon (1981) "An improved endpoint detector for isolated word recognition," *IEEE Trans. ASSP*, **ASSP-29**, 777–785.

91. J. Wilpon, L. Rabiner & T. Martin (1984) "An improved word-detection algorithm for telephone-quality speech incorporating both syntactic and semantic constraints," *AT&T Bell Labs Tech. J.* **63**, 479–497.

92. L. Rabiner & M. Sambur (1975) "An algorithm for determining the endpoints of isolated utterances," *Bell Syst. Tech. J.* **54**, 297–315.

93. P. de Souza (1983) "A statistical approach to the design of an adaptive self-normalizing silence detector," *IEEE Trans. ASSP*, **ASSP-31**, 678–684.

*94. W. Lea (1980) "Speech recognition: Past, present, and future," in L, pp. 39–98.

95. R. Zelinski & F. Class (1983) "A segmentation algorithm for connected word recognition based on estimation principles," *IEEE Trans. ASSP*, **ASSP-31**, 818–827.

96. H. Sakoe & S. Chiba (1978) "Dynamic programming algorithm optimization for spoken word recognition," *IEEE Trans. ASSP*, **ASSP-26**, 43–49; also in DM, pp. 194–200.

97. H. Sakoe (1992) "Dynamic programming-based speech recognition," in *Advances in Speech Signal Processing*, S. Furui & M. Sondhi (eds.) (Marcel Dekker: New York), pp. 487–507.

*98. H. Silverman & D. Morgan (1990) "The application of dynamic programming to connected speech segmentation," *IEEE ASSP Mag.* **7**, no. 3, 7–25.

99. J. Deller, J. Proakis & J. Hansen (1993) *Discrete-time Processing of Speech Signals* (Macmillan: New York), chaps. 11–12.

100. S. Furui (1986) "Speaker-independent isolated word recognition using dynamic features of speech spectrum," *IEEE Trans. ASSP*, **ASSP-34**, 52–59.

101. G. White & R. Neely (1976) "Speech recognition experiments with linear prediction, bandpass filtering & dynamic programming," *IEEE Trans. ASSP*, **ASSP-24**, 183–188.

102. H. Höhne, C. Coker, S. Levinson & L. Rabiner (1983) "On temporal alignment of sentences of natural and synthetic speech," *IEEE Trans. ASSP*, **ASSP-31**, 807–813.

103. C. Myers, L. Rabiner & A. Rosenberg (1980) "Performance tradeoff in dynamic time warping algorithms for isolated word recognition," *IEEE Trans. ASSP*, **ASSP-28**, 622–635.

104. L. Rabiner, A. Rosenberg & S. Levinson (1978) "Considerations in dynamic time warping algorithms for discrete word recognition," *IEEE Trans. ASSP*, **ASSP-26**, 575–582.

105. B. Yegnanarayana & T. Sreekumar (1984) "Signal-dependent matching for isolated word speech recognition systems," *Signal Processing* **7**, 161–173.

*106. L. Rabiner & S. Levinson (1981) "Isolated and connected word recognition—theory and selected applications," *IEEE Trans. Comm.* **COM-29**, 621–659.

107. S. Haltsonen (1985) "Improved dynamic time warping methods for discrete utterance recognition," *IEEE Trans. ASSP*, **ASSP-33**, 449–450.

108. C. Marshall & P. Nye (1983) "Stress and vowel duration effects on syllable recognition," *J. Acoust. Soc. Am.* **74**, 433–443.

109. P. Le Cerf & D. van Campernolle (1994) "A new variable frame rate analysis method for speech recognition," *IEEE Signal Proc. Lett.* **1**, 185–187.

110. C. Tappert & S. Das (1978) "Memory & time improvements in a dynamic programming algorithm for matching speech patterns," *IEEE Trans. ASSP*, **ASSP-26**, 583–586.

111. M. Kuhn & H. Tomaschewski (1983) "Improvements in isolated word recognition," *IEEE Trans. ASSP*, **ASSP-31**, 157–167.

112. M. Blomberg & K. Elenius (1986) "Nonlinear frequency warp for speech recognition," *Proc. IEEE Int. Conf. ASSP*, pp. 2631–2634.

113. C. Myers & L. Rabiner (1981) "Connected digit recognition using a level building DTW algorithm," *IEEE Trans. ASSP*, **ASSP-29**, 351–363.

114. H. Sakoe (1979) "Two-level DP-matching: A dynamic programming pattern matching algorithm for connected word recognition," *IEEE Trans. ASSP*, **ASSP-27**, 588–595.

115. L. Rabiner, J. Wilpon, A. Quinn & S. Terrace (1984) "On the application of embedded digit training to speaker independent connected digit recognition," *IEEE Trans. ASSP*, **ASSP-32**, 272–280.

116. J-P. Brassard (1985) "Integration of segmenting and nonsegmenting approaches in continuous speech recognition," *Proc. IEEE Int. Conf. ASSP*, pp. 1217–1220.

117. J. Bridle, M. Brown & R. Chamberlain (1982) "An algorithm for connected word recognition," *Proc. IEEE Int. Conf. ASSP*, pp. 899–902.

118. H. Ney (1984) "The use of a one-stage dynamic programming algorithm for connected word recognition," *IEEE Trans. ASSP*, **ASSP-32**, 263–271.

119. K. Greer, B. Lowerre & L. Wilcox (1982) "Acoustic pattern matching and beam searching," *Proc. IEEE Int. Conf. ASSP*, pp. 1251–1254.

120. L. Lamel & V. Zue (1982) "Performance improvement in a dynamic-programming-based isolated word recognition system for the alpha-digit task," *Proc. IEEE Int. Conf. ASSP*, pp. 558–561.

121. D. Burton, J. Shore & J. Buck (1985) "Isolated word speech recognition using multi-section vector quantization codebooks," *IEEE Trans. ASSP*, **ASSP-33**, 837–849.

122. K. Pan, F. Soong & L. Rabiner (1985) "A vector-quantization-based preprocessor for speaker-independent isolated word recognition," *IEEE Trans. ASSP*, **ASSP-33**, 546–560.

123. L. Rabiner, S. Levinson & M. Sondhi (1983) "On the application of vector quantization and hidden Markov models to speaker-independent, isolated word recognition," *Bell Syst. Tech. J.* **62**, 1075–1105.

124. M. Ackroyd (1980) "Isolated word recognition using the weighted Levenshtein distance," *IEEE Trans. ASSP*, **ASSP-28**, 243–244.

125. B. Landell, J. Naylor & R. Wohlford (1984) "Effect of vector quantization on a continuous speech recognition system," *Proc. IEEE Int. Conf. ASSP*, pp. 26.11.1–4.

126. L. Bahl & F. Jelinek (1975) "Decoding for channels with insertions, deletions, and substitutions with applications to speech recognition," *IEEE Trans. Info. Theory* **IT-21**, 404–411.

127. J. Baker (1975) "The DRAGON system—an overview," *IEEE Trans. ASSP*, **ASSP-23**, 24–29; also in DM, pp. 225–230.

*128. X. Huang, Y. Ariki & M. Jack (1990) *Hidden Markov Models for Speech Recognition* (Edinburgh University Press: Edinburgh).

129. K-F. Lee (1989) *Automatic Speech Recognition: The Development of the SPHINX System* (Kluwer: Boston).

*130. A. Poritz (1988) "Hidden Markov models: A guided tour," *Proc. IEEE Int. Conf. ASSP*, pp. 7–13.

131. J. Mariani (1989) "Recent advances in speech processing," *Proc. IEEE Int. Conf. ASSP*, pp. 429–440.

*132. L. Rabiner (1989) "A tutorial on hidden Markov models and selected applications in speech recognition," *Proc IEEE* **77**, no. 2, 257–286.

133. L. Rabiner, S. Levinson & M. Sondhi (1984) "On the use of hidden Markov models for speaker-independent recognition of isolated words from a medium-size vocabulary," *AT&T Bell Labs Tech. J.* **63**, 627–641.

134. F. Jelinek (1976) "Continuous speech recognition by statistical methods," *Proc. IEEE* **64**, 532–556.

135. T. Moon (1996) "The expectation-maximization algorithm," *IEEE Signal Proc. Mag.* **13**, no. 6, 47–60.

136. J. Hansen & B. Womack (1996) "Feature analysis and neural network-based classification of speech under stress," *IEEE Trans. Speech & Audio Proc.* **4**, 307–313.

137. R. Blahut (1985) *Fast Algorithms for Digital Signal Processing* (Addison-Wesley: Reading, MA).

138. H-L. Lou (1995) "Implementing the Viterbi algorithm," *IEEE Signal Proc. Mag.* **12**, no. 5, 42–52.

139. L. Liporace (1982) "Maximum likelihood estimation for multivariate observations of Markov sources," *IEEE Trans. Info. Theory* **IT-28**, 729–734.

140. S. Levinson, L. Rabiner & M. Sondhi (1983) "An introduction to the application of the theory of probabilistic functions of a Markov process to automatic speech recognition," *Bell Syst. Tech. J.* **62**, 1035–1074.

141. W. Turin (1998) "Unidirectional and parallel Baum-Welch algorithm," *IEEE Trans. Speech & Audio Proc.* **6**, 516–523.

142. A. Rosenberg, L. Rabiner, J. Wilpon & D. Kahn (1983) "Demisyllable-based isolated word recognition systems," *IEEE Trans. ASSP*, **ASSP-31**, 713–726.

143. L. Rabiner, A. Rosenberg, J. Wilpon & T. Zampini (1982) "A bootstrapping training technique for obtaining demisyllable reference patterns," *J. Acoust. Soc. Am.* **71**, 1588–1595.

144. A. Lazaridès, Y. Normandin & H. Kuhn (1996) "Improving decision trees for acoustic modeling," *Proc. Int. Conf. Spoken Lang. Proc.*, pp. 1053–1056.

145. A. Ljolje (1994) "High accuracy phone recognition using context-clustering and quasi-triphonic models," *Computer, Speech & Lang.* **8**, 129–151.

146. R. Rose (1995) "Keyword detection in conversational speech utterances using hidden Markov model based continuous speech recognition," *Computer, Speech & Lang.* **9**, 309–333.

147. L. Bahl, P. Brown, P. de Souza, H. Mercer & M. Picheny (1993) "A method for the construction of acoustic models for words," *IEEE Trans. Speech & Audio Proc.* **1**, 443–452.

148. L. Bahl, J. Bellegarda, P. de Sousa, P. Gopalakrishnan, D. Nahamoo & M. Picheny (1993) "Multonic Markov word models for large vocabulary continuous speech recognition," *IEEE Trans. Speech & Audio Proc.* **1**, 334–344.

149. B. Mak & E. Bocchieri (1998) "Training of subspace distribution clustering hidden Markov model," *Proc. IEEE Int. Conf. ASSP*, pp. 673–676.

150. X. Huang, H. Hon, M. Hwang & K. Lee (1993) "A comparative study of discrete, semicontinuous, and continuous hidden Markov models," *Computer, Speech & Lang.* **7**, 359–368.

151. C. Mitchell, M. Harper, L. Jamieson & R. Helzerman (1995) "A parallel implementation of a hidden Markov model with duration modeling for speech recognition," *Digital Signal Proc.* **5**, 43–57.

152. S. Levinson (1986) "Continuously variable duration hidden Markov models for speech analysis," *Proc. IEEE Int. Cont ASSP*, pp. 1241–1244.

153. H. Bourlard, Y. Kamp & C. Wellekens (1985) "Speaker dependent connected speech recognition via phonemic Markov models," *Proc. IEEE Int. Conf. ASSP*, pp. 1213–1216.

154. B. Strope & A. Alwan (1998) "Robust word recognition using threaded spectral peaks" *Proc. IEEE Int. Conf. ASSP*, pp. 625–628.

155. O. Siohan, Y. Gong & J-P. Haton (1996) "Comparative experiments of several adaptation approaches to noisy speech recognition using stochastic trajectory models," *Speech Comm.* **18**, 335–352.

156. Z. Hu & E. Barnard (1997) "Smoothness analysis for trajectory features," *Proc. IEEE Int. Conf. ASSP*, pp. 979–982.

157. L. Deng & M. Aksmanovik (1997) "Speaker-independent phonetic classification using hidden Markov models with mixtures of trend functions," *IEEE Trans. Speech & Audio Proc.* **5**, 319–324.

158. L. Deng & R. Chengalvarayan (1995) "A Markov model containing state-conditioned second-order non-stationarity: Application to speech recognition," *Computer, Speech & Lang.* **9**, 63–86.

159. M. Russell & W. Holmes (1997) "Linear trajectory segmental HMM's," *IEEE Signal Proc. Lett.* **4**, 72–74.

160. P. Hanna, J. Ming, P. O'Boyle & F. Smith (1997) "Modeling interframe dependence with preceding and succeeding frames," *Proc. Europ. Conf. Speech. & Tech.* pp. 1167–1170.

161. R. Sitaram & T. Sreenivas (1997) "Incorporating phonetic properties in hidden Markov models for speech recognition," *J. Acoust. Soc. Am.* **102**, 1149–1158.

162. K. Erler & G. Freeman (1996) "An HMM-based speech recognizer using overlapping articulatory features," *J. Acoust. Soc. Am.* **100**, 2500–2513.

163. K. Samudravijaya, S. Singh & P. Rao (1998) "Pre-recognition measures of speaking rate," *Speech Comm.* **24** 73–84.

164. L. Rabiner & J. Wilpon (1980) "A simplified, robust training procedure for speaker trained, isolated word recognition systems," *J. Acoust. Soc. Am.* **68**, 1271–1276.

165. S. Levinson, L. Rabiner, A. Rosenberg & J. Wilpon (1979) "Interactive clustering techniques for selecting speaker independent reference templates for isolated word recognition," *IEEE Trans. ASSP,* **ASSP-27**, 134–141.

166. L. Rabiner & J. Wilpon (1979) "Considerations in applying clustering techniques to speaker-independent word recognition," *J. Acoust. Soc. Am.* **66**, 663–673.

167. V. Gupta & P. Mermelstein (1982) "Effects of speaker accent on the performance of a speaker-independent, isolated-word recognizer," *J. Acoust. Soc. Am.* **71**, 1581–1587.

168. E. Scheirer & M. Slaney (1997) "Construction and evaluation of a robust multifeature speech/music discriminator," *Proc. IEEE Int. Conf. ASSP*, pp. 1331–1334.

169. X. Huang & K-F. Lee (1993) "On speaker-independent, speaker-dependent, and speaker-adaptive speech recognition," *IEEE Trans. Speech & Audio Proc.* **1**, 150–157.

170. Y. Zhao (1994) "An acoustic-phonetic-based speaker-adaptation technique for improving speaker-independent continuous speech recognition," *IEEE Trans. Speech & Audio Proc.* **2**, 380–394.

171. J. Kreiman (1997) "Speaker modeling for speaker adaptation in automatic speech recognition," in *Talker Variability in Speech Processing*, K. Johnson & J. Mullennix (eds.) (Academic Press: San Diego, CA), pp. 167–189.

172. S. Ahadi & P. Woodland (1997) "Combined Bayesian and predictive techniques for rapid speaker adaptation of continuous density hidden Markov models," *Computer, Speech & Lang.* **11**, 187–206.

173. V. Digalakis & G. Neumeyer (1996) "Speaker adaptation using combined transformation and Bayesian methods," *IEEE Trans. Speech & Audio Proc.* **4**, 294–300.

174. M. Padmanabhan, L. Bahl, D. Nahamoo & M. Picheny (1998) "Speaker clustering and transformation for speaker adaptation in speech recognition systems," *IEEE Trans. Speech & Audio Proc.* **6**, 71–77.

175. J-L. Gauvin & C-H. Lee (1994) "Maximum a posteriori estimation for multivariate Gaussian mixture observations of Markov chains," *IEEE Trans. Speech & Audio Proc.* **2**, 291–298.

176. J-T. Chien, C-H. Lee & H-C. Wang (1997) "A hybrid algorithm for speaker adaptation using MAP transformation and adaptation," *IEEE Signal Proc. Lett.* **4**, 167–169.
177. C. Leggetter & P. Woodland (1995) "Maximum likelihood linear regression for speaker adaptation of continuous density hidden Markov models," *Computer, Speech & Lang.* **9**, 171–185.
178. M. Gales (1998) "Maximum likelihood linear transformations for HMM-based speech recognition," *Computer, Speech & Lang.* **12**, 75–98.
179. J. Takahashi & S. Sagayama (1997) "Vector-field-smoothed Bayesian learning for fast and incremental speaker/telephone-channel adaptation," *Computer, Speech & Lang.* **11**, 127–146.
180. T. Kosaka, S. Matsunaga & S. Sagayama (1996) "Speaker-independent speech recognition based on tree-structured speaker clustering," *Computer, Speech & Lang.* **10**, 55–74.
181. R. Kuhn *et al* (1998) "Eigenvoices for speaker adaptation," *Proc. Int. Conf. Spoken Lang. Proc.*, pp. 1771–1774.
182. H. Jin, S. Matsoukas, R. Schwartz & F. Kubala (1998) "Fast robust inverse transform speaker adapted training using diagonal transformations," *Proc. IEEE Int. Conf. ASSP*, pp. 785–788.
183. T. Claes, J. Dologlou, L. ten Bosch & D. van Compernolle (1998) "A novel feature transformation for vocal tract length normalization in automatic speech recognition," *IEEE Trans. Speech & Audio Proc.* **6**, 549–557.
184. Q. Lin & C. Che (1995) "Normalizing the vocal tract length for speaker independent speech recognition," *IEEE Signal Proc. Lett.* **2**, 201–203.
185. L. Lee & R. Rose (1998) "A frequency warping approach to speaker normalization," *IEEE Trans. Speech & Audio Proc.* **6**, 49–60.
186. S. Umesh, L. Cohen & D. Nelson (1998) "Improved scale-cepstral analysis in speech," *Proc. IEEE Int. Conf. ASSP*, pp. 637–640.
187. E. Gouvêa & R. Stern (1997) "Speaker normalization through formant-based warping of the frequency scale," *Proc. Europ. Conf. Speech Comm. & Tech.* pp. 1139–1142.
188. S. Umesh, L. Cohen, N. Marinovic & D. Nelson (1998) "Scale transform in speech analysis," *IEEE Trans. Speech & Audio Proc.* **7**, 40–45.
189. C-H. Lee (1998) "On stochastic feature and model compensation approaches for robust speech recognition," *Speech Comm.* **25**, 29–47.
190. J-C. Junqua (1993) "The Lombard reflex and its role on human listeners and automatic speech recognizers," *J. Acoust. Soc. Am.* **93**, 510–524.
191. A. Acero (1980) *Acoustical and Environmental Robustness in Automatic Speech Recognition* (Kluwer: Boston, MA).
192. C. Mokbel & G. Chollet (1995) "Automatic word recognition in cars," *IEEE Trans. Speech & Audio Proc.* **3**, 346–356.
*193. J-C. Junqua & J-P. Haton (1996) *Robustness in Automatic Speech Recognition* (Kluwer: Dordrecht).
194. J. Hansen & L. Arslan (1995) "Robust feature-estimation and objective quality assessment for noisy speech recognition using the credit card corpus," *IEEE Trans. Speech & Audio Proc.* **3**, 169–184.
195. M. Cooke, A. Morris & P. Green (1997) "Missing data techniques for robust speech recognition," *Proc. IEEE Int. Conf. ASSP*, pp. 863–866.
196. S. Nakamura & K. Shikano (1997) "Room acoustics and reverberation: Impact on hands-free recognition," *Proc. Europ. Conf. Speech Comm. & Tech.*, pp. 2419–2422.
197. G. Faucon & R. Le Bouquin-Jeannes (1997) "Echo and noise reduction for hands-free terminals—state of the art," *Proc. Europ. Conf. Speech Comm. & Tech.*, pp. 2423–2426.

198. M. Omlogo, P. Svaizer & M. Matassoni (1998) "Environmental conditions and acoustic transduction in hands-free robust speech recognition," *Speech Comm.* **25**, 75–95.

199. A. Erell & M. Weintraub (1993) "Filterbank-energy estimation using mixture and Markov model recognition of noisy speech," *IEEE Trans. Speech & Audio Proc.* **1**, 68–76.

200. D. Mansour & B-H. Juang (1989) "A family of distortion measures based upon projection operation for robust speech recognition," *IEEE Trans. ASSP,* **ASSP-37**, 1659–1671.

201. M. Rahim & B-H. Juang (1996) "Signal bias removal by maximum likelihood estimation for robust telephone speech recognition," *IEEE Trans. Speech & Audio Proc.* **4**, 19–30.

202. M. Rahim, B-H. Juang, W. Chou & E. Buhrke (1996) "Signal conditioning techniques for robust speech recognition," *IEEE Signal Proc. Lett.* **3**, 107–109.

203. C. Nadeu, P. Pachès-Leal & A. Rosenberg (1997) "Filtering the time sequences of spectral parameters for speech recognition," *Speech Comm.* **22**, 315–332.

204. D. Mansour & B-H. Juang (1989) "The short-time modified coherence representation and its application for noisy speech recognition," *IEEE Trans. ASSP,* **ASSP-37**, 795–804.

205. H. Cung & Y. Normandin (1993) "Noise adaptation algorithms for robust speech recognition," *Speech Comm.* **12**, 267–276.

206. M. Gales (1998) "Predictive model-based compensation schemes for robust speech recognition," *Speech Comm.* **25**, 49–74.

207. F. Jelinek, R. Mercer & S. Roucos (1992) "Principles of lexical language modeling for speech recognition," in *Advances in Speech Signal Processing*, S. Furui & M. Sondhi (eds.) (Marcel Dekker: New York), pp. 651–699.

208. H. Ney, V. Steinbiss, R. Haeb-Umbach, B-H. Tran & U. Essen (1994) "An overview of the Philips research system for large-vocabulary continuous-speech recognition," *Int. J. Pattern Rec. & Artif. Intell.* **8**, 33–70.

209. M. Mohri (1997) "Finite-state transducers in language and speech processing," *Comp. Linguistics* **23**, 269–312.

210. S. Seneff (1992) "TINA: A natural language system for spoken language applications," *Comp. Linguistics* **18**, 61–86.

211. K. Church (1987) *Parsing in Speech Recognition* (Kluwer: Dordrecht).

212. T. Kawahara, C-H. Lee & B-H. Juang (1998) "Flexible speech understanding based on combined key-phrase detection and verification," *IEEE Trans. Speech & Audio Proc.* **6**, 558–568.

213. D. Jurafsky *et al* (1997) "Automatic detection of discourse structure for speech recognition and understanding," *IEEE Workshop on Speech Recognition*, pp. 88–96.

214. R. Kuhn & R. de Mori (1990) "A cache-based natural language model for speech recognition," *IEEE Trans. Pattern Anal. Machine Intell.* **PAMI-12**, 570–583; corrections: **PAMI-14**, 691–692.

215. W. Woods (1982) "Optimal search strategies for speech understanding control," *Artificial Intell.* **18**, 295–326.

216. R. Rosenfeld (1996) "A maximum entropy approach to adaptive statistical language modeling," *Computer, Speech & Lang.* **10**, 187–228.

217. F. Jelinek (1985) "The development of an experimental discrete dictation recognizer," *Proc. IEEE* **73**, 1616–1620.

218. P. Brown, V. Della Pietra, P. deSouza, J. Lai & R. Mercer (1992) "Class-based *n*-gram models of natural language," *Comp. Linguistics* **18**, 467–479.

219. S. Katz (1987) "Estimation of probabilities from sparse data for the language model component of a speech recognizer," *IEEE Trans. ASSP,* **ASSP-35**, 400–401.

220. M-Y. Hwang, X. Huang & F. Alleva (1996) "Predicting unseen triphones with senones," *IEEE Trans. Speech & Audio Proc.* **4**, 412–419.

221. R. Iyer, M. Ostendoff & H. Gish (1997) "Using out-of-domain data to improve in-domain language models," *IEEE Signal Proc. Lett.* **4**, 221–223.

222. J. Billa, K. Ma, J. McDonough, C. Zavaliagkos & D. Miller (1997) "Multilingual speech recognition: The 1996 Byblos Callhome system," *Proc. Europ. Conf. Speech Comm. & Tech.* pp. 363–366.

223. S. Young *et al* (1997) "Multilingual large vocabulary speech recognition: The European SQUALE project," *Computer, Speech & Lang.* **11**, 73–89.

224. G. Adda, M. Adda-Decker, J-L. Gauvin & L. Lamel (1997) "Text normalization and speech recognition in French," *Proc. Europ. Conf. Speech Comm. & Tech.*, pp. 2711–2714.

225. S. Martin, J. Liermann & H. Ney (1998) "Algorithms for bigram and trigram word clustering," *Speech Comm.* **24**, 19–37.

226. R. Iyer & M. Ostendoff (1999) "Modeling long-distance dependence in language: Topic in mixtures versus dynamic cache models," *IEEE Trans. Speech & Audio Proc.* **7**, 30–39.

227. P. Heeman & G. Damnati (1997) "Deriving phrase-based language models," *IEEE Workshop on Speech Recognition*, pp. 41–48.

228. J. Bellegarda (1998) "Exploiting both local and global constraints for multi-span statistical language modeling," *Proc. IEEE Int. Conf. ASSP*, pp. 677–680.

229. M. Russell (1997) "Progress towards speech models that model speech" *IEEE Workshop on Speech Recognition*, pp. 115–123.

230. R. Haeb-Umbach & H. Ney (1994) "Improvements in beam search for 10,000-word continuous speech recognition," *IEEE Trans. Speech & Audio Proc.* **2**, 353–356.

231. N. Nilsson (1980) *Principles of Artificial Intelligence* (Tioga: Palo Alto, CA).

232. S. Renals (1996) "Phone deactivation pruning in large vocabulary continuous speech recognition," *IEEE Signal Proc. Lett.* **3**, 4–6.

233. R. de Mori (1983) *Computer Models of Speech Using Fuzzy Algorithms* (Plenum: New York).

234. T. Kaneko & N.R. Dixon (1983) "A hierarchical decision approach to large-vocabulary discrete utterance recognition," *IEEE Trans. ASSP*, **ASSP-31**, 1061–1072.

235. S. Ortmanns & H. Ney (1997) "A word graph algorithm for large vocabulary continuous speech recognition," *Computer, Speech & Lang.* **11**, 43–72.

236. R. Schwartz, L. Nguyen & J. Makhoul (1995) "Multipass search strategies," in *Automatic Speech and Speaker Recognition*, C-H. Lee *et al* (eds.) (Kluwer: Dordrecht), chap. 18.

237. L. Rabiner & J. Wilpon (1981) "A two-pass pattern-recognition approach to isolated word recognition," *Bell Syst. Tech. J.* **60**, 739–766.

238. C-H. Lee, E. Giachin, L. Rabiner, R. Pieraccini & A. Rosenberg (1992) "Improved acoustic modeling for large vocabulary continuous speech recognition," *Comp., Speech & Lang.* **6**, 103–127.

239. E-F. Huang, H-C. Wang & F. Soong (1994) "A fast algorithm for large vocabulary keyword spotting application," *IEEE Trans. Speech & Audio Proc.* **2**, 449–452.

240. J. Wilpon, L. Rabiner, C-H. Lee & E. Goldman (1990) "Automatic recognition of keywords in unconstrained speech using hidden Markov models," *IEEE Trans ASSP*, **ASSP-38**, 1870–1878.

241. R. Christiansen & C. Rushforth (1977) "Detecting and locating key words in continuous speech using linear predictive coding," *IEEE Trans. ASSP*, **ASSP-25**, 361–367.

242. A. Higgins & R. Wohlford (1985) "Keyword recognition using template concatenation," *Proc. IEEE Int. Conf. ASSP*, pp. 1233–1236.

243. A. Manos & V. Zue (1997) "A segment-based word-spotter using phonetic filler models," *Proc. IEEE Int. Conf. ASSP*, pp. 899–902.

244. J. Foote, S. Young, G. Jones & K. Jones (1997) "Unconstrained keyword spotting using phone lattices with application to spoken document retrieval," *Comp., Speech & Lang.* **11**, 207–224.

245. M. Rahim, C-H. Lee & B-H. Juang (1997) "A study on robust utterance verification for connected digits recognition," *J. Acoust. Soc. Am.* **101**, 2892–2902.

246. D. Rumelhart, G. Hinton & R. Williams (1986) "Learning internal representations by error propagation," in *Parallel Distributed Processing, Vol. 1: Foundations*, D. Rumelhart & J. McClelland (eds.) (MIT Press: Cambridge, MA), chap. 8.

247. N. Morgan & H. Bourlard (1995) "Continuous speech recognition," *IEEE Signal Proc. Mag.* **12**, no. 3, 25–42.

248. N. Morgan & H. Bourlard (1995) "Neural networks for statistical recognition of continuous speech," *Proc. IEEE* **83**, 742–770.

249. A. Robinson (1994) "An application of recurrent nets to phone probability estimation," *IEEE Trans. Neural Networks* **NN-5**, 298–305.

250. A. Waibel (1992) "Neural network approaches for speech recognition," in *Advances in Speech Signal Processing*, S. Furui & M. Sondhi (eds.) (Marcel Dekker: New York), pp. 555–595.

251. P. Mermelstein (1975) "Automatic segmentation of speech into syllabic units," *J. Acoust. Soc. Am.* **58**, 880–883.

252. T. Schotola (1984) "On the use of demisyllables in automatic word recognition," *Speech Comm.* **3**, 63–87.

253. R. de Mori, P. Laface & Y. Mong (1985) "Parallel algorithms for syllable recognition in continuous speech," *IEEE Trans. Pattern Anal. Machine Intell.* **PAMI-7**, 56–68.

254. S. Haltsonen (1981) "Improvement and comparison of three phonemic segmentation methods of speech," *Proc. IEEE Int. Conf. ASSP*, pp. 1160–1163.

255. P. Regel (1982) "A module for acoustic-phonetic transcription of fluently spoken German speech," *IEEE Trans. ASSP*, **ASSP-30**, 440–450.

256. C. Weinstein, S. McCandless, L. Mondshein & V. Zue (1975) "A system for acoustic-phonetic analysis of continuous speech," *IEEE Trans. ASSP*, **ASSP-23**, 54–67; also in DM, pp. 314–327.

257. R. Schwartz & J. Makhoul (1975) "Where the phonemes are: Dealing with ambiguity in acoustic-phonetic recognition," *IEEE Trans. ASSP*, **ASSP-23**, 50–53.

258. K. Paliwal & P. Rao (1982) "Synthesis-based recognition of continuous speech," *J. Acoust. Soc. Am.* **71**, 1016–1024.

259. G. Doddington & T. Schalk (1981) "Speech recognition: Turning theory to practice," *IEEE Spectrum* **18**, no. 9, 26–32.

260. J. Chang & J. Glass (1997) "Segmentation and modeling in segment-based recognition," *Proc. Europ. Conf. Speech Comm. & Tech*, pp. 1199–1202.

261. H. Kuwabara (1985) "An approach to normalization of coarticulation effects for vowels in connected speech," *J. Acoust. Soc. Am.* **77**, 686–694.

262. V. Zue & R. Schwartz (1980) "Acoustic processing & phonetic analysis," in L, pp. 101–124.

263. R. Cole, R. Stern & M. Lasry (1986) "Performing fine phonetic distinctions: Templates vs. features," in *Invariance & Variability in Speech Processes*, J. Perkell & D. Klatt (eds.) (Erlbaum: Hillsdale, NJ), pp. 325–341.

264. J. Wolf (1976) "Speech recognition and understanding," in *Digital Pattern Recognition*, K. Fu, (ed.) (Springer-Verlag: Berlin), pp. 167–203.

265. P. Loizou, M. Dorman & A. Spanias (1995) "Automatic recognition of syllable-final nasals preceded by /ε/," *J. Acoust. Soc. Am.* **97**, 1925–1928.

266. J. Glass & V. Zue (1985) "Detection of nasalized vowels in American English," *Proc. IEEE Int. Conf. ASSP*, pp. 1569–1572.

267. L. Gerstman (1968) "Classification of self-normalized vowels," *IEEE Trans. Audio & Electroac.* **AU-16**, 78–80.

268. S. Disner (1980) "Evaluation of vowel normalization procedures," *J. Acoust. Soc. Am.* **67**, 253–261.

269. K. Nathan & H. Silverman (1994) "Time-varying feature selection and classification of unvoiced stop consonants," *IEEE Trans. Speech & Audio Proc.* **2**, 395–405.

270. P. Demichelis, R. de Mori, P. Laface & M. O'Kane (1983) "Computer recognition of plosive sounds using contextual information," *IEEE Trans. ASSP*, **ASSP-31**, 359–377.

271. P. Mermelstein (1977) "On detecting nasals in continuous speech," *J. Acoust. Soc. Am.* **61**, 581–587.

272. R. de Mori, R. Gubrynowicz & P. Laface (1979) "Inference of a knowledge source for the recognition of nasals in continuous speech," *IEEE Trans. ASSP*, **ASSP-27**, 538–549.

273. G. Vysotsky (1984) "A speaker-independent discrete utterance recognition system, combining deterministic and probabilistic strategies," *IEEE Trans. ASSP*, **ASSP-32**, 489–499.

274. J. Shoup (1980) "Phonological aspects of speech recognition," in L, pp. 125–138.

275. B. Oshika, V. Zue, R. Weeks, H. Neu & J. Aurbach (1975) "The role of phonological rules in speech understanding research," *IEEE Trans. ASSP*, **ASSP-23**, 104–112.

276. M. Hunt (1998) "Practical automatic dictation systems," **ELRA Newsletter 3**, no. 1, 4–7.

277. D. Klatt & K. Stevens (1973) "On the automatic recognition of continuous speech: Implications from a spectrogram-reading experiment," *IEEE Trans. Audio & Electroac.* **AU-21**, 210–217.

278. W. Lea (1980) "Prosodic aids to speech recognition," in L, pp. 166–205.

279. A. Waibel (1986) "Recognition of lexical stress in a continuous speech understanding system: A pattern recognition approach," *Proc. IEEE Int. Conf. ASSP*, pp. 2287–2290.

280. T. Lee, P. Ching, L. Chan, Y. Cheng & B. Mak (1995) "Tone recognition of isolated Cantonese syllables," *IEEE Trans. Speech & Audio Proc.* **3**, 204–209.

281. Y-R. Wang & S-H. Chen (1994) "Tone recognition continuous Mandarin speech assisted with prosodic information," *J. Acoust. Soc. Am.* **96**, 2637–2645.

282. J. Leggett & G. Williams (1984) "An empirical investigation of voice as an input modality for computer programming," *Int. J. Man-Machine Studies* **21**, 493–520.

283. R. Rose, S. Schroeter & M. Sondhi (1996) "The potential role of speech production models in automatic speech recognition," *J. Acoust. Soc. Am.* **99**, 1699–1709.

284. J. Elman & J. McClelland (1985) "An architecture for parallel processing in speech recognition: The TRACE model," in *Speech and Speaker Recognition*, M. Schroeder (ed.) (Karger: Basel), pp. 6–35.

285. J. Millar (1997) "Knowledge and ignorance in speech processing," *Proc. Int. Conf. Speech Proc.* pp. 21–27.

286. P. Niyogi & P. Ramesh (1998) "Incorporating voice onset time to improve letter recognition accuracies," *Proc. IEEE Int. Conf. ASSP*, pp. 13–16.

287. H. Kitano (1994) *Speech-to-Speech Translation* (Kluwer: Norwell, MA).

CHAPTER 11—SPEAKER RECOGNITION

*1. R. Mammone, X. Zhang & R. Ramachandran (1996) "Robust speaker recognition," *IEEE Signal Proc. Mag.* **13**, no. 5, 58–71.

2. O. Tosi (1979) *Voice Identification: Theory and Legal Applications* (University Park Press: Baltimore, MD).

3. K. Wu & D. Childers (1991) "Gender recognition from speech," *J. Acoust. Soc. Am.* **90**, 1828–1856.

4. L. Arslan & J. Hansen (1997) "New frequency characteristics of foreign accented speech," *Proc. IEEE Int. Conf. ASSP*, pp. 1123–1126.

5. M. Zissman (1996) "Comparison of four approaches to automatic language identification of telephone speech," *IEEE Trans Speech & Audio Proc.* **4**, 31–44.

*6. G. Doddington (1985) "Speaker recognition: Identifying people by their voices," *Proc. IEEE* **73**, 1651–1664.

7. K. Wu & D. Childers (1991) "Segmentation of speech using speaker identification," *Proc. IEEE Int. Conf. ASSP*, pp. I:161–164.

8. G. Yu & H. Gish (1993) "Identification of speakers engaged in dialog," *Proc. IEEE Int. Conf. ASSP*, pp. II:383–386.

*9. A. Rosenberg (1976) "Automatic speaker verification," *Proc. IEEE* **64**, 475–487.

*10. B. Atal (1976) "Automatic recognition of speakers from their voices," *Proc. IEEE* **64**, 460–475.

11. Q. Lin, E-E. Jan & J. Flanagan (1994) "Microphone arrays and speaker identification," *IEEE Trans. Speech & Audio Proc.* **2**, 622–628.

12. J. Oglesby (1995) "What's in a number? Moving beyond the equal error rate," *Speech Comm.* **17**, 193–208.

13. J. Koolwaaij & L. Boves (1997) "A new procedure for classifying speakers in speaker verification systems," *Proc. Europ. Conf. Speech Comm & Tech.*, pp. 2355–2358.

*14. H. Gish & M. Schmidt (1994) "Text-independent speaker identification," *IEEE Signal Proc. Mag.* **11**, no. 4, 18–32.

15. A. Higgins, L. Bahler & J. Porter (1993) "Voice identification using nearest neighbor distance measure," *Proc. IEEE Int. Conf. ASSP*, pp. II:375–378.

16. K. Yu, J. Mason & J. Oglesby (1995) "Speaker recognition models," *Proc. Europ. Conf. Speech Comm. & Tech.*, pp. 629–632.

17. B. Atal (1974) "Effectiveness of linear prediction characteristics of the speech wave for automatic speaker identification & verification," *J. Acoust. Soc. Am.* **55**, 1304–1312.

18. H. Hollien & W. Majewski (1977) "Speaker identification by long-term spectra under normal and distorted speech conditions," *J. Acoust. Soc. Am.* **62**, 975–980.

19. J. Markel & S. Davis (1979) "Text-independent speaker recognition from a large linguistically unconstrained time-spaced data base," *IEEE Trans. ASSP*, **ASSP-27**, 74–82.

20. K. Li & G. Hughes (1974) "Talker differences as they appear in correlation matrices of continuous speech spectra," *J. Acoust. Soc Am.* **55**, 833–837.

21. J. Schalkwyk, N. Jain & E. Barnard (1996) "Speaker verification with low storage requirement," *Proc. IEEE Int. Conf. ASSP*, pp. 693–696.

22. S. Furui (1981) "Comparison of speaker recognition methods using statistical features and dynamic features," *IEEE Trans. ASSP*, **ASSP-29**, 342–350.

*23. A. Rosenberg & F. Soong (1992) "Recent research in automatic speaker recognition," in *Advances in Speech Signal Processing*, S. Furui & M. Sondhi (eds.) (Marcel Dekker: New York), pp. 701–738.

24. S. Furui (1991) "Speaker-dependent-feature extraction, recognition and processing techniques," *Speech Comm.* **10**, 505–520.

25. D. Reynolds & R. Rose (1995) "Robust text-independent speaker identification using Gaussian mixture speaker models," *IEEE Trans. Speech & Audio Proc.* **3**, 72–83.

26. K. Li & E. Wrench, Jr. (1983) "An approach to text-independent speaker recognition with short utterances," *Proc. IEEE Int. Conf. ASSP*, pp. 555–558.

27. F. Soong, A. Rosenberg, L. Rabiner & B. Juang (1985) "A vector quantization approach to speaker recognition," *Proc. IEEE Int. Conf. ASSP*, pp. 387–390.

28. F. Soong & A. Rosenberg (1988) "On the use of instantaneous & transitional spectral information in speaker recognition," *IEEE Trans. ASSP*, **ASSP-36**, 871–879.

29. M-S. Chen, P-H. Lin & H-C. Wang (1993) "Speaker identification based on a matrix quantization method," *IEEE Trans. ASSP*, **ASSP-41**, 398–403.

30. D. Burton (1987) "Text-dependent speaker verification using vector quantization source coding," *IEEE Trans. ASSP*, **ASSP-35**, 133–143.

31. H. Matsui & S. Furui (1994) "Comparison of text-independent speaker recognition methods using VQ-distortion and discrete/continuous HMM's," *IEEE Trans. Speech & Audio Proc.* 2, 456–459.

32. P. Bricker & S. Pruzansky (1976) "Speaker recognition," in *Contemporary Issues in Experimental Phonetics*, N. Lass (ed.) (Academic: New York), pp. 295–326.

33. O. Kimball, M. Schmidt, H. Gish & J. Waterman (1997) "Speaker verification with limited enrollment data," *Proc. Europ. Conf. Speech Comm. & Tech.*, pp. 967–970.

34. L. Liu, J. He & G. Palm (1997) "A comparison of human and machine in speaker recognition," *Proc. Europ. Conf. Speech Comm. & Tech.*, pp. 2327–2330.

35. K. Fukunaga (1990) *Introduction to Statistical Pattern Recognition* (Academic: San Diego, CA).

*36. J. Campbell (1997) "Speaker recognition: A tutorial," *Proc. IEEE* **85**, 1437–1462.

37. S. Furui (1981) "Cepstral analysis technique for automatic speaker verification," *IEEE Trans. ASSP*, **ASSP-29**, 254–272.

38. J. Openshaw, Z. Sun & J. Mason (1993) "A comparison of composite features under degraded speech in speaker recognition," *Proc. IEEE Int. Conf. ASSP*, pp. II:371–374.

39. K. Assaleh & R. Mammone (1994) "New Lp-derived features for speaker identification," *IEEE Trans. Speech & Audio Proc.* 2, 630–638.

40. M. Zilovik, R. Ramachandran & R. Mammone (1997) "A fast algorithm for finding the adaptive weighting cepstrum for speaker recognition," *IEEE Trans. Speech & Audio Proc.* 5, 84–86.

41. M. Sambur (1976) "Speaker recognition using orthogonal linear prediction," *IEEE Trans. ASSP*, **ASSP-24**, 283–289.

42. R. Bogner (1981) "On talker verification via orthogonal parameters," *IEEE Trans. ASSP*, **ASSP-29**, pp. 1–12.

43. J. Fakotakis & J. Sirigos (1996) "A high performance text independent speaker recognition system based on vowel spotting and neural nets," *Proc. IEEE Int. Conf. ASSP*, pp. 661–664.

44. B. Necioglu, M. Clements & T. Barnwell (1996) "Objectively measured descriptors applied to speaker characterization," *Proc. IEEE Int. Conf. ASSP*, pp. 483–486.

45. J. Wolf. (1972) "Efficient acoustic parameters for speaker recognition," *J. Acoust. Soc. Am.* **51**, 2044–2056.

46. H. Matsumoto, S. Hiki, T. Sone & T. Nimura (1973) "Multidimensional representation of personal quality of vowels and its acoustical correlates," *IEEE Trans. Audio & Electroac.* **AU-21**, 428–436.

47. B. Walden, A. Montgomery, G. Gibeily, R. Prosek & D. Schwartz (1978) "Correlates of psychological dimensions in talker similarity," *J. Speech Hear. Res.* **21**, 265–275.

48. H. Kuwabara & T. Takagi (1991) "Acoustic parameters of voice individuality and voice-quality control by analysis-synthesis method," *Speech Comm.* **10**, 491–495.

49. M. Shridhar & N. Mohankrishnan (1982) "Text-independent speaker recognition: A review and some new results," *Speech Comm.* **1**, 257–267.

50. M. Sambur (1975) "Selection of acoustic features for speaker identification," *IEEE Trans. ASSP*, **ASSP-23**, 176–182.

51. U. Goldstein (1976) "Speaker-identifying features based on formant tracks," *J. Acoust. Soc. Am.* **59**, 176–182.

52. R. Cheung & B. Eisenstein (1978) "Feature selection via dynamic programming for text-independent speaker identification," *IEEE Trans. ASSP*, **ASSP-26**, 397–403.

53. F. Nolan (1983) *The Phonetic Bases of Speaker Recognition* (Cambridge University Press: Cambridge).

54. K. Paliwal (1984) "Effectiveness of different vowel sounds in automatic speaker identification," *J. Phonetics*, **12**, 17–21.

55. L. Su, K. Li & K. Fu (1974) "Identification of speakers by use of nasal coarticulation," *J. Acoust. Soc. Am.* **56**, 1876–1882.

56. Q. Lin, E-E. Jan, C. Che, D-S. Yuk & J. Flanagan (1997) "Selective use of the speech spectrum and a VQGMM method for speaker identification," *Proc. Europ. Conf. Speech Comm. & Tech.* pp. 2415–2418.

57. C. Jankowski, T. Quatieri & D. Reynolds (1996) "Fine structure features for speaker identification," *Proc. IEEE Int. Conf. ASSP*, pp. 689–692.

58. R. Lummis (1973) "Speaker verification by computer using speech intensity for temporal registration," *IEEE Trans. Audio & Electroac.* **AU-21**, 80–89.

59. A. Rosenberg & M. Sambur (1975) "New techniques for automatic speaker verification," *IEEE Trans. ASSP*, **ASSP-23**, 169–176.

60. B. Atal (1972) "Automatic speaker recognition based on pitch contours," *J. Acoust. Soc. Am.* **52**, 1687–1697.

61. C. Johnson, H. Hollien & J. Hicks (1984) "Speaker identification utilizing selected temporal speech features," *J. Phonetics* **12**, 319–326.

62. S. Das & W. Mohn (1971) "A scheme for speech processing in automatic speaker verification," *IEEE Trans. Audio & Electroac.* **AU-19**, 32–43.

63. M. Hunt (1983) "Further experiments in text-independent speaker recognition over communications channels," *Proc. IEEE Int. Conf. ASSP*, pp. 563–566.

64. A. Solomonoff, A. Mielke, M. Schmidt & G. Herbert (1998) "Clustering speakers by their voices," *Proc. IEEE Int. Conf. ASSP*, pp. 757–760.

65. A. Rosenberg, J. DeLong, C-H. Lee, B-H. Juang & F. Soong (1992) "The use of cohort normalized scores for speaker verification," *Int. Conf. on Spoken Lang. Proc.*, pp. 599–602.

66. A. Rosenberg & S. Parthasarathy (1996) "Speaker background models for connected digit password speaker verification," *Proc. IEEE Int. Conf. ASSP*, pp. 81–84.

67. H. Dante & V. Sarma (1979) "Automatic speaker identification for a large population," *IEEE Trans. ASSP*, **ASSP-27**, 255–263.

68. J. Millar & M. Wagner (1983) "The automatic analysis of acoustic variance in speech," *Language & Speech* **26**, 145–158.

69. D. Reynolds (1997) "Comparison of background normalization methods for text-independent speaker verification," *Proc. Europ. Conf. Speech Comm. & Tech.*, pp. 963–966.

70. D. Reynolds & R. Rose (1995) "Robust text-independent speaker identification using Gaussian mixture speaker models," *IEEE Trans. Speech & Audio Proc.* **3**, 72–83.

71. S. Everett (1985) "Automatic speaker recognition using vocoded speech," *Proc. IEEE Int. Conf. ASSP*, pp. 383–386.

72. A. Schmidt-Neilsen & K. Stern (1985) "Identification of known voices as a function of familiarity and narrow-band coding," *J. Acoust. Soc. Am.* **77**, 658–663.

73. C. McGonegal, A. Rosenberg & L. Rabiner (1979) "The effects of several transmission systems on an automatic speaker verification system," *Bell Syst. Tech. J.* **58**, 2071–2087.

*74. Y. Muthusamy, E. Barnard & R. Cole (1994) "Reviewing automatic language identification," *IEEE Sig. Proc. Mag.* **11**, no. 10, 33–41.

75. L. Lamel & J-L. Gauvin (1995) "A phone-based approach to non-linguistic speech feature identification," *Computer, Speech & Lang.* **9**, 87–103.

76. T. Hazen & V. Zue (1997) "Segment-based automatic language identification," *J. Acoust. Soc. Am.* **101**, 2323–2331.

77. E. Barnard & Y. Yan (1997) "Toward new language adaptation for language identification," *Speech Comm.* **21**, 245–254.

78. E. Parris & M. Carey (1996) "Language independent gender identification," *Proc. IEEE Int. Conf. ASSP*, pp. 685–688.

79. K. Kumpf & R. King (1997) "Foreign speaker accent classification using phoneme-dependent accent discrimination models," *Proc. Europ. Conf. Speech Comm. & Tech.*, pp. 2323–2326.

80. J. Kreiman (1997) "Listening to voices," in *Talker Variability in Speech Processing*, K. Johnson & J. Mullennix (eds.) (Academic: San Diego, CA), pp. 85–108.

81. G. Papçun, J. Kreiman & A. Davis (1989) "Long-term memory for unfamiliar voices," *J. Acoust. Soc. Am.* **85**, 913–925.

82. H. Hollien, W. Majewski & E.T. Doherty (1982) "Perceptual identification of voices under normal, stress and disguise speaking conditions," *J. Phonetics* **10**, 139–148.

83. D. Van Lancker, J. Kreiman & K. Emmorey (1985) "Familiar voice recognition: Patterns and parameters—Recognition of backward voices," *J. Phonetics* **13**, 19–38.

84. P. Ladefoged & J. Ladefoged (1980) "The ability of listeners to identify voices," *UCLA Working Papers in Phonetics* **49**, 43–51.

85. A. Reich & J. Duke (1979) "Effects of selected vocal disguises upon speaker identification by listening," *J. Acoust. Soc. Am.* **66**, 1023–1028.

86. A. Reich (1981) "Detecting the presence of vocal disguise in the male voice," *J. Acoust. Soc. Am.* **69**, 1458–1461.

87. R. Bolt, F. Cooper, E. David Jr., P. Denes, J. Pickett & K. Stevens (1973) "Speaker identification by speech spectrograms," *J. Acoust. Soc. Am.* **54**, 531–537.

88. A. Reich, K. Moll & J. Curtis (1976) "Effects of selected vocal disguises upon spectrographic speaker identification, *J. Acoust. Soc. Am.* **60**, 919–925.

*89. M. Hecker (1971) "Speaker recognition: An interpretive survey of the literature," *Am. Speech Hear. Assoc. Monographs* **16**.

*90. P. Corsi (1982) "Speaker recognition: A survey," in *Automatic Speech Analysis and Recognition*, J.-P. Haton (ed.) (Reidel: Dordrecht), pp. 277–308.

Index

filter bank, 186, 279, 280, 298, 373, 450
flap, 66, 110, 431
formant, 45–105, 121–224, 242, 250–304,
    319–384, 394, 412, 415, 427–458
  formant estimation, 213, 214
  formant synthesis, 349, 353, 354, 356, 358, 365
  formant vocoder, 190, 301
forward coarticulation, 96
  forward masking, 129–133, 222
  forward prediction, 203
Fourier series, 271
  Fourier transform, 92, 132, 142, 169–198,
      211–220, 278, 279, 296, 328, 335, 383,
      446, 447
frame rate, 175, 176, 270, 296, 330, 356
frequency domain, 173, 185, 278–333, 383
  frequency resolution, 113, 128, 132, 138,
      174–191, 215–217
  frequency response, 45, 68, 73, 78, 79, 92, 113,
      126, 176, 197, 252, 254, 281, 318, 333,
      376
fricative, 36–103, 121, 132–165, 181, 186, 223,
    272, 348–388, 409, 428–431, 451, 452
front end, 75, 364, 372
function word, 104, 106, 342, 362, 371
fundamental frequency, 36, 40, 124, 218, 333,
    335

G

gain, 95, 171, 193–209, 217, 247–284, 302–312,
    331–336, 351, 353, 375, 382, 456
geminate reduction, 432
glide, 41–65, 105, 122, 133, 152, 153, 169, 430
glottal, 36–106, 158, 159, 181–220, 265, 273, 299,
    300, 347–364
  glottal pulse, 44, 63, 65, 69, 88, 250, 273, 357,
      358, 452
  glottal stop, 53, 70, 148
  glottis, 40–98, 189, 193, 268, 301, 356–358
grammar, 374, 402, 417, 418, 420
granular noise, 263

H

hair cell, 110, 112, 113, 115, 118–120, 130, 138
half-wavelength resonator, 75, 76
Hamming window, 176, 178, 180, 225
hangover time, 315

hardware, 174, 210, 232, 318, 337, 392, 394, 433,
    434
harmonic, 36, 44, 57, 65, 121–136, 142, 158,
    169–221, 230, 250–278, 287–299, 310,
    319–337, 352–364
  harmonic coding, 295, 298
hearing threshold, 119–122, 127
helicotrema, 111–115
hidden Markov model, 359, 366
hierarchical vector quantization, 305
highpass, 64, 99, 135, 209, 222, 272–274, 351,
    457
  highpass filter, 87, 182, 274
histogram, 117, 118, 132, 208, 235, 268
HMM, 330, 335, 403–456
homorganic stop insertion, 431
hybrid coder, 273, 287
hypothesis, 420, 422, 432

I

impedance, 45–92, 111, 218, 351
impostor, 438, 439, 450, 455, 458
impulse, 92, 94, 179, 193, 207, 212–214, 222,
    254, 256, 279, 280, 298–300, 348, 357,
    358
  impulse response, 68, 136, 179, 180, 267, 280,
      308, 356
independence, 68, 88, 359, 379, 380, 412, 442
infinite peak clipping, 143, 220
ingressive sound, 55
inherent feature, 450
inner ear, 110, 111, 116, 125, 169, 377
  inner hair cell, 112
  inner spectrum, 128
inspiration, 38
instantaneous quantization, 246
integer-band sampling, 279, 283
integrated circuit, 433
integrator, 253, 261, 317
intelligibility, 50, 67, 121, 131, 136, 142, 148,
    168–174, 199, 208, 223, 240–272, 296,
    302, 310–339, 359–372
intensity, 35–67, 98, 111–167, 199, 231, 246, 280,
    328, 353–375
internal muscle, 38
interpolation, 208, 255, 260, 270–308, 314, 315,
    341, 353–377, 419
interstress interval, 103, 433
interval histogram, 117

About the Author

Douglas O'Shaughnessy has been a professor at INRS–Telecommunications (part of the University of Quebec) in Montreal, Canada, since 1977. For this same period, he has also taught as adjunct professor at McGill University in the Department of Electrical Engineering. His teaching and research work lies in the areas of speech communications (automatic speech synthesis, analysis, coding, and recognition) and digital signal processing. His research team is currently concentrating on voice dialogs in English and in French.

All his university study was at the Massachusetts Institute of Technology. He received Bachelor's and Master's degrees there in 1972 in electrical engineering and computer science (as well as a Bachelor's in mathematics). His master's thesis dealt with acoustic analysis and modeling of durations in speech, leading to his first *IEEE Transactions* publication in 1974. He was granted a Ph.D. from the same department at MIT in 1976, under the supervision of Professor Jon Allen. His doctoral thesis examined how speakers use fundamental frequency in speech.

Professor O'Shaughnessy is a senior member of the IEEE and was elected Fellow of the Acoustical Society of America in 1992. He has been an associate editor for the *IEEE Transactions on Speech and Audio Processing Society* since 1994, and is also an associate editor for the *Journal of the Acoustical Society of America*. For the period 1991–1997, he was program director at INRS–Telecom.

In addition to several book chapters published in recent years on speech processing, he was the author of the first edition of this book *Speech Communication: Human and Machine* (Addison-Wesley Publishing Co., 1987). He gave a tutorial on speech recognition at ICASSP-96, and is also a regular presenter at the major speech conferences of ICASSP, Eurospeech, and ICSLP.